EDWARD KUTLER

Public Opinion and Politics: A Reader

Public Opinion and Politics: A Reader

WILLIAM J. CROTTY, NORTHWESTERN UNIVERSITY

HOLT, RINEHART AND WINSTON, INC.

New York Chicago San Francisco Atlanta
Dallas Montreal Toronto London Sydney

Preface

This book of readings on public opinion is designed to be a selective presentation of reports that focuses on the political implications of the opinion process. The content of opinions, the agencies that influence opinion
formation, the distribution of opinions among populations, and the linkages
between mass and elite as they affect the political system are explored. In
addition, the functions that opinions serve for the individual as well as for the
system are treated. Considerably more emphasis is placed on the attitudinal
development process and less on the more obvious manifestations of views,
such as mass voting, the results of specific elections, or legislative behavior—
all of which are quite adequately treated in the available monographs and
texts.

The book is divided into five parts, preceded by an Introduction that
briefly places the opinion studies within a broader perspective, and represents
a framework that serves to interrelate the selections that follow with more
general questions of concern to the field. Part I consists of a series of reports
that explore the contribution of the principal socializing agents—the family
and the school—to the political awareness of the emerging adult. The comparative aspect of the volume is emphasized early with several selections that
analyze different child-training practices and their implications for socialization and inculcation of national behavior. Studies on schools include investigations of the elementary school, high school, and college. The place of
reference groups in reinforcing opinion development is indicated through a
follow-up study of college students designed to reveal the stability of attitudinal orientations that matured during the college years.

Part II is concerned with the content of opinions. The problems explored in the selections presented include the ability of citizens to think

conceptually in politically relevant terms, the consistency of beliefs, the levels of political information, and the contrasts between elite and mass in support of democratic values. The section concludes with an original article that contrasts the motivations and ideology of the contemporary new left and radical right movements.

The differences in opinion associated with such factors as social class, occupation, race, religion, and geographical location are examined in Part III. The comparative analysis of class voting patterns and partisan affiliations undertaken in this part includes an analysis of four Anglo-American countries; another study, published in its entirety here for the first time, compares political partisanship in West Germany and the United States. The concluding selection attempts to isolate and evaluate the independent contribution of political factors above and beyond demographic variables for an understanding of political actions.

Part IV focuses on the needs that attitudes fulfill for the individual and the personality characteristics associated with liberal and conservative political orientations. The section also includes a provocative essay concerning the implications that the ways agencies transmit systemic values to the individual have for adapting to the total political system, a particularly pressing concern for the newer nations. The final report reviews the psychological reactions to the unexpected death of a national leader, the adjustment mechanisms that arise, and the implications of these processes for the nation. The selection also evaluates the role of the mass media during a period of national crisis.

Part V directs attention to the two-way flow of communication between base-level opinion and those who conduct the affairs of state. One of the selections reviews in detail a presidential campaign and its consequences. The nomination fight, the national conventions, and the fall campaign are all discussed. The final selection examines the implications that the 1960 television-radio debates between the presidential contenders had for the election—who saw or heard the confrontation; how they reacted; of what consequence this was in the election; and how important and effective the mass media are in communicating information and shaping opinions.

This collection is intended as supplemental reading for political science courses in general, and for those that are concerned with public opinion in particular. The book can be used in public opinion courses in conjunction with the standard texts in the field, specifically with Harwood Child's *Public Opinion: Nature, Formation, and Role*, V. O. Key's *Public Opinion and American Democracy*, or Bernard Hennessy's *Public Opinion*. In combination with other readers and texts on public opinion, voting behavior, political parties or with political behavior courses, this collection should complement one or a series of standard works available in paperback. Among the latter would be such volumes as *The American Voter*, by Angus Campbell and his associates, *The Civic Culture*, by Gabriel Almond and Sidney Verba, and *Public Opinion*, by Robert Lane and David Sears.

W.J.C.

Evanston, Illinois
September 1969

Contents

PREFACE   v

INTRODUCTION: THE NATURE AND MEANING OF PUBLIC
  OPINION   1

I   OPINION-INFLUENCING AGENCIES: THE FAMILY
    AND THE SCHOOL   35
    1·The Family and the School as Agents of Socialization, *Robert
      D. Hess and Judith V. Torney*   39
    2·The Child's Image of Government, *David Easton* and *Jack
      Dennis*   59
    3·Civic Education, Community Norms, and Political Indoctrination,
      Edgar Litt   78
    4·Value-Outcomes of a College Education, *Philip E. Jacob*   86
    5·Factors Associated with Change: Social Support during Post-
      College Years, *Theodore M. Newcomb, Kathryn E. Koenig,
      Richard Flacks, and Donald P. Warwick*   99

II OPINION CONTENT   111
    6·Beliefs: A Neglected Unit of Analysis in Comparative Politics,
      Lester W. Milbrath   113
    7·The Nature of Belief Systems in Mass Publics, *Philip E. Converse* 129
    8·The Quality of the Electorate's Deliberation, *Morris Janowitz
      and Dwaine Marvick*   156
    9·Radical Right and New Left: Commitment and Estrangement in
      American Society, *Gilbert Abcarian*   168

III   STRUCTURAL DIMENSIONS OF OPINION EXPRESSION   **185**

10·The Geographical Distribution of Opinions, *V. O. Key, Jr.*   189
11·Class Voting in the Anglo-American Countries, *Robert R. Alford*   204
12·Social Structural Bases of Political Partisanship in West Germany
    and the United States, *David R. Segal*   216
13·Religion and Politics, *Gerhard Lenski*   236
14·Social Determinism and Electoral Decisions: The Case of Indiana,
    V. O. Key, Jr., and Frank Munger   250

**IV   THE PSYCHOLOGY OF OPINION HOLDING AND
       ITS FUNCTIONAL RELEVANCE**   **269**

15·Conservatism and Personality, *Herbert McClosky*   271
16·The Functional Approach to the Study of Attitudes, *Daniel Katz*   290
17·Political Socialization and Culture Change, *Robert LeVine*   303
18·The Assassination of President Kennedy: Public Reactions and
    Behavior, *Paul B. Sheatsley and Jacob J. Feldman*   320

**V   OPINIONS, LINKAGE AGENCIES, AND
       THE POLITICAL SYSTEM**   **343**

19·Registration and Voting: Putting First Things First, *Stanley Kelley,
    Jr., Richard E. Ayres, and William G. Bowen*   345
20·The 1964 Presidential Election: Further Adventures in Wonder-
    land, *Charles O. Jones*   374
21·The Kennedy-Nixon Debates: A Survey of Surveys, *Elihu Katz
    and Jacob J. Feldman*   409

Public Opinion and Politics: A Reader

INTRODUCTION: THE NATURE AND MEANING OF PUBLIC OPINION

Public opinion is a topic of concern to anyone who takes an interest in the affairs of his fellowman. It is of particular relevance to the governmental policy maker, the concerned businessman, the informed layman, and the various types of opinion leaders throughout the social structure. Yet, "public opinion" is a nebulous thing. It is difficult to identify and measure and even more challenging to interpret. Too often a reference to what an amorphous body of opinion is supposed to want or think is used to carry an argument, justify a policy, or defend inaction on social problems. What is meant by public opinion? how are opinions measured? of what significance are they in determining what a government does? and to what extent does an opinion actually reflect what a person is thinking? These questions represent a few of the areas explored in the following pages.

Public opinion can be defined as the expressed view of an individual or aggregation of individuals on a subject of broad social importance. A "public" opinion is a point of view shared by a number of people and relevant to a topic of general political significance. This definition is inclusive. The limits as to what constitutes an opinion of political relevance are determined by the situational factors present at the point in time that is in question. For example, an individual's opinion of the amount of money he pays the local grocer for food may represent an isolated expression of his own irritation with the cost of living or his life situation, or it may represent one manifestation of a generally irascible nature. If the view is shared by a sizeable number of other persons, then it is of potential political significance. If, in turn, the opinion is salient enough for the individuals concerned to communicate their dissatisfaction to the store owner, to distributors, to candidates for and incumbents of political office, then it becomes a fact of political life. A group can organize and bring pressure on those in a position to affect the situation. Distributors or sellers of grapes grown in nonunion California vineyards can be boycotted and picketed, or enforced negotiations can be brought about through the intervention of a third party, usually the government. More direct legal sanctions such as fair-pricing laws, limitations on profits, controls exerted on the manufacture and distribution of food, the enactment of health and safety measures, and other such regulations can be attempted if the public support is widespread and sufficiently intensive. All are intended to accommodate the prevailing situation in one way or another to the demands of the group. Thus, what in many circumstances would constitute a private feeling of no general relevance can be transformed into a recognizable point of view, shared by a sizeable number of people, and of potential political significance.

Exponents of a view can draw attention to their needs through a variety of stratagems, and in the process make their group opinions viable political demands. The intensity of a group's commitment to its stand can be dramatized. The shedding of garments in public by a militant sect of the Doukhobors in British Columbia strikingly demonstrated the strength of the group's reactions to governmental pressures to enroll their children in state-supported schools. These actions also commanded press attention that more conventional protest means could never achieve. The self-immolation of Buddist monks in Vietnam or students in Czechoslovakia vividly dramatized total dedication to a cause, again gaining attention from the mass media that less shocking actions could not rival. The burning of draft cards in demonstrations protesting an unpopular war, exposing the perpetrators to government prosecution, served similar ends—communicating to others the feelings of a committed few. Propaganda of the deed, of which these are examples, assist a small number of people who harbor strong feelings to convey their views to a larger population with great speed. The hope is that others will examine their own positions and eventually respond by supporting the movement.

A group can also strive to demonstrate the scope of its support, thus forcing authorities to recognize both the legitimacy of the ends sought and the political potency of the dissidents. The mass demonstrations in opposition to the Vietnam war, and in particular the 1967 march on the Pentagon, are good examples of one aspect of this strategy. The impressive mobilization of antiwar students and middle-income voters behind the candidacy of Senator Eugene McCarthy, a symbol of disaffection with the war, in the 1968 Democratic primaries in New Hampshire and elsewhere went far in convincing those still uncommitted as to the strength of the protest movement. The unsuspected strength of the dove candidates did much to alter the course of government policy in Vietnam.

Voting to put a candidate in office is one of the ways the political system provides for the registering of opinions. Voting is expressly designed to permit citizens to exercise a choice of decision makers and to influence policy making. The outcome of an election, however, can be ambiguous. A variety of groups support a candidate with a series of different objectives in mind. Evaluating the "mandate" symbolized by the winner is difficult. Each observer offers his own interpretation.

The referendum—a vote on a specific policy issue put before an electorate—was designed to clarify the intentions of an electorate as to opinions on prominent issues. It is infrequently used, and when employed is restricted primarily to the local level. Turnout is consistently low, because policy information represents the most difficult type of knowledge for voters to retain and evaluate. Highly organized, well-financed groups have a decided advantage in mobilizing support for their side of the issue. The apathy of the majority of people permits a relative few—about fifteen percent of the electorate in turnouts characteristic of most of these votes—to determine the outcome. Whether this practice is an improvement on more conventional voting contests is a moot point.

More personalized, and probably equally effective, means of communicating group or individual views to a policy maker include the telephone call to the city councilman or the financial contribution to a candidate for public office. The time and effort expended in trying to promote a cause or the political aspirations of an individual sympathetic to that cause can yield impressive returns. McCarthy's candidacy is but one example. The skill and perseverance of Barry Goldwater's supporters in the successful fight to gain him the 1964 Republican party nomination represents an effective testimonial to the impact that a relatively few people who determined to work through conventional political channels can have in promoting candidates or policies appealing to them.

Also of significance in drawing attention to social problems of great magnitude are the anomic violence and urban riots of the 1960s, products of cumulative grievances. The explosiveness of the outbursts, the sight of American cities in flames, and the reaction to the use of troops in restoring order resulted in a more profound investigation into the conditions contributing to the destruction.

As the foregoing general view indicates, public opinion is a complex topic. It can differ in content or emphasis in individuals or among groups. It can make itself visible and politically relevant in a variety of ways. And it can be channeled into the political decision-making structures at any of a series of critical entry points.

Figure 1 helps to simplify the scope of inquiry by presenting a diagram of the interaction process linking politically relevant opinions to the social institutions designed to respond to them. At one end of the continuum is the individual who holds a view on a subject of importance to him—an issue as global as atomic testing or as immediate as the price of food. The individual is a member of many groups—work, social, recreational, religious, and family groups, to name but a few—and interacts daily with other group members in various capacities. These groups contribute to the shaping of his opinions on subjects of importance to them. And depending on his own assertiveness and the firmness with which his views are held, the individual contributes to the development of their ideas.

Figure 1   Diagram of Opinion Interaction and Effect on the Political Process

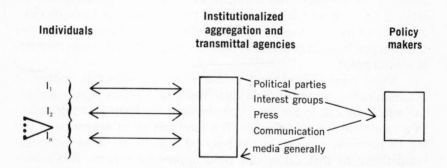

A group can be supportive of the individual's opinions, reinforcing them and providing a climate receptive to their expression. Group members also set limits as to what is acceptable and the views that the group as a whole can afford to tolerate comfortably. Individuals who persist in clinging to views that are unpopular and dysfunctional in the eyes of other members are ostracized.

Since a person holds membership in a series of groups, the standards of one can be in direct conflict with those of another. A peer group, for example, can have expectations as to what constitutes permissible behavior that are decidedly different from those of a parent of one of the members of the group. The political views of work associates or of one's boss can be dramatically opposed to those of friends or social acquaintances and in conflict with the beliefs of the family in which the individual matured. The multiple nature of group loyalties depresses the extremes of individual expression and channels influence along the lines of commonly held interest.

Through organized group efforts—interest group representation of specific views and the more diffuse consensual emphasis of the broader political party coalitions—or the publicizing of concerns and the educating of others through the media to support a policy position, pressure to respond can be directed toward those in official capacities. The intermediary agencies are the aggregation and transmittal institutions shown in Figure 1. The nature of the group's participation in the decision-making process and the effectiveness with which it can mobilize political resources to back its arguments determine the extent of its influence on policy deliberations.

OPINIONS AND ATTITUDE STRUCTURE

Opinions represent expressions of attitudes. Attitudes are, in turn, more fundamental predispositions (feelings of like or dislike) directed toward an object. There is a relationship among the basic drives involved in an individual's adjustment to his life conditions, the attitudes he develops, and the opinions he expresses. The pressures acting upon a person channel themselves into goal-directed motivations and are manifested in various types of response patterns.

Attitudes can be explored in terms of (1) their direction (for or against), (2) the intensity with which they are held, (3) their centrality within the individual's value structure, (4) their inclusiveness—the combination of elements and properties they encompass—and (5) the perceived ordering of stimulus objects by a person along dimensions (unidimensionality-multidimensionality). The complex interrelationship of these properties as they relate to political objects has been explored in a number of major works.[1]

Opinions, or their broader anchoring points attitudes, can serve any of a number of functions for an individual. A study by M. Brewster

[1] See also L. W. Milbrath, *Political Participation*, (Skokie, Ill.: Rand McNally, 1965); and Theodore M. Newcomb, Ralph H. Turner, and Philip E. Converse, *Social Psychology* (New York: Holt, Rinehart and Winston, Inc., 1965), pp. 47–79.

Smith, Jerome S. Bruner, and Robert W. White[2] conducted at the Harvard Psychological Clinic and concentrating on the function opinions fulfill for people helps to illustrate the processes at work. The researchers chose to examine opinions on post-World War II Russia— an area of views the authors expected to be well developed, independent of immediate environmental forces, and on which measurable differences should occur. Ten men with different occupational and social backgrounds were isolated for intensive analysis. The authors found that the respondents individually molded the object, Russia, to fit their own personalities. Certain dimensions were common to the individual conceptions, but each of the respondents had assimilated available information within a hierarchy of values, assigned it certain affective qualities, and then evaluated it within their highly idiosyncratic contexts. Consequently, their perceptions of the initial stimulus, as well as their opinions on it, exhibited a high degree of variation.

The interrelationship of the attitudes with an object and the opinions that result are difficult to analyze. The authors do conclude that opinions can serve at least three functions: (1) opinions represent a means of making explicit the relationship between an individual's own needs and the demands occasioned by outside forces—a mechanism for reducing the ambiguity in the world around him; (2) they provide a vehicle for adjusting to social relationships, for defining the social interactions which an individual will share with others; and (3) they attempt to resolve inner conflicts by projection onto external events and then dealing with the occurrence within the limits of the framework conditioned by the internal problem.

The difficulty inherent in ordering opinions and generalizing as to their implications is underscored by the researchers:

> . . . a man's opinions inevitably bear his personal stamp. His capacities for abstract or practical thinking, for intense feeling, for forthright action set limits on his response to public issues and, indeed, on what he makes of any significant event that impinges on him. His intellectual and temperamental qualities, general features of his behavior stabilized in the complex interaction of constitution and personal history, give distinctive form to his opinions about Russia no less than they do to his copings with a psychologist's ink blots. Even when his opinions serve the most minimal function in his life strategies—as when they are produced more or less *ad hoc* to satisfy the importunancies of an interviewer—they carry his signature.[3]

[2] M. Brewster Smith, Jerome S. Bruner, and Robert W. White, *Opinions and Personality* (New York: Wiley, 1956). Relevant commentaries are contained in M. Brewster Smith, "Opinions, Personality, and Political Behavior," *American Political Science Review*, 52 (March 1958), p. 1–17; and Alexander L. George, "Comment on 'Opinions, Personality, and Political Behavior,'" *American Political Science Review*, 52 (March 1958), pp. 18–26. See also the selection reproduced below by Daniel Katz, "The Functional Approach to the Study of Attitudes."

[3] M. B. Smith et al., *Opinions and Personality*, p. 259.

Others have grappled with the formidable difficulties implicit in relating idiosyncratic opinions to more fundamental and generalizable attitudinal sets directed at political objects. Robert Lane, in particular, has explored the conceptual frameworks employed by fifteen working class men, isolated for analysis in an eastern city, to order their political world.[4] His strategy was to establish the respondent's present perceptions of political consequences and then, through intensive psychological testing and depth interviewing, to develop the associations in the person's background that appear to fashion his more recent views and behavior. Lane was successful, for example, in illustrating how the four men in his study with strained father relationships exhibited, in contrast with the other respondents, negative orientations toward life in general that carried over into politics, characterized principally by authoritarian attitudes toward political figures and a restricted interest and involvement in political events.

The most ambitious, controversial, and stimulating of the attitudinal studies centered on the attempt by a group of researchers at the University of California at Berkeley to isolate the attitudinal syndrome common to a certain type of individual, the "authoritarian."[5] The research venture grew out of the climate surrounding World War II. The effort represented a seminal attempt by social scientists to deal with a contemporary problem of consequence: identifying the factors associated with prejudice and, more fundamentally, the attitudinal sets and environmental settings that lead to the formation of authoritarian and potentially antidemocratic behavior patterns. The social implications of the study are numerous and range from the assumed ramifications of childhood training procedures to the potentially disruptive influence of strongly prejudiced individuals within a political system, especially one that emphasized toleration of diversity and compromise among competitive groups.

The assumptions underlying the Berkeley research are complex. One of the most fundamental assumptions, of direct relevance to the present discussion, is the belief in a symbiotic relationship among an individual's attitudes. A person holds a series of opinions on diverse topics, such as, strangers, policy objectives, Jews, and democratic institutional procedures. His views are measurable and predict the more implicit attitudinal orientations. These orientations, in turn, reflect underlying dimensions of the individual's personality. Furthermore, it

[4] Robert E. Lane, *Political Ideology* (New York: Free Press, 1962). The following articles by Lane are also relevant: "The Fear of Equality," *American Political Science Review*, 53 (March 1959), pp. 35–51; and "Fathers and Sons: Foundations of Political Belief," *American Sociological Review*, 24 (August 1959), pp. 502–511.

[5] T. W. Adorno, Else Frenkel-Brunswick, D. J. Levinson, and R. N. Sanford, *The Authoritarian Personality* (New York: Harper & Row, 1950). R. Christie and Marie Jahoda, eds. *Studies in the Scope and Method of "The Authoritarian Personality"* (New York: Free Press, 1954) contains an extensive methodological critique of the study.

was assumed by the researchers that opinions were not only manifestations of fundamental attitudinal dimensions, but also were related to
behavior.

More specifically, it was anticipated in the study that distinctive
personality patterns would appear linking anti-Semitic attitudes with
other attributes, such as a tendency to distrust foreigners, a low tolerance for democratic means of problem solving, and specified types of
economic and political views, usually labeled "conservative." The researchers devised four scales to measure these dimensions of attitudes:
the Anti-Semitism Scale (A-S), the Ethnocentricism Scale (E), the Political
and Economic Conservatism Scale (PEC) and the Implicit Anti-democratic Trends Scale (F). The first three measures are based on an individual's reaction to ideological statements. The fourth and most famous
of the scales, the "Authoritarian" or "F-Scale," was conceived as a personality measure and scored a respondent on nine characteristics, including such qualities as uncritical, submissive attitudes toward authority
figures, rigid adherence to conventional values, hostility, and a disincli-
nation for subjective thinking. Data were collected through survey interviews, recorded case histories, clinical background examinations, and
projective techniques.

The researchers' assumptions as to the interrelationships to the
attitudes they measured was borne out by their analysis. The initial
version of the F-Scale had a mean correlation of 0.53 with the A-S
Scale, 0.65 with the E Scale, and 0.54 with the PEC Scale. Later refinements of the F-Scale eliminating the items with the weakest correlations improved the scores.

The methodology employed in the study introduced a series of
fundamental problems at critical points that were basic enough for
critics to argue that while the findings appear reasonable, the methods
employed in reaching them are suspect. The interrelationship of attitudinal sets and the covariation in views among the subjects as specifically explored in the research were well documented. Both represented assumptions crucial to the analysis. The nature of the relationship
among attitudinal dimensions was not developed. The unrepresentative nature of the sample of respondents also limited any ability to
generalize the findings to broader populations.

In a more recent study, Philip Converse, in reconstructing survey
data on national electorates in the United States, was unsuccessful in
establishing any strong associations among policy domains.[6] Also,
characterizations of a respondent's view of his policy orientation had
little relationship to the manner in which an individual described him-

---

[6] Philip E. Converse, "The Nature of Belief Systems in Mass Publics," in David
E. Apter, ed., Ideology and Discontent (New York: Free Press, 1964), pp. 206–261. A
portion of this research in reproduced in Selection 7.

self. For example, indices of policy choices that scored a respondent as liberal or conservative were not strongly associated with his own characterization of himself in these terms.

The data were not specifically collected for this analysis, and the measures employed are crude, reflecting the present state of social science analysis. Yet this research does not support, or for that matter refute, the broader findings of the earlier studies. It does, in concert with the others, suggest that the relationship among attitudes is highly complex and that it and the factors conditioning the association have yet to be established with reasonably acceptable precision or validity.

The number of respondents in each of the studies mentioned is too limited and too selective or unsystematic in representativeness to establish conclusively any relationships between the attributes of the attitudes explored and the political actions to be expected of more inclusive populations. The research findings are intriguing—and they do serve to emphasize the place of opinions within the individual's more general orientation toward the world in which he lives. They also direct attention to the forces acting upon the individual over time in conditioning the development of his views.

OPINION CHANGE

Once a person develops discernible opinions on a subject of political relevance, he normally perceives the environmental stimuli directed his way in such a selective manner as to reinforce his predispositions. This is especially true for those opinions with which he strongly identifies. A person deeply concerned about the brutality of war will expose himself to messages and speakers sympathetic to his position. He will also read newspapers or perceive television reports in a manner calculated to acquire documentation for his point of view. The informational stimuli he encounters are selectively screened and molded to fit his preconceived opinion structure.[7]

This reinforcement factor has even more explicitly political implications. Consider, for instance, the situation in which a candidate for public office addresses a mass of people at an election rally or delivers a nationwide television address. The majority of his audience consists of those who are already committed for varying reasons to support the candidate. They seek assurance that their inclinations are correct. They desire arguments as to why their candidate or party is superior, both to assuage any lingering doubts they may entertain and to enable them to justify their stand to others.

[7] Joseph Klapper, The Effects of Mass Communications (New York: Free Press, 1960).

One of the main advantages of televised campaign debates—and
the Kennedy-Nixon debates of 1960 are an outstanding example—is
that they enable both candidates to attract an audience to which they
normally would not have access. First, they can address the partisans
on the other side and those leaning in that direction. These viewers
have been attracted by their own candidate's appearance, but the less
committed at least are open to persuasion. Second, the voters with no
inclination either way are attracted by the drama of the occasion, the
well-publicized confrontation between the two principal contenders
on the great issues of the day. (No doubt, the less interested are drawn
to the debate also by the suspension of regular programming.) In this
situation, major, and possibly decisive, gains can be made by the candidate who can carry his appeal to the undecided voters. The opportunity is there for the candidate to argue his case convincingly, demonstrate his most attractive personal qualities, embarrass his opponent if
the opportunity arises, and debunk any stereotypes that might have
been associated with him previously (for instance, that he is too young,
too bland, not knowledgeable, inexperienced, or rich but vacuous).
The advantage, of course, is greater for the challenger who needs exposure or for the underdog in a contest than for the incumbent. The
perils to the front runner are obvious, and this is one reason for the
continuing argument among contenders at all levels of electoral contests as well as an explanation for the failure of the presidential candidates to enter into such televised exchanges during the 1964 and 1968
campaigns.

The principal purpose of a campaign is to convince the faithful
that their instincts to support a particular party and its nominees are
correct. A second purpose is to inspire partisans to the point that they
will make the effort necessary in casting a vote on election day. Attitudinal change during a campaign in the sense of conversion from one
party or candidate to another is rare.[8]

Still, attitudinal change does occur. Although the percentage of
individuals converted from one political party to another is small, the
party that records the net gain can realize the margin of victory in the
election. As suggested above, the image of Senator John Kennedy
among voters prior to the 1960 television debates was diffuse and generally negative. He was considered too rich, closely allied with a controversial father, too young, and with few visible qualifications for the
highest office in the country. In addition, he was a Roman Catholic, a
politically embarrassing religious affiliation at the time. The televised

But the Stat Results ??

---

[8] P. F. Lazarsfeld, B. Berelson, and H. Gaudet, *The People's Choice* (New York:
Duell, Sloan, and Pearce-Meredith Press, 1944). For a different perspective on voter
change in elections, consult V. O. Key, Jr., *The Responsible Electorate* (Cambridge,
Mass.: Harvard University Press, 1966).

debates gave Kennedy the opportunity to display his quick mind and his knowledge of policy questions. It also permitted him to confront Vice President Nixon, a considerably more experienced man, on equal footing in an intimate give-and-take. The change in the Kennedy image represented an important ingredient in his election, and possibly provided the margin of victory in a close contest.[9]

The change manifest in the perceptions of Kennedy stemming from the debates attests to several things. It reflects the candidate's own abilities and his performance in the first of the televised debates in particular. It also represents a testimonial to the power of television to reach large numbers of people, to communicate with them instantaneously, and to influence their thinking. Few viewers had experienced any direct contact with Kennedy prior to the campaign debates, with the exception of the Democratic National Convention and its bruising verbal battles between the principal contenders. It is probable that even among those who personally favored Kennedy his image was vague and the emotional ties to him weak. More than likely, most of the uncommitted spectators were simply curious. When an individual, in this case the television viewer, does not have strong feelings on a subject or when he has had limited information on or exposure to a topic, shaping his views is easier. This principle applies to advertising as well as to deciding between contenders for public office. The perception the individual has of the different types of automobiles, for instance, or of the contribution different brands of toothpastes can make to dental hygiene or to a happier social adjustment are largely products of mass media opinion formation in areas of relative unimportance to the individual.

Attitudinal change is less likely to occur when an individual's values are strongly held. Still, a person's unambiguous experience (that is, clearly favorable or unfavorable) with another group or his personal exposure to an incident can act as a catalyst in reshaping his thinking. A trip to an urban ghetto can result in a greater appreciation of the problems involved in living in such areas and more willingness to support social action programs intended to alleviate such conditions. If the exposure to those who live in a ghetto comes through an armed assault, a previously sympathetic individual may be found arguing for stricter law enforcement and little else.

The dislocation of a person's immediate environment also can

[9] See E. Katz and J. J. Feldman, "The Kennedy-Nixon Debates: A Survey of Surveys," *Studies in Public Communication,* 4 (Chicago: University of Chicago Press, 1962), pp. 127–163; Theodore H. White, *The Making of the President 1960* (New York: Atheneum, 1961); Bernard Rubin, *Political Television* (Belmont, Calif.: Wadsworth, 1967), pp. 43–68; and Earl Mazo, ed., *The Great Debates* (Santa Barbara, Calif.: Fund for the Republic, 1962). The Katz-Feldman article is reproduced in the readings below.

result in a reorientation of his attitudes. Political party identifications represent deep attachments formed early in life and remaining stable usually throughout the period of political involvement. Yet, the economic chaos resulting from the Great Depression and, rightly or wrongly, its association in the voter's mind with Republican control of political office made good Democrats of many former Republicans. The relationship between a party in power and "bad times" is highly complex: holding the party responsible for the economic conditions is a grossly oversimplified calculation, yet it is one that voters often make. Unfavorable conditions represent a *prima facie* case against the incumbents, often persuasive enough to result in a change of administrations. In the Great Depression, the desire for change went beyond the immediate election to provide the basis for the permanent reorganization of the two major political parties along more clearly discernible economic lives.

Such a basic attitudinal reorganization is rare. The more normal occurrence is for well-developed attitudes of importance to the individual to remain firm. Attitudes of less personal salience or of weak development are susceptible to change through the introduction of new considerations—additional information, personal experiences, a restructuring of environment, or communications from credible sources.[10]

POLITICAL PARTICIPATION

Opinions are communicated to policy makers in a variety of ways. An individual can call the Sanitation Department or write his state legislator; he can vote, possibly the most potent means for displaying support or disapproval; he can organize with others of similar disposition to gain an *ad hoc* measure or to maintain sustained pressures for the objectives he seeks; he can work on behalf of people he believes in sympathy with his views by contributing his time and money to convince others of the justness of his cause; or if these fail, he can offer himself for elective office. If the more conventional avenues appear unfruitful, the individual can engage in acts—parades, teach-ins, sit-ins, demonstrations, confrontations with police or authorities—designed to gain publicity and direct attention to the problems he wants considered.

Figures derived from nationwide samples of electorates indicate that the average citizen devotes relatively little time to any of these

[10] See Paul F. Secord and Carl W. Backman, *Social Psychology* (New York: McGraw-Hill, 1964); and Arthur R. Cohen, *Attitude Change and Social Influence* (New York: Basic Books, 1964).

activities. Voting is the most prevalent political activity. The vote represents the most visible and best understood means of transmitting opinions to policy makers. It is a crude shorthand for a complex set of attitudes, yet one of critical importance to the political system. The voter holds the power of continuing or replacing those officeholders ultimately responsible for official decisions.

Roughly three out of four individuals in any five-year period vote at least once.[11] Presidential contests produce the highest number of turnouts. Over 60 percent of those eligible participated in the presidential elections of 1960 and 1964. Voting declines, however, even in presidential years, for lesser offices. For example, the congressional vote in 1960 and 1964 was 59.4 percent and 58.0 percent respectively. In election years when there is no presidential contest to lead the ballot, the drop in turnout can be up to twenty percentage points for congressional seats and even more for state and local contests. The greatest apathy is evidenced in municipal and county elections and bond referenda with one-fifth to one-third of the eligible voters turning out. Nonpartisan elections and lack of competition also serve to depress involvement.[12]

Table 1 illustrates the disparities in turnout for President and U.S. House of Representatives for the years 1952–1966.

TABLE 1 PERCENTAGE OF VOTES CAST FOR PRESIDENT AND CONGRESSMEN BY YEAR, 1952–1966[a]

Year	OFFICE	
	President	U. S. Representative
1952	62.2%	58.1%
1954	———	42.1
1956	59.9	56.4
1958	———	43.2
1960	63.8	59.4
1962	———	46.5
1964	62.0	58.0
1966	———	45.6
	61.2%	51.2%

x = presidential years, 56.3%; off-years, 44.5%

[a] Percentage is based on the estimated number of voters eligible to participate.

Source: Congressional Quarterly Service, *Politics in America 1945–1966,* 2d. ed. (Washington, D. C.: Congressional Quarterly Service, 1967), p. 84.

[11] W. D. Burnham, "The Changing Shape of the American Political Universe," *American Political Science Review,* 59 (March 1965), pp. 7–28; and Julian L. Woodward and Elmo Roper, "Political Activity of American Citizens," *American Political Science Review,* 44 (December 1950), pp. 872–885.

[12] See Alvin Boskoff and Harmon Zeigler, *Voting Patterns in a Local Election* (Philadelphia: Lippincott, 1964) and the literature cited therein.

Even voting disproportionately represents the views of certain population groups: those with the interest and background sufficient to stimulate involvement. Participation in elections increases among the better educated and those with higher incomes and occupational achievements. It is more pronounced among whites, males, nonsoutherners, those who live in urban areas, and middle-aged and older citizens.[13]

Socioeconomic factors, in addition, correlate with such psychological qualities as sense of civic obligation, belief in the potency of the vote (political efficacy), interest in and importance attached to the election outcome, and partisan identification. Campbell, Converse, Miller, and Stokes have demonstrated the high correlation between such factors and political participation.[14] Lester Milbrath, in his overview of the evidence available, has correlated scores on these measures with a gauge of campaign activity devised by him, again reaffirming the strong associations.[15]

The relationship is illustrated in Table 2. The figures reproduced in the table employ those who scored highest and lowest on each of the psychological measures and relates these to whether or not the person voted.

TABLE 2 POLITICAL PERCEPTIONS AND VOTING

MEASURE AND SCORE	VOTE	NOT VOTE
Campaign interest		
high	87%	13%
low	58	42
Concern about election outcome		
high	84	16
low	52	48
Political efficacy		
high	91	9
low	52	48
Citizen duty		
high	85	15
low	13	87

Source: A. Campbell et al., The American Voter (New York: Wiley, 1960), pp. 101–110.

[13] See Angus Campbell, Philip E. Converse, Warren E. Miller, and Donald E. Stokes, The American Voter (New York: Wiley, 1960), pp. 333–401; Lester W. Milbrath, Political Participation, pp. 110–141; and Robert E. Lane, Political Life (New York: Free Press, 1959), pp. 220–234.

[14] A. Campbell et al., The American Voter, pp. 101–110.

[15] L. Milbrath, Political Participation, pp. 50–72.

The stronger one's ties to a political party, the more likely one is to vote. At present, in relation to party identification, Democrats have a decisive edge over Republicans. Approximately one-half of the electorate identify with the Democratic party (46 percent) and one-fourth to one-third with the Republican party (28 percent), with the remainder classified as Independents (22 percent). About one-half or more of the Independents, while claiming no tie to either party, "lean" toward either the Democrats (7 percent) or the Republicans (5 percent) in their voting behavior.[16]

Democratic candidates fail to control such offices as the presidency, however, because of the differential turnout—Republicans, drawn disproportionately from voters of higher socioeconomic status, are more likely to vote than Democrats—and the impact of shortrun campaign factors on any given election. Successful Republican candidates must demonstrate a substantial appeal to large numbers of Democrats. Dwight Eisenhower in 1952 (Table 3) epitomized Republican success in this regard, holding virtually all Republican party identifiers in his camp, showing great strength among Independents, and attracting one-third of the "weak" Democratic party identifiers and even some voters with "strong" Democratic party affiliations. Eisenhower repeated his performance in 1956, increasing his support among Independents to almost three out of four.

TABLE 3   EISENHOWER'S PRESIDENTIAL VOTE BY PARTY IDENTIFICATION

	STRENGTH OF PARTY IDENTIFICATION				
Year	Democrats Strong	Weak	Independents	Republicans Strong	Weak
1952					
Eisenhower	16%	38%	67%	94%	99%
Stevenson	84	62	33	6	1
1956					
Eisenhower	15	37	73	93	99
Stevenson	85%	63%	27%	7%	1%

Source: A. Campbell et al., *The American Voter* (New York: Wiley, 1960), p. 139.

Many of the Democrats who defected to Eisenhower maintained their Democratic party affiliation and continued to vote for other Democratic party contenders at the same time they cast their ballot in favor of the Republican presidential nominee. Most of those voters also

[16] Angus Campbell, Philip E. Converse, Warren E. Miller, and Donald E. Stokes, *Elections and the Political Order* (New York: Wiley, 1966), p. 13.

returned their support to the Democratic presidential candidates in succeeding elections.

The Republican party nominee for President in 1964 demonstrated the polar opposite to Eisenhower in appeal. Barry Goldwater attracted limited support in his bid for the presidency, failing even to hold many party identifiers with strong party attachments to their usual voting patterns.[17]

Those that fail to vote are drawn disproportionately from certain categoric groups: the poor, the less educated, those living in working class households, blacks, women, Southerners, and the young abstain from voting in greater numbers than other population groupings.[18] Their low turnout minimizes their impact on policy making.

The young, defined as those under thirty years of age, provide an interesting and timely example. Young people appear actively engaged at present in a variety of activities with political overtones: seeking policy goals, particularly in opposing wars such as that in Vietnam; supporting candidacies that they favor; and agitating for college-level educational reforms. Also, there is a movement underway to lower the voting age to eighteen in federal elections. However, the voting turnout of these seemingly hyperactive youth is low.

The number of college students who participate in the well-publicized confrontations with authorities or more avowedly political efforts is low, compared with the number of students in the population. Most students concern themselves with factors directly impinging on their own lives. They demonstrate less concern for public affairs and are less likely to make any sustained effort to vote than are other eligible groups. Elections occur while most students are away at college, maximizing the difficulty of registering and voting in their home localities. Many college communities, in turn, consciously attempt to restrict student participation in elections, especially through the enforcement of residence requirements. The unstated fear is of the impact of an unpredictable student vote on local races or questions. Noncollege youths are also more concerned with finding a job, with the demands of military service, and with beginning a family, than they are with more general public concerns. As both groups become increasingly settled, they demonstrate a livelier interest in community and national affairs and a higher rate of involvement in elections.

[17] Charles O. Jones, "The 1964 Presidential Election—Further Adventures in Wonderland," in Donald G. Herzberg, ed., American Government Annual, 1965–1966 (New York: Holt, Rinehart and Winston, Inc., 1965), pp. 1–30 (reproduced in Selection 20. See also Philip E. Converse, Aage R. Clausen, and Warren E. Miller, "Electoral Myth and Reality: The 1964 Election," American Political Science Review, 59 (June 1965), pp. 321–336.

[18] William H. Flanigan, Political Behavior of the American Electorate (Boston: Allyn and Bacon, 1968), pp. 20–25; and Angus Campbell, "The Passive Citizen," Acta Sociologica, 6 (1962), pp. 9–21.

Many arguments against lowering the voting age to eighteen fail to take these factors into account. Those who fight such a change also fear an impulsive, emotional vote by the younger voters. Actually, the first several votes of those youths just entering the electorate tend to follow the party preferences of their parents. Qualitatively, the patterns prevalent in the young vote would not be appreciably different from that of their elders. Lowering the voting age, however, would afford these individuals the opportunity to speak their minds in a manner calculated to hold the political decision-making processes directly accountable on issues of immediate personal concern to them.

Participation in presidential elections has steadily increased from the low percentage of the 1920s (only 44 percent of those eligible voted in both 1920 and 1924), which resulted from the doubling of the electorate through the adoption of the Nineteenth Amendment enfranchising women. This trend should continue. Educational achievements and income levels in the population generally continue to increase, the saturation media coverage of political events, especially presidential campaigns, stimulates political interest, and the competitive patterns associated with national races are penetrating other electoral contests. In particular, primary races and competition between political parties in the South are becoming more pronounced. Finally, the easing of legal barriers for voting, which range from seemingly innocuous residence requirements and literacy stipulations to the now-defunct (in national elections) poll tax, could also contribute to the impetus toward more political involvement.[19]

A variety of other activities afford the individual the opportunity to make his views count in policy making. Relatively few persons take advantage of these alternatives. Only one-fifth of the electorate communicate in person by telephone, or by mail in any given year with any public official. As few as one-third to one-fifth in presidential and off-

[19] According to the U.S. Civil Rights Commission report, "Political Participation" (Washington, D.C.: Government Printing Office, 1968), black voting has increased in the South from approximately 5 percent of those old enough to vote in 1940 to almost one-half (46 percent) in 1966. The change results in large part from the removal of such legal obstacles as the "white primary" and the stimulus provided by the civil rights legislation, in particular the Voting Rights Act of 1965, which insures equal application of registration procedures in the counties that fall under its provisions. The restrictions on voting that institutional forms can encourage are treated in: Stanley Kelley, Jr., Richard E. Ayres, and William G. Bowen, "Registration and Voting: Putting First Things First," *American Political Science Review*, 61 (June 1967), pp. 359–379 (reproduced in the readings below); Donald R. Matthews and James W. Prothro, "Social and Economic Factors and Negro Voter Registration in the South," *American Political Science Review*, 57 (March 1963), pp. 24–44, Donald R. Matthews and James W. Prothro, "Political Factors and the Negro Voter: Registration in the South," *American Political Science Review*, 57 (June 1963), pp. 355–367; and Lester W. Milbrath, "Political Participation in the States," Herbert Jacob and Kenneth N. Vines, eds., Politics in the American States: A Comparative Analysis (Boston: Little, Brown, 1965), pp. 25–60.

year elections respectively claim to discuss politics with others, at least to the extent of taking an active part in the conversation and attempting to influence the opinions of others.[20] As Table 4 shows, active political involvement is rare. An individual may place a sticker on his car in support of a candidate or party, or pin a campaign button on his lapel, but he is considerably less likely to donate money, attend meetings, work on behalf of a cause, or, most infrequent of all, belong to an active political organization.[21]

TABLE 4 POLITICAL INVOLVEMENT OF THE AMERICAN ELECTORATE

FORM OF ACTIVITY	1952	1956	1960	1962
Gave money	4%	10%	11%	11%
Attend political meetings	7	7	11	8
Work for a candidate or party	3	3	5	4
Belong to a political organization	2	3	3	4
Wear campaign button or have sticker	—%	—%	19%	13%

Source: 1952 and 1956 from A. Campbell *et al., The American Voter* (New York: Wiley, 1960), p. 91; 1960 and 1962 from Mark Wynn, "Political Participation in Midterm Elections," (Evanston: M. A. Thesis, Northwestern University, 1968).

Most Americans are aware of elections at least. Ninety-five percent are exposed to presidential campaigns, and a major portion of these people vote, at least at the presidential level. Otherwise, Americans do not overly involve themselves with politics. They appear content to let the politicians transact their affairs with a minimum of interference. Perhaps this apparent disinterest stems from absorption with more immediate problems and is rooted in an acceptance of the system and its ultimate stability and fairness, justified or not.

A curious paradox appears here. Apathy can result from contentment with policy directions and with one's position within the system. It can also be the product of frustration. Intense dissatisfaction with a life situation can nourish alienation from the system, through belief

[20] Mark Wynn, "Political Participation," (Evanston, Ill.: Unpublished Paper, Northwestern University, 1968); and J. L. Woodward and E. Roper, "Political Activity of American Citizens."

[21] The findings for blacks in the South provide an exception to these statements. Donald R. Matthews and James W. Prothro, *Negroes and the New Southern Politics* (New York: Harcourt, 1966), pp. 37–58. Southern white voters approximate the pattern that prevails in the nation as a whole, that is, a normal curve distribution that tapers off at both ends (no political activity and the most intensive forms of involvement). The curve peaks at voting. Southern blacks show a bimodal distribution pattern. The distribution peaks at discussing politics, dips at voting and increases again among the more demanding forms of participation such as involvement in campaigns. This represents an unusual pattern, suggesting the effectiveness of barriers to black voting participation.

that the system entertains little sympathy for one's problems and needs. Conventional means of communicating needs appear of limited utility. The political system does not respond. Yet, withdrawal from participation increases the probability of inaction. Political decision makers respond most readily to mobilized political resources. Apathy, for whatever psychological or environmental reasons, is too easily associated with a relative degree of satisfaction.

PUBLIC OPINION AND POLICY

The relationship among opinions, the manner in which they are fed into the political system, and policy outputs is extremely sophisticated. Attempts to unravel the association assume major significance for appreciating the operation of representative government.

One of the most impressive ventures along these lines was the study by Raymond Bauer, Ithiel de Sola Pool, and Lewis Dexter of the congruence of forces supporting foreign trade policies, and, in particular, the influences that resulted in the Kennedy Trade Expansion Act of 1962.[22] The focus of the study was on political communication, as against trade policies per se. It included nine hundred interviews with corporation executives, five hundred with policy decision makers and opinion representatives such as congressmen and their staffs, administrative officials, interest group advocates, journalists, and union leaders. The opinions of these people and their attitudes toward foreign trade were contrasted with those of the population in general, and a series of communities were isolated for case studies of their opinion structure. The relationships between the various strata of opinions, the mechanisms by which it was mobilized and communicated to policy makers, and the alternative policy courses followed were carefully explored. The result was a perceptive assessment of opinions and the forces that shape and channel these into policy objectives.

The findings cannot be reproduced here. Nonetheless, several of the author's major assumptions and their conclusions bear repeating. Bauer and his associates opted for a complex model in which to trace the activation of opinions within the individual and the linkage of these to policy concerns. They found in each individual a latent residue of previous beliefs formed by messages at different points in time. A trigger stimulus introduced into this setting to support restrictive trade policies, for example, may result in an activation of latent dispositions, producing just the opposite of the position sought. The structuring of

---

[22] Raymond A. Bauer, Ithiel de Sola Pool, and Lewis Anthony Dexter, *American Business and Public Policy* (New York: Atherton, 1963).

latent opinions within the individual's value hierarchy may prove more forceful in determining his eventual views than the immediate communication that provoked the processes into action. Once challenged by a newer or seemingly unpleasant alternative, a person in arguing for his present option may reinforce a commitment that previously was only tentative. Also, the nature of the individual's relationships with others and the opportunities afforded him partially determine the views that are expressed and thus reinforced. The social structure presents an added complication in evaluating opinion transmission, and one that refines the manner in which opinions influence any policy outcome.

A major advantage of the researchers' approach was the emphasis on social structures as independent forces affecting policy decisions. A knowledge of opinions themselves limits predictability of outcomes: it is necessary to have a clear appreciation of the operations of the transforming agencies into which the views are fed.

This institutional emphasis permits relating individual opinion formation and expression to the structural setting this society establishes for governing. Neither individual beliefs nor the operations of institutional agencies are examined independently. Within this context, the authors turned their attention to such social agencies of opinion transmittal as the individual businessman, the business community more generally, lobbies, Congress, and the social aspects of the policy-determining process.

Pressure groups are found to be less effective than popularly imagined. Multipurpose lobbies have too many constituent groups to allow them to take forthright stands on major issues. "One issue" lobbies encounter personnel and financial problems. Both frequently end up as more the tool of the public official than his boss, providing him with a vehicle through which to mobilize support for an issue he feels strongly on. Congressmen and administration figures assume the initiative in creating public opinion: they determine the issues on which national attention will focus.

Legislators, and public officeholders generally, also respond to public opinion. The authors make a convincing case that congressmen in framing policy alternatives and administrators in interpreting acts once passed have more leeway than is realized. Public opinion cannot anticipate issues or dictate specific technical solutions. The public official in calculating the influence of public opinion on a topic usually attempts to anticipate the public's reaction to a decision once made, rather than weighing its message in the predetermination phase.

Finally, the Bauer et al. study performs a service for the social science community by reemphasizing the complex nature of decision making and its place in a vortex of personal relations and social and political obligations, all essentially independent of the immediate issue under consideration. To trace the relationship between the individual's opinion and the policy outcomes, one must take into account all of these factors.

Other researchers have been less ambitious. In place of evaluating the total communication process, they have concentrated on more limited aspects of the broader problem: for example, the relationship between the social characteristics of a state's population and the proportion of funds expended in such special areas as education, welfare, highways, or health,[23] or the relationship between either a constituency's attributes or the vote in an electoral district (a critically important expression of an individual's views) and an elected representative's behavior as recorded in his roll-call votes. Unfortunately, the first approach fails to take into account the opinions associated with individuals or the processes that translate these opinions into government action.

There are many examples of the second genre of study.[24] One of the most successful in describing the association between mass voting and a legislator's decision making is that executed by Warren Miller and Donald Stokes.[25] The authors were primarily concerned with two dimensions of the problem: how a legislator construes his position, more specifically, the extent to which he believes he should be guided by the policy wishes of his constituents;[26] and whether there were any measureable acts of the legislator that could be correlated both with his own opinions and the attitudes of his supporters.

To answer these questions, Miller and Stokes correlated a congressman's views on policy and the preferences of his supporters with

[23] For an illustration of this approach, consult Thomas R. Dye, *Politics, Economics, and the Public: Policy Outcomes in the American States* (Skokie, Ill.: Rand McNally, 1966).

[24] See Lee F. Anderson, Meredith W. Watts, Jr., and Allen R. Wilcox, *Legislative Roll-Call Analysis* (Evanston, Ill.: Northwestern University Press, 1966) and the studies listed therein.

[25] Warren E. Miller and Donald E. Stokes, "Constituency Influence in Congress," *American Political Science Review*, 57 (March 1963), pp. 45–56. Also note the methodological refinements introduced into the analysis by Charles F. Cnudde and Donald J. McCrone in "Constituency Attitudes and Congressional Voting: A Causal Model," *American Political Science Review*, 60 (March 1966), pp. 66–72, and the companion piece to the original article by D. E. Stokes and W. E. Miller, "Party Government and the Saliency of Congress," *Public Opinion Quarterly*, 26 (Winter 1962), pp. 531–546.

[26] See Heinz Eulau, John C. Wahlke, William Buchanan, and Leroy C. Ferguson, "The Role of the Representative: Some Empirical Observations on the Theory of Edmund Burke," *American Political Science Review*, 53 (September 1959), pp. 742–756, and by the same authors, *The Legislative System* (New York: Wiley, 1962). For the voter's perspective, consult Carl D. McMurray and Malcolm B. Parsons, "Public Attitudes toward the Representational Roles of Legislators and Judges," *Midwest Journal of Political Science*, 9 (May 1965), pp. 167–185.

roll-call votes in three policy domains—social welfare measures, foreign involvement, and civil rights. Encouragingly, they found that a representative's voting was greatly influenced both by his own views and his perceptions of what his constituency wanted. The closest correlation between constituency views and a congressman's vote occurred on civil rights issues—the most visible of contemporary policy areas and potentially the most devisive. The least association between a district's preferences and the voting of its representative took place on foreign affairs items. Here the congressman was given great latitude and permitted to exercise his own independent judgment. Of the three areas examined, the latter is of the least immediate consequence to the voter, foreign affairs consistently ranking behind domestic issues in the hierarchy of voter interest.[27] The matters debated are complex, and with the emphasis on bipartisan foreign policy, the major political parties frequently do not take distinctive or opposing policy stands. These factors would contribute to the voter's disinterest in this particular issue area.

Miller and Stokes found the greatest unity between the representative and his party in roll-call voting on social welfare issues. In large part, this is a by-product of the realignment of forces during the period from 1928 to 1936, symbolized by the election of Franklin Roosevelt to the presidency in 1932. This era gave rise to the present party coalitions. The basic regrouping was along economic lines—the economically more disadvantaged aligning themselves with the Democrats, the more satisfied affiliating with the Republicans. The most consistent policy differences over time between the two parties have been on economic and social questions that reflect the group bases of party support.

This latter argument is borne out by a series of studies.[28] Research conducted by Herbert McClosky and associates into voter and party leader views[29] has shown that while the views of the majority of voters are close on most issues, the area in which they differ the most consistently relates to economic matters. Party leaders are more clearly divided on the same issues than are their followers. The balance of group support and the policy views espoused by the Republican and Democratic parties are distinguishable and, in contrast to frequently heard criticism, do offer the voter alternatives. A study on the state level—in contrast to the national orientation of the research by Mc-

[27] See Bernard R. Berelson, Paul F. Lazarsfeld, and William N. McPhee, *Voting* (Chicago: University of Chicago Press, 1954), and A. Campbell et al., *The American Voter.*

[28] The class differences in party support are analyzed in two of the selections that follow, those by Robert R. Alford and David R. Segal.

[29] Herbert McClosky, Paul J. Hoffman, and Rosemary O'Hara, "Issue Conflict and Consensus among Party Leaders and Followers," *American Political Science Review*, 54 (June 1960), pp. 406–429.

Closky and his associates—found similar identifiable disparities in party leadership opinions.[30]

In establishing associations between an electorate's policy positions and a congressman's voting, there is an implicit assumption that the voter has some interest in the subject and that he has a discernible view, intelligently arrived at—in effect, his opinion represents a belief on his part as to what should be done. Such assumptions are difficult to justify. The Miller and Stokes study can serve to illustrate the point. They found that congressmen had highly imperfect knowledge of their constituents' views. This could result from the physical obstacles present in attempting to communicate with the home district, as well as from the limited participation initiated by the voter as discussed above. It could also result from the fact that the individual's ideas on many subjects are poorly developed and that the majority of people remain unconcerned with political affairs or figures. The Miller and Stokes research, for example, illustrated that in the 1958 congressional election only 24 percent of their respondents had read or heard anything concerning the two candidates for office and one-half (46 percent) had been exposed to no information at all about either the incumbent or his opponent. A series of polls have demonstrated that the American public has little familiarity with political leaders below the level of President. Their factual knowledge of governmental procedures and institutions is sparse: 45 percent of the electorate in one poll could not tell how many United States senators are elected from one state, 60 percent did not know the number of justices on the United States Supreme Court, and, more disturbingly, 79 percent could not name anything contained in the Bill of Rights. The voter's knowledge of issues is weakest of all, ranking below name familiarity and textbook information on the mechanisms of government. There are many illustrations of respondents coming out solidly on both sides of an issue when the same question was put to them with slightly different wording; of respondents exhibiting little substantive knowledge of major policy debates well publicized by the media; and of respondents offering an opinion on an issue and then in a follow-up question being unable to communicate any sense of the measure's content or implications. The electorate can remain remarkably impervious to any information relevant to policy questions.[31]

On the other hand, and conceivably of greater significance, the overwhelming majority of citizens do accept fundamental democratic

[30] Thomas A. Flinn and Frederick W. Wirt, "Local Party Leaders: Groups of Like Minded Men," *Midwest Journal of Political Science*, 9 (February 1965), pp. 77–98.

[31] See the discussion of these points in Robert E. Lane and David O. Sears, *Public Opinion* (Englewood Cliffs, N.J.: Prentice-Hall, 1964), pp. 57–71, and the analysis below by Morris Janowitz and Dwaine Marvick, "The Quality of the Electorate's Deliberation."

values and the utility of democratic procedures. They do not, however, always agree on specific applications of these values or on the best means to achieve what are essentially long-term ideals.[32] All of these factors contribute to the difficulty of isolating and measuring public opinion and relating it intelligently to governmental outputs.

MEASURING PUBLIC OPINION

There are many ways of determining what the opinions of citizens are: intuitive assessments; various formalized manifestations of opinions, such as the vote; mass media commentaries, in particular the views of columnists and editorial writers and the opinions expressed in the letters-to-the-editor section of the newspaper; letters sent to legislators; the rise and fall of the stock market; and the opinions offered by knowledgeable people in a district and purporting to express the views of larger groups—labor representatives, church leaders, members of the business community, interest group officials, and civic association members. Possibly the most accurate and publicized means of determining what the electorate is thinking is the ubiquitous public opinion poll. Beginning with the 1936 presidential election, and despite several setbacks, public opinion polls have risen to a commanding place in contemporary American politics. Television, newspapers, and magazines employ them to ascertain citizen response to primary and general elections, to determine what the public thinks of various potential contenders, and to record the views of individuals as to policy questions and institutional reforms (for instance, Should Congress be reformed? Should the Electoral College be replaced?) Candidates employ them to plot their campaigns and as corrective devices feeding back information on what voters a candidate is reaching, what personal qualities of the candidate are admired or found unattractive by the citizens, and what issues that he is emphasizing the voters respond to or reject. They are also employed to predict election outcomes, although this was not their intention.[33]

[32] Herbert McClosky, "Consensus and Ideology in American Politics," *American Political Science Review*, 58 (June 1964), pp. 361–379; James W. Prothro and C. W. Grigg, "Fundamental Principles of Democracy: Bases of Agreement and Disagreement," *Journal of Politics*, 22 (Spring 1960), pp. 276–294; and the literature cited in William J. Crotty, "Democratic Consensual Norms and the College Student," *Sociology of Education*, 40 (Summer 1967), pp. 200–218.

[33] Polls can also be employed to predict public responses to the issues raised by candidates. See the discussion in Ithiel de Sola Pool, Robert Abelson, and Samuel L. Popkin, *Candidates, Issues, and Strategies: A Computer Simulation of the 1960 Presidential Election* (Cambridge: M.I.T. Press, 1964). For examples of their use in campaigning, consult Stanley Kelley, Jr., *Professional Public Relations and Political Power* (Baltimore: Johns Hopkins Press, 1956); and Murray B. Levin, *The Compleat Politician* (Indianapolis: Bobbs-Merrill, 1962).

Governor Nelson Rockefeller of New York attempted to use the polls as a weapon in his campaign for the 1968 Republican presidential nomination. Avoiding the primaries during the weeks preceeding the national conventions, Governor Rockefeller spoke directly to the American electorate through the mass media, attempting to acquaint them with his views and his personal qualifications. He gambled that their response to him would result in a more favorable showing in the national opinion polls—one sufficiently impressive to convince the delegates to the Republican nominating convention that he would make a more formidable presidential candidate than his adversary, the leading contender at the time, Richard Nixon. He lost his gamble. The polls did not indicate any change in his favor impressive enough to swing the convention delegates to his side. Also, the opinion transmission process from an electorate's stated preference to representation in national nominating conventions is at least as complex and indirect as the linkages between opinions and legislative policy.

Barry Goldwater's consistently poor showing in the polls both before the 1964 nominating conventions and after was a source of embarrassment to him and his supporters. In defense, Goldwater's backers claimed that the polls were incorrect and that they were not tapping a dimension of opinions that would result in a Goldwater vote in November. While not probable, this was a possibility. In this instance, the polls were correct. Roughly six out of ten voters chose Goldwater's opponent in the election.

The logic of polling is built on several assumptions. Opinion analysts have found that if you select a specified number of respondents —frequently only 1500 for a nationwide survey, a figure arrived at through experience—through probability sampling methods, they should represent an accurate picture of the views of the larger population from which they are drawn. Probability sampling means that no systematic bias enters into the choice of respondents: all individuals within the group being sampled have an equal, or at least known, chance of being chosen. Modifications of these procedures can be introduced for analytic purposes dictated by the nature of the study. Low-income voters or those of different religious persuasions or opponents to a particular course of action can be oversampled in order to supply enough respondents to satisfy the demands to be made in the analysis. Nonetheless, the assumptions underlying the original procedures must be conscientiously maintained. If these are violated, then the representativeness of the poll is in question and its usefulness diminished.

Reputable pollsters strive to neutralize the wording in their questions (for instance, the admirably terse question, "If the presidential election were being held today, would you vote for Johnson, for Goldwater, or for some other candidate?") and the bias that is introduced by interviewers through their appearance, their mannerisms, or their involvement with the respondent, each of which could threaten the validity of the interview situation. Polling agencies will also release their estimates of the confidence to be placed in the poll results (the range within which their predictions fall and the number of times— frequently ninety-five out of one hundred—their sample should be representative of the larger population).

Analogies are often advanced comparing polls to snapshots obtained by a camera—a picture of a continuing process at one point in time. If all goes well in designing the research and acquiring the information, the results should present an accurate representation of opinion distributions at the time of the sampling.

Problems do arise, however, in relating this static profile to actual behavior. Predicting actual turnout in elections—that is, precisely those who will vote—is difficult. Last-minute crises that cannot be anticipated may shift sentiment perceptibly in favor of one candidate or another (the Suez Crisis in 1956 is a good example). A large number of undecided voters or opinions in flux, which an analyst does not uncover in reviewing the findings, can threaten any predictions based on the poll.

Occasionally a poll in a primary election published either just before or on Election Day will show Candidate A leading Candidates B, C, and D. The poll is completed on the Friday or Saturday preceding the Tuesday election, a fact often misunderstood by the reader. When Candidate B, not A, wins the election (the 1964 Republican presidential primaries in New Hampshire, Oregon, and California, for instance), the question arises, Were the polls faulty? They could have been poorly conceived and executed, of course. Some pollsters engage in questionable survey practices, drawing unrepresentative samples, constructing weak questionnaire schedules, and employing inexperienced and poorly motivated interviewers. Even several of the better-known pollsters suffer occasional lapses.

More than likely, however, reputable polls accurately reflect voter choices as of the day they were taken. Factors unanticipated by the pollster can change the outcome. A large number of "undecideds" can make up their minds at the last minute, disproportionately favoring one candidate. This occurred during the 1968 Democratic presidential primaries and repeatedly favored Senator Eugene McCarthy. As a result, his vote was raised consistently above that expected. An electorate can also be experiencing a change in sentiment, a dynamic condition that the poll's analysts fail to weigh properly. Polls, then, have their weaknesses. Usually, despite momentary lapses, they are reasonably accurate within the set of limitations ordained. If their limits are appreciated (and most newspapers do not publish this information) they can be accepted for what they contribute to an understanding of opinions.

In 1964, the Harris and Gallup polls of nationwide electorates came within one percentage point of predicting President Johnson's vote, before corrections were introduced for the undecided voters. No acceptable distribution pattern has been devised for allocating the hard-core uncommitted voters among the contenders. In retrospect, most of these in 1964 appear to have supported Goldwater. The pollsters failed to identify this sentiment and divided the "undecideds" evenly between the two candidates. Even with the built-in bias, the two polls came within three percentage points of predicting both of the candidates' vote. In 1960, each of the three major polls, Gallup, Roper, and Kraft, had less than a two percent error in their predictions, and in an election that was extremely close, two of the polls (Gallup and Kraft) correctly foresaw a narrow Kennedy victory (the Democratic candidate edged the Republican with a 50.1 to 49.9 margin of the two-party vote).

The most publicized miscalculations in the polls occurred during the elections of 1936 and 1948. In 1936, at the height of the Great Depression, *Literary Digest* employed a preference poll chiefly as a means for boosting circulation. The poll had been successful in previous elections, beginning with tentative samplings in 1916 and 1920, and was looked to by commentators and the public alike to predict the election outcome. *Literary Digest* contacted up to twenty million people in its polls and in 1936 received a return ballot from approximately two million respondents, an unusually large number. On this basis, it calculated the election outcome, predicting that Governor Alfred Landon of Kansas, the Republican nominee, would win a majority of the electoral college vote and underestimating Franklin Roosevelt's popular vote by more than 19 percent. The election, of course, was won by Roosevelt in a landslide of historic proportions. The Democratic nominee captured 60.8 percent of the total vote and 523 electoral votes. Landon received 36.5 percent of the popular vote and eight electoral votes, doing well in Maine and Vermont.

With this poll, *Literary Digest* mercifully retired from polling. Within two years the magazine itself was out of business. What had happened was that several factors severely biased the results. First, the sample was weighted heavily in favor of the high-income, normally Republican voters. Large segments of the population, who voted heavily Democratic on Election Day, were not represented in the sample. Second, any subdivision of a sample not anticipated in the original study design is dangerous. In this case, the dividing of the returns from a nationwide electorate into state units in order to predict the electoral college distribution simply reinforced and illustrated the inadequacy

of the sampling techniques generally. Third, the use of a mail questionnaire assumes either a random response from those who submit
their ballot or some sort of weighting to equalize the returns. Those
who felt most deeply about the election submitted their questionnaires. This, in turn, increased the error built into the sample.[34]

The second major polling debacle took place in 1948. As Table 5
shows, in that year the principal national polls—Crossley, Gallup, and
Roper—overestimated the vote for Governor Thomas Dewey of New
York, the Republican presidential candidate, by from four to seven
percentage points and underestimated President Harry Truman's vote
by between five and twelve percentage points. The polls were also
unsuccessful in predicting the third-party share of the returns.

TABLE 5 THE PREDICTIONS OF THE MAJOR POLLS IN THE 1948 PRES-
IDENTIAL ELECTION

Polling Agency	ESTIMATED VOTE FOR			
	Dewey (R)	Truman (D)	Thurmond (SR)[a]	Wallace (P)[b]
Crossley	49.9%	44.8%	1.6%	3.3%
Gallup	49.5	44.5	2.0	4.0
Roper	52.2	37.1	5.2	4.3
Actual vote	45.1%	49.5%	2.1%	2.4%

[a] States' Rights (Dixiecrat) Candidate.
[b] Progressive Party Candidate.

Critiques of the 1948 miscalculations have pinpointed many probable causes for the error. Most voters decide early in a campaign whom
they will vote for. Approximately one-third know in late spring of an
election year how they will vote in November. Another third decide
during the national conventions when the parties settle on their nominees. Thus, roughly two-thirds—65 percent in 1964 as an illustration—
have determined whom they will support before the normal campaign
period begins. And when an incumbent is seeking reelection, the number of early deciders can be even greater. The election amounts to a
vote of confidence in the officeholder and his policies. Thus in 1956,
57 percent had decided their vote before the conventions, and three
out of four by the time the conventions were completed.

[34] Consult the discussion of these points and those on polling more generally in
Bernard C. Hennessy, *Public Opinion* (Belmont, Calif.: Wadsworth, 1965), pp. 39ff.
Properly handled, mail questionnaires can be very useful. On this see William J. Crotty,
"The Utilization of Mail Questionnaires and the Problem of a Representative Return
Rate," *Western Political Quarterly*, 19 (March 1966), pp. 44–53. For basic information
on surveys, Charles H. Backstrom and Gerald D. Hursh, *Survey Research* (Evanston,
Ill.: Northwestern University Press, 1963), and Mildred Parten, *Surveys, Polls, and
Samples* (New York: Harper & Row, 1950) are valuable.

Pollsters are aware of this. But in the 1948 election political factors alone appeared destined to bring certain defeat for President Truman. He was running against an able and well-known public figure, Governor Thomas E. Dewey of New York, the Republican presidential nominee of 1944. The country was restless, dissatisfied with the administration, uneasy about the Cold War and post-World War II international developments, and appeared ready for a change in leadership. President Truman was the unenthusiastic nominee of his party, a party divided by defections on the right and left. The Progressive Party was led by Henry A. Wallace, a former Vice-President under Franklin Roosevelt. A floor fight over a civil rights plank in the platform at the Democratic National Convention led to a walkout of Southern delegates and the formation of the States' Rights, or Dixiecrat, party, with Strom Thurmond as its standard-bearer.

The election outcome seemed foreordained. One of the leading pollsters, Elmo Roper, discontinued polling in September, predicting that Dewey was assured of a substantial victory. As a result, the Roper poll was well off the mark, doubling the totals of the third-party candidates, overestimating Dewey's vote by seven percentage points, and underestimating Truman's by over twelve percentage points.

The other polls ceased interviewing in mid-October, several weeks before the election. This practice was a necessity at the time for processing the information and getting it to the newspapers (a minimum of ten to twelve days was required). At present, this time lag has been reduced to two or three days because of the availability of high-speed digital computers and more standardized methods of data collection.

In 1948 the polls also employed a method called quota sampling in selecting respondents. After 1948 this was replaced because of the obvious bias it introduced into the selection procedures. The national headquarters would prejudge the number, or quota, of people in various population groupings—males and females, those of different religious affiliations, high- and low-income people of varying occupation distributions, urban and rural residents—that it wanted represented in its poll. Each of the interviewers was then assigned a number of individuals in each category that the headquarters wanted polled in specified geographical units. The interviewer could pick the specific individuals he wanted to question. Given this freedom, the tendency among interviewers was to ignore houses that looked threatening, to seek out people who wore business suits and would presumably be articulate and thus easier to question, and to avoid out-of-the-way places (isolated farms, for example) and unconventional or potentially unfriendly respondents. Today an interviewer has little discretion. In order to obtain the most accurate probability sample possible of a population, he is assigned the blocks he is to work, the residences on the block to be approached, and even the adult who is to be questioned in the house. All these decisions are calculated on a random basis to the extent practical.

In 1948 the pollsters also failed to distinguish a shift in sentiment by the electorate. President Truman had gone on the attack, calling back into session what he labeled the "do nothing" Congress (the Republican-controlled 80th); traveling widely and making a series of hardhitting speeches specifying the legislation he intended to enact; and promoting farm policies, repeal of Taft-Hartley (which had passed over his veto), public housing, and fair employment practices. His detailing of anticipated programs contrasted with the more general speeches of Dewey, and he began to pick up support. The polls did not catch this. Furthermore, there was an unusually large number of undecideds. One out of seven waited until the last week of the campaign to make a decision, an unusually late date. Of these, three out of four voted for Truman. Also, complicating matters was the low turnout— 51.5 percent of those eligible—another factor that the pollsters had not been able to anticipate.

The pollsters modified their procedures after 1948, and have since been successful in describing public sentiments and reestablishing public confidence. Along with the more intensive academic surveys, they continue as the principal means for gauging and reporting what the public thinks.

Questions continually arise as to the reliability of polls and their use. How good are they basically? Do people lie to interviewers? How are individuals chosen to be respondents. And, given the seemingly unlimited number of polls, why haven't I ever been interviewed? How can so few people in a national sample presume to speak for the nation as a whole? George Gallup of the American Institute of Public Opinion (Gallup poll) answers these and other questions in an interview recorded in *U.S. News and World Report*. The session is noteworthy both for the lucidity of the answers and the relevance in the choice of questions put to the dean of American pollsters.

An extended excerpt from the conversation follows:

Interviewer: Q. How accurate are the polls?
Dr. Gallup: A. I'm not an authority on all polls. There are polls and polls. There are postcard polls, there are polls of experts, street-corner
Interviewer: Q. How accurate are the polls?

In our own case, there have been 14 congressional and presidential elections since we started. We've been on the right side—that is our figures have pointed to the winner in a presidential year or to the winning party in a congressional year—13 of those 14 times.

Q. You missed in 1948—
A. Yes. The whole business of polling isn't designed to pick winners

or losers, and that's one of the great confusions that we've never been able to clear up. The mark we aim for is the actual division in the popular vote.

Now, since 1948, our average deviation has been in the neighborhood of about 1.7 percentage points, or 2 percentage points.

Strangely enough, that's better than we're entitled to be through the workings of the sampling system. We've always urged people to make an allowance of 3 or 4 percentage points of error in this sampling process, because error is inherent in any sampling procedure.

Q. Speaking of sampling: How big a sample do you take in a nationwide poll—how many people do you question?
A. We do it with a minimum of 1500. This is always a source of contention and amazement. But this whole system is based on the laws of probability.

Q. How did you arrive at 1500?
A. Empirically—simply through the years. We started with larger samples. There is an interesting thing about the laws of probability. This is that the size of the "universe," or total population group to be sampled, makes no difference at all in the necessary size of the sample. By this I mean that when we are polling the United States of America we don't need any bigger samples than if we are polling New York City, or Trenton, N.J.

Q. But, in using the law of probability, shouldn't you have a random sample?
A. Yes, and we do. What we've had to do is to break the country down by election districts—precincts. And we've picked those precincts, literally, out of a hat, so to speak. We just line them up and pick every x number of precincts, taking the various sizes into account. We do this right across the country. So we end up with a random selection of geographical areas. Now, having chosen the districts at random, we send an interviewer in and he follows a set pattern. He can't just go and pick people out himself. We actually give him a block assignment. He may be instructed to start with the third house from the northeast corner and then go to other dwelling units that assure a random selection. The selection of those interviewed is out of his hands.

Q. Since you pick the precincts at random, isn't there a risk that you'll get a sample that is weighted to a Democratic neighborhood or to a Republican neighborhood?
A. This is all part of the statistical process. You see, we have the past voting record in all these districts. So what we do is stratify within the sample, to make sure that we have the right percentage of people from New England, say, or from any area of the country.

Q. Dr. Gallup, how do you answer the question we hear so often: "Well, they've never polled me"?
A. Actually, there's a very simple answer. If we polled 10,000 persons every week—which we don't and wouldn't need to—it would take us over 200 years to get around to everybody. Now, if we polled 1500 every week—and we don't send out a ballot every week—it would take us over 1400 years, assuming a stable population. The chances of being interviewed are, as you can see, in a population of 110 million adults—

the chances of being in a sample of 1500 or even 15,000 are like a drop in a bucket.

The same principle operates when you go to get your blood tested. They don't draw gallons of blood—they take drops. The reason for this is that there's no point in going beyond, in getting a bigger sample. We could get samples of 3000 or 10,000, but we know from experience that, on a percentage basis, the answer wouldn't be much different.

Q. In polling, do you just ask a person how he would vote on that day?
A. Oh, no. An interview lasts approximately 40 minutes, and we ask a lot of questions in that time. . . . the best method of finding out how a person would vote is to ask him about issues, not the candidates. Well, this is something that we . . . have been doing since 1936, almost.

As a matter of fact, we've reached the point in this business where it wouldn't even be necessary to ask people directly how they are going to vote. By their answers to half a dozen issue questions, we could tell you how they were going to vote, and we wouldn't have to ask them their preference of candidates.

Q. Do you bring out issues in the same interview?
A. Oh, yes. In this forty-minute interview we include many questions about the voting intention, their interest in the campaign, the intensity of their preference, and we cover the issues.

In almost every interview and questionnaire, we ask the person to tell us what he regards as the most important problem facing the country. His answer may be the race issue—which is No. 1 at the present time— or it could have been Vietnam at the time of the PT-boat flare-up; it may be juvenile delinquency, or the lack of water in Western States. It can be anything that is in a person's mind.

Then we come along with a question which asks him to tell us which party he thinks can handle that particular problem better. Mind you, we haven't even mentioned candidates. We have found that, typically, the answer to that question gives a pretty good indication of how people are going to vote—how the vote will be divided between candidates.

Q. How can you be sure your returns are accurate and truthful? Do you have checks on that?
A. We have things we call "cheater questions" which catch the interviewer.

Q. The interviewer?
A. Yes. The interviewer is most important. Somebody, some interviewer, might be tempted to write up these long interviews by himself rather than actually conducting an interview. These "cheater questions" are put on the ballot for the specific purpose of tripping him up—and they can be pretty devastating.

Q. What happens when you catch one of these false interviews, where the interviewer fills in the answers?
A. We throw out that entire assignment.

Q. What does that do to your sample?
A. Typically, not very much, because we would have a minimum of about 180 precincts in the poll, and if you took out one it wouldn't distort the final result very much.

Q. Do people ever turn you down—refuse to answer?
A. Yes. It works out to about 4 or 5 percent. Incidentally, it is about the same percentage in every country of the world.

Q. You said an interview takes about 40 minutes. Is that typical?
A. Yes.

Q. Are all interviews conducted in the home?
A. In the homes. They start in late afternoon. We have made studies, and we have elaborate figures on exactly who is home at what time. We know, for example, how many males age 40 to 45 are home between 6:30 and 6:35 p.m. You have to know this because you have to work out a pattern.

By the way, the hardest man to find in the country is likely to be a young man, unmarried, who rushes home from work, changes clothes, and whips out of the house on a date or something.

Q. Do you ever take two people in the same household?
A. No, we interview only one person in a home.

Q. Do you give more weight to one response than another?
A. No, they are all weighted equally.[35]

CONCLUSION

Whatever the difficulties involved in the study, an understanding of opinions—who holds what beliefs, why, and what effect these have on policy determination—is fundamental for an appreciation of the operations of government. This would appear particularly crucial in a democratic society that theoretically seeks guidance and sanction from the will of the people. The selections in this volume are intended to shed some light on these basic concerns.

[35] "Do Polls Tell the Story?" *U.S. News and World Report*, 57 (October 5, 1964), pp. 52ff. Copyright © 1964 U.S. News and World Report, Inc. Public opinion polls do appear to stimulate interest in an event, thus increasing turnout. Presumably also, they influence voter perceptions and candidate support. The latter point is not well documented. On the first, and for a discussion of survey validity more generally, consult Aage R. Clausen, "Response Validity: Vote Report" (Ann Arbor: Mimeo., Survey Research Center, University of Michigan, 1967).

PART 1

OPINION-INFLUENCING AGENCIES: THE FAMILY AND THE SCHOOL

Political behavior is learned behavior. The first group of selections in the volume deals with the agencies that exert the principal impact on the individual in conditioning his response to his political environment. The last decade has witnessed an increasing awareness of the importance of studying the wide range of social institutions that act upon an individual to shape his political behavior. Previously, such agencies as the family, the school, and peer groups were treated as of indirect consequence for a study of political processes—at least, their impact on and ties to the political system were poorly understood and seldom explored.

Possibly the most ambitious and consistent research ventures in the area that has come to be called political socialization[1] have

[1] For reviews of the work to date, consult: Herbert Hyman, *Political Socialization* (New York: Free Press, 1959); Jack Dennis, "Major Problems of Political Socialization Research," *Midwest Journal of Political Science*, 12 (February 1968), pp. 85–114; Jack Dennis, *Recent Research on Political Socialization: A Bibliography of Published, Forthcoming, and Unpublished Works, Theses, Dissertations, and a Survey of Projects*

emerged from the pioneering efforts which originated from several social scientists at the University of Chicago. The work of these researchers is represented in the present volume by two selections. In the first (Selection 1), Professors Robert D. Hess and Judith V. Torney explore different characteristics of both the family and the school in developing political awareness and indicate the broader implications of these concerns. In the second piece (Selection 2), David Easton and Jack Dennis trace the evolution of the child from, in the author's words, a "political primitive"—an individual with a simple and benign perception of political authority—toward a more complex, sophisticated and realistic understanding of political institutions. Both studies deal with nationwide samples of children in grades two through eight.

Edgar Litt's analysis (Selection 3) is a highly imaginative piece of research focusing on high-school students in three communities with differing socioeconomic characteristics. Litt is concerned with the differences, if any, in the political views being transmitted to students through the varied community school systems. He concludes that the "students in the three communities are being trained to play different political roles, and to respond to political phenomena in different ways." The potential consequences of such training for the more inclusive political system merit attention by the student.

The college experience is frequently considered to be the first stage in the individual's intellectual growth in which views nurtured within the family and the school and reinforced by a supportive community environment undergo their first serious challenge. Folk wisdom, in part supported by academic research,[2] pictures the college years as a time of change. Many studies that employ education as a control variable have found basic differences in the attitudes and political practices of college educated groups in contrast with the population in general.[3]

Philip Jacobs, in synthesizing the results of a number of studies (Selection 4), attempts to reach a consensus as to what areas and in what ways the views of college students are modified. In general, he finds that those who have undergone the college experience are more tolerant of deviant ideas and behavior and more appraising of the world around them.

---

in Progress (Madison: Mimeo., University of Wisconsin, 1967); and Richard E. Dawson, "Political Socialization" in James A. Robinson, ed., *Political Science Annual: An International Review*, 1 (Indianapolis: Bobbs-Merrill, 1966), pp. 1–84.

[2] See Alex S. Edelstein, "Since Bennington: Evidence of Change in Student Political Behavior," *Public Opinion Quarterly*, 26 (Winter 1962), pp. 564–577.

[3] Consult, for example, the findings reported in Samuel A. Stouffer, *Communism, Conformity, and Civil Liberties* (Garden City, N.Y.: Doubleday, 1955), and any of the major voting studies.

In the 1950s, college students were criticized for their concentration on studies and vocational pursuits to the exclusion of participation in politics or movements of broad social concern. The students were dubbed by the press and popular commentators the "silent generation." The 1960s has witnessed a reversal of student orientations. Black students in the South have been actively engaged in civil rights movements—sit-ins, picketing, voter-registration campaigns—that added a new dimension to the integration drive. Other students throughout the country have joined in such activities. In addition, this hyperactive generation has participated in various forms of protest directed toward publicizing their views on the Vietnam war, promoting the presidential candidacy of Senator Eugene McCarthy in the 1968 Democratic nomination fight, and in questioning much of the impersonality and traditional practices of university administrations.

Do students generally change their views, and do they usually become more involved, because of the college experience? Theodore Newcomb and his associates address themselves to this problem in Selection 5. Newcomb executed the Bennington study[4] in the late 1930s, possibly the most renowned exploration of attitudinal change in college. In his research on students at Bennington College, Newcomb found significant change both in the areas mapped by Jacob and in those of more direct political consequence. The students were girls principally from high-income families and normally supporters of the Republican party. During their college years, the majority of the girls became more "liberal." That is, party identifications changed, favoring the Democrats; support for New Deal candidates and domestic policies increased; and a receptivity toward greater foreign involvement was evident.

In an attempt to discover how permanent these attitudinal changes were, Newcomb and associates conducted a followup study of the original respondents during the 1960s. The result, as reported in the selection, indicates that the women are still atypically Democratic in party affiliation and candidate preference and liberal in the nature of domestic and foreign policy views favored as contrasted with others of the same socioeconomic stratum. The authors suggest that the women have selectively molded their environment, choosing one in which they could operate comfortably and that is supportive of their political views.

The last research piece in this part sheds some light on the role of peer groups in reinforcing and supporting attitudes. The strength of the group ties and the relative importance of the group in the life of the

[4] Theodore M. Newcomb, *Personality and Social Change* (New York: Holt, Rinehart and Winston, Inc., 1943).

individual predetermine its role in shaping an individual's thinking. A person's friends or the members of work and recreational groups with which he interacts can supplement family or school influences and, in some cases, even supplant these. William Whyte's early research into the group bonds of street-corner gangs,[5] and in particular his description of the social reinforcement of status positions within the group as illustrated in the bowling competitions, serves to illustrate the profound impact a group's views can have on an individual's perception of himself and his own abilities relative to others.

More indirectly, the research done by Newcomb and his associates suggests some of the interaction that occurs between husbands and wives on political matters. Generally, politics is considered the province of the male. This is primarily a function of interest. Women (and this is most true of mothers in working class families) are more concerned with problems directly related to the home and the family and thus are more attuned to the cues provided by their husbands on more general political matters. The greater the interest of the woman in politics, the more likely she is to vote, make political decisions independent of her husband, and, in areas in which she has the greatest expertise, supply him with relevant information. One study[6] of women active in the League of Women Voters, chosen for analysis because of their obvious political concern, showed a good deal of agreement between the women and their husbands over the policy areas considered to be of principal interest to females and those considered of greater interest to males. The women appeared more involved with local government actions and educational activities and the men with labor relations and tax questions. Between these two sets of problems both males and females shared an interest in, and presumably interacted on a relatively equal basis on, questions relating to civil rights, foreign policy, administrative reform, and social welfare policies.

5 William Foote Whyte, *Street Corner Society* (Chicago: University of Chicago Press, 1955).

6 James G. March, "Husband-Wife Interaction Over Political Issues," *Public Opinion Quarterly*, 17 (Winter 1953–1954), pp. 461–470. See also William A. Glaser, "The Family and Voting Turnout," *Public Opinion Quarterly*, 23 (Winter 1959), pp. 563–570.

1

The Family
and the School
as Agents
of Socialization*

ROBERT D. HESS
JUDITH V. TORNEY

In the complex process of acquiring the behavior of the adult community in which he is reared, the child is influenced by several groups and individuals who do not necessarily agree in their attitudes toward political figures or public policy issues. There are some issues on which almost all groups in the community are united (such as respect for the flag, obedience to law, loyalty to country), but there are other issues on which a variety of views is presented to the child. Socialization of political behavior produces diverse attitudes on most of the topics with which this study dealt. . . .

Not all changes and individual differences occurring in children's political attitudes can be traced to direct socialization pressure. Socialization contexts are of three general types. The first type includes *institutions* of well-defined structure and organization—the family, the school, and the church —which influence children by direct teaching of political attitudes and values. . . . Such institutions also induct them into the behavior and roles appropriate to family, school, or church membership. These values, behavior, and roles may then be generalized to attitudes toward the political life of the

* Reprinted from Robert D. Hess and Judith V. Torney, *The Development of Political Attitudes in Children* (Chicago: Aldine Publishing Company, 1967), copyright © 1967 by Robert D. Hess and Judith V. Torney.

community and nation. A role may mediate between one situation or system in which learning takes place and another in which that learning is directly or indirectly applied. Particularly because a child does not have direct experience in the political arena, his experience in non-political roles is an important influence upon the later development of role relationships within the political system, assuming that transferral occurs. For example, parents teach children regard for authority and the rules of the family group, which are then translated into respect for law and political authority figures. This is illustrated by the tendency for children in early grades to confuse such family-imposed rules as, "Brush your teeth every morning," with more formal laws. Early experience in the family orients the child toward authority and law and in this way anticipates political socialization. Similiar illustrations apply to the child's experience in the school and church, where both formal teaching of values and concrete experience of participation give the child orientations which are transferred to behavior in the political system. This type of indirect learning . . . is especially significant in the formation of attachment to governmental figures and in compliance to laws.

The second type of socializing influence occurs in larger social settings. The most important of these social contexts are social class, ethnic origin, and geographical region. They are diffuse in the sense that the specific elements and experiences connected with them are numerous, subtle, and difficult to measure precisely. The social-class context has been described by several social scientists (Bronfenbrenner, 1958; Davis, 1948; Hess and Shipman, 1965; Kohn, 1959, 1963; Miller and Swanson, 1958; Warner, 1959) some of whom have analyzed the way in which social class influences behavior. This presentation assumes that a broad categorization, such as social class, is not a variable in the usual sense, but rather a general category indicating and subsuming several more specific influences, attitudes, interpersonal experiences, and types of roles. Because of the diffuse nature of the social class influence, the various models of socialization are all represented in the learning process.[1]

A third type of influence in the socializing process derives from the child's personal characteristics. These *individual characteristics* influence socializing efforts of the family, school, and other agents and limit the extent of learning. Socialization is not exerted upon a passive receptive object. Each child's emotional, intellectual, and physical properties modify the images, attitudes, and information transmitted to him by adults. The most salient influencing factor is intelligence. Much of political socialization occurs in school; the child's mental capacity mediates his comprehension of material presented in the classroom. Personal needs also play an important part. Individual differences in compliance and dependency needs may alter the child's perception of government's role in assisting and protecting the citizen. Children differ in characteristics which mediate their understanding of the world. Intelligence limits their comprehension of what is taught in school; sex role mediates other experiences.

[1] The socializing influence peculiar to a geographical region or to membership in an ethnic group is also diffuse, resulting from an interplay of many variables. Obviously, traditions and historical events are very powerful, as in differences within this country over the issues of integration and states' rights. . . .

Comprehensive examination of the ways in which a child transforms and selectively accepts teachings would require intensive case studies, such as those by Lane (1959) and by Smith, Bruner, and White (1956). Their studies illustrated and elaborated on the importance of internal, dynamic elements of personality in the socializing process. This project had somewhat different objectives; data were based on self-report and were drawn from relatively large research groups in order to examine group trends and differences. Hence, information about children's individual qualities is somewhat limited.

SYSTEMS ACTING AS AGENTS OF SOCIALIZATION

Role of the Family in Political Socialization

Introduction   Students of personality development and human behavior frequently regard the family as the most important agent of socialization, a unique context in which children acquire values and behavioral patterns. This view may be valid within certain areas of behavior, but it is not adequate as a model for the development of attitudes toward political objects or the growth of active political involvement. The data of this study raise several questions about the efficacy of the family as contrasted with other socializing agents, although there is certainly some family influence.

The family unit, especially the parents, participates in the socialization of political perceptions and attitudes in three ways. First, parents transmit attitudes which they consider valuable for their child to hold. The family may operate as one of several teaching agents imparting attitudes or values which reflect community consensus; that is, the family reinforces other institutions. Since the attitudes imparted are similar or identical to those transmitted by other groups and institutions, it is difficult to determine accurately the family's influence compared to that of other agents. Some attitudes which children acquire in these areas of high consensus are well known and perhaps taken for granted—feelings of loyalty, respect for the symbols of government (especially the flag, Statue of Liberty, and Uncle Sam), and the kind of behavior expected of the citizen (especially compliance to law). Also, the family transmits attitudes which represent differences of opinion existing within the community. In some cases this involves taking a position on a current issue (for example, civil rights, federal aid to education). In transmitting a position on a current issue, a family competes with some agents holding different views and is supported by other agents. This type of attitude transmission promotes and maintains the disagreement and division characteristic of our political life. The family may also transmit idiosyncratic attitudes; that is, those which do not correspond to any recognized or defined division within the community. . . .

The family also presents examples that children may emulate. . . . Probably the most significant socialization of this kind involves parental affiliation with a political party. Despite some variability in reported data, there is evidence that the family exerts an important influence upon the child's party preference (Hyman, 1959). Remmers and Weltman (1947), in studying preferences of high school youth and their parents, reported correlations of 0.8 and 0.9. Socialization of partisan preference is apparently well-established before voting age, and frequently follows that of the parents. These results are supported by retrospective studies of parents' party preferences which report the child's tendency to identify with his parents' party—or at least to report that he has done so (Campbell, Gurin, and Miller, 1954; Hyman, 1959; Maccoby, Matthews, and Morton, 1954). These results reaffirm the hypothesis that children follow the party preference of their parents in at least three-fourths of the cases in which both parents are affiliated with the same party. Also following the Identification Model, children may become politically active if their parents are active. Children may learn to value modes of political involvement which they observe in their parents (see Stark, 1957). Adults vary markedly in the extent of their political activity, a majority of them performing only the voting act and displaying little interest otherwise (Woodward and Roper, 1950). Children may therefore have only limited opportunity to observe their parents in political pursuits.

A third possibility is that expectations formed from experience in family relationships are later generalized to political objects. . . . The home provides the child's first and most lasting experience with interaction in a hierarchic social system. Through this experience, children develop relationships, expectations, and behavior patterns. A child becomes attached to the family unit through attachment to its individual members, relates to the hierarchy of authority and learns compliance to its regulations, thus establishing a frame of reference by which to approach systems he will later encounter.

The structure of family power not only influences the child's relationship to the system (Bronfenbrenner, 1961; Hoffman, 1961; Kagan, 1958) but also mediates class differences in personality and attitudes (Kohn, 1959, 1963). Families in which the father plays a strong, dominant role encourage in the child a different attitude toward authority than do mother-dominated families. Investigations of families from which the father is absent for long periods of time have indicated that personality differences may be expected, particularly in boys (Bach, 1946; Tiller, 1958). Here, the nature of transmitted attitudes and values does not necessarily differ, but specific experiences with an authority system do affect later relationships to governmental authority.

Data   The following types of analysis were performed to assess family influence on political socialization: (1) comparison of the attitudinal similarity among siblings with that occurring in pairs of unrelated children matched by social class and grade; (2) examination of the effect of absence of the father on attitude development; (3) analysis of the relationship between the children's perceptions of the family power structure and characteristics and certain political variables.

In examining these data, two questions were considered: (1) What evidence is there that the family socializes non-consensus attitudes, such as those toward a Presidential incumbent or party affiliation, by presenting models of partisan affiliation or political involvement? (2) What evidence is there that family structure or characteristics are important in creating orientations toward political affairs or political authority?

Role of the Family in Socialization of Division

Responses of sibling pairs were studied to assess the accumulated effect of family in transmitting attitudes. If the similarity between siblings was greater than that in pairs of children not from the same family, matched on relevant characteristics, it would be evidence for the effect of family influence. Sibling similarities should be particularly obvious in those attitudes which reflect well-defined variation between families (for example, party and candidate preferences). In areas where the family teaches attitudes shared by the community, the expectation was that siblings would not resemble one another more than they resembled unrelated children of the same grade, sex, social class, and school as their sibling.

Using school records, all the sibling pairs were identified among children tested in two cities of the study. The younger child of each pair was also matched with an unrelated child of the same school, sex, grade, and social status as his older sibling. To avoid confounding age trends with possible dissimilarities based on family teaching, the groups of siblings and random pairs were subdivided into four categories: sibling pairs with small age difference formed one group, those with large age differences another; this was done with the unrelated pairs as well. These groups were also subdivided by social class to control the possible difference in family influence attributable to parents' educational level or other class-related factors.

Similarities among children in the same family are confined to partisanship and related attitudes. Responses of the pairs in these groups were correlated for each of the 113 scaled items. The median coefficient for the total groups of siblings was 0.05, and that for the randomly chosen group was 0.01 (Table 1.1). For the total sibling group, only five correlations of 0.21 or above appeared; the sibling correlation on the item which inquired about feelings concerning Kennedy's election was 0.50.

From the perspective of political socialization, the family's primary effect is to support consensually held attitudes rather than to inculcate idiosyncratic attitudes. The presence of some family effect of a general nature upon atti-

TABLE 1.1 SIBLING RESEMBLANCES IN POLITICAL ATTITUDES

GROUP	NO. OF PAIRS	PROPORTION OF SIGNIFICANT CORRELATIONS[a]
Total sibling pairs	205	12.6
Total randomly matched pairs	205	2.7
Low-status sibling pairs	100	8.9
Low-status randomly matched pairs	100	7.1
High-status sibling pairs	100	12.5
High-status randomly matched pairs	100	5.7
Sibling pairs with small age difference (two grades or less)	135	16.1
Random pairs with small age difference	135	3.6
Sibling pairs with large age difference (more than two grades)	65	10.7
Random pairs with large age difference	65	5.4

[a] Based on 113 items; significance level $p < 0.05$. This analysis was done early in the study and did not include those indices on which later analyses were based.

tudes is indicated by the relatively greater number of sibling correlations that exceeded chance expectations. The number of correlations that appeared between matched unrelated pairs was close to the number expected by chance, over a series of such comparisons. The number of correlations appearing in the sibling pairs, while not large, nevertheless was consistently greater than the number in the unrelated group.

In one area the family does appear to transmit its own attitude. In four of the five groupings, the sibling correlation was 0.48 or above for the item which asked about feelings after learning of Kennedy's election.[2] This sibling similarity supplements other evidence that many children identify with their parents' party. The responses to this item reveal a familial similarity that goes beyond party affiliation to include competitive and emotional involvement with a candidate in a national election. The effect of this commitment on political attitudes is described elsewhere in this chapter. . . .

Interpersonal Transfer and Modeling: The Influence of Family Structure and Power Characteristics

Family Structure   Data concerning the direct effect of family structure upon socialization are limited and will be reported briefly. The testing instrument included an item inquiring about the presence or absence of a father or mother in the home. In very few families was the mother absent, but 12 percent of the children came from homes without fathers. On the hypothesis that attitudes toward authority stem, in part, from experience with paternal authority, children from father-absent homes were compared with children from homes with both parents present. This comparison showed no difference between the two groups that could not be attributed to chance.

Perceptions of the Family   It is apparent from extensive research (summarized by Schaefer, 1961) that two major dimensions order relationships within the family: attachment or support, and power or control. These also form the basic outline of the political relationships presented in this book. A factor analysis of correlations between the scale ratings of family and nonfamily figures was performed. An affect or attachment grouping of items (including "I like him," "He protects me," "He is my favorite") and a grouping of power items (including "Can make anyone do what he wants," "Can punish anyone," and "Makes important decisions") appeared clearly for ratings of the father. These item sets represent the separation of supportive and affective qualities from qualities of power and control. Similar item groupings appeared in the correlations of the scales for the President and the policeman. The child apparently learns to judge family members along these two dimensions of power and affection; he transfers these *dimensions of relationship* into perceptions of his relationships with figures of the larger political system.

Does the child transfer or generalize the content and direction of specific judgments of his father to perceptions of members of the political sys-

---

[2] No item inquiring directly about partisan affiliation was included in these correlations.

tem? Does he relate to the President as he relates to his father? Correlations of the father ratings with ratings of other figures indicate that the father items co-varied among themselves to a much greater extent than they co-varied with perceptions of other figures. This and other evidence (Torney, 1965) support the conclusion that there are essentially two groupings in the child's world: the family figure (father) and all non-family political figures. Although they are judged on the same basic dimensions, non-family political figures are viewed as considerably more similar to each other than they are viewed as similar to family figures.

Comparison of the father items with items for other figures, however, revealed that children who rated their father high also tended to rate non-family figures high. These differences must be interpreted cautiously because of the possibility that some children used the extreme response alternatives excessively. Because there was little difference among children in their attachment to their fathers (between 60 and 70 percent at all grade levels said that their father was their favorite of all), relationships are reported only between perceptions of the father's power and items of political orientation. This dimension was also chosen because there were four sources of information about fathers' power and the home atmosphere: the child's rating of whether his father "can make anyone do what he wants"; perception of who is "Boss in the family"; perception of the amount of interest his family has in current events; and perception of who teaches him most about citizenship.

Children from high-status families see their fathers as more powerful in the family and as more instrumental teachers of citizen attitudes than do lower-status children. The ratings of the father showed pronounced social-class differences; for example, lower-status children rated their fathers lower on ability to make others do what they tell them than upper-status children (Fig. 1.1).[3] This may result from the child's knowledge about his father's occupational role—an awareness that middle- and upper-class jobs carry more prestige and power. Perception of the parents' interest in government also varied by social class (Fig. 1.2). Children from homes of lower and middle social status viewed their parents as less interested in government and current events than did children from higher-status homes. These findings indicate differences in the home atmosphere in different social classes, particularly in the perceived political involvement and interest of the parents and the perception of the father's authority. Children of lower social status also tend to be oriented toward the school (represented by the teacher) as the agent of citizenship training, rather than toward the home (represented by the father; Fig. 1.3). Not only does the lower-class child perceive his father as lower in status (of lower power and less interested in politics), but these children do not regard their fathers as potential sources of information about politics and citizenship.

What other associations do these items show with political behavior

[3] The relatively small number which represents the lower limit of the Range of N in certain figures in this chapter and the next results from two factors: some questions were not administered at grade 3; the correlation between some independent variables meant that some group sizes were reduced. For all graphs, group sizes cluster at top not bottom of reported Range of N.

Figure 1.1 Comparison of Means of Social Status Groups in Rating Coercive Power of Fathers, within IQ and Grade

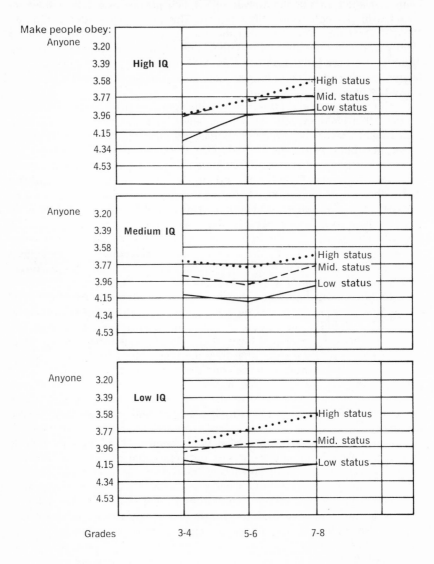

Item: My father can make *anyone* do what he wants.

Index Scale: 1—Anyone
                      6—Almost no one
Range of N:a 55—522
Significance Unit: 0.19

a The lower limit of the Range of N in certain figures results from two factors: some questions were not administered at grade 3; and the low correlation between some independent variables meant that some group sizes were reduced. For all graphs, group sizes cluster at top not bottom of reported Range of N.

Figure 1.2 Comparison of Mean of Social Status Groups in Reported Amount of Parents' Political Interest, within IQ and Grade

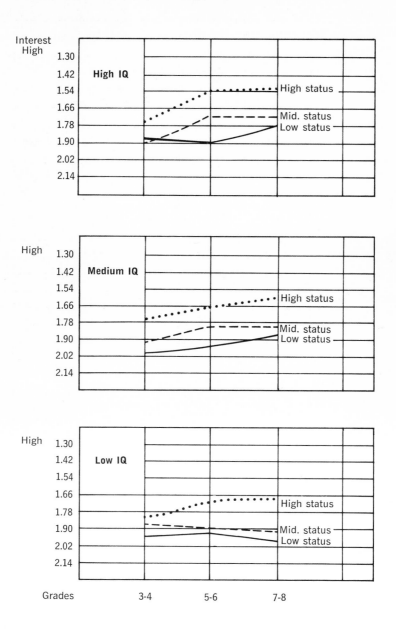

Item: How interested in the government are your parents?

Index Scale: 1—High
            4—Low
Range of N: 54—538
Significance Unit: 0.12

Figure 1.3 Comparison of Means of Social Status Groups in Differentiating Fathers' and Teachers' roles in Citizenship Training, within IQ and Grade

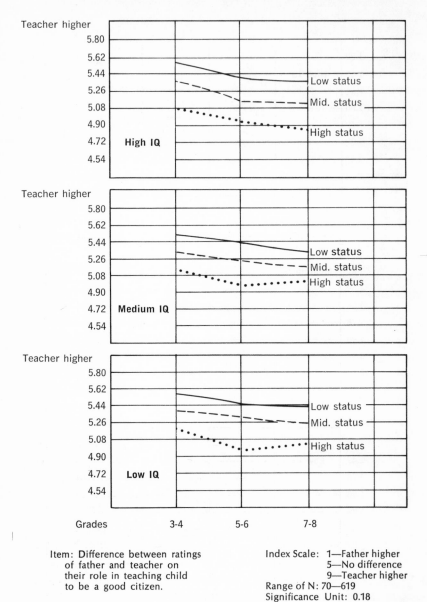

Grades   3-4   5-6   7-8

Item: Difference between ratings of father and teacher on their role in teaching child to be a good citizen.

Index Scale: 1—Father higher
             5—No difference
             9—Teacher higher
Range of N: 70—619
Significance Unit: 0.18

and attitudes? Briefly, the child who has a strong father tends to be more attached to figures and institutions in the political system, particularly the President and the policeman, than the child whose father is relatively weak. A set of items in the area of political participation and involvement also was related to these aspects of family atmosphere. In most cases, these political items also showed some social-class divergencies. The differences in family structure which are characteristic of the various classes may be one of the most important mediators of differences between socioeconomic groups.

Children who see their fathers as powerful tend to be more informed and interested in political maters. The citizen's role as a force in the political system is influenced by adult models within his family. Evidence for this is summarized in Table 1.2. The congruence of these trends, based on three different items used as indicators of family structure, shows that having active and powerful male role models is important in the development of active

TABLE 1.2   RELATION OF FAMILY CHARACTERISTICS TO REPORT OF POLITICAL INVOLVEMENT

	RELATIVE POSITION ON INDICES				
Family Characteristic	Sense of Efficacy	Political Interest	Participation in Political Discussion	Political Activities	Concern about Political Issues
Mother dominant [a]	Lower (in boys only)	Lower (in boys only)	Lower (in boys only)	Lower (in boys only)	Slightly lower (in boys only)
Father low in power [b]	Slightly lower (in both sexes)	Lower (in both sexes)	Lower (in both sexes)	Lower (in both sexes)	Lower (in both sexes)
Family interest low [c]	Lower (in all social classes)	Lower (in all social classes)	Lower (in all social classes)	Lower (in all social classes)	Lower (in all social classes)

[a] Item: Who is the boss in your family?
[b] Item: Think of *your father* as he really is: Can make people do what he wants.
[c] Item: Are your parents interested in current events and what happens in the government?

political involvement (particularly for boys). Having a father who asserts himself in family matters makes children more able to perceive themselves as active in the political world. More information about family perceptions is presented in Figures 1.4 and 1.5. Children who rated their fathers low and family interest low tended to give more "Don't Know" responses. That is, they had acquired fewer political attitudes. Families in which parents are distinctly uninterested in political affairs and where there is no active male figure have children who do not develop political orientations as rapidly as other children.

Cognitive Processes in Political Socialization: Role of the School

Teachers' Evaluation of the Politically Relevant Curriculum   The public school appears to be the most important and effective instrument of political socialization in the United States. It reinforces other community institutions and contributes a cognitive dimension to political involvement. As an

Figure 1.4   Coercive Power of Father and Acquisition of Political Attitudes[a]

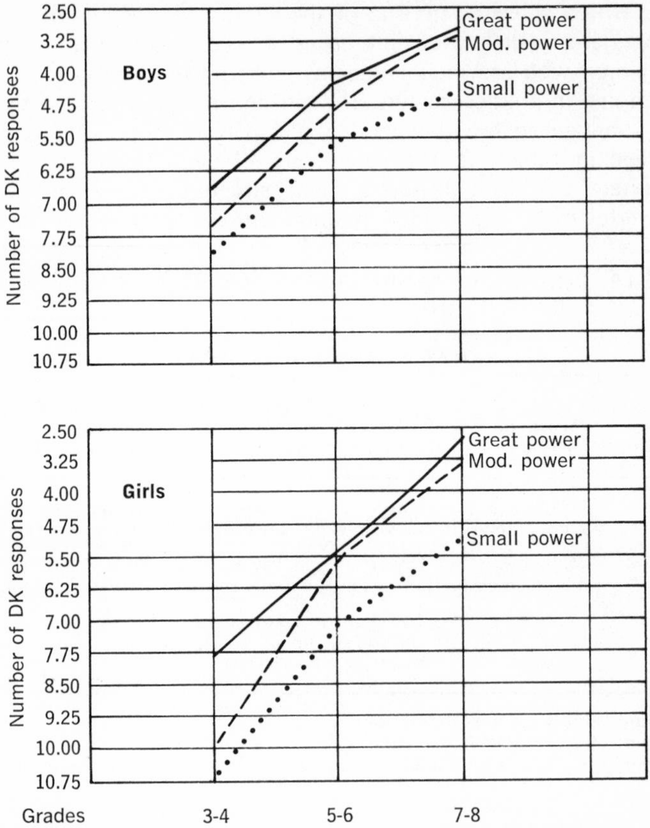

Item: Number of "Don't know"   Index Scale: 0—No DK
      responses to 32 questions   32—High DK
                                       Range of N: 181—565
                                       Significance Unit: 0.77

[a] Comparison (within sex and grade) of mean DK scores of three groups: children who rate their fathers' power as (1) great, (2) moderate, (3) small.

agent of socialization it operates through classroom instruction and cere-monies. It is important, therefore, to assess the impact of the school by an analysis of teachers' views of the civics curriculum and of its effects on the children whom they teach.

Socialization of Loyalty

The schools reinforce the early attachment of the child to the nation. This reinforcement of patriotism is accomplished in a number of ways in the schools in which we tested—displaying the flag, repeating the pledge of

Figure 1.5 Family Interest in Politics—Acquisition of Political Attitudes[a]

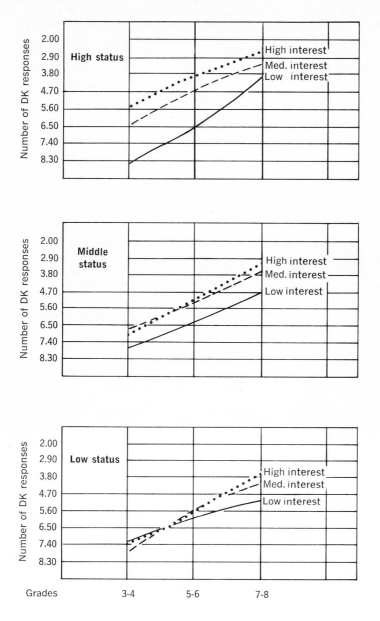

Grades 3-4 5-6 7-8

Item: Number of "Don't know" Index Scale: 0—No DK
responses to 32 items Range of N: 59—495
Significance Unit: 0.90

[a] Comparison (within social status and grade) of mean DK scores of three groups:
children who report their families' interest in politics to be (1) high, (2) medium, (3) low.

allegiance, and singing patriotic songs.[4] In addition, in the majority of class-rooms, pictures of historical figures, such as Washington and Lincoln, and of historic monuments or other symbols and sites of national interest were displayed. Many classrooms also contained a picture of Kennedy. The percentage of teachers who displayed these symbols and utilized these procedures as part of their daily classroom practice is shown in Table 1.3. It is interesting that rituals surrounding the flag and the pledge of allegiance are frequent throughout elementary school, while patriotic songs are less often a daily activity in classrooms for older pupils.

What is the effect of these patriotic rituals upon the young child? A typical first-grader does not understand the meaning of many words in the pledge of allegiance or the "Star-Spangled Banner." The questionnaire responses showed that a number of second-grade children believed the pledge of allegiance was a prayer to God. Whatever the child sees as the purpose of these daily routines, it is clear that they are highly valued by adults. (This is particularly evident whenever any group, such as Jehovah's Witnesses, refuses to pledge to the flag and also in recent incidents of flag burning.) The feeling of respect for the pledge and the national anthem are reinforced daily and are seldom questioned by the child. In addition to this basic tone of awe for government, two other elements are important. The first is the attitude

TABLE 1.3   COMPARISON OF TEACHERS OF EACH GRADE IN THEIR DISPLAY OF NATIONAL SYMBOLS AND PARTICIPATION IN PATRIOTIC RITUALS

GRADE-LEVEL TAUGHT	N	DISPLAY FLAG PERMANENTLY	N	PLEDGE ALLEGIANCE TO FLAG DAILY	N	SING PATRIOTIC SONG DAILY
2	24	100.0%	23	95.7%	24	58.3%
3–4	33	100.0	34	87.9	33	60.6
5–6	40	98.5	40	95.0	40	32.5
7–8	22	100.0	23	86.9	21	14.3

Note.—Items: In my classroom, we display the flag (choose one), (1) Permanently; (2) Only on special occasions; (3) Rarely or not at all. In my classroom, we say the Pledge of Allegiance (sing a patriotic song such as the "Star-Spangled Banner" or "America the Beautiful") (Choose one), (1) Every day; (2) Almost every day; (3) Once in a while; (4) Never.

of submission, respect, and dependence manifested in the gestures and words surrounding these acts, and the second is the group nature of the behavior. These rituals establish an emotional orientation toward country and flag even though an understanding of the meaning of the words and actions has not been developed. These seem to be indoctrinating acts that cue and reinforce feelings of loyalty and patriotism. This early orientation prepares the child for later learning and stresses the importance of loyalty for citizens of all ages.

[4] The analysis of curriculum practices is based on responses from 121 teachers in the cities in which testing was done.

The process of socialization in later years can best be understood in the context of this early establishment of unquestioning patriotism.

Socialization of Orientations toward
Governmental Figures and Institutions

The emphasis which teachers place upon topics other than patriotic observance is indicated in Figure 1.6. The importance assigned to topics dealing with governmental persons (President, mayor, senator) and institutions (Supreme Court, Congress) is of particular interest. Both topics were ascribed more importance by teachers of grades five and six than by teachers of younger children. According to their reports, the stress upon these topics was even greater at grades seven and eight. While teachers placed increasing importance at higher grade levels upon the child's regard for the President, children's personal feelings about the President declined with age, and the

Figure 1.6 Comparison of Teachers of Different Grade-Levels in View that Political Topics Are at Least as Important as Other Subjects Taught in Their Classrooms

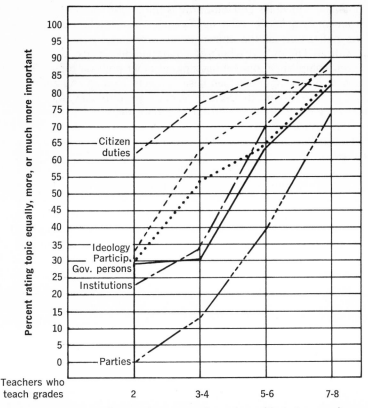

Item: How important are these topics compared to other subjects (e.g., reading, arithmetic)? (1)Much more, (2)more, (3)equal, (4)less, (5)much less.

rated attributes of the President's role increased only slightly. In addition, teachers of grades five through eight attributed approximately equal importance to teaching about the President and the senator, but children at all grade-levels expressed much less respect for the senator than for the President. Also, teachers of all grades viewed persons and institutions as approximately equal in importance as curriculum topics. Again, this did not coincide with children's orientations and attitudes as reported on the questionnaire. In contrast to the teachers' similar assessment of persons and institutions, older children attached greater importance to political institutions and a decreasing importance to persons. This disparity between children's responses and the importance teachers placed upon these subjects may indicate the role that the child's level of development plays in socialization. . . . On another point, there is also some disparity between the young child's interest in political figures and the teachers' relatively low emphasis upon these figures in the curriculum. This suggests that teachers do not recognize these figures as useful aids in teaching about the operation of the political system.

Socialization of Attitudes toward Duties of Citizens

Compliance to Rules and Authority is the Major Focus of Civics Education in Elementary Schools The significance which teachers attach to inculcating the obligations of the citizen is illustrated in Figure 1.6 by the line labeled "Citizen Duties." Teachers of young children place particular stress upon citizen compliance, de-emphasizing all other political topics. The three items rated as more important than basic subjects (reading and arithmetic) by a majority of second- and third-grade teachers were *the law, the policeman,* and the child's *obligation to conform* to school rules and laws of the community. This concern with compliance is characteristic of teachers of all grades and parallels most closely the importance placed upon national symbols at these grades.

The teachers' emphasis on the policeman is different from their treatment in the classroom of other governmental figures (President, senator, mayor) and is concurrent with their presentation of the citizen's duties. Perhaps teachers utilize the policeman to introduce the child to the compliance system. This supports the previous argument that children are initiated into behavior and relationship to a system (in this case, the system of laws) through relationships with personal representatives of that system, in this case, the policeman.

In summary, political socialization at early age levels emphasizes behavior that relates the child emotionally to his country and impresses upon him the necessity for obedience and conformity.

Socialization of Conceptions of Rights and Powers of Citizens

The citizen's right to participate in government is not emphasized in the school curriculum. The importance placed upon the citizen's active participation (his power, right to express opinion, effectiveness, voting) shows a pattern different from the emphasis placed upon attachment to country and compliance to law. The citizen's power to influence government is stressed very little until the fourth grade and is not given equal emphasis with the citizen's duties until the seventh and eighth grades. The role of political parties and partisanship receives less attention in the elementary school than any other topic. Orientation toward parties and politicians was considered less important than academic subjects by all second-grade teachers and by more than 85 percent of third- and fourth-grade teachers. There was a slightly greater emphasis in later grades, but its importance at grades seven and eight was still lower than any other area of political socialization.

The tendency to evade some realities of political life seems to be paralleled by the school's emphasis upon compliance with respect to both itself and the community—although teaching children to obey is certainly an important function of the school. For some children, the combination of complacency and compliance may contribute to political inactivity and the failure to progress from early levels of involvement (attachment to nation) to a more vigilant, assertive involvement in political activities.

The Teacher as a Model for Identification and Imitation   Teachers' evaluations of the importance of various political topics reveal their orientation toward teaching certain materials but do not indicate their own attitudes in these areas. In order to obtain information about the teachers' own orientations, teachers responded to the same questionnaire filled out by the children. This provided a group of adult attitudes against which to compare the children. Particularly in matters dealing with partisan conflict and disagreement, the teacher is obliged to refrain from expressing opinions to students in the classroom. The beliefs of the teacher in other attitude areas may be more readily apparent to the children in her class from direct expression of opinions and from indirect and subtle indications of feelings. The processes of identification and imitation apply to the transmission of political attitudes in the classroom; teachers' opinions play a role in the socialization of children's attitudes, even though evidence on the amount of such attitude transmission is neither readily available nor precise.[5]

The major question to be answered is whether school children come to share their teachers' attitudes before they graduate from the elementary school. These data show both the mean level of teacher responses, and attitude differences between teachers and the total group of eighth-grade children. Indirectly, they show the extent to which political socialization has been

[5] The teacher group which completed the children's questionnaire overlapped with that of teachers who evaluated the importance of various parts of the curriculum. Those completing the attitude questionnaire, however, constituted a larger group and included teachers in a majority of the classrooms where the the questionnaire was administered to children. Although this group did not represent a random sampling of teachers, it was one in which considerable diversity of opinion existed. There was relatively little difference in teachers' viewpoints between the several cities represented, however, except on a small number of topics which have particular regional significance. Other differences could easily be attributed to differences in political party preference. Differences between male and female teachers were relatively small. The most significant reason for using this group, of course, it that these teachers are responsible for teaching the children from whom we have gathered attitudinal data about political objects.

completed by grade eight. Conclusions drawn from these data must be tentative. Teachers, as an occupational group, are not representative of the general population and may be expected to hold dissimilar views in several important respects. Even in those areas of opinion which show the greatest similarity between teacher and pupil, there is no assurance that subsequent changes will not be made by these young people before they reach voting age.

These qualifications expressed, the results of the comparison show that eighth-graders hold attitudes highly similar to teachers on most items in the questionnaire. The magnitude of differences in mean response between eighth-graders and teachers on the rating scales for persons (including the President, policemen, and senators) for example, is very small. . . . In most cases, the difference which does exist is not larger than that existing between any two adjacent grades on the same items. These similarities occurred on the majority of items which expressed the child's attachment to persons, his beliefs about the role qualifications of these persons, and his statements about the power of these people to punish or to exercise control. The orientation of eighth-grade children to governmental figures is very similar to that of their teachers; the socialization accomplished by the school in this area appears to be completed by the eighth grade. The same is true for institutions; that is, attitudes concerning the Supreme Court and the more general conception of "the government" showed more marked similarities than differences between teachers and eighth-grade students.

Conceptions of the government showed somewhat less similarity between teachers and students. . . . One striking difference in response level between grade eight and the teacher group occurred in the choice of Congress or voting as giving the best picture of government, indicating that considerable change occurs in the conception of government between the eighth grade and adulthood. Although teachers have effectively imparted general orientations toward authorities, the greater appropriateness of institutions as symbols of government seems to have been less effectively communicated.

The ideal citizen's role was viewed in a similar fashion by eighth-grade children and teachers. . . . Despite marked age changes across grades, children grow to resemble their teachers in this area. This was especially true for the following qualities of citizens: "obey the laws," "is interested in the country," and "votes." These norms are learned even though children themselves are not necessarily as interested as their teachers, nor do they have the right to vote. Normative statements about the importance of adult party membership also showed similarity between teachers and children.

Teachers are more interested in political affairs and express less absolute trust in the operation of the political system than eighth-graders. A group of items dealing with global aspects of the political system and with parties in particular show marked differences between teachers and eighth-grade children. A number of items indicated greater cynicism on the part of teachers about the political system: considerably *less* tendency to agree that "people who break the law always get caught," that the government is "all for the best" . . . , that people run for political office in order "to keep things as good as they are in the country," and lower rating of the infallibility of government and its representatives. . . . In each of these items, children were more trusting and willing to vouch for the goodness of the system and for the status quo. A second area where student-teacher differences were marked concerned the perception of the influence of pressure groups, lobbies, and certain special interests on legislative processes. . . . Although the mean ratings given to pressure groups (unions, newspapers, churches, etc.) are rank-ordered similarly for teachers and children, teachers consistently assigned these groups more power in affecting legislation than did the children. Teachers attributed somewhat more power to these groups than to "the average citizen," which indicates their greater grasp of the realities of political life. In a third area, teachers tended to ascribe more positive value to conflict or disagreement between the political parties than children, who said that if the political parties disagree about many things it is "very bad" for the country. . . . Teachers, apparently, see the function of disagreement between the parties as promoting instructive dialogue in the political word.

In the sphere of political parties, teachers felt that independence, late choice of political party, and free choice with regard to alignment with parents' political party are ideal. . . . Although the differences in proportions of eighth-graders and teachers choosing these alternatives were marked, eighth-grade children tended to agree that independence is desirable and that one should vote for the best man rather for the political party. Forty-three percent of teachers felt that children should postpone choice of political party until after attainment of voting age; eighth-graders did not agree, only 25 percent endorsing this alternative. The figures on alignment with parents' political parties indicate that while a majority of teachers felt that students should not be committed to choosing their parents' party, eighth-graders did not agree. . . . There is considerable evidence that similarity in party commitment between parents and children is very great. It is conceivable that parents consciously or unconsciously attempt to socialize their children into partisanship, but that this is counteracted by teachers' socialization of independence.

In the area of political activities, teachers showed much more interest, more participation in political discussion, and demonstrated a more pronounced tendency to take sides on issues than did eighth-graders. . . . This is in contrast to two other indices of overt activity—sense of efficacy, and specific political activities—which showed very few differences between eighth-graders and teachers. . . . Specific factors in the indices themselves may account for this. The political activities inquired about did not include voting. Other types of activity—reading about current events, wearing buttons for candidates, and passing out literature—may reach a peak by the eighth grade. . . .

A listing of items on which teachers and eighth-graders are in relatively close agreement and of those where they are not would show that clear dissimilarity appears on few items. This result calls for an explanation of two features of the data—the meaning of this high degree of similarity and the significance to be attached to those topics on which disagreement is clear.

The extent of congruence in responses supports the conclusion that the school is a powerful socializing agent in the area of citizenship and political behavior. It also provides evidence that much of the basic socialization of political attitudes has taken place before the end of the elementary school years. While there is no doubt that attitudes and behavior change in some ways in the years following the eighth grade, from these data it may be argued that many of the basic orientations are established in the pre-high school years.

What of the areas in which this seems not to be true? Presumably not all of the sectors in which teachers and eighth-graders differ were tapped by this questionnaire. Within the attitude areas covered by this project, however, the dissimilarities may represent testing problems (items that may have been interpreted differently by teachers than by children), areas in which the school has less effect as a socializing agent, or behavior that shows great differences between adult and child levels. Where dissimilarities occur, there is likely to be specific participation by socializing agents and institutions of the community other than the school.

One of the items where teachers and eighth-graders are dissimilar can probably be explained on the ground of response appropriateness. The item dealing with the punitive power of authority figures, asking whether they could "punish anyone," may evoke a different interpretation of the word punish from the two groups. Teachers also have a different frame of reference concerning the prerogatives of authority figures to punish and may give answers affected by their own professional training and constraints upon their punishment of children. This is the only item where a case can be made for differences in the interpretation of an item.

The other items where teacher–eighth-grader dissimilarity is greatest fall into three areas: (1) trust vs. cynicism concerning the government; (2) interest in political affairs; (3) value placed upon affiliation with a political party. With respect to general values about partisanship and the specific choice of a party, it has already been established that this area of attitude is influenced strongly by family membership—one of the few political topics, although an important one, on which families seem to exert considerable influence. Differences in reported interest in public affairs and participation in political discussion are probably genuine differences between adults and children. However, the teachers as a group show relatively high interest when compared with other adults. Perhaps the children of the study are not greatly different from the general adult population of their social class and community. The items dealing with trust in government may represent another true adult-child difference. Teachers express considerable trust in the government, but not at the high level of these children; in addition to reflecting the realistic experience with government which adults have, this may also reflect the extreme wording of some of the questions on this topic. Persons of high education tend to avoid agreeing with extreme statements. This tendency was also apparent in the high status, highly intelligent group of children in this study, who appeared more like the teachers than did other groups.

2

The Child's Image
of Government*

DAVID EASTON
JACK DENNIS

Political socialization refers to the way in which a society transmits political orientations—knowledge, attitudes or norms, and values—from generation to generation. Without such socialization across the generations, each new member of the system, whether a child newly born into it or an immigrant newly arrived, would have to seek an entirely fresh adjustment in the political sphere. But for the fact that each new generation is able to learn a body of political orientations from its predecessors, no given political system would be able to persist. Fundamentally, the theoretical significance of the study of socializing processes in political life resides in its contribution to our understanding of the way in which political systems are able to persist,[1] even as they change, for more than one generation.

THE THEORETICAL SETTING

A society transmits many political orientations across the generations, from the most trivial to the most profound. One of the major tasks of research is to formulate criteria by which we may distinguish the significant from the

* Reprinted by permission from *The Annals of the American Academy of Political and Social Science*, 361 (September 1965), pp. 40–57.

[1] For the idea that persistence includes change, see D. Easton, *A Framework for Political Analysis* (Englewood Cliffs, N.J.: Prentice-Hall, 1965) and *A Systems Analysis of Political Life* (New York: John Wiley & Sons, 1965).

less important. Once we posit the relationship between socialization and system persistence, this compels us to recognize that among many theoretical issues thereby raised, a critical one pertains to the way in which a society manages or fails to arouse support for any political system, generation after generation. In part, it may, of course, rely on force or perception of self-interest. But no political system has been able to persist on these bases alone. In all cases, as children in society mature, they learn through a series of complicated processes to address themselves more or less favorably to the existence of some kind of political life.

But socialization of support for a political system is far too undifferentiated a concept for fruitful analysis. As has been shown elsewhere,[2] it is helpful to view the major objects towards which support might be directed, as the political community, the regime, and the authorities (or loosely, the government). The general assumption is that failure to arouse sufficient support for any one of these objects in a political system must lead to its complete extinction.

This paper seeks to illuminate one of the numerous ways in which the processes of socialization in a single political system, that of the United States, manages to generate support for limited aspects of two political objects: the regime and the government (authorities). Ultimately, comparable studies in other systems should enable us to generalize about the processes through which members learn to become attached to or disillusioned with all the basic objects of a system.

Within this broad theoretical context our specific problems for this paper can be simply stated: How does each generation born into the American political system come to accept (or reject) the authorities and regime? As the child matures from infancy, at what stage does he begin to acquire the political knowledge and attitudes related to this question? Do important changes take place even during childhood, a time when folklore has it that a person is innocent of things political? If so, can these changes be described in a systematic way?

GOVERNMENT AS A LINKAGE POINT

In turning to the political socialization of the child, we are confronted with a fortunate situation. The area that the theoretical considerations of a systems analysis dictate as central and prior—that of the bond between each generation of children and such political objects as the authorities and regime—happens to coincide with what research reveals as part of the very earliest experiences of the child. As it turns out empirically, children just do not develop an attachment to their political system, in the United States, in some random and unpatterned way. Rather, there is evidence to suggest that the persistence of this system hinges in some degree on the presence of some readily identifiable points of contact between the child and the system. From

[2] See Easton, *A Framework for Political Analysis* and *A Systems Analysis of Political Life.*

this we have been led to generalize that in one way or another every system will have to offer its maturing members objects that they can initially identify as symbolic or representative of the system and toward which they feel able to develop sentiments and attitudes deemed appropriate in the system. If a system is to persist, it will probably have to provide each new age cohort with some readily identifiable points of contact with the system. But for this, it would scarcely be likely that children could relate in any meaningful way to the various basic objects in a system.

In this respect our point of departure diverges markedly from the few past studies in the area of political socialization. In these it has been customary to take for granted the object towards which the child does, in fact, become socialized. Thus, following the pattern of adult studies, efforts have been made to discover how the child acquires his party identification, his attitudes towards specific issues, or his general political orientations on a liberal-conservative or left-right axis. But such research has adopted as an assumption what we choose to consider problematic. How, in fact, does a child establish contact with the broad and amorphous political world in which he must later take his place as an adult? What kind of political objects do, in fact, first cross his political horizon? Which of these does he first cathect?

For the American democratic system, preliminary interviewing led us to conclude that there are two kinds of initial points of contact between the child and the political system in its broadest sense. One of these is quite specific. The child shows a capacity, with increasing age, to identify and hold opinions about such well-defined and concrete units among the political authorities as the President, policeman, Congress, and Supreme Court. But we also found that simultaneously another and much more general and amorphous point of contact is available. This consists of the conglomeration of institutions, practices, and outcomes that adults generically symbolize in the concept "government." Through the idea of government itself the child seems able to reach out and at a very early age to establish contact both with the authorities and with certain aspects of the regime. In a mass society where the personnel among the authorities changes and often remains obscure for the average person, the utility of so generalized and ill-defined a term as "the government" can be readily appreciated. The very richness and variability of its meaning converts it into a useful point of contact between the child and the system.

But the discovery of the idea of "government" as an empirically interesting point of reference for the child brings with it numerous complications for purposes of research. In the first place, any awareness of government as a whole is complicated by the necessary diffuseness of the idea; it applies to a broad and relatively undifferentiated spectrum of disparate events, people, structures, and processes. Government speaks with a cacophony of voices. It takes innumerable actions both large and small, visible and virtually invisible; and these locate themselves at the national as well as the local level, with many strata in between. Furthermore, the usual child is not likely to place *res publica* very high among his daily concerns.

Thus, the child's marginal interest in things political combined with the complexities of the object itself discourages a clear perception of the over-all nature of government. This enormously complicates the task of isolating the specific image and attitudes that children do acquire. However, the points of contact between maturing members of the system and its basic parts are not so numerous that we could allow these obvious difficulties to discourage a serious effort to explore the nature of this connection and the part it may play in the growth of supportive or negative attitudes towards the authorities and regime.

OUR DATA

The children whom we have surveyed concerning what they think and feel about government, as well as about a number of other political orienta-tions (which we will report elsewhere), are for the most part children in large metropolitan areas of the United States. They are, with few exceptions, White, public school children, in grades two through eight, and were selected from both middle-class and working-class neighborhoods. We have con-ducted many individual interviews and administered a series of pencil-and-paper questionnaires. The latter we read out to the children in their regular classrooms while they individually marked their answers.

The data to be reported below are some fairly uncomplicated examples of these responses; we use them to illustrate the kinds of developments of greatest interest about orientations towards "the government." In some we are attempting to discern the pattern of cognitive development about govern-ment as a whole; in others there is some mixture of cognitive and affective elements; and in a third type, the affective or supportive aspects dominate.

PREVIEW OF FINDINGS

The findings which grew out of this analysis will, perhaps, surprise those readers who are accustomed to think of children as innocent of politi-cal thought. For not only does the child quite early begin to orient himself to the rather remote and mystical world of politics, but he even forms notions about its most abstract parts—such as government in general. Our data at least suggest this. The political marks on the *tabula rasa* are entered early and are continually refurbished thereafter.

We will, perhaps, disappoint as well those readers who are accustomed to think of the American as one who is brought up on the raw meat of rug-ged individualism, which supposedly nourishes our national frame. We find that the small child sees a vision of holiness when he chances to glance in the direction of government—a sanctity and rightness of the demigoddess who dispenses the milk of human kindness. The government protects us, helps us, is good, and cares for us when we are in need, answers the child.

When the child emerges from his state of nature, therefore, he finds himself a part of a going political concern which he ordinarily adopts imme-diately as a source of nurturance and protection. His early experience of gov-

TABLE 2.1   DEVELOPMENT OF A SENSE OF CONFIDENCE IN UNDERSTANDING
THE CONCEPT OF GOVERNMENT (RESPONSES OF CHILDREN BY
GRADE LEVEL)[a]

GRADE	PERCENT	N
2	27.29	1655
3	19.01	1678
4	17.61	1749
5	11.15	1803
6	12.41	1749
7	8.36	1723
8	9.79	1695

[a] The questionnaire which contained this item was administered to a purposively selected group of 12,052 white, public school children in regular classrooms in eight large metropolitan areas (100,000 and over) in four major geographic regions (South, Northeast, Midwest, and Far West) in late 1961 and early 1962. The children were in grades two through eight and from both middle- and working-class areas. We will refer to this questionnaire hereinafter as simply "CA–9," which is our code name for Citizenship Attitude Questionnaire #9.

ernment is, therefore, analogous to his early experience of the family in that it involves an initial context of highly acceptable dependency. Against this strongly positive affective background the child devises and revises his cognitive image of government. Let us first turn to some empirical evidence bearing upon this cognition.

THE CHILD'S EARLY RECOGNITION OF GOVERNMENT

In earlier studies of the child's growing awareness of political objects and relationships, it was found that the President of the United States and the policeman were among the first figures of political authority that the child recognized.[3] In part, at least, we would expect that attitudes towards political authority would begin to take shape in relationship to these objects. They are clearly the first contact points in the child's perception of wider external authority. In general, data collected since the early exploratory studies have supported these findings, as will be reported in later publications.

We can, however, now raise a question which takes us beyond these findings. Does the child also establish some early perceptual contact with the more amorphous, intangible abstraction of government itself, that is, with the more general category of political authority among whose instances are counted presidents and policemen? Is the child's cognitive development such that he is likely to work immediately from a few instances to the general class of objects? This would then put him in a position to apply his concept to new instances, as well as to refurbish it as the experiences of its in-

[3] David Easton, with R. D. Hess, "The Child's Changing Image of the President," 24 *Public Opinion Quarterly*, pp. 632–644; "Youth and the Political Systems," *Culture and Social Character*, ed. S. M. Lipset and L. Lowenthal (New York: Free Press, 1961); and "The Child's Political World," 6 *Midwest Journal of Political Science* (1962), pp. 229–246.

stances grow. If this is so, we can anticipate that, in addition to such points of contact as the policeman and the President, in the American political system the child will also be able to orient himself to political life through perceptions of and attitudes towards the more generalized and diffuse object that we call "the government."

The Crystallization of the Concept

When do our respondents first begin to recognize the general category of things labeled "government"? One simple way of exploring this is to see whether the child himself thinks he knows what the word "government" means, even if no verbalization of his understanding is called for. On this simple test we would contend that even the seven- or eight-year-old child is likely to feel that he has attained some rudimentary grasp of this general concept. This test is met in a question we asked on our final questionnaire which read as follows: "Some of you may not be sure what the word *government* means. If you are not sure what government means, put an X in the box below." The changing pattern of response to this question over the grades is shown in Table 2.1.

What we find from these simple data is that 27 percent of the second-grade children feel some uncertainty about the concept. This proportion declines rather regularly over the grades, however, so that for the eighth-grade children, less than 10 percent express this uncertainty. In general, these data suggest that a considerable portion of the youngest children had already crystalized some concept of government prior to our testing, and with each higher grade level the likelihood that they had not formed some concept decreases. With these data—and similar data from other protocols—as a background, it is plausible for us to proceed to a more detailed consideration of the content of the child's understanding of government.

Symbolic Associations of the Concept "Government"

Since it appears that the child is rather likely to develop some working conception of government in these early years, we can move on to ask: Is there any specific content to this concept, especially of a kind that is political in character? We might well expect that because of the inherent ambiguity and generality of the term, even for adults, considerable differences and disjunctiveness would characterize this concept for aggregates of children. Our findings do, in part, support this expectation. Yet there are clear patterns of "dominance" in these collective conceptions, and these patterns vary to a large degree with the age and grade level of the children.

One way we have devised for getting fairly directly at which patterns are dominant in this period and at how these patterns change involves a pictorial presentation of ten symbols of government. These are symbols which appeared strongly in our extensive pretest data when children were asked either to define government or to "free associate" with a list of words, one of which was government.

What we asked in our final instrument was the following: "Here are

TABLE 2.2 DEVELOPMENT OF A COGNITIVE IMAGE OF GOVERNMENT: SYM-
BOLIC ASSOCIATIONS (PERCENT OF CHILDREN AND TEACHERS
RESPONDING)[a]

| | GRADE | | | | | | | |
	2	3	4	5	6	7	8	Teachers
Policeman	8.15	4.09	5.74	2.74	2.36	3.03	1.66	1.00
George Washington	39.47	26.77	14.19	6.93	4.94	3.44	1.72	1.00
Uncle Sam	15.63	19.01	18.02	19.40	16.78	18.26	16.40	5.00
Voting	4.32	8.36	10.83	19.23	27.99	39.44	46.77	72.00
Supreme Court	4.51	6.38	10.25	16.77	16.84	13.54	15.87	13.00
Capitol	13.65	16.13	16.57	11.57	9.94	9.39	6.93	5.00
Congress	5.93	12.94	28.97	49.08	49.66	44.22	49.14	71.00
Flag	15.75	16.49	13.33	11.57	11.38	12.84	11.78	6.00
Statue of Liberty	12.11	14.26	12.92	11.18	17.07	18.61	19.60	8.00
President Kennedy	46.26	46.81	37.25	38.51	30.52	27.89	22.91	15.00
I Don't Know	15.69	12.94	13.15	4.86	4.66	2.98	1.54	1.00
N Responding	1619	1662	1726	1789	1740	1714	1689	390
N Not Responding	36	16	23	14	9	9	6	1

[a] (1) Percentages should add to 200 due to the two-answer format, but do not, because of the failure of some children to make two choices. This is especially the case for
those answering "I don't know." (2) 113 children failed to respond to this question. Thus
the N at each grade are those responding and the percentages are of that number. (3) We
have added, at the right, the responses of the teachers of these children, for the sake of
comparison. The teachers were given a similar questionnaire at the time of administration
of the children's questionnaire.

some pictures that show what our government is. Pick the two pictures that
show best what our government is." This instruction was then followed for
the balance of the page by ten pictures plus a blank box for "I don't know."
Each of the ten pictures represented a salient symbol of the United States
government and was accompanied by its printed title underneath the picture.
The options in order were: (1) Policeman; (2) George Washington; (3) Uncle
Sam; (4) Voting; (5) Supreme Court; (6) Capitol; (7) Congress; (8) Flag; (9)
Statue of Liberty; (10) President (Kennedy); (11) I Don't Know. The pattern of
response to these ten symbols of government is shown in Table 2.2.

Several interesting facts emerge from this table. If we take 20 percent
as a rough guide to what we might expect purely by chance as a maximum
level of response to each of the ten symbol options (for two-answer format),
we see that only four of these pictures were chosen with a frequency greater
than chance. These four are George Washington, Voting, Congress, and
President Kennedy. These four are considerably more dominant than any of
the others, but this dominance varies by grade level. For the youngest children, the two most popular options are the two Presidents, Washington and
Kennedy. But these choices drop in the later grades. In Figure 2.1, the developmental curves for the four dominant options are plotted over the grade
span in order to interpret more easily the major changes that are taking place.

It would appear that, in terms of these symbols, the youngest child's
perception of government is quite likely to be framed by the few personal
figures of high governmental authority that cross his cognitive horizon, probably both in the school (where the portraits of presidents are often promi-

Figure 2.1 Development of a Cognitive Image of Government: The Four Dominant Symbolic Associations (the Number of Children Responding at Each Grade Level Varies from 1619 to 1789)

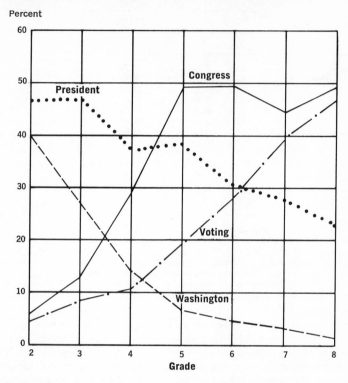

nently displayed) and outside. The young child focuses most directly upon personal or perhaps "charismatic" aspects of political authority for his interpretation of what government is. But as he moves into the middle years, there is a greater likelihood that his attention will be turned to rather different, prominent aspects of the authorities.

First, he revises his notions to include the Congress and drops George Washington—who suffers a precipitous decline after his initial showing. Undoubtedly, the growing adoption of Congress reflects an awareness of several things, and these are supported by various other data. First, the older children become more aware of the group character of government rather than simply identifying it with single persons. Second, the more frequent choice of Congress probably also reflects a greater awareness of governmental institutions—particularly the ongoing organizations engaged in *law-making* (as suggested undoubtedly in the beginning social studies, history, or civics texts). Children move, in a sense, from a very personalized conception of governmental authority to one better characterized as "legal-rational," institutionalized, or impersonal political authority, to continue the Weberian parallel.

Third, children appear to reflect a greater awareness of the representative character of these institutions. Impersonalization of authority is coincident with some growth in the recognition of regime norms, in this case of the rules of behavior that contribute to representation. This conclusion is borne out to some degree by the third marked shift which occurs—that concerning the older child's greater tendency to pick "voting" as the best picture of our government. Thus, by grade eight nearly half the children choose voting. This suggests some beginning awareness of the regime rules associated with popular democracy and the role of ordinary people in it.

The child's conception of government is, therefore, brought in stages from far to near, from one small set of persons to many people, from a personalistic to an impersonalized form of authority, and toward an awareness of the institutionalization in our system of such regime norms as are embodied in the idea of a representative, popular democracy. There are obviously a number of further tests we would wish to make on these hypotheses. We would also wish to keep in mind that by no means all of these children appear to be going through these stages of cognitive development. But the patterns which emerge seem to us at least very striking, and they are supported in various ways from our other data.[4]

Generally, therefore, in these data about the cognitive development of this rather abstract category of the individual's political thought, we detect more than a mere glimmering of a concept. Furthermore, the emergent conception in this instance seemingly reflects some fairly wide and regularly changing comprehension for aggregates of children.

This suggests that considerable societal efforts are probably being made to transmit a concept deemed appropriate in the American political system. If we compare children with their teachers, for example, we find that the latter most roundly endorse the two options dominant for the eighth-grade children. The proportions are even higher for the teachers, however, so that in terms of the statistical norms, they stand perhaps closer to the end-state suggested by the direction of movement of the children. Thus the teachers—who are highly salient agents of the child's political and general conceptual development—have a concept that is quite in line with the child's apparent maturational tendencies. One could hypothesize, therefore, that a part of society's efforts to inform the child is reflected in the teacher's responses.

The Concept of Government and the Law-Making Function

A supporting piece of evidence which is connected to the above, but supplements it from the standpoint of governmental functions (rather than from the structural aspects of the concept alone), has to do with the child's changing awareness of the chief law-makers in our system of government. One thing we find is the fact that, of the various kinds of political or other functions that the child most readily associates with government, the making of laws is very prominent. That is, when the child is asked, "What does the government do?" he is quite likely to answer that he, it, or they make the laws.

A questionnaire item that we presented in this connection reads as follows: "Who makes the laws? Put an X next to the *one* who does the most to

---

[4] Some of these supporting data will be presented below; other kinds of data will be shown in other publications.

make the laws." The options were: (1) Congress, (2) President, (3) Supreme Court, (4) I Don't Know. The same pictures as before were used. In Table 2.3 we see the patterns of change over the grade span for this aspect of the child's understanding.

Here the President's early dominance is apparent, but Congress gradually supplants him by grade five. Thus, by the middle grades the child is both increasingly prone to identify Congress as the chief source of lawmaking as well as a more representative symbol of our government than the President.

If this trend should continue into adulthood, we would expect great support for Congress as the primary institution of government vis-à-vis the

TABLE 2.3   DEVELOPMENT OF AN AWARENESS OF THE CHIEF LAW-MAKER (PERCENT OF CHILDREN AND TEACHERS RESPONDING)[a]

GRADE	CONGRESS	PRESIDENT	SUPREME COURT	I DON'T KNOW	N RESPONDING	N NOT RESPONDING
2	4.79	75.55	11.49	8.17	1627	28
3	11.41	66.14	16.93	5.52	1648	30
4	27.51	44.11	21.07	7.31	1723	26
5	57.39	19.35	19.85	3.40	1793	10
6	65.06	13.25	18.30	3.38	1743	6
7	72.14	8.88	16.41	2.57	1712	11
8	85.33	5.44	7.87	1.36	1690	5
Teachers	96.00	1.00	3.00	0.00	1339	5

[a] CA-9, item 33.

President. We would expect that, of the opposing observations of Max Lerner and Robert Lane, for example, those of Lane would be given support. Lerner observed (as cited by Lane) that "when the American thinks of his government, he thinks first of the President as its symbol."[5] If "first" means while he is a second or third grader, then Lerner is correct. But this does not appear to be the sense in which he is using the word.

In light of the developmental trends we see in our data, our respondents seem to resemble more closely the "common men" in Lane's Eastport study. Lane found that his respondents were more likely to perceive government in terms of its legislative functions than its administrative or judicial ones.[6] As far as the common men in Eastport were concerned, Congress was the most important focus of their concept of government. Lane also found that government (and Congress) are thought of in terms of their products, namely, the laws they make.[7] His subjects consider government and Congress as benign, helpful, and responsive—an organization "working for the people, not merely restraining them."[8]

[5] Max Lerner, *America as a Civilization* (New York: Simon and Schuster, 1957), p. 377.

[6] Robert Lane, *Political Idealogy* (New York: Free Press, 1962), p. 146.

[7] Lane, pp. 147–148.

[8] Lane, pp. 145, 149.

All of these findings converge with our data as far as the developmental trends are concerned. The oldest children in our test group are those who most resemble the common men of Eastport. One can therefore interpret what we find as an indication that this image of government is one not confined to the period of Lane's study but seems to have more general application. Our respondents tend over the grades toward the adoption of a vision of government which puts great emphasis upon Congress as the center of government, upon law as its most visible product, and upon benign, helpful, protective, and responsive qualities as those most appropriately describing its manner of operation. The latter, more affective image will be discussed shortly after we present some further findings concerning cognitive development.

Differentiation of the Public Sector

Even though the children tested assert a growing awareness of government as an idea and object, are they, in fact, able to distinguish it as a sphere separate from other areas of social life? If attitudes towards the authorities as an object are to have relevance for later ties to the system, we need some evidence indicating that even in their earliest years children are, in fact, able to recognize some minimal difference between that which is governmental and that which is not. Only under such conditions could we infer that attitudes towards government—to which we shall turn in a moment—refer to distinctively political bonds.

To discover whether the child's declared knowledge of what government means includes a capacity to discriminate governmental from nongovernmental objects, we chose to test his awareness of the difference between what we normally view as the public and private sectors of life. A variety of contexts could be used to test for this differentiation—activities of various kinds, organizations, symbols, or personnel. We have chosen for our test the last because we found that the formulation, "people who do various jobs to help the community," is a rather familiar context for the child who has been exposed to the beginning social studies texts. The child learns that a variety of "community helpers" exist, ranging from doctors and nurses to firemen and street sweepers.

What we asked was very simple. Taking various occupations—milkman, policeman, soldier, judge, postman, and teacher—we said: "Here are some people. Which ones work for the government?" Then followed six questions with an appropriate picture for each such as: "Does the MILKMAN work for the government?" The options were: (1) Yes. (2) No. What we found is shown in Table 2.4.

Only the first of these people was considered by us to be clearly outside the governmental system as determined by his occupation.[9] Of the rest two were more directly local government workers—the policeman and the teacher; two were clearly national government workers—the soldier and

[9] Pretesting had indicated that "the milkman" was as good an indicator as numerous other private roles.

TABLE 2.4   DEVELOPMENT OF AN AWARENESS OF THE PUBLIC AND PRIVATE
SECTORS (PERCENT OF CHILDREN AND TEACHERS REPONDING)[a]

GRADE	MILK-MAN	POLICE-MAN	SOLDIER	JUDGE	POST-MAN	TEACHER	N RESPONDING (VARIES BY ITEM)
2	29.12	86.04	68.33	86.42	56.87	48.01	1601–1626
3	30.77	89.11	79.16	88.35	62.74	54.95	1627–1656
4	28.03	90.98	83.17	88.70	71.35	58.29	1702–1730
5	20.54	88.99	90.18	90.45	80.02	62.65	1778–1792
6	16.24	87.84	93.28	91.70	85.53	64.48	1730–1747
7	12.85	82.47	95.52	94.16	89.02	64.03	1697–1718
8	8.38	80.95	98.11	93.72	93.20	59.31	1681–1692
Teachers	1.00	77.00	100.00	91.00	99.00	45.00	330–341

[a] CA-9, items 49–54.

the postman; and one was indeterminate as among levels—the judge.

Several things are apparent from the table. Of these workers, the milk-man is the one (as we would expect) who is least often identified as a member of the public sector. Around 70 percent of the youngest children were able to make an accurate assessment of his nongovernmental status. From grade four on, this proportion steadily increased so that by grade eight, less than 10 percent were in error.

For the rest, the policeman and the judge are most easily recognized as belonging in the governmental system by the youngest children. Then come the soldier, postman, and teacher in that order. Both the soldier and the postman—the more nearly exclusively national government workers—increase in the proportions of children endorsing them at successively higher grade levels, until, by grade eight, they are the ones who, with the judge, get the greatest governmental identification.

The teacher, on the other hand, does not really make any major gains over the grades, but remains somewhat ambiguous with respect to her governmental status. And this effect holds for the teacher respondents as well. Somehow the status of the teacher is a more complex one.

That something else is probably at work is seen when we compare with the others the perception over the grades of the teacher and the policeman—both local-governmental status. Both, over the grades, suffer some net decline in the proportions of children endorsing their governmental status while the other government workers show gains. Possibly the older child is more likely to direct his attention to the national level for his image of government, and, therefore, his differentiation is conflicted for local government workers. This would fit, at least, other somewhat similar findings about the child's greater awareness of the national than of the lower levels of government.[10] It also explains the markedly lower percentage of teachers who identify policemen and teachers as working for the government.

In general, the child in his elementary years attains the capacity to differentiate the governmental system of behavior from nongovernmental systems. This does not mean that he is able to do so in every conceivable way. Our data suggest only that he is increasingly able to do this for the

[10] See Fred Greenstein, *Children and Politics* (New Haven: Yale University Press, 1965), pp. 60–61.

personnel of government. His concept of government, therefore, does become a differentiated one, at least in these terms. Again, this suggests a development beyond that of only a rudimentary grasp of this complex object in these early years of political awareness.

There is thus sufficient content in the child's perception of government for us to have some confidence that when we now come to talk about his attitudes toward this object, it will reflect affect towards a genuinely political (that is, public) authority. It will also prove significant for our interpretation that there is even a tendency to think of government at the national rather than at the local level.

Summary of Findings on the Child's
Developing Cognitive Image of Government

As a possible object toward which affect might be directed, the idea of government undergoes far-reaching changes in the cognitive development of the child as represented in our test group. As he passes through grades two to eight, he begins with a rudimentary notion in which government is personal in character, represented by a few high-ranking and visible leaders. But as he grows older, the child sees government in less personal terms. He becomes increasingly aware of its group character and its major institutions; he learns something about the norms (voting) of a representative and popular democracy. In addition, it is crucial that the child proves increasingly able to identify government as something that is different from the private sector of life, however the latter may be defined in different epochs of society. All of these things suggest that, aside from any feelings that may be associated with government, the efforts by society to convey an adequate representation of this abstract object are by no means in vain.

THE CHILD'S AFFECTIVE RESPONSE TO GOVERNMENT

Although analytically we are able to separate the cognitive aspects of the image of government from accompanying feelings towards it, empirically they go hand in hand. For an understanding of the way in which the American political system stimulates diffuse support for the political authorities, it is critical to appreciate the fact that from the very beginning of his awareness—at its conceptually most rudimentary stage—the child interprets government as something provided to further his welfare and that of the people around him. The benevolent, protective, helpful, and otherwise good qualities of government constitute the first and continuing overall context of evaluation. Even at the end of this period—when the child is thirteen or fourteen years of age, and government and individual authorities, such as the President and the policeman, are beginning to be seen more realistically and less ideally—the child still regards them as great blessings, if slightly mixed ones.

The child thus continues to endorse government even though what he understands it to be is changing. Having started off his evaluation in highly positive terms, he seems reluctant to give it up. In this we see, perhaps, the early formation of a bond that is hard to loosen. It is a bond that entails future diffuse support for the governmental system.[11]

[11] For the concept "diffuse support," see D. Easton, *A Systems Analysis of Political Life.*

The Child's Approval of Government's Role

In our pilot data, we found such a uniformly favorable affective image of government, from the earliest grades onward, that we felt no special large-scale effort was necessary to deal with this in our final instrument. Yet we do have some data from our eight cities which bear upon the question. First, however, we shall present a few examples of our considerable body of pilot data in order to show how highly consensual our young children's approval of government is over the whole grade range.

In an instrument administered to children in the Chicago area, we proposed that the children either agree or disagree with statements such as these:

1. The government is getting too big for America
2. The government meddles too much in our private lives.
3. The government has too much power.
4. The United States government usually knows what is best for the people.
5. The government ought to give money and food to people out of work.
6. The government should have more power over the people.[12]

We attempted as far as possible to retain the original wording of statements of children in our pretest interviews—but reversing the items in several cases. The patterns of response to these statements are shown in Table 2.5.

What we see is that children at all of these grade levels roundly approve of government. They reject, at a fairly high level of agreement (75 percent or more), the first three statements about the scope of government becoming too large. Statements four and five, on the other hand, reflect approval of the role of government in guiding and caring for the people, and these statements elicit a high level of agreement. Only for the last statement do we see any impetus toward restricting the role of government; that is, the children like it the way it is.

The overall response is one which is better characterized as collectivist endorsement than individualistic disapproval of government. In spite of the great myth of rugged individualism which is supposed to pervade the American consciousness, these children, at least, seem to be inclined toward the opposite kind of feeling about government. Thus the child begins as something of a natural collectivist, and whatever individualistic tendencies he may exhibit are developed later on.

The sixth item suggests, moreover, that the child is likely to be a "conservative collectivist" in that he is not much in favor of extending the scope of government beyond its present limits. He is rather happy with government as it stands and would not give it "more power over the people." Thus, the child's early contentment with government is fairly complete, and it is one which exhibits the characteristics of a high acceptance of government as a given, necessary part of the natural environment. If the child is to develop discontent and a desire for change, it is undoubtedly yet to be learned. It thus will be overlaid upon an early base of high regard for the government.

---

[12] These questions are from our pilot questionnaire "In My Opinion—# III," items 50, 125, 169, 170, and 151, respectively.

TABLE 2.5 ATTITUDES TOWARD THE ROLE OF GOVERNMENT

| | 1 | | 2 | | 3 | | 4 | | 5 | | 6 | |
| | "The government is getting too big for America." | | "The government meddles too much in our private lives." | | "The government has too much power." | | "The government usually knows what is best for the people." | | "The government ought to give money and food to people out of work." | | "The government should have more power over the people." | |
Grade	% Agree	N	% Agree	N	% Agree	N	% Agree	N	% Agree	N	% Agree	N
3	16	113	28	108	36	116	80	69	70	69	22	69
4	14	125	21	118	19	122	77	119	84	119	33	120
5	10	118	17	116	22	118	87	117	80	117	24	117
6	7	146	19	145	10	146	84	145	78	143	13	145
7	13	143	19	139	12	139	91	139	71	139	20	138
8	11	149	14	148	15	147	84	147	77	145	19	145

The Child's Rating of Government's Qualities

The early positive regard for the government is shown, as well, over a larger group of respondents in some ratings of the government in our final "eight cities" questionnaire. Using five role attributes and qualities of government as descriptions, we asked the child to "think of the Government as it really is." The items (CA-9, items 32–36) read as follows:

"Think of the Government as it really is . . ." (Circle the number of your choice)

1	2	3	4	5	6
Almost never makes mistakes	Rarely makes mistakes	Sometimes makes mistakes	Often makes mistakes	Usually makes mistakes	Almost always makes mistakes

1	2	3	4	5	6
Would always want to help me if I needed it	Would almost always want to help me if I needed it	Would usually want to help me if I needed it	Would sometimes want to help me if I needed it	Would seldom want to help me if I needed it	Would not usually want to help me if I needed it

1	2	3	4	5	6
Makes important decisions all the time	Makes Important decisions a lot of the time	Makes Important decisions sometimes	Makes Important decisions seldom	Almost never makes important decisions	Never makes important decisions

1	2	3	4	5	6
Can punish anyone	Can punish almost anyone	Can punish many people	Can punish some people	Can punish a few people	Can punish no one

1	2	3	4	5	6
Knows more than anyone	Knows more than most people	Knows more than many people	Knows less than many people	Knows less than most people	Knows less than anyone

TABLE 2.6 RATING OF THE QUALITIES OF GOVERNMENT (PERCENT OF CHILDREN RESPONDING)

1 "Makes mistakes"

Grade	1 Almost Never	2 Rarely	3 Some-times	4 Often	5 Usually	6 Almost Always	Mean Rating	N Respond-ing	N Not Re-sponding
4	29.75	42.70	25.02	1.13	.87	.53	2.02	1499	250
5	23.95	45.72	27.87	1.90	.39	.17	2.10	1787	16
6	22.18	47.93	27.18	1.67	.40	.63	2.12	1740	9
7	16.78	48.89	31.59	2.21	.12	.41	2.21	1716	7
8	13.44	45.51	38.25	2.26	.18	.36	2.31	1681	14

2 "Would want to help me if I needed it"

Grade	1 Always	2 Almost Always	3 Usually	4 Some-times	5 Seldom	6 Not Usually	Mean Rating	N Respond-ing	N Not Re-sponding
4	25.27	31.72	23.92	11.63	5.17	2.28	2.47	1488	261
5	16.60	31.01	27.80	16.26	5.29	2.98	2.72	1777	26
6	16.60	31.12	28.36	16.43	4.50	3.00	2.70	1735	14
7	15.64	29.00	30.92	15.99	5.72	2.74	2.75	1714	9
8	13.66	28.82	32.34	15.93	6.26	2.98	2.81	1676	19

3 "Makes important decisions"

Grade	1 All the Time	2 A Lot of the Time	3 Some-times	4 Seldom	5 Almost Never	6 Never	Mean Rating	N Respond-ing	N Not Re-sponding
4	35.01	47.93	13.92	2.21	.54	.40	1.87	1494	235
5	38.75	46.89	12.00	1.63	.45	.28	1.79	1783	20
6	47.70	40.39	9.78	1.32	.35	.46	1.68	1738	11
7	54.32	35.06	8.75	1.46	.06	.35	1.59	1714	9
8	57.81	35.16	5.72	.83	.18	.30	1.51	1678	17

4 "Can punish"

Grade	1 Anyone	2 Almost Anyone	3 Many People	4 Some People	5 A Few People	6 No One	Mean Rating	N Respond-ing	N Not Re-sponding
4	13.90	29.28	24.11	19.01	9.13	4.57	2.94	1489	260
5	13.68	33.67	25.45	16.61	6.53	4.05	2.81	1776	27
6	19.83	31.82	23.29	14.47	6.22	4.38	2.69	1735	14
7	22.46	31.79	23.75	13.43	5.34	3.23	2.57	1705	18
8	26.44	30.58	21.28	12.83	5.52	3.36	2.50	1668	27

5 "Knows"

Grade	1 More Than Anyone	2 More Than Most People	3 More Than Many People	4 Less Than Many People	5 Less Than Most People	6 Less Than Anyone	Mean Rating	N Respond-ing	N Not Re-sponding
4	13.68	44.67	36.35	2.88	1.41	1.01	2.37	1491	258
5	11.35	52.11	33.56	1.46	.79	.73	2.30	1779	24
6	14.02	52.05	29.95	2.25	.75	.98	2.27	1733	16
7	16.05	54.09	27.34	1.65	.53	.35	2.18	1701	22
8	15.34	58.24	23.83	1.56	.60	.42	2.15	1662	33

We asked for these ratings at grades four to eight. The results are shown in Table 2.6.

Over-all on these five ratings[13] approval of government is high across the grades. There is some decline for two of these ratings, however, and an increase on three. The most apparently affectively loaded item, "would want to help me if I needed it," for example, shows a greater tendency for the older child to rate the government's willingness to help him "almost always" or "usually" rather than "always." And the same is true for the somewhat affectively loaded item "makes mistakes." The more cognitively directed, role-relevant items show steady increases in the more positive categories, although the perception of government's capacity to punish is seemingly never as high as the other two—"makes important decisions" and "knows more than other people."

Perhaps the most interesting observation is that the most directly affective item, "would want to help me if I needed it," elicits a high regard for government over the whole span of grades, with a small drop of this support for the older children.

Summary of the Child's Affective Response to Government

The child's affect in this context begins high but diminishes somewhat as he learns more about the political world. He begins with deep sympathy for government, and this early aura of approval is likely to remain at the base of his acceptance of the government, whatever later modifications and limitations he puts on his trust and approval. These limited data, at least, suggest that he certainly begins with highly supportive feelings.

CONCLUSION

To maintain a social construct as varied, extensive, and demanding of social resources as government, a broad panoply of forces need to be set in motion to provide the requisite support. The political socialization of new members is one of the most far-reaching and most consequential of these forces. The political system must somehow provide a flow of information about and continuously create deep feelings of loyalty and obedience for its basic forms. One of these is its government or authorities. Government is a primary focus for the generation of politically supportive or disaffective orientations. Our data suggest that in the United States a supportive image of government is being widely and regularly reproduced for young new members. The average grade school child of our test group appears to experience some rather basic changes in his conception of government—changes which move him toward a cognitive image that conforms to the requirements of a democratic political system.

---

[13] We have the same five ratings, as well as others, for the President, the child's father, the policeman, the average United States senator, and the Supreme Court. We will present comparisons of these ratings in a later report.

He begins, as a "political primitive," with a vision of government as the embodiment of a man or a small set of men who constitute a yet dimly recognized form of external authority. This authority applies to the immediate environment of the child in a rather abstract way as well as to the wider world beyond. Probably the first recognizable shadow that flickers across the wall of the cave of the child's unformed political mind is that of the President. He forms the initial visible object of the political world, and, from him, the child builds down, gradually incorporating more and more objects below him until the image becomes rounded and complex.

The child, moving down toward a plural, complex, and functional conception of government (as our unpublished data show) runs upon representative and popular institutions. He raises Congress and voting in his mind's eye to positions of dominance as symbolic associations and thus elicits democracy in his interpretation of what our government is. At the same time, he is beginning to sharpen his knowledge about the boundaries of government by sorting what is outside the realm of government from what is within it.

This finally adds up to a picture supportive of a democratic interpretation and evaluation, a picture that becomes rapidly and forcefully exhibited in these years, as other data, not reported as yet, confirm. The child is initiated into a supportive stance by what is probably high exposure to cues and messages about government, even while he is essentially unconcerned with such matters and too young to do much about them even if he wished. He learns to like the government before he really knows what it is. And as he learns what it is, he finds that it involves popular participation (voting) and that this is a valuable part of its countenance. It is further reason for liking it; and liking it is what the child continues to do. The child has somehow formed a deep sympathy for government even before he knows that he is in some way potentially part of it.

We know of course that such a process of changing understanding and feeling must go beyond these early years. And later experiences may upset these earlier formed images. Yet we know as well, from what little evidence there is directly about support for government *per se*, that adult Americans are also highly supportive of their government, whatever exaggerations may exist about their belief in limited government.[14] In these exploratory data that we have presented, we think we see growing the deep roots of this supportive sentiment.

Furthermore, our data enable us to link up our discussion of the cognitive and affective aspects of the child's image of government, at least in a speculative way. Two things stand out in our data. First, the child begins with a view of government as composed of palpable, visible persons—such as the President or a past President, Washington. Second, as he makes his initial contact with government, it becomes a symbol of orientation to politi-

[14] See V. O. Key, Jr., *Public Opinion and American Democracy* (New York: Knopf, 1961), pp. 28–32; M. Janowitz, D. Wright, and W. Delaney, *Public Administration and the Public: Perspectives toward Government in a Metropolitan Community* (Ann Arbor: Bureau of Government, University of Michigan, 1958), pp. 31–35; and Donald E. Stokes, "Popular Evaluation of Government: An Empirical Assessment," *Ethics and Bigness*, eds. Harlan Cleveland and Harold D. Lasswell (New York: Harper & Row, 1962), pp. 61–72.

cal life that is charged with positive feelings. If we now make the plausible assumption that a child of seven or eight is not likely to develop such feelings about *impersonal* organizations or institutions, we can appreciate the significance of the fact that his first glimpse of government is in the form of the President. It permits the child to express toward a figure of political authority sentiments that he is already accustomed to displaying to other human beings in his environment.

From this we would draw the hypothesis that the personalizing of the initial orientation to political authority has important implications for the input of support to a political system as the child continues through his early years into adolescence. As he fills in his picture of government, adding, to leading figures, such institutions as Congress and such regime rules as voting, we would suggest that the affect originally stimulated by his personalized view of government subtly spills over to embrace other aspects of government and the regime itself.

But for this process it is difficult to see how impersonal, remote, and complex organizations such as Congress or practices such as voting could possibly catch the imagination of a child and win his affection. Yet our data do show that positive sentiment towards government, even after the child has begun to see it in impersonal terms, is so high as to approach a consensual level. When we add to this the fact that children tend to view government as national rather than local in its scope, we can appreciate the unifying force that this image must have in a system such as the United States.

This interpretation carries us far beyond its immediate significance for socialization into the American political system. In effect, we may have encountered here a central mechanism available to many political systems in building up diffuse support in each wave of children as they enter a political system through birth into it. In many ways a child born into a system is like an immigrant into it. But where he differs is in the fact that he has never been socialized to any other kind of system. That is to say, he is being socialized politically for the first time rather than resocialized as for an immigrant. The fact that the new member is a child rather than an adult with a pre-existing set of attitudes towards political life, creates a need for special devices to build support for the regime and authorities. Each system will, of course, have its own specific mode of personalization. It may take the form of a monarch, a paramount chief, a renowned elder or ancestor, a charismatic leader, or a forceful dictator. But the pattern of making government a warm and palpable object through its initial symbolization as a person, the high affect that this permits for a child, and the possible subsequent overflow of this feeling to cold and impersonal institutions and norms may form a complex but widespread mechanism for attaching to the system those members who are new to it by virtue of their birth in it.

3

Civic Education, Community Norms, and Political Indoctrination*

EDGAR LITT

"All national educational systems," observes V. O. Key, Jr., "indoctrinate the coming generation with the basic outlooks and values of the political order."[1] But this indoctrination is not uniform. Do different socioeconomic communities, for instance, differ in the kinds of textbooks they employ in civic education? Do differing political attitudes and norms in these communities affect the process of indoctrination? To answer these questions, we analyzed textual material in civic education programs, attitudes of leaders in the school's political and educational milieu, and changes in political attitudes accompanying participation in civic education classes.

PROCEDURE

The study was conducted in the major secondary school in each of three communities in the Boston metropolitan area (to be referred to as

* Reprinted by permission from the *American Sociological Review*, 28 (February 1963), pp. 69–75.
  [1] V. O. Key, Jr., *Public Opinion and American Democracy* (New York: Knopf, 1961), p. 316.

Alpha, Beta, and Gamma).[2] The three communities differ in socio-economic and political characteristics: Alpha is an upper middle-class community with much political activity; Beta is a lower middle-class community with moderate political activity; and Gamma is a working-class community with little political activity.

A content analysis, described in the Appendix, was made of all textbooks used in the civic education programs in Alpha, Beta, and Gamma schools over the past five years (ten texts were investigated in Alpha, eight in Beta, and seven in Gamma). A random sample of paragraphs was selected in each text and classified, where applicable, along one of the following five dimensions.[3]

1. Emphasis on citizen political participation—references to voting, norms of civic duty, political activity, and the effectiveness of citizen action in influencing the behavior of public officials.

2. Political chauvinism—references to the unique and nationalistic character of "democracy" or "good government" as an American monopoly, and glorified treatment of American political institutions, procedures and public figures.

3. The democratic creed—references to the rights of citizens and minorities to attempt to influence governmental policy through non-tyrannical procedures.

4. Emphasis on political process—references to politics as an arena involving the actions of politicians, public officials, and the use of power and influence contrasted with references to government as a mechanistic set of institutions allocating services to citizens with a minimum of intervention by political actors.

5. Emphasis on politics as the resolution of group conflict—references to political conflicts among economic, social, and ethno-religious groupings resolved within an agreed-upon framework of political rules of the game.

A second measure of civic education norms consisted of a series of interviews with a pool of "potential civic and educational influentials" in each of the three communities.[4] The interviews included a sample of all school administrators who were responsible for the school's civic education program; all teachers of civic education; the president and vice-president of each

[2] Course titles of civic education instruction vary in the three communities. A control group was available in the same schools of Alpha and Gamma where the civic education course was not required. For Beta, a control group was selected from a school in an adjoining, and comparable community. From *American Sociological Review*, 28 (February 1963), 69–75.

[3] Based on procedures developed in Bernard B. Berelson, *Content Analysis in Communications Research* (New York: Free Press, 1952), and Lloyd Marcus, *The Treatment of Minorities in Secondary School Textbooks* (New York: B'nai B'rith Anti-Defamation League, 1961).

[4] The distinction "potential civic and educational leaders or influentials" is used because we have no data on overt attempts to influence the school's civic education program. Our immediate concern is with their attitudes toward the political themes in the program. This distinction between manifested and imputed political influence is drawn in Raymond Wolfinger, "Reputation and Reality in the Study of Community Power," *American Sociological Review*, 25 (October 1960), 636–644.

school's Parent and Teachers Association or Home and School Association over the past five years; and the current and most recent presidents and vice-presidents of ten major civic groups in each community. Interviewees included leaders of business, fraternal, labor, patriotic, religious, and civic betterment associations, and the chairman of the local Republican and Democratic party organizations. A total of 66 leaders were interviewed in Alpha, 57 in Beta, and 63 in Gamma.[5]

The interview schedule was designed to tap the intensity of the respondent's attitudes toward the proper orientation of the community school's civic education program in each of the five political dimensions. The content, reliability, and sources of the items are presented in the Appendix.

A third measure involved the effects of exposure to a formal course in civic education. A civic education class in each community was matched with a control group in age, academic attainment, parental social class, parental political affiliation, and ethno-religious affiliation. The control group, which did not take a course in civic education, was used to measure the changes in attitudes along the five political dimensions.

These dimensions were adapted for a questionnaire given to the three civic education classes, and their corresponding control groups, before and after a semester's exposure to the course (see Appendix). Thus we can compare attitudinal changes attributable to the school's "official version" of political phenomena, and the differential effects of the course in each community.

FINDINGS

The content analysis of textbooks in the civic education programs of Alpha, Beta, and Gamma schools revealed no substantial differences in references to elements of the democratic creed, or in chauvinistic treatment of American political procedures and institutions. Few references in the material employed by the three schools connoted an insular view of American politics; the isolationist and jingoist orientation of civic education texts observed in Pierce's pioneer study were absent in this sampling.[6] Nor does the textual material differ in references endorsing the political rights of minorities and political procedures available to them. Indeed, the endorsement of the democratic creed far exceeds the other political dimensions. The blandness of the Gamma texts should be noted; they contain a large number of descriptive references (dates of major political events, anatomical presentations of po-

---

[5] Wherever possible, civic leaders were selected from comparable organizations in each community, such as the Chamber of Commerce and political party organizations. Differences in social structure made complete matching impossible. For example, labor union leaders were included in the Gamma sample, but not in the Alpha or Beta pools. There were 8 nonrespondents or 12 percent of the sample in Alpha, 7 (13%) in Beta, and 11 (18%) in Gamma.

[6] Bessie L. Pierce, *Civic Attitudes in American Schools* (Chicago: University of Chicago Press, 1930).

litical procedure) that could not be classified along one of the five political dimensions (See Table 3.1).

Differences do exist in the formal exposure to norms supporting political participation, in the view of politics as process, and in the functions of the political system. Unlike Alpha and Beta texts, Gamma texts contain only a few references to norms that encourage voting, feelings of political effectiveness,

TABLE 3.1 REFERENCES ON SALIENT POLITICAL DIMENSIONS IN CIVICS TEXTBOOKS

POLITICAL DIMENSION	ALPHA	BETA	GAMMA
Emphasis on democratic creed	56%	52%	47%
Chauvinistic references to American political institutions	3	6	2
Emphasis on political activity, citizen's duty, efficacy	17	15	5
Emphasis on political process, politicians, and power	11	2	1
Emphasis on group conflict-resolving political function	10	1	2
Other	3	26	43
Totals	100%	100%	100%
Number of paragraphs	(501)	(367)	(467)

and a sense of civic duty. References to the political process as a conduit involving political actors and the use of political power—rather than the workings of an invisible hand of governmental institutions—are also sparse in the Gamma texts.

Both Beta and Gamma texts are short on references to politics as a mechanism for settling competing group demands. Table 3.1 reveals that only Alpha schools indicate to some degree a political process in which politicians and power are the main ingredients, and through which a political group struggle is periodically ameliorated.

How do the norms of civic education that prevail among the potential civic and educational influentials of each community compare with the formal classroom material designed to shape student political attitudes? Are salient themes in the curriculum reinforced, opposed, or ignored by community norms?

Potential community influentials do support the inculcation of basic democratic principles (the democratic creed) and the avoidance of chauvinistic references to American political institutions—attitudes that were stressed in the texts. They also support material encouraging political activity and competence in young citizens, an attitude that is less reinforced in the Gamma school texts.

[Other data] indicates, however, that the potential influentials in the three milieux differ about the presentation of politics as a process involving the resources of politicians and power, and the conflict-alleviating goal of politics. Alpha leaders endorse these "realistic" political themes; and attempts to impart elements of political reality are present only in the Alpha civic education program. In Beta and Gamma the low level of support for these themes reinforce the contextual material of their school programs which ignores or avoids these perspectives on political phenomena.

It would be useless to talk about the effects of civic education programs without considering changes in political attitudes as functions of different textual emphasis and norms of community leaders. Comparisons of attitude changes in the schools do not uncover any reversal of beliefs along the five political dimensions that can be attributed to the school's indoctrination.

Several patterns, however, relate the effects of the civic education program on student attitudes to its material and the community's potential political support. Based on the "before" and "after" questionnaires administered to the three classes and matched control groups, the data in Table 3.2 reveals that students in the civic education classes were more likely to endorse aspects of the democratic creed and less likely to hold chauvinistic political sentiments than students not exposed to the program. But none of the three "exposed" classes was more likely to favor political participation than their control group. And only in Alpha were perceptions of politics as group conflict involving politicians and political power strengthened through exposure to civic education.

In Alpha, Beta, and Gamma, we observe (Table 3.2) that exposure to the course strengthened support for democratic processes and negated chauvinistic sentiment, thus reinforcing the material presented in the civic education program and supporting attitudes of community leaders. The result is to level the socio-political differences among the communities and their school populations. Training in the tenets of democratic fair play and tolerance is sustained by civic education courses within a supporting educational and political milieu.

But civic education does not affect the varying positive attitudes toward citizen political participation manifested by the school population of the three communities. Despite the positive references of civic education material in Alpha and Beta, and the supporting community norms in all three communities, different attitudes—based on socio-political cleavages—remain about the citizen's role in public affairs. Apparently attitudes toward political activity are so strongly channeled through other agencies in each community that the civic education program's efforts have little independent effect.

Attitudes toward political process and function are related to other variables in the classroom and community climate.[7] In Alpha, where community attitudes and texts are supportive, a positive change in views of political process and function occurs among students in civic education. In Beta and Gamma, where attitudes and texts are relatively non-supportive little change in such views occurs; politics is treated and learned as a formal, mechanistic set of governmental institutions with emphasis on its harmonious and legitimate nature, rather than as a vehicle for group struggle and change.

---

[7] A comparable investigation of this problem in advancement to college has been made by Natalie Rogoff, "Public Schools and Equality of Opportunity," *Journal of Educational Sociology*, 33 (February 1960), 252–279.

TABLE 3.2 EFFECT OF SEMESTER COURSE IN CIVIC EDUCATION ON POLITICAL
ATTITUDES IN THREE COMMUNITIES (IN PERCENTAGES)

| | ALPHA | | | |
| | Class | | Control | |
Political Attitude	Before	After	Before	After
Support of democratic creed	62[a]	89	57	61
Political chauvinism	23	8	19	18
Support of political participation	70	72	79	76
Politics a process of power, politicians	59	72	53	58
Function of politics to resolve group conflict	32	59	39	34
Number of cases	(38)		(44)	

| | BETA | | | |
| | Class | | Control | |
Political Attitude	Before	After	Before	After
Democratic creed	56	74	53	50
Political chauvinism	31	19	29	27
Political participation	55	56	54	49
Political process	23	21	27	26
Political group conflict	17	21	19	17
Number of cases	(51)		(46)	

| | GAMMA | | | |
| | Class | | Control | |
Political Attitude	Before	After	Before	After
Democratic creed	47	59	38	44
Political chauvinism	29	10	33	38
Political participation	32	29	31	33
Political process	12	15	16	14
Political group conflict	9	12	8	6
Number of cases	(59)		(63)	

[a] Denotes percent of sample strongly holding political attitude. See Appendix for indices.

CONCLUSIONS

The civic education program does not simply reinforce the prevailing sentiments and political climate of the community. Nor are attitudes about political participation and varying levels of political activity affected by courses in civic education. Even a combination of numerous textual references and support from community leaders fails to result in attitude changes about the role of the citizen in public life.

Nevertheless, without some degree of reinforcement from its material and the political environment, the school system's effort at political indoctrination also fails. The materials, support, and effects of civic education differ in the three communities, and it is the nature of these differences that are crucial in evaluating the political role of citizenship training.

All three classes are instructed in the equalitarian ground rules of democracy. Agreement with the maxims of the democratic creed and rejection of political chauvinism are increased in the civic education programs of all three communities. But the material and effects of the working-class community, Gamma, and its civic education program, do not encourage a belief in the citizen's ability to influence government action through political participation. And only the texts and community support of Alpha are related through its civic education course to a developed awareness of political processes and functions.

In sum, then, students in the three communities are being trained to play different political roles, and to respond to political phenomena in different ways. In the working-class community, where political involvement is low, the arena of civic education offers training in the basic democratic procedures without stressing political participation or the citizen's view of conflict and disagreement as indigenous to the political system. Politics is conducted by formal governmental institutions working in harmony for the benefit of citizens.

In the lower middle-class school system of Beta—a community with moderately active political life—training in the elements of democratic government is supplemented by an emphasis on the responsibilities of citizenship, not on the dynamics of public decision-making.

Only in the affluent and politically vibrant community (Alpha) are insights into political processes and functions of politics passed on to those who, judging from their socio-economic and political environment, will likely man those positions that involve them in influencing or making political decisions.

APPENDIX

The content analysis of the 27 civic education textbooks was conducted in the following manner. A random sample of paragraphs, as the content unit, was selected from each text. The text was entered by use of a random table of numbers to select page and paragraph. Every twentieth paragraph was read and classified by the writer and two other judges. The criteria of classification are noted in the text. In case of disagreement among the judges, a paragraph was classified in the "other" category. Dominant emphasis, based on sentence counts within paragraphs, was determining when a paragraph contained more than one politically relevant theme. In this manner, 1235 paragraphs were classified.

Five indices were used in the questionnaire administered to the student populations, and the interview with community leaders. Responses ran across a five-point scale from "agree strongly" to "disagree strongly." Unlike the students, the community leaders were asked whether or not each statement should be included in the civic education program. The content, reliability, and source of the political indices follow.

1. The Democratic Creed: (coefficient of reliability $= 0.911$)

Every citizen should have an equal chance to influence government policy.

Democracy is the best form of government.

The minority should be free to criticize government decisions.

People in the minority should be free to try to win majority support for their opinions.

(Adapted from James W. Prothro and Charles M. Grigg, "Fundamental Principles of Democracy: Bases of Agreement and Disagreement," *The Journal of Politics,* 22 (1960), 276–294).

2. Political Chauvinism: (cr $= 0.932$)

The American political system is a model that foreigners would do well to copy.

The founding fathers created a blessed and unique republic when they gave us the constitution.

Americans are more democratic than any other people.

American political institutions are the best in the world.

(Index constructed for this study.)

3. Political Activity: (cr $= 0.847$)

It is not very important to vote in local elections.

It is very important to vote even when so many other people vote in an election.

Public officials do care what people like me think.

Given the complexity of issues and political organizations there is little an individual can do to make effective changes in the political system.

People like me do not have any say about what the government does.

Politics is often corrupt and the interests of the underworld are looked after by some public officials.

(Adapted from the civic duty and sense of political effectiveness measures of the Michigan Survey Research Center, and Agger's index of political cynicism. See Angus Campbell, Gerald Gurin, and Warren E. Miller, *The Voter Decides,* Evanston: Harper & Row, 1954, pp. 187–204, and Robert E. Agger, Marshall N. Goldstein, and Stanley A. Pearl, "Political Cynicism: Measurement and Meaning," *The Journal of Politics,* 23 (1961), 447–506.)

4. Political Process: (cr $= 0.873$)

The use of political power is crucial in public affairs.

Many political decisions are made by a minority of political activists who seek to secure the agreement of the majority to the decisions.

Politics is basically a conflict in which groups and individuals compete for things of value.

Differences of race, class, and income are important considerations in many political issues.

Governmental institutions cannot operate without politicians.

(Index constructed for this study.)

5. Political Function: (cr $= 0.919$)

Politics should settle social and other disagreements as its major function.

Since different groups seek favorable treatment, politics is the vehicle for bargaining among these competing claims.

Politics is not a means of insuring complete harmony, but a way of arriving at temporary agreements about policies within agreed-upon rules.

The politician is the key broker among competing claims made within society.

(Index constructed for this study.)

4

Value-Outcomes
of a College Education*

PHILIP E. JACOB

What happens to the values of American students when they go to college? How different are the outlook and standards of behavior of the man or woman who has been "higher-educated"? Does the experience seem to change in any significant way the beliefs and the character which a freshman brings with him when he enrolls?

The overall conclusion of this study is that college does make a difference—but not a very fundamental one for most students. Basic values remain largely constant through college.

The changes which do occur bring greater consistency into the value-patterns of the students and fit these patterns to a well-established standard of what a college graduate in American society is expected to believe and do. But the college student is not front-runner in a broad forward movement of values within the culture at large. If anything the "typical" college graduate is a cultural rubber-stamp for the social heritage as it stands rather than the instigator of new patterns of thought and new standards of conduct.

College socializes, but does not really liberalize the student.

These generalizations do not hold for all students and all colleges. There are wide differences both among and within institutions. The point made by a leading authority on psychological studies of values is well taken that the exact role of colleges in value development remains undefined. . . .

THE CHANGES WHICH COLLEGE MAKES

Three bodies of evidence indicate something of the scope and character of the changes which occur in the values held by college students. First, the attitudes of college graduates have been contrasted with those held by the general population on a number of issues. Second, the beliefs and opinions of freshmen have been compared with those of upperclassmen and alumni at several institutions. Third, some "longitudinal" studies have been conducted, showing the differences in outlook of the same individuals at various stages of their education. . . .

FROM DIVERSITY TO UNIFORMITY— ACQUIRING THE COLLEGE OUTLOOK

Seniors as they emerge from college are far more in agreement among themselves on many issues than when they entered. They have given up extreme views, or at least views which set them apart from the "normal" upperclassman at their institution.

This uniformity of outlook among seniors is so pronounced that one can even design a scale which aptly indicates how much any particular student is like a senior at his college. For instance an intensive study of the intellectual and personality development of students at Vassar . . . revealed some 150 traits which were significantly characteristic of seniors but not of freshmen. Combined, these constituted a "Vassar Developmental Scale" which has been statistically validated.[1]

Among value judgments more typical of seniors than of freshmen at Vassar are:

> **Freedom from compulsiveness:** The senior, compared with the freshman, would rather be a brilliant but unstable worker than a steady and dependable one, doesn't particularly care how people dress, or feel the need to plan far ahead.

> **Tolerant, impunitive attitudes toward others:** The senior is not so critical as the freshman of persons who become intoxicated, who don't vote, who have intercourse before marriage, are lawbreakers, or don't take things seriously enough. She tends not to set arbitrary standards of right and wrong conduct, and judge others by them.

> **Critical attitudes toward parents and family:** The senior is more independent of her family, critical of its habits, under less sense of obligation.

[1] The total scale was found to have a reliability of 0.84 (KR = 20)

Critical or rebellious attitudes toward the state, laws, rules, etc.: The senior more often than the freshman justifies the breaking of rules on occasion, including civil disobedience; questions whether "communism is the most hateful thing in the world today" or whether the American way of life should be preserved unchanged; would prefer to betray country rather than best friend.

Religious liberalism: The senior goes to church and prays less than the freshman, and is less likely to believe in the second coming of Christ, a life hereafter and even that there is a God.

Unconventionality: The senior is more likely than the freshman to admit to conduct and attitudes contrary to conventional moral taboos concerning drinking, telling the truth, sexual propriety, and even theft. She feels people would be happier if sex experience before marriage were taken for granted in both men and women, and that in illegitimate pregnancies abortion is in many cases the most reasonable alternative. She thinks she would probably get into a movie without paying if sure she would not be seen.

These particular views, it should be emphasized, are not unanimously shared by the Vassar seniors, nor would they necessarily be representative of college seniors everywhere. But they do indicate what is apparently the lodestone towards which the values of girls coming to Vassar are attracted. Students tended to shed divergent attitudes which they may have brought with them as they became "seniorized."

A study of changing beliefs at Antioch, Colgate and Michigan State illustrates the same process, with the principal readjustment apparently taking place during the first two years. . . . In the first two institutions the Inventory of Beliefs (ACE Cooperative Study) was taken by freshmen when they entered and retaken by the same students later (at the end of the freshman year at Antioch, and the end of the sophomore year at Colgate). At Michigan State, the Inventory was given simultaneously to freshmen and to a sample of upperclassmen. The results show that in each case there was much more agreement on the various items among the students when they had been at college some time than when they just arrived. Most freshmen tended (1) to keep their views if they coincided with the prevailing sentiment of upperclassmen, (2) to change their views if they did not so coincide. The net result was to encourage greater uniformity of outlook as the students progressed through college.

In general these attitudinal changes resulted at the institutions concerned in a well-defined upperclass "model" of beliefs which emphasized (a) a free market place for ideas, based on respect for intelligence and acceptance of a wide diversity of opinions and beliefs, (b) a free melting pot of peoples and cultures, rejecting racial and ethnic stereotypes and discriminatory social barriers, (c) a self-critical approach to the national American culture based on a recognition of world interdependence and rejection of chauvinism, (d) a tolerance of unconventional behavior in social relations and a less repressive attitude toward moral taboos, (e) skepticism of the supernatural as a determining force in human affairs.

TABLE 4.1 STUDENT VALUES—UPPERCLASS MODEL (FRESHMAN DIVERSITY VS. UPPERCLASS UNIFORMITY ON SELECTED ITEMS FROM THE INVENTORY OF BELIEFS)

	ANTIOCH		COLGATE		MICHIGAN STATE	
	Freshmen					
PERCENTAGE WHO REJECTED THE FOLLOWING BELIEFS AT:	At Entrance	At End of Year	Fresh-men	Soph-omore	Fresh-men	Upper-class
a. Freedom of Thought						
We are finding out today that liberals really are soft-headed, gullible and potentially dangerous.					67	83
Being a successful wife and mother is more a matter of instinct than of training.	58	81				
Modern paintings look like something dreamed up in a horrible nightmare.			58	83		
Ministers who preach socialistic ideas are a disgrace to the church.			63	81	55	79
A lot of teachers, these days, have radical ideas which need to be carefully watched.			53	83		
b. Racial Tolerance						
One trouble with Jewish businessmen is that they stick together and prevent other people from having a fair chance in competition.			63	79	64	78
There may be a few exceptions, but in general Jews are pretty much alike.			64	79	59	78
c. Rejecting Ethnocentrism						
Anything we do for a good cause is justified.	67	80			41	76
Voting determines whether or not a country is democratic.					52	89
Americans may tend to be materialistic, but at least they aren't cynical and decadent like most Europeans.	68	81	54	79	51	68
Europeans criticize the United States for its materialism but such criticism is only to cover up their realization that American culture is far superior to their own.	77	87	67	91	50	78
No world organization should have the right to tell Americans what they can or cannot do.			69	77	53	82
d. Moral Permissiveness						
Books and movies should start dealing with entertaining or uplifting themes instead of the present unpleasant, immoral or tragic ones.	57	80				
Literature should not question the basic moral concepts of society.					63	78

(Continued on next page)

TABLE 4.1   STUDENT VALUES—UPPERCLASS MODEL *(CONTINUED)*

PERCENTAGE WHO REJECTED THE FOLLOWING BELIEFS AT:	ANTIOCH		COLGATE		MICHIGAN STATE	
	Freshmen					
	At Entrance	At End of Year	Fresh-men	Soph-omore	Fresh-men	Upper-class
Our rising divorce rate is a sign that we should return to the values which our grandparents held.			55	77	47	74
People who say they're religious but don't go to church are just hypocrites.	74	91	65	82		
A sexual pervert is an insult to humanity and should be punished severely.	72	87	60	88	49	79
e. Skepticism of the Supernatural Miracles have always taken place whenever the need for them has been great enough.			61	80	47	69

It is apparent that in most respects a majority of the freshmen were already inclined to accept this model, so that the person who did not was out of step not only with the upperclassmen but with the preponderent sentiment of his classmates as well. To maintain his idiosyncracy against these twin pressures, plus whatever influence in the same direction might come from his instruction would require a sturdy character indeed, or extremely strong countervailing forces from family or other sources. As a matter of fact, most students (at least those that did not drop out) did make the adjustment.

The classic demonstration of the phenomenon of adaptation to a college norm is Newcomb's prewar study of the transformation of attitudes of Bennington College girls. . . . He found that most of these students took on, in greater or less degree, the pattern of values acknowledged in the college community even though it fundamentally opposed (especially in its "radical" approach to economic and social questions) the basic assumptions with which they had grown up in a family environment of wealth and economic power. The mark of a student leader usually was his championship of the outlook and values of the community. He was "like his class, only more so." Of course Bennington's model was quite unrepresentative of college values generally, but the process of change which went on is probably similar to what happens elsewhere.

TOWARDS FLEXIBILITY AND SOCIABILITY

If the thesis just suggested is sound, one would expect that most of the changes in student values would tend in the direction of the overall profile set forth in the previous chapter, unless certain special personality, institutional or other influences intervened. Students who at first differed from the common values prevailing among students would come to accept them more and more. But on issues which divided the general student population, the division would be perpetuated as the student took sides with those who espoused the values he brought with him to college.

The evidence reviewed largely confirms this expectation. The movement of values during college is generally along the lines witnessed at Vassar, Colgate, and Michigan State. Students become somewhat less rigid, dogmatic and absolute in the standards and beliefs they hold, more critical of authority *per se*, more self-confident and self-reliant, also more self-centered, less prejudiced towards people of different races and more tolerant of those who do not conform to traditional mores.

Students Become Less Dogmatic

Total scores made on the Inventory of Beliefs, which gauge the overall acceptance of "authoritarian" stereotypes and clichés, show that students tend to reject such concepts more at the end of college than when they entered. There is some variation among institutions in the amount of change recorded, and in few cases is the average change for an entire student body breathtaking. But the trend is clearly and customarily towards increased flexibility of belief. Change is usually greatest with students who start with the most rigid attitudes. (1)

The most important significance of the changes recorded is not the modification of attitudes on particular issues but the increased tendency of students to reject dogmatism *per se*. It is apparent that students often accept

TABLE 4.2 CHANGES IN STUDENT DOGMATISM DURING COLLEGE[a]

COLLEGE	PRE-TEST	POST-TEST	DIFFERENCE
1	75.9	87.1	11.0
5	59.0	70.0	11.2
6	60.1	62.5	2.4
7	58.4	63.7	5.3
10	58.5	62.1	3.6
11	57.0	55.1	1.9
14	57.1	61.6	4.5
12	57.0	63.3	6.3
15	59.4	66.8	7.4
16	61.5	69.3	7.8
18	71.3	73.9	2.6
19	61.8	65.3	3.5

[a] Scores reported are the means for each college sample taking the Inventory of Beliefs developed by the American Council on Education Cooperative Study of Evaluation in General Education. As the circumstances under which the pretest and post-test were administered were not always identical (including some differences in the elapsed time between the two at various institutions) those responsible for the study caution against precise comparisons among the institutions. The pre-tests were usually administered at college entrance and the post-tests towards the end of the freshman year.

A high score indicates a rejection of the authoritarian stereotypes of which the inventory was composed, in other words a disposition towards "liberality" or flexibility of belief. Maximum score—120.

or disagree with certain of the items because of the categorical way in which they are expressed rather than because of their intrinsic meaning. To the extent that the Inventory of Beliefs measures the degree of dogmatism in personality, the results of its use show that some change in student character, beyond the expressed opinions, may be under way in college. . . .

Students' Capacity to Think Critically Increases

Tests of "critical thinking in social science" show students acquiring greater capacity to reach judgments by reasoned thought instead of blind opinion or on the basis of someone's unchallenged authority. Again, the improvement is modest on an overall basis at most institutions, and is greatest with those who need it most. . . . One study does show specifically that those who have had a year's residence in college make a greater gain than those who have not. . . .

TABLE 4.3 DEVELOPMENT OF CRITICAL THINKING IN SOCIAL SCIENCE[a]

COLLEGE	PRE-TEST	POST-TEST	DIFFERENCE
1	33.1	36.9	3.8
6	25.6	29.4	3.8
7	21.9	24.8	2.9
8	22.9	30.7	7.8
12	24.1	33.8	9.7
14	23.1	24.9	1.8
15	22.7	28.9	6.2
17	23.8	26.6	2.8
18	32.1	36.8	4.7
19	24.0	28.2	4.2

[a] Scores reported are the means for each college sample on the Critical Thinking in Social Science test developed by the American Council on Education Cooperative Study in General Education. As the circumstances under which the tests were administered varied among institutions, those responsible for the study caution against precise institutional comparisons. A high score indicates a high capacity for critical thinking.

The College-Educated are Less Prejudiced

Studies of prejudice show that more highly educated persons tend to have less prejudice toward racial and ethnic groups and to be more tolerant of political nonconformists. On racial attitudes, the difference in favor of college graduates as against those with less education is in the order of 10 percent–20 percent. . . . Regarding civil rights for communists and radicals in general, the definitive study made for the Fund for the Republic establishes that a clear majority of those with a college education can be considered among the more tolerant third of the whole population, and only a very small percentage among the least tolerant fifth. This tendency persists in all groups and regardless of sectional, religious or other differences. . . . The Cornell survey and the Inventory of Beliefs confirm the view that students become progressively less prejudiced at college.

TABLE 4.4 THE TOLERANCE OF THE EDUCATED[a]

SCHOOLING	LESS TOLERANT	IN-BETWEEN	MORE TOLERANT
College graduate	5%	29%	66%
Some college	9	38	53
High school graduate	12	46	42
Some high school	17	54	29
Grade school only	22	62	16

	YEAR IN COLLEGE[b]				
	1	2	3	4	5
Anti-civil liberties	49	48	41	34	31
Pro-civil liberties	51	52	59	66	69

[a] Data from *Communism, Conformity and Civil Liberties* by Samuel A. Stouffer (New York: Doubleday and Co., 1955). Scores on the "tolerance scale" developed in this survey were used to differentiate the "more tolerant" segment of the population (31%), the "less tolerant" (19%) and the in-between group (50%). The findings are reported in terms of the percentage of each educational group whose scores placed them in one of these three segments.

[b] Data from the Cornell survey. Percentage of students in each college year (including graduate school) who, on a scale of attitudes toward civil liberties, tended toward suppressing, or maintaining them.

But these conclusions are subject to several important reservations. The educational variable does not seem to govern all forms of prejudice with equal force. It influences some opinions more than others, especially those which hinge largely on the possession of knowledge or information. Where *emotional* attitudes are involved, the amount of a person's education plays a lesser part. For instance, the influence of education is less marked regarding attitudes towards the *social* rights of Negroes—willingness to eat in restaurants where Negroes are served, to reside with them or accept them in fraternities—than in regard to opinions concerning racial differences in intelligence, cultural contribution or moral character. . . .

Furthermore, the differentiating influence of education tends to work *with the grain* of the movement of social attitudes in the country at large, rather than against it. That is, if the point of view of their contemporaries shifts—towards lesser prejudice or towards greater—the attitudes of the college graduate shift also and in the same direction. There is thus no *fundamental* effect of education on prejudice but only a modest tempering of the prevailing mood. For instance, in the years from 1945–1953 Americans became much less tolerant of Communists. The shift in opinion among the college educated was just as marked as among the less educated, even though a somewhat larger proportion of the college group started—and remained—tolerant. Among the college educated, those who would deny freedom of speech to a Communist increased from 31 percent to 71 percent; among the less educated from 42 percent to 78 percent. The tide of the national opinion thus swept the college educated along just as easily. Their tolerance was just as volatile. . . .

This same conclusion is implied in the data showing that the younger a person is, regardless of education, the more tolerant he is likely to be. The older college graduates tend to share the prejudice of their generation, rather than the tolerance of the "educated." For instance, among college graduates 60 and over, only 31 percent are included in the "more tolerant" category, whereas among those below 40, 75 percent or more are "more tolerant." This compares with 29 percent of high school graduates over 60 who are "more tolerant" and 44 percent under 40 who are so inclined. . . . Thus, as the whole pattern of American culture moved towards tolerance, during the last twenty-five years, the college experience made for even greater tolerance. The college student acquired—or perhaps anticipated—the outlook of his generation, only more so. But the fact of having had a college education, did *not* make the older generation either more disposed towards a tolerant outlook *per se*, or more flexible than others of their age in changing their original mind set to accord with the trend of the times.

There is further evidence to the effect that the influence of college in diminishing prejudice depends on operating within a favorable cultural context. Before the Second World War, studies of attitude changes in college frequently showed little or no change in regard to racial prejudice. . . . Since the War, however, increased racial tolerance is one of the most characteristic changes. During that period, of course, the United States had mounted a major ideological crusade against the doctrines of racial inequality and discrimination as propounded and practiced by the Nazis, and in the process had to reevaluate its own conceptions and conduct *vis-à-vis* its Negro, Jewish, and other minorities. The main "thrust" of the American disposition regarding racial differences shifted as segregation was abandoned in the Army, fair employment practices legislation increasingly ruled out economic discrimination, and even social and educational discrimination came under concerted attack as antidemocratic. College students quickly discovered if they had not before that prejudice was now considered unbecoming an "enlightened" American citizen. College thus became an effective medium of communication for a newly prescribed social value.

Students Become More Permissive in Human Relations

The college student is less prone than those with less education to categorize people as "weak" or "strong" and to adopt inflexible beliefs regarding human nature and capabilities. Here, as with racial prejudice, youth and education go hand in hand. The older generation and the less educated are the more likely to be "rigid categorizers." . . .

Greater flexibility is characteristic of college students' attitudes towards family relations and the bringing up of children. 15 percent to 25 percent more of the college graduates than of high school graduates depending on their age) would allow children to talk back to their parents. . . .

Students seem to become less dogmatic and critical in judging human conduct as they progress through college, also more sensitive to human qualities such as tolerance, cooperativeness, and broad-mindedness. Findings of a pre-war study at Ohio State using the Pressey Interest-Attitude Test anticipate those of the much more exhaustive inquiry at Vassar. Far fewer seniors than freshmen disapproved of such activities as "talking back," "playing hookey," "shooting craps," petting, divorce, or being an atheist. Seniors, more than freshmen, admired people who were tolerant, sympathetic, democratic, impartial, cooperative. (They also valued more highly such qualities as enthusiasm, resourcefulness, inventiveness and competence and having initiative. The senior prototype was thus a strong human as well as a friendly one). . . .

THE MYTH OF COLLEGE LIBERALISM

When all is said and done, the value changes which seem to occur in college and set the college alumnus apart from others are not very great, at least for most students at most institutions. They certainly do not support the widely held assumption that a college education has an important, general, almost certain "liberalizing" effect.

This conclusion admittedly is at variance with the findings of a sizeable number of attitude studies, indicating a clear "trend toward liberalism with increasing exposure to academic influence." . . . However, the following considerations warrant a revised estimate.

(1) Most of the studies reporting significant change by students towards liberal beliefs in college were conducted in the 1930s when exceptional social and economic distress was prompting the most drastic reorientation of public philosophy experienced in American society. It would have been extraordinary indeed if this culture-wide social revolution had not penetrated the campus to some extent. But did the change of outlook on the campus move in front of the change in the country, or merely keep pace with it?

Unfortunately, none of these studies was in a position to compare the amount of change in the social and economic attitudes of college students with that occurring among youth not in college, or for that matter, among the population as a whole. Recent studies which do compare college graduates with others find the difference in outlook negligible on many questions. On economic issues the college man is likely to be more *conservative* than the others.

Looked at from another standpoint—in the perspective of time rather than of cultural context—a *long-run* shift in some values was under way, a "secular trend" to borrow the economists's concept. This ran parallel to many of the changes in student attitudes in the 1930s and therefore accounts for at least part of the influence which has heretofore been attributed specifically to the college experience. For instance, a comparison of three undergraduate generations at Ohio State, in 1923, 1933, and 1943, showed that the modern student was freer from social and moral taboos, and had less anxiety connected therewith. . . . Also, a much larger proportion of the war generation approved of war, than did their depression predecessors. On the other hand, students changed little in their disapproval of divorce, strikes and socialism. Within each college generation the movement of attitudes followed the long-run trend, though the change from generation to generation was greater than from freshman to senior in the same generation. The persistence of these trends through depression and war lends weight to the conclusion suggested by the director of the study that the "general tone or climate of life" has changed, at least in regard to liberalizing the conventions of social conduct. If this be so, college students were merely keeping up with their times, rather than responding to a particular impetus from their educational environment.

2. Such liberalizing influence as college does exert beyond the secular trend, probably operates upon a superficial rather than a fundamental level, upon voiced attitudes toward broad, impersonal social policies rather than upon the decisive standards of personal conduct and human relationships.

The term "liberalism" (or "radicalism") as used in most of the studies does not refer to a well-defined, consistent pattern of values. It has been attached on a blanket and largely a *priori* basis to approval of social legislation, defense of the "freedoms," rejection of racial discrimination, and skepticism of a supernatural God holding a personal relationship to man. Do these various attitudes really hang together and distinguish a "liberal personality" or do they indicate only what some researcher (or his panel of consultants and "judges") personally conceives to be liberal?

Some of the very attitudes which might in the 1930s have marked a man as an independent thinker, and even a non-conformist, are today thoroughly conventional. What undoubtedly appears to many students' families as thoroughly unconventional thinking and behavior, is the sophistication, flexibility and social aplomb which will enable these students to get along easily with the kind of people who will be their own neighbors and associates after graduation. A liberal attitude, in the sense that a student will not let fixed moral standards or ingrained prejudices govern his relations with other people is almost an imperative "convention" of a society in which good business requires everyone to be treated with respect as a prospective customer.

Furthermore, some of the data cited above in regard to civil rights show how much and how quickly so-called liberal attitudes can shift with the current of popular opinion or public policy. Another example is the evaporation of "liberal" pacifism as the United States became progessively involved in the Second World War. If liberalism were a way of life, a fundamental organization of values that a student had acquired during college, one would expect greater steadiness.

The "liberalism" which was detected in these attitude studies, therefore, was not a liberalism of character, but only a random collection of opinions in vogue during a particular generation. The studies do not show that the student became a more liberal *person* in college, but only that he acquired, temporarily perhaps, some social and political attitudes that were representative of the outlook of his own time, rather than of his father's. As perceived by an admirably candid analyst qualifying the results of his own research, the attitude tests perhaps were measuring "verbalized liberality of attitudes rather than socially functioning personality." . . .

3. Still a further qualification must be entered concerning the significance of attitude changes during college. A selective process to a considerable

extent foreordains that only students will come to college and succeed in staying through college who are already somewhat inclined towards the prevailing "college attitudes," or whose views are most susceptible to change in this direction. One study showed that high school students expecting to go to college tended to be less racially prejudiced and more devoted to civil rights than those who were not planning to go on to higher education. But politically and economically the college group was more conservative. . . . This corresponds exactly to the difference we have seen between college graduates and the rest of the population—the college man is to the right on politics and economics, and "liberal" on social and moral issues. Comparisons of students who drop out of college with those who stay on find the same contrast—the former could not or at least did not sufficiently liberalize their attitudes at the proper points in order to fit in. . . .

In conclusion, college has a socializing rather than a liberalizing impact on values. It softens an individual's extremist views and persuades him to reconsider aberrant values. It increases the tolerance potential of students towards differing beliefs, social groups and standards of conduct so that they can move about with minimum friction in a heterogeneous culture. It strengthens respect for the prevailing social order.

THE CONSTANCY OF BASIC VALUES

The changes which have been observed—moving students towards a greater uniformity and at the same time somewhat more flexibility of social outlook—are mainly changes on the surface of personality. They do not really involve the fundamental values which shape a student's life-pattern. The weight of evidence indicates that actually very little change occurs during college in the essential standards by which students govern their lives. The values with which they arrive and which are integral elements of their personality, are still there when most students leave. They may have modified their opinions on a lot of questions and have learned how to tolerate and to get along more easily with people of differing hues and views. They may have become more self-reliant. They may have changed vocational plans. But most students remain fundamentally the same persons, with the same *basic value-judgments.*

At Syracuse University, for instance, practically no difference in religious beliefs emerged as between freshmen and seniors. In regard to social values, seniors tended to avoid extreme positions more than the freshmen, but the differences were not profound. . . . Most of the surveys made of student "citizenship"—attitudes towards politics and political participation—show little if any change from freshman to senior year. At one college, renowned for its positive interest in encouraging students to undertake active political and civic responsibilities, seniors exhibited a more *negative* view than freshmen of politics and *less* interest in personal participation. . . .

The overall constancy of student values is convincingly demonstrated in several studies which compared freshmen and senior responses on the Allport-Vernon Study of Values. A number of these were able to test the same individuals when they entered college and again when they were about to graduate. With few exceptions, the differences between freshmen and seniors were so small as to be of little or no statistical significance. . . .

An intensive study of the effect on individual students of transition from high school to college came to much the same conclusion for the period up to the sophomore year. . . . While some shifts in emphasis occurred, the individual's basic pattern of values remained unchanged. For the group as a whole, the religious and the political values somewhat declined, and the aesthetic and economic values rose slightly. The amount of change in certain values for some individuals was considerable. But close examination of each case revealed that the pattern was set *before* college, and that the direction of the change which occurred was consistent with the student's previous bent. Thus the values of the religiously inclined student became even more clearly and consistently pivoted around a religious hub; the student who started with a strong value for wealth became more devoted to this end during college, and subordinated or adjusted his other values accordingly. College—or maturity—contributed consistency, but did not effect a reorientation of values.

This is the broad conclusion, too, of the values survey conducted by the Cornell Social Science Research Center, both at Cornell itself and elsewhere. The upperclassmen by and large have achieved a synthesis of their values which reinforces their principal original motivations. College has firmed up their attitudes on most issues, and given them more definiteness. Fewer students straddle. But most of them have not changed the fundamental value-orientation with which they came to college. They have simply worked out a greater internal consistency within their value-system. . . .

5

Factors Associated
with Change: Social Support
during Post-College Years*

THEODORE M. NEWCOMB
KATHRYN E. KOENIG
RICHARD FLACKS
DONALD P. WARWICK

This chapter is devoted mainly to the human environments of our interview respondents since graduation from college. We shall, in general, be comparing women who showed noticeable changes during this period with those who did not.

We had predicted that those women who had experienced a large change in political attitudes while in college would tend to maintain that change. The assumption was that large changes during the college years were likely to have been accompanied by a reorganization of important values sufficiently extensive to support persistence. It was further assumed that this new value system would be important enough to influence post-college interests, jobs, community participation, and the choice of friends, including those from whom husbands were selected. If so, these students would tend to create for themselves a social environment which would nurture and reinforce the value systems with which they left college.

To the extent that we can assess the characteristics of post-college social environments, it appears that most of the women had just this sort of

* Reprinted by permission from Theodore M. Newcomb, Kathryn E. Koenig, Richard Flacks, and Donald P. Warwick, *Persistence and Change: Bennington Students after 25 Years* (New York: John Wiley & Sons, 1967), pp. 53–66.

experience, though in varying degrees. Those who were able to maintain attitudes similar to the ones with which they left college were, by and large, women who lived in social environments which supported those attitudes, and those who changed their attitudes since college were primarily individuals who associated with others who held different opinions. The data presented in this chapter in support of these conclusions were obtained in interviews with the graduates of 1938, 1939, and 1940.

We look first at the prediction that those women, among the 129 interviewed, who had experienced a large change in political attitudes while in college would tend to maintain that change after college. Of these, 43 had scored at least 13 points lower on the PEP scale as seniors than as freshmen in college. This represents a relatively large drop in "conservatism," amounting to a change of one standard deviation or more. Even with such a large change, 10 of these 43 still had higher scores on the PEP scale as seniors than most of their peers in college. In 1960–1961, 28 of these 43 (65 percent) were below the median on conservatism, and 15 (35 percent) were above the median. Of the 15 who became much less conservative in college and were relatively conservative in 1960–1961, 11 were married to someone who was conservative, or, if not married, had mainly conservative friends. For the other four, the political attitudes of husbands or friends were not ascertained.

Of the 28 who became much less conservative in college and were relatively nonconservative in 1960–1961, 24 were married to someone who was nonconservative, or, if not married, had friends who were predominantly nonconservative. For three of them, the political attitudes of friends and husbands were not ascertained. Only one woman from this group of 28 was known to be married to someone who was relatively conservative.

These figures suggest first that the majority who experienced a large change toward nonconservatism while in college held nonconservative political attitudes when surveyed in 1960–1961. Second, the data suggest that those who maintained nonconservative attitudes over the years lived in social environments which supported their nonconservatism; and, conversely, those who became more conservative again after college lived in social environments which supported conservatism.

The rest of the chapter will be devoted to exploring the relationship between political attitudes and social support for all of the women in the study. Eighty-six others were included in the study who, as college students, did not experience such large changes in political attitudes as the 43 just described. We shall also examine their current political attitudes, as related to the points of view of their husbands and their associates.

ATTITUDES OF HUSBANDS

The most important and influential member of the social environment for most of these women is her husband. Ideally, we would have interviewed the husbands, independently of the wives, but it was economically impractical and too difficult to arrange. Instead, each woman was asked to report how her husband felt about various political questions, what he thought about the issues, his opinion of the public figures, and how he had voted in the last 20 years. In some cases, the wives did not know how their husbands felt about the issues, and a few of them refused to answer for their husbands.

Since all of our information about the husband's political attitudes comes from the wife's report, there is a possibility of bias and distortion. There may be a tendency for the respondents to underestimate the differences in opinion between themselves and their husbands. In any case there is close agreement between the political attitudes of the women in our sample and reported political attitudes of their husbands. The product-moment correlation between the 1960 Conservatism Index reported for the husband and the 1960 Conservatism Index of the wife is 0.85. Ninety-one percent of 113 married couples, according to respondents, voted for the same candidate in the 1960 election, and 90 percent of 103 in 1964; 58 percent of the couples voted for the same candidate in all of the six presidential elections from 1940 through 1960.

Husbands' Attitudes as Related to Wives' Histories

Table 5.1. shows the relationship between the husband's political conservatism and the change or persistence of the wife's attitude since leaving college. The mean conservatism score of the husbands of the 30 women who

TABLE 5.1   RELATIONSHIP OF WIFE'S CHANGE IN ATTITUDE AND HUSBAND'S POLITICAL CONSERVATISM

Final PEP Score in College[b]	1960 Conservatism Index[b]	HUSBAND'S 1960 CONSERVATISM INDEX[a]			
		Above Median	Below Median	Total	Mean
a. Above median	Above median	29	1	30	29.8
b. Above median	Below median	1	13	14	17.2
c. Below median	Above median	15	1	16	27.2
d. Below median	Below median	6	24	30	18.1
		51	39	90	

[a] The husband's attitudes were reported by the wife.
[b] The median of final PEP scores is that of the total population of students replying in college. The median for 1960 Conservatism Index is that of interviewees only.

remained conservative after college (Group a) is 29.8 as compared to score of 17.2 for the husbands of the 14 women who became less conservative since college (Group b); $t = 6.6$, $p < 0.001$.

The average score of the husbands of the 16 women who became more conservative since college (Group c) is significantly higher than the mean score of the husbands of the 30 who remained nonconservative (Group d); $t = 4.7$, $p < 0.001$. The difference in mean scores of the husbands whose wives became more conservative (Group c) and the husbands of those who became less conservative (Group b) is also statistically significant; $t = 4.8$, $p < 0.001$. It is clear from Table 5.1 that the woman who became less conservative after college were married to men who were on the average less conservative than the husbands of those who remained conservative over the years. Similarly, the women who became more conservative since college were married to men who were reported as more conservative than the husbands of the women who remained nonconservative after college. . . .

Although there is a statistically high degree of agreement between spouses, such differences as do exist turn out not to be random. A pair-by-pair comparison shows that wives tend to report their husbands as more conservative than themselves. The mean difference in scores on the 1960 Political Conservatism Index is 1.4; $t = 3.51$, and $p < 0.001$ with 89 df.

When the sample is broken down into the four groups—those who remained conservative, those who remained nonconservative, those who became conservative, and those who became nonconservative after college— one finds some differences in the tendency to attribute greater conservatism to their husbands than to themselves. Table 5.2 shows that the husbands of

TABLE 5.2   DEGREE OF HUBANDS' CONSERVATISM RELATIVE TO FOUR GROUPS OF WIVES

	MEAN DIFFERENCE	t-VALUE	p	N
a. Wife conservative in college, also in 1960–1961	1.6	2.11	.05	30
b. Wife conservative in college, not conservative in 1960	0.3	0.42	n.s.	14
c. Wife not conservative in college, conservative in 1960	1.9	1.88	.10	16
d. Wife not conservative in college, nor in 1960	1.4	2.19	.05	30
				90

those who remained conservative and the husbands of women who remained nonconservative are reported by their wives to be more conservative than themselves, on the average. It is only with the group of women who become less conservative after college that we find virtually no such differences. The fact remains, however, that the attitudes reported for husbands were relatively nonconservative. The average differences in scores were small, even though statistically significant.

Each wife was also asked to report how her husband felt about a number of public figures; these responses were scored in the same manner as for the women themselves. Using the median obtained from the combined distribution of the couples' scores, the men were divided into two groups, those who scored above this median and those who scored below this median on favorability to conservative figures. As shown in Table 5.3, a relatively high proportion of the husbands of the women who remained conservative favor the conservative public figures (for Groups a and b; chi-square = 19.5, $p < 0.001$). Other differences in this table are not significant.

Table 5.4, in similar fashion, shows the relationship between husbands' voting preferences in 1960 and the relative stability of their wives' attitudes since college. A greater proportion of the husbands of the women who remained conservative since college preferred Nixon than of the husbands of those who became less conservative; chi-square $= 18.4$, $p < 0.001$. And the husbands of the women who became more conservative since college (Group c) were more likely to prefer Nixon than the husbands of the wives in Group d who remained nonconservative; chi-square $= 6.9$, $p < 0.01$.

TABLE 5.3   HUSBAND'S FAVORABILITY TO CONSERVATIVE FIGURES, AS RE-LATED TO WIFE'S CHANGE IN ATTITUDE

Final PEP Score in College	1960 Conservatism Index	HUSBAND'S FAVORABILITY TO CONSERVATIVE FIGURES[a]					
		Above Median[b]		Below Median[b]		Total	
a. Above median	Above median	31	(97%)	1	(3%)	32	(100%)
b. Above median	Below median	5	(33%)	10	(67%)	15	(100%)
c. Below median	Above median	11	(55%)	9	(45%)	20	(100%)
d. Below median	Below median	12	(37%)	20	(63%)	32	(100%)
		59		40		99	

[a] The husband's attitudes were reported by the wife.
[b] Median was determined from the combined distribution of scores for men and women.

This relationship is true not only of the 1960 election, but of the other elections from 1940 through 1960, as shown in Table 5.5, in which exactly the same pattern appears as in Table 5.4.

TABLE 5.4   HUSBAND'S CHOICE IN 1960 ELECTION AS RELATED TO WIFE'S CHANGE IN ATTITUDE

Final PEP Score in College	1960 Conservatism Index	HUSBAND'S CHOICE IN 1960 ELECTION[a]					
		Nixon		Kennedy		Total	
a. Above median	Above median	29	(88%)	4	(12%)	33	(100%)
b. Above median	Below median	3	(20%)	12	(80%)	15	(100%)
c. Below median	Above median	11	(55%)	9	(45%)	20	(100%)
d. Below median	Below median	6	(19%)	25	(81%)	31	(100%)
		49		50		99	

[a] The husband's choice is reported by the wife.

Similar results are found when a switch in party preference is used as the indicator of change in political point of view. Thus the husbands of the women who switched from the Republican to the Democratic party are much less conservative than the husbands of those who were Republican in 1938 and also in 1960. Likewise the husbands of the women who were Democrats in 1938 and Republicans in 1960 are much more conservative than the husbands of the wives who remained Democrats over the years.

TABLE 5.5   RELATIONSHIP OF WIFE'S CHANGE IN ATTITUDE AND THE VOTING
PATTERN OF HUSBAND

Final PEP Score in College	1960 Conservatism Index	NUMBER OF TIMES HUSBAND VOTED REPUBLICAN[a] 1940–1960			
		0–1	2–4	5–6	Total
a. Above median	Above median	3 (9%)	8 (24%)	22 (67%)	33 (100%)
b. Above median	Below median	8 (54%)	5 (33%)	2 (13%)	15 (100%)
c. Below median	Above median	9 (45%)	3 (15%)	8 (40%)	20 (100%)
d. Below median	Below median	22 (71%)	6 (19%)	3 (10%)	31 (100%)
		42	22	35	99

Chi-square = 33.7, $p < 0.001$, 6 df.
Comparison of Groups a and b; chi-square = 14.6, $p < 0.001$, 2 df
Comparison of Groups c and d; chi-square = 6.6, $p < 0.05$, 2 df

[a] The voting pattern of the husband is reported by the wife.

Spouses' Influence upon Each Other

One cannot safely infer from close agreements that wives changed their political attitudes to agree with their husbands' points of view. It is also possible that (1) the women married men of the same political orientation as themselves; or (2) the wives changed their political opinions after marriage; or (3) the husbands changed their political opinions after marriage. By comparing the voting preferences of the women before and after marriage with the reported voting preferences of the husband before and after marriage, a more detailed picture of their interaction regarding political attitudes can be obtained.

Complete information about voting preferences is available for only 68 couples. In this subsample, 63 percent (43) of the women married men with the same voting preferences as themselves; 37 percent of the women (25) married men with a preference for the opposing party. The subsequent data on these two groups are shown in Table 5.6. The same data, differently organized, appear in Table 5.7, in which women who remained in the same political party are compared with those who changed.

Among the 68 couples for whom full information is available, all but five were in agreement in 1960–1961, although 25 of them had differed at the time of marriage. Fourteen wives changed to agree with husbands, eight husbands to agree with wives, and two wives in initial agreement changed although their husbands did not. Considering also the three couples who continued to differ, it may be concluded that wives "followed" husbands in 14 instances (category 4 in Table 5.7), and were "independent" in 18 instances (categories 2, 3, 6, 8), whereas 41 couples were "collaborative." Of the 27 wives who changed party preferences, 22 changed to agree with their husbands—14 after marriage and 8 before (although we cannot be sure that the premarriage shifts represent influence by financés).

TABLE 5.6 CHANGE AND STABILITY OF PARTY PREFERENCE ON THE PART OF HUSBANDS AND WIVES

I. Married Man with Same Party Reference		43
1. Neither wife nor husband changed parties after marriage	39	
2. Both husband and wife changed parties after marriage	2	
3. Wife changed parties after marriage, husband did not	2	
II. Married Man with Different Party Preference		25
4. Wife changed to husband's party after marriage (7 Democratic, 7 Republican)	14	
5. Husband changed to wife's party after marriage (6 became Democratic, 2 Republican)	8	
6. Husband and wife continued to have different party preferences (wives Democratic, husbands Republican in all cases)	3	

TABLE 5.7 HUSBAND-WIFE SIMILARITY IN PARTY PREFERENCE

I. Women Who Remained in the Same Party 1940–1960		41
1. Married man of same party preference	31	
2. Married man of different party preference, husband changed to wife's party	7	
3. Married man of different party preference, husband and wife continued with different parties (husband Republican, wife Democratic, in all cases)	3	
II. Women Who Changed Party Preference 1940–1960		27
4. Wife changed to same party as husband after marriage (7 Democratic, 7 Republican)	14	
5. Wife changed before marriage, married man who shared new party preference	8	
6. Wife changed before marriage, married man of opposite party, husband changed to wife's new party preference	1	
7. Married man who shared party preference, both switched after marriage	2	
8. Married man of some party, wife changed, husband did not change	2	

Wives' Attitudes in College as Related to Husbands' Present Attitudes

Husbands' attitudes in 1960–61 are also related to their wives' attitudes as of more than 20 years earlier. Thus, for example, 67 percent of the women who scored above the median on conservatism in college were married to men who preferred Nixon in the 1960 election, whereas only 33 percent of the women who scored below the median on conservatism in college were married to men who preferred Nixon. The chi-square value of this relationship is 9.04, with a p value of less than 0.005. Thus in two-thirds of all cases it would have been possible to predict correctly, 20-odd years ago, whether a future husband's attitudes would be in the more or the less conservative half of the 1960–1961 distribution, simply by knowing in which half of the distribution the future wife belonged in the 1930s.

This rather strong relationship rests, of course, *both* upon the persistence of most women's attitudes over the years and upon their tendency to select and be selected by men having attitudes like their own. These two processes, as many lines of evidence suggest, are interdependent. That is, the persistence of their attitudes during late college and early post-college years had something to do, directly or indirectly, with their "choice" of husbands who, typically, in turn helped to provide an environment supportive of those attitudes.

ATTITUDES OF FRIENDS

We hypothesized that friends were another important influence upon respondents' attitudes. It was not possible to interview their friends (with rare exemptions later noted). Hence our information about friends' attitudes comes only from respondents, each of whom was asked how most of her close friends felt about the several current issues and public figures. About 40 percent of the interviewees reported that they did not know how their friends felt, and were not willing to guess. An analysis of responses by the 60 percent who did reply shows that in all four groups—those who had remained conservative, remained nonconservative, become more conservative, or become less conservative since college—women reported significantly more conservatism on the part of their friends than on their own part. . . .

Table 5.8 shows a distribution of scores on the 1960 Political Conservatism Index for the friends of the women in each of the four groups of attitude change or persistence. Respondents who became less conservative after college report attitudes for their friends that are significantly lower on conservatism than those reported for the friends of the women who remained con-

TABLE 5.8 RELATIONSHIP OF RESPONDENT'S CHANGE IN ATTITUDE AND FRIENDS' POLITICAL CONSERVATISM

		FRIEND'S 1960 CONSERVATISM INDEX[a]		
Final PEP Score in College	1960 Conservatism Index	Above the Respondents' Median	Below the Respondents' Median	Mean
a. Above median	Above median	27	0	30.2
b. Above median	Below median	5	10	22.0
c. Below median	Above median	14	0	27.3
d. Below median	Below median	11	20	19.7
		57	30	

[a] The friends' attitudes are reported by the respondent.

servative ($t = 4.16$, $p < 0.005$). Also women who became more conservative after college report attitudes for their friends that are significantly more conservative than the attitudes of the friends of those who remained nonconservative ($t = 3.37$ $p < 0.005$).

Even though most of the women report attitudes for their friends that are more conservative than their own, they do tend to see some similarity between their own and their friends' beliefs. Friends of women who are not conservative are reported to be much less conservative than are the friends of the women who are conservative (chi-square $= 37.9$, $p < 0.001$). The ability of the respondents to report accurately how their friends feel about various issues probably varies with the frequency with which they discuss political issues, how important politics is to them, and how important it is for them to find support and agreement for their own points of view among their associates. Whether or not the reports are accurate, they are useful indicators of how the respondents perceive their friends. Only 8 percent of the women reported attitudes for their friends that were less conservative than their own.

Some of the close friends of the women in the study were other Bennington College alumnae who were also participants in the follow-up study. It is therefore possible to compare the attitude scores of the respondents with those of these friends. On the basis of the 1960 Conservatism Index our procedure was to classify the respondents in three groups: (1) those more than half of whose friends scored above the median on conservatism; (2) those more than half of whose friends scored below the median on conservatism; (3) those half of whose friends scored above the median and half below the median on conservatism. The proportion of women whose friends were classified in each of these groups is shown in Table 5.9. There is a tendency for those who became conservative since college to have friends from Bennington who are also conservative and for the women who became less conservative to have friends from Bennington who are not conservative. These findings are independent of respondents' judgments.

The relationship between respondents' conservatism and that of their Bennington friends in 1960 can most easily be shown by combining the first and third rows of Table 5.9, and comparing them with the second and fourth rows, assigning half of the cases in the third column to the first and half to the second column, as follows:

	Friends at or below Median	Friends at or above Median	Total
Respondents above median	34	24	58
Respondents below median	20.5	29.5	50
	54.5	53.5	108

The chi-square value of this distribution is 4.06, significant at less than 0.05. Thus there is a clear tendency, although not a marked one, for the respondent's own degree of conservatism to be associated with similar attitudes on the part of her Bennington friends.

This finding has special importance since it provides the only evidence we have that attitude scores obtained by report from the respondent about her friends and from those friends themselves tend to be congruent. All other comparisons of attitudes between the respondent and significant members of her social environment are based on the respondents' report alone. Thus it appears that there is both an actual and a perceived congruence in political attitudes among the respondent and members of her social environment.

For the most part it appears that the graduates of the classes of 1938, 1939, and 1940 selected and moved into—and perhaps in some degree, created—a social environment which tended to support and reinforce the

TABLE 5.9 RELATIONSHIP OF RESPONDENT'S ATTITUDE CHANGE TO THE ATTITUDES OF THE MAJORITY OF HER BENNINGTON FRIENDS

Final PEP Score in College	1960 Conservatism Index	ACTUAL SCORES OF FRIENDS FROM BENNINGTON ON THE 1960 CONSERVATISM INDEX						
		More than Half of Friends above Median		More than Half of Friends below Median		Half above, Half below Median		Total
a. Above median	Above median	18	(46%)	15	(38%)	6	(15%)	39	(99%)
b. Above median	Below median	3	(19%)	8	(50%)	5	(31%)	16	(100%)
c. Below median	Above median	12	(63%)	5	(26%)	2	(11%)	19	(100%)
d. Below median	Below median	13	(38%)	17	(50%)	4	(12%)	34	(100%)
		46		45		17		108

value systems with which they had left college. However, as we have seen, some of these women did not find support for their points of view in the associations they made after college. In some instances, too, their political attitudes were presumably not important enough to them or well enough developed to have influenced their post-college interests, selection of friends, or participation in activities.

SELF-REPORTS OF INTERESTS AND INFLUENCES

One of the ways in which the students who maintained conservative political attitudes in college during the 1930s differed from the students who became less conservative is that many of them were not as interested in politics and were not involved at that time. The women who were interviewed in 1960 were asked how frequently they discussed politics. Sixty-eight percent of the women who became *less* conservative after college said that they discussed politics frequently, whereas only 47 percent of the women who remained conservative said that they discussed politics that often. On the other hand, 61 percent of the women who became *more* conservative after college discussed politics frequently, and 71 percent of those who remained nonconservative said that they discussed them as often. There is thus some tendency for the people who remained conservative to discuss politics less frequently than any others, suggesting either personal indifference or a social environment of indifference, or both.

Each woman was asked why she had changed her political attitudes, or, if she had not changed them, what were the important influences which helped to shape her political point of view.

The most frequently mentioned reason for becoming more conservative was "getting older," and the most frequently mentioned reason for becoming less conservative was "I'm better informed now." From the relationships reported earlier in the chapter it appears that the husbands were an important influence on the women's political attitudes. However, only a small percentage of the women interviewed mentioned their husbands as an important influ-

—Sure that could be
the true case

ence on their political thinking. They felt that the major influences had been new information and new responsibilities.

The women were also asked to indicate the important influences on their political points of view. About 20 percent of them mentioned their husbands, 27 percent mentioned other relatives, 26 percent mentioned friends, and 25 percent mentioned work associates. Twenty percent mentioned their education at Bennington, Bennington classmates, or faculty. Almost everyone mentioned some interpersonal influence.

OVERVIEW: SUPPORTIVE SOCIAL ENVIRONMENTS

Change in political attitude after college is associated with many interpersonal and intrapersonal factors. In some instances, the changes in point of view were quite self-conscious, the result of much thinking, and something felt to be very important. In other cases, the person had changed her point of view without being aware of it, and was not involved with political orientations, nor did she consider politics an important part of her life.

Husbands' influence upon wives' attitudes most frequently appears to be indirect—by way of providing support for wives existing attitudes—rather than direct, in the sense of influencing wives to change. Spouses' histories of stability and change suggest "independence" from their husbands about as often as "dependence" upon them, although more of the wives (about one-fifth) changed toward agreement with their husbands than the other way around (about one-eighth). Very few couples, as of 1960–1961, held opposing preferences for political parties.

Women who had friends who were interested in public affairs and who agreed with their own points of view tended to maintain their previous political orientations. Those who had friends who disagreed with them tended to defend and question their points of view, and sometimes changed them. In general, respondents tended to report that most of their friends had political orientations similar to their own. When the attitudes of the respondents who named each other as friends were compared, most pairs of ex-Bennington friends expressed similar attitudes about public issues.

The women who had not changed their political attitudes since college had, to a greater extent, moved into a social environment which supported their existing political viewpoints. In some instances, change was deliberate and self-conscious; in others, we have no evidence that change was determined by their interest in public affairs. On the other hand, those who changed their attitudes after college had moved into social environments which tended to oppose their points of view, or at least not support them. However, lack of social support was not sufficient to produce changes in attitudes in some women, and some of them changed their points of view even though there was a good deal of support for their original attitudes; events, new information, and new problems had arisen which initiated a re-evaluation of their positions.

PART II

OPINION CONTENT

The next two sections deal less with the contributions of various social institutions to the molding of political opinions and more with the consistency and order imposed on them by individuals and their structural distribution among populations. In Selection 6 Lester Milbrath stresses the importance individual belief systems have for understanding the actions of and differences among nations. Milbrath reviews the problems inherent in the analysis of an individual's opinion organization. In particular, he offers some insight into the complex relationship between a state's political institutions and predominant ideologies and the cruder and more simplified notions that a person acts upon. Philip Converse, in Selection 7, is concerned with examining an individual's attitudinal orientations to discover which political views he holds to be the most consequential and what functional interdependence, if any, exists among his opinions. For example, it is often assumed that a "conservative" or "liberal" possesses a general attitudinal predisposition toward the government and its policies. A conservative would be in favor of the status quo, gradual change, and, within the contemporary political context, less government involvement in economic and social affairs. A liberal might favor change in general, active government participation in the redistribution of wealth, regulation of business in the name of the public interest, and the consistent advancement of social causes. Whatever the policy consequence, there is implicit in the use of these labeling terms an assumption that the individual maintains some consistency among his views, possibly relating to a more basic view of the nature of man and the role of government. In turn, his policy choices should be relatively stable over time. Converse examines these questions in his attempt to map the cognitions of the voter and the ideas he employs to order his political world. The author finds a fairly low level of conceptual development in the electorate and little predictability or relationship among views.

Opinion content and its role in electoral decision making is also the focus of the research piece (Selection 8) by Morris Janowitz and Dwaine Marvick. The authors examine the issues of concern to Democratic and Republican voters in a presidential campaign and the relationship between these and the positions taken by the political parties. Next, they assess the image of the presidential candidates as held by the voters and then they attempt to judge the relative contribution of each to the voting decision. Crudely put, Which is more important to the voter, the candidate's personality or pertinent campaign issues? The authors find a close link between a positive image of a contender for office and an individual's vote for him. However, one-fifth of the respondents had conflicting or undeveloped candidate perceptions and correspondingly employed other criteria for decisions. Party changers—those who voted for another party in a previous election— were found to be motivated less by policy considerations than the consistent party supporters.[1] The authors end by arguing that the campaign does not provide an effective means of associating party positions with an individual's policy desires and both with his vote.

Finally, in Selection 9, an article previously unpublished and specifically written for inclusion within the present volume, Gilbert Abcarian identifies the place of unconventional political groups within the total political system. The author discusses the purpose of a group's own political doctrines and, in detail, the motivating beliefs of the contemporary movements, the radical right and the new left. The Students for a Democratic Society (SDS), an organization immersed in social action programs on many university campuses, represents the focal point for the discussion of radical left groups. Abcarian concludes by examining the movements within the context of conventional explanations of personal involvement.

[1] The ideological insensitivity of "swing" voters as illustrated here and in the major voting studies has been challenged more recently by the late V. O. Key, Jr., in his last work, *The Responsible Electorate* (Cambridge: Harvard University Press, 1966).

6

Beliefs: A Neglected
Unit of Analysis
in Comparative Politics *

LESTER W. MILBRATH

If one were to make a catalog of important unanswered questions in the field of comparative politics, the list probably would include the following: Why do governmental arrangements that work well in one nation or culture work poorly or fail in another? Why is government slowly evolving and stable in some nations and volatile and unstable in others? Why do nations which have similarities in their resource bases develop at radically different economic rates? Why do nations with goals that are amenable to one another still see events in different lights, have difficulties in negotiating and communicating with each other, and choose courses of action which bring them into conflict?

One explanation normally offered attributes these differences to differences in "culture." But, having said that, what has been explained? The thorough scholar would wish to know: What is different about the cultures? What aspects of a culture support governmental institutions? What kinds of cultural changes lead to what kinds of changes in institutions and procedures?

Considerable time must elapse before scholars will have answers to the

* Reprinted by permission of the University of North Carolina Press. From Edward L. Pinney, ed., *Comparative Politics and Political Theory: Essays Written in Honor of Charles Baskervill Robson* (Chapel Hill: University of North Carolina Press, 1966), pp. 44–66.

questions posed above. It is my contention, however, that the quest for answers would be significantly aided if greater attention were paid to beliefs as a unit of analysis when comparing the characteristics of nations. Culture is expressed and is transmitted via beliefs. When parents teach their children the significant parts of their culture, they are essentially teaching them what to believe; and this is especially true when children are taught to react to and to approach the institutions of government. A child must learn a set of beliefs about what he is to do for the government and what the government should do for him. In this way a set of beliefs is inculcated in a child concerning appropriate times of obedience and disobedience to governmental authorities, and concerning government structure and the way government performs its functions.

Before proceeding further, a definition of "beliefs" would be appropriate, distinguishing this from related terms such as cognition, value, attitude, opinion, and ideology. Cognition incorporates the broadest range of phenomena because it is a component of that included in all the other concepts. One can cognize without either valuing or believing, whereas the reverse is not true. To a cognition may be attached two kinds of feeling, either separately or together. One kind of feeling is a valence; i.e., a person may be positively attracted toward or negatively repulsed from the object being cognized. Both values and attitudes are cognitions with attached valences.

We have no widely used generic term in the English language for the other kind of feeling that can attach to a cognition. It is a feeling that the object being cognized is credible (believable) or incredible (not believable), so that a belief is a cognition to which credulity is attached. This feeling varies in strength, being neither totally present nor totally absent, and in direction, since we disbelieve as well as believe. Both strength and direction are abstractly illustrated in Figure 6.1.

Figure 6.1   Range of Credulity

Strong disbelief	Non-belief	Unshakable belief
100	0	100

It is important to note here that it is the feeling about the cognition which makes it believable or not; credulity is not inherent in the cognition itself. A cognition which is credible to some persons will be incredible to others, and some cognitions stimulate strong credulity while others stimulate such feelings very weakly. In one setting or at one time in one's life a cognition may prompt incredulity, but in another setting or at another time the same cognition may prompt credulity.

Another important point about these two kinds of feeling (valence and credulity) is that although they are distinctive analytically, they often attach simultaneously to the same cognition. The relationship between the two kinds of feelings is spatially illustrated in Figure 6.2. Cognitions with a valence

Figure 6.2 Spatial Relationship of Credulity and Valence

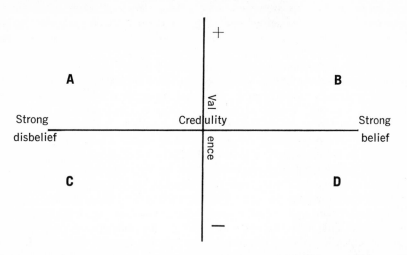

only fall on the vertical axis. Those with a credulity only fall on the horizontal axis. If neither feeling is present the cognition will be located in the center of the diagram. If the cognition is believed and liked, it will fall in quadrant B; if believed and disliked, in quadrant D; if disbelieved and liked, in quadrant A; and if disbelieved and disliked, in quadrant C.

The two kinds of feeling also have interactive effects on each other. Research has shown repeatedly that we tend to believe what we like (many cognitions fall in quadrant B) and disbelieve what we dislike (quadrant C). This tendency is not always evident, however, for we believe many things we dislike (my enemy is strong than I) and like many things we do not believe (I am flying like a bird). Neither is it always so that both feelings attach to a single cognition. We sometimes feel a valence without deciding whether or not we believe (listening to music or looking at a painting), and sometimes we believe without feeling a valence (two plus two equals four).

At times we have valences on two levels for a complex cognition, and sometimes these valences go in opposite directions. For instance, we have all experienced negative revulsion from the pain of an inoculation or a dentist's drill, yet, on another level and at the same time, we have a positive attraction to such temporary pain because we believe it will bring future pleasure (or at least avoid worse pain). Because we believe certain means-ends relationships to be true (inoculations prevent disease), we can readily choose to do painful things for the moment in anticipation of future benefits. Lacking the necessary means-ends beliefs, a child reacts only to the pain of the moment (runs from the shot). The superimposition of beliefs on valences enables us to choose mature courses of action.

The characteristics of these two kinds of feeling have some important research consequences. In everyday life both feelings often attach to cognitions and are often spoken of as a single feeling. Researchers writing items for survey studies must use everyday language and usually cannot communicate pure belief items or pure value items. The belief format can be used for both kinds of feelings, however, since most instances of valence toward an object can be restated as a belief. ("I like constitutional government" becomes "I believe that I like constitutional government," or "I hate Castro" becomes "I believe I hate Castro.")

Although the belief-value distinction is difficult to maintain for single items, it has some utility for directing the focus of categories of items. One can, for example, identify some items that focus on what a person actually does and then direct other items to discovering what a person thinks he ought to do. More importantly, the distinction alerts us to areas of inquiry that might be overlooked if we did not distinguish the two kinds of feeling. One's belief system generally is larger than one's value system, and by focusing only on statements with valences a research study might miss many things of importance. For example, a respondent's beliefs about how his government functions may be much more important for understanding his political behavior than knowing whether he likes or dislikes the way it functions. An impoverished understanding of what an individual can do vis-à-vis the government will not only be highly determinative of an individual's political behavior but may well shape his general attitude toward the government. If one focuses on a study of beliefs, he is likely to pick up both valences and beliefs, whereas an exclusive focus on values or attitudes increases the likelihood that important beliefs will be overlooked.

Conceptual distinctions can now be stated somewhat more precisely. *Cognitions* are common to all the concepts considered here. They can exist separately from a valence or from a feeling of credulity (although that is unlikely). Credulity or incredulity attached to a cognition make it a *belief* or a *disbelief*. A valence attached to a cognition makes it an attitude or a value. *Attitudes* may be thought of as preferences, whereas *values* carry a normative component. If we value something we not only feel that the norm applies to us but that it applies to others as well (we all must value peace). Conversely we are not so distressed if others do not share our attitudes (I do not mind if others do not share my liking for ice cream).

Opinions are a somewhat larger structure than the simple feelings discussed above; they typically combine beliefs, attitudes, and values. Although an opinion may focus on a single object (e.g., I disapprove of Medicare), it usually is embedded in a larger structure of related beliefs, attitudes, and values. If this larger structure is elaborated and differentiated into a somewhat consistent hierarchy with application to a wide variety of specific objects, it may be called an *ideology*. Ideologies are important aids to making decisions, by having a hierarchy of values to be served and by containing a set of beliefs which suggest that certain institutional arrangements and patterns of action are most likely to realize those values. A proposed policy can be judged for its fit with ideological prescriptions and can then be readily accepted, or rejected, as the case may be.

Unfortunately, ideologies with a common name (e.g., Marxism) may not be uniform in structure from person to person, and grave errors of interpretation and prediction can be made by assuming that from adherence to a common ideological label the same patterns of action will follow. Ideologies need to be broken down into component beliefs and values, as felt by specific adherents, before analysis and explanation can be very effective. Two important findings have come from some recent studies of these more specific beliefs: (1) few people have a logically consistent ideological structure, and (2) many people have such impoverished cognitions and beliefs about government and public affairs as to preclude their holding an ideology.[1] A person lacking beliefs about whether or not a policy will lead to the outcome he desires, or who has no ideas about what actions to take to try to get a policy adopted, is a person whose beliefs are insufficiently linked to form a hierarchical structure.

THE ACT OF BELIEVING

How does one decide if a cognition is credible or not? Fundamentally, we all depend on our five senses; and by sensing a cognition directly we are likely to believe that it is so. Things we have learned to believe from direct sensory experience form the center of our belief structure, and they tend to be firm and unshakable. More peripheral beliefs, which we have had to accept on the recommendation of others, are less firmly held but can sometimes be tested by our own sensory experience. There is a good chance that our beliefs will change about something we have cognized, but not sensed, when we finally get the opportunity to sense it (e.g., cognizing Eastern Europe via the public media produced a set of beliefs in myself quite different from those based on my direct experience while living there.)

On reflection, it is striking how small a proportion of the totality of our beliefs is based on information picked up directly by our senses. For the most part we depend on information provided by others for the things we believe. But we cannot believe everything we are told; we have had to learn, sometimes bitterly, that we must question and doubt all new information. But how do we decide if the new information is credible or not? By far the most important factor is our *feeling* about the authoritativeness of the information. This tendency to accept as credible the information provided by authority figures is conditioned in children by their parents almost from the day of birth. The trend is continued by teachers, clergy, writers, scientists, and so forth throughout one's life. A second factor is the unanimity with which a belief is held by the people around us. Most of us are disinclined to doubt the veracity of something that everyone around us takes for granted as true. A third factor is our valence toward the cognition; if we want something to be true, we are much more inclined to believe it than if we do not want it to be true.

We cannot directly sense those things that are the subject of most religious beliefs. Yet most religious people hold their beliefs very firmly, perhaps because all three of the above-mentioned factors pull in the same

[1] Angus Campbell, Phillip Converse, Warren Miller, and Donald Stokes, *The American Voter* (New York: Wiley, 1960), Chap. 9; Herbert McClosky, "Consensus and Ideology in American Politics," *American Political Science Review*, LVIII (June 1964), 361–382; James W. Prothro and Charles M. Grigg, "Fundamental Principles of Democracy: Bases of Agreement and Disagreement," *Journal of Politics*, XXII (May 1960), 276–294.

direction. Children are told that religious beliefs are true by the highest authorities (their parents, the clergy, and the very "word of God"), most of the people around them believe the same thing, and religious believers want desperately to believe. At the same time there is no evidence available to their senses which might challenge or contradict the belief so authoritatively handed to them. Furthermore, the authorities claim there is something virtuous about believing *in* something; that is, one is fulfilled as a person by believing in a cause, and doubts or questions are inadmissible (or sinful).

When we speak of believing *in* something we suggest that extra emotional investment has been given to the belief. Usually this means that the belief has become a part of the security system of the believing individual. As such, it cannot be altered or abandoned without seriously disturbing that system. Because of this emotional dependence on the belief, a person will go to considerable lengths to defend a belief against assault, developing elaborate rationalizations to counter any possible challenging argument. It is the belief itself which is important, not a dispassionate test of its truth or falsity. This extra emotional investment characterizes not only religious beliefs, but many political, economic, and social beliefs as well. Most political ideologies, for example, are objects of just as strong a belief as are religious ones. It is as futile to use rational argument against one as against the other.

There are additional sources for the feeling of credulity which are especially necessary for those who are inclined to doubt beliefs handed down by tradition and authorities, and who are suspicious of the beliefs to which their own desires might lead them. Building on a base of central beliefs, many of which are confirmed by direct sensation, we all judge the credibility of new information by its "fit" with the existing structure of beliefs. Milton Rokeach tells of hearing on the radio one day that a camera had been invented that could take a picture of something that wasn't there. This did not fit with the pattern of already accepted beliefs which he used to judge new information, and he did not believe. Later he learned that it was an infrared camera, which was so sensitive that it could take pictures of the traces of heat left by an object even though the object had been moved before the picture was taken. This "new" information fit with Rokeach's belief structure, and it was now possible to believe that such a camera had been invented. . . .[2]

One can extrapolate some characteristics of national belief-holding from this examination of the sources of beliefs. Because most beliefs are bestowed by authorities and are strongly supported by being widely shared, one tends to find a uniformity of belief in a given national culture. Because most nations or cultures have had somewhat unique historical experiences, they tend to develop a certain uniqueness in their national beliefs. If the nation has a unique language this uniqueness of beliefs tends to be enhanced, and national myths about the history and destiny of the nation can usually be found. Certain ways of deciding whether or not a problem exists and certain methods for problem solution come to be accepted as the only reliable methods. Certain patterns of relationship between the individual and the government come to be accepted as the only proper ones.

[2] Milton Rokeach, *The Open and Closed Mind* (New York: Basic Books, 1960), p. 48.

Students of comparative politics traditionally have tended to look at institutions, social functions, social structure, developmental rates and patterns, and ideologies as units of analysis. The major point of this paper is that the belief structure of a nation undergirds and partially explains all of these factors. Now that technical know-how enables us to study national beliefs systematically and thoroughly,[3] it is perhaps time to end their neglect as a unit of analysis. In the next section I shall suggest some analytical possibilities for cross-cultural research using beliefs as the primary focus of inquiry.

SOME ANALYSIS POSSIBILITIES

The suggestions which follow derive partly from my personal experience while living in Eastern Europe and in Scandinavia, and partly from a pretest which I conducted in the Chicago metropolitan area, during the summer of 1963, for a cross-cultural study of beliefs. The pretest sample was designed for wide variance and it utilized random selection only within certain social strata. Half of the persons were chosen from the city of Chicago and half from Evanston. All ranges of socioeconomic status were included; seventeen residents of Negro slums in Chicago were interviewed by a Negro interviewer. About twenty precinct captains, randomly chosen from the same neighborhoods as the other respondents, also were interviewed. The total size of the pretest sample was sixty-five. This sample is not representative of any territorially-defined population; it was designed primarily to test the workability of various methods. Yet some of the findings turned up by the pretest were so interesting that they are reported here to suggest possibilities for further analytical exploration. The reader is cautioned not to take them as representative of beliefs held by American citizens.

Sense of Boundaries on Rulers

Although they may have been taught certain things about a constitution, ordinary citizens seldom indicate much concern over constitutional matters. In fact, one could hypothesize that the better the constitution works, the less likely they are the citizens who live under it to give it much thought. If one puts constitutional questions to them, as we did in the Chicago pretest, they are inclined to grope ineffectively for responses. (These were not questions about the fine points of constitutionalism, but simple questions about the rights and responsibilities citizens have under the Constitution.) For example: most could see no instance in which they might justifiably disobey a government order; most did not see the Constitution as a higher law, and would not disobey a law that violated the Constitution if they did; most disapproved of civil disobedience as a means of keeping rulers within bounds; most were unclear as to how a citizen can stand up to the government; and when confronted with hypothetical situations in which

---

[3] A five-nation study conducted by Almond and Verba is an important first step in that direction. Gabriel Almond and Sidney Verba, *The Civic Culture* (Princeton: Princeton University Press, 1963).

the government does something in violation of the Constitution, they could usually recognize the violation but were unable to imagine that it could occur or what they would do if it should occur.

Despite this inability readily to manifest their understanding of the need to keep rulers within bounds, some of the data suggest that a latent sense of boundary does exist. I would hypothesize that this sense of boundary is present in all nations or cultures, developed or underdeveloped, dictatorship or democracy. In oppressive regimes the leadership may prevent the sense of boundary from finding meaningful expression, but I would hypothesize that it is present nevertheless. In the Chicago pretest this sense was manifested by the ability of respondents to recognize instances of improper action by officials, even if they were unable to prescribe some means for boundary enforcement. Some small group experiments, conducted in conjunction with the survey interviews, suggest that group discussion sharpens this sense of boundary and enhances the probability that the group can decide on an effective course of action for attempting to enforce the boundary.

In these experiments, small discussion-groups (4–6 persons) were presented with a hypothetical situation in which some part of the government violates the Constitution (a clear-cut violation if judged by the tradition of Anglo-Saxon constitutional law). The group was asked first if the governmental action was proper or not and, if they decided it was improper, they were asked to choose a course of action to rectify the situation. (Although somewhat artificial, such group discussions are probably closer to a "real-life" situation than questions put to an individual respondent; most people, if confronted with a constitutional violation, would discuss it with their friends and neighbors and would choose a course of action in concert with them.) As the discussions proceeded, the participants found their conceptualization being sharpened; in addition, they almost always found themselves in eventual agreement about what is proper and improper. Although there was less unanimity about what should be done to counter the unconstitutional action, the group was usually able to select a common course. In one set of these discussions a short test of constitutional principles was administered both before and after the discussions; and the gain shown on the after tests suggests that the discussions were important learning occasions. Experimental controls, according to a complex Solomon design, were applied to make certain the gain was not just an artifact of the testing itself.

It would be useful to find out if this sense of boundaries is readily discoverable in other countries, especially in those which do not have a written constitution. I would hypothesize that such a sense exists and can be found. A reasonable expectation is that the position of the boundary varies from country to country; knowledge of this variance could be an important aid to understanding differences in the functioning of political systems. Probably a very important variation to be appreciated is the extent to which the people believe they can do something to hold their rulers in check should the boundaries be overstepped. The fact that in some nations the people believe they can do nothing because of an oppressive state apparatus does not mean that they have no sense of boundary. They may still believe that certain actions are improper, but are unwilling to pay the high cost of enforcing the boundary. Unfortunately, it is difficult to obtain data on what people would do to keep their rulers within bounds. In a stable constitutional system most persons have not confronted the situation and cannot effectively imagine what they would do. In a police state the authorities would be unlikely to allow researchers to go about asking people what they could do to check their rulers; and even if they did, one could not be confident of the respondents' candor.

Input and Demand Structure Linking the Individual to the State

Closely related to an individual's sense of boundaries are his beliefs about what he should do for the government and what the government should do for him. In the Chicago pretest we labeled these "inputs" and "outtakes"; they were called outtakes rather than outputs because we wanted to place emphasis on what the individual took from the government rather than on government performance. The pattern of these beliefs for a society shapes into what might be called its input and demand structure vis-à-vis government.

In the pretest individual input and outtake items were placed on small cards. In the first (or reality) sorting of the input cards, respondents were asked to sort them into three piles according to what they actually did: (1) those things they did regularly, (2) those things they did occasionally, and (3) those things they never did at all. In the second (or ideal) sorting of the same cards respondents were asked to sort them into three piles according to their sense of responsibility: "(1) important responsibility to do, (2) medium responsibility to do, and (3) no responsibility at all." A similar "ideal" and "real" comparison was devised for the outtake items. An examination of the differences between the reality and idea sorts discloses aspiration and rejections and carries a suggestion as to how well people believe their government is doing in specific programs.

Responses on the input and outtake items from the Chicago pretest were subjected to factor analysis. It may be interesting to look at some of the general findings even if the data cannot be taken as representative of American beliefs on these matters. As the individual factors and items are discussed an arithmetic mean will sometimes be reported, but this should be taken as characteristic of nothing more than this pretest sample. The cards were scored according to the numbers given above; thus, the lower the mean, the more regularly the activity was done or the more important it was believed to be. The input items shaped into four factors which were labeled: (1) keeping rulers within bounds, (2) political activity, (3) teaching children about government, and (4) citizen duties.

Most respondents reported that they seldom did (mean range 2.4–2.8) the things that fell in the first factor, keeping rulers within bounds. They acknowledged a medium responsibility to "protest vigorously and publicly if the government oversteps its boundaries" (1.88) and to "send messages of support or protest to party leaders between elections as well as at election time" (1.94). Still, they felt it was less important to "question the legitimacy of regulations issued by authorities before obeying them" (2.03), and rejected "join public demonstrations" (2.63) as well as "belong to a party or group trying to change the constitution" (2.54). These items show little support for vigorous defense of boundaries.

The general pattern on the second factor, political activity, was to acknowledge a somewhat stronger responsibility to be active in politics than was actually carried out. Especially strongly felt was the responsibility to "keep informed about politics" (1.215), and to "vote in elections" (1.00), both of which were so uniformly endorsed as to constitute a duty. Respondents also expressed a fairly strong responsibility to "engage in political discussion" (1.63), to "take an active part in a campaign" (1.66), and to "join a political party" (1.58), but in practice they fell a little short of this aspiration. Respondents felt little responsibility to "be a candidate for public office" (2.46) and it was hardly ever done (2.71).

On the third factor, teaching children about government, respondents said they had a strong responsibility to "teach my children the importance of give-and-take in the democratic way of life" (1.015) and to "personally see to it that my children understand and accept the responsibilities of citizenship" (1.015); they also reported doing these things fairly regularly (1.3). They reported only a medium responsibility to "teach my children to be active in politics" (1.69), and did it only occasionally (1.92).

Certain items were so uniformly considered important and so regularly done as to be considered duties. Voting and discussing have already been mentioned. Other items were: "pay all taxes," "have undivided loyalty and love for my country," and "perform military or national service."

The activities which individuals in this sample felt they had to do were fairly narrowly defined. Inputs are also a function of how potent or efficacious individuals believe their actions to be. To a considerable extent this sense of potency depends on an individual's beliefs about how the government functions. If he makes a demand, does the government respond? If he has been mistreated, does he receive justice? If he approaches bureaucracy, does he receive his rights without having to fight for them or curry favor? There are probably important differences in national beliefs about individual potency in these matters. Perhaps especially important to look for would be a belief that one can use one part of the government (e.g., one's representative) to get another part to take action. In the pretest, respondents were asked if their individual actions could affect the system. Somewhat over half felt some sense of efficacy, but only one-third felt a clear sense of individual efficacy, while nearly another third felt no sense of efficacy at all. On another question most respondents believed they would eventually receive justice even if some official treated them unfairly.

On the reality sort of the outtake cards, respondents were again asked to sort into three piles: "(1) those things the state does an efficient or active job of providing here, (2) those things the state does a moderately active job of providing, and (3) those things the state does ineffectively or not at all." On the ideal sort the instructions read: "(1) those things the state has a strong or important responsibility to do for you, (2) those things you would like the state to provide but you don't feel quite as strongly about it, and (3) those things you believe the state should not attempt to provide at all." The outtake items shaped into five factors given the following names: (1) maintaining an open society, (2) economic opportunity, (3) efficiency and rectitude in government, (4) justice, and (5) less important outtakes.

Respondents generally appraised the items that fell in the first factor, maintaining an open society, as being moderately well done and being moderately to very important (range 1.33–1.73). The five items in this factor were "insuring equal opportunity for citizens to participate in making political decisions," "insuring adequate channels of expression for all citizens," "making available means or facilities to resolve conflict between private parties," "intervening to stop an individual or group from persecuting another individual or group," and "providing stability in society even if it means slowing down the rate of progress."

There was less uniformity in appraising the items that tell in the economic opportunity factor. "Providing a chance to make a good living" was judged as being moderately well done (1.692) and quite important (1.262). "Arranging things so it is easy for citizens to move from place to place, job to job, class to class" was judged as being a bit less well done (1.985) and moderately important (1.68). "Seeing to it that every man who wants a job can have a job" was considered not very well done (2.03) but quite important (1.31). "Providing welfare services" was perceived as reasonably well done (1.26) and somewhat less important (1.43). In other words, this sample felt the government could relax a little here, although the importance rating was still fairly high. "Providing free university education for all who can qualify" was perceived as not very well done (2.05) but moderately important (1.69). "Arranging things so that business is left alone" was perceived as not very well done (2.09) and moderately important (1.60). Generally, this sample said that they wished the government to provide jobs and university education, more effectively to leave a little more freedom to business, and to relax on providing welfare benefits.

The outtakes in the third factor, efficiency and rectitude in government, were all considered important (range 1.00–1.13), and most were believed to be well done: "taking actions that make one proud of his country" (1.49), "providing protection and security" (1.25), "providing public order" (1.20), and "providing strong leadership" (1.385). Two outtakes were believed to be only moderately well done, but still important: "being careful in using public money and trust" (1.72), and "competently handling foreign affairs" (1.72).

Only two items loaded heavily on the fourth factor, justice. "Securing civil rights and liberties for all" was believed to be only moderately well done (1.74) but important (1.11). "Providing justice for all" was thought of as somewhat better than moderately well done (1.57) and very important (1.00).

The outtakes considered least important fell in the fifth factor. "Trying to even out differences in wealth and prestige" was not only believed to be not well done (2.05), but also to be not very important (2.12). Rejection was even more pronounced for "adopting one official religion supported by the state" (2.63). Providing celebrations, holidays, and parades" was believed to be reasonably well done (1.40) but not so important (1.80).

These findings suggest the kind of information that is available. Similar studies on adequate samples in several countries, carefully done, would produce some interesting comparisons and would provide partial answers to such questions as the following: How do the input and demand structures of societies with stable governments differ from those with unstable governments? How do the two structures differ for socialist and capitalist countries? How do the two structures differ for developed and underdeveloped countries? What minimal inputs are necessary to keep a government functioning adequately? What pattern of demands must minimally be met for a government to maintain support? When the minimal pattern of demands is better understood, what is the ratio of emotional to material outtakes among them? How do input and demand patterns differ across different strata of a society? Does the maintenance of constitutionalism (keeping rulers within bounds) require a minimal level of scrutiny and protest from the broad body politics, or is it satisfactory if this minimal level is provided only by the elite of the society? How does an individual's belief about his own potency (vis-à-vis the government) affect the pattern of his inputs and outtakes?

Popular Conceptions of Government, Politics, and the Constitution

A belief about a general concept may be a many-faceted complex of feelings. We attempted to measure some of this complexity in the Chicago area pretest by using Osgood's "semantic differential."[4] For each of three central concepts (government, politics, constitution) about 25 polar adjectives were presented; each pair of adjectives was separated by seven spaces allowing the respondent to judge which space best characterized the central concept (for example: giving—demanding, or dirty—clean). By checking one position between each of the 25 pairs a respondent displays a many-faceted semantic conceptualization. This over-all pattern also can show how positively or negatively he feels about the general concept. To avoid a set to respond either to the left or to the right side of the check sheet, and thus bias the over-all pattern, the presumably positive adjectives (clean, for example) were alternately placed on the right and the left side of the sheet.

Prior to systematic investigation, it was easy to suppose from many bits of evidence (letters to the editor, exposé-type newspaper stories, charges of corruption between antagonistic parties and candidates, etc.) that most Americans had negative feelings toward politics and government. The Almond and Verba five-nation study, however, showed that Americans generally had more positive feelings toward their government than did citizens from the other countries (England, Germany, Italy, and Mexico).[5] To see if feelings about politics differed from those toward government, respondents in the Chicago pretest were given the identical set of paired adjectives for the two concepts. The over-all results support the findings of the five-nation study: this sample had very positive feelings toward both politics and govern-

[4] Charles E. Osgood, G. J. Suci, and P. H. Tannenbaum, *The Measurement of Meaning* (Urbana: University of Illinois Press, 1957).

[5] Almond and Verba, *The Civic Culture.*

ment. We hypothesized that they would have stronger positive feelings toward government than toward politics; this was true to a very slight extent, but none of the differences between means was significant for this sample. This finding may be biased by the fact that about one-third of the sample were precinct captains. Obviously research on a much more adequate sample is needed.

The semantic picture can be presented simultaneously for the two concepts, politics and government. The adjectives seemed to cluster into four factors: evaluative, activity, potency, and essentiality. Under the evaluative factor respondents saw politics and government as largely honest, clean, attractive, honorable, open, straight, deep, good, creative, and leaning more toward happy than sad. Government was seen as a bit more unselfish than grasping, but the mean was equal between the poles for politics.

In the activity factor the respondents saw the two concepts as leaning toward friendly, many, giving, hot, uniting, exciting, and a shade noisier than quiet. Government was a bit more old than young, but the mean was equal between the poles for politics. In the potency factor the direction was very clear: they were seen as powerful, big, strong, and leaning more toward hard than soft. Under the essentiality factor they were seen as very necessary, serious, and everlasting.

A somewhat different set of paired adjectives was presented for the central concept of "constitution" than was administered for politics and government. The new set could be grouped into five factors: evaluation, majesty and essentiality, potency, activity, and flexibility. Respondents were highly positive in their evaluation of the constitution; they saw it as good, attractive, democratic, open, uniting, beautiful, and clean. The majestic-essentiality factor also showed highly positive connotations: majestic, deep, everlasting, necessary, fundamental, serious, and leaning toward long and old. Like politics and government, constitution was perceived as very potent: strong, powerful, leaning toward hard. On the activity factor it was seen as friendly, leaning toward quiet and giving, but equally slow and fast. No direction appeared for the flexibility factor; the constitution was perceived as equally rigid and flexible, equally innovative and traditional, and equally restraining and freeing.

Clearly displayed in all three of these semantic descriptions is great faith in the constitutional and political system of the United States. Possessing this kind of faith, it is understandable that this sample should feel little urgency to keep rulers within bounds. It also corresponds with the general vote of confidence given the government on the "reality outtake sort" where governmental performance on certain outtakes was judged. Possibly this positive feeling about political institutions, in this sample, stems from a greater than normal faith in the goodness of human nature. A semantic differential and an open-ended question used in the pretest both showed a very positive appraisal of the capacity of human nature to improve. Yet there was no correlation between this belief and seeing the political system as dirty or clean. Clearly missing from this analysis are comparable data from several other countries (as well as more complete data for the United States). With more complete data one could see if semantic conceptions affect patterns of inputs and outtakes, if they affect belief in the need to keep rulers within bounds, if they affect governmental stability, if they affect the pattern and rate of social change, and so forth.

Tolerance of Deviation and Change

It is inherent in the nature of believing to seek sustenance for our credulity by looking for the people around us to believe the same thing. So strong is this need for belief-support from others that there is a natural tendency in all societies to cast out those who believe differently from the dominant belief. Toleration of deviant beliefs does not come naturally, it must be learned—often-times only after bitter experience with the cost of intolerance. To become tolerant a person has to accept the possibility that his own beliefs may not be absolutely true. This is difficult for many persons because such doubts frequently constitute a serious threat to their systems of personal security. Frequently found supplementing this natural tendency in many countries of the world are government policies descouraging the expression of beliefs contrary to the officially accepted views of the government. Whatever the rationale (build national unity, create support for policies, protect the people from false doctrines, etc.), it is likely that the mass of people find some comfort in enforced belief uniformity.

In studying comparative politics one should not expect to find easy acceptance of deviation, but should look instead for ways in which a society tolerates deviation and accommodates itself to abberations. It seems that deviants are more easily accepted when they are relatively few in number. Respondents in the Chicago pretest believed there were only a few extremists in the United States, and perceived little danger from them. Most respondents believed there was ample room for the expression of extreme opinions. Two-thirds of them believed minority rights should be protected even if the will of the majority should be frustrated, but two-thirds also said it would be proper for the government to outlaw an extremist group like the fascists or communists. The pattern of these answers suggests that this sample has very little concern about the problem of extremists and the protection of their rights, despite a profession of belief in minority rights. Other studies have shown high agreement on the principle of minority rights but little mass support for concrete applications to despised situations (for instance, allowing a communist to speak in your town).[6] The educated elite, however, is willing to protect both the right to deviate and its concrete applications. These studies suggest the hypothesis that in order for extremists and civil disobedience to be tolerated in a society, the right of peaceful expression must be stipulated in a basic law which the ruling elite believes it is important to protect.

The society's general level of tolerance probably affects its reaction to change as well as to deviation. Adherence to custom is a defense against the challenge of alien beliefs. I would hypothesize that strong adherence to

---

[8] Prothro & Grigg, *Journal of Politics*, XXII (May 1960), 276–294; McClosky, *American Political Science Review*, LVIII (June 1964), 361–382.

custom and a low level of tolerance are positvely correlated. It is possible, however, for societies to learn both to welcome change and to question customary ways. A nation's beliefs about change may be an important determinant of its ability to develop economically. Data on beliefs about change from countries at several stages of development would disclose whether a relationship exists between beliefs about change and rate of development.

The ability of a nation to tolerate alien beliefs may also affect its ability to get on well with its neighbors. A country that tolerates new beliefs is less likely to be defensive in contacts with foreigners, and it will be more likely to open its borders to commercial transactions and to tourist visits. It will look upon visitors from abroad more as persons to learn from than as possible spies. A country that feels it must defend its ideology from the intrusion of alien beliefs pays a high cost in greater friction with its neighbors and in losing a certain ability to learn.

Problem Definition and Modes
for Problem Solution

In the sphere of activities in which government is involved, problems are socially defined and socially solved. Societies develop in their belief-structure typical ways of recognizing what constitutes a problem. A state of affairs that would be recognized as a problem in one culture may not be recognized as such in another culture. In Eastern Europe, for example, people are often required to stand in line to do certain things. The lines develop not so much because there is a shortage of goods or of personnel to wait on those in line, but because administrative concerns are not oriented to the reduction of lines. Lines simply are not recognized as a serious problem. In the USA, in contrast, thousands of people wasting thousands of hours standing in line would be considered a serious problem. It is not altogether clear why this situation is seen so differently in the two cultures, but a fair guess might be a different valuation placed on time and efficiency in each culture.

Even if a few individuals recognize a situation as a problem requiring solution, they are often stymied because the existence of the problem must be socially recognized. Lines in Eastern Europe are one example. Another example is the sacred cow in India; some Indians recognize the sacredness of the cow as a serious drain on the economy, a drain which must be removed before India can increase her standard of living. Yet their recognition that this is a problem is shared by only a small percentage of Indians and, until it receives widespread social recognition, little societal action to change the situation can be expected.

A society may not be able to define the nature of a problem even if it recognizes that a problematical situation exists. It is typical to escape from such a situation by declaring that it is impossible to solve the problem. (This is different from assigning low priority to a problem.) The impossibility, however, lies more with the inability to define the problem than with the inability to solve the problem once defined. Generally speaking, once a problem has been properly defined it can be solved. An emphasis on problem definition is itself a cultural belief. In many cultures people do not go about looking for problems to define and to solve. In the United States, by contrast, there is a national belief that nothing is so good that it cannot be improved, a perspective which seems relatively rare in the rest of the world.

Nations or culture also have beliefs about preferred or "good" ways to arrive at social decisions. One such norm is, "The more persons involved in the decisional process, the better the decision." A contrasting norm emphasizes division of labor and allocates certain decisions to certain people (experts, for example), or to a leadership elite. Some norms emphasize time and efficiency at the cost of consensus: "Take a vote and let's get on with it." Others emphasize consensus: "We must discuss until we all agree." In some societies it is normal to have a smaller work-group canvass the alternative solutions and lay these before the full decisional body; debate is often confined to these alternatives. In other societies the definition of alternatives is left unstructured prior to debate.

Modes for problem definition and solution probably affect the assignment of responsibility. A collective or consensual decision often leads to collective responsibility for its execution. Collective responsibility generally is more uncertain and erratic in execution than is individual assignment to a task for which the individual is then held responsible. Assignment and enforcement of individual responsibility is a culturally-learned behavioral norm which is much stronger in some cultures than in others.

Hopefully, the above examples are sufficient to suggest the importance of a comparative study of beliefs about problem definition and solution. . . .

7

The Nature
of Belief Systems
in Mass Publics*

PHILIP E. CONVERSE

Belief systems have never surrendered easily to empirical study or quantification. Indeed, they have often served as primary exhibits for the doctrine that what is important to study cannot be measured and that what can be measured is not important to study. In an earlier period, the behaviorist decree that subjective states lie beyond the realm of proper measurement gave Mannheim a justification for turning his back on measurement, for he had an unqualified interest in discussing belief systems.[1] Even as Mannheim was writing, however, behaviorism was undergoing stiff challenges, and early studies of attitudes were attaining a degree of measurement reliability that had been deemed impossible. This fragment of history, along with many others, serves to remind us that no intellectual position is likely to become obsolete quite so rapidly as one that takes current empirical capability as the limit of the possible in a more absolute sense. Nevertheless, while rapid strides in the measurement of "subjective states" have been achieved in recent decades, few would claim that the millennium has arrived or that Mann-

* Reprinted with permission of the Macmillan Company from *Ideology and Discontent,* edited by David E. Apter, Copyright © The Free Press of Glencoe, a Division of the Macmillan Company, 1964. The report is from pp. 206–231 and has been edited slightly.

[1] Karl Manheim, *Ideology and Utopia* (New York, 1946), especially pp. 39 ff.

heim could now find all of the tools that were lacking to him forty years ago.

This article makes no pretence of surpassing such limitations. At the same time, our substantive concern forces upon us an unusual concern with measurement strategies, not simply because we propose to deal with belief systems or ideologies, but also because of the specific questions that we shall raise about them. Our focus in this article is upon differences in the nature of belief systems held on the one hand by elite political actors and, on the other, by the masses that appear to be "numbered" within the spheres of influence of these belief systems. It is our thesis that there are important and predictable differences in ideational worlds as we progress downward through such "belief strata" and that these differences, while obvious at one level, are easily overlooked and not infrequently miscalculated. The fact that these ideational worlds differ in character poses problems of adequate representation and measurement.

The vertical ordering of actors and beliefs that we wish to plumb bears some loose resemblance to the vertical line that might be pursued downward through an organization or political movement from the narrow cone of top leadership, through increasing numbers of subordinate officials, and on through untitled activists to the large base formally represented in membership rolls. It is this large base that Michels noted, from observations of political gatherings, was rarely "there," and analogues to its physical absence do not arise accidentally in dealing with belief systems. On the other hand, there is no perfect or necessary "fit" between the two orderings, and this fact in itself has some interest.

That we intend to consider the total mass of people "numbered" within the spheres of influence of belief systems suggests both a democratic bias and a possible confusion between numbers and power or between numbers and the outcomes of events that power determines. We are aware that attention to numbers, more or less customary in democratic thought, is very nearly irrelevant in many political settings. Generally, the logic of numbers collides head on with the logic of power, as the traditional power pyramid, expressing an inverse relation between power and numbers, communicates so well. "Power" and "numbers" intersect at only one notable point, and that point is represented by the familiar axiom that numbers are one resource of power. The weight of this resource varies in a systematic and obvious way according to the political context. In a frankly designed and stable oligarchy, it is assumed to have no weight at all. In such a setting, the numbers of people associated with particular belief systems, if known at all, becomes important only in periods of crisis or challenge to the existing power structure. Democratic theory greatly increases the weight accorded to numbers in the daily power calculus. This increase still does not mean that numbers are of overriding importance; in the normal course of events it is the *perception* of numbers by democratic elites, so far as they differ from "actual" numbers, that is the more important factor. However this may be, claims to numbers are of some modest continuing importance in democratic systems for the legitimacy they confer upon demands; and, much more sporadically, claims to numbers become important in nondemocratic systems as threats of potential coercion.

SOME CLARIFICATION OF TERMS

A term like "ideology" has been thoroughly muddied by diverse uses.[2] We shall depend instead upon the term "belief system," although there is an obvious overlap between the two. We define a *belief system* as a configuration of ideas and attitudes in which the elements are bound together by some form of constraint or functional interdependence.[3] In the static case, "constraint" may be taken to mean the success we would have in predicting, given initial knowledge that an individual holds a specified attitude, that he holds certain further ideas and attitudes. We depend implicitly upon such notions of constraint in judging, for example, that, if a person is opposed to the expansion of social security, he is probably a conservative and is probably opposed as well to any nationalization of private industries, federal aid to education, sharply progressive income taxation, and so forth. Most discussions of ideologies make relatively elaborate assumptions about such constraints. Constraint must be treated, of course, as a matter of degree, and this degree can be measured quite readily, at least as an average among individuals.[4]

In the dynamic case, "constraint" or "interdependence" refers to the probability that a change in the perceived status (truth, desirability, and so forth) of one idea-element would *psychologically* require, from the point of view of the actor, some compensating change(s) in the status of idea-elements elsewhere in the configuration. The most obvious form of such constraint (although in some ways the most trivial) is exemplified by a structure of propositions in logic, in which a change in the truth-value of one proposition necessitates changes in truth-value elsewhere within the set of related propositions. Psychologically, of course, there may be equally strong constraint among idea-elements that would not be apparent to logical analysis at all, as we shall see.

We might characterize either the idea-elements themselves or entire belief systems in terms of many other dimensions. Only two will interest us here. First, the idea-elements within a belief system vary in a property we shall call *centrality*, according to the role that they play in the belief system as a whole. That is, when new information changes the status of one idea-element in a belief system, by postulate some other change must occur as well. There are usually, however, several possible changes in status elsewhere in the system, any one of which would compensate for the initial change. Let us imagine, for example, that a person strongly favors a particular policy; is very favorably inclined toward a given political party; and rec-

---

[2] Minar has compiled a useful if discouraging survey of this diversity. See David W. Minar, "Ideology and Political Behavior" *Midwest Journal of Political Science*, V (November 1961), No. 4, 317–331.

[3] Garner uses the term "contraint" to mean "the amount of interrelatedness of structure of a system of variables" when measured by degree of uncertainty reduction. Wendell R. Garner, *Uncertainty and Structure as Psychological Concepts* (New York, 1962), pp. 142ff. We use the term a bit more broadly as relief from such polysyllables as "interrelatedness" and "interdependence."

[4] Measures of correlation and indices of the goodness of fit of a cumulative scale model to a body of data are measures of two types of constraint.

ognizes with gratification that the party's stand and his own are congruent. (If he were unaware of the party's stand on the issue, these elements could not in any direct sense be constrained within the same belief system.) Let us further imagine that the party then changes its position to the opposing side of the issue. Once the information about the change reaching the actor has become so unequivocal that he can no longer deny that the change has occurred, he has several further choices. Two of the more important ones involve either a change in attitude toward the party or a change in position on the issue. In such an instance, the element more likely to change is defined as less central to the belief system than the element that, so to speak, has its stability ensured by the change in the first element.[5]

In informal discussions of belief systems, frequent assumptions are made about the relative centrality of various idea-elements. For example, idea-elements that are logically "ends" are supposed to be more central to the system than are "means." It is important to remain aware, however, that idea-elements can change their relative centrality in an individual's belief-system over time. Perhaps the most hackneyed illustration of this point is that of the miser, to whom money has become an end rather than a means.

Whole belief systems may also be compared in a rough way with respect to the *range* of objects that are referrents for the ideas and attitudes in the system. Some belief systems, while they may be internally quite complex and may involve large numbers of cognitive elements, are rather narrow in range: Belief systems concerning "proper" baptism rituals or the effects of changes in weather on health may serve as cases in point. Such other belief systems as, for example, one that links control of the means of production with the social functions of religion and a doctrine of aesthetics all in one more or less neat package have extreme ranges.

By and large, our attention will be focused upon belief systems that have relatively wide ranges, and that allow some centrality to political objects, for they can be presumed to have some relevance to political behavior. This focus brings us close to what are broadly called *ideologies*, and we shall use the term for aesthetic relief where it seems most appropriate. The term originated in a narrower context, however, and is still often reserved for subsets of belief systems or parts of such systems that the user suspects are insincere; that he wishes to claim have certain functions for social groupings; or that have some special social source or some notable breadth of social diffusion.[6] Since we are concerned here about only one of these limitations—the question of social diffusion—and since we wish to deal with it by hypothesis rather than by definition, a narrow construction of the term is never intended.

---

[5] Definitions of belief systems frequently require that configurations of ideas be stable for individuals over long periods of time. The notion of centrality fulfills this requirement in a more flexible way. That is, once it is granted that changes in the perceived status of idea-elements are not frequent in any event and that, when change does occur, the central elements (particularly in large belief systems) are amply cushioned by more peripheral elements that can be adjusted, it follows that central elements are indeed likely to be highly stable.

[6] Minar, "Ideology and Political Behavior."

SOURCES OF CONSTRAINT ON IDEA-ELEMENTS

It seems clear, however logically coherent a belief system may seem to the holder, the sources of constraint are much less logical in the classical sense than they are psychological—and less psychological than social. This point is of sufficient importance to dwell upon.

Logical Sources of Constraint

Within very narrow portions of belief systems, certain constraints may be purely logical. For example, government revenues, government expenditures, and budget balance are three idea-elements that suggest some purely logical constraints. One cannot believe that government expenditures should be increased, that government revenues should be decreased, and that a more favorable balance of the budget should be achieved all at the same time. Of course, the presence of such objectively logical constraints does not ensure that subjective constraints will be felt by the actor. They will be felt only if these idea-elements are brought together in the same belief system, and there is no guarantee that they need be. Indeed, it is true that, among adult American citizens, those who favor the expansion of government welfare services tend to be those who are more insistent upon reducing taxes "even if it means putting off some important things that need to be done."[7] . . .

Psychological Sources of Constraint

Whatever may be learned through the use of strict logic as a type of constraint, it seems obvious that few belief systems of any range at all depend for their constraint upon logic in this classical sense. . . . What is important is that the elites familiar with the total shapes of . . . belief systems have *experienced* them as logically constrained clusters of ideas, within which one part necessarily follows from another. Often such constraint is quasi-logically argued on the basis of an appeal to some superordinate value or posture toward man and society, involving premises about the nature of social justice, social change, "natural law," and the like. Thus a few crowning postures— like premises about survival of the fittest in the spirit of social Darwinism— serve as a sort of glue to bind together many more specific attitudes and beliefs, and these postures are of prime centrality in the belief system as a whole.

Social Sources of Constraint

The social sources of constraint are twofold and are familiar from an extensive literature in the past century. In the first place, were we to survey

[7] See A. Campbell, P. E. Converse, W. Miller, and D. Stokes, *The American Voter* (New York, 1960), pp. 204–209. See also William J. McGuire, "A Syllogistic Analysis of Cognitive Relationships," in Milton J. Rosenberg, Carl I. Hovland, William J. McGuire, Robert P. Abelson, and Jack W. Brehm, *Attitude Organization and Change*, Yale Studies in Attitude and Communication, Vol. 3 (New Haven, 1960), pp. 65–111.

the combinations of idea-elements that have occurred historically ..., we should undoubtedly find that certain postures tend to co-occur and that this co-occurrence has obvious roots in the configuration of interests and information that characterize particular niches in the social structure.... The middle-class temperance movement in America, for example, which now seems "logically" allied with the small-town Republican right, had important alliances some eighty years ago with the urban social left, on grounds equally well argued from temperance doctrines.[8] Nonetheless, there are some highly reliable correlations of this sort, and these correlations can be linked with social structure in the most direct way. Developmentally, they have status similar to the classic example of the spurious correlation—two terms that are correlated because of a common link to some third and prior variable. In the case of the belief system, arguments are developed to lend some more positive rationale to the fact of constraint: The idea-elements go together not simply because both are in the interest of the person holding a particular status but for more abstract and quasi-logical reasons developed from a coherent world view as well. It is this type of constraint that is closest to the classic meaning of the term "ideology."

The second source of social constraint lies in two simple facts about the creation and diffusion of belief systems. First, the shaping of belief systems of any range into apparently logical wholes that are credible to large numbers of people is an act of creative synthesis characteristic of only a miniscule proportion of any population. Second, to the extent that multiple idea-elements of a belief system are socially diffused from such creative sources, they tend to be diffused in "packages," which consumers come to see as "natural" wholes, for they are presented in such terms ("If you believe this, then you will also believe that, for it follows in such-and-such ways"). Not that the more avid consumer never supplies personal innovations on the fringes—he is very likely to suppress an idea-element here, to elaborate one there, or even to demur at an occasional point. But any set of relatively intelligent consumers who are initially sympathetic to the crowning posture turns out to show more consensus on specific implications of the posture as a result of social diffusion of "what goes with what" than it would if each member were required to work out the implications individually without socially provided cues.

Such constraint through diffusion is important, for it implies a dependence upon the transmission of information. If information is not successfully transmitted, there will be little constraint save that arising from the first social source. Where transmission of information is at stake, it becomes important to distinguish between two classes of information. Simply put, these two levels are what goes with what and why. Such levels of information logically stand in a scalar relationship to one another, in the sense that one can hardly arrive at an understanding of why two ideas go together without being aware that they are supposed to go together. On the other hand, it is easy to know that two ideas go together without knowing why. For example, we can expect that a very large majority of the American public would somehow have ab-

8 Joseph R. Gusfield, "Status Conflicts and the Changing Ideologies of the American Temperance Movement," in Pittman and Snyder, eds., Society, Culture and Drinking Patterns (New York, 1962).

sorbed the notion that "Communists are atheists." What is important is that this perceived correlation would for most people represent nothing more than a fact of existence, with the same status as the fact that oranges are orange and most apples are red. If we were to go and explore with these people their grasp of the "why" of the relationship, we would be surprised if more than a quarter of the population even attempted responses (setting aside such inevitable replies as "those Communists are for everything wicked"), and, among the responses received, we could be sure that the majority would be incoherent or irrelevant.

The first level of information, then, is simple and straightforward. The second involves much more complex and abstract information, very close to what Downs has called the "contextual knowledge" relevant to a body of information.[9] A well informed person who has received sufficient information about a system of beliefs to understand the "whys" involved in several of the constraints between idea-elements is in a better position to make good guesses about the nature of other constraints; he can deduce with fair success, for example, how a true believer will respond to certain situations. Our first interest in distinguishing between these types of information, however, flows from our interest in the relative success of information transmission. The general premise is that the first type of information will be diffused much more readily than the second because it is less complex.

It is well established that differences in information held in a cross-section population are simply staggering, running from vast treasuries of well organized information among elites interested in the particular subject to fragments that could virtually be measured as a few "bits" in the technical sense. These differences are a static tribute to the extreme imperfections in the transmission of information "downward" through the system: Very little information "trickles down" very far. Of course, the ordering of individuals on this vertical information scale is largely due to differences in education, but it is strongly modified as well by different specialized interests and tastes that individuals have acquired over time (one for politics, another for religious activity, another for fishing, and so forth).

Consequences of Declining Information for Belief Systems

It is our primary thesis that, as one moves from elite sources of belief systems downwards on such an information scale, several important things occur. First, the contextual grasp of "standard" political belief systems fades out very rapidly, almost before one has passed beyond the 10 percent of the American population that in the 1950s had completed standard college training.[10] Increasingly, simpler forms of information about "what goes with what"

[9] Anthony Downs, *An Economic Theory of Democracy* (New York, 1957), p. 79.

[10] It should be understood that our information dimension is not so perfectly correlated with formal education as this statement implies. Since educational strata have a more ready intuitive meaning, however, we shall use them occasionally as convienient ways of meuring off levels in the population. In such cases, the reader may keep in mind that there are always some people of lesser education but higher political involvement who are numbered in the stratum and some people with education befitting the stratum who are not numbered there because their interests lie elsewhere and their information about politics is less than could be expected.

(or even information about the simple identity of objects) turn up missing. The net result, as one moves downward, is that contraint declines across the universe of idea-elements, and that the range of relevant belief systems becomes narrower and narrower. Instead of a few wide-range belief systems that organize large amounts of specific information, one would expect to find a proliferation of clusters of ideas among which little constraint is felt, even, quite often, in instances of sheer logical constraint.[11]

At the same time, moving from top to bottom of this information dimension, the character of the objects that are central in a belief system undergoes systematic change. These objects shift from the remote, generic, and abstract to the increasingly simple, concrete, or "close to home." Where potential political objects are concerned, this progression tends to be from abstract, "ideological" principles to the more obviously recognizable social groupings or charismatic leaders and finally to such objects of immediate experience as family, job, and immediate associates. . . .[12]

ACTIVE USE OF IDEOLOGICAL DIMENSIONS OF JUDGMENT

Economy and constraint are companion concepts, for the more highly constrained a system of multiple elements, the more economically it may be described and understood. From the point of view of the actor, the idea organization that leads to constraint permits him to locate and make sense of a wider range of information from a particular domain than he would find possible without such organization. One judgmental dimension or "yardstick" that has been highly serviceable for simplifying and organizing events in most Western politics for the past century has been liberal-conservative continuum, on which parties, political leaders, legislation, court decisions, and a number of other primary objects of politics could be more—or less—adequately located.[13]

[11] There is a difference, of course, between this statement and a suggestion that poorly educated people have no systems of belief about politics.

[12] This observation is valid despite the fact that surveys showing ignorance of crucial political facts are much more likely to run in a range from 40–80 percent "unaware." At the height of the 1958 Berlin crisis, 63 percent of the American public did not know that the city was encircled by hostile troops. A figure closer to 70 percent is a good estimate of the proportion of the public that does not know which party controls Congress.

In this regard, it was enlightening to read the stunned reactions of the political columnist Joseph Alsop when, during the 1960 presidential primaries, he left the elite circuits of the East Coast and ventured from door to door talking politics with "normal" people in West Virginia. He was frank to admit that the change in perceived political worlds was far greater than anything he had ever anticipated, despite his prior recognition that there would be some difference.

[13] The phrase "less adequately" is used to show recognition of the frequent complaint that the liberal-conservative dimension has different meanings in different politics at different times. More importantly, it takes into account the fact that in most politics new issues are constantly arising that are difficult before the fact to relate to such a yardstick. Some of these intrinsically "orthogonal" issues may remain unrelated to the dimension, and, if they become of intense importance, they can split existing parties and redefine alignments. More typically however, elites that are known on some other grounds to be "liberal" or "conservative" ferret out some limited aspect of an issue for which they can

The efficiency of such a yardstick in the evaluation of events is quite obvious. Under certain appropriate circumstances, the single word "conservative" used to describe a piece of proposed legislation can convey a tremendous amount of more specific information about the bill—who probably proposed it and toward what ends, who is likely to resist it, its chances of passage, its long-term social consequences, and, most important, how the actor himself should expect to evaluate it if he were to expend further energy to look into its details. The circumstances under which such tremendous amounts of information are conveyed by the single word are, however, twofold. First, the actor must bring a good deal of meaning to the term, which is to say that he must understand the constraints surrounding it. The more impoverished his understanding of the term, the less information it conveys. In the limiting case—if he does not know at all what the term means—it conveys no information at all. Second, the system of beliefs and actors referred to must in fact be relatively constrained: To the degree that constraint is lacking, uncertainty is less reduced by the label, and less information is conveyed.

The psychological economies provided by such yardsticks for actors are paralleled by economies for analysts and theoreticians who wish to describe events in the system parsimoniously. Indeed, the search for adequate overarching dimensions on which large arrays of events may be simply understood is a critical part of synthetic description. Such syntheses are more or less satisfactory, once again, according to the degree of constraint operative among terms in the system being described.

The economies inherent in the liberal-conservative continuum were exploited in traditional fashion in the early 1950s to describe political changes in the United States as a swing toward conservatism or a "revolt of the moderates." At one level, this description was unquestionably apt. That is, a man whose belief system was relatively conservative (Dwight D. Eisenhower) had supplanted in the White House a man whose belief system was relatively liberal (Harry Truman). Furthermore, for a brief period at least, the composition of Congress was more heavily Republican as well, and this shift meant on balance a greater proportion of relatively conservative legislators. Since the administration and Congress were the elites responsible for the development and execution of policies, the flavor of governmental action did indeed take a turn in a conservative direction. These observations are proper description.

The causes underlying these changes in leadership, however, obviously lay with the mass public, which had changed its voting patterns sufficiently

---

argue some liberal-conservative relevance and begin to drift to one of the alternative positions in disproportionate numbers. Then, either because of the aspect highlighted or because of simple pressures toward party competition, their adversaries drift toward the opposing position. Thus positions come to be perceived as "liberal" or "conservative," even though such alignments would have been scarcely predictable on logical grounds. After the fact, of course, the alignments come to seem "logical," by mechanisms discussed earlier in this paper. Controversy over British entry into the European Common Market is an excellent example of such a process. Currently the conservatives are officially pro-entry, and Labour leadership has finally declared against it, but the reverse of this alignment had frequently been predicted when the issue was embryonic.

to bring the Republican elites into power. And this change in mass voting was frequently interpreted as a shift in public mood from liberal to conservative, a mass desire for a period of respite and consolidation after the rapid liberal innovations of the 1930s and 1940s. Such an account presumes, once again, that constraints visible at an elite level are mirrored in the mass public and that a person choosing to vote Republican after a decade or two of Democratic voting saw himself *in some sense or other* as giving up a more liberal choice in favor of a more conservative one.

On the basis of some familiarity with attitudinal materials drawn from cross-section samples of the electorate,[14] this assumption seems thoroughly implausable. It suggests in the first instance a neatness of organization in perceived political worlds, which, while accurate enough for elites, is a poor fit for the perceptions of the common public. Second, the yardstick that such an account takes for granted—the liberal-conservative continuum—is a rather elegant high-order abstraction, and such abstractions are not typical conceptual tools for the "man in the street." Fortunately, our interview protocols collected from this period permitted us to examine this hypothesis more closely, for they include not only "structured" attitude materials (which merely require the respondent to choose between prefabricated alternatives) but also lengthy "open-ended" materials, which provided us with the respondent's current evaluation of the political scene in his own words. They therefore provide some indication of the evaluative dimensions that tend to be spontaneously applied to politics by such a national sample. We knew that respondents who were highly educated or strongly involved in politics would fall naturally into the verbal shorthand of "too conservative," "more radical," and the like in these evaluations. Our initial analytic question had to do with the prevalence of such usage.

It soon became apparent, however, that such respondents were in a very small minority, as their unusual education or involvement would suggest. At this point, we broadened the inquiry to an assessment of the evaluative dimensions of policy significance (relating to political issues, rather than to the way a candidate dresses, smiles, or behaves in his private life) that seemed to be employed *in lieu of* such efficient yardsticks as the liberal-conservative continuum. The interviews themselves suggested several strata of classification, which were hierarchically ordered as "levels of conceptualization" on the basis of a priori judgments about the breadth of contextual grasp of the political system that each seemed to represent.

In the first or top level were placed those respondents who did indeed rely in some active way on a relatively abstract and far-reaching conceptual dimension as a yardstick against which political objects and their shifting policy significance over time were evaluated. We did not require that this dimension be the liberal-conservative continuum itself, but it was almost the only dimension of the sort that occurred empirically. In a second stratum were placed those respondents who mentioned such a dimension in a periph-

14 All American data reported in this paper, unless otherwise noted, have been collected by the Survey Research Center of The University of Michigan under grants from the Carnegie Corporation, the Rockefeller Foundation, and the Social Science Research Council.

eral way but did not appear to place much evaluative dependence upon it or who used such concepts in a fashion that raised doubt about the breadth of their understanding of the meaning of the term. The first stratum was loosely labeled "ideologue" and the second "near-ideologue."

In the third level were placed respondents who failed to rely upon any such over-arching dimensions yet evaluated parties and candidates in terms of their expected favorable or unfavorable treatment of different social grouping in the population. The Democratic party might be disliked because "it's trying to help the Negroes too much," or the Republican party might be endorsed because farm prices would be better with the Republicans in office. The more sophisticated of these group-interest responses reflected an awareness of conflict in interest between "big business" or "rich people," on the one hand, and "labor" or the "working man," on the other, and parties and candidates were located accordingly.

It is often asked why these latter respondents are not considered full "ideologues," for their perceptions run to the more tangible core of what has traditionally been viewed as ideological conflict. It is quite true that such a syndrome is closer to the upper levels of conceptualization than are any of the other types to be described. As we originally foresaw, however, there turn out to be rather marked differences, not only in social origin and flavor of judgmental processes out in overt political reactions as well, between people of this type and those in the upper levels. These people have a clear image of politics as an arena of group interests and, provided that they have been properly advised on where their own group interests lie, they are relatively likely to follow such advice. Unless an issue directly concerns their grouping in an obviously rewarding or punishing way, however, they lack the contextual grasp of the system to recognize how they should respond to it without being told by elites who hold their confidence. Furthermore, their interest in politics is not sufficiently strong that they pay much attention to such communications. If a communication gets through and they absorb it, they are most willing to behave "ideologically" in ways that will further the interests of their group. If they fail to receive such communication, which is most unusual, knowledge of their group memberships may be of little help in predicting their responses. This syndrome we came to call "ideology by proxy."

The difference between such narrow group interest and the broader perceptions of the ideologue may be clarified by an extreme case. One respondent whom we encountered classified himself as a strong Socialist. He was a Socialist because he knew that Socialists stood four-square for the working man against the rich, and he was a working man. When asked, however, whether or not the federal government in Washington "should leave things like electric power and housing for private businessmen to handle," he felt strongly that private enterprise should have its way, and responses to other structured issue questions were simply uncorrelated with standard socialist doctrine. It seems quite clear that, if our question had pointed out explicitly to this man that "good Socialists" would demand government intervention over private enterprise or that such a posture had traditionally been viewed as benefiting the working man, his answer would

have been different. But since he had something less than a college education and was not generally interested enough in politics to struggle through
such niceties, he simply lacked the contextual grasp of the political system
or of his chosen "ideology" to know what the appropriate response might be.
This case illustrates well what we mean by constraint between idea-elements
and how such constraint depends upon a store of relevant information. For
this man, "Socialists," "the working man," "non-Socialists" and "the rich"
with their appropriate valences formed a tightly constrained belief system.
But, for lack of information, the belief system more or less began and ended
there. It strikes us as valid to distinguish such a belief system from that of
the doctrinaire socialist. We, as sophisticated observers, could only class this
man as a full "ideologue" by assuming that he shares with us the complex
undergirding of information that his concrete group perceptions call up in our
own minds. In this instance, a very little probing makes clear that this assumption of shared information is once again false.

The fourth level was, to some degree, a residual category, intended to
include those respondents who invoked some policy considerations in their
evaluations yet employed none of the references meriting location in any of
the first three levels. Two main modes of policy evaluation were characteristic of this level. The first we came to think of as a "nature of the times"
response, since parties or candidates were praised or blamed primarily because of their temporal association in the past with broad societal states of
war or peace, prosperity or depression. There was no hint in these responses
that any groupings in the society suffered differentially from disaster or
profited excessively in more pleasant times: These fortunes or misfortunes
were those that one party or the other had decided (in some cases, apparently, on whim) to visit upon the nation as a whole. The second type included those respondents whose only approach to an issue reference involved
some single narrow policy for which they felt personal gratitude or indignation toward a party or candidate (like social security or a conservation program). In these responses, there was no indication that the speakers saw programs as representative of the broader policy postures of the parties.

The fifth level included those respondents whose evaluations of the
political scene had no shred of policy significance whatever. Some of these
responses were from people who felt loyal to one party or the other but confessed that they had no idea what the party stood for. Others devoted their
attention to personal qualities of the candidates, indicating disinterest in
parties more generally. Still others confessed that they paid too little attention to either the parties or the current candidates to be able to say anything
about them.[15]

The ranking of the levels performed on a priori grounds was corrobo-
rated by further analyses, which demonstrated that independent measures of
political information, education, and political involvement all showed sharp
and monotonic declines as one passed downward through the levels in the
order suggested. Furthermore, these correlations were strong enough so that

[15] This account of the "levels of conceptualization" is highly abbreviated. For a
much more detailed discussion and rationale, along with numerous illustrations drawn at
random from interviews in each stratum, see Campbell et al., Chapter 10.

each maintained some residual life when the other two items were controlled, despite the strong underlying relationship between education, information, and involvement.

The distribution of the American electorate within these levels of conceptualization is summarized in Table 7.1. The array is instructive as a por-

TABLE 7.1 DISTRIBUTION OF A TOTAL CROSS-SECTION SAMPLE OF THE AMERICAN ELECTORATE AND OF 1956 VOTERS, BY LEVELS OF CONCEPTUALIZATION

	PROPORTION OF TOTAL SAMPLE	PROPORTION OF VOTERS
I. Ideologues	2.5%	3.5%
II. Near-ideologues	9	12
III. Group interest	42	45
IV. Nature of the times	24	22
V. No issue content	22.5	17.5
	100%	100%

trait of a mass electorate, to be laid against the common elite assumption that all or a significant majority of the public conceptualizes the main lines of politics after the manner of the most highly educated. Where the specific hypothesis of the "revolt of the moderates" in the early 1950s is concerned, the distribution does not seem on the face of it to lend much support to the key assumption. This disconfirmation may be examined further, however.

Since the resurgence of the Republicans in the Eisenhower period depended primarily upon crossing of party lines by people who normally considered themselves Democrats, we were able to isolate these people to see from what levels of conceptualization they had been recruited. We found that such key defections had occurred among Democrats in the two bottom levels at a rate very significantly greater than the comparable rate in the group-interest or more ideological levels. In other words, the stirrings in the mass electorate that had led to a change in administration and in "ruling ideology" were primarily the handiwork of the very people for whom assumptions of any liberal-conservative dimensions of judgment were most farfetched.

Furthermore, within those strata where the characteristics of conceptualization even permitted the hypothesis to be evaluated in its own terms, it was directly disproved. For example, the more sophisticated of the group-interest Democrats were quite aware that Eisenhower would be a more pro-business president than Stevenson. Those of this group who did defect to Eisenhower did not, however, do so because they were tired of a labor oriented administration and wanted a business-oriented one for a change. Quite to the contrary, in the degree that they defected they did so *in spite of* rather than *because of* such quasi-ideological perceptions. That is, their attitudes toward the respective interests of these groups remained essentially constant, and they expressed misgivings about an Eisenhower vote on precisely these grounds. But any such worries were, under the circumstances, outweighed by admiration for Eisenhower's war record, his honesty, his good family life, and (in 1952) his potential for resolving the nagging problem of the Korean War. Among respondents at higher levels (ideologues and near-ideologues), there was comparable attraction to Eisenhower at a personal level, but these people seemed more careful to hew to ideological considerations, and rates of Democratic defection in these levels were lower still. In short, then, the supposition of changing ideological moods in the mass public as a means of understanding the exchange of partisan elites in 1952 seems to have had little relevance to what was actually going on at the mass level. And once again, the sources of the optical illusion are self-evident. While it may be taken for granted among well educated and politically involved people that a shift from a Democratic preference to a Republican one probably represents a change in opinion from liberal to conservative, the assumption cannot be extended very far into the electorate as a whole.

RECOGNITION OF IDEOLOGICAL DIMENSIONS OF JUDGMENT

Dimensions like the liberal-conservative continuum, as we have observed, are extremely efficient frames for the organization of many political observations. Furthermore, they are used a great ideal in the more ambitious treatments of politics in the mass media, so that a person with a limited understanding of their meaning must find such discussions more obscure than enlightening. Aside from active cognitive use, therefore, the simple status of public comprehension of these terms is a matter of some interest.

It is a commonplace in psychology that recognition, recall, and habitual use of cognized objects or concepts are rather different. We are capable of *recognizing* many more objects (or concepts) if they are directly presented to us than we could readily *recall* on the basis of more indirect cues; and we are capable of recalling on the basis of such hints many more objects (or concepts) than might be *active* or *salient* for us in a given context without special prompting. In coding the levels of conceptualization from free-answer material, our interest had been entirely focused upon concepts with the last status (activation or salience). It had been our assumption that such activation would be apparent in the responses of any person with a belief system in which these organizing dimensions had high centrality. Nevertheless, we could be sure at the same time that if we presented the terms "liberal" and "conservative" directly to our respondents, a much larger number would recognize them and be able to attribute to them some kind of meaning. We are interested both in the proportions of a normal sample who would show some recognition and also in the meaning that might be supplied for the terms.

In a 1960 reinterview of the original sample whose 1956 responses had been assigned to our levels of conceptualization, we therefore asked in the context of the differences in "what the parties stand for," "Would you say that either one of the parties is more *conservative* or more *liberal* than the other?"

(It was the first time we had ever introduced these terms in our interviewing of this sample.) If the answer was affirmative, we asked which party seemed the more conservative and then, "What do you have in mind when you say that the Republicans (Democrats) are more conservative than the Democrats (Republicans)?" When the respondent said that he did not see differences of this kind between the two parties, we were anxious to distinguish between those who were actually cynical about meaningful party differences and those who took this route to avoid admitting that they did not know what the terms signified. We therefore went on to ask this group, "Do you think that people generally consider the Democrats or the Republicans more conservative, or wouldn't you want to guess about that?" At this point, we were willing to assume that if a person had no idea of the rather standard assumptions, he probably had no idea of what the terms meant; and indeed, those who did try to guess which party other people thought more conservative made a very poor showing when we went on to ask them (paralleling our "meaning" question for the first group), "What do people have in mind when they say that the Republicans (Democrats) are more conservative than the Democrats (Republicans)?" In responding to the "meaning" questions, both groups were urged to answer as fully and clearly as possible, and their comments were transcribed.

The responses were classified in a code inspired by the original work on levels of conceptualization, although it was considerably more detailed. Within this code, top priority was given to explanations that called upon broad philosophical differences. These explanations included mentions of such things as *posture toward change* (acceptance of or resistance to new ideas, speed or caution in responding to new problems, protection of or challenge to the *status quo*, aggressive posture towards problems versus a *laissez-faire* approach, orientation toward the future or lack of it, and so forth); *posture toward the welfare state, socialism, free enterprise, or capitalism* (including mention of differential sensitivity to social problems, approaches to social-welfare programs, governmental interference with private enterprise, and so forth); *posture toward the expanding power of federal government* (issues of centralization, states' rights, local autonomy, and paternalism); and *relationship of the government to the individual* (questions of individual dignity, initiative, needs, rights, and so forth). While any mention of comparably broad philosophical differences associated with the liberal-conservative distinction was categorized in this top level, these four were the most frequent types of reference, as they had been for the full "ideologues" in the earlier open-ended materials.

Then, in turn, references to differences in attitude toward various interest groupings in the population; toward spending or saving and fiscal policy more generally, as well as to economic prosperity; toward various highly specific issues like unemployment compensation, highway-building, and tariffs; and toward postures in the sphere of foreign policy were arrayed in a descending order of priority, much as they had been for the classification into levels of conceptualization. Since respondents had been given the opportunity to mention as many conservative-liberal distinctions as they wished, coding priority was given to the more "elevated" responses, and all the data that we shall subsequently cite rests on the "best answer" given by each respondent.[16]

The simple distributional results were as follows. Roughly three respondents in eight (37 percent) could supply no meaning for the liberal-conservative distinction, including 8 percent who attempted to say which party was the more conservative but who gave up on the part of the sequence dealing with meaning. (The weakest 29 percent will, in later tables, form our bottom stratum "V," while the 8 percent compose stratum "IV.") Between those who could supply no meaning for the terms and those who clearly did, there was naturally an intermediate group that answered all the questions but showed varying degrees of uncertainty or confusion. The situation required that one of two polar labels (conservative or liberal) be properly associated with one of two polar clusters of connotations and with one of two parties. Once the respondent had decided to explain what "more conservative" or "more liberal" signified there were four possible patterns by which the other two dichotomies might be associated with the first. Of course, all four were represented in at least some interviews. For example, a respondent might indicate that the Democrats were the more conservative because they stood up for the working man against big business. In such a case, there seemed to be a simple error consisting in reversal of the ideological labels. Or a respondent might say that the Republicans were more liberal because they were pushing new and progressive social legislation. Here the match between label and meaning seems proper, but the party perception is, by normal standards, erroneous.

The distribution of these error types within the portion of the sample that attempted to give "meaning" answers (slightly more than 60 percent) is shown in Table 7.2. The 83 percent entered for the "proper" patterns is artificially increased to an unknown degree by the inclusion of all respondents whose connotations for liberalism-conservatism were sufficiently impoverished so that little judgment could be made about whether or not they were making proper associations (for example, those respondents whose best explanations of the distinction involved orientations toward defense spending). The error types thus represent only those that could be unequivocally considered "errors." While Table 7.2 does not in itself constitute proof that the error types resulted from pure guesswork, the configuration does resemble the portable results if 20–25 percent of the respondents had been making random guesses about how the two labels, the two polar meanings, and the two parties should be sorted out. People making these confused responses might or might not *feel* confused in making their assessments. Even if they knew that they were confused, it is unlikely that they would be less confused

---

[16] Some modest internal support for the validity of the distinction between those who spoke in terms of broad philosophy and those who offered narrower explanations may be seen in the fact that only 5 percent of the former category had previously judged the Democrats to be more conservative than the Republicans. Among those giving less elevated "best answers," 14 percent deemed the Democrats the more conservative party. And, to give some sense of the "continental shelf" being explored here, among those who had responded that a certain party was more conservative than the other but who subsequently confessed that they did not know what the distinction implied, 35 percent had chosen the Democrats as the more conservative, a figure that is beginning to approach the 50–50 assignment of sheer guesswork.

TABLE 7.2 ASSOCIATION OF IDEOLOGICAL LABEL WITH PARTY AND MEANING

IDEOLOGICAL LABEL	MEANING	PARTY	PROPORTION OF THOSE GIVING SOME ANSWER
Conservative	Conservative	Republican	83%
Liberal	Liberal	Democrat	
Conservative	Liberal	Republican	
Liberal	Conservative	Democrat	5
Conservative	Conservative	Democrat [a]	
Liberal	Liberal	Republican	6
Conservative	Liberal	Democrat	
Liberal	Conservative	Republican	6
			100%

[a] While this pattern may appear entirely legitimate for the southern respondent reacting to the southern wing of the Democratic party rather than to the national party, it showed almost no tendency to occur with greater frequency in the South than elsewhere (and errors as well as lacunae occurred more frequently in general in the less well educated South). Data from a very different context indicate that southerners who discriminate between the southern wing and the national Democratic party take the national party as the assumed object in our interviews, if the precise object is not specified.

in encountering such terms in reading or listening to political communications, which is the important point where transmission of information is concerned. If on the other hand, they were wrong without realizing it, then they would be capable of hearing that Senator Goldwater, for example, was an extreme conservative and believing that it meant that he was for increased federal spending (or whatever other more specific meaning they might bring to the term). In either case, it seems reasonable to distinguish between the people who belong in this confused group at the border of understanding and those who demonstrate greater clarity about the terms. And after the confused group is set aside (stratum III in Tables 7.3–7.6, we are left with a proportion of the sample that is slightly more than 50 percent. This figure can be taken as a maximum estimate of reasonable recognition.

We say "maximum" because, once within this "sophisticated" half of the electorate, it is reasonable to consider the quality of the meanings put forth to explain the liberal-conservative distinction. These meanings varied greatly in adequacy, from those "best answers" that did indeed qualify for coding under the "broad philosophy" heading (the most accurate responses, as defined above) to those that explained the distinction in narrow or nearly irrelevant terms (like Prohibition or foreign-policy measures). In all, 17 percent of the total sample gave "best answers" that we considered to qualify as "broad philosophy."[17] This group was defined as stratum I, and the remainder, who gave narrower definitions, became stratum II.

Perhaps the most striking aspect of the liberal-conservative definitions supplied was the extreme frequency of those hinging on a simple "spend-save" dimension vis-à-vis government finances. Very close to a majority of

[17] In all candor, it should probably be mentioned that a teacher grading papers would be unlikely to give passing marks to more than 20 percent of the attempted definitions (or to 10 percent of the total sample). We made an effort, however, to be as generous as possible in our assignments.

all "best" responses (and two-thirds to three-quarters of all such responses in stratum II) indicated in essence that the Democratic party was liberal because it spent public money freely and that the Republican party was more conservative because it stood for economy in government or pinched pennies. In our earlier coding of the levels of conceptualization, we had already noted that this simple dimension seemed often to be what was at stake when "ideological" terms were used. Frequently there was reason to believe that the term "conservative" drew its primary meaning from the cognate "conservation." In one rather clear example, a respondent indicated that he considered the Republicans to be more conservative in the sense that they were ". . . more saving with money and our *natural resources*. Less apt to slap on a tax for some nonessential. More conservative in promises that can't be kept." (Italics ours.)

Of course, the question of the proportion of national wealth that is to be spent privately or channeled through government for public spending has been one of the key disputes between conservatives and liberal "ideologies" for several decades. From this point of view, the great multitude of "spend-save" references can be considered essentially as accurate matching of terms. On the other hand, it goes without saying that the conservative-liberal dialogue does not exhaust itself on this narrow question alone, and our view of these responses as an understanding of the differences depends in no small measure on whether the individual sees this point as a self-contained distinction or understands the link between it and a number of other broad questions. On rare occasions, one encounters a respondent for whom the "spend-save" dimension is intimately bound up with other problem areas. For example, one respondent feels that the Republicans are more conservative because ". . . they are too interested in getting the budget balanced—they should spend more to get more jobs for our people." More frequently when further links are suggested, they are connected with policy but go no further:

> [Republicans more conservative because] "Well, they don't spend as much money." [What do you have in mind?] "Well, a lot of them holler when they try to establish a higher interest rate but that's to get back a little when they do loan out and make it so people are not so free with it."

Generally, however, the belief system involved when "liberal-conservative" is equated with "spend-save" seems to be an entirely narrow one. There follow a number of examples of comments, which taken with the preceding citations, form a random drawing from the large group of "spend-save" comments:

> [Democrats more conservative because] "they do more for the people at home before they go out to help foreign countries. They are truthful and not liars."
>
> [Republicans more liberal judging] "by the money they have spent in this last administration. They spent more than ever before in a peace time. And got less for it as far as I can see."
>
> [Republicans more conservative because] "Well, they vote against the wild spending spree the Democrats get on."
>
> [Republicans more conservative because] "they pay as you go."

[Democrats more conservative because] "I don't believe the Democrats will spend as much money as the Republicans."

[Republicans more conservative because] "it seems as if the Republicans try to hold down the spending of government money." [Do you remember how?] "Yes," [by having] "no wars."

From this representation of the "spend-save" references, the reader may see quite clearly why we consider them to be rather "narrow" readings of the liberal-conservative distinction as applied to the current partisan scene. In short, our portrait of the population, where recognition of a key ideological dimension is concerned, suggests that about 17 percent of the public (stratum I) have an understanding of the distinction that captures much of its breadth. About 37 percent (strata IV and V) are entirely vague as to its meaning. For the 46 percent between, there are two strata, one of which demonstrates considerable uncertainty and guesswork in assigning meaning to the terms (stratum III) and the other of which has the terms rather well under control but appears to have a fairly limited set of connotations for them (stratum II). The great majority of the latter groups equate liberalism-conservatism rather directly with a "spend-save" dimension. In such cases, when the sensed connotations are limited, it is not surprising that there is little active use of the continuum as an organizing dimension. Why should one bother to say that a party is conservative if one can convey the same information by saying that it is against spending?

Since the 1960 materials on liberal-conservative meanings were drawn from the same sample as the coding of the active use of such frames of reference in 1956, it is possible to consider how well the two codings match. For a variety of reasons, we would not expect a perfect fit, even aside from coding error. The earlier coding had not been limited to the liberal-conservative dimension, and, although empirical instances were rare, a person could qualify as an "ideologue" if he assessed politics with the aid of some other highly abstract organizing dimension. Similarly, among those who did employ the liberal-conservative distinction, there were no requirements that the terms be defined. It was necessary therefore to depend upon appearances, and the classification was intentionally lenient. Furthermore, since a larger portion of the population would show recognition than showed active use, we could expect substantial numbers of people in the lower levels of conceptualization to show reasonable recognition of the terms. At any rate, we assumed that the two measures would show a high correlation, as they in fact did (Table 7.3).

Of course, very strong differences in education underlie the data shown in Table 7.3. The 2 percent of the sample that occupy the upper left-hand cell have a mean education close to seven years greater than that of the 11 percent that occupy the lower right-hand cell. Sixty-two percent of this lower cell have had less formal education than the least educated person in the upper corner. The differences in education show a fairly regular progression across the intervening surface of the table (see Table 7.4). Although women have a higher mean education than men, there is some sex bias to the table, for women are disproportionately represented in the lower right-hand quadrant of the table. Furthermore, although age is negatively correlated with

TABLE 7.3 LEVELS OF CONCEPTUALIZATION (1956) BY RECOGNITION AND UNDERSTANDING OF TERMS "CONSERVATISM" AND "LIBERAL-ISM" (1960)

		LEVELS OF CONCEPTUALIZATION				
	Stratum	Ideologue	Near Ideologue	Group Interest	Nature of the Times	No Issue Content
	I	51%	29%	13%	16%	10%
Recognition	II	43	46	42	40	22
and	III	2	10	14	7	7
understanding a	IV	2	5	6	7	12
	V	2	10	25	30	49
		100%	100%	100%	100%	100%
Number of cases		(45)	(122)	(580)	(228)	(290)

a The definitions of the strata are: I. recognition and proper matching of label, meaning, and party and a broad understanding of the terms "conservative" and "liberal"; II. recognition and proper matching but a narrow definition of terms (like "spend-save"); III. recognition but some error in matching; IV. recognition and an attempt at matching but inability to give any meaaning for terms; V. no apparent recognition of terms (does not know if parties differ in liberal-conservative terms and does not know if anybody else sees them as differing).

education, there is also rather clear evidence that the sort of political sophistication represented by the measures can accumulate with age. Undoubtedly even sporadic observation of politics over long enough periods of time serves to nurture some broader view of basic liberal-conservative differences, although of course the same sophistication is achieved much more rapidly and in a more striking way by those who progress greater distances through the educational system.

It is not surprising that political sophistication goes hand in hand with political activism at the "grass roots" (Table 7.5). The relationship is certainly not perfect: About 20 percent of those in the most sophisticated cell engaged in none of the forms of participation beyond voting that were sur-

TABLE 7.4 LEVELS OF CONCEPTUALIZATION (1956) AND TERM RECOGNITION (1960) BY MEAN YEARS OF FORMAL EDUCATION

		LEVELS OF CONCEPTUALIZATION				
	Stratum	Ideologue	Near Ideologue	Group Interest	Nature of the Times	No Issue Content
Recognition	I	14.9 a	14.2	12.3	11.1	11.9
and	II	13.9	11.9	10.7	10.7	11.5
understanding b	III	*	11.1	10.6	9.8	9.6
	IV	*	*	10.4	9.9	10.3
	V	*	10.0	9.5	8.5	8.2

* Inadequate number of cases.

a The cell entry is mean number of years of formal education. Partial college was arbitrarily assumed to represent an average of 14 years, and work toward an advanced degree an average of 18 years.

b See Table 7.3 for definitions of the five strata.

TABLE 7.5 AMOUNT OF 1956–1960 POLITICAL ACTIVITY BY LEVEL OF CON-
CEPTUALIZATION (1956) AND TERM RECOGNITION (1960)

		LEVEL OF CONCEPTUALIZATION			
	Stratum	Ideologue	Near Ideologue	Group Interest	Nature of the Times	No Issue Content
	I	3.8 [a]	2.6	2.5	2.6	2.2
Recognition	II	3.4	3.0	1.7	1.8	1.3
and	III	*	2.5	2.2	1.5	1.1
understanding [b]	IV	*	*	1.9	1.5	.8
	V	*	1.7	1.0	.8	.4

* Inadequate number of cases.

[a] Both five-by-five matrices are those employed in Tables 7.3, 7.4, 7.5. Aside from exclusive of voting reported for the two presidential campaigns of 1956 and 1960. For 1956, a point as awarded to each respondent for party membership, campaign contributions, attendance at political rallies, other party work, attempts to convince others through informal communication, and displaying campaign buttons or stickers. In 1960, essentially the same scoring applied, except that on two items more differentiated information was available. A point was awarded for attending one or two political rallies, two points for three to six rallies, and three points for seven or more. Similarly, a second point was awarded for people who reported having attempted in 1960 to convince others in more than one class (friends, family, or coworkers). A total score of 15 was possible, although empirically the highest score was 14. Only about 1 percent of the sample had scores greater than 9.

[b] See Table 7.3 for definitions of the five strata.

veyed (see note a, Table 7.5) in either the 1956 or 1960 election campaigns, and there is more "stray" participation than has sometimes been suspected among those who express little interest in politics or comprehension of party differences yet who may, for example, happen on a political rally. Furthermore, even the active hard core is not necessarily sophisticated in this sense: Two of the thirteen most active people fall in the lower right half of the table, and their activism is probably to be understood more in terms of mundane social gratifications than through any concern over the policy competition of politics.

Nonetheless, persistent and varied participation is most heavily concentrated among the most sophisticated people. This fact is important, for much of what is perceived as "public reaction" to political events depends upon public visibility, and visibility depends largely upon forms of political participation beyond the vote itself. Anyone familiar with practical politics has encountered the concern of the local politician that ideas communicated in political campaigns be kept simple and concrete. He knows his audience and is constantly fighting the battle against the overestimation of sophistication to which the purveyor of political ideas inevitably falls prey. Yet, even the grass-roots audience that forms a reference point for the local politician is, we suspect, a highly self-selected one and quite sophisticated relative to the electorate as a whole.

Since we have 1960 information on the number of political rallies attended by each of our respondents, we may simulate the "sophistication composition" of the typical political gathering. "Typical" is loosely used here, for real gatherings are various in character: A dinner for the party faithful at $15 a plate obviously attracts a different audience from the one that comes to the parade and street rally. Nonetheless, the contrast between the electorate and an hypothetical average rally is instructive (Table 7.6). People located in the three upper left-hand corner cells of the matrix (6 percent of the electorate) form more than 15 percent of the composition of such rallies, and probably, in terms of further rally participation (vocal and otherwise), seem to form a still higher proportion. Yet on election day their

TABLE 7.6   THE SOPHISTICATION COMPOSITION OF A "TYPICAL" POLITICAL RALLY, COMPARED TO THE COMPOSITION OF THE TOTAL ELECTORATE[a]

	A RALLY					THE ELECTORATE				
	High			Low		High			Low	
High	5%	5%	11%	11%	2%	2%	3%	6%	3%	2%
	6	8	11	11	4	1	4	18	9	5
	0	5	9	0	*	*	1	6	1	2
	*	0	1	*	*	*	*	3	2	3
Low	*	2	7	1	0	*	1	11	7	11

* Less than half of 1%.

[a] Both five-by-five matrices are those employed in Tables 7.3, 7.4, 7.5. Aside from rounding error, the proportions entered in each matrix total 100 percent. The table should be read by observing differences between proportions in the same regions of the two tables. For example, the three least sophisticated cells in the lower right-hand corner constitute 21 percent of the electorate and 1 percent of a typical rally audience.

vote (even with a 100 percent turnout) is numerically outweighed by those votes mustered by people in the single cell at the opposite corner of the table who do not attend at all.

One of the most intriguing findings on the surface of the matrix is that strength of party loyalty falls to one of its weakest points in the upper left-hand corner cell of the matrix. In other words, among the most highly sophisticated, those who consider themselves "independents" outnumber those who consider themselves "strong" partisans, despite the fact that the most vigorous political activity, much of it partisan, is carried on by people falling in this cell. If one moves diagonally toward the center of the matrix, this balance is immediately redressed and redressed very sharply, with strong partisans far outnumbering independents. In general, there is a slight tendency (the most sophisticated cell excepted) for strength of party loyalty to decline as one moves diagonally across the table, and the most "independent" cell is that in the lower right-hand corner.[18]

This irregularity has two implications. First, we take it to be one small

[18] This cell is laden, of course, with people who are apathetic and apolitical, although more than half of them vote in major elections. Flanigan, working with the total sample, set aside those who never vote as politically inconsequential and then set about comparing the remainder of self-styled independents with strong partisans. Some of the customary findings relating political independence with low involvement and low information then became blurred or in some cases reversed themselves altogether. Our highly sophisticated independents contribute to this phenomenon. See William H. Flanigan, "Partisanship and Campaign Participation" (Unpublished doctoral dissertation, Yale University, 1961).

and special case of our earlier hypothesis that group-objects (here, the party as group) are likely to have less centrality in the belief system of the most sophisticated and that the centrality of groups as referents increases "lower down" in the sophistication ordering. We shall see more handsome evidence of the same phenomenon later. Second, we see in this reversal at least a partial explanation for the persistence of the old assumption that the "independent voter" is relatively informed and involved. The early cross-section studies by Lazarsfeld and his colleagues turned up evidence to reverse this equation, suggesting that the "independent voter" tends instead to be relatively uninformed and uninvolved. Other studies have added massively to this evidence. Indeed, in many situations, the evidence seems so strong that it is hard to imagine how any opposing perceptions could have developed. The perception is somewhat easier to understand, however, if one can assume that the discernment of the informed observer takes in only 5, 10 or 15 percent of the most sophisticated people in the public as constituting "the public." This "visible" or "operative" public is largely made up of people from the upper left-hand corner of our preceding tables. The illusion that such people are the full public is one that the democratic sample survey, for better or for worse, has destroyed.

CONSTRAINTS AMONG IDEA-ELEMENTS

In our estimation, the use of such basic dimensions of judgment as the liberal-conservative continuum betokens a contextual grasp of politics that permits a wide range of more specific idea-elements to be organized into more tightly constrained wholes. We feel, furthermore, that there are many crucial consequences of such organization: With it, for example, new political events have more meaning, retention of political information from the past is far more adequate, and political behavior increasingly approximates that of sophisticated "rational" models, which assume relatively full information.

It is often argued, however, that abstract dimensions like the liberal-conservative continuum are superficial if not meaningless indicators: All that they show is that poorly educated people are inarticulate and have difficulty expressing verbally the more abstract lines along which their specific political beliefs are organized. To expect these people to be able to express what they know and feel, the critic goes on, is comparable to the fallacy of assuming that people can say in an accurate way why they behave as they do. when it comes down to specific attitudes and behaviors, the organization is there nonetheless, and it is this organization that matters, not the capacity for discourse in sophisticated language.

If it were true that such organization does exist for most people, apart from their capacities to be articulate about it, we would agree out of hand that the question of articulation is quite trivial. As a cold empirical matter, however, this claim does not seem to be valid. Indeed, it is for this reason that we have cast the argument in terms of constraint, for constraint and organization are very nearly the same thing. Therefore when we hypothesize that constraint among political idea-elements begins to lose its range very rapidly once we move from the most sophisticated few toward the "grass

TABLE 7.7   CONSTRAINT BETWEEN SPECIFIC ISSUE BELIEFS FOR AN ELITE SAMPLE AND A CROSS-SECTION SAMPLE, 1958[a]

	DOMESTIC				FOREIGN			
	Employment	Education	Housing	FEPC	Economic	Military[b]	Isolationism	Party Preference
Congressional Candidates								
Employment	—	0.62	0.59	0.35	0.26	0.06	0.17	0.68
Aid to education		—	0.61	0.53	0.50	0.06	0.35	0.55
Federal housing			—	0.47	0.41	—0.03	0.30	0.68
F.E.P.C.				—	0.47	0.11	0.23	0.34
Economic aid					—	0.19	0.59	0.25
Military aid						—	0.32	0.18
Isolationism							—	0.05
Party preference								—
Cross-Section Sample								
Employment	—	0.45	0.08	0.34	—0.04	0.10	—0.22	0.20
Aid to education		—	0.12	0.29	0.06	0.14	—0.17	0.16
Federal housing			—	0.08	—0.06	0.02	0.07	0.18
F.E.P.C.				—	0.24	0.13	0.02	—0.04
Economic aid					—	0.16	0.33	—0.07
Soldiers abroad [b]						—	0.21	0.12
Isolationism							—	—0.03
Party preference								—

a Entries are tau-gamma coefficients, a statistic proposed by Leo A. Goodman and William H. Kruskal in "Measures of Association for Cross Classifications," *Journal of the American Statistical Association,* 49 (December 1954), No. 268, 749. The coefficient was chosen because of its sensitivity to constraint of the scalar as well as the correlational type.

b For this category, the cross-section sample was asked a question about keeping American soldiers abroad, rather than about military aid in general.

roots," we are contending that the organization of more specific attitudes into wide-ranging belief systems is absent as well.

Table 7.7 gives us an opportunity to see the differences in levels of constraint among beliefs on a range of specific issues in an elite population and in a mass population. The elite population happens to be candidates for the United States Congress in the off-year elections of 1958, and the cross-section sample represents the national electorate in the same year. The assortment of issues represented is simply a purposive sampling of some of the more salient political controversies at the time of the study, covering both domestic and foreign policy. The questions posed to the two samples were quite comparable, apart from adjustments necessary in view of the backgrounds of the two populations involved.[19]

For our purposes, however, the specific elite sampled and the specific beliefs tested are rather beside the point. We would expect the same general contrast to appear if the elite had been a set of newspaper editors, political

19 As a general rule, questions broad enough for the mass public to understand tend to be too simple for highly sophisticated people to feel comfortable answering without elaborate qualification. The pairing of questions, with those for the mass public given first, are as follows:

writers, or any other group that takes an interest in politics. Similarly, we
would expect the same results from any other broad sampling of political
issues or, for that matter, any sampling of beliefs from other domains: A set
of questions on matters of religious controversy should show the same pattern
between an elite population like the clergy and the church members who
form their mass "public." What is generically important in comparing the two
types of population is the difference in levels of constraint among belief-
elements.

Where constraint is concerned, the absolute value of the coefficients in
Table 7.7 (rather than their algebraic value) is the significant datum. The first
thing the table conveys is the fact that, for both populations, there is some
falling off of constraint *between* the domains of domestic and foreign
policy, relative to the high level of constraint *within* each domain. This result is to be expected: Such lowered values signify boundaries between belief
systems that are relatively independent. If we take averages of appropriate
sets of coefficients entered in Table 7.7 however, we see that the strongest
constraint *within* a domain for the mass public is less than that *between*
domestic and foreign domains for the elite sample. Furthermore, for the
public, in sharp contrast to the elite, party preference seems by and large to be
set off in a belief system of its own, relatively unconnected to issue positions
(Table 7.8).[20]

Employment "The government in Washington ought to see to it that everybody who
wants to work can find a job." "Do you think the federal government ought to sponsor programs such as large public works in order to maintain full employment, or do you think that
problems of economic readjustment ought to be left more to private industry or state and
local government?"
Aid to Education "If cities and towns around the county need help to build more
schools, the government in Washington ought to give them the money they need." "Do you
think the government should provide grants to the states for the construction and operation of
public schools, or do you think the support of public education should be left entirely to
the state and local government?"
Federal Housing "The government should leave things like electric power and housing
for private businessmen to handle." "Do you approve the use of federal funds for public housing, or do you generally feel that housing can be taken care of better by private effort?"
F.E.P.C. "If Negroes are not getting fair treatment in jobs and housing, the government
should see to it that they do." "Do you think the federal government should establish a
fair employment practices commission to prevent discrimination in employment?"
Economic Aid. "The United States should give economic help to the poorer countries of
the world even if those countries can't pay for it." "First, on the foreign economic aid
program, would you generally favor expanding the program, reducing it, or maintaining it
about the way it is?"
Military Aid "The United States should keep soldiers overseas where they can help
countries that are against Communism." "How about the foreign military aid programs?
Should this be expanded, reduced, or maintained about as it is?"
Isolationism "This country would be better off if we just stayed home and did not
concern ourselves with problems in other parts of the world." "Speaking very generally,
do you think that in the years ahead the United States should maintain or reduce its commitments around the world?"

[20] We are aware that drawing an average of these coefficients has little interpretation from a statistical point of view. The averages are presented merely as a crude way of
capturing the flavor of the larger table in summary form. More generally, it could be argued that the coefficients might be squared in any event, an operation that would do no
more than heighten the intuitive sense of contrast between the two publics. In this format,
for example, the elite-mass difference in the domestic-issue column of Table 7.8 would
shift from 0.35 versus 0.23 to 0.28 versus 0.05. Similarly, that in the party column would become 0.15 versus 0.01.

TABLE 7.8 SUMMARY OF DIFFERENCES IN LEVEL OF CONSTRAINT WITHIN
AND BETWEEN DOMAINS, PUBLIC AND ELITE (BASED ON TABLE
7.7)

	AVERAGE COEFFICIENTS			
	Within Domestic Issues	Between Domestic and Foreign	Within Foreign Issues	Between Issues and Party
Elite	0.53	0.25	0.37	0.39
Mass	0.23	0.11	0.23	0.11

It should be remembered throughout, of course, that the *mass* sample
of Tables 7.7 and 7.8 does not exclude college-educated people, ideologues,
or the politically sophisticated. These people, with their higher levels of
constraint, are represented in appropriate numbers, and certainly contribute
to such vestige of organization as the mass matrix evinces. But they are
grossly outnumbered, as they are in the active electorate. The general point
is that the matrix of correlations for the elite sample is of the sort that would
be appropriate for factor analysis, the statistical technique designed to reduce
a number of correlated variables to a more limited set of organizing dimensions. The matrix representing the mass public, however, despite its realistic
complement of ideologues, is exactly the type that textbooks advise against
using for factor analysis on the simple grounds that through inspection it is
clear that there is virtually nothing in the way of organization to be discovered. Of course, it is the type of broad organizing dimension to be suggested by factor analysis of specific items that is usually presumed when observers discuss "ideological postures" of one sort or another.

Although the beliefs registered in Table 7.7 are related to topics of controversy or political cleavage. McClosky has described comparable differences in levels of constraint among beliefs for an elite sample (delegates to
national party conventions) and a cross-section sample when the items deal
with propositions about democracy and freedom—topics on which fundamental consensus among Americans is presumed.[21] Similarly, Prothro and
Grigg, among others, have shown that, while there is widespread support for
statements of culturally familiar principles of freedom, democracy, and tolerance in a cross-section sample, this support becomes rapidly obscured when
questions turn to specific cases that elites would see as the most direct applications of these principles.[22] In our estimation, such findings are less a demonstration of cynical lip service than of the fact that, while both of two inconsistent opinions are honestly held, the individual lacks the contextual
grasp to understand that the specific case and the general principle belong
in the same belief system: In the absence of such understanding, he maintains psychologically independent beliefs about both. This is another impor-

[21] Herbert McClosky, "Consensus and Ideology in American Politics" *American Political Science Review*, 58 (June 1964), No. 2.

[22] James W. Prothro and C. W. Grigg, "Fundamental Principles of Democracy: Bases
of Agreement and Disagreement," *Journal of Politics*, 22 (May 1960), No. 2, 276–294.

tant instance of the decline in constraint among beliefs with declining information.

While an assessment of relative constraint between the matrices rests only on comparisons of absolute values, the comparative algebraic values have some interest as well. This interest arises from the sophisticated observer's almost automatic assumption that whatever beliefs "go together" in the visible political word (as judged from the attitudes of elites and the more articulate spectators) must naturally go together in the same way among mass public. Table 7.7 makes clear that this assumption is a very dangerous one, aside from the question of degree of constraint. For example, the politician who favors federal aid to education could be predicted to be more, rather than less, favorable to an internationalist posture in foreign affairs, for these two positions in the 1950s were generally associated with "liberalism" in American politics. As we see from Table 7.7, we would be accurate in this judgment considerably more often than chance alone would permit. On the other hand, were we to apply the same assumption of constraint to the American public in the same era, not only would we have been wrong, but we would actually have come closer to reality by assuming no connection at all.

All the correlations in the elite sample except those that do not depart significantly from zero exhibit signs that anybody following politics in the newspapers during this period could have predicted without hesitation. That is, one need only have known that Democrats tended to favor expansion of government welfare activities and tended to be internationalists in foreign affairs, to have anticipated all the signs except one. This exception, the 0.18 that links advocacy of military aid abroad with the Republican party, would hold no surprises either, for the one kind of international involvement that Republicans came to accept in this period limited foreign aid to the military variety, a view that stood in opposition to "soft" liberal interests in international economic welfare. If these algebraic signs in the elite matrix are taken as the culturally defined "proper" signs—the sophisticated observer's assumption of what beliefs go with other beliefs—then the algebraic differences between comparable entries in the two matrices provide an estimate of how inaccurate we would be in generalizing our elite-based assumptions about "natural" belief combinations to the mass public as a whole. A scanning of the two matrices with these differences in mind enhances our sense of high discrepancy between the two populations.

To recapitulate, then, we have argued that the unfamiliarity of broader and more abstract ideological frames of reference among the less sophisticated is more than a problem in mere articulation. Parallel to ignorance and confusion over these ideological dimensions among the less informed is a general decline in constraint among specific belief elements that such dimensions help to organize. It cannot therefore be claimed that the mass public shares ideological patterns of belief with relevant elites at a specific level any more than it shares the abstract conceptual frames of reference. . . .

8

The Quality
of the Electorate's
Deliberation*

MORRIS JANOWITZ
DWAINE MARVICK

The election of a president as a result of a two-party campaign means in effect that the electorate has only one real decision to make. Nevertheless, meaningful deliberation in any presidential campaign requires voters to weigh two types of considerations. This was especially true in the 1952 campaign.

On a rational level, deliberation centered around the issues and the political rhetoric of the campaign. The quality of such deliberation could be judged by the extent to which voters become involved in debating and weighing those issues. What patterns of attitudes toward campaign issues could be found in the various strata of the voting population? A sample survey, with its emphasis on the scientific neutral investigation of discrete issues, rules out any extensive analysis of the dynamics of political deliberation. Perhaps with a more argumentative approach to respondents, more appropriate data could have been gathered. But such an emphasis would have meant the sacrifice of other basic objectives. Actually, only a few of the central issues could be investigated, namely those on which the parties were known to divide. Moreover, the survey was necessarily confined to collecting a concise expression of attitude on each issue.

* Reprinted by permission from Morris Janowitz and Dwaine Marvick, *Competitive Pressure and Democratic Consent* (2d ed; Chicago: Quadrangle Books, 1964), pp. 40–56.

On an emotional level, the campaign deliberation focused heavily on the public personality and imagery of the opposing candidates. Voters were called upon to make a deliberate choice between the candidates as political leaders, as standard bearers of their party, and as human beings. Although deliberations about candidates can involve overtones of irrationality and emotionalism, such deliberations are still relevant to a theory of competitive democracy. Again, the sample survey method of research has only limited opportunities for probing deeply into the respondent's images and subjective evaluations of candidates as symbols of authority. But a content analysis of the interview enabled us to distinguish generalized attitudes toward Eisenhower and Stevenson and to relate such attitudes to voting preferences.

The quality of citizen deliberation on issues had also to be judged indirectly. A pattern of attitudes on key campaign issues which was consistent with the announced position of one party could be viewed as a meaningful basis for a voting decision. A pattern of attitudes which either revealed no basis for preferring one party's position over another's, or which indicated preference for one party's position as often as the other's, could be construed as providing no meaningful basis for a voting decision. To what degree, then, were attitudes on party-framed issues of public policy related to voting alignments in 1952? Indirectly, it was the answer to this question which enabled us to assess the quality of deliberation during the campaign.

Since the relative importance of political issues as compared with candidate appeal has long preoccupied practical politicians, it likewise promised to supply a basis for analysis of campaign deliberation. Throughout the campaign, strategists of both parties apparently were concerned with a proper emphasis and balance. Communications via the mass media during the campaign, the appeals pressed by the local party organizations, and the arguments that took place in intimate face-to-face groups fell, in good measure, on one side or the other of this central dichotomy: the merits of the men and the merits of the issues.

Likewise, a theory of competitive democracy requires some a priori judgment about what is a proper concern by the electorate over political issues verses the character of the candidates. If the election is a process of arriving at consent which must endure post-election realities, how is the final agreement aided or hindered by the electorate's over-emphasis or under-emphasis of either issues or candidates? The problem takes on particular meaning within the American constitutional system, where the relationship between the President and Congress is not mediated by explicit and formal parliamentary institutions. In the 1952 election, since General Eisenhower was without previous political commitment, such considerations were of added importance.

According to the premises of traditional democratic theory, it is issues that are crucial. After rational analysis based on self-interest, the electorate selects officeholders who within reasonable limits are committed in their political program. It is precisely this aspect of the process of consent which the critics of democracy consider most susceptible to "mass manipulation." Broad segments of the population, they argue, are unable to formulate their self-interest in clear political terms. Often, too, when these segments are able to formulate self-interest, it lacks even a rudimentary political consistency and so cannot be related to alternatives posed by the two major parties.

The criteria of competitive democratic elections also require a minimum consistency between issues and political choice in an election. However, this relationship is now seen as secondary. Instead, greater emphasis is placed on the competition between candidates and on the imagery of candidates as sponsored by the rival parties. The election is primarily a means by which officeholders are selected. Only in a secondary sense is it appropriate as a means of expressing self-interest on public issues. Therefore, less consistency between issue orientation and voting behavior was to be expected. In theory, moreover, more inconsistency can be tolerated as compatible with competitive democracy.

In the simplest terms, a two-step analysis (of voting behavior, attitudes toward issues and attitudes toward candidates) was expected to throw light on the quality of campaign deliberation and the quality of consensus it developed. First: What patterns of attitudes toward key issues were found among Eisenhower voters as opposed to Stevenson voters? No causal analysis was directly envisioned; yet it was necessary to chart how extensively each set of voters held attitudes that were clear cut and consistent with their party's position. Second: Was there evidence, as might be expected, of a closer link between candidate imagery and voting choice than between party-framed ideology and voting choice?

CAMPAIGN ISSUES AND THE 1952 VOTE

Specific controversies did, of course, present powerful appeals to particular segments of the population. Individual campaign issues were almost certain to divide a considerable number of Republicans from Democrats. Some of these issues were peculiar to the campaign of 1952; others were of long standing.

For example, the corruption issue, embodied in part in the slogan, "Time for a Change," was heavily underscored throughout the campaign. Our data, however, indicate that it was an issue that aroused the concern of only a minority of the electorate. No specific or direct question dealing with corruption was contained in the interview schedule. Concern over this issue was measured by a content analysis of spontaneous mentions, since the interview was repeatedly so structured as to bring comment on that topic. In all, 389 respondents (24.2 percent of the total sample) made spontaneous mention of corruption and, by implication, indicated it was a factor to be weighed in their choice. Only 51 (13.1 percent) took a position on the corruption issue that could be characterized as pro-Democratic; by contrast, 338 (86.9 percent), more than six times as many, expressed a pro-Republican attitude.

Of those who took a pro-Republican viewpoint on the corruption controversy, over three-quarters (76.9 percent) voted Republican, while of those who took a pro-Democratic stand, only half (50 percent) voted for Stevenson. The implications of the corruption controversy as a conditioner of Republican voting behavior will be amplified later, when a fuller analysis is made of the other key campaign issues.

By contrast with the corruption issue, spontaneous expressions of concern with internal communism were considerably fewer. Only 59 respondents (3.7 percent of the sample) mentioned it spontaneously, less than one-sixth as many as spoke of corruption in government. The political implication was almost completely one-sided; all but four respondents took a pro-Republican stand. Crude though these measures may be, they are a useful guide to the relative weight of the two controversies in the deliberations of the electorate.

While these two issues were specific for the 1952 campaign, a core of long-standing issues was presented to the voters reflecting years of strategic competition between the two parties. During the last two decades, the Democratic party had sponsored a wide range of social welfare policies. How did the vote for Stevenson and for Eisenhower relate to the major elements of the New Deal heritage? One would expect at least a preponderantly favorable orientation toward these issues on the part of Stevenson voters. Foreign policy was more complex, since the Republicans had developed a stake in bipartisanship and since Eisenhower had not in effect repudiated the goals of bipartisan foreign policy. Nevertheless, even in the area of foreign policy, a difference in attitudes was to be expected between Eisenhower and Stevenson voters.

Seven questions—three on domestic policy and four on foreign affairs—were used in the pre-election schedule to gauge attitudes on party-framed issues. The three domestic issues dealt with: (1) social welfare activities of the national government; (2) legislative action to ensure fair employment practices; and (3) legislative revision of the Taft-Hartley labor law. The four issues of foreign policy were concerned with: (1) the extent of United States involvement in world affairs, (2) the degree of American responsibility for the loss of China to the Communists, (3) the correctness of the United States entry into the Korean war, and (4) the best current policy to pursue in Korea.

Tables 8.1 and 8.2 classify the Eisenhower and Stevenson vote according to the voter's attitude on the specific issues. These data highlight the proportion of the electorate whose opinions had crystallized in favor of one party's stand, and simultaneously measure the divergence on these issues between Eisenhower and Stevenson voters. Since opinions were gathered largely in October, prior to actual voting, the attitudes reported may be taken to represent in good part the relevance of these issues to voting decisions.

It is perhaps a mark of America's acceptance of its role in world politics that rudimentary ideological patterns on questions of foreign policy were at least as firmly crystallized as on matters of domestic policy. Moreover, despite the efforts of Eisenhower and his leading followers to narrow the range of competition on foreign issues, the ideology of his supporters diverged from that of Stevenson in foreign policy to a degree equal to, if not greater than, that encountered in domestic politics.

On the question of social welfare activity by the national government, only a very small percentage had no opinion (8.4 percent of the total sample and 6.3 percent of those who voted; see Table 8.1). The extent of consensus on the developments of the New Deal was reflected by the finding that more than half of the Eisenhower supporters were willing to accept Demo-

TABLE 8.1   THE 1952 PRESIDENTIAL VOTE AND DOMESTIC CAMPAIGN ISSUES
(PERCENT)

	EISENHOWER VOTERS	STEVENSON VOTERS	NON-VOTERS
Governmental Social Welfare Activity			
Should do more (alternative formulations)	19.5	34.0	22.6
About right; O.K. as is	37.8	54.6	51.5
Should do less (alternative formulations)	31.7	5.4	10.3
More on some, less on others	3.9	.7	1.2
Don't know; not ascertained	7.1	5.3	14.4
Revision of Taft-Hartley Law			
Completely repealed	6.7	28.1	8.6
Changed in favor of labor (alternative formulations)	2.6	5.1	1.4
Changed in favor of management, with minor pro-labor changes	36.0	12.5	10.7
Other changes	6.5	5.5	2.6
No knowledge of Taft-Hartley Law.	48.2	48.8	77.7
FEPC			
National government should legislate	18.5	30.5	25.0
State government should legislate	15.9	14.8	13.6
Government should take an interest, not ascertained how	4.9	5.1	10.0
Government non-legislative action only	7.6	8.5	7.4
National government should stay out but state government should take action	19.8	13.4	10.3
National and state government should stay out entirely	20.7	16.6	16.9
Favor restrictive action	5.7	4.5	5.3
Don't know; not ascertained	6.9	6.6	11.5
Number	(687)	(494)	(419)

cratic social welfare policies. Likewise, almost 90 percent of the Stevenson supporters were willing to accept the social welfare policies of the Administration as sufficient to meet their needs. On the other hand, 31.7 percent of the Eisenhower voters demanded a retrenchment of social welfare activity while only 5.4 percent of the Democrats had that attitude.

The ideological outlook with respect to labor problems presented a markedly different pattern. Slightly less than a majority of the voters had no crystallized opinions on modification of the Taft-Hartley Act (48.2 percent of the Eisenhower voters and 48.8 percent of the Stevenson voters). Of the Eisenhower voters, 6.7 percent were in favor of complete repeal, while among Stevenson supporters the percentage was 28.1.

Specific responses to the FEPC issue need to be evaluated with great care since the same response had markedly different political overtones in differen regions of the country. The range of responses was rather highly differentiated in general, with only moderate differences between Republican supporters and Democratic supporters as compared with their responses on other domestic issues of social policy. This reflects the complex character of opinion on the FEPC issue.

Attitudes toward the level of U.S. foreign involvement divided Eisenhower voters from Stevenson voters almost as much as any single domestic issue (see Table 8.2). Of the Eisenhower voters, 65.6 percent expressed

TABLE 8.2   THE 1952 PRESIDENTIAL VOTE AND FOREIGN POLICY CAMPAIGN ISSUES (PERCENT)

	EISENHOWER VOTERS	STEVENSON VOTERS	NON-VOTERS
U.S Foreign Involvement			
Country has not gone too far	28.2	43.3	26.5
Pro-con	1.6	3.0	2.6
Country has gone too far	65.6	45.8	50.6
Don't know; not ascertained	4.6	7.9	20.3
U.S. Entry into Korean War			
Yes, we did the right thing	34.6	52.8	33.7
Pro-con	6.7	3.8	5.0
No, we should have stayed out	46.2	32.7	42.7
Don't know; not ascertained	12.5	10.7	18.6
1952 U.S. Korean Policy			
Keep trying for a peaceful settlement	36.8	52.4	51.8
Pull out of Korea entirely	9.5	6.5	11.7
Take a stronger stand and bomb Manchuria and China	46.4	35.2	27.2
Don't know; not ascertained	7.3	5.9	9.3
U.S. China Policy			
Nothing we could do	38.4	61.5	48.7
It was our fault	38.5	18.2	11.0
Don't know; not ascertained	23.1	20.3	40.3
Number	(687)	(494)	(419)

agreement with the anti-Administration proposition that "this country has gone too far in concerning itself with problems in other parts of the world." Only 45.8 percent of the Stevenson voters were of this opinion. Attitudes were crystallized in party-framed terms to the extent that a relatively low concentration of Eisenhower voters and Stevenson voters alike fell into the "no opinion" category (4.6 percent and 7.9 percent respectively).

Korea emerged as a most crucial aspect of the campaign deliberation. Despite Eisenhower's pronouncements, the initial intervention of the United States in Korea remained a controversial subject. His supporters included 46.2 percent who believed that the United States should not have intervened. Current (1952) policy in Korea divided the electorate in a similar pattern. The data suggest that Eisenhower represented a compromise position on Korea acceptable to citizens whose views were markedly different. A majority of his supporters (55.9 percent) voiced opposition to the Truman Administration's policy of continuing to work for an armistice. They consisted of two highly divergent blocs. One bloc wished the United States to pull out of Korea entirely (9.5 percent) while the larger group (46.4 percent) wanted to take a stronger stand, bombing Manchuria and China. Eisenhower's promise of a personal inspection of the Korean battlefield apparently appealed to both groups of voters dissatisfied with the stalemated situation. In particular, he was appealing to persons who had low levels of personal tolerance for the ambiguous struggle and who desired clear-cut action.

Finally, on the issue of U.S. responsibility for the loss of China, on which more people had "no opinion" than any other foreign issue investigated, there was a similar differentiation between Eisenhower and Stevenson supporters. Of the Stevenson vote, 61.5 percent took a pro-Administration view on this matter, while only 38.4 percent of the Eisenhower vote absolved the Truman Administration.

THE IDEOLOGICAL BASIS
OF POLITICAL COMPROMISE

By combining attitudes on specific domestic and foreign issues, we were able to evaluate the quality of campaign deliberation in terms of broader political ideology. Ideology was conceived of as a pattern of attitudes toward a range of fundamental issues, using expressed party platforms as the basic criteria. In constructing this measure of ideology, only five of the seven issues were used.[1] For the purposes of this analysis, responses to these issues were coded as pro-Democratic Administration, neutral or no opinion, and anti-Democratic Administration. Although there were disadvantages to such an analysis, it did measure ideological deviation from the 1952 Administration policy.

Four categories of ideological orientation were employed:

"Stalwarts"—those who supported the party position on all or almost all of the issues

"Compromisers"—those who supported the party position in a majority of the issues

"Weak Compromisers"—those whose support was limited to a minority of the issues, with a tendency to have no opinions or contradictory opinions on the remainder

"Ambivalent or Neutralized"—those who were divided on the majority of the issues, neutral on almost all of the issues, and in some cases with no opinion[2]

Thus, in Table 8.3, the presidential vote is classified by the electorate's compromise position on these two domestic and three foreign issues.

We recognize that these issues represented only a sample of the range of policy alternatives on which the parties were divided. We also recognized that arbitrary definitions were used to establish meaningful categories of political orientation. But given these limitations, it was still felt that the categories contributed to a more meaningful analysis of a competitive theory of democracy.

From the outset, it was clear that to find a large segment of the electorate in the "stalwart" category was neither to be expected nor even desired if the election was to be a process of consensus and compromise. In general, it is necessary to underline the contributions to the competitive

[1] In the foreign affairs sphere, the question of U.S. intervention in Korea was eliminated as being repetitious of the issue of the 1952 policy in Korea FEPC was eliminated from the domestic issues, since the responses were widely scattered and linked to overriding regional interpretations that made evaluation on a national basis overly complex.

[2] See Technical Appendix Section 8, "Ideological Orientation toward Campaign issues," in Janowitz and Marvick, *Competitive Pressure and Democratic Consent,* 2d ed. for details of the classification scheme and the operational definitions of the category system.

TABLE 8.3   THE 1952 PRESIDENTIAL VOTE AND IDEOLOGICAL ORIENTATION (PERCENT)

	EISENHOWER VOTERS	STEVENSON VOTERS	NON- VOTERS	TOTAL[a]
Republican stalwarts	16.7	1.1	3.0	8.3
Republican compromisers	26.2	8.4	8.4	16.0
Weak Republican compromisers	17.2	11.0	18.8	16.0
Ambivalent or neutralized	16.5	20.2	22.0	19.0
Weak Democratic compromisers	11.1	20.4	27.5	18.0
Democratic compromisers	10.4	21.7	16.6	15.4
Democratic stalwarts	1.9	17.2	3.7	7.3
Number	(687)	(494)	(419)	(1600)

[a] Total excludes fourteen cases for which no basis for classification was available.

arena of "compromisers" and even "weak compromisers." In this type of analysis, simple negative value judgments toward voters who show a relative lack of opinion on crucial issues gives way to a clearer understanding of how compromise may develop. "No opinion" is therefore not regarded as an inherent evil, per se; danger only arises when exceptionally high levels of "no opinion" or contradictory opinion prevent meaningful consensus. In any case, one must avoid the simplistic fallacy of assuming that the holding of fixed party-framed opinions on all subjects is the desirable criterion for evaluating political deliberation in a campaign.

It was found that only 16.7 percent of the Eisenhower votes were Republican "stalwarts" in that they supported the Republican party position on all or almost all of the issues. The percentage of Stevenson voters who were Democratic party "stalwarts" was about the same, 17.2 percent. Any assumption that the Republican voters had a decidedly higher ideological consistency than the Democratic voters is dispelled by this and subsequent observations from the data. Since the party stalwarts represented heavy and therefore rigid commitment to the "party line," a greater concentration of voters in these categories could have hindered the process of consent through elections. Nevertheless the major political parties must draw much of their stable support and organizational strength, as well as intellectual vitality, from the ranks of these party stalwarts.

A party's stalwarts must be augmented by the less doctrinaire "compromisers"—those who at polling time show an explicit position of compromise on which they base their candidate preference. In a society as dynamic and diverse as that of the United States, these compromisers represent important components of the electorate. Thus, of Eisenhower's voters, 26.2 percent were Republican "compromisers," while Stevenson's voters included 21.7 percent Democratic "compromisers." It seems reasonable to assume that the bulk of the Republican compromisers would vote persistently for the Republican candidate, and the same would be expected of Democratic compromisers. Nevertheless, the image of the candidate, campaign pressure, and other considerations led small but important minorities to vote for the candidate opposed to their ideological inclination.

However, those voters classified as "weak compromisers", reflect an ideological orientation that seems too undefined for effective political competition. They were the individuals who, by and large, saw little fundamental difference between the alternatives posed by the two principal parties competing for the right to rule. In all, 29.5 percent of those who cast a vote for president were of this type in 1952. Yet the fact remains that weak Republican compromisers voted two-to-one for the Republican candidate, while weak Democratic compromisers voted for Stevenson only to a slightly greater extent than for Eisenhower. Thus, while the voting behavior of these groups was not random, both parties seem likely to have extended their claims by over-simplification and extremism in order to appeal to such groups, which, in this sense, constitute a potential pressure for at once over-intensifying and weakening the competitive process.

The range of ideological orientations is completed by the neutrals, who constituted 16.5 percent of the Eisenhower voters and 20.2 percent of the Stevenson voters. For the members of this group, campaign competition seems to have failed to create a link between party-framed alternatives and their personal ideological demands.

The pattern of linkage between voting behavior and ideological orientation can be summarized in another way by comparing persistent party voters with party changers. These data confirm previous findings, based on the analysis of political predispositions, that the political competition reached the periphery of the electorate. Those voters who were pro-Republican changers (between 1948 and 1952) appeared markedly less explicit in their ideology than persistent Republican voters. Thus, for example, the combined incidence of Republican stalwarts and Republican compromisers among regular Republican voters was 53.3 percent; the combined incidence among the pro-Republican changers was only 24.8 percent. The extent to which the shift to Eisenhower was based on considerations other than issues is further delimited by the fact that 18.9 percent of the pro-Republican changers were Democratic compromisers and 3.6 percent of them were even Democratic stalwarts. A similar but somewhat narrower gap was present between pro-Democratic changers and regular Democratic voters in their ideological orientations.

Finally, these patterns of ideological orientation afforded an over-all device for making inferences about how significantly certain campaign issues affected voting behavior.[3] In particular, there was the question of how much impact lay in the corruption controversy. As mentioned earlier, almost a quarter of the sampled electorate expressed concern about the corruption issue, and this concern rested on attitudes which were exploitable by Republicans. Those who expressed concern were characterized by an overwhelmingly pro-Republican orientation (86.9 percent to 13.1 percent).

In order to gauge how far the "corruption issue" was able to offset

---

[3] A breakdown of the over-all ideological patterns into the groups of domestic and foreign issues revealed similar results in both cases to those of the combined analysis. One noteworthy difference, however, was the higher concentration of ambivalents and those Without orientation in foreign policy matters, as compared with that of weak compromisers. The concentration was almost equal for both parties.

ideological orientation which was otherwise pro-Democratic, persons with similar ideological leanings who expressed no concern with this issue were contrasted with those who did (see Table 8.4). The results lead to the inference that in 1952 corruption was an important Republican appeal which served to motivate a small group of persons who might otherwise have been

TABLE 8.4 IDEOLOGICAL ORIENTATION, CORRUPTION, AND THE 1952 PRESIDENTIAL VOTE (PERCENT)

	REPUBLICAN STALWARDS	REPUBLICAN COMPROMISERS[a]	NEUTRALS	DEMOCRATIC COMPROMISERS[a]	DEMOCRATIC STALWARDS	TOTAL[b]
No Concern about the Corruption Issue						
Eisenhower voters	76.2	48.4	29.9	23.3	11.3	34.1
Stevenson voters	8.9	24.0	34.4	93.3	72.7	34.7
Nonvoters	14.9	27.6	35.7	37.4	16.5	31.2
Number	(67)	(362)	(247)	(442)	(97)	(1215)
Pro-Republican Concern about the Corruption Issue						
Eisenhower voters	85.1	86.5	72.9	57.0	26.6	77.1
Stevenson voters	1.6	6.4	18.7	23.6	66.7	13.7
Nonvoters	3.3	7.1	8.4	19.4	6.7	9.2
Number	(61)	(141)	(48)	(72)	(15)	(337)

[a] Includes both compromisers and weak compromisers.

[b] Excludes sixty-two cases for which no basis for classification was available.

expected to vote for Stevenson. In all ideological groups, a pro-Republican concern with the corruption issue mobilized a higher Eisenhower vote, even at that end of the ideological continuum most heavily committed to the Democrats. The greatest impact was among the ideologically neutral, as might have been expected.

COMPETITION AND CANDIDATE IMAGERY

As opposed to the complex relations between ideology and presidential vote, the linkage between candidate imagery and presidential vote was almost "one-to-one." The endless preoccupation of the mass media with the human interest aspects of the candidates undoubtedly contributed to the formation of these images.

Charting the electorate's imagery of the two candidates is a tedious and complex matter. The more direct the approach, the less likelihood that the interview will produce candid and revealing insight into the underlying and emotionally charged imagery and stereotypes about Eisenhower and Stevenson. Therefore, the data on imagery were not gathered as responses to direct or "structured" questions, but from the two interview sessions which lasted about one hour each and covered a wide range of political topics; this gave ample opportunity for those interviewed to reveal spontaneously and indirectly their images of the two candidates. The verbatim records of the interviews were carefully analyzed for content, and responses were classified in a range from strongly pro-Eisenhower to strongly pro-Stevenson (see Table 8.5). The classification scheme depended on the balance of positive to negative (favorable to unfavorable) references accorded to one candidate or another. Thus, this operationalization is different from that presented in the Survey Research Center's basic report, The Voter Decides.

The expected correspondence between imagery and presidential vote was not only extremely high, but there were no significant exceptions or revealing deviations. To be sure, the incidence of those who held a strongly favorable image of their candidate was somewhat higher among Eisenhower voters than among Stevenson voters (39.0 percent to 32.7 percent). But if those voters who had mildly favored imagery of their candidates are included in order to arrive at over-all totals of favorable imagery, both candidates were quite equal. However, additional light on the impact of Eisenhower's

TABLE 8.5   THE 1952 PRESIDENTIAL VOTE AND CANDIDATE IMAGE (PERCENT)

	EISENHOWER VOTERS	STEVENSON VOTERS	NON-VOTERS	TOTAL[a]
Strongly pro-Eisenhower	39.0	5.2	21.0	24.0
Mildly pro-Eisenhower	21.2	3.2	4.6	11.3
Ambivalent or neutralized	22.8	17.8	15.4	19.3
Mildly pro-Stevenson	4.0	30.9	12.1	14.4
Strongly pro-Stevenson	2.0	32.7	21.0	16.4
None [b]	11.0	10.2	25.9	14.6
Number	(687)	(494)	(419)	(1600)

[a] Total excludes fourteen cases for which no basis for classification was available.

[b] Since the categorization of imagery depended on the balance expressed between the two candidates, the "None" category included 6.7 percent who revealed an image of only one candidate.

public personality is shown by the fact that about twice as many voters who held ambivalent images of both candidates voted for Eisenhower as for Stevenson. In the past, the United States has had civilian presidential leadership during all of its armed conflicts. Military heroes as presidential candidates have assumed power in periods after the military conflict or crisis. In 1952, while military operations were being carried on, the persistence of international tension apparently resolved the old ambivalence toward military candidates in Eisenhower's favor.

Moreover, the concentration of ambivalent or neutral imagery among Eisenhower supporters was not only greater than among Democratic supporters, but also exceeded the concentration among nonvoters. Here was a form of cross pressure which, apparently because of its character, did not lead to nonvoting. And finally, nonvoters included the highest concentration of those who held no imagery. Apparently, favorable imagery toward Stevenson was more compatible with nonvoting than favorable imagery toward

Eisenhower, an additional criterion affirming the impact of Eisenhower's public personality.

The third criterion for evaluating the election hinged on the consequences of the political deliberation stimulated by the campaign. The measure was not "political man," fully and consistently committed to one party on all campaign issues. Rather, did the political deliberation create a meaningful basis on which citizens could make their voting decisions? Both issues and candidates had to be considered.

The analysis, in summary, demonstrated that the presidential vote was closely and consistently linked to images of the presidential candidates. Nevertheless, almost one-fifth of the electorate revealed a candidate imagery that was neutral or ambivalent, suggesting that they made their voting decision from other bases.

Furthermore, the political deliberation over central campaign issues must be evaluated as failing to develop a basis for some particular groups on which to ground their decision. A range of campaign issues—domestic and foreign—make possible a classification of the voters into "stalwarts," "compromisers," "weak compromisers," and "ambivalent neutrals" with respect to Republican and Democratic party programs. Each group had a contribution to make to the functioning of the electoral process and thereby to the form of consensus that emerged. Even the weak compromisers had some notion about the style of government they preferred. However, for the ambivalent neutrals—16.5 percent of the Eisenhower vote and 20.2 percent of the Stevenson vote—the campaign failed to link party-framed alternatives, personal ideological demands, and voting behavior. Though it cannot be said that this group acted without any deliberation as to its self-interest, its members were most vulnerable to the manipulative aspects of the campaign. The dynamics and limitations of the deliberative process can be stated alternatively: the pro-Republican changers between 1948 and 1952—those who effected a change in political power—showed markedly lower levels of ideological orientation than did the persistent Republican voters.

9

Radical Right and New Left: Commitment and Estrangement in American Society*

GILBERT ABCARIAN

It is characteristic of American politics that its democratic ideology is invoked by all radical movements in their efforts to secure legitimation and power. Through their particular ideologies each of these movements seeks to attach a distinctive normative interpretation to the abstractions expressed in the nation's reigning ideology. One consequence of the ensuing ideological conflict is persistent tension in the larger society over the proper location and institutionalization of behavior control boundaries.

Deviance from certain norms of the larger society is legitimized by the ideology of the radical group since support of the latter is believed to constitute the highest expression of political loyalty and moral behavior. The social control system operating within the group serves both as a substitute for that of the larger society, and as the basis for legitimized retreat from threatening involvements in the external world.[1]

* An original selection prepared for this volume.

[1] See, for example: Hadley Cantrill, *The Psychology of Social Movements* (New York: Wiley, 1941); Norman Cohn, *The Pursuit of the Millennium* (London, 1957; H.T. Dohrman), *California Cult* (Boston: Beacon, 1958); Leon Festinger et. al., *When Prophecy Fails* (Minneapolis: University of Minnesota Press, 1956); Mark Holloway *Heavens on Earth: Utopian Communities in America, 1680–1880* (New York: Hilary House, 1951); Ernest B. Koenker, *Secular Salvations* (Philadelphia: Fortress Press, 1965); John Loftland, *Doomsday*

Current efforts to specify the nature and generative conditions of radical right and new left ideologies have important implications from the standpoint of social control perspectives. In clarifying the ideological dimensions of both movements we may learn a great deal about their own particular and idealized conception of social control. But more than this, by viewing radical ideologies as a set of propositions containing diagnostic as well as prescriptive elements, we may perceive more clearly those elements in the prevailing control system with which Right and Left are in deepest conflict and which appear to precipitate selective commitment to political protest movements.

Radical right and new left ideologies are mechanisms for organizing and routinizing political beliefs and behavior patterns of members and supporters. Through zealous propagation of ideology, each movement seeks to influence a number of strategically placed individuals and groups potent enough to ensure some role in the authoritative allocation of social values. Ideology facilitates that goal by providing members of the right and left with special verbal systems of action-oriented communications.

There is a popular though vaguely defined view that in essentials "extremists" or "radicals" are interchangeable, that there is, in effect, a convergence of intent, values and consequences among radical political movements. This view is held not only by members of the general public but also by a sizable group of social scientists. Political scientists may be reminded of three recent expressions of the interchangeability hypothesis: first, the literature developed before and during World War II, in which Naziism and Communism were presented as two evils sharing in a common set of reality misconceptions and institutional perversions; second, Eric Hoffer's development of the thesis that "When people are ripe for a mass movement, they are usually ripe for any effective movement, and not solely for one with a particular doctrine or program;"[2] and third, the current view that radical right and left in American society constitute a unidimensional aberration, a common threat, or in one version, "deadly parallels."[3]

The purpose of the present essay is chiefly to explore the interchangeability hypothesis in the context of a model of ideology that this author is currently employing in empirical research into radical movements. Additional analytical foci to which the hypothesis of interchangeability will be related are those of alienation and mass society. Other aspects of radicalism bearing on the hypothesis such as structure, functions and consequences, are not detailed here.

A distinctive feature of contemporary political radicalism is its ideological protest against the moral and political consequences of the existing social

---

Cult (Englewood Cliffs, N.J.: Prentice-Hall, 1966); Vernon L. Parrington, Jr., American Dreams: A Study of American Utopias (Providence: Brown University Press, 1947); Sylvia Thrupp (ed.), Millennial Dreams in Action (The Hague, 1962); Hans Toch, The Social Psychology of Social Movements (Indianapolis: Bobbs-Merrill, 1965); Bryan R. Wilson, "An Analysis of Sect Development," American Sociological Review, 24 (February 1959).

[2] The True Believer (New York: Mentor Books, 1951), p. 25.

[3] Alan F. Westin, "The Deadly Parallels: Radical Right and Radical Left," Harper's Magazine (April 1962), 25–32.

system. In the case of the radical right, what began in the 1950s as a schism within the Republican party now has assumed the proportions of a national phenomenon that openly challenges the normative and structural control system of American society. In the case of the new left, disillusionment with progress in civil rights triggered approximately the same challenge. Defenders of the system, in reply, refer to both expressions of radicalism variously as "extremist," "paranoid," "irrational," or "nihilistic," in themselves terms of no little ideological import.

It is appropriate then to begin with a model defining the nature and consequences of political ideology per se[4] before proceeding to evaluation of the interchangeability hypothesis.

I

We may speak of ideology as an integrated system of observations and prescriptions whose ultimate intent is to provide individuals with a conceptual basis for faith, evaluation and action in life.

Political ideology may be understood as referring to a coherent system of values, definitions and imperatives containing diagnostic and prescriptive statements that undertake to interpret, conceal, defend, or alter the political order by inspiring action-oriented movements or organizations. Hence political ideology encompasses (1) symbolic unity, (2) social perspectives, (3) power preferences, and (4) public strategies.

Though different in specific content, political belief systems exhibit certain common functional features that characterize each as "ideology." A brief explanation of these features will help us understand the nature of ideological politics as it bears on the two movements under analysis.

Perceptual selectivity refers to the tendency of ideologies to incorporate certain limited, incomplete aspects of social life. Political ideologies are hence highly selective sets of perceptions drawn out of a much larger political universe. They customarily present themselves as objective reflections of political realities. Adherents of a given ideology tend to believe that their perceptions and the political principles derived from them constitute objective knowledge. Political ideologies consequently distort and oversimplify events. The capacity of an ideology to present a unified, coherent account of political life may strengthen it as a movement by intensifying the faith of its members and attracting new followers who crave prefabricated interpretations.

Rationalization is characteristic of political ideologies in that it offers

---

[4] Fundamental issues and aspects of political ideology in its conceptual context are treated in the following: Daniel Bell, *The End of Ideology* (New York: Free Press, 1960), William E. Connolly, *Political Science and Ideology* (New York: Atherton, 1967); Charles Madge, *Society in the Mind* (New York: Free Press, 1964); Karl Mannheim, *Ideology & Utopia* (New York: Harcourt, n.d.); Arne Naess, *Democracy, Ideology and Objectivity* (Oslo: Oslo University Press, 1956); Gustave Bergmann, "Ideology," *Ethics* (1951), 205–218; George Lichtheim, "The Concept of Ideology," *History and Theory*, 4 (1965), 164–195; Colwyn Williamson, "Ideology and the Problem of Knowledge," *Inquiry*, 10 (Summer 1967), 121–138.

elaborate justifications in defense of existing political arrangements or proposed new ones. These justifications serve as abstract, public explanations for political preferences by investing them with legitimacy and objective merit. Rationalization is rarely on the level of conscious motivation. Indeed, it is typical for political activists to believe themselves guided purely by the requirements of God, Justice, Class, or the People.

Scripturalism is encountered in political ideologies in the form of appeal to a special body of literature believed to contain impeccable and exclusive propositions. The basic "scripture" of an ideology frequently evokes a quasireligious response from its adherents, who may regard its content and author(s) as unique or even sacred.

Normative certitude signifies the moral sense of purity and validity that is associated with the norms of a political ideology. From this standpoint, an ideology may confer on the believer a feeling of commitment to principles whose validity is beyond challenge. The sense of certitude conveyed by political ideologies may be described alternatively as political fundamentalism in much the same way that certain religious writings are believed to contain "fundamentals" of literal validity in the spiritual life of the individual. The cultivation of normative certitude has the very important purpose of mobilizing political strength by displacing personal tensions arising from feelings of uncertainty and normlessness.

Transcendentalism is the process through which political ideologies provide their supporters with a gratifying sense of moral and political uplift, of elevation from the imperfect and disturbing aspects of prevailing political life. Every political ideology thus seeks to provide a transcendent vision and a set of goals against which the existing order can be assessed. In its milder form, this process may lead to reform efforts, in its more radical expression, to utopian schemes, and to revolutionary acts. Whatever the degree, ideologies promise to revitalize political systems by creating a mood of progress, change, and renewed hope.

Political ideology may be viewed not only as a system of ideas, but also as a vehicle for generating conditions that may ensure its own success in the political arena. In this context we may refer to the characteristic tactical operations of political ideologies.

The success or failure of an ideological movement is determined partly by the extent to which public receptivity is shaped through a program of *political socialization*. The social structure of any society contains a variety of institutions playing a critical role in the formation of popular political attitudes. Such institutions "socialize" particular viewpoints when individuals are taught to accept some as authoritative and to reject others as deviant. From a tactical point of view it is essential that the doctrines of an ideology are incorporated into the value systems of these social institutions. Hence political socialization in desired directions depends upon the extent to which dominant social institutions legitimize the central tenets of a political ideology, or at the very least tolerate an atmosphere in which such tenets may thrive.

The degree of acceptance of a political ideology is closely linked to the intensity of personal faith it is able to inspire. Organizational leaders commonly attempt to maximize a movement's likelihood of success through propaganda programs aimed at *emotional arousal*. In the case of those individuals already committed, it is important to sustain and reinforce ideological orthodoxy. For those outside the movement who are indifferent to its message, it is imperative to generate political emotions that promise eventual affiliation or support. The most persistent form of emotional arousal consists in attacks on those individuals, groups, norms, agencies, and policies regarded as threats to the values and influence of the movement. A specific aim of such attacks is to create an atmosphere of doubt, confusion, and distrust sufficient to weaken the degree of public support enjoyed by rival ideological movements.

Political ideologies must cope with events that for many persons appear overwhelmingly complex or meaningless. Successful propagation of an ideological position requires considerable skill in presenting the public with a relatively simple framework of interpretation that will substitute order for experienced chaos. The employment of such an interpretive framework may be termed *reductionism*, the process through which a comparatively simple thesis purports to "explain" political intracacies to the bewildered public. A political ideology bent on expanding its power requires a diagnostic theory which appears to "make sense" of political events in terms of principles and properties easily grasped by the average citizen.

Political movements frequently engage in *personification*, through which spokesmen are presented to the public as symbols of ideological integrity. If the persons so presented command a high degree of public prestige and respect, authority and credibility may be lent to the political ideas presented, hopefully inducing others to adopt them. Some movements are able to call upon the services of leaders who are perceived by segments of the public as possessing charisma—powers of knowledge and wisdom denied ordinary persons. An ideology may begin as a cult in which a charismatic leader attracts a number of disciples who devote themselves to the institutionalization and propagation of his ideas.

To one degree or another, political ideologies engage in warfare. The arena of battle, whether a nation or the world itself, is perceived in terms of friendly and hostile forces. Accordingly, a crucial function of ideology is *strategic assessment*, the articulation of techniques to discriminate between friends and enemies in the power arena. The ideology itself provides a series of guidelines for making strategic assessments. Persons supporting its doctrines are friends, those opposing them are enemies. Much of the time of ideological movements is taken up with the task of gathering political information deemed pertinent to the development of strategic assessments.

The final, and perhaps decisive, tactical element is *political action*, the process through which abstract ideas inspire active involvement in the political arena where the struggle for power takes place. That struggle characteristically involves competing demands for access to power roles. In this instance it is typical for the challengers to employ highly moralized slogans and programs aimed at establishing "justice," "public welfare," "national honor," "peace," and so on.

Before suggesting several implications that emerge from the model of ideology just sketched, we may turn for the moment to an analysis of radical right and new left ideologies as exemplifications of that model.

II

The political ideology of the radical right comprises five principal dimensions.[5]

1. Conspiracy reflects the belief that "communists," "fellow travelers" and "dupes" have penetrated, effectively control, and are systematically undermining "the American way of life." Virtually all top public leaders are presumed to be witting or unwitting accomplices in a variety of interrelated plots. Political events that on the surface appear chaotic and meaningless to the average citizen are believed to "cloak" the designs of conspirators who are extraordinarily skilled at public deception and political betrayal.

2. Failure of Foreign policy assumes American calamities around the world owing to accommodation of subversive and alien ideologies at the highest levels of decision-making. The right wing sees the nation plunged into international humiliation and national dishonor through policies geared to appeasement and leading to national extinction.

3. Fundamentalism expresses the conviction that the universe is characterized by norms of absolute moral validity, but norms that have been betrayed. Americans are implored to return to the eternal truths, divine and secular, that are embodied in the teachings of the scriptures as a perfect and godly reflection of absolute reality, as an "inerrant" source of truth. The secular version of fundamentalism takes the form of a call to "Americanism" by a small, dedicated body of true patriots and moral leaders who will initiate a "return" to the universal moral principles that once guided and ennobled the American "republic."

4. Distrust of democracy conveys the belief that the political system is dominated by demagoguery, mob-rule, ideological heresy and vulgarizing mass values. Distrust of this sort reveals the expectancy that the masses are highly gullible and that their inclusion in the governing process, as with most interest groups, leads to erosion of "constitutional government." The ultimate expression of the democratic process is seen as the emergence of the omnipotent State, which "collectivizes" and "enslaves" the individual while arrogantly proclaiming the glories of individual freedom.

5. Anticollectivism completes the repertoire of right wing ideological dimensions and is expressed typically in the warning that Americans face an

[5] A fuller treatment of the discussion that follows will be found in Gilbert Abcarian and Sherman M. Stanage, "Alienation and the Radical Right," *The Journal of Politics*, 27 (November 1965), 776–796. Other works dealing with ideological attributes of the radical right include: Daniel Bell (ed.), *The Radical Right* (New York: Doubleday, 1963); B.R. Epstein and A. Forester, *The Radical Right* (New York: Anti-Defamation League, 1967); Richard Hofstadter, *The Paranoid Style in American Politics* (New York: Knopf, 1965); David Danzing, "The Radical Right and the Rise of the Fundamentalist Minority," *Commentary*, 38 (April 1962); Everett C. Ladd, Jr., "The Radical Right: The White-Collar Extremists," *South Atlantic Quarterly*, (Summer 1966), 314–324; Seymour M. Lipset, "The Radical Right," *British Journal of Sociology*, 6 (June 1955), 176–209; Raymond E. Wolfinger, "America's Radical Right: Politics and Ideology," in David E. Apter (ed.), *Ideology and Discontent* (New York: Free Press, 1964), 281–283.

either/or choice between a "free" and a "collectivistic" political destiny. It is believed that American individualism, once the hallmark of a great nation, has virtually disappeared in proportion to the growth of governmental regimentation and "coddling" in nearly all aspects of national life. Through centralization, government ostensibly has grown remote from the genuine needs and aspirations of the people by imposing alien ideals and programs that have taken this nation into socialism, the stage leading "inevitably" to communistic "slavery."

The rightist ideological mood reflects intense feelings of estrangement from contemporary American society and from the political processes shaping the future. From the diagnostic perspective of rightist ideology, traditional "absolutes" have all but disappeared in modern life and thus destroyed the likelihood of the individual living a life of significance, worth, belongingness and rootedness. The political system—perceived as alien, evil, punitive, intractable, and above all manipulated by a nearly-omnipotent elite—is regarded as unresponsive to individual merit as defined in the nation's own sacred heritage. With that heritage repudiated by the "forces" exercising "real power," impersonality, emptiness and distrust appear the logical price of modern life as the gulf widens between the defenders and the enemies of "our way of life."

The prescriptive aspect of rightist ideology reflects the conviction that politics require the simple extension into governmental affairs of moral propositions possessing absolute and self-evident validity. For at bottom, the rightist say, social problems are moral problems, which means that political understanding cannot be attained nor political solutions devised through primary reliance on science or intellect.

Political salvation accordingly lies in the hands of the few "natural" leaders possessing the highest degree of moral insight and courage. This charismatic tendency derives in part from the idea that the political destiny of a nation is determined by epic struggles between the forces of good and evil as embodied in the political activities of a few great or evil men of power. All else in politics and political analysis is regarded as secondary and illusory. The final hope in politics is that men of divine charisma, those who possess extraordinary understanding and resources, might be found and assume their "rightful" positions of highest authority in order to crush those men of evil charisma whose diabolical machinations threatens all that is sacred.

Political events are hence believed to derive from the clash of wills among a tiny number of powerful men. The exclusion of impersonal environmental circumstances as shaping forces in the political sphere leads the radical rightist to the view that the political process is dominated by superactivists through whose efforts the rest of society is led either to salvation or damnation.

The ideology of the radical right reinforces certain personal and organizational needs.

On the personal side, the impulse for certainty is supported insofar as rightist ideology provides a relatively simple framework of interpretation through which events on the personal, national and world levels are invested with clarity, meaning and directionality. The image of self-righteousness receives impetus since, through ideological commitment, displacement of guilt feelings and a mood of self-gratification are achieved by dedication to the crusade to destroy the "enemy." Such commitment also reinforces the need for compensatory superiority through which an individual may overcome status frustration through identification with a movement deemed on the "right" side of a universal struggle against evil and corruption. Finally, since the enemy must be treated mercilessly, the tendency toward rationalized aggression receives reinforcement through affiliation with a movement that has identified an absolute, intolerable adversary against which all hostile measures are sanctioned by the principles of morality and the requirements of the public interest.

On the organizational side several needs served by right-wing ideology are worth noting. The ideology helps create relational linkages among actual and potential members. These are of sufficient importance to give the movement a sense of organic life and activity apart from the inviduals constituting it. Solidarity of the group structure is buttressed by singling out leaders who are regarded as possessing charismatic powers that include an unexcelled, quasi-religious understanding of the ideology, and a moral vision of the future to which the movement is dedicated.

A major concern of the radical right research just summarized was a search for antecedent or generative conditions of ideology. The perspective employed for this purpose, and tested through empirical correlations, was alienation.

The alienation perspective[6] emphasizes the severance of man from certain historic and moral certitudes in the age of the mass society.[7] Mass society has instrumentalized and depersonalized individual relationships in such a way as to produce highly estranged persons. Alienation therefore suggests the loss of community, of the sense of belongingness in an age of enveloping bureaucracy and technology. The alienated man feels unrelated to others in a world in which people and events have become mechanized. The result is a loss of self, one response to which is the compulsion to locate and conform to a movement promising authentic freedom.

Empirical application of the alienation perspective to right wing extremism has involved the use of four alienation dimensions operationalized through measurement scales.

Meaninglessness is the feeling that because current and historical events seem overwhelmingly complex, purposeless, and unpredictable, one is

---

[6] The empirical and philosophic dimensions of alienation are fruitfully explored in: Lewis Feuer, "What is Alienation? The Career of a Concept," in M. Stein and A. Vidich (eds.), *Sociology on Trial* (Englewood Cliffs, N.J.: Prentice-Hall, 1963), 133–135; Daniel Bell, "The Debate on Alienation," in Leopold Labedz (ed.), *Revisionism: Essays on the History of Marxist Ideas* (London: Allen Unwin, 1962); Igor S. Kon, "The Concept of Alienation in Modern Sociology," *Social Research, 34* (Autumn 1967), 507–528; Dwight Dean, "Alienation: Its Meaning and Measurement," *American Sociological Review, 26* (October 1961), 753–758; Gwyn Nettler, "A Measure of Alienation," *American Sociological Review, 22* (December 1957), 670–677; Melvin Seeman, "On the Meaning of Alienation," *American Sociological Review, 24* (December 1959), 783–791.

[7] A comprehensive discussion of this concept is found in William Kornhauser's *The Politics of Mass Society* (New York: Free Press, 1956).

losing or has lost the feeling of significance, commitment, meaning of personal thought, and behavior within group life. Robert Welch of the John Birch Society, for example, refers to a "loss of faith" in the individual's "reasons for existence, in his purposes, and his hopes." *Normlessness* is experienced as the loss of a personal center of values and standards of certitude leading to the conviction that socially unapproved behavior is required for goal attainment since moral standards have seemingly lost their hold over individual conduct. Right-wing expressions about "the breakdown of law and order" often reflect this dimension. *Powerlessness* is the feeling that one is unable to control the outcome of events that are decisive in his life, the felt loss of one's personal efficacy and ability to act influentially and with satisfying significance within the social community. Typically, we encounter the rightist demand for a "return" to the sacred "heritage" of "true Americanism." *Social isolation*, lastly, refers to the experience of estrangement or detachment from society, producing an impulse either to withdraw from or deliberately protest against a society that has bred experiences of apartness, loneliness, and solitariness with respect to interpersonal life. This sentiment produces a strong inclination to distinguish between "friends" and "enemies" in social and political life.

Alienation may be treated then as a generative condiiton of right wing political commitment. As we have seen, the alienated man feels unrelated to others in a confusing, mechanized social system. His response may take the form of apathy and indifference at one extreme or, as in the case of the radical right, political obsessiveness, and stylized protest at another.[8]

III

Analysis of the new left poses certain hazards.[9] Whether that movement possesses an identifiable political ideology, apart from the pseudo-analyses of the mass media, is a hotly debated question among Movement members and external observers.[10] For other elements aside, what seems new about the new left ". . . is its ecumenical mixture of political traditions that were

[8] It is a weakness of current alienation theory that it fails to account satisfactorily for the intervening variables through which alienation leads, alternatively, to both political retreatism and activism.

[9] One of these is definition of the movement in terms of constituent organizations. Leaving the "hereditary" young left groups to one side, characteristic elements within the movement would include the Student Non-Violent Coordinating Committee, the Southern Christian Leadership Conference, the Southern Student Organizing Committee and, of course, Students for a Democratic Society.

[10] Jack Newfield, *A Prophetic Minority* (New York: New American Library, 1966); J. L. Simmons and Barry Winograd, "The New Politics," in *It's Happening* (Santa Barbara: Marc-Laird Publications, 1966), 120–138; David Greenwald, "The Ideology of the New Left: An interpretation," *The Intercollegiate Review*, 3 (Sept.–Oct. 1966), 14–22; Dennis Hale, "The Problem of Ideology," *New Politics*, 4 (Spring 1965), 91–94; Michael Harrington, "The Mystical Militant," *The New Republic* (Feb. 9, 1966), 20–22; Irving Howe, "New Styles in 'Leftism,' " *Dissent* (Summer 1965), 295–323; Sidney Lens, "The New Left—and the Old," *The Progressive* (June 1966), 19–24; M.J. Sklar and James Weinstein, "Socialism and the New Left," *Studies on the Left*, 6 (March–April 1966), 62–70; Howard Zinn, "The Old Left and the New: Emancipation from Dogma," *The Nation* (April 4, 1966), 385–389; Tom Hayden, "The Politics of the 'The Movement,' " in Irving Howe (ed.), *The Radical Papers* (New York: Doubleday, 1966), 362–377; Paul Jacobs and Saul Landau, *The New Radicals* (New York: Random House, 1966); Andrew Kopkind (ed.), *Thoughts of the Young Radicals* (New York: New Republic, 1966).

once murderous rivals in Russia, Spain, France, and the United States. It contains within it, and often within individuals, elements of anarchism, socialism, pacifism, existentialism, humanism, transcendentalism, bohemianism, Populism, mysticism, and black nationalism."[11]

Fortunately, we may concentrate upon one major segment of the new left that encompasses most of its relevant characteristics and tendencies, namely, Students for a Democratic Society.[12]

Most SDS members are poorly read in radical literature, are predominantly middle class in origin, seek understanding of one another through highly unstructured meetings and psychological interaction, and are strongly committed to action programs and therefore anti-cool. Members avoid complex verbalizations through the use of a simple vocabulary; are apprehensive about the pitfalls of leadership, authority, organization, and bureaucracy; believe in social transformation through face to face relationships; and assess American society primarily in terms of power elites rather than classes, problem solving rather than analytical detachment.

Like the new left itself, SDS membership embraces several distinguishable but overlapping categories of persons: political idealists with a Populist outlook who view supermilitants and apathetics with equal disdain; organizational old guardists who performed the function of founding fathers; anarcho-hipsters skeptical of all organized power and decisions by formal voting processes; ghetto workers who devote their entire time to programs aimed at alleviating the misery of the poor; and liberal intellectuals, a large segment of career-oriented professionals scattered around the nation.

The closest approximation of an "official" statement of values of the group is to be found in *The Port Huron Statement* of 1962, from which is drawn its critique of university education, mass culture, party politics, the economic system, discrimination, anticommunism, and foreign policy.[13] The following statements are typical:

> We regard men as infinitely precious and possessed of unfulfilled capacities for reason, freedom, and love. In affirming these principles we are aware of countering perhaps the dominant conceptions of man in the twentieth century: that he is a thing to be manipulated, and that he is inherently incapable

[11] Jack Newfield, *A Prophetic Minority* (New York: New American Library, 1966), p. 22.

[12] SDS is a direct descendent of the Student League for Industrial Democracy (SLID), originated in 1930 by the League for Industrial Democracy, itself a group with a Fabian orientation and closely associated with the Socialist Party. In view of the current charge that SDS has a cavalier attitude toward communist membership, it is noteworthy that SLID functioned as an opponent of the communist-dominated National Student Union. SLID and NCU later merged into the American Student Union, dying a few years later because of internal struggles between socialist and communist factions.

After World War II, SLID was revived under James Farmer, later to become national chairman of the Congress of Racial Equality, but by the end of the 1950s membership declined sharply in the wake of campus McCarthyism. In 1960 SLID became SDS when a group of activist radicals, mostly from the University of Michigan, revived the organization and gave it a distinct action orientation. In early 1966, formal links with the League for Industrial Democracy were severed as SDS became disenchanted with what it viewed as the LID's cautious trade unionism and emotional anti-communism.

[13] SDS's aversion to fixed ideological scripture is reflected, for example, in an internal committee recommendation that ". . . a political insert be drawn up explaining the historical position of the Port Huron Statement and explaining that it no longer represents SDS's view of the society. The dialectic applied to consciousness seems to be at work within SDS." *New Left Notes*, 2 (Nov. 6, 1967), p. 8.

of directing his own affairs. We oppose the depersonalization that reduces human beings to the status of things. . . .

Loneliness, estrangement, isolation describe the vast distance between man and man today. These dominant tendencies cannot be overcome by better personnel management, nor by improved gadgets, but only when a love of man overcomes the idolatrous worship of things by a man. . . .

As a social system we seek the establishment of a democracy of individual participation, governed by two central aims: that the individual share in those social decisions determining the quality and direction of his life; that society be organized to encourage independence in men and provide the media for their common participation. . . .

SDS has ambivalent feelings about the role of ideology. In rejecting Marxian metaphysics SDS expresses its anti-ideological posture, believing that its own ideology, if needed at all, must emerge from experience in the form of action programs rather than through interminable debates over antecedent universal propositions. The ambivalence is still there, reflecting antipathy to dogma at one time, but the need for some kind of theoretical anchorage at another.

In social life a man may be known by his friends, but in politics a movement may be understood by its enemies. It is a fact of no little psychological significance that the primary target of the radical right is the conservative, rather than the liberal, socialist or communist. For SDS the enemy is "corporate liberalism," not the conservative, the reactionary or the fascist. The "liberal establishment" bears the responsibility for American injustice, alienation and imperialism.

The SDS analysis goes something like this: Supreme political power— for good or evil—rests in the hands of political liberals for whom the large corporation is taken as the desired model for organizing the entire social system. Their presumed goal is to achieve harmony among the dominant strata of society by distributing just enough rewards throughout the system to discourage the lowest segments from producing forces of disequilibrium. Except in rhetoric, however, that goal is never reached, hence millions of citizens are doomed to poverty, futility and embitterment. For this reason, say SDS activists, the vanguard for restructuring society is the organized poor, for they alone constitute a force capable of compelling structural change. It is believed that corporate liberals work diligently to prevent an alliance from developing between the very poor and the unorganized workers since such an alliance might challenge the traditional leadership and power of the trade unions and civil rights organizations which the liberals actually control. Liberal leftists who fret because the SDS brand of radicalism minimizes the traditional electoral process are reminded of "this quadrennial spasm of the body politic [presidential elections] that puts purchasable men in the low places and purchasers in the high. . . ."[14]

The link between SDS diagnosis and action is provided by the concept of "participatory democracy," or decentralized decision making through which every man would have an equal voice in decisions that effect him. Such democratic participation ostensibly will help the poor develop a sense

[14] Carl Oglesby, "Democracy Is Nothing if not Dangerous," reprinted from *The Peacemaker* (n.d.).

of group solidarity that must precede legitimate demands for a role in making public policies:

> The central issue must be understood. . . . It is neither in the nature of the state that it can give political freedom nor in the nature of political freedom that it can be given. . . . Political freedom is in political man, in his life, and it exists when he claims it. . . . *Any decision not made by the people in free association, whatever the content of that decision, cannot be good.* . . .[15]

SDS members manifest a rather intense degree of indignation and hostility toward the American political system. That response derives from the experience disparity between democratic ideology and social realities, from the conviction that the reigning credo promises far more than its guardians are willing to deliver. The tension felt between promise and performance is bitter to endure, for the young radical tends to identify himself with moral imperatives rather than with the politics of necessity. Hence the "credibility gap" he experiences is not merely a temporary loss of faith in the honesty of specific public officials, but also alienation from the structural elements producing them.

The SDS quarrel with conventional political ideologies is not so much that they have declined or become irrelevant, but they continue to command widespread rhetorical support even while they refer loftily to problems their adherents have no intention of confronting. In this sense, these ideologies are believed to have corrupted and undermined civic mindedness, at least for the older generations, by breeding apathy, hypocrisy and social insensitivity. But even worse, these qualities have been passed off as moral responsibility and political "realism."

On a superficial level of analysis, the new left often sounds like a convocation of deaf prophets, a babble of many ideological voices. It is true that the rhetoric of several traditional ideologies is found within the movement. But if verbal style of the moment is distinguished from deeply-rooted, recurrent concepts, a meaningful approximation of new left ideology is possible. That ideology embraces the following major dimensions:

> **1. Romanticism** reflects the rejection of political "realism" by viewing politics as a venture in moral values rather than power mechanics. It springs from the leftists' deep faith in human nature, character, and aspirations, especially among the poor and the oppressed. Above all, romanticism is reflected in the demand for the strict adaptation of political resources, values, programs and behavior to the implementation of a utopian vision, unencumbered by concessions to "practicality."

> **2. A-historicism** is expressed in detachment from the past and from presumably spurious "lessons of history." There is a refusal to adjudicate among or accept any of the traditional ideologies, a fundamental skepticism toward closed orthodoxies. The result is a considerable degree of both antidogmatism and anti-intellectualism, but above all a vehement anti anticommunism.

> **3. Revitalization** expresses the demand for social reconstruction through a spirit of insurgency, and through acts of disaffiliation and detachment from

---

[15] Carl Oglesby, "Vietnam Crucible: An Essay on the Meanings of the Cold War," in C. Oglesby and Richard Shaull, *Containment and Change* (New York: Crowell-Collier-Macmillan pp. 164–165.

practices or institutions deemed corruptive of one's normative commitments. Society must be radicalized by preventing cooptation of the young by corporate liberalism. It must be purified by avoiding the politics of coalition and by creating counter institutions or parallel structures that will precipitate authentic "confrontations."

4. Communitarianism calls for a de-alienation through the creation of smaller communities that will offset the evils of mass society by making participatory democracy a reality for those at the bottom layers of the social system.

5. Disengagement, finally, conveys the belief that the U.S. is the great disturber and imperialist of the world, and should therefore withdraw from political, economic and military intervention in the affairs of foreign countres. Before the U.S. can resume a constructive role in world politics, it must rebuild and humanize its own institutions.

IV

In the context of political radicalism, the interchangeability hypothesis is a cluster of specific theories operating on several different levels of analysis. It will be useful to identify these theoretical components of the hypothesis before assessing its relevance for comparative analysis of the radical right and the new left.

The *theory of personality* holds that radical movements indiscriminately attract persons suffering identity crises, persons who seek attenuation of feelings of estrangement and inauthenticity through identification with groups bent on transforming society or the world. A common experience is presumed to be that of "conversion" from a lower to a higher self, a transcendence from experiences of frustration and meaninglessness to experiences of dedication, integration, and normative certitude.

The *theory of authoritarianism* suggests that radical movements are functional equivalents of one another with respect to the anti-democratic orientations of their doctrines, structures, leaders, and programs. In this perspective, radicals of all hues, despite superficial distinctions, possess a common, authoritarian denominator. That is, each is believed to embody the underlying unidimensionality of all radical movements.

The *theory of pathology* centers on a clinical interpretation of radicalism. Its most characteristic form is the imputation to paranoia to those who allegedly have lost touch with "reality" and hence live in a fantasy world of mysterious forces, perpetual evil, betrayal and martyrdom.

The *theory of extremism* emphasizes the adoption by all radical groups of a common style of public protest typified by contempt for existing forms of authority and communication, rejection of the ameliorative approach to problem solving, and a strong inclination toward the adoption of illegal or immoral means of goal attainment.[16]

16 These five theories receive varying degrees of emphasis in the following works: T.W. Adorno and others, *The Authoritarian Personality* (New York: Harper & Row, 1950); Gabriel Almond and others, *The Appeals of Communism* (Princeton: Princeton University Press, 1964); Hannah Arendt, *The Origins of Totalitarianism* (New York: Harcourt, 1951); Daniel Bell (ed.), *The Radical Right* (New York: Doubleday, 1963);

The *theory of defection*, finally, stresses the transient nature of radical affiliation patterns, particularly the rather free migration from one radical group to another. The classic instance cited is the defection of some left-wingers to right-wing extremist values and organizations.

How do these theoretical components of the interchangeability hypothesis apply to radical right and new left? Do they apply more or less uniformly to right and left as the hypothesis requires? From the standpoint of empirical evidence presently available, the following highly tentative observations seem warranted: Regarding the theory of personality, there is little evidence of unusual gravitation of persons suffering identity crises to one movement rather than another. While the incidence of such crises appears to be just as high, or low, in non-radical strata of society, the distribution seems random. The hypothesis is supported. Comparison on the basis of authoritarian predilections suggests a higher tendency for the radical right than the new left. In the context previously suggested, the new left manifests few of the blatantly authoritarian features of the radical right. The hypothesis is not supported. As to pathological dimensions, the members of neither movement may be said to possess a unique monopoly of delusions so serious as to justify one sided clinical inferences. The hypothesis is supported. In the extremist context, it appears that while both movements occasionally engage in extralegal, illegal, or immoral activity, the new left exhibits a significantly greater tendency toward such activity. The hypothesis is not supported. Finally, the type of freewheeling political migration suggested by the defection theory of radical movements is not to be observed to any appreciable degree to or from both movements. The hypothesis is not supported.

J. Allen Broyles, *The John Birch Society: Anatomy of a Protest* (Boston: Beacon, 1964); Hadley Cantrill, *The Psychology of Social Movements* (New York: Wiley, 1941); Richard Crossman (ed.), *The God That Failed* (New York: Harper & Row, 1949); H. J. Eysenck, *The Psychology of Politics* (London: 1954); Erick Fromm, *Escape From Freedom* (New York: Holt, Rinehart and Winston, Inc., 1941); Richard Hofstadter, *The Paranoid Style in America Politics* (New York: Knopf, 1965); Arnold Kaufman, *The Radical Liberal* (New York: Atherton, 1968); J. C. Flugel, *Man, Morals and Society* (London: Duckworth, 1945); Harold D. Lasswell, *Psychopathology and Politics* (Chicago: University of Chicago Press, 1931); Edwin Lemert, "Radicalism and Radicals," in *Social Pathology* (New York: McGraw-Hill, 1951); I. A. Taylor, *Similarities in the Structure of Extreme Social Attitudes*, Psychological Monographs, 74 (1960), 1–36; Milton Rokeach, *The Open and Closed Mind* (New York: Basic Books, 1960); Sylvan Tompkins, "Left and Right: A Basic Dimension of Ideology and Personality, in Robert W. White (ed.), *The Study of Lives* (New York: Atherton, 1963).

"American Political Extremism in the 1960s," *Journal of Social Issues*, XIX (April 1963); M. Geltman, "The New Left and the Old Right," *National Review*, 19 (June 13, 1967), 632; Fred I. Greenstein, "Personality and Political Socialization: The Theories of Authoriarian and Democratic Character," *Annals of the American Academy of Political and Social Science*, 361 (September 1965), 81–95; William Haythorn et al., "Behavior of Authoritarian and Equalitarian Personalities in Groups," *Human Relations*, 9 (February 1956), 57–73; Nathan Leites, "Psycho-Cultural Hypotheses About Political Acts," *World Politics*, 1 (October 1948), 102–119; Herbert McClosky, "Conservatism and Personality," *American Political Science Review*, 52 (March 1958), 27–45; Herbert McClosky and John Schaar, "Psychological Dimensions of Anomy," *American Political Science Review*, 30 (February 1965), 14–40; Thelma H. McCormack, "The Motivation of Radicals," *The American Journal of Sociology*, LVI (July 1950), 17–24; M. Sanai and P.M. Pickard, "The Relation Between Politico-Economics Radicalism and Certain Personality Traits," *The Journal of Social Psychology*, 30 (November 1949), 217–227; D. Steward and T. Hoult, "Social-Psychological Theory of the Authoritarian Personality," *American Journal of Sociology*, 65 (November 1959), 274–279; Cushing Strout, "Fantasy on the Right," *New Republic*, 144 (May 1, 1961), 13–15; Alan F. Westin, "The Deadly Parallels: Radical Right and Radical Left," *Harper's Magazine* (April 1962), 25–32.

We conclude, then, that the interchangeability hypothesis largely fails to demonstrate the functional equivalence of the radical movements under discussion, though that conclusion must be qualified with respect to apparent confirmation of the personality and pathology theories.

The persistent notion that radicals are all "basically the same" would appear to involve some combination of these, and possibly other, components of the interchangeability hypothesis. But if we shift our analysis to those employing the hypothesis, we find that it may express the serious concern of the moderate intellectual who regards all radicals as threats to the prevailing system of social control with which he has generally identified himself. Yet there is considerable evidence that variations in ideological commitment among radicals lead to variations in behavior systems and political consequences. If this is so, we must conclude that the consequences of radical ideologies for the social system are hardly equivalent. This is particularly evident if one undertakes to trace out radical right and new left manifestations of the common features and tactical uses of ideology discussed earlier. Thus the standardized portrait of the radical expressed by the interchangeability hypothesis has several serious flaws: it fails to account for variations in those aspects of the social system under attack; it obscures the political potential and impact of specific movements; and it minimizes the degrees and sources of public sympathy and hostility. The persistence of the portrait may be understood, then, as itself performing an ideological function in principle hardly distinguishable from the movements under attack. A classic illustration of antiradicalism as ideology is the regrettable tendency among some social scientists to reduce all political movements and ideologies to simple "democratic" and "totalitarian" archetypes.

Imputations about right and left radicalism frequently reflect and serve ideological purposes, though such imputations may originate with persons and groups that consider themselves "nonideological," "moderate," or "pragmatic." In terms of ideological tactics, the repudiation of "radicals" often serves to maximize efforts toward middle of the road political socialization and emotional arousal in order to protect or enhance power positions. Antiradicalism as ideology does call attention to a fundamental problem: can one speak of any political ideology that is not "radical" in the sense of providing what is regarded by its adherents as a root interpretation of political life? Probably not. Perhaps certain ideologies are described as radical in the sense of assuming that commitment to them results in deviant behavior patterns and disruptive social consequences. The weakness in this interpretation is the assumption of predictable congruence between political ideas and political behavior, an assumption not sustained by the available evidence. To say that ideology influences behavior is a tenable proposition; to say that ideology determines behavior is not.

Further exploration of the five theories mentioned earlier is needed. The defection theory of interchangeability, for example, points to a significant aspect of radical politics. Empirical studies of political conversion, of drastic migration from one end of the political continuum to the other, are virtually nonexistent. Interestingly enough, what little data we have about the presumed free-floating quality of radical affiliation suggests that in this country the major direction of defection is from left to right. Why there is a negligible degree of movement in the opposite direction, that is from right to left, remains a fascinating question though one beyond the scope of this essay. The immediate point, however, is that defection in both directions seemingly expresses one of the necessary consequences of the interchange-ability hypothesis, an assumption that is not presently supported by a convincing body of evidence.

Distinctions among radical movements are sometimes blurred through hasty invocation of the concept of "mass society." As Kornhauser suggests, the concept all too often "becomes merely a shorthand expression for the modern world."[17] If radical groups have their origins in certain conditions of mass society, it is useful to assess their own images of society as a manifestation of such conditions. On this score, one may observe quite different sets of images projected by the radical right and new left.

For the radical right, the struggle in mass society is defined as resistance to corruptive groups that have dispossessed certain traditional and legitimate elites from their rightful political prerogatives. For example, the idea of conspiracy conveys the sense of illegitimate elites "selling out" to the demands of "lawless elements" in a "sick society." For the new left, on the other hand, the struggle in mass society is perceived as resistance to elite pressures exerted on the lowest, most helpless and powerless segments of the public. This image is expressed, for example, through the principle of revitalization, which calls for "radical confrontation" with the controlling "establishment."

Alienation analysis may be helpful in accounting for these divergent perceptions of contemporary mass society. It is worth knowing whether or not differences in types and intensities of alienation may help explain public attraction to one rather than another radical movement. Empirical research in this direction would not only provide a much-needed assessment of the interchangeability hypothesis, but might also provide new insights into the relevance of alienation analysis for understanding of political behavior more generally. While alienation analysis has proven useful in illuminating certain consequences of mass society, it has yet to be employed in a systematic attempt to reach verifiable generalizations regarding the principal components of the interchangeability hypothesis.

The available data suggests that radical right experiences of society are strongest on the normlessness and social isolation dimensions of alienation, while new left experiences emphasize meaninglessness and powerlessness. Hence it is not surprising that radical right ideology stresses immorality and impersonality in its political indictment, while the new left stresses drift and illegitimate power.

Assuming widespread alienation from mass society among members of radical groups, efforts are needed to determine whether specific types of alienation are significantly correlated with particular radical ideologies. Inquiry into the major forms of political alienation requires the development of measures of political radicalism possessing sufficient reliability to determine the extent to which political alienation pervades non-radical populations, and to determine the conditions under which feelings of alienation do or do not express themselves through radical commitment.

[17] Kornhauser, p. 13.

III

STRUCTURAL DIMENSIONS OF OPINION EXPRESSION

The readings in this section introduce the demographic correlates of opinion representation. V. O. Key, Jr. (Selection 10), establishes the differences in opinion on a series of issues of political relevance by contrasting the policy views expressed in different regions of the country and the views held by inhabitants of cities of different sizes, by suburbanites, and by those in rural areas. Key indicates that the latter differentiations may be replacing the early emphasis on regional clusters of opinions.

Robert Alford (Selection 11) concentrates on identifying and comparing differences in class voting in the United States, Great Britain, Canada, and Australia. He examines the social structure of the societies and their historical development, and puts forth some explanations for the dissimilarities in class representation in the four countries. Alford illustrates the level of class voting in each of the countries—from the high class representation in Britain to the virtual nonexistence of similar patterns in Canada—and the correlates of such political behavior: urbanization, education, labor force characteristics, income, and mobility. Both the cultural cleavage in Canada and an emphasis on representation through regional governments possibly explain the low amount of class voting observed in that country.

David R. Segal, in a paper published in its entirety in this volume for the first time,[1] explores a related problem, but with a different emphasis (Selection 12). The author continues the comparative emphasis by contrasting developments in the United States and West Germany. He illustrates the differences in the social underpinnings of the party systems in two highly developed economic and political systems. Despite the congruence of economic factors within the systems, disparities remain, and these can be traced to the historical evolution of political practices within each of the countries.

Segal introduces a discussion of religion as a factor influencing political behavior. A more extended analysis of the differences among religious adherents in their political beliefs on domestic welfare measures, civil rights, and morality issues is provided by Gerhard Lenski (Selection 13). He finds that, despite controlling for such variables as education, class, and race, differences in opinions traceable to religious affiliation consistently emerge. Jews, for example, are the strongest supporters of welfare-state measures, although they have less to gain in terms of tangible reward. Catholics are less consistent in their backing of such measures, and Protestants are the least enthusiastic. Protestants were more pronouncedly sympathetic to individual guarantees of free speech. In this latter analysis, Lenski suggests that the introduction of more controls—specifically in relation to race and sectionalism—within the presentation of the Stouffer findings on democratic beliefs based on a nationwide sampling of respondents[2] would have resulted in a more accurate representation of who does and who does not support specified democratic values and with what intensity. Questions relating to both social problems and public ethics—gambling, drinking, birth control—uncovered differences both among the religions and within the religious groupings. In the area of international affairs, little disparity in view occurred among the four major socioreligious groups analyzed. There was greater agreement on these issues than on any others examined.

In Selection 14, which concludes the chapter, V. O. Key, Jr., and Frank Munger examine some implications of the major voting studies. In particular, they isolate one of the major contentions of the first

[1] A modified version of the Segal paper has appeared as "Classes, Strata, and Parties in West Germany and the United States" in *Comparative Studies in Society and History*, 10 (October 1967), pp. 66–84.

[2] S. A. Stouffer, *Communism, Conformity, and Civil Liberties* (New York: Doubleday, 1955).

principal work on voter decision making,[3] *The People's Choice* (1944) by Paul Lazarsfeld, Bernard Berelson, and Hazel Gaudet, that the social climate in which an individual operates is the decisive factor in his political behavior. Key and Munger supplement this argument by examining, through the use of aggregate electoral data, patterns of voting behavior in Indiana over long periods of time. The authors would like, in their words, to reintroduce political considerations into the study of electoral decision making. In their longitudinal analysis of voting patterns, they succeed in demonstrating that party support persists beyond attempts to explain it through socioeconomic factors. There is, in short, a residue of behavior that social characteristics cannot account for. Supplemental analyses of political institutions, attachments to the system and political parties, and the role of political groups and politicians in investing social questions with political significance expand available knowledge of the electoral decision-making process.

[3] The principal voting works are introduced and reviewed in: Peter H. Rossi, "Four Landmarks in Voting Research," in Eugene Burdick and Arthur J. Brodbeck, eds., *American Voting Behavior* (New York: Free Press, 1959), pp. 5–54; P. H. Rossi, "Trends in Voting Behavior Research: 1933–1963"; in Edward C. Dreyer and Walter A. Rosenbaum, eds., *Political Opinion and Electoral Behavior* (Belmont, Calif.: Wadsworth, 1966), pp. 67–77; and Robert T. Golembiewski, William A. Welsh, and William J. Crotty, *A Methodological Primer for Political Scientists* (Stokie, Ill.: Rand McNally, 1969), pp. 389–424.

10

The Geographical Distribution of Opinions*

V. O. KEY, JR.

SECTIONALISM

The South: The Place of the Negro and Other Questions

The South remains the most distinctive region in political opinion; yet its most notable contrast with the rest of the country is in attitudes about national policy toward the Negro. Though the South is often assumed to be conservative on matters of domestic economic policy, its appearance of conservatism results from imperfect representation of its views rather than from a peculiar mass opinion. Even with respect to the Negro the unity of the South varies from aspect to aspect of race policy. Southerners take a far stronger position on school segregation than on such questions as the protection of the economic rights of Negroes.

Southern spokesmen in Congress have been virtually unanimous in their opposition to school integration. That solidarity is a result of the fact that regional majorities, as they flow through the representative system, ap-

* Reprinted with omissions by permission of Alfred A. Knopf, Inc. from *Public Opinion and American Democracy* by V. O. Key, Jr. Copyright, © 1961 by V. O. Key, Jr.

Figure 10.1 "The Government in Washington Should Stay out of the Question of Whether White and Colored Children Go to the Same School."

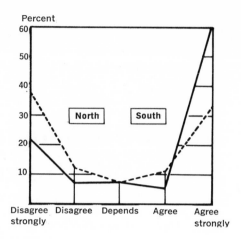

SOURCE: Survey Research Center, University of Michigan, 1956. Percentage base excludes those with no opinion.

pear to be far larger than they actually are. The small southern minority unopposed to integration practically disappears when southern sentiment is filtered through the representative system. Of the southerners questioned by the Survey Research Center in 1956, 22 percent disagreed strongly with the proposition: "The government in Washington should stay out of the question of whether white and colored children go to the same school"; 59 percent agreed strongly; another 5 percent expressed a less-intense agreement.[1] The contrast between southern and nonsouthern opinion distributions on this question appears in Figure 10.1, which incidentally indicates that southern opponents of school integration had a sizeable number of allies outside the South.[2]

Southerners show considerably less solidarity about the economic rights of Negroes than they do on the school integration question. Almost as many southerners as nonsoutherners (67 percent against 71 percent) expressed agreement in 1956 with the proposition: "If Negroes are not getting fair treatment in jobs and housing, the government in Washington should see to it that they do." The conditional form of the proposition doubtless enabled

[1] The percentages are not affected materially by the inclusion of Negroes in the southern sample.

[2] The AIPO in July 1959 asked: "The U.S. Supreme Court has ruled that racial segregation in the public schools is illegal. This means that all children, no matter what their race, must be allowed to go to the same schools. Do you approve or disapprove of this decision?" In the South 22 percent approved; in the North 72 percent. This phrasing of the issue attracted a much higher northern approval than did the 1956 Survey Research Center formulation. Hyman and Sheatsley find some softening of Southern opinion toward school integration from 1942 to 1956. See their "Attitudes towards Desegregation," *Scientific American*, December 1956.

some persons to agree with it and at the same time to feel that Negroes were already "getting fair treatment." And conceptions of fairness may vary. Nevertheless, the resemblance at this verbal level of equity between the South and the remainder of the country deserves attention.[3]

On domestic economic policy the image of the South that appears in the public prints is one of a soundly conservative region ever ready to ally itself in Congress with northern Republicans. That image itself involves misrepresentation, for some southern Senators and Representatives are conservatives and others are liberals on economic issues, at least as those terms are popularly defined in these days. At the level of mass opinion, however, the conservatism of the South disappears once its opinions are compared with those of the remainder of the country. If southern opinion corresponded to the popular caricature, it would frown on governmental endeavors to maintain employment, it would take a low view of the influence of trade unions, and it would perhaps look with tolerance on the influence of big corporations. In fact, southern opinion on these matters, as is shown in Table 10.1, closely resembles that of the rest of the country. On some questions the South turns out to be a shade more "liberal" than other regions. More southerners than midwesterners, for example, agree that the government "ought to help people get doctors and hospital care at low cost" (68 percent against 54 percent), a finding not inconsistent with the spectacle of the late Senator Walter George of Georgia chiding AMA representatives at a Senate hearing about the high cost of medical care and calling to their attention the prospect that their tactics might assure governmental intervention.

Withal, apart from its attitudes on the Negro question, the South takes positions in mass opinion on broad questions of policy remarkably similar to those of the nation. It may still possess some intangible characteristics that give its policies a distinctive style. On some specific moral issues, too, it

TABLE 10.1   REGION, SOUTH AND NON-SOUTH, IN RELATION TO OPINION ON JOB GUARANTEE, BIG BUSINESS INFLUENCE, UNION INFLUENCE, AND POWER AND HOUSING

OPINION	JOB GUARANTEE		BIG BUSINESS		UNION		POWER AND HOUSING	
	S	N	S	N	S	N	S	N
Agree strongly	53%	46%	55%	52%	50%	51%	43%	43%
Agree but not very strongly	16	14	16	18	16	16	13	16
Not sure; depends	9	7	9	7	8	7	11	9
Disagree but not very strongly	9	13	9	11	13	11	11	11
Disagree strongly	13	20	11	12	13	15	22	21
	100%	100%	100%	100%	100%	100%	100%	100%
N	456	1131	348	924	341	976	332	917

SOURCE: Survey Research Center, University of Michigan, 1956.

[3] In these tabulations of Survey Research Center data, the South includes those states commonly regarded as border states. For the definition of regions employed in Survey Research Center data, see the map at the front flyleaf of Angus Campbell, Gerald Gurin, and Warren E. Miller: *The Voter Decides* (New York: Harper & Row, 1954).

tends to differ.[4] Its people have far lower levels of political participation than do other Americans. Yet on broad substantive issues its opinions have been largely captured by the same forces that prevail over the nation.

How can the similarity in opinions between the South and the rest of the country be reconciled with the conservative outlook of many southern Senators and Representatives? The marked differentials in levels of political participation among occupational groups in the South, as compared with the North, probably contribute a part of the explanation. In the South the classes that tend to be conservative approach in their levels of political participation comparable groups outside the South. On the other hand, southern blue-collar workers (both white and black) are far less active in politics than non-southern blue-collar workers. In 1956 59 percent of southern blue-collar

TABLE 10.2   OCCUPATION, SOUTH AND NON-SOUTH, IN RELATION TO PO-LITICAL PARTICIPATION

Level of Participation		OCCUPATION AND REGION					
		White-collar		Blue-collar		Farmers	
		S	N	S	N	S	N
High	4	34%	39%	19%	28%	27%	24%
	3	36	48	22	48	27	61
	2	5	3	8	5	8	0
Low	1	25	10	51	19	38	15
		100%	100%	100%	100%	100%	100%
	N	166	414	203	571	64	100

SOURCE: Survey Research Center, University of Michigan, 1956.

workers did not vote in the presidential election; the comparable nonsouthern figure was only 24 percent. (Table 10.2.) If the blue-collar vote in the South should double, southern conservatives in Congress would probably become less numerous. The bias of the active, as contrasted with the potential, elec-torate in the South impresses on many southern Representatives outlooks not compatible with what might be expected from the opinion data. Of course, other factors contribute to the conservatism of some southern Representa-tives. The regional figures conceal the fact that in the South, as elsewhere, opinions are not uniformly spread geographically; southern suburban areas

[4] A Gallup question of April, 1938, read: "Would you favor lotteries in this state to help pay the cost of government?" The "Yes" replies were: South, 37 percent; New Eng-land, 59 percent. On sex, though, the Midwest seems to talk, if not act, with a special re-gional accent. Elmo Roper & Associates put the question: "Do you think it is all right for either or both parties to a marriage to have had previous sexual experience?" Not all right: Midwest, 70 percent; South, 44 percent. The pollers add the caution: "No one can tell pre-cisely how the words articulate with the deeds,"—*The Public Pulse*, November 1959. In a May 1960, AIPO poll 46 percent of the southerners favored prohibition of the "sale of all beer, wine and liquor throughout the nation"; only 15 percent in the East took that posi-tion. In May, 1959, the AIPO reported results on the question: "If your party nominated a generally well-qualified man for President, and he happened to be a Catholic, would you vote for him?" In the South 53 percent of the respondents said they would vote for such a nominee; outside the South, 73 percent.

may have views not unlike northern suburbs. These and other such variations are mirrored by the representative system in the South just as they are elsewhere.

The Midwest:
Erstwhile Stronghold of Isolationism

The Midwest was long regarded as the stronghold of isolationism. Between World Wars I and II American foreign policy was supposedly held in check by the disposition of this great region to avoid involvement in the affairs of other parts of the world. Such interpretations probably exaggerated the role of midwestern opinion or rested on an elastic definition of the Midwest. The great spokesmen for the isolationist position included such men as Senator William E. Borah of Idaho and Senator Hiram Johnson of California.[5] Yet within the conventionally defined Midwest opinion surveys during the preliminaries to World War II showed the people of this region to be far more opposed to aid to England and other such measures than were people in other sections of the country.

The impact of World War II in large degree erased regional differences in mass opinion on broad foreign-policy problems. On question after question put by survey organizations during World War II and afterward the Midwest divided in about the same way as did the rest of the country. In 1944, for example, when discussion of America's role in the postwar period was rife, the AIPO put the question: "Do you agree with those people who think that the United States should take an active part in world affairs after the war, or with those people who think we should stay out of world affairs?" Seventy-two percent of the midwestern sample and 73 percent of the national cross section agreed that an active American role in world affairs was desirable. Though not all questions produce the same degree of similarity, the region of isolationism has lost its marked contrast with the rest of the country.[6]

Probably on some specific policy questions regional peculiarities exist and will exist, but on the broad question of toleration of, if not zealous support for, American participation in world affairs regional contrasts seem to have disappeared. An attitude measure that bundles up opinions on several questions by Guttman scaling techniques indicates that only a slight residue of the old midwestern isolationism remains. On that scale (Table 10.3) 53 percent of midwesterners ranked high in willingness to support involvement in international affairs in 1956, in contrast with 59 percent in the Northeast,

[5] Ralph Smuckler has shown that isolationism, as measured by the voting records of Senators and Representatives, formed a broad but not solid band across the northern half of the country—"The Region of Isolationism," *American Political Science Review*, XLVII (1955), 336–401.

[6] For regional breakdowns of national polls on questions of foreign policy, see Gabriel Almond: *The American People and Foreign Policy* (New York: Harcourt, 1950), pp. 131–135; W. A. Scott and S. B. Withey: *The United States and the United Nations* (New York: Manhattan, 1958), pp. 129–133; F. W. Williams, "Regional Attitudes on International Cooperation," *"Public Opinion Quarterly,"* IX (1945), 38–50.

TABLE 10.3   REGION IN RELATION TO DISTRIBUTION ALONG SCALE MEASUR-
ING ATTITUDES TOWARD AMERICAN INVOLVEMENT IN FOR-
EIGN AFFAIRS

INTERNATIONALISM	MIDWEST	NORTHEAST	FAR WEST	SOUTH
High	15%	59%	58%	56%
Medium	27	25	24	26
Low	20	16	18	18
	100%	100%	100%	100%
N	372	469	177	398

SOURCE: Survey Research Center, University of Michigan, 1956.

not an impressive difference.[7] At the other end of the scale, 20 percent of midwesterners ranked low in internationalism in contrast with 16 percent of those in the Northeast. If opinion data were available for smaller areas, states and districts would doubtless be found with opinion patterns supportive of isolationist Representatives and Senators, especially on matters of foreign aid, but they would certainly not all be in the Midwest.[8]

Regional Similarities and Shadings in Differentiation

Save for the special position of the South on the Negro question, the salient characteristic of regional distributions of opinion on many questions in 1952 and 1956 is their similarity. One must search for small differentiations from region to region to account for the appearances of sectionalism that emerge from time to time. Small differences within the public may create marked contrast in Congress when the popular vote happens to fall in precisely the right manner.

The Far West, whose population is heavily concentrated in such centers as Los Angeles, San Francisco, Seattle, and Denver, cultivates a style of distinction that reveals itself in shadings in the opinion data. Though that style cannot readily be described, it probably consists of the old western tradition of progressivism reinforced by the New Deal, all fortified by the presence and acceptance on every hand of governmental economic activities on a scale unknown in the East. A more marked concern for civil liberties also seems to characterize the West. Stouffer found from the application of his scale to measure tolerance of deviate political behaviors—such as the making of

[7] In this tabulation the Midwest was defined as the region from Ohio to Kansas to North Dakota, including these states as corners of the triangle.

[8] Contrary to general belief, the South probably has long had a strain of isolationist sentiment susceptible of activation under appropriate conditions. In 1956 a larger proportion of southerners than of the people of any other region (34 percent against 22 percent in the Far West) agreed with this proposition: "This country would be better off if we just stayed home and did not concern ourselves with problems in other parts of the world," The chances are that southern isolationists are especially heavily represented among the region's nonvoters, a factor facilitative of internationalism among southern representatives. Since 1952, without the spur of Democratic presidential leadership, southern representatives have moved away from internationalism. See Charles O. Lerch, Jr.: "Southern Congressmen and the 'New Isolationism,' " *Political Science Quarterly*, LXXV (1960), 321–337.

speeches in favor of government ownership—that the proportions ranked as "more tolerant" ranged from 48 percent in the West down to 16 percent in the South.[9] The proportions of "less tolerant" ranged from 13 percent in the West to 27 percent in the South. The 1956 Survey Research Center sample confirmed these differences by another question: 61 percent in the Far West, against 46 percent in the South, strongly disagreed with the proposition that the "government ought to fire any government worker who is accused of being a communist even though they don't prove it."

The Far West takes a notably more permissive attitude toward government participation in power projects than does the rest of the country. In 1956 42 percent of the Survey Research Center respondents in the Far West disagreed with the statement that "government should leave things like electric power and housing for private businessmen to handle." Only 28 percent of the Northeast were so adamant in their doubts about laissez faire. While the West is not populated predominantly by rabid advocates of public ownership, their numbers suffice to give western congressional representation a distinctive coloration. Perhaps strangely, this attitude is mixed with a degree of hard-headedness on taxation. Fewer westerners felt in 1956 that taxes should be cut even if it meant "putting off some important things that need to be done." Only 22 percent in the Far West accepted this absurdity, as against 38 percent in the Northeast.[10]

The odds are that the Far West has an attitudinal differentiation on foreign policy that turns attention westward rather than toward Europe, with a corresponding assignment of priority of effort. Though information on the point is scant, in 1952 50 percent of far westerners in the Survey Research Center sample thought a stronger stand, even to the bombing of Manchuria, was in order in the Korean War, while only 40 percent of the entire country took so bellicose a stance. Other measures of views on international policy indicate that the pedestals of opinion from which William Borah and Hiram Johnson thundered their isolationism have long since worn away.[11]

Significance of Interregional Consensus

Although on a few vexing questions fairly sharp sectional differences in mass attitudes prevail, the similarities, not the differences, in a distribution of opinions from region to region attract attention. On most broad issues for which the data are available the mass of the people of all sections divide in approximately the same manner. If we were to draw the J-curves of consensus . . . for each of the sections of the country, they would closely resemble each other on most major issues. Thus, on such questions a concurrent consensus prevails among the geographical regions of the nation. This fact is fundamental for the nature of American politics; and, it must be recognized,

[9] *Communism, Conformity, and Civil Liberties* (New York: Doubleday, 1955), p. 112.

[10] For analyses of opinions in the Far West based on the 1952 campaign study by the Survey Research Center, see Alfred de Grazia: *The Western Public* (Stanford: Stanford University Press; 1954).

[11] Only 26 percent in the Far West disagreed in 1956 with the proposition that the United States should give economic aid to the poorer countries "even if they can't pay for it." In the South 33 percent disagreed (23 percent "strongly").

the practice of American politics has had something to do with building interregional similarities of attitude. Concurrent interregional consensus on most issues assures that political conflict will occur on lines other than geographical. In the grand architecture of politics the multiplication of issue cleavages along geographical lines threatens national unity; when divisions are nongeographical, the proponents of any major point of view in one region are allied with those having a similar outlook in other sections.

These comments must be reconciled with the fact that a flavor of sectionalism indubitably pervades the discussion of some concrete questions in the councils of government. One phase of such reconciliation consists in the simple fact that the media commonly exaggerate the degree of sectional cleavage that actually prevails. Yet genuine interregional conflict remains. To some extent this is attributable to the magnification of local majorities as they are projected into representative bodies under systems of geographical representation; 51 percent in popular opinion may become 100 percent in Congress. By the same token, the popular 49 percent of today becomes the congressional 100 percent of tomorrow, so narrow are many of our popular pluralities. Popular differences between geographic areas need not be wide to support marked differences between their representatives.

Another line of reconciliation between sectionalism in Congress and interregional homogeneity of opinion is one for which little evidence is available. Much of our sectionalism is about issues on which probably few people have interest, awareness, or opinion; yet politically influential persons may share a lively sense of sectional concern. Thus, western Senators and Congressmen make common cause in the promotion of silver policy and other mining interests. If we had public opinion data on this issue and on many lesser matters of sectional concern, the chances are that concentrated distributions . . . would be found to exist. That is, relatively small numbers of persons would be possessed of an opinion, either pro or con, and they would probably be concentrated geographically. Much sectional conflict may be, in the main, a conflict among relatively narrow political elites who do not enlist much mass support in their respective bailiwicks. Such limited popular involvement may mute sectional conflict. At any rate such an inference might be drawn from contrast with sectional differences on the place of the Negro, a matter on which general involvement of the population seems to mold the behavior of representatives into rigid, rather than muted, patterns of conflict.[12]

METROPOLIS, CITY, TOWN, COUNTRYSIDE

It is common in political discourse to speak of the interests of the metropolitan centers, of the concerns of the smaller cities and towns, and of the individuality of rural America. To a large extent the special orientations of

[12] Another, perhaps extremely significant, fact is that few persons seem to think of politics in sectional terms. In the inquiries by the Survey Research Center in 1952 and in 1956 the respondents were asked: "Is there anything in particular that you like about the Democratic party?" The same questions were asked about the Republican party. As people responded to these open-ended inquiries, few indicated that they saw the political parties as dedicated to the cause of any geographical section. Only three or four comments out of several thousand could be so interpreted.

these areas are not the corporate concerns of metropolis, village, or town but are the views of those types of people that predominate within these political units: the workers of the metropolis, the farmers of the countryside, the bourgeoisie of the small towns. Yet the differentials in opinion among places of differing population size and destiny deserve attention, for the geographical system of representation assures for them special recognition in the governmental process.

These opinions interact with the representative process in a dual fashion. Representatives of geographical areas in which a particular shade of opinion or interest predominates may be relied upon to promote that interest with devotion. On the other hand interests shared across class and occupational lines within representative units—states or districts—may also be given special emphasis through the geographical system of representation. Opinions on this second type of question—such as, Shall a dam be built in the district?—remain largely unmeasured by opinion surveys. Most of the

TABLE 10.4   SIZE OF PLACE IN RELATION TO OPINION ON JOB-GUARANTEE QUESTION[a]

ISSUE POSITION	METRO[b]	METRO FRINGE[c]	CITIES OVER 50,000[d]	CITIES 10,000– 50,000	TOWNS 2500– 10,000	COUNTRY[e]
Agree strongly	58%	46%	53%	34%	47%	46%
Agree but not strongly	13	11	12	16	17	16
Depends	5	6	7	15	5	9
Disagree but not strongly	8	16	11	12	14	11
Disagree strongly	16	21	17	23	17	18
	100%	100%	100%	100%	100%	100%
N	268	171	234	163	295	455

SOURCE: Survey Research Center, University of Michigan, 1956.

[a] The question was as follows: "The government in Washington ought to see to it that everybody who wants to work can find a job."

[b] The 12 largest cities and their suburbs of 50,000 or more.

[c] Metropolitan fringe consists of the suburbs, with populations of from 2500 to 50,000, of the 12 metropolitan cities plus some urban fringe and rural suburban territory.

[d] That is, cities over 50,000 not suburban to metropolitan centers.

[e] Includes places under 2500 not elsewhere classified.

data bear on the concerns of classes of people whose opinions might be expected to be about the same wherever they live. Yet even on such questions the fact of residence in a metropolis may give a special cast to opinions, a tenor that would be lacking among similar persons resident in small cities. Thus, blue-collar workers in a metropolis may develop outlooks that differ in degree from those of blue-collar workers in towns and small cities.

The detailed evidence on gradations of opinion among places of different population size indicates that even the country is not often set off sharply from the metropolis. Rather, people of all shades of opinion inhabit both the

city and the country. The opinion distributions in the two types of areas overlap; only the averages differ.[13] Moreover, on many questions differences in
opinion patterns are not related with regularity to size of community. For
example, the people of villages and countryside are not on all issues the most
conservative of population groups. An illustration of the opinion variations
among places of different population size appears in Table 10.4, which indicates direction of 1956 opinion on the proposition: "The government in
Washington ought to see to it that everybody who wants to work can find a
job." The table also serves as a step in the explanation of a means for a more
comprehensive comparison between types of communities.

As a preliminary to the presentation of data on other questions, we can
by an arithmetical maneuver make the data of Table 10.4 more compre-
hensible. Let us ignore the differences in strength of opinion on the job-
guarantee proposition. Then 71 percent of the metropolitan sample agrees
and 24 percent disagrees; these figures contrast sharply with the 50 percent
agreement and 35 percent disagreement in the small cities of 10,000 to
50,000 population. If, taking another step, we use as a single indicator the
difference between the percentage that agrees and the percentage that disagrees, we lose some detail but obtain simpler measures of position on the
issue. By these operations Table 10.4 can be reduced to the index in the right-
hand column below:

	(1) AGREE	(2) DISAGREE	(3) (1)MINUS(2)
Metropolitan	71	24	47
Metropolitan fringe	57	37	20
Cities over 50,000	65	28	37
Cities, 10,000–50,000	50	35	15
Towns, 2500–10,000	64	31	33

If we treat several issues in the same manner, we obtain the contrasts in
opinion division among places of different size that appear in Table 10.5.

The gradations of opinion among types of communities shown by Table
10.5, fit in part the common suppositions. The metropolitan centers stand at
the extreme "liberal" position on each of the domestic issues analyzed.
Relatively more people in these centers look approvingly on public enterprise
in housing and in power, more regard medical care as a proper subject of
governmental action, fewer wish to restrict the influence of unions, and more
believe the government should see to it that every one who wants to work
can find a job. The table also confounds some political folklore. The stronghold of conservatism, at least on these issues, rests in small cities of from
10,000 to 50,000 population and not in the rural areas. That conservatism,
though, is mixed with a sense of fiscal responsibility. Far fewer persons in the
small cities agree that taxes should be cut even if it means putting off some
important "things that need to be done." In public services the tastes of small
cities are simple, but their citizens seem to be more willing to pay for what

---

[13] For an extensive compilation of poll results comparing farmers with other sectors
of the population, see Howard W. Beers: "Rural-Urban Differences: Some Evidence from
Opinion Polls," *Rural Sociology*, XVIII (1953), 1–11.

they want than do metropolitan residents. The thorough control of the politics of these smaller cities by business and professional men is reflected both in popular attitudes and in the generally conservative tendency of Representatives, be they Democratic or Republican, from districts dominated by such communities. Although these small cities account for only about 10

TABLE 10.5   INDICES OF OPINION CLEAVAGE IN PLACES OF DIFFERENT SIZE ON SELECTED ISSUES[a]

ISSUE	METRO	CITIES OVER 50,000	TOWNS 2500– 10,000	COUNTRY	METRO FRINGE	CITIES 10,000– 50,000
Power and housing	+17	+21	+23	+28	+39	+43
Union influence	+22	+36	+45	+46	+50	+47
Medical care	+48	+37	+29	+32	+21	+16
Job guarantee	+47	+37	+33	+33	+20	+15
Cut taxes	− 8	−15	−22	−25	−30	−35

SOURCE: Survey Research Center, University of Michigan, 1956.

[a] The entries, explained in the text, are the differences between the percentage agreeing and the percentage disagreeing with the issue proposition, something of an index of the size of relative pluralities in places of different size. The figure is affected by the proportions of "it depends" responses as well as by the size of the proportions in agreement and in disagreement. In reading the figures the precise form of the question must be kept in mind.

percent of the national sample, the intensity of their opinions, compounded by their overrepresentation in Congress and in state legislatures, may give them a disproportionate strength in the political process. The hard-headed opinion of the small city represents a strain of politics that probably once was far more typical of America than it now is.

Some common suppositions about the conservatism of the country and of the small towns under 10,000 are in error, at least as measured by opinions on the issues in Table 10.5. In the main people of small towns, villages, and of the country stand between those of the metropolis and those of the small cities. On other questions places of various sizes would probably arrange themselves in a different order, but the distribution of attitudes on this series of questions indicates that the villages and countryside occupy a middle position. Their swings in attitude over time may contribute to the settlement of conflicts involving the extremes in the small and great cities.

On questions of involvement of the United States in international politics communities arrange themselves in an order different from that prevailing on domestic issues. On a scale designed to measure willingness to see the United States involved in international affairs variations among types of places are not striking, as Table 10.6 shows. While people of all kinds of places rank, on the average, high on the scale, the most marked deviation occurs in the open country and in villages under 2500, which have relatively about twice as many persons ranking low on the scale of internationalism as do the suburbs. This deviation may not be attributed solely to conditions of

TABLE 10.6 SIZE OF PLACE IN RELATION TO OPINION DISTRIBUTION ON INTERNATIONALISM SCALE[a]

INTER-NATION-ALISM	CITIES OVER 50,000	METRO FRINGE	CITIES 10,000–50,000	METRO	TOWNS 2500–10,000	RURAL
High	60%	53%	58%	61%	59%	51%
Medium	27	34	28	22	24	25
Low	13	13	14	17	17	24
	100%	100%	100%	100%	100%	100%
N	217	159	148	223	260	408

SOURCE: Survey Research Center, University of Michigan, 1956.
[a] See Table 10.4 for definition of place categories.

rural life, for substantial numbers of metropolitan residents also rank low on the scale. In any case, rural dwellers turn up in relatively large numbers on most questions that seek to tap isolationist attitudes.[14]

Minor Tempests: Rural versus Urban

In American politics several issues of style, morals, and convenience are notorious sources of urban-rural cleavage. The survey data support the popular impressions on these matters. Regularly, for example, the question of daylight-saving time taxes the ingenuity of statesmen for its solution. Farmers, supposedly bound by their way of life to rise early anyway, do not wish to start their day even earlier for the convenience of city dwellers who want more daylight left free for golfing. Mr. Gallup in April 1957 found the following percentages to favor daylight-saving time.[15]

Farm population	24%
Towns under 10,000	54
Towns 10,000–99,999	54
Cities over 100,000	73

Mr. Gallup also found in 1950 that farmers had little use for the proposal to have all holidays, except Christmas, celebrated on Mondays in order to have a few long week ends. Dwellers in cities of over 100,000 approved the scheme by 58 percent, but only 37 percent of the farmers favored it.[16]

---

[14] On the average those persons who grew up on farms but were residing in urban places in 1956 ranked lower on the internationalism scale than did their fellow citizens who had not grown up on farms. Substantially more of those who grew up on farms had so few opinions that they could not be placed on the internationalism scale.

[15] The figures do not reveal certain urban sources of opposition to daylight-saving time. On occasion an urban utility has made a modest contribution to those campaigning against fast time; to move the clocks up reduces the consumption of electricity for illumination.

[16] What cosmic import to attach to the farmers' views is hard to say. One farmer explained: "My wife's folks are always coming out here as it is, but now, at least, they have to pack up and go home Sunday nights."

Rural concentration of prohibition sentiment has long given battles over policy on the sale of alcoholic beverages the flavor of conflict between city and country. To some degree at least the urban-rural cleavage on prohibition masks differences in religious doctrine on the liquor question. Yet the conditions of life in small towns and the countryside may generate community opinions less tolerant of deviate behavior than is the impersonal metropolis. Whatever the basis for the attitude differences, their uneven geographical distribution projects the prohibition issue into the governmental mechanism as friction between metropolis and countryside. In February 1942 the AIPO found the sentiment in favor of national prohibition to be:[17]

	FOR
Farmers	50%
Towns under 10,000	43
Cities 10,000 to 100,000	31
Cities over 100,000	23

Variations in attitudes toward prohibition are paralleled by, and perhaps connected with, urban-rural differences found by Stouffer by the application of his scale of willingness to tolerate nonconformists. Of his sample in the metropolitan areas 14 percent were rated as "less tolerant"; this proportion increased in smaller cities and in towns under 2500 and reached 29 percent in the farm population. Similarly, the proportion rated as "more tolerant" was over twice as great in the metropolitan areas (39 percent) as among farmers (18 percent).[18]

Community Size, Social Structure, and Opinion

The fact of variation, or similarity, in the distribution of opinions within metropolitan areas, other urban communities, and the open country alone has its political significance. The further problem remains whether size of community may itself be important in the shaping of opinion. The hypothesis has been suggested that the metropolis—with its neighborhood segregation of income, class, and occupational groupings, with its multiplicity of centers of information and propaganda, and with its *modus vivendi* permitting all kinds of people to live together yet apart—may facilitate the development of diversity in opinion. In contrast, the intimate relations of the small town, the hypothesis goes, may induce a greater homogeneity of opinion, a condition perhaps enforced by the monopolization of the positions of respectability and prestige by a unified and visible norm-setting community leadership. To a degree, the argument is that in smaller communities, lesser peoples without the aid of organization and opinion-forming centers beholden to them, may be dominated in their views to a higher degree by community leadership.

[17] Readers may have encountered truly imposing rustic tipplers, but, if we are to believe what people tell interviewers, imbibers are relatively fewer on the farms than in the cities. In 1939 the AIPO asked: "Do you ever drink any alcoholic beverages such as wine, beer, cocktails, highballs?" The yes response among farmers was 43 percent; the urbanites confessed at the rate of 63 percent.

[18] Stouffer: p. 112.

Such evidence as is available on these plausible arguments relates to voting rather than to policy opinions. Epstein, from an analysis of Wisconsin cities, suggested that the smaller Democratic vote in medium-sized cities, in comparison with that in large cities, might be a function of community size.[19] In a more extended analysis in Michigan, Masters and Wright found that a substantial proportion of the variation in Democratic vote among cities of different sizes could be accounted for by differences in the occupational composition of the cities. Yet laborers in small cities were distinctly less inclined to vote Democratic than were laborers in large cities. Factors present in the larger cities and absent in the smaller ones mobilized workers for the Democrats; the relative absence of labor organization in cities under 10,000 seemed to be the most important of these factors.[20] MacRae, in a correlational analysis of congressional voting and occupations, arrives at similar general findings. In congressional districts with high percentages of farmers—that is, primarily rural and small-town districts—he found little or no correlation

TABLE 10.7   PERCENTAGES OF OCCUPATIONAL GROUPS IN METROPOLITAN CENTERS AND IN SMALL CITIES AGREEING STRONGLY WITH SELECTED POLICY PROPOSITIONS

	METROPOLITAN		SMALL CITY[a]	
ISSUE	Blue-collar	White-collar	Blue-collar	White-collar
Union influence	36%	47%	45%	50%
Power and housing	33	43	45	47
Job guarantee	60	51	37	26
Medical care	55	50	42	31

SOURCE: Survey Research Center, University of Michigan, 1956.
[a] Cities of 10,000–50,000.

between occupation and vote. In urban districts occupations tended to divide in their voting along the expected party lines.[21] Berelson observed that in Elmira the community norms, more favorable to middle-class and business groups, solidified the middle-class vote, while the workers showed "less political solidarity and more political ambivance."[22]

If community pressures in the small town discourage voting dissent from the dominant party, the question remains of whether a similar process

[19] "Size of Place and the Two-Party Vote," Western Political Quarterly, IX (1956), 138–150.

[20] Nicholas A. Masters and Deil S. Wright: "Trends and Variations in the Two-Party Vote: The Case of Michigan," American Political Science Review, LII (1958); 1078–1090.

[21] Duncan MacRae, Jr.: "Occupations and the Congressional Vote, 1940–1950," American Sociological Review, XX (1955), 332–340.

[22] Bernard Berelson et al.: Voting (Chicago: University of Chicago Press; 1954), pp. 56–57. Relevant also is Warren Miller's finding that one-party dominance in counties hampers the minority party in the mobilization of its potential vote; see his "One-Party Politics and the Voter," American Political Science Review, L (1956), 707–725. Consistent with the assumption that more interaction occurs among people in small communities are the findings by Stuart C. Dodd in "A Power of Town Size Predicts an Internal Interacting," Social Forces, XXXVI (1957), pp. 132–137.

operates with respect to policy outlooks. Some evidence indicates that it does. If we single out those persons who "agree strongly" with policy propositions that might be expected to affect white-collar and blue-collar workers differentially, we obtain suggestive contrasts. Table 10.7 shows the percentages of occupational groups in metropolitan centers and in small cities "agreeing strongly" with the indicated policy statements. In each instance blue-collar workers of the small cities differ sharply from their metropolitan brethren, and in each instance that difference moves them toward the position of the white-collar classes of the small cities.[23]

Whether the facts mean that small-city elites impose upon blue-collar groups their own conservative views one cannot say. Whatever the processesses of opinion formation may be, small-city workers tend toward the views of their white-collar fellow citizens and away from the like occupational strata of the metropolis. Table 10.7 may provide a clue to a problem entirely different from that raised in this immediate discussion. At earlier points we have groped toward the identification of leadership groups that set opinion patterns. Perhaps in the professional and business classes of the small cities we can isolate a comparatively small and well-knit elite which, because of its solidarity and the size and nature of the political unit within which it operates, exerts exceptional powers in opinion formation.[24]

[23] Similar gradations do not appear on every issue. Small-city white-collar people, for example, feel strongly, even more frequently than metropolitan blue-collar workers, that the government ought to see to it "that big business corporations don't have much to say about how the government is run." This may reflect the greater importance of small business and the professions in smaller places.

[24] The hypothesis that social structure accounts for these differences, though, remains on shaky ground. The processes of equalization of opinion across occupational groups by community pressure do not, for example, seem to operate in so marked a way, as might be expected, in places of less than 10,000. The possibility also remains that the occupational categories in the metropolis and in the cities of from 10,000–50,000 may not be precisely comparable. For example, a higher proportion of skilled craftsmen in the smaller places might be associated with the opinion differential, a possibility that cannot be checked because of the sample size.

11

Class Voting
in the Anglo-American
Countries*

ROBERT R. ALFORD

... Survey data from four Anglo-American countries have shown that clear and consistent differences between the countries exist, regardless of whether class voting is examined for the total electorate divided into manual and non-manual occupations, for the same division within various demographic groups, or for a more rigorous definition of classes. Great Britain and Australia have higher levels of class voting than the United States and Canada. Some of the correlates of different levels of class voting which may be casual factors are discussed in the next section.

In none of these countries is the voting of one stratum for "its" party unanimous. Political consensus in these countries is shown by the constant shifting back and forth from Right to Left, but never does the vote by manual workers for the Right party, or non-manual workers for the Left party, drop below about 20 percent. Never does the index of class voting rise above 60 percentage points (80 percent of the manual workers voting Left, 20 percent of the non-manual workers voting Left, for example) even when ... classes are defined more narrowly than by occupation only. This narrower definition leaves out so much of the potential electorate that it is meaningless as an

* Reprinted by permission from Robert R. Alford, *Party and Society: The Anglo-American Democracies* (Skokie, Ill. Rand McNally, 1963), pp. 107–122.

over-all measure of class voting. The imperfect "status crystallization" of these four countries produces a high level of "cross-class" voting, no matter how class is defined. The fairly even impact of politically relevant events upon the classes is also shown clearly by the parallel moves to the Right or Left in most election periods. . . .

POSSIBLE CAUSES OF THE DIFFERENCES IN CLASS VOTING

A search for political and social differences between the Anglo-American countries which parallel the differences in class voting and which might account for them suggests four possibilities: (1) the parties in countries where class voting is higher might more consistently *represent* class interests; (2) the parties in countries where class voting is higher might more consistently *appeal* to class interests; (3) the parties where class voting is higher might simply possess the historical loyalties of certain classes, regardless of how they appeal to or represent class interests; (4) regardless of historical loyalties or the actions of parties, the social classes in these societies might be differently exposed to situations in which the political relevance of class interests becomes apparent; i.e., the social structure of these countries might be sufficiently different (despite similarities in the range and number of class positions, in the prestige of different occupations, and in the level of social mobility) that a high level of class voting is more likely in one country than another.

Whether the parties in Australia and Great Britain more consistently represent or appeal to class interests is a crucial problem for an adequate understanding of the emergence of class patterns of support for the parties. That all of the parties in each country strive to win support from all social classes does not contradict the existence of real differences between parties in their appeals and representativeness. Only a few speculative suggestions can be offered here.

The historical links of the trade unions in Great Britain and Australia to the Labor parties certainly suggest that the Labor parties there are more likely both to appeal to and to represent working-class interests than the Left parties of the United States and Canada. Upon that assumption, Table 11.1 suggests a connection between the differences in class voting actually

TABLE 11.1 CLASS VOTING AND REPRESENTATION OF OR APPEALS TO SPECIFIC CLASS INTERESTS

COUNTRY	PARTIES REPRESENTING CLASS INTERESTS	PARTIES APPEALING TO SPECIFIC CLASS INTERESTS	LEVEL OF CLASS VOTING
Great Britain	+	+	High
Australia	+ —	+	Medium high
United States	+	—	Medium low
Canada	—	—	Low

found and possible differences of appeal and representation. Parties in Great Britain both appeal to and represent class interests; voters rationally respond by dividing their support more clearly along class lines. Parties in Australia appeal to, but less clearly represent, class interests (this is only speculation). Parties in the United States represent class interests as much as the Australian parties but do not specifically appeal for support in class terms. Last, the parties in Canada neither consistently represent distinctive class interests nor appeal to different class bases for support.

Two characteristics of working-class ideology in these countries might affect the level of class voting, other things being equal: the level of class consciousness and the degree of equalitarianism. Qualitative evidence suggests that the countries should be differentiated as shown in Table 11.2.

TABLE 11.2   CLASS IDEOLOGIES

COUNTRY	CLASS CONSCIOUSNESS	EQUALITARANISM
Australia	+	+
Great Britain	+	—
United States	—	+
Canada	—	—

Table 11.2 suggests that Australian workers have a sharp working-class consciousness and strong feelings of equalitarianism. Their leaders are not seen as "any better" than they are. British workers, in contrast, are class-conscious but accept the leadership of the aristocrats and the well-educated. (Obviously these are relative statements.) American workers are not particularly class-conscious but are equalitarian; Canadian workers are neither class-conscious, nor equalitarian in this sense. If such a schema accurately sums up differences between the countries (and assuming that the middle class is similarly differentiated), we would expect the level of class voting to be in line with them, given similar class structures, and therefore that class voting should be higher in Australia than in Britain. Since it is not, other social and economic differences to be discussed may be more crucial explanatory factors than ideological differences.

These differences between the parties and the prevalent ideologies of social classes in the four countries might completely account for the differences in class voting, but because the interest here is in class voting as a structural fact of their socio-political systems, we may look further for correspondences of the rank order of class voting with other characteristics of the four societies.[1] Do we find correspondences of the order of class voting with other social characteristics of these societies?

At first glance this might seem unlikely. These four societies were

---

[1] The last possible cause of differences in class voting—historic loyalties—is, for our purposes, merely a residual category; if neither social-structural differences nor differences in party appeals and representation of class interests are correlated with class voting, we could ascribe differences between the countries to historical loyalties of certain strata to certain parties. Traditionalism of one kind or another—class-based traditionalism in Great Britain, non-class traditionalism in the United States or Canada—may be a historical factor of great importance.

picked precisely because they were similar in political and social type. On any measure of economic and social development—urbanization, wealth, industrialization—all four countries will be included in the first ten nations.[2] Their similarity of political culture, party systems and parliamentary systems has also been documented. But precisely because of this great similarity, correlations between class voting and certain other social characteristics are more plausible as casual relationships, since the correlations cannot be ascribed to gross differences of social or political structure.

For comparative purposes, some of these socio-economic measures are given for the other European or English-speaking stable democracies as well (for Belgium, Denmark, Ireland, New Zealand, the Netherlands, Norway, Sweden, and Switzerland).[3] Although the comparisons with these other countries will not be discussed separately, it may be noted that in almost every instance, each of the four Anglo-American countries here analyzed is more urbanized, has a higher per capita income, and a higher percentage of employed males in the non-agricultural labor force, than the average of the other stable European democracies. Since the European and English-speaking democracies are far more "developed" than any other group of countries in turn, it is clear that these four countries are among the most economically developed and wealthy countries in the world.

In spite of the gross similarities of wealth and industrialization, even differences in the level of economic growth and development seem to be consistent with differences in the level of class voting. The countries with higher levels of class voting are expanding more slowly—which may reduce opportunities, restrict mobility, and therefore maintain the solidarity of classes to a greater degree. On four related measures of economic growth, the rank order was Australia (lowest), Great Britain, the United States, and Canada.[4]

All other factors being equal, we might expect that more urbanized societies (and societies which had been urbanized for a longer period of time) would have higher levels of class voting than less urbanized societies. A considerable amount of sociological and political research has indicated that urbanism breaks down loyalties to community, region, and religion, and substitutes class loyalties as the basis for political behavior.[5] We might also

[2] See, for example, Thomas O. Wilkinson, "Urban Structure and Industrialization," *American Sociological Review*, XXV (June 1960), 358, in which data from forty-nine nations are compared.

[3] For other indexes of wealth, urbanization, industrialization, and education, including figures for Latin-American and European unstable democracies and dictatorships, see Seymour M. Lipset, *Political Man* (New York: Doubleday, 1960), pp. 51–54.

[4] The measures showed the rise per year (in the post-World War II years) in gross domestic product, gross national product, net domestic product, and net national product. Measures of investment and savings rates were also fairly consistent for both the late nineteenth and early twentieth century periods, but ratios indicating net capital formation were not consistent with class voting. See Simon Kuznets, "Quantitative Aspects of the Economic Growth of Nations," V: "Capital Formation Proportions: International Comparisons for Recent Years" and VI: "Long-Term Trends in Capital Formation Proportions," *Economic Development and Cultural Change*, VII, Part II (July 1960), 1–96, and IX, Part II (July 1961), 1–124.

[5] The works of the political scientist A. N. Holcombe are the American classics taking this point of view. See his *The New Party Politics* (New York: Norton, 1933), and *The Middle Classes in American Politics* (Cambridge: Harvard University Press, 1940).

expect that relatively poorer societies with a relatively larger working class would have higher levels of class voting, simply on the grounds that class interests would be more explicit, and working class parties more easily organized.

Also, more "closed" societies—societies with lower levels of educational opportunities, less chance for upward social mobility, and less chance for individuals to "escape" via a frontier—might have a higher level of class voting. In these four societies, where education is a real symbol of class status, lack of educational opportunities for bright working-class children might strongly reinforce class voting (and this might be the case even though in actual fact as many workingclass children move up into nonmanual positions) for both manual and non-manual voters. Manual workers would be more likely to vote Left out of resentment; nonmanuals would be more likely to vote Right as a symbol of their privilege. If, in addition, there were important differences in the character of social mobility (despite the similarities in over-all rates. . . .), the objective gap between social classes might be greater in one society than another.

Another aspect of a "closed" society—the lack of a frontier—also should increase class voting. Where no escape is possible from the urban class struggle, manual workers stay and fight. Where open land is available, many who might form the leadership of working-class organizations leave.

Clearly these factors are not necessarily independent, and where they all exist, class voting should be reinforced accordingly. Relatively poor, highly urbanized societies where manual workers have little educational opportunity and few avenues for escape should have high levels of class voting. And in fact such is the case. It is impossible here to explore these relationships deeply and establish in fact their independent effect upon class voting, but the data available are highly suggestive. Statistics on each of the factors mentioned show that the rank order on each factor is almost the same as the rank order of class voting.

The extent of urbanization of a society is itself an index of many other social processes, which can be interpreted in various ways, but the statistics are quite consistent both for recent times and in the late nineteenth century. If urbanization is an index of the extent to which the population is freed from traditional ties to locality and church, and therefore is rendered susceptible to class appeals, then at least as far back as 1890 the British have been less traditionalist in these respects than any of these other three peoples. The striking fact about these statistics is that on every index of urbanization, the rank order is almost exactly the same as that of class voting. Several indexes of urbanization are given, and the consistency for several such measures shows that the result is not an artifact of the particular way of computing the urban proportion of the population. See Table 11.3.

Another measure of lack of traditionalism associated with urbanization is the birth rate. In countries which have lost the rural traditions of big families and the exclusively family-centered pattern of social life, birth rates have dropped fairly consistently. And persons less exposed to such traditional family controls—more willing to restrict their family size—are presumably less likely to respond to political appeals in traditional, non-class

TABLE 11.3 CUMULATIVE PERCENTAGE OF THE POPULATION LIVING IN CITIES OF DIFFERENT SIZES, 1890 AND C. 1950

	CUMULATIVE PERCENTAGE OF POPULATION IN CITIES, BY SIZE				
	1890				
COUNTRY	2000+	10,000+	20,000+	20–100,000	100,000+
England and Wales	72.0	61.7	53.6	21.8	31.8
Scotland	65.4	49.9	42.4	12.6	29.8
Australia (7 colonies)	—	41.4	38.8	9.7	29.1
United States	37.7	27.6	23.8	8.3	15.5
Canada	27.3	17.1	14.2	6.0	8.2

	1950				IN METRO-POLITAN AREAS
COUNTRY	2000+	10,000+	20,000+	100,000+	
United Kingdom (1951)	79.7	74.0	66.9	36.1	77.0
Australia (1947)	71.5	55.4	43.9	51.4	55.4
United States (1950)	59.8	49.0	43.0	29.4	55.9
Canada (1951)	50.7	40.2	35.1	23.3	45.5
Other European stable democracies	—	—	38.0	23.3	33.7

SOURCES: The 1890 figures are from Adna F. Weber, *The Growth of Cities in the 19th Century* ("Columbia Studies in History, Economics and Public Law," Vol. XI [New York: Macmillan, 1891]), p. 144. The *circa* 1950 figures are taken from Jack P. Gibbs and Kingsley Davis, "Conventional versus Metropolitan Data in the International Study of Urbanization," *American Sociological Review*, XXIII (October 1958), 506–507.

ways. If such a relationship holds for the Anglo-American countries, it is even more likely to be significant, because these countries are already among the least traditional countries in which the birth rate is already lower than in most countries of the world. But, in fact, the Anglo-American countries with the lowest birth rates have the highest levels of class voting. See Table

TABLE 11.4 RANGE OF CRUDE BIRTH RATE, 1947–1955[a]

COUNTRY	RANGE OF CRUDE BIRTH RATE
Great Britain	15.4–20.7
Australia	22.5–24.1
United States	23.5–25.8
Canada	27.1–28.9

SOURCE: United Nations, *Demographic Yearbook* (New York, 1956), Table 20, pp. 610–621.

[a] The consistency over a period of eight years in the differences between the countries shows that the differences are not due to some yearly variation. Since differences in the age structure of these countries are not great, the crude birth rate may be used here. The same rank order is found when measures which control for age and sex composition (either the intrinsic birth rate or the net reproduction rate) are computed.

11.4. It may be noted that the sharpest difference in birth rates is between the "Old World" and the "New" even though the rank order is the same.

The differences in per capita income between these countries show that the poorer countries—Australia and Great Britain—have higher levels of class voting. See Table 11.5. Further research might show that the pattern of *distribution* of wealth is also more uneven in those countries than in the United States and Canada.

TABLE 11.5　PER CAPITA INCOME, c. 1950

COUNTRY	PER CAPITA INCOME (United States Dollars)
Great Britain	773
Australia	679
United States	1453
Canada	870
Other European stable democracies	658

SOURCE: United Nations, Statistical Office, *National and Per Capita Income in 70 Countries* 1949 (Statistical Papers, Series E, No. 1 [New York, 1950]), pp. 14–16.

The relative size of the middle class in the Anglo-American countries may also be related to class voting. It would seem natural that a country with a larger middle class would have less class voting. Regardless of the level of Left voting of manual workers, the middle class is more likely to vote Left in such a country (and therefore reduce the gap between the Left vote of manual and non-manual strata) for two reasons. First, in a country with a small middle class, the members are more likely to think of themselves as occupying a favored position vis-à-vis workers and therefore are more likely to vote Right. Second, in a country with a large middle class, many members are "fresh" from the working class and might be expected to retain their traditional Left allegiances for a certain period of time. These two factors would tend to raise the Left vote among persons in non-manual occupations. Therefore, we should expect that the Anglo-American countries with higher

TABLE 11.6　MALES IN THE NON-AGRICULTURAL LABOR FORCE IN TERTIARY INDUSTRY, 1950

COUNTRY	MALES IN TERTIARY INDUSTRY[a] (Percent)
Great Britain	42
Australia	47
United States	50
Canada	48

SOURCE: International Urban Research, Berkeley, California.

a "Tertiary industry" includes workers in commerce and finance, transport and communication services, and other service industries. The term "tertiary" is taken from Colin Clark, The *Conditions of Economic Progress* (New York: St. Martin's Press, 1940).

levels of class voting—Australia and Great Britain—should have a smaller middle class proportionately.

Some evidence of this does exist, again although these four countries are very highly industrialized and urbanized and therefore very much alike ... where the industrial distribution of their popoulations was given. This table does show slight differences between the countries, however, which are in almost the same order as the level of class voting. Combining the "tertiary" industries ..., the obtained results are as shown in Table 11.6. The United States has the highest proportion of workers in tertiary industries; otherwise the rank order is the same as the order of class voting. (It may be noted also ... that the percentage of males in the non-agricultural labor force is also almost in the rank order of class voting.)

Another indicator of the proportion of middle-class or white-collar workers is the proportion of salaried employees to wage-earners in manufacturing establishments. Table 11.7 shows that the countries with higher levels of class voting have a lower proportion of salaried workers to wage-earners. Admittedly, the rank order here is not the same as that of class voting, but in none of these correlations do the two countries highest in class voting change positions with either of the countries lowest in class voting.

TABLE 11.7   RATIO OF SALARIED WORKERS TO WAGE-EARNERS IN MANUFAC-
TURING ESTABLISHMENTS, 1954–1957

COUNTRY	MANUFACTURING ESTABLISHMENTS (000's)	WAGE-EARNERS (000's)	SALARIED	RATIO
Great Britain	57.2	6,216	1,406	0.22
Australia	52.8	870	135	0.16
United States	300.0	13,135	4,044	0.30
Canada	37.4	1,052	301	0.28

SOURCE: United Nations, *Statistical Yearbook* (New York, 1958), pp. 157–63. Data from previous years are given in the same table. The British data are for the other countries are for 1956–1967.

Educational opportunities are quite different in the four countries, and again, in the same direction as the level of class voting. The countries with higher class voting have fewer students per 1000 in the population in either higher education or primary education, as Table 11.8 shows, and Great Britain and Australia are below the other European democracies in this respect.

The greater opportunities for education in the United States and Canada than Britain and Australia suggest that the character of social mobility must be quite different in the former countries, in spite of the gross similarity of movement. ... Possibly, "... the distance moved occupationally is commensurately greater [in the United States and Canada]; or, because of increased educational achievement in the United States, manual to non-manual occupational mobility involves traversing a greater social distance than a com-

TABLE 11.8   STUDENTS IN HIGHER EDUCATION AND IN PRIMARY EDUCATION, 1000 POPULATION, c. 1950

COUNTRY	STUDENTS PER 1000 POPULATION IN	
	Higher Education	Primary Education
Great Britain	1.6	90
Australia	2.9	131
United States	17.8	124
Canada	5.4	138
Other European stable democracies	3.2	113

SOURCE: Figures on higher education are from UNESCO, *World Survey of Education* (Paris, 1955), pp. 24–25. Figures on primary education are from United Nations, *A Preliminary Report on the World Social Situation* (New York, 1952), pp. 86–98.

parable move in Western Europe.[6] In spite of the similarity of over-all rates of social mobility, it is possible that such differences as exist may help account for differences in the level of class voting—if mobility is relatively low where class voting is high. Unfortunately few truly comparable data exist.[7] However, more elaborate distinctions between types of mobility and directions of movement show some international variations which may be of significance in interpreting the data on class voting.

While upward mobility (the movement of sons of fathers in manual—including farming and working-class urban—occupations into non-manual occupations) is fairly similar in Great Britain and the United States, downward mobility of the sons of non-manual fathers is far higher in Britain. Of the "manual" British fathers, 25 percent have "non-manual" sons. The comparable figure is 29 percent in the United States. However, 42 percent of the sons of non-manual fathers are in manual positions in Britain, as compared to only 25 percent of the sons of non-manual fathers in the United States.[8]

The greater downward rate of mobility in Great Britain—the replenishing of the manual working class from the non-manual strata—may be a significant cause of the higher level of class voting in that country. Miller raises the question: "Is it true that the easier the drop, the more the concern with status and social distance?" If such a constant interchange between strata

[6] H. Feldman, "Economic Development and Social Mobility," *Economic Development and Cultural Change*, VIII (April 1960), 316. This hypothesis is only one of several suggested by Feldman to account for the seeming contradiction between the findings that mobility rates are equal in highly industrialized countries, that education is a key path for upward mobility, and yet that educational opportunities are so different.

[7] One study comparing a British with an American study found that mobility was actually slightly higher in Britain for each of three occupational status categories (the proportion of sons remaining in their father's status), However, the authors note that the American sample was urban, the British sample national, and that "the biases almost certainly produce an artificially high index of association" of sons' and fathers' occupations for the United States. See J. R. Hall and W. Ziegel, "A Comparison of Social Mobility Data for England and Wales, Italy, France and the U.S.A." in David Glass, ed., *Social Mobility in Britain* (London: Routledge & Kegan Paul, 1953), p. 265.

[8] See S. M. Miller, "Comparative Social Mobility," *Current Sociology*, IX, No. 1 (1960), p. 36.

occurs, then downwardly mobile Britishers must become Labour voters very quickly (and vice versa). . . .[9]

If, regardless of how *many* of the manual workers achieve non-manual status in a given generation, there is a relatively large drop-back of non-manual persons into the manual strata, the impetus for class voting would seem to be reinforced. Recent recruits to the non-manual strata might feel that they had an insecure hold upon their new status and try to adopt the political attitudes they felt to be appropriate to their position; whereas the manual workers, both those in stable positions and those recently downwardly mobile, might react negatively to their experiences by higher rates of Left voting.

The only Canadian study of intergenerational mobility was done in the province of Quebec. The authors did find, however, that urban French-Canadians had about the same rate of mobility as was found in national studies in France, England, and the United States. This conclusion may or may not be generalizable to Canada as a whole.[10]

Comparison of Britain with the United States in the level of "elite mobility" indicates that in this respect also mobility is higher in the United States. Miller analyzed the rate of movement into "elite" occupations (the higher business and independent professional occupations) and found that the rate of movement of *both* manual and non-manual strata into the highest occupational positions was higher in the United States than in Britain.[11] Thus, both a crude measure of intergenerational mobility from "manual" to "non-manual" occupations, and a more refined measure of movement into the highest positions indicate differences between Britain and the United States that seem consistent with the variation between countries in class voting patterns.[12]

Political appeals on class lines may evoke a more homogeneous response in Britain and Australia than in the other countries—if there is greater objective stratification *within* working-class occupations where class voting is lower. Some evidence for this is found in the smaller gap between the

[9] Miller. p. 33. Australia also had the pattern of high upward mobility and high downward mobility, but data were available only for Melbourne, not for national samples as in Britain and the United States. Two United States studies found the pattern of high upward mobility and low downward mobility. No study was available to Miller for Canada, and therefore it is impossible to determine whether the patterns of mobility are completely consistent with the level of class voting.

[10] Yves de Jocas and Guy Rocher, "Inter-Generation Occupational Mobility in the Province of Quebec," *Canadian Journal of Economics and Political Science,* XXIII (February 1957), 66. English-Canadians had a much higher rate of mobility than French-Canadians in this study. Unfortunately, the Quebec data were only for an urban sample. If urban mobility rates are higher than rural rates in such societies, as seems likely, then the over-all national rates might be quite similar. An important area for further research is a comparison of rural vs. urban mobility rates. International gross similarities may conceal sharp internal differences in rural-urban rates, differences related to the speed and direction of industrialization and the rates of internal migration to small areas (urbanization).

[11] Miller, p. 38.

[12] Miller, (p. 36) computed an index of "inequality of opportunity," which showed that opportunities were most unequal in Britain, less in Australia, and least in the United States. On the other hand an index of "equality of opportunity" was almost the same, reflecting the fact that the life-chances of middle-class sons in Great Britain were lower than in any of the eighteen countries for which data were available.

wages of skilled workers and those of unskilled workers in the United Kingdom and Australia than in Canada and the United States.[13] A difference in the
wage-rates of skilled and unskilled workers might be expected to have political consequences—skilled workers being less likely to vote Left in countries
where the skilled are much more highly paid than the unskilled, and vice
versa where the income differential is small. Lack of differentiation of the
working class might also demarcate the line between worker and middle
class more sharply, since it seems unlikely that the similarity of wages of
skilled and unskilled would bring them both closer to the non-manual level
rather than farther from it.[14]

The almost complete absence of class voting in Canada cannot be explained by relatively greater economic security of the working classes if a
gross measure of unemployment can be considered a rough criterion. A
careful compilation of available statistics on unemployment rates in the three
Commonwealth countries between 1916 and 1950 shows that while unemployment rates were lower in Canada than in either Australia or the United
Kingdom for thirteen of the sixteen years between 1916 and 1931, unemployment was actually higher in Canada than in either of the other countries in
sixteen of the nineteen years between 1932 and 1950.[15] Unless it be argued
that the non-class character of the Canadian parties was determined prior to
the Great Depression, and that therefore the present lack of class differentiation is a "cultural lag," the low level of Canadian class voting cannot be explained by any great insulation of Canadian workers from the vicissitudes of
the business cycle . . . cultural factors largely account for the Canadian
pattern.

The extent to which these countries have "frontiers" which offer an
escape from intense class struggles and a safety valve reducing the strains of
political conflict (and therefore class voting) is difficult to judge. According
to most historians, the United States and Canada are the classic frontier
countries, having great expanses of land to the west. Their lower levels of
class voting are therefore understandable for yet another reason. Great Britain,
enclosed within its island, clearly is not a frontier country, and therefore its

[13] A comparison of the average wage of unskilled urban laborers with the average
wage of five types of skilled workers (furniture-makers, engineers, garage mechanics, construction workers, and truck drivers) found that the gap was almost uniformly narrower in
1953 in both Britain and Australia than in either the United States or Canada. Fifteen of eighteen possible comparisons were in this direction. See Colin Clark, *The Conditions of Economic Progress*, 3d ed. (New York: St. Martin's Press, 1957), pp. 526–531. Similar figures
are given for over forty other countries. It may be noted that the pattern was the same in New
Zealand, where class voting is also apparently high, as in Britain and Australia.

[14] In 1940, at least, the average wage of unskilled laborers was lower in Britain and
Australia than in the United States and Canada. See Karl Deutsch, *Nationalism and Social
Communications* (New York: Wiley, 1953), p. 36. The real question, however, may be
whether wages of manual workers are *relatively* lower than others. Political reactions may
be due largely to relative, not absolute, deprivation.

[15] Walter Galenson and Arnold Zellner, "International Comparison of Unemployment
Rates" in National Bureau of Economic Research, *The Measurement and Behavior of Unemployment* (Princeton: Princeton University Press, 1957), pp. 455–56. The monograph deals
with six other countries as well, and over a slightly longer period of time for some of the
nine, and contains extensive methodological discussion. Data were not available for the
United States.

high level of class voting is reinforced on this score also. Australia is perhaps the more puzzling case because of its wide areas of uninhabited land.

Yet Australia is not a "frontier" country in any acceptable sense of the word. Its unpopulated areas have practically no rainfall and are not really available for "frontier" purposes. Australia is actually an urban country, par excellence. It has the highest proportion of its population of any of the four countries in six cities of over 100,000 population—the capitals of the six states. It is second only to Great Britain in the proportion of the population in cities over 20,000, and only a shade under the United States (but considerably under Great Britain) in the proportion of its population in "Standard Metropolitan Areas." Canada, by contrast, is lowest on all of the urbanization indexes. This high level of urbanization, combined with the lack of real opportunities in the unpopulated areas, imply that Australia is not a true frontier country. Its relatively high level of class voting is therefore not inconsistent with this factor.

In the search for possible causes of the differences in class voting between the Anglo-American countries, a number of fairly consistent correlations have fit our expectations as to factors which should affect class voting. In general, the poorer and more urbanized societies also have a slightly smaller proportion of the labor force in "middle-class" occupations, have lower educational and other opportunities, and offer less opportunity to escape via the frontier. They also have higher levels of class voting, which seems rather understandable.

SUMMARY

Consistent and striking differences between the Anglo-American countries in the level of class voting . . . have been found. These differences exist despite similarities of class and political structure and the maintenance of consensus on the parties and the form of government. Correlations between the level of class voting and various social factors such as: (1) the degree of urbanization, (2) the proportion of middle-class persons in the labor force, (3) the per capita income, (4) educational opportunities, (5) mobility, (6) income stratification among workers, and others are consistent with expectations concerning possible causes of class voting.

12

Social Structural Bases
of Political Partisanship
in West Germany
and the United States*

DAVID R. SEGAL

INTRODUCTION

As a major sociopolitical doctrine in the industrializing West, Marxism has had great impact on the research and theory of political sociology and behavioral political science.[1] Particularly, a great deal of research energy has been expended on establishing the nature and degree of relationship between social class and political partisanship in Western democracies.[2] Historical developments have made the study of Communist Party organizations per se less relevant in such countries. In Italy, for example, the Communists have increasingly tried to elicit a base of support among that portion of the bourgeoisie not involved in industrial monopolies,[3] while in West Germany, the Communist

---

* Reprinted, by permission of the Editors, from *Comparative Studies in Society and History,* Vol. X, No. 1 (October 1967), pp. 66–84. The present paper is an extension of the article which appeared as "Classes, Strata and Parties in West Germany and the United States."

[1] For a discussion of the role of Marxist thought in political sociology, see Morris Janowitz, "Political Sociology," *International Encyclopedia of the Social Sciences* (forthcoming).

[2] See for example, Bernard R. Berelson et al., *Voting* (Chicago: University of Chicago Press, 1954), pp. 55–56; Angus Campbell et al., *The American Voter* (New York: Wiley, 1960), pp. 333 ff.; Robert R. Alford, *Party and Society* (Skokie, Ill.: Rand McNally, 1963).

[3] See Joseph LaPalombara, "Decline of Ideology: A Dissent and an Interpretation," *American Political Science Review,* Vol. LX, No. 1 (March 1966), pp. 5–16.

party was outlawed in 1956, and in recent years, the Social Democratic party has tried to change its public image from a workers' party to that of a popular party. The Bad Godesberg program was one manifestation of this effort.

Nonetheless, the relevance of traditional Marxian class-conflict categories is still argued by some, although most current debate in the field is focused on the implications for Marxist sociology of trends in the industrial sphere that Marx did not foresee—notably high rates of mobility into the middle class, separation of ownership from management in capitalist enterprise, and the increased power of labor both in a bargaining relationship with management and directly in production decisions.[4] The arena of debate is defined largely by the difference between the "middle-mass" theories and the "consensus and cleavage" approach to political partisanship, and this difference is more one of degree than of kind. The "middle-mass" theorists argue that as the labor force becomes concentrated in the upper-working class and lower-middle class, and management as well as labor becomes separated from capital ownership, the life styles of the two classes will become homogenized, ideological politics will decline, and political life will become increasingly consensual.[5] The "consensus and cleavage" orientation acknowledges the changing social structure of Western society, but argues for recognition of emergent bases of political cleavage and ideological dissensus unrelated to traditional social class notions.[6]

Studies that utilize the concept of class, whether they base their definition on broad occupational position (blue collar versus white collar) or on subjective class identification, continue to show that some relationship exists between real or perceived economic position and political partisanship.[7] Specifically, membership in or identification with the working class is found to be associated with affiliation with the "left" major party: the Democratic party in the United States, the Social Democratic party in West Germany, the Labour party in England, and so on. Indeed, Hamilton has demonstrated that at equivalent income levels, the political choices of members of the German working class and middle class were quite different, the workers being more similar to other lower-paid workers than to members of the middleclass of similar income.[8] It is our assumption, however, that such studies do not di-

[4] George Lichtheim argues for the applicability of Marxian categories in "Class and Hierarchy: A Critique of Marx," *Archives Européenes de Sociologie*, Tome 5, numéro 1 (1964), pp. 101–112. Changes in industrial society that make Marx appear less relevant are discussed in Ralf Dahrendorf, *Class and Class Conflict in Industrial Society* (Stanford: Stanford University Press, 1959), pp. 36–71; Joseph Schumpeter, *Capitalism, Socialism and Democracy* (New York: Harper & Row, 1962), pp. 59 ff.

[5] See for example Seymour Martin Lipset, "The Changing Class Structure and Contemporary European Politics," *Daedalus*, Vol. 93 (Winter 1964), pp. 271–303, and Robert E. Lane, "The Politics of Consensus in an Age of Affluence," *American Political Science Review*, Vol. LIX, No. 4 (December 1965), pp. 875–894.

[6] For a discussion of these issues see Morris Janowitz and David R. Segal, "Social Cleavage and Party Affiliation," *American Journal of Sociology*, Vol. 72, No. 6 (May 1967), pp. 601–618.

[7] See Alford, *Party and Society*, pp. 225–231; Campbell et al., *The American Voter*, pp. 346 ff.

[8] Richard F. Hamilton, "Affluence and the Worker: The West German Case." *American Journal of Sociology*, Vol. 71, No. 2 (September 1965), p. 150. For other indications of this phenomenon in Germany and in other Western democracies see Hamilton, *The Social*

rectly confront the hypothesized relationship between economic substructure and political superstructure because while they accept the methodology of Marxist sociology and choose economic indicators as independent variables, they reject Marxist economics, and choose indicators other than those specified in Marx's theory. A reevaluation of class as a historical as well as a sociological concept should enable us to explain differentials in the persistence of class-based politics in Western democracies as well as differentials in the emergence of alternative bases of social cleavage.

Class conflict, for Marx, was not a product of capitalist society, but an enduring state of human organization. "The history of all hitherto existing society is the history of class struggles."[9] The class conflict of industrial society, in the Marxian view, is seen as a stage in the historical progression of conflict in which the "manifold gradation of social rank" prevalent under feudalism is simplified into a dichotomization of social rank based upon ownership of the means of production. We would thus, at a minimum, expect differences in the extent of class based politics among Western democracies to be related to differences in the structural complexity of the feudal organization that existed prior to capitalist industrialization. Since Marxism postulates a continuity of classes through the dialectical process of history, with the capitalist bourgeoisie developing out of the burgher classes in the earliest towns, and these in turn springing from the serfs in the Middle Ages, class politics in this instance must be seen in terms of capital ownership relations. However, as we shall see below, industrial authority relations serve as bases of political differentiation both in the industrial West and in modern Communist states despite the bifurcation of ownership and management in these systems.[10] We therefore reject the assumption that census occupational categories or crude differentiations of white-collar and blue-collar jobs are operationalizations of the Marxian notion of class.

Central to the Marxian notion of class conflict is the concept of class consciousness. Class, to Marx, did not imply consciousness. Indeed, prior to the revolution of the proletarians, the wage-workers existed as a social class. It was the development of class consciousness that transformed the wage earner class into a politically relevant proletariat. The extent to which social class identification as measured in contemporary social surveys is a reflection of ownership of productive facilities is an empirical question. We know that working-class men tend to aspire to self-employment.[11] Insofar as middle-class identification is associated with selfemployment, some degree of blue-

---

Bases of French Working Class Politics (unpublished Ph.D. dissertation, Columbia University, 1963), chapter 8; Juan J. Linz, The Social Bases of West German Politics (unpublished Ph.D. dissertation, Columbia University, 1959), chapter 9; Seymour Martin Lipset, Political Man (New York: Doubleday, 1960), pp. 239–240.

[9] Karl Marx and Friedrich Engels, The Manifesto of the Communist Party.

[10] These issues are discussed by Dahrendorf, Class and Class Conflict in Industrial Society, pp. 241 ff.; Schumpeter, Capitalism, Socialism and Democracy, pp. 72 ff.; A. A. Berle and Gardner Means, The Modern Corporation and Private Property (New York: Crowell-Collier-Macmillan, 1963); Talcott Parsons and Neil J. Smelser, Economy and Society (New York: Free Press, 1965) pp. 252–255; Rinehard Bendix, Work and Authority in Industry (New York: Harper & Row, 1963); Milovan Djilas, The New Class (New York: Praeger, 1957).

[11] See for example Seymour Martin Lipset and Reinhard Bendix, Social Mobility in Industrial Society (Berkeley: University of California Press, 1960), p. 178.

collar identification with the party of the right may be explicable in terms of Marx's theory. It has been previously demonstrated that independent small businessmen support the parties of the right.[12] Our test of the Marxian hypothesis then must define class in terms of property relations, and must deal with the questions of historical continuity and the bases of class identi-fication. These, in turn, may be rooted in the histories of labor movements in the nations involved. It is thus necessary for us to consider the relationship between union affiliation and subjective class identification, and the degree to which organized labor opposed the social order rather than attempting to improve the worker's lot within it.

Similarly, the role of religion in political life must must be viewed in an historical context if one is to consider the relevance of Marxian proposi-tions to the analysis of Western politics. Marx's condemnation of religion as the opiate of the people was not a rejection of the religious institution per se any more than his analysis of capitalism was a rejection of economic princi-ples. Rather, he viewed the alliances between specific churches and the bourgeoisie as bases for false ideologies that left the workers complacent with their exploited condition. To the extent that such historical alliances do not exist, however, religious bodies may be seen as representing the interests of the working class or as an emergent basis of political cleavage independent of social class considerations.[13]

While one of our primary concerns here is in empirically testing, with behavioral data, the propositions of historical materialism, bases of political differentiation other than class must be identified and studied if only be-cause industrial social structures have changed in ways unforeseen by Marx. At a minimum, we may differentiate between social cleavage based upon class and that based upon status. Here we utilize Weber's definition of status as determined by social estimation of honor.[14] Unlike class, social status is not necessarily based upon market position, but upon style of life. The proposi-tion that social honor may be independent of market position is supported by studies of occupational prestige in the United States. On the basis of data collected by the National Opinion Research Center, Hodge and his associates found that scientists, government officials and professionals have higher social status than do members of the boards of directors of large corporations, and that these relations have been relatively constant since at least 1947. Among blue-collar workers there was no indication that prestige was based upon owning one's own business. The owner-operator of a printing shop had the same status as a trained machinist, and the owner-operator of a lunchstand had the same prestige rating as barbers, factory machine operators, corporals in the regular army, and garage mechanics.[15] There is evidence however, that these relations do not hold cross-nationally. A comparative

---

12 See for example Stanley Hoffman, *Le Mouvement Poujade* (Paris: Colin, 1956).

13 The current dialogue between the Catholic Church and leading Communist theoreticians in Western Europe is indicative of the willingness of neo-Marxists to accept theology as something other than class-based ideology. See Roger Garaudy, *From Anathema to Dialogue* (New York: Herder and Herder, 1966).

14 Max Weber, *Wirtschaft und Gesellschaft*, Part III, chapter 4, p. 635.

15 Robert W. Hodge, Paul M. Siegel and Peter H. Rossi, "Occupational Prestige in the United States: 1925–1963," in Reinhard Bendix and Seymour Martin Lipset, eds., *Class, Status and Power*, 2d ed. (New York: Free Press, 1966), pp. 322–334.

study that included data from the United States and Germany revealed that while the prestige structures were similar in the two countries for white-collar occupations ($r^2 = 0.85$), the relative ranking for blue-collar occupations yielded the smallest relationship in the entire study ($r^2 = 0.42$).[16] This differential in an area that both over time and cross-nationally yields little variation suggests that, at least for blue-collar workers, Marxian notions of class relations may be more important in the understanding of social position in Germany than in the United States. It should be noted that while we argue for the potential independence of status from class, we do not fully accept the notion that social strata, as the aggregates of individuals sharing given social statuses, are merely categories for "describing hierarchical systems at a given point in time."[17] Indeed, we are prepared to argue that status differences may serve as bases of persisting political differentiation, and even of ideological cleavage.

BACKGROUND AND PROPOSITIONS

Our choice of West Germany and the United States as units for comparative analysis was based upon both pragmatic and theoretical considerations. In the first instance, they are the nations with which the researcher had the most intimate knowledge. Secondly, we were familiar with large data archives available for secondary analysis in each country.[18] Finally, we had collaborated earlier on a more limited attempt at comparative analysis along the present lines, and felt that our accomplishments in that earlier effort justified further research.[19]

On the other hand, the histories of these two nations differ in precisely those respects that will enable us to consider the relationships between historical variations and contemporary partisan structures. We are not arguing here that such relationships can be ultimately tested on the basis of the experiences of these two nations. Indeed, it should be possible to test these notions using data from a large number of nations. The present effort, however, exemplifies the kind of comparative analysis that can be undertaken through the juxtaposition of historical and survey data. Moreover, we argue specifically for the utilization of paired comparisons, with analyses carried out *within* countries and comparisons *between* them. The alternate strategy—

---

[16] Robert W. Hodge, Donald J. Treiman and Peter H. Rossi, "A Comparative Study of Occupational Prestige," in Bendix and Lipset, *Social Mobility in Industrial Society*, pp. 309–321.

[17] Dahrendorf, *Class and Class Conflict in Industrial Society*, p. 76.

[18] The German data were collected by the Institut für angewandte Sozialwissenschaft between January 1963 and April 1964. I am grateful to Klaus Liepelt for access to these data. The American data were collected by the Survey Research Center, University of Michigan, and were made available to us through the Inter-University Consortium for Political Research.

[19] See Morris Janowitz, Klaus Liepelt and David R. Segal, "An Approach to the Comparative Analysis of Political Partisanship," paper given at the Sixth World Congress of Sociology, Evian, France, September 1966.

that of carrying out multivariate analyses among *nations*, as though they were elements of a sample—obscures the very historical idiosyncracies that we are trying to preserve.

The Feudal Backgrounds

It is difficult to imagine two Western nations that differ more in their historical backgrounds. Germany was the center of the Holy Roman Empire at least as far back as 824 A.D., and while the Empire as a political form can be said to have terminated with the revolt of the Church against political domination in the early eleventh century, or with the beheading of Konradin in 1268, feudalism remained the dominant form of social organization in the German domains at least through the sixteenth century, although the formal institutions of feudalism, primarily vassalage and the law of the fief, were less bound up in the structure of society here than in other areas of Europe.[20] It might be argued that feudalism was in fact stronger following the collapse of the Empire, since highly centralized authority probably mitigated against the full utilization of feudal privilege at the local level. Under the Hohenzollerns, class relations in Prussia were feudal in form into the nineteenth century, and it was common for peasants to owe compulsory service on the estates of the nobility. One of the major legacies of this agrarian feudal organization was that Germany did not develop a large commercial middle class until relatively late in its history—after the middle of the nineteenth century. Thus, the "middle-mass", so important to contemporary theories of consensus politics, is a recent phenomenon in Germany.

The social structure of the United States, on the other hand, had a very different history. A much younger country, America was born with a large middle class. A great majority of the population were small property owners. At the same time, the wealthier class held a much smaller proportion of the national wealth than has been the case in more recent times, and a very small proportion of the population were wageworkers.[21]

We are not arguing here that all historical differences must necessarily be related to differences in present day patterns of partisanship. Rather we argue that the effects of historical patterns on contemporary phenomena may be seen through two manifest linkages. On the first hand, despite convergences in the technologies of industrialized Western nations, the present social structure of any single country must be seen in part as the product of historical trends within that country. Table 12.1 presents the industrial distributions of the labor forces of West Germany and the United States. While certain similarities are evident, particularly in the areas of transportation, utilities and construction, there are several important differences. The legacy of the peasant agricultural past of Germany is reflected in the proportion of its current population that is involved in agriculture; a figure more than twice

---

[20] For a discussion of German feudalism, see Marc Bloch, *Feudal Society*, trans. by L. A. Manyon, Vol. 1 (Chicago: University of Chicago Press, 1964), pp. 179 ff. Note that the Empire existed as a social entity until 1806, when it was destroyed by Napoleon.

[21] See Jackson T. Main, "The Class Structure of Revolutionary America," in Bendix and Lipset, *Social Mobility in Industrial Society*, pp. 111–121.

TABLE 12.1   PERCENTAGE DISTRIBUTION OF LABOR FORCES OF WEST GERMANY AND THE UNITED STATES, BY INDUSTRY

INDUSTRY	WEST GERMANY	UNITED STATES
Agriculture	13.4	6.6
Manufacturing	37.2	26.9
Construction	7.5	6.2
Utilities, sanitary services and mining	3.0	2.4
Commerce	13.4	21.9
Transport	5.5	5.4
Service	8.5	20.4
Unclassified	11.5	10.2
Total	100.0%	100.0%
N	26,821,112	68,877,476

SOURCE: United Nations, *Demographic Yearbook, 1964* (New York: Statistical Office of the United Nations, 1965), 255–256, 275.

as large as the same parameter for the United States. The United States, with a commercial heritage, still has a larger proportion of its population engaged in commerce than does Germany. The fact of America's earlier industrialization is reflected in the shift of its labor force into the tertiary service industries.[22] The German labor force is more heavily concentrated in secondary manufacturing industries. This difference has important implications for the degree to which authority relations in the two countries are class-based. Germany, with a greater agricultural and manufacturing labor force has a proportionately larger group of manual workers, while the United States, with its concentration in commerce and in service industries has a preponderance of white-collar functionaries. Therefore, industrial authority relations are more likely to cross manual-nonmanual lines in Germany than in the United States. We hypothesize that because of this difference, the German major party of the left, the Social Democratic party (SPD), is more likely to have a traditional working-class base than the American major party of the left, the Democratic party.

Secondly, because class relations have historically been more strongly polarized in Germany than the United States, we suggest that class identifications are likely to persist longer through the generations in the former than in the latter. Lipset and Bendix found that the proportion of sons of manual workers who achieved nonmanual positions was between 26 and 30 percent in Germany, and between 31 and 35 percent in the United States.[23] This rather minimal difference, we suspect, is amplified by the fact that an American upwardly mobile from the working class is more likely to assume a middle-class identification than is an upwardly mobile German, who is more likely to retain an identification with the class of his origin. We hypothesize then that the social class of one's father will prove to be a more important determinant of partisanship in Germany than in the United States.

[22] See Harold L. Wilensky and Charles N. Lebeaux, *Industrial Society and Social Welfare* (New York: Free Press, 1965), pp. 93 ff.

[23] See Lipset and Bendix, *Social Mobility in Industrial Society,* pp. 17–23.

Religious Cleavages

The meaning of religious differences in Germany and the United States is also a function of historical experiences. In Germany, there was a historical alliance between the feudal nobility and the Catholic Church, dating at least as far back as the tenth century, when counties were granted as fiefs to bishops. At this time, there was no religious cleavage because there was no religious differentiation. In the sixteenth century, however, the German peasantry, largely in response to Martin Luther's criticisms of the Roman Church, revolted against the Empire and the Church. While Luther disclaimed responsibility for the uprising, and sharply criticized the peasants, and despite the fact that the peasants suffered a tremendous military defeat, Luther's new theology succeeded in leading the peasants of northern Germany out of the Church.[24] In Germany today, approximately 51 percent of the electorate is Protestant, 46 percent is Catholic, and the remainder is unaffiliated. Assuming historical continuity, we would expect the Catholics to support the major party of the right, the Christian Democratic Union (CDU), and indeed they do. Roman Catholics in the German Federal Republic account for at least 60 percent of the CDU vote. Among Catholics in Germany, moreover, support of the CDU is directly proportional to church activity, since the Catholic Church and its lay organizations actively encourage their members to vote for the CDU. Protestants, for their part, disproportionately support the SPD. Interestingly, the Protestant population in Germany has experienced more rapid social mobility than has the Catholic population, so that the German middle class today is disproportionately Protestant.[25] There are thus a large number of cross-pressured individuals—people who on the basis of religion would be expected to vote for one party, and on the basis of social class for another. Because of the greater political involvement of the Catholic Church, as compared to the Protestant churches, we hypothesize that for such cross-pressured individuals, the Church will have more influence in the partisan choice of Catholics than of non-Catholics, and that among Catholics, the influence of the Church will be directly proportional to the church-related activity of the individual.

The relationship between religion and politics in America is somewhat different. First of all, while the Catholic Church was the established church in Europe, America was settled by religious deviants who established Protestant churches in the new world. The American upper-class churches were Episcopalian in the South and the Congregationalist in New England. Secondly, although it has been common to regard "Protestants" in America as a homogeneous aggregate supporting the Republican party, the dissenting sects—the Methodists and the Baptists—supported the Democrats in the

[24] For insightful if unorthodox analyses of the revolt against the Church and feudal nobility in Germany see Erik H. Erikson, *Young Man Luther* (New York: Norton, 1962), pp. 234–287, and Frederick Engels, *The Peasant War in Germany* (Moscow: Foreign languages Publishing House, 1956). Note that although the conversion of German Peasants to Protestantism can be viewed as a class-struggle phenomenon, there was a significant degree of conversion among the nobility as well which resulted in part in the Schmalkaldic War against Charles V, resolved by the Religious Peace of Augsburg in 1555.

[25] See Morris Janowitz "Social Stratification and Mobility in West Germany," *American Journal of Sociology*, Vol. 64, No. 1 (July 1958), pp. 10–15.

early years of the Republic while the "high" churches supported the Federalists,[26] and partisan cleavage is still evident among Protestants in the United States. Recent studies have placed the Baptists in the Democratic camp along with Catholics and Jews—largely, it should be noted, because of the preponderance of Baptists in the South.[27]

Third, in America we have seen the upward mobility not only of individuals, but of denominations as well. Thus, for example, as the social status of members of the Presbyterian Church has risen, it has not been necessary for them to join new churches to find religious affiliations congruent with their status. The status of the church has risen with them. Baltzell argues against the hegemony of the Establishment churches in the American upper class, and puts forth the thesis that if the American upper class is going to retain any legitimacy, it must become representative of the population as a whole.[28]

Fourth, it should be noted that cleavages exist within religious groupings other than the Protestants. Because successive waves of Catholic immigrants to America arrived at different times, they were differentially able to elicit the representations of American political parties. In the case of New Haven, Connecticut for example, Dahl points out that because the Democratic party represented the Irish-Catholics, it could not represent the interests of the more recent Italian-Catholic arrivals as well. The Republican party was therefore able to elicit the support of this latter community.[29]

We hypothesize, than, that in general, in the American case, core protestant churches will support the Republican party while the neofundamentalist churches, the Catholics, and the Jews will support the Democratic party. We anticipate however, that there may be cleavages within any of these groups on the basis of socioeconomic or ethnic differences. As between America and West Germany, we hypothesize that religious cleavage will be sharper in the latter than in the former, and operate in greater relative freedom from other factors in determining political partisanship.

Trade Unions

The comparison of the political effects of trade unions in Germany and in the United States is especially interesting because while industrial development was similar in the two countries, the ongoing authority relations upon which trade unionism was superimposed differed greatly.

In both Germany and the United States, the technological bases of industrialism were similar, for both required means of transporting heavy mineral resources from inland locations. The railroads fulfilled this need. This common technology, however, appeared in the German case in the

---

[26] See Seymour Martin Lipset's metaphorical chronology, The First New Nation (New York: Basic Books, 1963), pp. 79–82.

[27] Janowitz, Liepelt and Segal, "An Approach to the Comparative Analysis of Political Partisanship."

[28] E. Digby Baltzell, The Protestant Establishment: Aristocracy and Caste in America (New York: Random House, 1964).

[29] Robert A. Dahl, Who Governs (New Haven: Yale University Press, 1961), p. 39.

context of a society with a rigid class system, in which the state, the military and private concerns were highly bureaucraticized, and in which guild organizations already had a niche in the social structure.[30] Trade unions as such were born in the latter part of the nineteenth century, with the approval of the Catholic Church. Through the Weimar period the non-Catholic unions with their strong social democratic bent, and the more conservative Catholic unions remained independent of each other. Unionism had been used as an effective political weapon as, for example, the general strike at the time of the Kapp *putsch* indicated. However, there was an avoidance of radical politics, and at times, an unwillingness to act in accord with their own political interests. In 1932, for example, when the government of Prussia was overthrown by von Papen, the trade unions did not resist forcefully.[31] It might be argued that the unionists felt that in a time of mass unemployment, a strike could not have been effective. Nonetheless, the unions bore part of the cost of the toppling of democracy in Germany. In 1933 the offices of the unions were occupied by storm troopers, and the unions were replaced by the Nazi-run German Work Front (DAF).

In the postwar years, the unions have regained an important position in the German social structure. About 35 percent of the wage-earning class, as well as 85 percent of the civil servants and more than 20 percent of the white-collar employees are unionized. The most important labor organization is the German Confederation of Trade Unions (DGB) which, unlike the Weimar period, unites the social democratic unions with the Christian Trade Unions. Because of the Catholic factions within the organization, the DGB cannot make a strong partisan commitment to the SPD. Indeed, very much in keeping with the propositions of the "middle-mass" theory of partisanship, the DGB stresses the common interests of wage-earners, civil servants and white-collar employees. This is not to say that the unions have moved completely to the right. Indeed, there still exist historical affinities between the policies of the SPD and the interests of the non-Catholic trade unions. We therefore hypothesize that in studying the relationship between unionism and partisanship in Germany, we will find an interaction effect between religion and union membership, with Catholic unionists leaning toward the CDU and non-Catholic unionists favoring the SPD. Moreover, we would expect people involved in unions during the Weimar period to be more likely to support the SPD than would members of the labor force who affiliated with the unions at a later period. Thus, in a sense, we anticipate a generation difference.

In the American case, the political stance of labor unions has been different. In fact, the basic cleavage among unions has been political rather than religious. Evolving in a society in which egalitarianism rather than class differentiation prevailed, the labor movement in America emphasized advancement within the established social structure, rather than basic changes in that structure.[32] The preeminence of the American Federation of Labor

---

[30] See William H. McNeill, *The Rise of the West* (New York: Mentor, 1965), pp. 806 ff.

[31] See Fritz Erler, *Democracy in Germany* (Cambridge: Harvard University Press, 1965), p. 65.

[32] See Lipset, *The First New Nation,* pp. 170–204.

(AFL), resulting from a conflict which started in the 1890s and extended until World War I, signalized the dominance of Gompers' pragmatic orientation to politics. The AFL emphasized the role of the unions as integral social elements with a voice in policy debates but a commitment to no party. "Defeat labor's enemies and reward its friends," Gompers admonished. While labor has most frequently been aligned with the Democratic party, as early as the 1900s the AFL demonstrated its nonpartisanship by joining the Republican-dominated National Civic Association. As early as 1874, the approach taken by the AFL was opposed by the more radical unions, which were concerned with altering the social structure rather than improving the workers' lot within it. The Socialist Labor party—a product of the First International—attempted to form a rival body to the AFL in 1895, and starting in 1901, socialists concerned with winning American labor to their cause without resorting to "dual unionism" formed the Socialist party and tried to change the AFL from within. These efforts, and later efforts by the International Workers of the World, failed to win American labor's support for socialist ideologies, and the dominant political orientation of American labor today is pragmatic and nonideological.[33]

In terms of the political relevance of trade unions, two parameters are important for present consideration. First, in terms of membership, American labor unions are not particularly strong. Roughly 30 percent of the nonagricultural labor force is affiliated with unions. This percentage is not large enough to win national elections in its own right. On this basis alone we would expect unionism to be a less important determinant of partisanship in the United States than in Germany. Secondly, we know that historically, while American unions have to some extent been able to exercise a veto over candidates unacceptable to labor, particularly in urban areas where union members are concentrated, the combined factors of traditional nonpartisanship, cross-pressures upon union members, and nonresponsiveness of members to union political advice have minimized the relevance of union appeals in American elections. There are indications, however, that the import of union membership in determining political style is increasing.[34]

In summary, labor unions today are associated strictly with the major party of the left in neither West Germany nor the United States. In the former case, this is due to the recent marriage of the Catholic and non-Catholic unions, while in the latter it is due to traditional nonpartisanship. Despite this similarity, German unions—particularly the non-Catholic unions—have a history of class consciousness and alliance with socialist political interests. We would expect historical continuities to lead to a closer association between unionism and left partisanship in Germany than in the United States. Moreover, because of the relatively higher level of unionization in Germany than in the United States, we suggest that this relationship has important social structural implications.

See Daniel Bell, *The End of Ideology* (New York: Collier Books, 1962), chap. 12. "The Failure of American Socialism."

[34] Arthur Kornhauser, Harold L. Sheppard and Albert J. Mayer, *When Labor Votes* (New York: University Books, 1956).

Emergent Bases of Political Cleavage

While we are arguing for the continuity of historical influences on social structure, and for the sociological relevance of historical experience, we regard history as an ongoing process. Therefore, it is important to attend to the effects of recent events both for their contemporary significance, and because they will affect party alignments of the future. On the basis of increased military capabilities and the potential for wars of total annihilation, attitudes toward warfare, which cut across class lines, have become increasingly polarized.[35] Evidence from the United States, for example, indicates that more people want to withdraw from military commitments in Asia *and* that more people want to increase our military activities there in the interest of containing the spread of communism than was the case during the Korean police action.[36] Similarly, domestic policy issues may have important implications for party alignments and partisan strength. Thus, in the United States, the increasing integration of the black in American society has been accompanied by the alignment of the black vote with the Democratic party. Indications are that the distinctiveness of a racial vote will be maintained for some time.[37] In the German case, there seems in recent months to have been an increase in support for nationalistic right-wing politics, during a period when the relative strength of the SPD in government was on the increase. While the increased strength of the SPD seems in part to be a function of the domestic policies pursued by the CDU, the increase in nationalistic sentiment may be more a reflection of Gaullist ideas than a reaction of domestic political issues. Thus, in both Germany and the United States, new political alignments are emerging on the basis of both domestic and international events.

THE DATA

Contrary to the usual practice of working with national samples of 1500 to 2000 respondents, we were concerned with cumulating large case bases in the interest of minimizing the relative amount of error variance in our data. This was accomplished through the collapsing of a series of national surveys. We assume that our indicators are not sensitive to the points in time at which our data were collected.[38]

The analysis of partisanship in Germany is based upon 9493 interviews conducted by the Institut für angewandte Sozialwissenschaft between January

[35] See Philip E. Converse, "The Shifting Role of Class in Political Attitudes and Behavior," in Harold Proshansky and Bernard Seidenberg, eds., *Basic Studies in Social Psychology* (New York: Holt, Rinehart and Winston, Inc., 1965), p. 346.

[36] Glenn Harvey, "Sex as an Attitudinal Variable: The X Factor in Opinions on Policy Alternatives in Korea and Vietnam" (unpublished paper: University of Michigan, February 1967).

[37] David R. Segal and Richard Shaffner, "Class, Party and the American Negro" (forthcoming).

[38] "The benefits of large numbers and broadly based coverage proved to be greater than the benefits of timeliness," Ithiel de Sola Pool, Robert P. Abelson and Samuel L. Popkin, *Candidates, Issues and Strategies* (Cambridge, M.I.T. Press, 1964), pp. 65–67.

1963 and April 1964. In our earlier analysis of American data, we ran into problems of comparability from one survey to another because major American survey research agencies deal with the same variables in different ways, and a single agency is in fact likely to alter its codes over a short period of time. In the present instance, we were able to get comparable data for 5551 respondents who were interviewed in presidential election surveys conducted by the Survey Research Center, University of Michigan, in 1952 through 1964.[39] The statistical technique used was the so-called tree-analysis, based upon the nonsymmetric splitting of social groups. Because of the different data-processing machinery available, somewhat different procedures were used in the two countries. The German data were analyzed using a program written by Stouthart and Seegers for the IBM 1401 computer.[40] The American data were handled with the AID program, developed by Morgan and Sonquist for the IBM 7090.[41] The basic differences in the two approaches are the amount of man-machine interaction required and the handling of the dependent variable: AID requires less operator intervention and deals with the dependent variable as a continuous attribute. Comparison of preliminary analyses of the American data with tabulations made earlier in Germany suggest that there are no essential differences in the results generated by the two programs.

Table 12.2 presents the results of the nonsymmetric splitting of the German data. Slightly less than one-third of the sample constituted what we would consider a traditional left vote. The individuals in this group were members of the working class, were non-Catholic or nonpracticing Catholic, and tended to belong to trade unions or to identify with the working class. Of the individuals with these characteristics, 71.5 percent supported the SPD. An additional 9 percent of the sample were middle-class people who were affiliated with trade unions and tended to support the SPD. Here we have an example of the persistent effect of union affiliation regardless of objective social position.

At the other extreme, comprising 22 percent of the sample, are the traditional Catholic voters. All of the individuals in this group are practicing Catholics, and at a minimum either hold middle-class occupations or are not affiliated with trade unions. Only 17.7 percent of this group supported the SPD. Note that even among middle-class practicing Catholics, union affiliation was related to important differentials in SPD support.

The CDU also gained support from the traditional middle-class voters—those who were non-Catholic or nonpracticing Catholic, but who had middle-class occupations and were not affiliated with trade unions. This group accounted for 22 percent of the sample, and only slightly more than 25 percent of its members claimed SPD affiliation.

[39] We are grateful to the Inter-University Consortium for Political Research for making these data available to us. The analysis of the American data was carried out at the Computing Center. University of Michigan. I am indebted to Allen J. Rubin for his efficient handling of these data.

[40] J. H. G. Seegers, "De Contrasgroepen-Methode: Nadere Uitwerking en een Tweetal Toepassingen," *Social Wetenschappen*, No. 3 (1964), pp. 194–225.

[41] John A. Sonquist and James N. Morgan, *The Detection of Interaction Effects* (Survey Research Center, University of Michigan, 1964)

TABLE 12.2 SOCIAL STRUCTURAL CLEAVAGE IN THE GERMAN POPULATION

CATEGORY	N	PERCENT	PERCENT SPD
1. Traditional Left			
1.1 Working class, non-Catholic or nonpracticing Catholic trade union affiliation	1707	18	77.4
1.2 Working class, non-Catholic or nonpracticing Catholic, trade union affiliation fication	1335	14	63.5
2. Left-Oriented			
2.1 Middle class, non-Catholic or nonpracticing Catholic, trade, union affiliation	813	9	62.1
3. Middle-Class-Oriented			
3.1 Middle class, non-Catholic or nonpracticing Catholic, no trade union affiliation, working-class social origins	497	5	52.5
3.2 Working class, non-Catholic or nonpracticing Catholic, no trade union affiliation, middle-class identification	440	5	49.3
4. Catholic-Oriented			
4.1 Practicing Catholics, working class, trade union affiliation	531	5	41.0
5. Traditional Middle Class			
5.1 Middle class (including self-employed), non-Catholic or nonpracticing Catholic, no trade union affiliation, middle-class social origin	940	12	18.6
5.2 Middle class (including clerical), non-Catholic or nonpracticing Catholic, no trade union affiliation	1125	10	32.0
6. Traditional Catholic			
6.1 Working class, practicing Catholic, no trade union affiliation	678	7	28.7
6.2 Middle class, practicing Catholic, trade union affiliation	297	3	21.5
6.3 Middle class, practicing Catholic, no trade union affiliation	1130	12	9.9
Total	9493	100%	

There are, then, three dominant factions in the German population: the middle class and the practicing Catholics supporting the CDU, and the traditional working-class left supporting the SPD. Each of these factions has its counterpart in the middle of the electoral spectrum. We have mentioned above the left-oriented middle class. There are in addition a Catholic-oriented group, composed of working-class people affiliated with trade unions, who due to the influence of the Church are affiliated with the SPD in only 41 percent of the cases, and a middle-class-oriented group, composed of people in middle-class occupations who are influenced neither by trade union membership nor by the Catholic Church, and who tend to identify with the middle class.

The American data are presented in Table 12.3. Note that here, the dependent variable is expressed not as a percentage of the vote cast for the major parties, as in the German case, but rather as a mean, $\overline{Y}$. Partisanship in the American case was recorded on a six-point scale, ranging from Strong Democrat (0.1) to Strong Republican (0.7). By including party strength in our measure, we are able to deal with those people in our sample who call themselves Independents, but who favor one or the other of the major American parties. A mean score ($\overline{Y}$) of less than 0.4000, then, indicates a tendency to-

TABLE 12.3 SOCIAL STRUCTURAL CLEAVAGE IN THE AMERICAN POPULATION

CATEGORY	N	PERCENT	$\overline{Y}$
1. Traditional Left			
1.1 Working-class or lower-class identification; working-class or farm origins; South, West, Alaska or Hawaii	997	18	0.2487
2. Negro Democratic Bloc			
2.1 Working-class or lower-class identification; New England, northeast, north-central, midwest, mountain states, Appalachian states or northwest; Protestant, Orthodox (other than Catholic) or no religious preference; black	160	3	0.2606
2.2 Upper-class or middle-class identification; New England, northeast, north-central, West, southwest, Alaska or Hawaii; Protestant, Orthodox (other than Catholic), nontraditional Christian, non-Judeo-Christian; not union members; all occupational groups except self-employed businessmen and housewives; black	17	a	0.2647
3. Minority Religions			
3.1 Working-class or lower-class identification; New England, northeast, north-central, midwest, mountain states, Appalachian states, southwest, Catholic or Jewish.	777	14	0.2640
3.2 Upper-class or middle-class identification, New England, northeast, north-central, West, southwest, Alaska or Hawaii; Catholic, Jewish or no religious preference.	498	9	0.3299
4. Southern Democrat			
4.1 Upper-class or middle-class identification; Southern and Appalachian states; ceneral cities and rural areas	549	10	0.2872
5. Union-Oriented			
5.1 Upper-class or middle-class identification; New England, northeast, north-central, West, southwest, Alaska or Hawaii, Protestant, Orthodox (other than Catholic), nontraditional Christian or non-Judeo-Christian; union member	59	1	0.3203
6. Working-Class-Oriented			
6.1 Working-class of lower-class identification; Protestant or Orthodox (other than Catholic); white; midwest, north-central, Appalachian states, mountain states or southwest; not regular church attenders	757	14	0.3482
6.2 Working-class or lower-class identification; South, West, Alaska or Hawaii; middle-class origins	98	2	0.3510
7. Southern-Oriented			
7.1 Upper-class or middle-class identification; South and Appalachian states; suburban	40	1	0.4175
8. Protestant-Oriented			
8.1 Working-class or lower-class identification; north-central, midwest, southwest, mountain states or Appalachian states; Protestant or Orthodox (other than Catholic); white; attend church regularly	300	5	0.4160
8.2 Working-class or lower-class identification; New England or northeast; Protestant, Orthodox (other than Catholic), or no religious preference; white	315	6	0.4749

TABLE 12.3 SOCIAL STRUCTURAL CLEAVAGE *(CONTINUED)*

CATEGORY	N	PERCENT	$\overline{Y}$
9. Middle-Class Protestant			
9.1 Upper-class or middle-class identification; Protestant, Orthodox (other than Catholic), nontraditional Christian or non Judeo-Christian; New England, northeast, north-central, West, southwest, Alaska or Hawaii; not a union member; all occupations except self-employed businessmen and housewives; white	460	8	0.4700
9.2 Upper-class or middle-class identification; Protestant, Orthodox (other than Catholic), nontraditional Christian or non-Judeo-Christian; not union member; self-employed businessmen and housewives; north-central, mountain states, West, southwest, Alaska or Hawaii.	203	4	0.4823
9.3 Upper-class or middle-class identification; Protestant, Orthodox (other than Catholic), nontraditional Christian or non-Judeo-Christian; not union member; self-employed businessmen or housewives; northeast, New England, midwest	321	5	0.5684
Total	5551	100%	

a Less than 1 percent

ward the Democratic party, while a mean on greater than 0.4000 indicates support for the Republican party.

The group that we would consider the traditional left in the United States, composed of working-class people from working-class origins, is slightly more than half as large as its German counterpart. Only 18 percent of our sample fell into this group. An additional 3 percent of the sample was included in the Democratic camp by virtue of being black. Social class identification had little impact on the party choices of American blacks, although it was the single most important variable in the determination of partisanship for the sample as a whole. The minority religions—Catholics and Jews—were also included as Democratic supporters, although here there was clearly differentiation on the basis of class identification. The 9 percent of the sample that was Catholic or Jewish and had middle-class or upper-class identifications leaned more toward the Republican party than did the 14 percent that identified with the lower class or working class.

Although their brand of Democratic politics differs somewhat from that in the nation as a whole, people in the South and Appalachian states who consider themselves upper class or middle class added strength to the Democratic ranks to the tune of 10 percent of the sample, and an additional one percent of the sample was tied to the Democrats by union membership, despite upper-class or middle-class identification.

At the other end of the political spectrum, as the most strongly Republican groups in our sample, we find self-employed businessmen and housewives predominantly Protestant, who consider themselves to be upper class or middle class, and who live in areas outside the South. These groups account for 9 percent of the total sample. An additional eight percent of the sample shared these characteristics save for the occupational specification, and was only slightly less pro-Republican.

As in the German case, we again find groups in the middle of the political spectrum who lean toward one or the other of the political parties. Thus, 16 percent of the sample is composed of people primarily from white Protestant backgrounds or from middle-class social origins who identify with the working class or lower class and favor the Democratic party.

Very close to the center of our scale was the 5 percent of our sample characterized by suburban residence in the South, and by upper-class or middle-class identification. Indeed, this is not the first indication that Republican areas do exist in the South, and did so before the 1964 presidential election.[42] In the present instance, this group was shown to be more strongly Republican than the Southern urban and rural middle-class groups, but not as strongly as middle-class groups outside the South.

Finally, 11 percent of the sample was composed primarily of white Protestants who either lived in the northeastern part of the United States or who attended church regularly who, although they identified with either the working class or the middle class, favored the Republican party.

OVERVIEW

These data argue for the persistence of historical influences upon contemporary political alignments, and in fact, for historical materialism as an important focus, although we reject the Marxian postulates both of unicausalism and the dialectic. In Germany with its traditionally more rigid class relations, partisanship is clearly related both to objective economic status, notably occupation, and to membership in the Catholic Church, which body has historically been associated with political authority. Note especially that the self-employed appear in one of the social groupings that is least supportive of the SPD. In America, on the other hand, class identification, rather than occupation, was dominant in determining political partisanship. Although class identification does not correlate perfectly with occupational position, we reject the Marxian notion of false consciousness and argue that because America is the more consensual of the systems under consideration, and because of American emphases on egalitarianism and the Protestant Ethic, in America, being a member of the working-class is not disvalued,[43] and is at best ambiguous in its connotations. Occupation did appear as an important variable in the American case among Protestants not affiliated with unions who identified with the upper or middle classes and lived outside the South. Here, as in Germany, self-employed businessmen emerged as the most con-

[42] See Bernard Cosman, *Five States for Goldwater* (University: University of Alabama Press, 1966), p. 49.

[43] See Robert E. Lane, *Political Ideology* (New York: Free Press, 1962), pp. 57 ff.

servative group (in partisan terms), accompanied in the American case by housewives. The conservatism of housewives in Western democracies has been documented elsewhere.[44]

While religion served as an indicator of partisanship in America, both among the Protestant plurality and the Catholic and Jewish minorities, there was significant differentiation on the basis of social class. Moreover, only among white Protestants outside of New England and the South who identified with the working class was there any partisan differentiation on the basis of religious attendance. These results support Lenski's propositions that the political differences among American religious groups are based upon status rather than class struggles, and that it is involvement in the religious subcommunity, rather than attachment to the church, that provides the linkage between religious affiliation and partisan choice.[45]

The impact of trade-union membership is also differentially felt in the two systems in question. Even among non-Catholics in Germany, trade-union affiliation is clearly related to SPD support, and in addition causes practicing Catholics and people with middle-class occupations to lean less strongly toward the CDU than would otherwise be the case. In America, on the other hand, union membership was shown by our analysis to be important in only one instance. Among Protestants outside the South who identified with the middle class or upper class, those who were union members— roughly 1 percent of the total sample—favored the Democratic party while nonunion members leaned toward the Republican party. Insofar as union politics is indicative of political interests based upon economic classes, here, as elsewhere in this analysis, partisanship in America is shown to be less class-based than is partisanship in Germany.

While lines of cleavage based upon unionization, social class and religion seem sharper in Germany than in the United States, there remains one historical source of cleavage that our data show to still be relevant in the analysis of American politics. In the early days of the American republic, political cleavages between frontier farmers and the financial and commercial interests of the coastal cities existed along Federalist-Republican lines. The conservative preference of the North-Atlantic seaboard has been retained among Protestants who identify with all social classes. The South, for its part, has retained the conservative Democratic coloration that it took on during the post-civil War years, although here there is reason to believe that the issue of civil rights will serve as a base for the reemergence of a two-party system in this region.

Although there has been some slight trace of reemergent nationalism in the German population, no recent political events in that country can account for as much variance in partisanship as does the Negro vote in the United States. Here, we find a bloc of voters solidly behind the Democratic

[44] See for example Robert McKenzie and Allan Silver, "Conservatism, Industrialism and the Working Class Tory in England." *Transactions of the Fifth World Congress of Sociology,* Vol. III (1964), pp. 191–202.

[45] See Gerhard Lenski, *The Religious Factor* (New York: Anchor, 1963), pp. 173, 181 ff.

party regardless of social class. Given the increase in black voting turnout in the United States over the last decade, this homogeneous vote promises to be an important political tool in the hands of the black community.

CONCLUSION

The late Otto Kirchheimer has characterized German political opposition as "vanishing," arguing that in the post-World War II period, the SPD has constantly retreated from the position of offering meaningful alternatives to the policies of the CDU. This situation has been aggravated by the necessity of the SPD to disclaim the radical roots it is accused by both Communists in East Germany and the CDU in the Federal Republic of having. The goal of the SPD in competing for public office is not opposition, in Kirchheimer's terms, but unconditional participation in government.[46] Certainly the SPD as a party organization has assumed a more consensual political style in recent years. However, political analysis must not be cast in organizational terms alone. The present data indicate that despite the current ideological stance of the party, which repudiates class conflict politics, the artifactual remnants of just such a political style are still present in the electorate. While ownership of business explains the conservatism of only a small segment of the sample, economic variables such as union membership and occupation underlie most political differences. To characterize the system as wholly consensual then would at best be premature.

In the American case, we find that no single base of cleavage is pervasive, unionization and occupation have little import, and political discourse is not cast in the rhetoric of class and ideology. However, multiple bases of political differentiation do exist. "European (and American) observers have often underestimated the pervasiveness of conflict in American politics because political conflict in the United States does not follow the expected patterns of class and ideological politics."[47] The difference between the United States and Germany, however, is more than just one of historical versus emergent sources of cleavage. The degree to which authority within the system is superimposed is also important here.

Because of the historical linkages between the Catholic Church and the upper classes on the one hand, and the Protestant churches, the working class and the labor unions on the other, Germany is just emerging from a history of high superimposition of authority. That is, those people who were Protestant, working-class and union members were subordinated in the arenas of religious, occupational, and industrial authority. The increased upward mobility of Protestants, of course, has alleviated the subordination of these groups in recent years, and while long-term trend data are not available, we would expect that the trend from superimposition to pluralism

---

[46] Otto Kirchheimer, "Germany: The Vanishing Opposition," in Robert A. Dahl, ed., *Political Oppositions in Western Democracies* (New Haven: Yale University Press, 1966), pp. 237–259.

[47] Robert A. Dahl, "The American Oppositions: Affirmation and Denial," in Dahl, ed., *Political Oppositions in Western Democracies*, p. 48.

would reduce the intensity of political opposition since political alignments, rather than being fixed, would shift as a function of issue salience. This same argument, however, does not predict the elimination of opposition.

In the United States, on the other hand, lines of cleavage may be defined as pluralistic. The cumulation of subordinate roles, save in the case of the black, is not as relevant here. For this reason, alignments on political issues are not highly interrelated, and the polarization of political interests along class-conflict lines is inhibited.

These differences in polarization are reflected in the view of Americans and Germans toward the parties that they *do not* support. Almond and Verba found that in well over half the cases, Democrats in America described the Republican party in positive terms, and vice-versa. In Germany, on the other hand, supporters of the CDU view the SPD favorably in less than half the cases, and SPD supporters view the CDU in positive terms in less than one-quarter of the cases.[50] We would suspect, however, that these latter figures are greater than they have been in the past, and, with increased cooperation between the parties in the running of the Federal Republic, will continue to rise in the future.

In brief, the data here indicate that despite convergences in social structure due to similar technologies and economic systems, important differences remain between the political alignments of the American and German populations, and these may be attributed to different historical backgrounds. While we suggest that the import of these historical differences is decreasing, there seems to be no basis for the argument that ideological politics are disappearing. Rather, as demonstrated by the black vote in the United States, the unfolding of history generates new cleavages which can themselves be ideological. Thus, while perhaps in the long run one may speak of a convergence of political styles in Western democracies, this convergence, of necessity, will be asymptotic.

[48] See Dahrendorf, *Class and Class Conflict in Industrial Society*, pp. 213 ff., for a discussion of superimposition and pluralism.

[49] Dahl, *Political Oppositions in Western Democracies*, p. 54.

[50] Gabriel A. Almond and Sidney Verba, *The Civic Culture* (Princeton: Princeton University Press, 1963), p. 131.

13

Religion and Politics*

GERHARD LENSKI

ATTITUDES TOWARD THE WELFARE STATE

In any complex society where there are only two political parties, party affiliation can never be a reliable indicator of the total range of political attitudes of individuals or of groups. Because of the multiplicity of political issues, and because these issues divide men in so many different ways, one inevitably finds people with divergent viewpoints on a given issue rallying under the same party banner. Simultaneously, one finds people sharing the same viewpoint on a given issue affiliated with different political parties. Because it is impossible for mass parties such as the Republicans and Democrats to achieve internal unity on all important issues of the day, it is desirable to look behind party preferences and examine the attitudes of group members on specific issues.

In so doing, however, we run a calculated risk. Many individuals have never seriously considered many of the issues confronting American society, yet when questioned about them in an interview are likely to voice some

* From *The Religious Factor*, by Gerhard Lenski. Copyright © 1961 by Gerhard Lenski. Reprinted by permission of Doubleday & Company, Inc.

opinion, no matter how hastily arrived at. Obviously such opinions are likely to be somewhat random or hit-and-miss. The more obscure the issue, the more pronounced this randomizing effect which blurs the evidences of group influences on individual thought and action.[1] For this reason we tried to confine our questions to issues of some importance. Nevertheless, it is clear that to some degree the randomizing effect has been at work, especially on issues not currently "in the news."

The first of the issues with which we dealt was the critical issue of how broad the powers of government should be in contemporary American Society. This is, of course, the issue which is central to all arguments for and against the modern welfare state. To discover how our respondents viewed this subject, we asked:

> Some people say the government should do more than it has in connection with problems such as housing, unemployment, education, and so on. But others say the government is already doing too much along these lines. *On the whole*, would you say that what the government is doing now is too much, about right, or not enough?[2]

We expected that white Protestants would be most inclined to say that the government was doing too much, and that members of other groups would be more inclined to say the government was not yet doing enough. If a given respondent said he felt the government was not yet doing enough, we then went on to ask him the following question:

> Would you like to see the government go so far as to take over and run the big industries in this country such as the railroads, or the steel industry, or would you not be in favor of this?

Among our sample as a whole, only 8 percent said that they felt the government is already doing too much. From comments made by respondents it seems clear that the inclusion of education in the question confused the issue for many people. A number told us that they thought the government was doing too much in areas such as public housing, but not enough in the area of education. Such persons were classified as responding that on the whole the government is now doing what it should do, neither too much, nor too little.

Forty-five percent believed the government is not yet doing enough; the remainder either said that the *status quo* is satisfactory, or that they were

---

[1] To illustrate how this phenomenon operates, one might imagine two groups which influence their members in diametrically opposed ways on a given issue, with the result that all of the individuals in Group A who have given serious thought to the issue are in favor of policy X, while all of the members of Group B who have given the matter thought are opposed to this policy. If, however, half of the members of each group have not given thought to the matter prior to the interview, and respond on the spur of the moment and in completely random fashion, with half favoring policy X and half opposing it, when the analyst relates group membership to attitudes toward policy X, he will find that only 75 percent of the members of Group A are in favor of this policy, and that 25 percent of the members of Group B are also in favor of it. In short, spur-of-the-moment decisions made while the interview is in progress cause one to *underestimate* the divergence between groups.

[2] Emphasis present in interview schedule.

uncertain. In answer to the second question, 7 percent of the total sample said they would like to see the government run the big industries, and another 5 percent said they were uncertain. The other 33 percent who had previously stated that they felt that the government was not yet doing enough in areas such as housing, unemployment, and education, indicated that nevertheless they were opposed to the nationalization of basic industries.

As Table 13.1 reveals, white Protestants were the most likely to feel that the government is already intervening more than it should in our economy, and they were the least likely to favor nationalization of basic industries. Especially noteworthy was the low percentage of white Protestant members of the working class who were favorably disposed to; or even uncertain about, the idea of nationalizing basic industries. This idea found even less favor with them than it did with *middle*-class members of the other three socio-religious groups.

TABLE 13.1   PERCENTAGE OF RESPONDENTS EXPRESSING SELECTED ATTITUDES TOWARD GOVERNMENTAL INTERVENTION IN THE ECONOMY IN THE 1958 SURVEY, BY SOCIO-RELIGIOUS GROUP, AND CLASS

CLASS: SOCIO-RELIGIOUS GROUP	GOVT. DOING TOO MUCH	PREFER STATUS QUO	GOVT. NOT DOING ENOUGH: OPPOSE NAT'L'N.	FAVOR OR UNCERTAIN RE NAT'L'N.	TOTAL	NO. OF CASES
Middle Class						
White Protestants	16	49	34	1	100	110
White Catholics	14	40	39	7	100	85
Negro Protestants	8	50	33	8	99	12
Jews	0	35	47	18	100	17
Working Class						
White Protestants	8	44	42	6	100	130
White Catholics	5	33	40	23	101	115
Negro Protestants	1	32	26	41	100	78

Catholics ranked second both in the frequency with which they said that the government has already moved too far towards the welfare state, and in the infrequency with which they favored the nationalization of industry. Negro respondents ranked third in both respects, and, among middle-class respondents at least, the Jews ranked fourth. In fact, *middle*-class Jews were more likely to express the view that the government is doing too little than were *working*-class members of either the white Protestant or Catholic groups.

Since our control for differences in the class position of respondents does not completely control for differences in income, education and family background, we sought to determine whether these other factors might account for some of the differences between groups. To do this we set up simultaneous controls for the class level of the respondent, the class level of his parents, his education, and the income of the head of the family in which he currently lived. Needless to say, with such stringent controls the number of cases in each comparison was very small. However (as shown in Table

13.2), when comparisons were limited to those cells in which there were at least five persons in each group, it was found that Catholics still were more likely to favor broadening governmental powers than were white Protestants in nine out of ten comparisons.[3] But what is even more significant, the magnitude of the differences was greater than when the simple class control was used in Table 13.1. The mean difference between white Protestants and Catholics was only 13 percentage points in the former table, but in Table 13.2 it is 23 points, or nearly twice as great (figures are based on the percentage favoring broader governmental powers).

As a further check on these relationships we examined data from the 1952 and 1957 surveys which bear on this same problem. In the 1952 survey, for example, half of the respondents were asked whether they thought it was a good thing for the government to play a bigger part in dealing with problems like "unemployment, education, the extension of social security, and so on." In the same survey they were also asked how they felt on the subject of price controls: should they be strengthened, should they be eliminated, or should they be retained as they were at the time? Finally, they were asked whether they favored a system of National Health Insurance operated by the government. At the time, this subject, like the subject of price controls, was much in the news. In the 1957 survey respondents were again questioned about their views on governmental aid in the area of medical care. This time, however, the question was phrased a bit differently, and they were asked whether they thought the government should help people get doctors and hospitals at low cost.

TABLE 13.2 PERCENTAGE OF RESPONDENTS FEELING THAT THE GOVERNMENT IS NOT DOING ENOUGH WITH RESPECT TO HOUSING, UNEMPLOYMENT, EDUCATION, AND SIMILAR MATTERS, BY SOCIORELIGIOUS GROUP, CLASS, CLASS ORIGINS, EDUCATION, AND INCOME OF FAMILY HEAD

CLASS LEVEL OF R: CLASS ORIGIN OF R: EDUCATION OF R: [a] INCOME OF FAMILY HEAD	WHITE PROTESTANTS		WHITE CATHOLICS		NEGRO PROTESTANTS	
	%	N	%	N	%	N
Mid-Mid-Coll—$8000 plus	29	14	38	8	—	0
Mid-Mid-H.S.—$8000 plus	13	8	60	5	—	0
Mid-Wkg-H.S.—$8000 plus	50	12	57	7	—	1
Mid-Wkg-H.S.—$5000–7999	35	17	60	20	—	0
Mid-Wkg-H.S.—$0–4999	0	5	33	6	—	2
Wkg-Mid-H.S.—$5000–7999	60	5	50	6	—	2
Wkg-Wkg-H.S.—$5000–7999	51	39	56	43	67	6
Wkg-Wkg-H.S.—$0–4999	46	37	63	27	89	18
Wkg-Frm-H.S.—$5000–7999	30	10	67	6	60	5
Wkg-Frm-H.S.—$0–4999	23	14	87	8	58	26

[a] The abbreviation H.S. refers to persons with a high school education or less.

[3] The probability of this occurring by chance in nine out of ten independent samples is slightly over 0.01.

As Table 13.3 indicates, there was considerable stability in the patterns of responses to these questions dealing with various proposals for the extension of governmental powers. For example, in the ten comparisons among groups, with class controlled, white Protestants proved to be the most opposed to any expansion in the powers of government in eight instances, and in the two ranked second in degree of opposition. At the other extreme, Negro Protestants proved to be the most favorably disposed toward increased governmental powers in four of the six comparisons in which they were involved, and tied for this position in one other instance. The Catholic

TABLE 13.3 PERCENTAGE OF DETROITERS FAVORING EXPANSION OF GOVERNMENTAL POWER IN VARIOUS AREAS, BY CLASS AND SOCIORELIGIOUS GROUPS (DATA FROM 1952, 1957, AND 1958 SURVEYS)

CLASS: SOCIO-RELIGIOUS GROUP	1952 SURVEY				1957 SURVEY		1958 SURVEY		Mean Percentage Consistent with Welfare State Philosophy
	Percent Favoring Greater Governmental Powers in Unemployment, Education, and Social Security	Percent Favoring Stronger Price Controls	Percent Favoring National Health Insurance	N	Percent Favoring Government Aid in Medical Care	N	Percent Favoring Greater Governmental Powers in Housing, Unemployment, and Education	N	
Middle Class									
Wh. Prots.	57	41	20	57	42	125	35	110	39
Wh. Caths.	65	66	52	49	62	79	46	85	58
Jews	83	58	67	12	38	16	65	17	62
N. Prots.	—	—	—	4	94	16	41	12	—
Working Class									
Wh. Prots.	82	70	57	99	69	193	48	130	65
Wh. Caths.	86	71	50	78	79	152	63	115	70
N. Prots.	91	71	80	37	90	99	67	78	80

group rather consistently occupied an intermediate position. Of the ten comparisons in which it was involved, it ranked second in seven, and in only three instances occupied either of the extreme positions.

The Jewish group was the most erratic, though usually it was very favorably disposed toward the principle of the welfare state. The only serious exception to this pattern occurred in the 1957 survey, and this may reflect nothing more than sampling error. In short, data from these other surveys confirm the conclusions based on the 1958 survey.

The Jewish advocacy of the welfare state deserves special attention. [Earlier] . . . we saw that the Jewish group had an affinity for certain classical capitalistic patterns of thought and action, and enjoyed remarkable success within the context of the capitalist system. One would therefore expect them to be staunch supporters of *laissez-faire* capitalism, and vigorous opponents *possibly less valid now; upper SES Jews more secure in status; whereas lower SES types becoming more conservative*

of the welfare state, much as the white Protestants are. Yet this is clearly not the case. This curious combination of traits deserves closer examination.

As many differences as there may be between capitalism and welfare statism, both systems have one important element in common—both involve *rational*, rather than *traditional*, forms of organization. In capitalism the locus of rationality lies in the business enterprise, while in the welfare state it lies in the governmental system. Hence, the modern Jewish advocacy of the welfare state is not a rejection of rationality, but rather the rejection of one type of rational organization in favor of another more inclusive, and more extreme, form.

This, then, leads us to ask the question of *why* Jews should prefer welfare statism (or democratic socialism) to classical capitalism. The answer here seems to be that under the capitalist system it has become evident to Jews that economic victories do not insure status victories.[4] The successes of the Jews in capitalist societies have not won them comparable social recognition and acceptance. On the contrary, despite their remarkable successes, even the wealthiest Jews frequently find themselves excluded from private clubs and organizations by their economic peers, and from high administrative posts in many corporations dominated by Gentiles. Hence, despite their success, American Jews have not developed any sense of solidarity with the American economic elite, and have, in fact, reacted against this elite, their political values, and the social institutions on which they depend.

Democratic socialism, from its inception, has contained a strong utopian element which holds out the promise of social justice to all. It is a form of social organization which promises almost all of the advantages of capitalism, but none of its disadvantages. Based on rational principles, it promises rewards (both material and psychic) in proportion to the ability of individuals to contribute to its rationally defined goals. It promises that these rewards will be based on universalistic criteria of performance, rather than particularistic criteria of status group membership. Hence, it has a strong appeal for American Jews.[5]

Undoubtedly there are other factors involved in the Jewish commitment to the welfare state. This historic Jewish concern with social justice has surely contributed to this end,[6] but had the Jews been accepted fully into the inner circles of the American economic elite, would their concern with social justice be any greater than that which motivates wealthy Gentiles? One cannot help wonder whether the Jewish commitment to social justice would, under such circumstances, express itself in anything more pronounced than generous private contributions to charity.[7]

[4] See Max Weber's discussion of the distinction between class and status in *From Max Weber*, pp. 189–94.

[5] The fact that democratic socialism promises a more general application of universalistic criteria of evaluation than found in capitalism is undoubtedly a major factor promoting Jewish support. All available evidence indicates that American Jews are highly resentful of discriminatory practices which ignore their abilities and judge them solely on the grounds that they are Jews.

[6] See Lawrence H. Fuchs, "Sources of Jewish Internationalism and Liberalism," in Marshall Sklare, pp. 595–613.

[7] Undoubtedly the persecutions of Jews abroad in the last generation have also served as a stimulus keeping alive Jewish concern for social justice and reform.

FOREIGN AFFAIRS

... In general, differences between the four major socio-religious groups [in foreign affairs] were minor. In only two instances were differences of any magnitude found. First, less than 40 percent of the Negro Protestants favored foreign aid when this is not required in the interests of national defense, while half of the members of other groups did so. Second, Jews were the most likely to endorse the United Nations and the idea of world government. For example, 70 percent of the Jews, but only 55 percent of the members of other groups, said they favored American participation in a world government. Or, all of the Jews, but only 90 percent of the members of other groups, thought American participation in the UN a good thing.

The lack of support for foreign aid among Negro Protestants seems clearly linked with their group's economic difficulties. Negroes in Detroit tend to feel that this country has serious problems at home and should deal with these before attempting to solve the world's problems.

The Jewish tendency toward internationalism is something which has been noted many times before by friends and foes alike.[8] As the victims of nationalistic enthusiasm in countless countries for centuries, Jews have naturally developed a distrust of nationalism, and have come to pin their faith on international institutions as the only practical alternative. Our findings in this area, therefore, are hardly surprising.

But more important than these differences is the remarkable uniformity in outlook on international issues found among the four major socio-religious groups. In no other major area of political behavior were differences generally so small and agreement so great.

CIVIL RIGHTS: FREEDOM OF SPEECH

A third important area of political controversey involves the issue of *civil rights*. How broadly should the Bill of Rights be interpreted? What rights should, and what rights should not, be guaranteed to American citizens? Should the right of free speech be extended to Communists, Fascists, and others who desire to destroy the traditional structure of American society, or should it be limited only to those willing to work within the framework of American democratic institutions? Or, in a somewhat different area, should Negro children be permitted to attend the same schools as white children, or should they be assigned to segregated schools? Finally, should the coercive power of the law be used to support standards of morality which are not generally shared by the American people, as in such areas as gambling, drinking, birth control, and so forth? These are questions which have repeatedly confronted us in recent years, and they seem likely to remain a source of controversy for years to come.

[8] See, for example, Lawrence H. Fuchs, *The Political Behavior of American Jews* (New York: Free Press, 1956), or the essays by J. O. Hertzler and Talcott Parsons in Isaque Graeber and S. H. Britt, eds., *Jews in a Gentile World* (New York: Crowell-Collier-Macmillan, 1942).

On the subject of freedom of speech, we asked Detroiters four questions. These were as follows:

1. In our country the Constitution guarantees the right of free speech to everyone. In your opinion, does this include the right for someone to make speeches criticizing what the President does?

2. In your opinion, does the right of free speech include the right for someone to make speeches against religion?

3. In your opinion, does the right of free speech include the right for someone to make speeches in favor of Fascism or dictatorship?

4. In your opinion, does the right of free speech include the right for someone to make speeches in favor of Communisim? (that is, speeches only).

The first of these practices was the only one which the majority of Detroiters felt was protected by the Bill of Rights. Even then, one quarter of our respondents answered that they did not feel that the right of free speech covered criticism of presidential actions. In general, conservatism in this area was linked with limited education, advanced age, and a rural background. However, even among those who had attended college, one eighth did not believe that criticism of presidential actions was a right guaranteed by the Constitution.

Comparing the four major socio-religious groups, one finds several noteworthy differences, especially in the middle class (see Table 13.4). White Protestants were generally the most likely to adopt a liberal interpretation of the Bill of Rights; Negro Protestants the least likely. Comparing the two

From McCarthy holdowr: ?'s 2,3,4 weighted

TABLE 13.4 PERCENTAGE OF DETROITERS EXPRESSING BELIEF THAT VARIOUS PRACTICES ARE PROTECTED BY THE BILL OF RIGHTS, BY CLASS AND SOCIO-RELIGIOUS GROUP

CLASS: SOCIO-RELIGIOUS GROUP	PERCENTAGE BELIEVING SPECIFIED PRACTICE PROTECTED					
	Criticism of President	Attacks on Religion	Fascist Speeches	Communist Speeches	N	Mean
Middle class						
Wh. Prots.	88	65	53	46	117	63
Jews	89	53	47	37	19	57
Wh Caths.	77	52	43	34	92	52
N. Prots.	77	54	23	23	13	44
Working class						
Wh. Prots.	69	40	35	33	150	44
Wh. Caths.	70	40	32	32	138	44
N. Prots.	46	28	30	27	87	33

largest groups, middle-class white Protestants were from one quarter to one third more likely than middle-class white Catholics to adopt the liberal position on all except the issue of criticism of presidential actions. Among members of the working class, no difference was observed between white Catholics and Protestants, though Negro Protestants were a good bit more likely than either of these groups to adopt a conservative position.[9]

As students of American politics have long recognized, members of the middle and upper classes are much more likely to have the financial means, intellectual skills, and social contacts required to influence governmental institutions. Hence, their attitudes and values tend to be far more influential than those of the working class. Differences in attitudes toward freedom of speech among persons of middle-class status are therefore likely to be far more important than similarities among members of the working class. For this reason, the differences observed between the two very large middle-class groups, white Catholics and Protestants, may be very important. One should not exaggerate these differences, since they are modest proportions, but neither should one minimize them. These are differences which could well have important consequences for the formation of public policy.

One might suppose that these differences are due to factors other than religion which remain uncontrolled in Table 13.4. In particular, education suggests itself as a possible alternative explanation: if middle-class Catholics are less well educated than middle-class Protestants, this might account for the difference. To check this possibility we compared the 34 middle-class Catholics in our sample who had a college education with their 45 white Protestant counterparts Not only was there no reduction in the magnitude of the differences between the two groups, but on the question dealing with religion there was a substantial increase. Whereas 80 percent of the college-trained, middle-class, white Protestants took the liberal position on this question, only 59 percent of their white Catholic counterparts shared this view. On the other three questions the size of the difference remained the same. From this evidence we can only conclude that variations in degree of education are not the explanation for the difference in attitudes toward freedom of speech observed between middle-class white Catholics and Protestants— despite the fact that attitudes on this subject are clearly influenced by the extent of an individual's education.

A second explanation of the difference might be that relatively more of the Catholics in the middle class are first- and second-generation immigrants. While it is true that this is the case, and also that first- and second-generation immigrants are less committed to the principle of freedom of speech than those who are more Americanized, it does not follow that this is the explanation for Catholic-Protestant differences in the middle class. When we controlled for immigrant generation, the mean difference between middle-class Catholics and Protestants decreased to 7 percentage points for third- (or more) generation Americans. These figures do involve a drop compared with the figure shown in Table 13.4 when immigrant generation was not controlled (the figure there was 11 points), but it is significant that when immigrant generation is controlled, there is *no evidence that the groups are converging.* On the contrary, there is a slight hint that the trend may be in the opposite direction.

---

[9] Robert C. Angell reports a similar pattern of findings based on his analysis of the 1956 Detroit Area Study. See "Preferences for Moral Norms in Three Problem Areas," *American Journal of Sociology,* 67 (May 1962), pp. 650–660.

On the surface the findings of our study appear to differ from those of an important earlier study of this subject made on a national scale. The results of this study (conducted by Professor Stouffer of Harvard, and sponsored by the Fund for the Republic) appeared to indicate that there were no differences between Catholic and Protestant attitudes toward freedom of speech.[10] However, in his analysis Stouffer failed to separate Negro and white Protestants. Had we not separated these two groups, we would have come to the same conclusion as he. The simple fact is that even when one controls for both class and education, Negro and white Protestants differ considerably in their views on freedom of speech, and an indiscriminate mixing of the groups blurs the important differences between white Catholics and Protestants.

Stouffer's analysis also fails to take proper account of other important differences between the major faiths. To begin with, the average level of education of American Jews is substantially higher than that of Protestants and Catholics, as shown by various national surveys. Since education is so highly correlated with liberalism in the realm of civil rights, it seems unwise to draw conclusions about the relative liberalism of the three groups without such a control.

Second, and perhaps even more important, there are major differences in the geographical distribution of Protestants, Catholics, and Jews. Jews are heavily concentrated in the urbanized, eastern section of the country, which is the most liberal part of the nation. Catholics are also heavily represented in this section. Protestants, on the other hand, are heavily concentrated in the rural sections of the country and in the South, the centers of civil rights conservatism.

One might be tempted to postulate a cause-and-effect relationship as a result of such findings, attributing the conservatism of the rural areas and South to the influence of Protestantism, but other evidence makes it clear that the matter is not so simple. When controls are introduced, and comparisons limited to persons similarly situated with respect to region and community size, the pattern shifts. For example, as Stouffer's own figures indicate, among persons living in the North, Protestants prove more liberal than Catholics (and this despite the absence of any control for community size). Thus it appears that Stouffer's analysis of the religious problem must be regarded as incomplete, and his conclusions questionable.

CIVIL RIGHTS: THE RIGHTS OF MINORITY GROUPS

A second aspect of the problem of civil liberties concerns the extension of the full rights and privileges of American citizenship to various minority groups. One of the most controversial issues today revolves around the efforts of northern liberals to integrate public schools, especially in the southern states. However, not even all northerners subscribe to the principle of racial integration in their own communities. Substantial resistance to integration in

[10] Samuel A. Stouffer, *Communism, Conformity, and Civil Liberties* (New York: Doubleday, 1955), p. 143.

the North is revealed by our 1958 survey. One third of the white respondents said white and Negro children should attend separate schools. . . . An additional 5 percent were uncertain.

White Protestants and Catholics were the most likely (34 percent) and Jews the least likely (8 percent) to advocate segregated schools. These figures are partly a reflection of the differing percentages of southern-born whites in the various groups. Fifty-five percent of the southern-born whites favored segregated schools, compared with 30 percent of those born elsewhere. Since 90 percent of the southern-born whites were Protestants, this obviously affected the percentage of Protestants favoring segregated schools. When the comparison is limited to those born outside the South, the three groups rank as follows in terms of the percentage of persons advocating segregated schools:

White Catholics	33 percent (N = 215)
White Protestants	27 percent (N = 210)
Jews	8 percent (N = 26)

The differences between Catholics and Protestants were greater among those in the middle class and those with a college education than among persons in the working class and those with no more than a high school education.

CIVIL RIGHTS: THE LEGISLATION OF MORALITY

A great deal of public controversy in the area of civil liberties springs from the divergent conceptions of morality prevailing in various groups within the population. Each group has a tendency to seek the sanction of law for its own distinctive standards, with the result that bitter controversies often ensue. To explore this problem, we designed a series of questions relating to areas in which we expected to find divergent moral standards. We then followed each of these questions with a second question designed to determine whether individuals upholding a controversial standard felt that it should be enforced by the government. Needless to say, this is a most important aspect of the larger problem of civil liberties.

We explored five basic areas of moral controversy in this connection: (1) gambling; (2) moderate drinking; (3) birth control; (4) divorce; and (5) Sunday business activity. With respect to each of these we asked Detroiters whether "from the moral standpoint [the practice in question] is always wrong, usually wrong, sometimes wrong, or never wrong."

As even a cursory examination of Table 13.5 reveals, the major religious groups differ substantially in their views of these five practices. Protestants are the most strongly opposed to gambling and drinking; Catholics to birth control, divorce, and Sunday business. On this item, however, differences between Protestants and Catholics are relatively small. The Jewish group is the least critical of drinking, divorce, and Sunday business, and relatively uncritical also of gambling and birth control. On the whole, the patterns are what one would expect in the light of public pronouncements by leaders of the various groups.

One notable surprise was the finding that a large percentage of the Negro Protestants, especially those in the working class, oppose birth control on moral grounds. Why they take this position is not altogether clear, but one authority in this area, Professor Ronald Freedman, has suggested to us that many working-class Negroes with limited education may be confusing birth control with abortion. While we could find no direct evidence of this in the records of the interviews, we did find ample evidence that many working-class Negroes did not understand what birth control is. On a number of occasions interviewers made a marginal notation indicating that they were not at all sure that the respondent understood the question. In one instance a Negro Baptist janitor said birth control is always wrong, but then added, "What do that mean?"

If it was surprising to find so many Negro Protestants opposing birth control, it was also surprising to find so many white Catholics favoring it. Only three fifths of the Catholics interviewed were willing to say that birth control is always or usually wrong from the moral standpoint. Here again there is the possibility that some misunderstanding occurred. Some Catholics may have thought the question included the practice of the rhythm method, which has found conditional approval on the part of Catholic leaders. Perhaps these persons answered that birth control is only "sometimes wrong,"

TABLE 13.5 PERCENTAGE OF DETROITERS EXPRESSING THE VIEW THAT VARIOUS PRACTICES ARE ALWAYS OR USUALLY WRONG FROM THE MORAL STANDPOINT, BY CLASS AND SOCIO-RELIGIOUS GROUP

CLASS: SOCIO-RELIGIOUS GROUP	PERCENTAGE BELIEVING PRACTICE ALWAYS OR USUALLY WRONG					
	Gambling	Moderate Drinking	Birth Control	Divorce	Sunday Business	N[a]
Middle Class						
White Protestants	50	21	8	34	58	117
White Catholics	17	10	63	66	63	92
Jews	32	5	21	11	17	19
Negro Protestants	77	23	25	38	54	13
Working Class						
White Protestants	55	25	22	35	51	150
White Catholics	39	12	56	63	62	138
Negro Protestants	67	25	48	25	57	87

[a] The Ns shown here are the totals for each category. In a very small number of instances responses were not ascertained and these cases were omitted in the calculation of percentages. The total N is listed here, as in other complex tables of this type, to avoid the addition of four more columns of figures

but this seems somewhat unlikely. Even if one takes the rhythm method into account, a proper Catholic response to this question would seem to be that birth control is usually wrong, since it is clear that the majority of Americans who engage in this practice do not rely on the rhythm method.

Judging from comments made by Catholics who amplified their views on birth control, it is clear that many, if not most, of those who did *not* condemn it were thinking in terms of the forbidden methods. For example, a young Catholic housewife who never attends Mass any more said: "It's against my religion, but I believe in it." A young Catholic man working in his parents' store told us: "I was brought up to believe it's wrong, but personally I don't believe this." There was also the case of an Irish policeman who attended Mass every Sunday, and who had been married for fifteen years but had no children. Although he answered all of the other questions, he refused to answer this one. In short, our evidence suggests that most Catholics understood our question as referring to those methods of birth control which are condemned by their church.

The questions dealing with drinking and gambling were especially interesting since they were among the handful of questions in the whole study which uncovered sharp differences *within* the white Protestant group. Only 25 percent of the Episcopalians said gambling was always or usually wrong from the moral standpoint. By contrast, more than half of those in other groups opposed it. On the question of drinking, both Lutherans and Episcopalians diverged from the rest of the Protestant group. Only 7 percent of the Lutherans and 12 percent of the Episcopalians said that moderate drinking is always or usually wrong. By contrast, 46 percent of the Baptists and 41 percent of the Methodists were opposed to drinking even in moderation.

In this study we were less concerned with differences in moral standards than with the implications these differences have for the political life of the nation. As noted previously, differences in moral standards frequently give rise to serious political controversies. Those who oppose a given practice as being immoral frequently seek the support of legal sanctions, while others who do not share their views fight to prevent this. Conflicts which arise out of struggles of this type are frequently bitter and protracted.

To determine how prone Detroiters are to seek governmental sanction for controversial moral norms, we asked all those who said that gambling, moderate drinking, birth control, or Sunday business were "always" or "usually" wrong, whether the government should have laws against this practice. As an inspection of Table 13.6 reveals, no group has a monopoly on the tendency to seek governmental support for its moral standards. Men of every faith seem inclined to do this with considerable frequency. However, this is hardly surprising since conformity to basic moral norms is usually assumed to be prerequisite to order and stability in human society. The problem arises, of course, because people cannot agree in their definitions of morality. Some define gambling as gross immorality, while others condone it. Some define the use of certain methods of limiting family size as gross immorality, while others define the failure to plan and limit family size as immoral. Some define racial segregation in schools as a breach of basic morality, while others with equal fervor view integration as immoral.

We found that middle-class white Protestants are the least likely to seek governmental support for standards of morality in which they believe, and working-class Negro Protestants the most likely. Although our data tell us nothing directly about *why* this should be, much can be inferred from a knowledge of American history. Throughout the history of this country minority groups have repeatedly won rights and privileges through governmental action. This has been especially true of the Negro group, which has probably gained more in this way than any other group. Often governmental action has succeeded where appeals to individual conscience have failed. As a consequence, Negro Protestants in particular seem to have developed a faith in the efficacy of governmental action, and perhaps simultaneously some distrust of reliance on individual ideals.

TABLE 13.6 PERCENTAGE OF THOSE DETROITERS WHO BELIEVE VARIOUS PRACTICES ARE ALWAYS OR USUALLY WRONG FROM THE MORAL STANDPOINT WHO BELIEVE THAT THE GOVERNMENT SHOULD HAVE LAWS TO FORBID THE PRACTICE, BY CLASS AND SOCIO-RELIGIOUS GROUP

CLASS: SOCIO-RELIGIOUS GROUP	PERCENTAGE OF THOSE BELIEVING SPECIFIED PRACTICE IS WRONG WHO FAVOR GOVERNMENTAL RESTRAINT[a]								
	Gambling		Moderate Drinking		Birth Control		Sunday Business		
	Percent	N	Percent	N	Percent	N	Percent	N	Mean
Middle Class									
Wh. Prots.	61	56	26	23	(11)	9	48	65	27
Wh. Caths.	67	15	(50)	8	15	53	75	52	52
N. Prots.	70	10	—	3	—	5	(57)	7	—
Working Class									
Wh. Caths.	71	51	33	15	32	72	62	82	50
Wh. Prots.	67	82	64	33	21	33	68	75	55
N. Prots.	76	58	45	20	60	40	76	46	64

[a] This question was not asked in the case of divorce.

14

Social Determinism
and Electoral Decision:
The Case of Indiana*

V. O. KEY, JR.
FRANK MUNGER

The style set in the Erie County study of voting, *The People's Choice*,[1] threatens to take the politics out of the study of electoral behavior. The theoretical heart of *The People's Choice* rests in the contention that "social characteristics determine political preference." Professor Lazarsfeld and his associates, prudent as they are, do not let so bald a statement stand without qualification or exception. Yet almost inevitably from this basic view, which is usually not put so explicitly, there develops a school of analysis that tends to divert attention from critical elements of electoral decision. The focus of analysis under the doctrine of social determinism comes to rest broadly on the capacity of the "nonpolitical group" to induce conformity to its political standards by the individual voter.

At bottom the tendency of the theory of group or social determinism is to equate the people's choice with individual choice. Perhaps the collective electoral decision, the people's choice, is merely the sum of individual

* Reprinted with permission of The Macmillan Company from *American Voting Behavior*, edited by Eugene Burdick and Arthur J. Brodbeck. Copyright © The Free Press of Glencoe, a Division of The Macmillan Company, 1959.

[1] P. F. Lazarsfeld, B. R. Berelson, and Hazel Gaudet, *The People's Choice*, 2d ed. (New York: Columbia University Press, 1948).

choices. If enough were understood about individual decisions, by addition the collective political decision of the electorate would be comprehended. Yet when attention centers on the individual elector as he is led to decision by the compulsion of his nonpolitical group, the tendency is to lose sight of significant elements that both affect and relate individual decisions to the political aggregate. The study of electoral behavior then becomes only a special case of the more general problem of group inducement of individual behavior in accord with group norms. As such it does not invariably throw much light on the broad nature of electoral decision in the sense of decisions by the electorate as a whole.

The purpose here is not to dissent from *The People's Choice*. It is rather to raise the question whether its fundamental propositions do not provide a base on which, if enough effort were devoted to the matter, a supplementary theoretical structure might be erected that would bring politics into the study of electoral behavior. A few of the possible directions of development are here indicated through questions suggested by an examination of the voting record of Indiana. The simplest of techniques permits the analysis of a variety of types of electoral situations and suggests interpretations not so likely to emerge from the close observation of a single campaign. Parenthetically, it ought to be made explicit that such crude manipulation of aggregate electoral data is not urged as a substitute for the refined techniques of observation and analysis employed in *The People's Choice*.

TRADITIONAL PARTISAN ATTACHMENTS:
A BENCH MARK FOR ANALYSIS

Almost any pioneer inquiry is inevitably beset by the peril of generalization that requires modification after a series of analyses has been made. What seemed a plausible general finding turns out to have been only a characteristic of the peculiar case cast in general terms. Similarly, the inspection of a cross section at a particular moment of a society existing through time may divert attention from characteristics that would be revealed by deliberate attention to the time dimension. Voting decisions made prior to the campaign itself may differ radically from those occurring during the campaign, both in the kinds of voters involved and in the factors associated with decision. Moreover, the factors relevant to decision may differ from time to time.[2]

Explicit attention to the time dimension of electoral decision would probably bring to light a variety of characteristics not readily perceptible by the observation of a single case. Illustrative is the difficulty of obtaining a satisfactory estimate of the nature and significance of traditional or habitual

[2] A basic contribution of *The People's Choice* was, of course, its development of a technique for observation of at least short segments of the time dimension of decision, and its authors manifest an awareness of the significance of this factor not common among electoral sociologists.

partisan attachments by interviewing a sample at a particular point in time. Often electoral decision is not an action whose outcome is in doubt but a reaffirmation of past decisions, at least for the community as a whole. For generations the Democrats may carry this county and the Republicans may predominate in an adjacent county.

The potency of these traditional attachments may be inferred from the maps in Figure 14.1 which show the distribution of Indiana presidential vote by counties in 1868 and 1900. Although the pattern of 1868 did not move unchanged from election to election to 1900, an astonishing parallelism appears in the county-by-county division by party strength at the two widely separated points in time. Thirty-six of the state's ninety-two counties were over 50 percent Democratic at both elections; forty-five were under 50 percent Democratic at both elections.[3]

Apparently the persistent pattern of party division represented a crystallization of attitudes at the time of the Civil War mainly along lines separating areas with different sources of settlement. The southern half of the state, peopled chiefly from the southern states, contained in 1868 and 1900 most of the Democratic strongholds. Other Democratic areas find a partial explanation in the greater attractiveness of that party to newcomers from abroad. Dearborn, Franklin, Adams, Allen, and Pulaski counties all had large German populations as did Dubois in the south. The Republicanism of certain blocks of counties was related also to the sectional origins of settlers. The block of 1868–1900 Republican counties in east central Indiana was settled by Quakers, whose cultural center was Richmond in Wayne County. Their antislavery sentiments and perhaps other reasons as well made them early converts to Republicanism. Other strongly Republican areas in the northern part of the state had drawn heavily from Federalist and Whig areas of the Northeast. Many of the oddities in detail of the territorial distribution of party strength find explanation in like terms.[4]

From 1868 to 1900 the potency of traditional party attachments may have been much greater than now, yet such community traits persist as is demonstrated by the scatter-diagram in Figure 14.2. The diagram relates the Republican percentage of the total presidential vote by county in 1920 to the corresponding percentage in 1948. Although most counties were more Democratic in 1948 than in 1920, a substantial correlation, +0.689, existed between the Republican percentages for the two elections. Generally where the Re-

---

[3] The similarity between two such maps drawn with the same class intervals in the distribution of counties depends somewhat on the elections chosen for comparison. Since most counties tend to fluctuate in unison, the comparison of elections at which the division of the entire state's vote is approximately the same maximizes the similarities of the county-by-county pattern.

[4] Thus, the Republican county of Jefferson in the southeast is surrounded by Democratic territory. In the first decades of the nineteenth century the county seat, Madison, was the metropolis of the state and a flourishing river trading center. The county was peopled, the local histories say, by the "educated" and "upper strata of society" from Philadelphia and Baltimore, some of whom built magnificent residences that still stand as monuments to the erstwhile glory of Madison. Long since the river trade virtually disappeared. Dreams of metropolitan grandeur came no longer to haunt the county's declining population. Yet so firmly did the old Whig traders fix the political tradition that the county ranked low in Democratic strength even after 1900.

publicans were strong in 1920, they were relatively strong in 1948; where the Democrats were weak in 1920, they were relatively weak in 1948.[5]

The analytical model that centers attention on the campaign as a period of decision obviously obscures a significant dimension of the electoral process. In fact, there tends to be a standing decision by the community, although as a descriptive term "decision" has connotations of deliberate choice that are apt to be misleading. The "decision" may simply represent the balance between two opposing party groups each with striking powers of self-perpetuation. Their original formation may have in some instances represented a simple transplantation of partisan attachments. In others the dominant classes of the community allied themselves with the party whose policies of the moment were most akin to their inclinations. Doubtless great contests and stirring events intensified and renewed partisan loyalties.[6] The clustering of interests, career lines, and community sentiments about the dominant party gives it a powerful capacity for survival.

The relevance of all this to the theoretical problem is that it raises the question whether one needs to supplement the doctrine that "social characteristics determine political preference." May there not also be a political group with to some extent an independence of exterior determinants of membership and attachment? Obviously a simple reconciliation of the persistence of party groupings and the notion of social determinism would be to assert that the stability of "interests" and people associated with geography produces a parallel continuity of partisan attachment. Yet the long persistence of county patterns of party affiliation despite changes in "interest" and the disappearance of issues that created the pattern, and the existence of contrasting patterns in essentially similar counties, point toward a "political" grouping at least to some extent independent of other social groupings.[7] It may be also that the continuity of the life of the party group is not a smooth and uninterrupted flow, as might be inferred from electoral analysis alone. Each election may be accompanied by considerable churning about and crossing of party lines in both directions. From election to election varying proportions of the electorate may be affected by indecision and inner conflict. Yet the net effect over long periods is the maintenance of similar party divisions. Aggregate figures do not, of course, tell us whether this net result is accomplished by stability of individual party attachments or by the power of party

---

[5] A word of caution is in order about both the maps and the scatter-diagram. The maps convey an erroneous impression in that they make no allowance for differences in population density. The significance of a metropolitan center in the entire picture is thus minimized. Similarly, one dot on the diagram may represent a rural county of small population; another a densely populated metropolitan county. Moreover, differentials in behavior within subgroups of the population of large counties are concealed by this sort of analysis.

[6] If one plots on the map of Indiana clusters of underground railroad stations and points at which Union authorities had difficulties in drafting troops, he separates, on the whole, Republican and Democratic counties. Whether the sort of animosities associated with such long-past events project themselves far through time in lending strength to political groupings, perhaps, unbeknownst to succeeding generations, raises an interesting question.

[7] Some evidence pointing in this direction has been presented by George Belknap and Angus Campbell, "Political Party Identification and Attitudes Toward Foreign Policy," *Public Opinion Quarterly*, XV (1951–1952), 601–623.

Figure 14.1 The Traditional Vote: Democratic Percentage of the Two-Party Presidential Vote in Indiana, 1868 and 1900

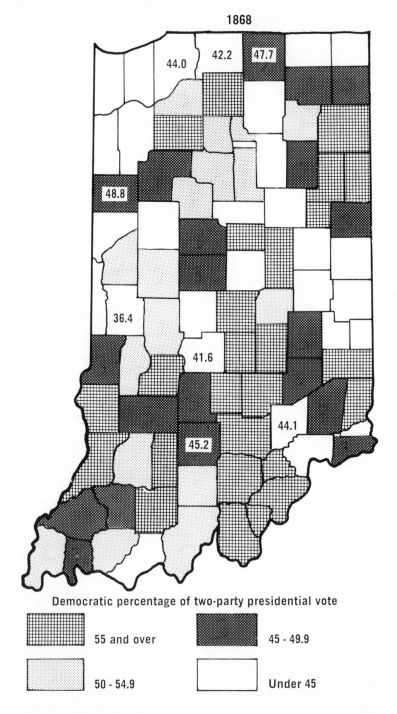

1868

Democratic percentage of two-party presidential vote

55 and over		45 - 49.9	
50 - 54.9		Under 45	

Figure 14.1 The Traditional Vote *(Continued)*

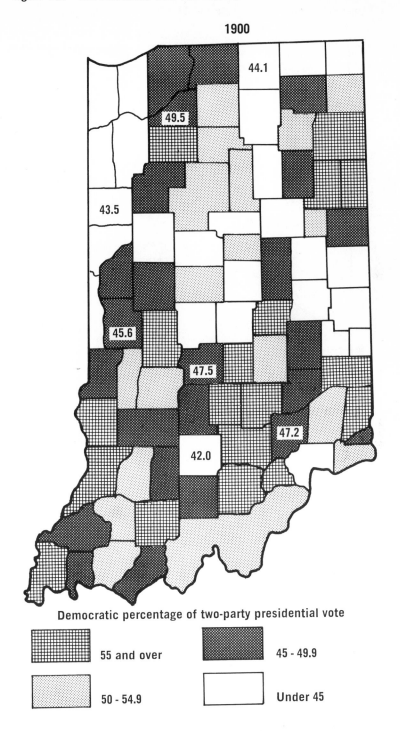

1900

Democratic percentage of two-party presidential vote

55 and over

50 - 54.9

45 - 49.9

Under 45

Figure 14.2 The Traditional Vote: Relation between Republican Percentage of Total Presidential Vote in 1920 and 1948 by Counties in Indiana

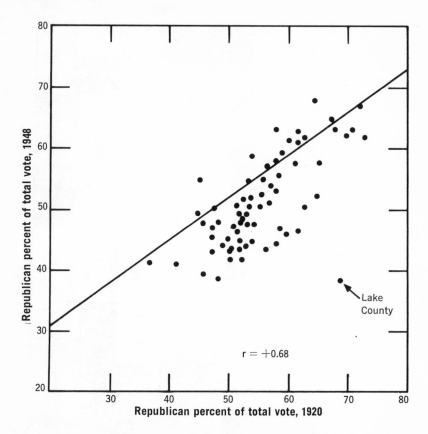

groups to maintain their being through a combination of the retention of individual loyalties and the recruitment of new adherents.[8]

Recognition of the time dimension of "decision" suggests the plausibility of an analytical model built on the assumption that political groupings manage to exist, as majorities or minorities, over long periods of time.[9] Their persistence suggests that they may represent, not mere derivatives from other social groupings, but political groups with a life of their own.[10] To be properly understood these groupings would probably have to be analyzed in their

---

[8] See S. J. Eldersveld, "The Independent Vote: Measurement, Characteristics, and Implications for Party Strategy," *American Political Science Review*, XLVI (1952), 732–753.

[9] How one converts this kind of proposition into a problem susceptible of neat empiracle testing presents another question.

[10] This factor may partially explain the frustration that almost invariably accompanies attempts to identify party characteristics by correlation of votes with demographic characteristics. One element of the variance unexplained by such analysis may lie in variables in the behavior of "political" man, such as persistence of partisan attachment, which may be quite independent of the so-called determinants.

behavior *vis-à-vis* the institutions of local government as well as in relation to national issues.

Focus on the time dimension of voting behavior compels recognition of the more or less standing nature of electoral decision, at least for a substantial part of the electorate. Yet the traditional vote does not by any means decide all elections nor govern the decisions of all individual voters. The traditional party divisions apparently fix a line of seige which moves to and fro with the fortunes of individual political battles. The balance of electoral strength varies from community to community and is disturbed in varying degrees by the impact of events and of campaigns. In any case the traditional pattern of voting provides a bench mark for the identification and analysis of particular electoral shifts. Electoral decision may be fundamentally a question of whether to depart from preexisting decision. Under what circumstances does the electorate, or parts of it, choose to deviate from old habits of action? Does the nature of these "decisions" differ from election to election, situation to situation?

DURABLE ALTERATIONS IN PARTISAN DIVISION

Even the most cursory analysis of shifts in party strength from the more or less viscous pattern of traditional behavior suggests that an understanding of the process of electoral decision (and of popular government must rest on a differentiation of types of electoral decision in the sense of elections as collective decision. It also suggests lines for the supplementation of the theory that "social characteristics determine political preference" to make it a more useful tool for political analysis.

Evidently one type of electoral decision consists in a more or less durable shift in the traditional partisan division within a community. The manner in which such realignments occur should be instructive to advocates of party reconstruction as well as suggestive for speculation about the nature of the party system. This type of alteration is not the work of a moment but may take place in a series of steps spread over a considerable period of time. Or at least such would be the conclusion if the Indiana data mean anything beyond the particular situation.

To identify areas undergoing a secular change in party division one must separate the electoral movements that occur from election to election from those that seem to represent a long-term trend. The long-term tendency of the areas undergoing durable realignment presumably will be retarded or accelerated by those factors peculiar to each election which affect them as well as those areas not touched by the secular trend. A crude separation of short-term movements and long-term trends is accomplished by the arrangement of the data in Figure 14.3. From 1920 to 1948 in fifteen Indiana counties the Democratic proportion of the two-party presidential vote increased by 10 percentage points or more.[11] In the chart the average Democratic per-

---

[11] Obviously the manifestation of a secular trend in particular counties depends to some extent on the terminal points chosen for identifying them. Further, it would be erroneous to suppose that all areas moving in a secular manner either begin that movement at the same time or proceed at the same rate.

Figure 14.3 Secular Shift in Partisan Attachment: Mean Democratic Percentage of Two-Party Presidential Vote for All Indiana Counties and for Fifteen Counties with the Most Marked Democratic Growth, 1920–1952

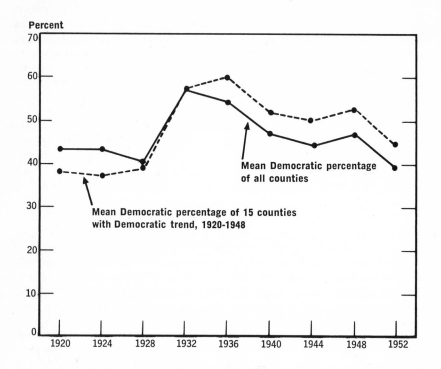

centage of these counties is plotted alongside the average Democratic percentage of all counties of the state. Although the fifteen counties evidently felt the election-to-election influences common to all counties, their long-term divergence as a group from the mean of all counties moved them in a sequence of steps over sixteen years from a Republican position to a new and relatively stable pattern of division above the Democratic average for all counties. The shifting counties were more affected by the LaFollette candidacy in 1924 than were the rest of the state's counties.[12] As a group, they withstood the general trend toward Hoover in 1928. In 1932 they moved Democratic as did all other counties but at a slightly higher rate. In 1936 their divergent trend continued and apparently that election fixed a new equilibrium in partisan division. In effect, the analysis segregates out areas undergoing a secular trend that creates a "new traditional" pattern. If the cyclical component of the fifteen-county series in Figure 14.3 were to be removed, the residual secular trend would show a gradual upward movement from 1924 to 1936 after which the series would flatten out.

[12] The mean LaFollette percentage of the total vote in the fifteen counties was 9.0; in all counties the mean was 4.8

The phenomenon recorded in the chart has interest purely for its isolation of a secular movement from one party toward the other. Only a panel study over a long period could determine the detailed nature of the secular change, yet from the aggregate statistics some surmises are possible. To the extent that the shift reflected a net change in partisan attachment rather than differentials in accretions to the two parties,[13] it probably occurred by the cumulation of individual shifts. Some persons became disenchanted with the major parties in 1924 and voted for LaFollette. Others were recruited by the Democrats on liquor and religious issues in 1928. The depression made permanent as well as temporary Democratic converts in 1932. The impact of the New Deal program completed the process in 1936. Party realignment may be accomplished under some circumstances by a series of steps.[14]

If this aggregate analysis identifies a type of electoral shift, can it be brought under the doctrine that "social characteristics determine political preference" or do we need a supplementary theory? If social characteristics determine political preference, it would be supposed that a set of secular social changes occurred in our fifteen counties and guided their political reorientation. Most of the fifteen counties either included within their limits considerable cities or were within the zone of influence of such cities.[15] Yet not all counties containing such cities underwent enough partisan change to be included in the group.[16] Most of the counties enjoyed a continuing growth of urban population and of industry, and in some instances notable addition to the electorate occurred with the coming of age of sons and daughters of immigrants.

[13] The great upswing in Democratic strength in Indiana from 1920 to 1936 may have represented principally Democratic success in recruiting new voters rather than in the conversion of erstwhile Republicans. With 1920 as 100, the total presidential vote, the Republican vote, and the Democratic vote from 1920 to 1936 were as follows.

	TOTAL	REPUBLICAN	DEMOCRATIC
1920	100.0	100.0	100.0
1924	100.8	100.9	96.3
1928	112.5	121.8	110.0
1932	124.7	97.2	168.6
1936	130.7	99.3	182.8

Apart from their temporary expansion in 1928, the Republicans only about held their own from 1920 to 1936, while the Democrats almost doubled their vote. These figures do not prove that the Democrats had greater success in winning new voters. Yet from what is known of the stability of voting attachments, the figures strongly suggest that such an interpretation provides at least a partial explanation.

[14] One should cover himself against the possibility that the apparent secular trend of the fifteen counties is not a secular divergence from the movement of the state but a cyclical fluctuation with a wider amplitude than the cyclical movement of the state as a whole.

[15] The fifteen counties were Blackford (near Muncie), Clark (which falls within the Louisville metropolitan district), Delaware (Muncie), Elkhart (Elkhart), Howard (Kokomo), Knox (Vincennes), Lake (Gary), LaPorte (Michigan City), Madison (Anderson), Porter (adjacent to Lake), Starke (in northeastern Indiana, the home of Henry Schricker, important Indiana Democratic leader), St. Joseph (South Bend), Vanderburgh, (Evansville), Vermillion (a marginal coal mining county), Vigo (Terre Haute). The range of the 1920 Democratic percentages was from 21.3 (Lake) to 51.0 (Clark). The 1948 range was from 36.7 (Porter) to 61.0 (Clark). Of the fifteen counties, eleven were over 50 percent Democratic in 1948; only one was over 50 percent Democratic in 1920.

[16] For example, Marion (Indianapolis) and Allen (Fort Wayne).

It seems most improbable that changes in social characteristics occurred as rapidly as did political change during the period 1924–1936. To fill in one theoretical gap one could posit the existence of a lag in the adjustment of political preference to social characteristics, that is, that it took some time for political attitude to catch up with urbanization and industrialization. Under some circumstances the process of social determinism may encounter formidable friction in remolding political orientation.

The perspective of time also suggests the utility of taking into account other elements of the field within which the voter acts. Over the period 1920–1948 the political parties and the voter's perceptions of political parties probably changed more than did his social characteristics. The pronouncements of political leadership and alternatives in program tendencies of the parties played upon the voter. Moreover, the group affiliations of the people of our fifteen counties and of the state changed but little in the period 1924–1936, but through the differential effects of depression and party appeals those memberships and characteristics, if they were determinative of political preference, took on a new meaning. Social characteristics do not operate in a political vacuum. It is quite as meaningful, perhaps more, to assert that changes in the structure of political alternatives govern electoral choice as it is to say that social characteristics determine political preference.

All this discussion points, of course, to the proximate relation of group discipline to individual electoral decision. To explain the more or less durable secular shift in partisan loyalty identified here one must go beyond group theory to an analysis of factors that bring particular social characteristics to the level of political consciousness, to changes that alter radically the distribution of the electorate among categories of persons differentiated by politically significant characteristics. Collective electoral decision, at least at times, may be a product of such changes in the aggregate with group determinism functioning more or less as an accessory after the fact.

SHORT-TERM DISTURBANCES OF PARTISAN PATTERNS: THE RELATIVITY OF SOCIAL DETERMINISM

Another elaboration of the doctrine of social determinism is suggested by observation of the short-term shifts in partisan strength. Evidently at some moments in time these shifts are associated with a particular social characteristic; at other times that characteristic will be unimportant as a determinant. At one time one social characteristic may seem to fix election results; at another time another will predominate.

Again rough analyses of the Indiana data may illustrate the argument. The charts in Figure 14.4 indicate the movement of the mean of the Republican percentage of the total presidential vote from 1924 to 1928 in four types of counties. In the urban counties with relatively small proportions of their population Roman Catholic, the Republicans gained sharply while their proportion of the vote declined in urban counties with the highest proportions of

Figure 14.4 Impact of the 1928 Campaign: Shift from 1924 to 1928 in the Republican Percentage of Total Presidential Vote in Four Types of Indiana Counties

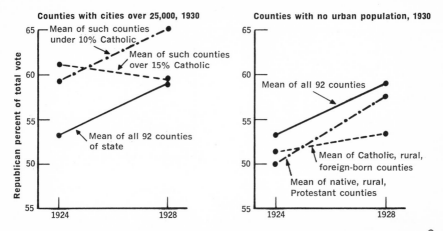

Roman Catholic population.[17] In the rural counties with the highest proportions of native-born Protestant population, a much sharper Republican gain occurred than in rural counties with relatively high proportions of Catholic and foreign-born.[18]

Obviously these aggregate figures do not establish that Protestants moved from Democratic to Republican ranks from 1924 to 1928. Nevertheless, it is most probable that a shift associated with religion and related factors occurred. To the extent that the data indicate electoral decisions associated with such social attributes, they point toward an additional elaboration of the theory of social determinism. The social characteristics of our contrasting counties changed very little over the period 1924–1928. If these characteristics determined political preference, they acquired a political significance, at least for some people, in 1928 that they lacked in 1924.

The same sorts of propositions find further illustration in the voting behavior of German and non-German counties. Although most Indiana counties from 1936 to 1940 shifted to some degree away from the Democrats, the supposition is that voters of German origin were especially antagonized by Roosevelt's policy toward the Reich.[19] In 1940 Henry Schricker ran as the Democratic candidate for governor. Of German origin, he was reputed

[17] Those counties containing cities of over 25,000 and witth less than 10 percent Roman Catholic population were Delaware, Elkhart, Howard, Madison, Marion, Vigo, Wayne. Those with over 15 percent Catholic population were Lake, LaPorte, St. Joseph.

[18] Completely rural counties with under 5 percent Catholic population and under 5 percent of their population foreign-born or of foreign or mixed parentage were Brown, Carroll, Crawford, Hendricks, Orange, Owen, Parke, Scott, Switzerland. The other group consisted of rural counties with over 10 percent Catholic population and over 10 percent foreign-born or of foreign or mixed parentage. These were Benton, Pulaski, Starke, Franklin, Spencer. It scarcely need be said that the available census data provide no satisfactory differentiation of counties according to the national origin of their population.

[19] This is the thesis of Louis Bean *How to Predict Elections* (New York: Knopf, 1948), pp. 93–99.

Figure 14.5 National Origin and the Vote: Democratic Percentage of the Two-Party Vote for President and Governor in Dubois and Clark Counties, Indiana, 1936–1948

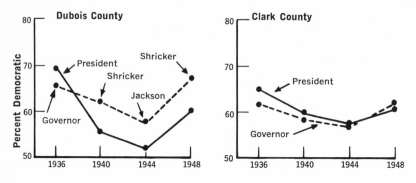

to have a potent appeal to voters of that nationality. If the social characteristic of national origin moved in higher degree into the zone of political relevance in 1940, it would be supposed that German voters would support Schricker in higher degree than Roosevelt while the non-German groups would probably give about the same proportion of their vote to both gubernatorial and presidential candidates.

Insofar as election returns give a clue to group voting behavior the graphs in Figure 14.5 support the proposition. The chart compares Dubois County, in high degree Germanic in origin, with Clark County, an area with relatively fewer citizens of German origin. Dissatisfaction with foreign policy presumably accounted for the especially sharp drop in Dubois in the vote for the Democratic presidential candidate in 1940. The higher vote in that county for Democratic candidates for governer probably reflected primarily a loyalty to the state Democratic ticket unaffected by national policy and perhaps to some extent the special appeal of Henry Schricker, who ran in both 1940 and 1948. On the other hand, in Clark County the Democratic presidential and gubernatorial candidates polled more nearly the same percentages of the vote.

The relativity of social determinism is further illustrated by a type of fluctuation in party strength in which voters are apparently drawn away from their usual party preference by the issue or events of a particular campaign only to return to the fold when the repelling peculiarities of the election disappear.[20] It might be supposed, for example, that in 1928 some persons who usually voted Democratic supported Hoover in preference to Smith yet returned to their party when the commotion subsided. A rough test of the proposition is provided by the data in Figure 14.6, which shows the mean Republican percentage of the total vote for President and for Lieutenant-Governor of another pair of contrasting groups of counties from 1920 to 1932. Note in particular that the predominantly Protestant rural counties reported about twice as wide a net splitting of tickets to the advantage of

[20] The possibility should not be excluded that a series of "peculiar" elections may have cumulative effects productive of a secular growth of one party.

Figure 14.6 Mean Republican Percentage of the Total Vote for President and Lieutenant Governor in Selected Protestant and Catholic Counties in Indiana, 1920–1932

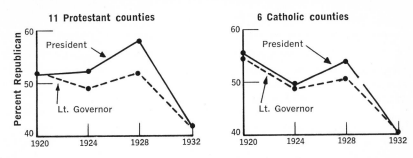

Hoover as did otherwise comparable counties with relatively large Catholic populations.[21] In both types of counties the gaps between the state and national votes disappeared in 1932. Such aggregate figures, of course, do not tell us who crossed party lines, whether gross ticket splitting was greater in one set of counties than in the other, or whether ticket splitting was higher at one election than another.[22] Yet the differentials strongly suggest that Protestant Democrats and perhaps Catholic Republicans responded to the situation in 1928 by splitting their tickets. After the religious issue subsided, national and local party appeals were more nearly congruent and ticket splitting declined.

The data have an incidental utility in sharper definition of the "independent" voter. Insofar as ticket splitting is regarded as a manifestation of "independence," one type of independence apparently is not a generalized objectivity of judgment but a response of particular classes of voters to the particular issues of the day. The quantity and incidence of this type of voting would be expected to differ from time to time with the issues and personalities of the moment.[23]

All these illustrative analyses in a sense support the doctrine of social

[21] The counties compared were drawn from those counties with 20–29.0 percent urban population in 1930 and with no cities of over 10,000. The differentiation of Catholic and non-Catholic counties was based on the percentage of the 1930 total population reported as Roman Catholic by the Census of Religious Bodies of 1936. The counties under 2 percent Catholic were: Boone, Clay, Fulton, Greene, Hamilton. Johnson, Kosciusko, Morgan, Putnam, Wells. Those over 12 percent Catholic were Daviess, Decatur, Dubois, Perry, Porter, Warrick. It scarcely needs be said that the data on religious composition are not very reliable.

[22] Which, of course, points to one of the great advantages of the sample survey over the analysis of election returns.

[23] The phenomenon of departure and return to party suggests the question whether the pattern of party division among the counties of the state could be regarded as something of an equilibrium which may be disturbed by the impact of particular campaigns yet tends to restore itself when the next campaign comes along. To test the notion the county-by-county Republican percentage in 1916 was regarded as the "normal" pattern. A rank order correlation was made with succeeding elections with the following results: 1920, 0.862; 1924, 0.775; 1928, 0.634; 1932, 0.754. Through 1928 the correlations steadily declined. Each election marked a further departure from the 1916 pattern. The 1928 election showed the sharpest deviation as the crosscurrents of that campaign played havoc with past voting patterns. Yet in 1932, the counties moved back toward their pre-existing ranking.

determinism of political preference yet they also point to the need for correlative theory. Social characteristics gain a political significance when political alternatives tend to parallel differentials in social attribute. One attribute may be of political significance at one time and another at another. That significance may well be the product of events and actions entirely outside the group concerned. Politicians may, in effect, invest group attributes with political significance. Appeals to group interest, prejudice, and pride are part of the stock-in-trade of the politician who often labors mightily to make the voter conscious of his social characteristics in order that they may determine his political preference.

To gain a broader understanding of electoral choice, it is necessary to account for the circumstances associated with variations in the relevance of social characteristics for electoral decision. That inquiry must lead beyond the nexus of group and individual voter to those factors associated with the political activation of groups or to those factors that bring social characteristics into the zone of political relevance. The data examined suggest such factors as the differentials in impact of market forces on different groups, the changing structure of political alternatives, the interaction of group memories of past and contemporary events. Undoubtedly many types of factors contribute to group tensions and frictions. Their identification permits one to go a step beyond the proximate relations involved in the focus on relationship of group and individual toward a more complete identification of the nature of electoral decision. Unless we can make some such step, we are left more or less with the proposition that those social characteristics that happen to be relevant at a particular time and place determine, or are associated with, political preference.[24]

UNEXPLAINED ELEMENTS OF DECISION: THE GENERAL DRIFT OF SENTIMENT

While the interaction of the structure of political alternatives and cleavages in social characteristics undoubtedly bears significantly on electoral decision, the preceding analyses implicitly suggest that social determinism may account for only part of the movement of the electorate from party to party over each four-year period. Social groups that move into the zone of political relevance in a particular campaign may transfer their loyalties in a relatively high degree, but it seems not unlikely that in many elections most groups move in the same direction. If this could be demonstrated, it would

[24] Tests of the index of political predisposition of the Erie County study of 1940 against national samples in the elections of 1944 and 1948 illustrate the problem. (See Lazarsfeld, Berelson, and Gaudet, pp. xi-xviii; and Morris Janowitz and W. E. Miller, "The Index of Political Predisposition in the 1948 Election," *Journal of Politics*, XIV [1952], 710–727). An index descriptive of the association between particular social characteristics and political preference among the electors of a particular locality at a particular election did not fit so well national samples at other elections. To round out the theory of the determinism of social characteristics, it would be necessary to devise a scheme to account for the shifting political significance of these characteristics. If they do change in significance, no index in terms of particular characteristics could be expected to have much predictive value save under conditions of a highly stable politics or over the relatively short run.

suggest the existence of some political *X* factor or factors which may, in most elections, play the determinative role in political decision.

The evidence on the proposition is extremely thin. Obviously the facts differ from election to election, yet it seems fairly plain that in many four-year periods a general drift of sentiment occurs that is shared to some degree by people of all sorts of social characteristics. Some of the charts point in that direction. Some broader possibilities are suggested by the data in Table 14.1,

TABLE 14.1 NUMBER OF INDIANA COUNTIES WITH INCREASING OR DECLIN-
ING DEMOCRATIC PERCENTAGE OF TWO-PARTY PRESIDENTIAL
VOTE, 1928–1952

PERIOD	INCREASING DEMOCRATIC PERCENTAGE	DECINING DEMOCRATIC PERCENTAGE	NO PER-CENTAGE CHANGE	TOTAL
1928–1932	92	0	0	92
1932–1936	23	68	1	92
1936–1940	0	92	0	92
1940–1944	3	89	0	92
1944–1948	87	5	0	92
1948–1952	0	92	0	92

which shows the direction of movement from presidential election to presidential election from 1928 to 1952 of all the counties of Indiana. It will be observed that the more common pattern was for most of the counties to move in the same direction. A sharp deviation from this uniformity occurred in 1936 which was a crucial election in reshaping the traditional composition of the Democratic following, as was indicated by Figure 14.1.

The figures of Table 14.1 only show, of course, that the people of geographical units as a whole moved in the same direction in most elections. Only insofar as social differentiation is associated with geography do the figures give ground for supposing that various sorts of social groups moved in the same direction. A series of sample surveys covering the same period as the table would be necessary to determine the answer to that question. Yet scattered evidence suggests that it is not uncommon for people of the most diverse social groups to shift their political sentiments in the same direction. Decisions, for instance, to change, may well be conditioned, at least in some elections, by factors more or less independent of social characteristics. It could be that persons of different characteristics shift in the same direction for different reasons, yet that seems inadequate to account for the drastic shifts affecting all types of persons in some elections. Whatever the explanations may be, it seems clear that the search has to extend beyond the tendency of nonpolitical groups to enforce their norms on their members.

COMMENT

A major burden of the argument has been that the isolation of the electorate from the total governing process and its subjection to microscopic analysis tends to make electoral study a nonpolitical endeavor. That isolation tends, perhaps not of necessity but because of the blinders on perception associated with the method, to divorce the subjects of microscopic examination from their place in the larger political situation. Hence, all the studies of so-called "political behavior" do not add impressively to our comprehension of the awesome process by which the community or nation makes decisions at the ballot box.

It has been suggested that a fruitful avenue of development might be to seek to bridge the gap between microanalysis and macroanalysis, to the improvement of both. Much further refinement of our knowledge of the place of social characteristics in electoral decision, for example, would probably quickly follow once the setting of political alternatives and the matrix of objective conditions within which these determinants operate were brought more specifically into the field of observation. It seems apparent that social characteristics move into and out of the zone of political relevance, that they "explain" the actions of some people and not those of others, and that insofar as social characteristics determine political preference they encounter considerable friction.

Some of the difficulties of theory and analysis will be solved in due course, doubtless in a serendipitous manner, as the number of studies multiplies. New types of election situations will be analyzed; provisional generalizations will be modified to account for new situations; and the process will be repeated. By the observation of a greater variety of types of situations it may be possible to tie the study of electoral behavior more directly to the workings of the state. Such a linkage might enable us to talk with a bit more information about the conditions under which an electorate can most effectively perform its decision-making role in the governing process. What are the consequences, for example, of the subjection of differing proportions of the vote to determination by specified social characteristics? Of the existence of a greater or lesser proportion of the electorate loyal to party? Of the intensification of particular types of group loyalties? Of the decay of others? Of the introduction of particular types of issues into the electoral arena? Of integration or atomization of the structure of leadership? Of variations in the range of electoral indifference and in the intensity of electoral involvement.[25]

Another point that recurs is a note of doubt about the doctrine that social characteristics determine political preference. There can be no doubt that there is at times a high degree of association between readily identifiable social characteristics and political preference. At the extreme position it might be argued that political preference is a hitchhiker or social characteristics. Yet there seems to be always a very considerable part of the electorate for which no readily isolable social characteristic "explains" political preference. The query may be raised whether a rather serious void does not exist in the theory. Is there some sort of political order or system of loyalties more or less independent of the identifications of citizens and electors with these nonpolitical groups to which we have an index in their social characteristics? The identification and analysis of the political role of the voter may

25 For a statement of other directions of development, see B. R. Berelson, "Democratic Theory and Public Opinion," Public Opinion Quarterly, XVI (1952), 313–330.

present considerable difficulty in research design, yet if there is no political community, if citizens, or many of them, have no political role more or less autonomous from their other roles, a good many centuries of political speculation, both hortatory and otherwise, has been beside the point. Some of the considerable variance unaccounted for by social determination might be removed by attempts to analyze the nature of the individual's identification with the community and the nation, the character of his identification with political party, his perception of the political world, his general orientation toward complexes of policy questions, his conception of his role as a voter and as a citizen. There may well be, for a part of the electorate at least, roles, identifications, and preferences of a purely political nature with quite as much reality as his "social characteristics." Perhaps some common denominator ties together the archetype Republican and the Republican unskilled laborer who always turns up in the survey.

In research the answers one gets depend in part on the kinds of questions he asks. If one inquires about social characteristics and political preference, he finds out about social characteristics and political preference. If one puts other sorts of questions into the research mill, he might well bring out other and more complex characteristics of the process of electoral decision. It might well turn out that the emerging picture would be one of an electorate, or at least of a great many electors, now struggling with great questions, now whipped into a frenzy or into fear by the demagogue, now voting against its own imputed short-term interest, now acting without check or restraint, now weighing as best it may the welfare of the community, all more or less in accord with classical democratic theory.[26]

---

[26] It should be noted for the record that this essay was completed essentially in its present form in June, 1953. It, therefore, does not take into account the theoretical advances by Berelson, Lazarsfeld, and McPhee in their *Voting* (Chicago: University of Chicago Press, 1964). Moreover, since the essay was drafted Mr. Munger has completed an intensive analysis of Indiana politics reported in *Two-Party Politics in the State of Indiana* (MS dissertation, Harvard University, 1955). Full utilization of his detailed findings would permit considerable refinement of the factual data underlying the argument.

IV THE PSYCHOLOGY OF OPINION HOLDING AND ITS FUNCTIONAL RELEVANCE

The readings in this part reverse the priorities emphasized in the previous sections. In place of structural aggregations of opinions and their contribution to understanding political questions, the selections in Part IV examine the psychological aspects of opinion expression.

In Selection 15, Herbert McClosky attempts to isolate "conservatives" and "liberals" and then to compare such individuals as to their attitudes toward government and human nature and the personality attributes they manifest, such as dominance, alienation, pessimism, and guilt. McClosky also relates his typologies to clinical psychological traits such as paranoia, hostility, rigidity, and intolerance. The study finds numerous psychological characteristics that appear to distinguish the conservative personality. The translation of these characteristics into politically relevant belief systems is also treated.

In a broadly related work (Selection 16), Daniel Katz explores the needs that patterns of opinions serve for the individual. Katz identifies the four principal functions that attitudes perform for the individual personality as the adjustive function, the ego-defensive function, the value-expressive function, and the knowledge function. He elaborates on each category and the contribution it makes in accommodating the individual to his world.

While the McClosky and Katz papers focus mainly on the micro-level of behavior, Robert LeVine's article (Selection 17) concentrates on the potential relationships among an individual's motives, habits, and values and the behavior patterns of nations. The essay is broad and thought-provoking. For example, LeVine reviews the implications of family child-rearing practices for the values assimilated by the individual, and in turn the individual's attitudinal orientations toward the state. He examines the early work on political socialization—specifically that of Easton, Hess, and Newcomb—and explores the complex psychological interrelationship between the individual and the governing system and the attitudinal climates appropriate for change in the newer nations. The broader political implications of the opinion-formation process in all varieties of settings are well illustrated by this selection.

The last paper in Part IV, by Paul Sheatsley and Jacob Feldman (Selection 18), reviews the implications of the assassination of a President. The selection introduces some understanding of how important news is communicated and of the role of the mass media in keeping citizens informed. It also indicates the fundamental psychological dislocations that individuals undergo upon the brutal loss of a national leader and the manner in which people attempt to adjust to such an unexpected event. The consequences of such political murders for a nation are grave, for the President personifies the values and programs of a country. In the literature on political socialization, the President has been identified as the image that forms one of the child's earliest and warmest ties to the political system. In the crisis period following the assassination of President Kennedy, the grief was shared by both friend and foe and apparently served to bring all closer together for at least the immediate duration of the upheaval. Seldom do specific events touch all citizens with such an impact. The manner in which the individual psychologically adjusts to the news has importance for the vitality and perseverance of the total political system.

15

Conservatism and Personality *

HERBERT McCLOSKY

If justification were needed for taking notice once again of the liberal-conservative distinction, it would be sufficient, I suppose, merely to observe that this division has been injected into the politics of Western nations for at least two centuries and, depending on the nature of one's criteria, perhaps longer.

INTRODUCTION

The distinction between the two camps has not always been sharply drawn, of course, for both have been compelled, as a condition for survival, to hold important beliefs in common. Moreover, each has reversed itself on certain issues, such as government regulation of the economy, casting off old views in favor of beliefs previously cherished by the other. Competing for popular support in elections, and succeeding one another in office, the two camps have, of necessity, taken on many values in common, tempering their programs and adjusting their courses to the practical requirements of political

* Reprinted by permission from *The American Political Science Review*, 52 (March 1958), pp. 27–45.

contest. In a system like ours, where the parties have functioned less as ideological movements than as brokerage organizations hoping to attract majority support from almost every segment of the electorate, the distinction has tended to be dulled even further, until, at the actual scenes of daily political struggle, it has often faded entirely. Even in political systems abroad where doctrinal parties are more frequently in evidence, the differences between liberals and conservatives have become operationally more obscure as the parties have shared office, confronted the reality of common problems, and competed for the support of the waverers at the middle ranges of the ideological spectrum.

We would be mistaken, however, to infer from this that all distinctions between the liberal and conservative tendencies are spurious, or that they are mere inventions of office-seekers or publicists. Not only do our Minnesota studies find many of the differences to be genuine, but the two camps bear a remarkable continuity with the patrilineal doctrines from which they have descended. For example, the credo of the "New Conservatives" (as distinguished from the shifting programs of conservative parties) includes few notions not already expressed by Edmund Burke, whose writings, despite seeming inconsistencies, are generally considered the fountainhead of modern conservative thought. The political writings of Russell Kirk, Clinton Rossiter, John Hallowell, or Richard Weaver, of the refurbished Southern Agrarians like Donald Davidson, the poets of nostalgia like T. S. Eliot, or of magazines like *Measure*, the *National Review*, the *American Mercury*, and *Modern Age*— express with varying degrees of intensity and spiritual violence the principles and doctrines which have enjoyed currency among self-styled conservatives for generations. Thus, despite modifications imposed by political exigency and despite even the sharp reversals that have occasionally developed on specific issues, the outlook of conservatism has, like liberalism, remained fairly firm through recent centuries. This suggests that both conservatism and liberalism may be "natural" or polar positions around which individuals of certain habitual outlooks, temperaments, and sensibilities can comfortably come to rest and be united with others of like disposition.

Many people, of course, do not exhibit the patterns of mind and personality that are fully identified with either of the polar positions, but embrace elements of both, in varying proportions. Nevertheless, it is reasonable to believe that a characteristic conservative focus exists, not only because of the historical continuity already noted, but also because liberal and conservative values would not, in the absence of such focus, fall into pattern, but would instead be distributed randomly throughout all sections of the population; that is, even if one knew some of the beliefs a given individual possessed, one could not predict by better than chance what other beliefs or values he held.

The data I will present show, however, that there is considerable regularity and coherence not only in the body of norms professed but in the relation between certain casts of character and personality on the one side and the degree of conservatism or liberalism expressed on the other.

Before proceeding to the body of the paper bearing on this relation, I should point out that we have had less interest in the conservative-liberal distinction as such than in the example it offers for the further study of political preference, belief, and affiliation—the subjects with which we have been centrally concerned in our research. Hence we have not been occupied with many of the questions about conservatism which have commanded the attention of political scientists and essayists. It has not been our purpose, for example, to explore the historical unfolding of conservative thought; to describe conservative movements of the past; to present the case for embracing or rejecting conservatism as a doctrine; to estimate the truth of its essential propositions or the validity of its claims; to ascertain the excellence or shabbiness of its moral outlook; or to resolve the question of its "real" definition. It has not been our intention either to challenge or support its assumptions, to make policy recommendations, or to exhort anyone for or against its doctrines. Admittedly, we have opinions and biases on these matters, and we are not blind to the possibility that they may influence the interpretation of our findings. Indeed, we assume that they will, no matter how disinterested our original intention. We should be very disappointed, nevertheless, if the controversial nature of the subject matter or the heat that may be generated by the findings were to obscure the scientific validity we have worked so hard to achieve.

A prefatory note concerning our interest in personality may also be helpful. Although certain assumptions about the nature of man were implicit in the thought of many of the classic political writers (Plato, Machiavelli, Hobbes, Locke, and Bentham come immediately to mind), the relation of personality to politics has, I think, received less attention from contemporary political scientists than it deserves. Spurred, however, by the injunctions of Graham Wallas that we must "deal with politics in its relation to the nature of man," and stimulated by the progress of academic, as well as Freudian, psychology, attention has here and there begun to be focused upon personality as an important dimension for the study of politics. In recent years the work of Lasswell, Fromm, the authors of *The Authoritarian Personality*, Almond, and a few others offer cases in point, and these have stimulated others. For my own part, I should like to make it clear that while I believe the study of personality to be extremely valuable, it would be naive to suppose that it could possibly serve as a universal device for the study of every problem encountered in political research. It cannot be substituted for certain other types of investigation which have interested political scientists, such as the study of institutional and legal structures, descriptions of political process, or the formal analysis of normative propositions. Rather, the study of personality offers one more category of explanation to accompany those already familiar to us, thereby adding an important new dimension to our understanding of political phenomena, and helping us to clarify or correct certain propositions about politics that have never been put to adequate empirical test.

THE CONSERVATISM MEASURE:
DEFINITION AND VALIDITY

Because it is a key term in the language of political conflict, choked with emotive connotations, "conservatism" has naturally evoked controversy over its meaning. The problem of defining it has, furthermore, been confused in recent decades by the already mentioned switch in the economic attitudes of both conservatives and liberals, and by the rise of movements of the "radical right" of which the fascist parties are the most extreme example but which are also represented in somewhat milder form by such groups as the Conservative Citizens' Committees. Some prefer to reserve the "conservative" label for the advocates of laissez-faire capitalism, for critics of the New Deal, or for Republicans of whatever ideological persuasion; for some it mainly signifies intemperate right-wing values of the McCarthy or *Chicago Tribune* type; while for others, it recalls the somewhat romanticized image of a Boston Brahmin—genteel, cultivated, practical, a gentleman of exquisite sensibilities and manners, a critic of the vulgarities of mass society, saddened by, though resigned to, the heavy price of equalitarian democracy.

Arguments occur as well over more esoteric questions: whether conservatism is a full-blown ideology or only a state of mind; whether it is a social posture found among the defenders of every type of society or a clutch of prejudices appropriate to a specific social class at a given historical stage; whether it is a set of empirically settled propositions about man and society or a body of self-evident truths, intuitively prized by persons of sufficient character to grasp their significance; and so on.

In the face of these diverse opinions, we cannot hope that the definition employed in our research, and the measure or "scale" that we constructed from this definition, will satisfy everyone. We have made an earnest effort, however, to extract from the tradition of self-styled conservative thought, and especially from the writings of Edmund Burke, a set of principles representing that tradition as fairly as possible. We have concentrated upon those attitudes and values that continually recur among acknowledged conservative thinkers and that appear to comprise the invariant elements of the conservative outlook. By the same token, we have tried to avoid attitudes or opinions that seemed to us situationally determined and which, for that reason, appear to be secondary and unstable correlates of liberal or conservative tendencies. Many attitudes that arise mainly from party or class affiliation fall into this category, for instance, attitudes toward free enterprise, toward trade unions, toward expansion of government functions, toward the New Deal and its welfare measures, toward tariffs, farm supports, and a number of similar issues that have featured prominently in political campaigns.

In spite of the differences, there is astonishing agreement among the disciples, and among disinterested scholars as well, that the following are characteristic, if not quintessential elements of the conservative outlook.[1]

> **1.** Man is a creature of appetite and will, "governed more by emotion than by reason" (Kirk), in whom "wickedness, unreason, and the urge to violence lurk always behind the curtain of civilized behavior" (Rossiter). He is a fallen creature, doomed to imperfection, and inclined to license and anarchy.

[1] The doctrines expressed in these paragraphs have been drawn from the writings of such acknowledged conservative spokesmen as Edmund Burke, *Reflections on the Revolution in France*; F. J. C. Hearnshaw, *Conservatism in England* (London, 1933); R.J. White, ed., *The Conservative Tradition* (London, 1950); Quentin Hogg, *The Case for Conservatism* (Harmondsworth, 1947); Russell Kirk, *The Conservative Mind* (Chicago, 1953); Clinton Rossiter, *Conservatism in America* (New York, 1955); Francis G. Wilson, *The Case for Conservatism* (Seattle, 1951); Peter Viereck, *Conservatism: From John Adams to Churchill* (New York, 1955); and others. In addition, books and articles by numerous commentators were consulted, including such recent articles as Samuel P. Huntington, "Conservatism as an Ideology," *American Political Science Review*, Vol. 51 (June 1957), 454–473.

2. Society is ruled by "divine intent" (Kirk) and made legitimate by Providence and prescription. Religion "is the foundation of civil society" (Huntington) and is man's ultimate defense against his own evil impulses.

3. Society is organic, plural, inordinately complex, the product of a long and painful evolution, embodying the accumulated wisdom of previous historical ages. There is a presumption in favor of whatever has survived the ordeal of history, and of any institution that has been tried and found to work.

4. Man's traditional inheritance is rich, grand, endlessly proliferated and mysterious, deserving of veneration, and not to be cast away lightly in favor of the narrow uniformity preached by "sophisters and calculators" (Burke). Theory is to be distrusted since reason, which gives rise to theory, is a deceptive, shallow, and limited instrument.

5. Change must therefore be resisted and the injunction heeded that "Unless it is necessary to change it is necessary not to change" (Hearnshaw). Innovation "is a devouring conflagration more often than it is a torch of progress" (Kirk).

6. Men are naturally unequal, and society requires "orders and classes" for the good of all. All efforts at levelling are futile and lead to despair (Kirk and Rossiter), for they violate the natural hierarchy and frustrate man's "longing for leadership." The superior classes must be allowed to differentiate themselves and to have a hand in the direction of the state, balancing the numerical superiority of the inferior classes.

7. Order, authority, and community are the primary defense against the impulse to violence and anarchy. The superiority of duties over rights and the need to strengthen the stabilizing institutions of society, especially the church, the family, and, above all, private property.

Some of the points in the conservative creed are, unfortunately, distinguished more for their rhetoric than for the clarity and crispness of their content. Nevertheless, owing to the fact that they comprise an integrated outlook, we were able to construct a scale that makes it possible to measure the strength of conservative belief in individuals and groups, and thus to classify persons according to the degree of conservatism they exhibit.

In constructing this scale, we began with an initial pool of 43 items, the majority of which were fairly straightforward statements of the various conservative beliefs just discussed. Here, for example, are some typical items from the original set of 43:

> If something grows up over a long time there is bound to be much wisdom in it.
> If you start trying to change things very much, you usually make them worse.
> It's not really undemocratic to recognize that the world is divided into superior and inferior people.
> All groups can live in harmony in this country without changing the system in any way.
> You can usually depend more on a man if he owns property than if he does not.
> Our society is so complicated that if you try to reform parts of it you're likely to upset the whole system.
> I prefer the practical man anytime to the man of ideas.

A man doesn't really get to have much wisdom until he's well along in years.

I'd want to know that something would really work before I'd be willing to take a chance on it.

No matter how we like to talk about it, political authority comes not from us but from some higher power.

Private ownership of property is necessary if we are to have a strong nation.

It is never wise to introduce changes rapidly, in government or in the economic system.

It's better to stick by what you have than to be trying new things you don't really know about.

Together with the items from a number of other scales we were simultaneously trying to build, the 43 items in the conservatism pool were submitted, through survey methods, to a large general sample of persons in the vicinity of the Twin Cities who were asked to state, in relation to each item, whether they agreed or disagreed. The patterns of their responses were then analyzed, with a three-fold purpose in mind: (1) to select from each pool those items which, by reproducibility and other statistical tests, clustered sufficiently to convince us that they belonged to the same universe; (2) to reduce the number of items in each scale to manageable proportions (we began with more than 2300 items, and over 80 pools of scale items); and (3) to ensure that every item selected for a given scale was in fact measuring some degree of the same attitude dimension or, in other words, that all the items in the final scale were consistent with each other.

Altogether, the responses of over 1200 persons were sampled and analyzed in this preliminary scale-construction stage, a procedure that took more than two years to complete. Some 539 items, comprising an inventory of 53 separate scales, survived this stage. The remaining thirty item pools failed to meet our scale standards and were dropped. Conservatism emerged as a twelve-item scale, tighter, more refined, and with greater internal consistency than was found in the original 43-item pool, with which, however, it correlated +0.83. Although the twelve-item scale did not encompass as wide a range of values as were contained in the initial item pool, its ranking of people from extreme conservatism on the one end to liberalism on the other was very close to the rank order yielded by the original 43 items, as the high correlation attests. Empirically, then, the shorter scale may be taken as an adequate, if not actually a superior and more refined substitute for the initial set of "conservative" items. (The scale has subsequently been refined further in a succeeding study, and the items reduced in number to nine.)

The validation of a scale, i.e., determining the degree to which it in fact measures the thing it purports to measure, is at best a difficult and frustrating affair. Although we have not yet exhausted all the validation procedures planned for this scale, several considerations bearing on its validity can be offered. For one thing, the scale possesses a certain amount of "face validity," which is to say that the items it includes express on their face the values which most knowledgeable people would designate as conservative. In one validation procedure employed, we submitted subsets of items from the twelve-item conservatism scale to an advanced senior-graduate class in political theory, whose members had no prior knowledge of the study or its purposes. Each student was asked to supply a name or label for the group of statements and to write a paragraph explaining or justifying the label he had chosen. Of 48 students participating, 39 volunteered the word *conservatism* as best describing the sentiments expressed in the statements, five offered names that were virtually synonymous with conservatism (e.g., *traditionalism*), while two supplied other names and two did not answer.

Thus, over 90 percent of an informed group recognized that the items expressed values characteristic of conservatism, and were able to supply explanations consistent with the labels they chose.

The conservatism scale correlated highly, and in the predicted direction, with several related measures that were being tested at the same time. For example, persons who scored as strongly conservative in the preliminary runs also proved, by comparison with the low scorers, to hold extremely conventional social attitudes, to be more responsive to nationalistic symbols, and to place greater emphasis upon duty, conformity, and discipline.

We also checked a number of individual statements that were not included as part of the conservatism scale but which nevertheless, express sentiments or opinions that would be widely recognized as related to conservatism. In all but a few instances, the persons who score as extreme conservatives agree with these statements far more frequently than do those who score as liberals. The following are a few examples:

	PERCENT AGREE	
	Liberals	Extreme Conservatives
	(N = 258)	(N = 282)
Duties are more important than rights.	32%	63%
The world is too complicated to be understood by anyone but experts.	26%	51%
You can't change human nature.	30%	73%
People are getting soft and weak from so much coddling and babying.	31%	68%
The heart is as good a guide as the head.	22%	58%
We have to teach children that all men are created equal, but almost everyone knows that some are better than others.	35%	73%
No matter what the people think, a few people will always run things anyway.	33%	63%
Few people really know what is in their best interest in the long run.	77%	43%

By reason of such criteria, we believe that the conservatism scale possesses the properties of a valid measure, and that it can be used with confidence in group studies or in research involving large samples. Similar procedures were employed in the development of the 52 other scales used in the original study (referred to as the *P A R* study, the initials standing for political participation, awareness, and responsibility); and the process was repeated in the development of 18 additional scales employed in a subsequent study of persons with extreme or "marginal" political beliefs (the *Marginal Believer* study). In constructing and validating some of the personality and social attitude scales, we were able to build on a great deal of previous work by clinical and social psychologists interested in the classification and measurement of personality traits; while in the case of other scales, such as Dominance and Social Responsibility, we were compelled to start afresh and to undertake elaborate empirical procedures to develop measures that fitted these concepts.[2]

The *P A R* study was carried out on a sample of 1211 persons in the Twin City area (not to be confused with the 1200 subjects previously employed in developing and pre-testing the inventory of scales). The *Marginal Believer* study drew upon a cross-section sample of 1082 persons from the entire state of Minnesota,[3] together with two special samples of extreme Right-Wing and Left-Wing believers, numbering almost 300 each. The data from the cross-section sample of the *Marginal Believer* project have confirmed in virtually every detail the findings relative to conservatism yielded by the *P A R* study. Hence the results described below have been borne out by two separate studies, carried out six years apart, on entirely different samples of the adult population. Most of the findings presented in this paper are drawn from the general population data of the *Marginal Believer* study, although we have equivalent results that could as easily be reported from the *P A R* project.

In each study, we broke the entire sample into quartiles of several hundred persons each, assigning subjects to one quartile or another according to their scores on the conservatism scale. Subjects scoring 7–9 on the conservatism scale were thrown into the uppermost or Extreme Conservative quartile; those with scores of 5–6 were labelled Moderate Conservatives; with scores of 3–4, Moderate Liberals; and the lowest quartile, with scores of 0–2, were called Liberals.

With these classifications, we next computed the scores of the four groups on each of the remaining scales used in the two studies, as well as on a large number of personal background characteristics for which we had also collected data in the course of the two surveys. A variety of tabulating and statistical procedures were then employed to check hypotheses, to note differences and similarities between groups, and to ascertain patterned or prototypic responses. In addition, all major tabulations were re-run with controls introduced for such factors as education, occupation, socio-economic status, and possible response set bias,[4] in order to be certain that the findings were not the spurious product of some hidden or disguised factor which, conceivably, we had been failing to take into account. We discovered, how-

[2] We have described the procedures employed in the development of these scales in the *Journal of Abnormal and Social Psychology*, Vol. 6 (1951), pp. 360–366; and Vol. 47 (1952), pp. 73–80.

[3] I should like to acknowledge the generous assistance of the *Minnesota Poll* and of its director, Sidney Goldish, for assistance in selecting this sample and administering the questionnaire.

[4] Among the most important and interesting of such response sets is the tendency exhibited by some respondents to agree—or to disagree—with statements regardless of their content. This tendency obviously distorts the response scores of the individuals who possess it. A number of special procedures were introduced to correct for this phenomenon, and to eliminate, as far as possible, the spurious influence of this factor.

ever, that even with such factors partialled out or otherwise accounted for, the tendency to affirm or to reject conservative doctrines was significantly related to social and personality characteristics.

RESULTS

In turning now to some of the outcomes of the research, I will confine myself in the main to the data that bear most immediately on personality and related attributes, omitting, for reasons of space, the material on political and social attitudes with which both studies have been greatly concerned.

Intelligence

One of the clearest findings in both studies is that, contrary to claim, conservatism is not the preferred doctrine of the intellectual elite or of the more intelligent segments of the population, but the reverse. By every measure available to us, conservative beliefs are found most frequently among the uninformed, the poorly educated, and so far as we can determine, the less intelligent. The following table sets out a few of these relationships:

The Awareness scale, referred to in the table, is a test not only of actual knowledge but also of the clarity of one's grasps of the social process, past and present. It serves, to some extent, as a crude intelligence test. The same can be said, though less authoritatively, for the Intellectuality scale, which

TABLE 15.1 COMPARISON OF CONSERVATIVES AND LIBERALS BY EDUCATION AND KNOWLEDGE, MINNESOTA SAMPLE[a]

	LIBERALS (N = 190)	MODERATE LIBERALS (N = 316)	MODERATE CON- SERVATIVES (N = 331)	EXTREME CON- SERVATIVES (N = 245)
Education				
Percent with grade school education	9	14	29	49
Percent with some college education	47	33	21	12
Awareness				
Percent scoring low	9	25	45	66
Percent scoring high	54	32	21	9
Intellectuality				
Percent scoring low	7	20	34	56
Percent scoring high	62	43	26	11

[a] In this and the following tables *high* always means a score in the upper third of the scale named; *low* always means a score in the lower third of the scale named. The middle third is omitted from these tables. The table should thus be read across, as follows: Whereas 54 percent of the Liberals score among the upper (or "high") third of the distribution on the Awareness scale, 32 percent of the Moderate Liberals, 21 percent of the Moderate Conservatives and only 9 percent of the Extreme Conservatives have "high" scores on Awareness. It should also be noted that the differences between the extreme groups in this table, and in all the subsequent data reported, are statistically significant beyond the 1 percent level of significance, which is to say that the probability is less than one in 100 that differences of these magnitudes could be occurring by chance, given the size of our samples.

assesses the degree to which intellectual habits have been formed and are perceived as attractive. The findings on these measures make plain that there is a sharp decline in the level of information and intellectual grasp as one moves from the more liberal to the more conservative sections of the population. Similarly, an increase in the level of knowledge is usually accompanied by a corresponding decrease in the incidence of conservatism. Individual items correlated with intelligence bear out the same general tendency. Thus, the item "I was a slow learner in school" is answered yes by 34 percent of the Extreme Conservatives but by only 14 percent of the Liberals. These differences on Awarness and Intellectuality remain large and statistically significant even when education and other status factors are controlled.

Of course, not all conservatives are uninformed, not all liberals are knowledgeable, and not all the unlearned are conservative. The data show clearly, nevertheless, that the most articulate and informed classes in our society are preponderantly liberal in their outlook. Procedures carried out with a special sample of civic and political leaders in the *P A R* study bear this out even further, regardless of party preference or of other affiliations that might ordinarily be expected to have an influence upon liberal-conservative tendencies.[5]

Social-Psychological Attributes

Related to status and intelligence are a set of traits that reflect the interrelation of personality and life-style, and especially the degree to which people feel themselves to be the masters or victims of their immediate environment and of themselves. These traits have to do with one's sense of security, with the sense of belonging, isolation, and social support, with feelings of worthlessness, submissiveness, inferiority, timidity, self-assurance, personal strength, and the like. In the preceding table are some of the scales we developed to assess this universe of feelings and attitudes, together with the scores registered by liberals and conservatives for each of these traits.

As these figures make plain, the Conservatives tend to score at the more "undesirable" end of the distributions on every one of the above traits. Uniformly, every increase in the degree of conservatism shows a corresponding increase in submissiveness, anomie, sense of alienation, bewilderment, etc. To some extent, the vast differences appearing in this table are a function of the somewhat higher status and education of the liberals in the sample. But the differences remain almost as large even when we control for these factors. Conservatism, in our society at least, appears to be far more characteristic of social isolates, of people who think poorly of themselves, who suffer personal disgruntlement and frustration, who are submissive, timid, and wanting in confidence, who lack a clear sense of direction and purpose, who are uncertain about their values, and who are generally be-

TABLE 15.2 COMPARISON OF CONSERVATIVES AND LIBERALS BY PERSONALITY TRAITS—SOCIAL

	LIBERALS (N = 190)	MODERATE LIBERALS (N = 316)	MODERATE CON-SERVATIVES (N = 331)	EXTREME CON-SERVATIVES (N = 245)
Dominance				
Percent low	9	19	37	51
Percent high	72	50	29	14
Anomie				
Percent low	71	48	32	10
Percent high	4	16	30	59
Alienation				
Percent low	57	47	35	18
Percent high	11	20	27	45
Bewilderment				
Percent low	61	40	33	10
Percent high	9	20	34	57
Pessimism				
Percent low	44	35	31	19
Percent high	25	35	42	53
Social Responsibility				
Percent low	12	25	36	62
Percent high	47	31	23	8
Self-Confidence				
Percent low	18	23	32	35
Percent high	46	38	24	20
Guilt				
Percent low	62	42	36	18
Percent high	16	18	28	47

wildered by the alarming task of having to thread their way through a society which seems to them too complex to fathom.

Readers of Eric Hoffer will recognize in these findings support for his brilliant, intuitive characterization of the conservative and of the conditions which give rise to him.[6] Far from being the elite or the masters or the prime movers, conservatives tend on the whole to come from the more backward and frightened elements of the population, including the classes that are socially and psychologically depressed. The significance of this, and of other findings reported in this section, will be considered in the evaluation section shortly to follow.

Clinical-Personality Variables

Turning now to a set of traits that are more straightforwardly clinical and psychological, conservatives and liberals are found to be sharply distinguished from each other in many of these characteristics as well. The differences, furthermore, are consistent with those cited in the personality-life style group. Scores on the more important of the clinical variables are shown in the following table.

[6] Eric Hoffer, The True Believer (New York, 1951), chap. 1, and passim.

TABLE 15.3 COMPARISON OF CONSERVATIVES AND LIBERALS BY PERSONALITY TRAITS—CLINICAL

	LIBERALS (N = 190)	MODERATE LIBERALS (N = 316)	MODERATE CON- SERVATIVES (N = 331)	EXTREME CON- SERVATIVES (N = 245)
Hostility				
Percent low	59	38	26	9
Percent high	18	37	46	71
Paranoid Tendencies				
Percent low	56	42	28	13
Percent high	16	27	37	62
Contempt for Weakness				
Percent low	61	33	21	5
Percent high	8	18	29	55
Need Inviolacy (Ego Defense)				
Percent low	68	58	36	17
Percent high	11	20	38	60
Rigidity				
Percent low	58	43	29	14
Percent high	18	32	41	60
Obsessive Traits				
Percent low	47	40	29	22
Percent high	24	31	43	55
Intolerance of Human Frailty				
Percent low	52	30	17	6
Percent high	8	16	23	54

The figures demonstrate with overpowering effect that conservatives tend once more to score on the more "undesirable," poorly adapted side of these personality variables. Of the four liberal-conservative classifications, the extreme conservatives are easily the most hostile and suspicious, the most rigid and compulsive, the quickest to condemn others for their imperfections or weaknesses, the most intolerant, the most easily moved to scorn and disappointment in others, the most inflexible and unyielding in their perceptions and judgments. Although aggressively critical of the shortcomings of others, they are unusually defensive and armored in the protection of their own ego needs. Poorly integrated psychologically, anxious, often perceiving themselves as inadequate, and subject to excessive feelings of guilt, they seem inclined to project onto others the traits they most dislike or fear in themselves.

If space permitted, these data could be buttressed by numerous other related findings in our studies, and the relationships so briefly presented here could be elaborated in dozens of ways. We must, however, move on to evaluate the data just offered and to analyze, in particular, their relation to conservatism as a political and social outlook.

ANALYSES

If we may trust the evidence just presented, there seems little doubt that support for conservative doctrines is highly correlated with certain distinct personality patterns. The quantitative data do not immediately make plain, however, the nature of the connection between the two or the reasons for the particular relationships found. These questions take us into realms that are somewhat more theoretical and speculative.

In the explanations that follow I have proceeded from the view that most of the propositions fundamental to the conservative creed (as well as to the liberal creed) are in reality normative rather than empirical statements. Hence, they can neither be demonstrated nor refuted by experience or observation of the external world. The universe to which conservative doctrines refer is so ambiguous that it is often possible to assert with equal validity a given proposition or its contrary. For example, which can we demonstrate more firmly, that men are naturally equal or unequal? Anarchic or law-abiding? Essentially wicked or essentially good? Which is it correct to believe, that man is governed more "by emotion than by reason," or the reverse? Which generalization can best be supported by evidence, that change is a "devouring conflagration," destructive of mankind, or a boon that prevents stagnation and the withering of the human spirit? As for statements which claim—or for that matter deny—that society is ruled by "divine intent" and that power is made legitimate by Providence, one would be hard put to decide what manner of data would be needed before one could rationally embrace or reject either view.

If the assertions contained in the conservative creed cannot be referred to the world of experience for proof or refutation, we may conclude that one is led to conservatism not by the fact as such, but only by the way one happens to perceive or "structure" the facts. There are, I think, three main ways in which such structures are developed:

First, one may impose structure on an ambiguous field of phenomena by logical procedures. Conservative doctrines might, for example, be formally derived from some set of postulates or from another system of beliefs or cognitions. Many of us like to think that our beliefs are carefully reasoned out in this way, and that our several outlooks and attitudes are internally consistent, dispassionately arrived at, and valid. The practice of reasoning out and forming attitudes on complex social questions in this purely disinterested way is, however, rare. It may occasionally be found in a few intellectuals of unusual philosophic inclination, but it is not likely to be the essential element in determining most people's convictions. As Graham Wallas observed, even the methods of reasoning about social affairs are fixed by habit and by subjective leanings. Numerous psychological studies have shown, moreover, that judgments thought to have been derived analytically, or sometimes even from observation, become notoriously more unreliable as the ambiguity of the stimulus field increases.

A second possibility is that one's views of man and society are learned through indoctrination and group influence, so that an individual reared in an environment of conservative belief absorbs its attitudes unconsciously and with no particular awareness of alternatives. While such learning is obviously important in the formation of opinions and doubtless accounts for a great number of conservative (and liberal) believers, it cannot by itself adequately explain the personality differences revealed in our research. One should also keep in mind that Americans appear mainly to have been exposed to a liberal rather than a conservative tradition.[7] Then, too, it is difficult for anyone in a society as mobile and as literate as ours to escape all contact with alternative doctrines; hence individuals reared in an environment of conservative belief are likely to have had *some* contact with liberal sentiments as well. Some measure of choice has probably been exercised, therefore, even by those whose beliefs have been determined chiefly by indoctrination.

This brings us to a third process by which cognitions of the external world may be structured, namely, through projection of the personality of the observer himself. In this way, an individual creates a set of perceptions that express, or that are consonant with, his own needs and impulses. The more ambiguous the thing observed, the greater the likelihood that he will fashion his perceptions of it to accord with his own inner feelings. In other words, conservatives believe what they do not because the world is the way it is but because they, the observers, are the way *they* are. Liberals, observing the same world, arrive at quite different judgments about it. Thus, conservative doctrines may tell us less about the nature of man and society than about the persons who believe these doctrines. Although we cannot explain all our findings by reference to these projective processes, they do, I think, provide a key to the explanation of a good many of the results.

Even the data on intellectuality, knowledge, and intelligence bear some relation to these processes. The conservative, as we have seen, is psychologically timid, distrustful of differences, and of whatever he cannot understand. He fears change, dreads disorder, and is intolerant of nonconformity. The tendency of the prototypic conservative to derogate reason and intellectuality, and to eschew theory, seems in some measure to be an outgrowth of these and related elements in his personality. He is inclined to regard pure intellectual activity as dangerous to established arrangements, for in his view of the world such activity often gives way to utopian "schemes" or unrealistic "plans." Intellectuals are likely to be impractical dreamers and potential radicals, unstable people whose theories may weaken the foundations of the social order. The conservative tends, furthermore, to perceive intellectuals as bohemians, as deviants and nonconformists who flaunt the requirements of convention and who lack respect for property or religion. Excessive intellectual activity is thought to lead to skepticism and rationalism and, consequently, to the destruction of faith. Like Cassius, the intellectual thinks too much and is therefore very dangerous.

It will be obvious that this manner of perceiving intellectuals has little to do with the characteristics of the class of people being observed and much to do with the anxieties and torments of the observer.

Related to this is the tendency for conservatives to be attracted to

---

[7] For a full scale development of this thesis, cf., for example, Louis Hartz, *The Liberal Tradition in America* (New York, 1955). Interestingly enough, a belief in the predominance of a liberal tradition in America has frequently been advanced by new conservative writers, who point to it as an obstacle to a victory for conservatism. For example, Clinton Rossiter, 68, asserts that: "The American political tradition is basically a liberal tradition, an avowedly optimistic idealistic way of thinking about man and government. It is stamped with the mightly name and spirit of Thomas Jefferson, and its articles of faith, an American Holy Writ, are perfectibility, progress, liberty, equally, democracy, and individualism."

sentiments that would have to be described as mystical, and even obscuran-tist. One comes upon this not only in the writings of Russell Kirk, Eric Voegelin, or other spokesmen for the "New Conservatism," but also in the responses of conservatives throughout our samples. To cite but one illus-tration among dozens, over 67 percent of the Extreme Conservatives score in the upper third of the Mysticism scale compared with only 15 percent of the liberals. Similarly the conservatives show a far greater tendency to agree or to say yes to items that are sweeping in nature and somewhat obscure in meaning. To judge from their responses, they apparently set far less store upon rigor or precision of thought, and allow less scope to the critical faculties. They also tend to score higher on the more extreme religious items and on the Religiosity scale itself.

To some extent, the findings on intellectuality are the result of the lower average education of conservatives. In the United States, at least, education is likely to lead to liberal rather than conservative tendencies. For one thing, it exposes the student to the American inheritance which, as we have noted, is primarily liberal. For another, education trains people in some measure to demand greater precision in speech and thought, to be more open-minded and tolerant, to be intellectually flexible and receptive to sci-entific modes of discourse, to reject mystical or non-natural explanations, and so on. These are traits which we find to be negatively correlated with con-servatism; or, put another way, we find that individuals who learn to think in the ways just described are, other things being equal, far more likely to become liberals than conservatives.

If we turn next to the connection between conservatism and the variables reflecting hostility and suspicion, the role of personality in the formation of social beliefs becomes even more striking. In many ways hos-tility is a principal component of the conservative personality, as it is a principal component of conservative doctrine. It does not seem accidental, considering the data on hostility, that conservatives prefer to believe in man's wickedness, that they choose to see man as fallen, untrustworthy, law-less, selfish, and weak. Expressed as political doctrine, these projections of aggressive personality tendencies take on the respectability of an old and honored philosophical position. These tendencies may also lie at the root of the conservative inclination to regulate and control man; to ensure that he will not violate the conditions necessary for order; to train him to value duty, obedience, and conformity; and to surround him with stabilizing in-fluences, like property, church, and the family. The high values placed on authority, leadership, and natural hierarchy, and on an elite to guide and check the rest of mankind, apparently derive from the same set of psy-chological impulses.

These personality needs can also be discerned in the scores registered on several of our other social attitude measures, as well as on many indi-vidual items. It may be noted, for example, that only 11 percent of the Liberals scored at the high end of our ethnocentric prejudice measure,[8]

---

[8] Adapted and revised from the California Ethnocentrism scale, the original version of which is reported in T. W. Adorno et al., The Authoritarian Personality (New York, 1950), chap. 4.

compared with 71 percent of the extreme Conservatives. Similarly, 45 percent of the Liberals but only 12 percent of the Extreme Conservatives were high on a measure of Faith in People. A scale dealing with Political Suspiciousness showed conservatives to be far more mistrustful of others in this respect as well (55 percent of the Extreme Conservatives were high, but only 14 percent of the Liberals). From whatever direction we approach him, the prototypic conservative seems far more impelled to contain, to reject, and to take precautions against, his fellow creatures.

The data on psychological rigidity offer additional support for these interpretations. It will be recalled that conservatives showed up as relatively inflexible and far more inclined than the rest of the sample to exhibit compulsive-obsessive traits. Not only are they less able to tolerate human foibles or weaknesses, but they are less tolerant of any and all differences between themselves and others. On a Tolerance scale developed for these studies, 55 percent of the Liberals fell into the highest third of the distribution, compared with only 25 percent of the Extreme Conservatives. An item asserting that "A man oughtn't to be allowed to speak if he doesn't know what he is talking about" was answered affirmatively by 55 percent of the Extreme Conservatives, but by only 8 percent of the Liberals. Seventy-seven percent of the Conservatives say that "It is wrong ever to break a law," while only 38 percent of the Liberals assert this. As we have seen, 32 percent of the Liberals but 63 percent of the Extreme Conservatives think that "Duties are more important than rights." In a measure of the ability to tolerate ambiguity —a scale which expresses a need for certainty and for having all matters neatly pegged and ordered—the Extreme Conservatives appear considerably less able than others to live with uncertainty or ambiguity (67 percent of the conservatives, but only 12 percent of the Liberals, score high on this measure).

These are a few of the many supplementary findings which lend support to the hypothesis that the inflexible and exacting features of conservative social doctrine are related to the prototypic personality attributes of conservative believers. The connection does not seem surprising, so soon as one thinks about it. The extreme emphasis on order and duty; the elaborate affection for the tried and familiar; the fear of change and the desire to forestall it; the strong attachments to the symbols and rituals of in-group culture; the hope for a society ordered and hierarchical in which each is aware of his station and its duties; the unusual concern for law, authority, and stability—all these can easily be understood as doctrinal expressions of a personality pattern that has strong need for order and tidiness; that adjusts only with difficulty to changes in the environment; that cannot bear the uncertainty of questions left open, and requires answers; that is made uncomfortable by the give-and-take of free inquiry and the open society; that yearns for consensus, harmony of values, unequivocal definitions of the norms, and conclusive specifications of the sources of authority.

It may seem ironic, in light of these traits, that conservatives also tend to exhibit the submissive, indecisive, retiring, and somewhat spiritless demeanor noted in our discussion of the social-psychological variables. I cannot pretend to follow, if indeed anyone can, the complex threads by which these several personality configurations are somehow held together. One can, nevertheless, observe (without explaining it) that persons who feel inadequate and who for one reason or another dislike themselves are often the quickest to aggress against others and to demand perfection of them. Similarly, by a process which psychologists have labelled "reaction formation," the disgruntled often seem to venerate the very society which frustrates them. It is almost as though, disliking themselves, they seek solace and support in an overdefense of society and in the overinstitutionalization of life. Conservatives make a fetish of community, although it is apparent that in many ways they are more alienated from the community than most. This conclusion is suggested not only by their scores on such measures as anomie, alienation, and social responsibility, but by their unusually high scores on political cynicism, feelings of political impotence, and status frustration. In the same vein, although the intensity of their patriotism exceeds that of any other group, their faith in democracy (American or otherwise), is lowest of the four groups, while their scores on the totalitarian, elitist, and authoritarian values (which for the most part, the American creed rejects) are the highest of the four.[9]

CAUTIONS AND QUALIFICATIONS

Impressive though the conservatism data may be, we must take note of several important qualifications and problems bearing upon their interpretation, to which fuller attention will eventually have to be given. Here, for reasons of space, I can only comment briefly upon a few of these points.

1. The findings refer to aggregates, not to specific individuals. Doubtless, many of us know individual conservatives whose personalities differ in key ways from the prototypic pattern described here. In our research, some conservatives have been turned up who, in personality and other attributes, essentially resemble liberals. These, however, are exceptions, since the probabilities are strong that a conservative selected at random from the general population will resemble the conservative profile that emerges from the preceding data.

2. A question might also be raised about the propriety of classifying highly informed, upper status conservatives in the same category with uneducated conservatives of low status. Conceivably, the "elite" and the "mass" conservatives are motivated by very dissimilar influences and could be scoring high on conservatism for quite different reasons. This possibility cannot be dismissed lightly, especially when one considers that status and education factors account, by themselves, for a significant share of the total variance found in our data. Subsequent analyses will make it possible, we hope, to settle this matter conclusively; but for the present, at least one

[9] For a fascinating set of data on *conformity* as measured in an experimental group situation that fit, even in detail, with the findings presented here on conservatism, see Richard S. Crutchfield, "Conformity and Character," *American Psychologist,* Vol. 10 (1955), pp. 191–198.

important consideration can be noted: when education and other status factors are controlled, we find that informed, upper status conservatives differ from informed, upper status liberals in precisely the same ways that conservatives in general differ from liberals in general; or, for that matter, in the same ways that "mass" conservatives differ from "mass" liberals. While the *range* of the scores varies as occupation, education, or knowledge varies the *direction* and *magnitude* of the differences between liberals and conservatives remain very much the same for all status and education levels. In short, personality factors seem to exercise a fairly uniform influence on the formation of conservative or liberal outlooks at all social levels.

3. The association between conservatism and the traits outlined exists in the form of correlations, which only tell us that the two go together. *How* they go together, and which is antecedent to which, is a more difficult and more elusive problem. Conservative doctrines appear, in some measure, to arise from personality needs, but it is conceivable, at least, that both are the product of some third set of factors. Both, for example, may have been learned or acquired simultaneously, through family indoctrination, in which case the connection between the two would be more epiphenomenal than causal. I do not think that this explanation can account for most of our results, but it will need to be checked out further.

4. The terms employed in the description of traits must be seen as relative and as having been mainly defined by the items in the scales themselves. Satisfactory external validation has not always been available. Also, although clinical terms have been employed that might be used in the diagnosis of psychotics, we have used the terms only as terms of tendency within the normal population. one of them is intended to signify the presence of a pathological mental state.

5. One must be careful to avoid the reductivist fallacy of assigning all significance in the problems considered to personality factors. Equally, one must avoid the temptation to "psychologize" problems to such an extent as to strip them of their significance as genuine political or philosophical problems.

6. The term liberalism has been inadequately defined in our study so far. We have tended to call someone liberal if he rejected the values of conservatism. While our findings suggest that most of these people would in fact meet the definition of a liberal, our present classification of liberals is crude and needs to be refined. All persons who reject conservatism may not be liberals, for, as in the case of the "authoritarian-democratic" dimension, liberalism-conservatism may not be variables, paired in such a way that a high score on one necessarily signifies a low score on the other.

7. The connections between classical conservatism (or liberalism) and such factors as party affiliation, attitude on economic issues, and liberal-conservative self-designation have been extensively explored in our research, but could not be reported in the present paper. The correlation between them tends, however, to be fairly low, suggesting that for the present, at least, many Americans divide in their party preferences, their support of candidates, their economic views, their stands on public issues, or their political self-identifications without reference to their beliefs in liberalism or conservatism. The

latter have influence, of course, especially among some of the more articulate groups; for the general population, however, political divisions of the sort named appear to be more affected by group membership factors than by personality.

8. Some readers may be inclined to identify our "conservatives" with "right-wing authoritarians," in the belief that we are measuring the latter rather more than the former. This view would be difficult to support, however, for not only have we defined conservatism by reference to its most frequently articulated values (which are by no means identical with right-wing values), but we have also found that while right-wing authoritarians are in some respects a more extreme version of our conservatives, there are also significant differences between the two.

9. Finally, our findings have so far been drawn entirely from Minnesota samples, and the degree to which the conclusions can be generalized to conservatives everywhere and at all times is open to debate. We shall soon have comparable data on a national cross-section sample, which I have reason to think will bear out the present results. In fact, I am inclined to believe that the connections between conservatism and the personality configurations presented in the foregoing would very likely prevail wherever, and whenever, the members of a society are free to choose between conservatism and alternative, liberal systems of belief. But this is a subject for future research.

16

The Functional Approach to the Study of Attitudes*

DANIEL KATZ

The study of opinion formation and attitude change is basic to an understanding of the public opinion process even though it should not be equated with this process. The public opinion process is one phase of the influencing of collective decisions, and its investigation involves knowledge of channels of communication, of the power structures of a society, of the character of mass media, of the relation between elites, factions and masses, of the role of formal and informal leaders, of the institutionalized access to officials. But the raw material out of which public opinion develops is to be found in the attitudes of individuals, whether they be followers or leaders and whether these attitudes be at the general level of tendencies to conform to legitimate authority or majority opinion or at the specific level of favoring or opposing the particular aspects of the issue under consideration. The nature of the organization of attitudes within the personality and the processes which account for attitude change are thus critical areas for the understanding of the collective product known as public opinion.

* Reprinted by permission from *The Public Opinion Quarterly*, 24 (Summer 1960), pp. 163–176.

EARLY APPROACHES TO THE STUDY
OF ATTITUDE AND OPINION

There have been two main streams of thinking with respect to the determination of man's attitudes. The one tradition assumes an irrational model
of man: specifically it holds that men have very limited powers of reason
and reflection, weak capacity to discriminate, only the most primitive self-
insight, and very short memories. Whatever mental capacities people do
possess are easily overwhelmed by emotional forces and appeals to self-
interest and vanity. The early books on the psychology of advertising, with
their emphasis on the doctrine of suggestion, exemplify this approach. One
expression of this philosophy is in the propagandist's concern with tricks and
traps to manipulate the public. A modern form of it appears in *The Hidden
Persuaders*, or the use of subliminal and marginal suggestion, or the devices
supposedly employed by "the Madison Avenue boys." Experiments to support this line of thinking started with laboratory demonstrations of the power
of hypnotic suggestion and were soon extended to show that people would
change their attitudes in an uncritical manner under the influence of the prestige of authority and numbers. For example, individuals would accept or reject the same idea depending upon whether it came from a positive or a
negative prestige source.[1]

The second approach is that of the ideologist who invokes a rational
model of man. It assumes that the human being has a cerebral cortex, that
he seeks understanding, that he consistently attempts to make sense of the
world about him, that he possesses discriminating and reasoning powers
which will assert themselves over time, and that he is capable of self-
criticism and self-insight. It relies heavily upon getting adequate information
to people. Our educational system is based upon this rational model. The
present emphasis upon the improvement of communication, upon developing more adequate channels of two-way communication, of conferences and
institutes, upon bringing people together to interchange ideas, are all indications of the belief in the importance of intelligence and comprehension in
the formation and change of men's opinions.

Now either school of thought can point to evidence which supports
its assumptions, and can make fairly damaging criticisms of its opponent.
Solomon Asch and his colleagues, in attacking the irrational model, have
called attention to the biased character of the old experiments on prestige
suggestion which gave the subject little opportunity to demonstrate critical
thinking.[2] And further exploration of subjects in these stupid situations does
indicate that they try to make sense of a nonsensical matter as far as possible.
Though the same statement is presented by the experimenter to two groups,
the first time as coming from a positive source and the second time as
coming from a negative source, it is given a different meaning dependent
upon the context in which it appears.[3] Thus the experimental subject does

[1] Muzafer Sherif, *The Psychology of Social Norms* (New York: Harper, 1963).

[2] Solomon E. Asch, *Social Psychology* (Englewood Cliffs, N.J.: Prentice-Hall, 1952).

[3] Asch, pp. 426–427. The following statement was attributed to its rightful author,
John Adams, for some subjects and to Karl Marx for others: "those who hold and those

his best to give some rational meaning to the problem. On the other hand, a large body of experimental work indicates that there are many limitations in the rational approach in that people see their world in terms of their own needs, remember what they want to remember, and interpret information on the basis of wishful thinking. H. H. Hyman and P. Sheatsley have demonstrated that these experimental results have direct relevance to information campaigns directed at influencing public opinion.[4] These authors assembled facts about such campaigns and showed conclusively that increasing the flow of information to people does not necessarily increase the knowledge absorbed or produce the attitude changes desired.

The major difficulty with these conflicting approaches is their lack of specification of the conditions under which men do act as the theory would predict. For the facts are that people do act at times as if they had been decorticated and at times with intelligence and comprehension. And people themselves do recognize that on occasion they have behaved blindly, impulsively, and thoughtlessly. A second major difficulty is that the rationality-irrationality dimension is not clearly defined. At the extremes it is easy to point to examples, as in the case of the acceptance of stupid suggestions under emotional stress on the one hand, or brilliant problem solving on the other; but this does not provide adequate guidance for the many cases in the middle of the scale where one attempts to discriminate between rationalization and reason.

RECONCILIATION OF THE CONFLICT
IN A FUNCTIONAL APPROACH

The conflict between the rationality and irrationality models was saved from becoming a worthless debate because of the experimentation and research suggested by these models. The findings of this research pointed toward the elements of truth in each approach and gave some indication of the conditions under which each model could make fairly accurate predictions. In general the irrational approach was at its best where the situation imposed heavy restrictions upon search behavior and response alternatives. Where individuals must give quick responses without adequate opportunities to explore the nature of the problem, where there are very few response alternatives available to them, where their own deep emotional needs are aroused, they will in general react much as does the unthinking subject under hypnosis. On the other hand, where the individual can have more adequate commerce with the relevant environmental setting, where he has time to obtain more feedback from his reality testing, and where he has a

---

who are without property have ever formed distinct interests in society." When the statement was attributed to Marx, this type of comment appeared: "Marx is stressing the need for a redistribution of wealth." When it was attributed to Adams, this comment appeared: "This social division is innate in mankind."

[4] Herbert H. Hyman and Paul B. Sheatsley, "Some Reasons Why Information Campaigns Fail," *Public Opinion Quarterly*, Vol. 11 (1947), pp. 413–423.

number of realistic choices, his behavior will reflect the use of his rational faculties.[5] The child will often respond to the directive of the parent not by implicit obedience but by testing out whether or not the parent really meant what he said.

Many of the papers in this issue, which describe research and theory concerning consistency and consonance, represent one outcome of the rationality model. The theory of psychological consonance, or cognitive balance, assumes that man attempts to reduce discrepancies in his beliefs, attitudes, and behavior by appropriate changes in these processes. While the emphasis here is upon consistency or logicality, the theory deals with all dissonances, no matter how produced. Thus they could result from irrational factors of distorted perception and wishful thinking as well as from rational factors of realistic appraisal of a problem and an accurate estimate of its consequences. Moreover, the theory would predict only that the individual will move to reduce dissonance, whether such movement is a good adjustment to the world or leads to the delusional systems of the paranoiac. In a sense, then, this theory would avoid the conflict between the old approaches of the rational and the irrational man by not dealing with the specific antecedent causes of behavior or with the particular ways in which the individual solves his problems.

In addition to the present preoccupation with the development of formal models concerned with cognitive balance and consonance, there is a growing interest in a more comprehensive framework for dealing with the complex variables and for bringing order within the field. The thoughtful system of Ulf Himmelstrand, presented in the following pages, is one such attempt. Another point of departure is represented by two groups of workers who have oganized their theories around the functions which attitudes perform for the personality. Sarnoff, Katz, and McClintock, in taking this functional approach, have given primary attention to the motivational bases of attitudes and the processes of attitude change.[6] The basic assumption of this group is that both attitude formation and attitude change must be understood in terms of the needs they serve and that, as these motivational processes differ, so too will the conditions and techniques for attitude change. Smith, Bruner, and White have also analyzed the different functions which attitudes perform for the personality.[7] Both groups present essentially the same functions, but Smith, Bruner, and White give more attention to perceptual and cognitive processes and Sarnoff, Katz, and McClintock to the specific conditions of attitude change.

---

[5] William A. Scott points out that in the area of international relations the incompleteness and remoteness of the information and the lack of pressures on the individual to defend his views result in inconsistencies. Inconsistent elements with respect to a system of international beliefs may, however, be consistent with the larger system of the personality. "Rationality and Nonrationality of International Attitudes," *Journal of Conflict Resolution*, Vol. 2 (1958), pp. 9–16.

[6] Irving Sarnoff and Daniel Katz, "The Motivational Bases of Attitude Change," *Journal of Abnormal and Social Psychology*, Vol. 49 (1954), pp. 115–124.

[7] M. Brewster Smith, Jerome S. Bruner, and Robert W. White, *Opinions and Personality* (New York: Wiley, 1956).

The importance of the functional approach is threefold.

1. Many previous studies of attitude change have dealt with factors which are not genuine psychological variables, for example, the effect on group prejudice of contact between two groups, or the exposure of a group of subjects to a communication in the mass media. Now contact serves different psychological functions for the individual and merely knowing that people have seen a movie or watched a television program tells us nothing about the personal values engaged or not engaged by such a presentation. If, however, we can gear our research to the functions attitudes perform, we can develop some generalizations about human behavior. Dealing with nonfunctional variables makes such generalization difficult, if not impossible.

2. By concerning ourselves with the different functions attitudes can perform we can avoid the great error of oversimplification—the error of attributing a single cause to given types of attitude. It was once popular to ascribe radicalism in economic and political matters to the psychopathology of the insecure and to attribute conservatism to the rigidity of the mentally aged. At the present time it is common practice to see in attitudes of group prejudice the repressed hostilities stemming from childhood frustrations, though Hyman and Sheatsley have pointed out that prejudiced attitudes can serve a normative function of gaining acceptance in one's own group as readily as releasing unconscious hatred.[8] In short, not only are there a number of motivational forces to take into account in considering attitudes and behavior, but the same attitude can have a different motivational basis in different people.

3. Finally, recognition of the complex motivational sources of behavior can help to remedy the neglect in general theories which lack specification of conditions under which given types of attitude will change. Gestalt theory tells us, for example, that attitudes will change to give better cognitive organization to the psychological field. This theoretical generalization is suggestive, but to carry out significant research we need some middle-level concepts to bridge the gap between a high level of abstraction and particularistic or phenotypical events. We need concepts that will point toward the types of motive and methods of motive satisfaction which are operative in bringing about cognitive reorganization.

Before we attempt a detailed analysis of the four major functions which attitudes can serve, it is appropriate to consider the nature of attitudes, their dimensions, and their relations to other psychological structures and processes.

NATURE OF ATTITUDES: THEIR DIMENSIONS

Attitude is the predisposition of the individual to evaluate some symbol or object or aspect of his world in a favorable or unfavorable manner. Opinion is the verbal expression of an attitude, but attitudes can also be expressed in nonverbal behavior. Attitudes include both the affective, or feeling core of liking or disliking, and the cognitive, or belief, elements which describe

---

[8] Herbert H. Hyman and Paul B. Sheatsley, "The Authoritarian Personality: A Methodological Critique," in Richard Christie and Marie Jahoda, editors, *Studies in the Scope and Method of the Authoritarian Personality* (New York: Free Press, 1954), pp. 50–122.

the object of the attitude, its characteristics, and its relations to other objects. All attitudes thus include beliefs, but not all beliefs are attitudes. When specific attitudes are organized into a hierarchical structure, they comprise *value systems.* Thus a person may not only hold specific attitudes against deficit spending and unbalanced budgets but may also have a systematic organization of such beliefs and attitudes in the form of a value system of economic conservatism.

The dimensions of attitudes can be stated more precisely if the above distinctions between beliefs and feelings and attitudes and value systems are kept in mind. The *intensity* of an attitude refers to the strength of the *affective* component. In fact, rating scales and even Thurstone scales deal primarily with the intensity of feeling of the individual for or against some social object. The cognitive, or belief, component suggests two additional dimensions, the *specificity* or *generality* of the attitude and the *degree of differentiation* of the beliefs. Differentiation refers to the number of beliefs or cognitive items contained in the attitude, and the general assumption is that the simpler the attitude in cognitive structure the easier it is to change.[9] For simple structures there is no defense in depth, and once a single item of belief has been changed the attitude will change. A rather different dimension of attitude in the *number and strength of its linkages to a related value system.* If an attitude favoring budget balancing by the Federal government is tied in strongly with a value system of economic conservatism, it will be more difficult to change than if it were a fairly isolated attitude of the person. Finally, the relation of the value system to the personality is a consideration of first importance. If an attitude is tied to a value system which is closely related to, or which consists of, the individual's conception of himself, then the appropriate change procedures become more complex. The *centrality* of an attitude refers to its role as part of a value system which is closely related to the individual's self-concept.

An additional aspect of attitudes is not clearly described in most theories, namely, their relation to action or overt behavior. Though behavior related to the attitude has other determinants than the attitude itself, it is also true that some attitudes in themselves have more of what Cartwright calls an action structure than do others.[10] Brewster Smith refers to this dimension as policy orientation[11] and Katz and Stotland speak of it as the action component.[12] For example, while many people have attitudes of approval toward one or the other of the two political parties, these attitudes will differ in their structure with respect to relevant action. One man may be prepared to vote on election day and will know where and when he should vote and will go to the polls no matter what the weather or how great the

[9] David Krech and Richard S. Crutchfield, *Theory and Problems of Social Psychology* (New York: McGraw-Hill, 1948), pp. 160–163.

[10] Dorwin Cartwright, "Some Principles of Mass Persuasion," *Human Relations,* Vol. 2 (1949), pp. 253–267.

[11] M. Brewster Smith, "The Personal Setting of Public Opinions: A Study of Attitudes toward Russia," *Public Opinion Quarterly,* Vol. 11 (1947), pp. 507–523.

[12] Daniel Katz and Ezra Stotland, "A Preliminary Statement to a Theory of Attitude Structure and Change," in Sigmund Koch, editor, *Psychology: A Study of a Science,* Vol. 3 (New York: McGraw-Hill, 1959), pp. 423–475.

inconvenience. Another man will only vote if a party worker calls for him in a car. Himmelstrand's work is concerned with all aspects of the relationship between attitude and behavior, but he deals with the action structure of the attitude itself by distinguishing between attitudes where the affect is tied to verbal expression and attitudes where the affect is tied to behavior concerned with more objective referents of the attitude.[13] In the first case an individual derives satisfaction from talking about a problem; in the second case he derives satisfaction from taking some form of concrete action.

Attempts to change attitudes can be directed primarily at the belief component or at the feeling, or affective, component. Rosenberg theorizes that an effective change in one component will result in changes in the other component and presents experimental evidence to confirm this hypothesis.[14] For example, a political candidate will often attempt to win people by making them like him and dislike his opponent, and thus communicate affect rather than ideas. If he is successful, people will not only like him but entertain favorable beliefs about him. Another candidate may deal primarily with ideas and hope that, if he can change people's beliefs about an issue, their feelings will also change.

FOUR FUNCTIONS WHICH ATTITUDES PERFORM FOR THE INDIVIDUAL

The major functions which attitudes perform for the personality can be grouped according to their motivational basis as follows:

1. The instrumental, adjustive, or utilitarian function upon which Jeremy Bentham and the utilitarians constructed their model of man. A modern expression of this approach can be found in behavioristic learning theory.

2. The ego-defensive function in which the person protects himself from acknowledging the basic truths about himself or the harsh realities in his external world. Freudian psychology and neo-Freudian thinking have been preoccupied with this type of motivation and its outcomes.

3. The value-expressive function in which the individual derives satisfactions from expressing attitudes appropriate to his personal values and to his concept of himself. This function is central to doctrines of ego psychology which stress the importance of self-expression, self-development, and self-realization.

4. The knowledge function based upon the individual's need to give adequate structure to his universe. To search for meaning, the need to understand, the trend toward better organization of perceptions and beliefs to provide clarity and consistency for the individual, are other descriptions of this function. The development of principles about perceptual and cognitive structure have been the contributions of Gestalt psychology.

[13] Ulf Himmelstrand, "Verbal Attitudes and Behavior: A Paradigm for the study of Message Transmission and Transformation," *Public Opinion Quarterly,* Vol. 24 (1960), pp. 224–250.

[14] Milton J. Rosenberg, "A Structural Theory of Attitude Dynamics," *Public Opinion Quarterly,* Vol. 24 (1960), pp. 319–340.

Stated simply, the functional approach is the attempt to understand the reasons people hold the attitudes they do. The reasons, however, are at the level of psychological motivations and not of the accidents of external events and circumstances. Unless we know the psychological need which is met by the holding of an attitude we are in a poor position to predict when and how it will change. Moreover, the same attitude expressed toward a political candidate may not perform the same function for all the people who express it. And while many attitudes are predominantly in the service of a single type of motivational process, as described above, other attitudes may serve more than one purpose for the individual. A fuller discussion of how attitudes serve the above four functions is in order.

The Adjustment Function

Essentially this function is a recognition of the fact that people strive to maximize the rewards in their external environment and to minimize the penalties. The child develops favorable attitudes toward the objects in his world which are associated with the satisfactions of his needs and unfavorable attitudes toward objects which thwart him or punish him. Attitudes acquired in the service of the adjustment function are either the means for reaching the desired goal or avoiding the undesirable one, or are affective associations based upon experiences in attaining motive satisfactions.[15] The attitudes of the worker favoring a political party which will advance his economic lot are an example of the first type of utilitarian attitude. The pleasant image one has of one's favorite food is an example of the second type of utilitarian attitude.

In general, then, the dynamics of attitude formation with respect to the adjustment function are dependent upon present or past perceptions of the utility of the attitudinal object for the individual. The clarity, consistency, and nearness of rewards and punishments, as they relate to the individual's activities and goals, are important factors in the acquisition of such attitudes. Both attitudes and habits are formed toward specific objects, people, and symbols as they satisfy specific needs. The closer these objects are to actual need satisfaction and the more they are clearly perceived as relevant to need satisfaction, the greater are the probabilities of positive attitude formation. These principles of attitude formation are often observed in the breach rather than the compliance. In industry, management frequently expects to create favorable attitudes toward job performance through programs for making the company more-attractive to the worker, such as providing recreational facilities and fringe benefits. Such programs, however, are much more likely to produce favorable attitudes toward the company as a desirable place to work than toward performance on the job. The company benefits and advantages are applied across the board to all employees and are not specifically relevant to increased effort in task performance by the individual worker.

Consistency of reward and punishment also contributes to the clarity

---

[15] Katz and Stotland, pp. 434–443.

of the instrumental object for goal attainment. If a political party bestows recognition and favors on party workers in an unpredictable and inconsistent fashion, it will destroy the favorable evaluation of the importance of working hard for the party among those whose motivation is of the utilitarian sort. But, curiously, while consistency of reward needs to be observed, 100 percent consistency is not as effective as a pattern which is usually consistent but in which there are some lapses. When animal or human subjects are invariably rewarded for a correct performance, they do not retain their learned responses as well as when the reward is sometimes skipped.[16]

The Ego-Defensive Function

People not only seek to make the most of their external world and what it offers, but they also expend a great deal of their energy on living with themselves. The mechanisms by which the individual protects his ego from his own acceptable impulses and from the knowledge of threatening forces from without, and the methods by which he reduces his anxieties created by such problems, are known as mechanisms of ego defense. A more complete account of their origin and nature will be found in Sarnoff's article in this issue.[17] They include the devices by which the individual avoids facing either the inner reality of the kind of person he is, or the outer reality of the dangers the world holds for him. They stem basically from internal conflict with its resulting insecurities. In one sense the mechanisms of defense are adaptive in temporarily removing the sharp edges of conflict and in saving the individual from complete disaster. In another sense they are not adaptive in that they handicap the individual in his social adjustments and in obtaining the maximum satisfactions available to him from the world in which he lives. The worker who persistently quarrels with his boss and his fellow workers, because he is acting out some of his own internal conflicts, may in this manner relieve himself of some of the emotional tensions which beset him. He is not, however, solving his problem of adjusting to his work situation and thus may deprive himself of advancement or even of steady employment.

Defense mechanisms Miller and Swanson point out, may be classified into two families on the basis of the more or less primitive nature of the devices employed.[18] The first family, more primitive in nature, are more socially handicapping and consist of denial and complete avoidance. The individual in such cases obliterates through withdrawal and denial the realities which confront him. The exaggerated case of such primitive mechanisms is the fantasy world of the paranoiac. The second type of defense is less handicapping and makes for distortion rather than denial. It includes rationalization, projection, and displacement.

[16] William O. Jenkins and Julian C. Stanley, "Partial Reinforcement: A Review and Critique," *Psychological Bulletin,* Vol. 47 (1950), pp. 193–234.

[17] Irving Sarnoff, "Psychoanalytic Theory and Social Attitudes," *Public Opinion Quarterly,* Vol. 24 (1960), p. 251–279.

[18] Daniel R. Miller and Guy E. Swanson, *Inner Conflict and Defense* (New York: Holt, Rinehart and Winston, Inc. 1960), pp. 194–288.

Many of our attitudes have the function of defending our self-image. When we cannot admit to ourselves that we have deep feelings of inferiority we may project those feelings onto some convenient minority group and bolster our egos by attitudes of superiority toward this under-privileged group. The formation of such defensive attitudes differs in essential ways from the formation of attitudes which serve the adjustment function. They proceed from within the person, and the objects and situation to which they are attached are merely convenient outlets for their expression. Not all targets are equally satisfactory for a given defense mechanism, but the point is that the attitude is not created by the target but by the individual's emotional conflicts. And when no convenient target exists the individual will create one. Utilitarian attitudes, on the other hand, are formed with specific reference to the nature of the attitudinal object. They are thus appropriate to the nature of the social world to which they are geared. The high school student who values high grades because he wants to be admitted to a good college has a utilitarian attitude appropriate to the situation to which it is related.

All people employ defense mechanisms, but they differ with respect to the extent that they use them and some of their attitudes may be more defensive in function than others. It follows that the techniques and conditions for attitude change will not be the same for ego-defensive as for utilitarian attitudes.

Moreover, though people are ordinarily unaware of their defense mechanisms, especially at the time of employing them, they differ with respect to the amount of insight they may show at some later time about their use of defenses. In some cases they recognize that they have been protecting their egos without knowing the reason why. In other cases they may not even be aware of the devices they have been using to delude themselves.

The Value-Expressive Function

While many attitudes have the function of preventing the individual from revealing to himself and others his true nature, other attitudes have the function of giving positive expression to his central values and to the type of person he conceives himself to be. A man may consider himself to be an enlightened conservative or an internationalist or a liberal, and will hold attitudes which are the appropriate indication of his central values. Thus we need to take account of the fact that not all behavior has the negative function of reducing the tensions of biological drives or of internal conflicts. Satisfactions also accrue to the person from the expression of attitudes which reflect his cherished beliefs and his self-image. The reward to the person in these instances is not so much a matter of gaining social recognition or monetary rewards as of establishing his self-identity and confirming his notion of the sort of person he sees himself to be. The gratifications obtained from value expression may go beyond the confirmation of self-identity. Just as we find satisfaction in the exercise of our talents and abilities, so we find reward in the expression of any attributes associated with our egos.

Value-expressive attitudes not only give clarity to the self-image but also mold that self-image closer to the heart's desire. The teenager who by dress and speech establishes his identity as similar to his own peer group may appear to the outsider a weakling and a craven conformer. To himself he is asserting his independence of the adult world to which he has rendered child-like subservience and conformity all his life. Very early in the development of the personality the need for clarity of self-image is important—the need to know "who I am." Later it may be even more important to know that in some measure I am the type of person I want to be. Even as adults, however, the clarity and stability of the self-image is of primary significance. Just as the kind, considerate person will cover over his acts of selfishness, so too will the ruthless individualist become confused and embarrassed by his acts of sym-pathetic compassion. One reason it is difficult to change the character of the adult is that he is not comfortable with the new "me." Group support for such personality change is almost a necessity, as in Alcoholics Anonymous, so that the individual is aware of approval of his new self by people who are like him.

The socialization process during the formative years sets the basic out-lines for the individual's self-concept. Parents constantly hold up before the child the model of the good character they want him to be. A good boy eats his spinach, does not hit girls, etc. The candy and the stick are less in evidence in training the child than the constant appeal to his notion of his own character. It is small wonder, then, that children reflect the acceptance of this model by inquiring about the characters of the actors in every drama, whether it be a television play, a political contest, or a war, wanting to know who are the "good guys" and who are the "bad guys." Even as adults we persist in labeling others in the terms of such character images. Joe McCarthy and his cause collapsed in fantastic fashion when the telecast of the Army hearings showed him in the role of the villain attacking the gentle, good man represented by Joseph Welch.

A related but somewhat different process from childhood socialization takes place when individuals enter a new group or organization. The indi-vidual will often take over and internalize the values of the group. What accounts, however, for the fact that sometimes this occurs and sometimes it does not? Four factors are probably operative, and some combination of them may be necessary for internalization.

    1. The values of the new group may be highly consistent with existing values central to the personality. The girl who enters the nursing profession finds it congenial to consider herself a good nurse because of previous values of the importance of contributing to the welfare of others.

    2. The new group may in its ideology have a clear model of what the good group member should be like and may persistently indoctrinate group members in these terms. One of the reasons for the code of conduct for mem-bers of the armed forces, devised after the revelations about the conduct of American prisoners in the Korean War, was to attempt to establish a model for what a good soldier does and does not do.

    3. The activities of the group in moving toward its goal permit the indi-vidual genuine opportunity for participation. To become ego-involved so that he can internalize group values, the new member must find one of two conditions. The group activity open to him must tap his talents and abilities so that his chance to show what he is worth can be tied into the group effort. Or else the activities of the group must give him an active voice in group decisions. His particular talents and abilities may not be tapped but he does have the opporunty to enter into group decisions, and thus his need for self-determination is satisfied. He then identifies with the group in which such opportunities for ego-involvement are available. It is not necessary that opportunities for self-expression and self- determination be of great magnitude in an objective sense, so long as they are important for the psychological economy of the individuals themselves.

4. Finally, the individual may come to see himself as a group member if he can share in the rewards of group activity which includes his own efforts. The worker may not play much of a part in building a ship or make any decisions in the process of building it. Nevertheless, if he and his fellow workers are given a share in every boat they build and a return on the proceeds from the earnings of the ship, they may soon come to identify with the shipbuilding company and see themselves as builders of ships.

The Knowledge Function

Individuals not only acquire beliefs in the interest of satisfying various specific needs, they also seek knowledge to give meaning to what would otherwise be an unorganized chaotic universe. People need standards or frames of reference for understanding their world, and attitudes help to supply such standards. The problem of understanding, as John Dewey made. clear years ago, is one "of introducing (1) *definiteness* and *distinction* and (2) *consistency* and *stability* of meaning into what is otherwise vague and wavering."[19] The definiteness and stability are provided in good measure by the norms of our culture, which give the otherwise perplexed individual readymade attitudes for comprehending his universe. Walter Lippmann's classical contribution to the study of opinions and attitudes was his description of stereotypes and the way they provided order and clarity for a bewildering set of complexities.[20] The most interesting finding in Herzog's familiar study of the gratifications obtained by housewives in listening to daytime serials was the unsuspected role of information and advice.[21] The stories were liked "because they explained things to the inarticulate listener."

The need to know does not of course imply that people are driven by a thirst for universal knowledge. The American public's appalling lack of political information has been documented many times. In 1956, for example, only 13 percent of the people in Detroit could correctly name the two United States Senators from the state of Michigan and only 18 percent knew the name of their own Congressman.[22] People are not avid seekers after

[19] John Dewey, *How We Think*, (New York: Crowell-Collier-Macmillan, 1910).

[20] Walter Lippmann, *Public Opinion* (New York: Crowell-Collier-Macmillan, 1922).

[21] Herta Herzog, "What Do We Really Know about Daytime Serial Listeners?" in Paul F. Lazarsfeld and Frank N. Stanton, editors, *Radio Research 1942–1943* (New York: Duell, Sloan & Pearce-Meredith Press, 1944), pp. 3–33.

[22] From a study of the impact of party organization on political behavior in the Detroit area, by Daniel Katz and Samuel Eldersveld, in manuscript.

knowledge as judged by what the educator or social reformer would desire. But they do want to understand the events which impinge directly on their own life. Moreover, many of the attitudes they have already acquired give them sufficient basis for interpreting much of what they perceive to be important for them. Our already existing stereotypes, in Lippmann's language, "are an ordered, more or less consistent picture of the world, to which our habits, our tastes, our capacities, our comforts and our hopes have adjusted themselves. They may not be a complete picture of the world, but they are a picture of a possible world to which we are adapted." [23] It follows that new information will not modify old attitudes unless there is some inadequacy or incompleteness or inconsistency in the existing attitudinal structure as it relates to the perceptions of new situations.

[23] Lippmann, p. 95.

17

Political Socialization
and Culture Change*

ROBERT LEVINE

With the growing recognition that political behavior is an aspect of culture and as such is regularly transmitted from generation to generation, social psychologists and political scientists have been paying increasing attention to *political socialization*, that is, the means by which individuals acquire motives, habits, and values relevant to participation in a political system. The concept of political socialization covers topics as diverse as the effect of parent-child relationships on images of authority and the role of the army in building national loyalties in youth. Although systematic research on such topics is just beginning and for the most part has not been cross cultural in scope, its implications for the comparative analysis of new nations are many and varied. In this chapter, the concept of political socialization and research pertaining to it will be explored from a comparative point of view in the context of the new and changing nations of Asia and Africa.

* Reprinted with permission of The Macmillan Company from *Old Societies and New States* edited by Clifford Geertz. © The Free Press of Glencoe, a Division of The Macmillan Company, 1963. An earlier version of this article was presented at the meeting of the Society for Applied Anthropology, Pittsburgh, May 1960.

THE ROLE OF SOCIALIZATION IN POLITICAL
STABILITY AND CHANGE IN NEW NATIONS

In his book on political socialization, Hyman[1] attempts to explain why, in surveys of American youth and adults, party affiliation seems established earlier in life than political ideology and why parent-child correlations in party preferences are higher than such preferences in political attitudes. His explanation, in brief, is that political issues change over the years while parties endure. An American parent who attempts to give his child an ideological orientation cannot anticipate the issues that will be meaningful by the time he reaches adulthood; whereas socializing the child with respect to party preference gives him not only a loyalty to a stable organization but also an organizing principle for coping with new issues as they emerge.[2] The hypothesis behind this interpretation has some interesting comparative implications that Hyman does not discuss. It would predict, for example, that in those Western European nations where ideological issues concerning church and state and class conflict are more enduring than political parties, attitudes concerning these issues should be formed earlier in life than party affiliation, and parent-child correlations on these attitudes should be higher than on party preference.

It is interesting to speculate on the application of this hypothesis to other areas. If any general characterization is possible, how do parents in the new nations of Asia and Africa socialize their children with respect to politics? What enduring aspect of the political system do they prepare their children to respond to? While there are few detailed empirical studies, it seems likely that the majority of such parents socialize their children for participation in the local authority systems of the rural areas rather than for roles in the national citizenry. The local system, compounded of traditional political patterns, forms introduced during colonial administration, and changes wrought under the pressure of contemporary economic conditions, is not only more enduring but also more familiar to the rural parent in a country where mass communication and mass education are not highly developed. The national government is not only more fluctuating and unstable, if only by virtue of the transition from colonial to independent status, but it is also in many cases an urban phenomenon, isolated from the rural population by a huge cultural gap. The national government was created by the colonial power and greatly affected by independence; the local authority systems antedate colonization, were less affected by it, and have been less affected by self-government at the national level. In this situation it is reasonable to assume that the socialization process typical of the rural majority in new nations is functionally integrated to a greater degree with local authority systems than it is with the national political system. Such a picture may be overdrawn for a few of the older postcolonial nations of Asia, but it is not for most of Africa—where only a small fraction of the population live in cities and where many rural people are unaware of the nation in

[1] Herbert Hyman, *Political Socialization* (New York: Free Press, 1959).
[2] Hyman, pp. 46–47, 74–75.

which they reside—and it is a fair working approximation of the general situation in new nations of both continents.

It must be recognized that local authority systems in the nations under discussion, while they may be generally referred to as "traditional" and "particularistic," often vary greatly from one ethnic group to another along many important dimensions: concentration of authority in decision-making units, institutionalization of leadership roles at various structural levels, the use of supernatural sanctions, the importance of social stratification in community decision-making, deferential behavior, and so forth. There are, for example, numerous African nations that contain, side by side, groups that were large independent monarchies eighty years ago and groups that had no political units larger than the village of several hundred persons. There is even considerable diversity in values concerning authority among the traditionally stateless ethnic groups which might seem at first glance to have had roughly the same political orientations; some tend in an authoritarian direction, while others are clearly egalitarian in their local decision-making patterns.[3] In terms of the theoretical framework on which this chapter is based, the variation in authority systems among the ethnic groups of the new nations means that there should be concomitant variations in the socialization patterns of the groups. In so far as such concomitant variations are revealed by empirical research, this theoretical framework will have received confirmation.

A possible key to the ontogenesis of authority values among the peoples of new nations is the domestic group (such as the extended family) and the wider kin groupings of which it is part, which serve to introduce the child into the political system by acting as models of authority roles as well as by more direct training. In America we often pay little attention to the family as a source of our ideologies concerning authority because neolocality and the emotional and economic independence of adult children from their parents tend to relegate parental influence to childhood memories. In those Asian and African societies that have extended family units, however, an adult male often lives with and is dependent emotionally and economically on his father or on another elder kinsman who legitimately exercises some degree of control over him. Norman M. Bradburn (personal communication) has noted that in Turkish cities the patrilocal extended family is maintained as a residential unit in apartment houses, with married sons occupying separate apartments in the same building as their parents; this is also found in India and elsewhere, and indicates that modern housing does not necessarily terminate traditional family relationships. In such situations parental influences on attitudes toward authority are not left behind in childhood but are reinforced many times over in adult life. The use of extended family (that is, father-son and elder brother-younger brother) relations as models for emperor-subject relations was explicitly encouraged in the Confucian doctrine of traditional China, but such modeling appears to be widespread even where it is not overtly recognized. Bradburn also finds that factory organiza-

[3] Cf. the comparison of the Nuer of Sudan and the Gusii of Kenya in Robert A. Le-Vine, "The Internalization of Political Values in Stateless Societies," *Human Organization*, Vol. 19, pp. 51–58.

tion in Turkey is patterned after the extended family in considerable detail, with employer-employee relations conforming to norms derived from the traditional father-son relationship.[4] This kind of evidence suggests a correlation between domestic group authority patterns and local community authority patterns that should be carefully investigated in comparative research.[5]

To return to the picture of political socialization in the majority of families as being geared primarily to local political systems rather than national ones in new nations, this appears likely to persist for a long time. This assertion is based on the following considerations:

> **1.** The population explosion means that, in countries with relatively undeveloped industrial economies, families of basically traditional orientation are multiplying and transmitting their own cultural orientations more rapidly than the rate at which the nation has the capacity to "modernize" them through industrialization and mass education.

> **2.** The disparity in Western education and acculturation between the sexes in many (though not all) new nations presents obstacles to the development of a self-perpetuating, endogamous, "modernized" elite. Where Westernized males must marry traditionally oriented females, the children are likely to acquire traditional orientations from their mothers.

> **3.** The assumption that urbanization per se leads to dissolution of traditional cultures is an untenable one. In a symposium on urbanization at the 1959 American Anthropological Association meetings, reports from Nigeria, Indonesia, India, and Mexico[6] all seemed to point to the conclusion that traditional values can persist in an urban setting, in one case because the cities are themselves traditional, in another because of the formation of ghetto communities, and in yet another because of traditional relations between village and city. This may be a short-range phenomenon but it is a striking one. Urbanization combined with the political competition of new nationhood sometimes intensifies interethnic rivalries and hostilities that had been dormant in the rural setting.

This emphasis on factors making for persistence of local, village, or traditional orientations may represent an anthropological bias. It should be noted, however, that there are indications apart from anthropological perspectives that support this point of view. For example, no new nation population is undergoing more intensive cultural homogenization than immigrant groups did in the United States, yet American ethnic groups, including their second- and third-generation members, show significant differences in patterns of family interaction, achievement motivation, religious values, social mobility, political behavior, forms of psychoses, rates of alcoholism, and so on. If it takes something like a century to wipe out these effects of transmission of tradi-

---

[4] Norman M. Bradburn, "Interpersonal Relations within Formal Organizations in Turkey," paper presented at meeting of Society for Social Research, University of Chicago, May 1961.

[5] For a more extensive theoretical discussion of this hypothesized correlation, see Robert A. LeVine, "The Role of the Family in Authority Systems: A Cross-Cultural Application of Stimulus-Generalization Theory," *Behavioral Science*, Vol. 5 (1960), pp. 291–296.

[6] The papers were by William R. Bascom, Edward M. Bruner, Stanley Freed, and Oscar Lewis, respectively.

tional orientations in the United States, it will take considerably longer in the new nations of Asia and Africa unless they adopt the coercive measures involved in China's direct assault on traditional family life. Where such drastic measures are not used, the dual problems of heterogeneity and traditionalism in political life will probably remain for many years.

The persistence over generations of behavioral dispositions acquired in the milieu of the family or ethnic enclave, even when they are no longer reinforced by the broader cultural environment, can be understood in terms of individual development. Brunner, on the basis of American Indian studies, proposed the general hypothesis that culture patterns learned early in life are more resistant to change in contact situations.[7] Values and kinship behavior comprised the kinds of patterns he found to be learned early. The same general assumption has been made independently by linguists working in the field of lexicostatistics, who distinguish between basic vocabulary, which changes at a slow and constant rate, and "cultural" vocabulary, which is highly susceptible to borrowings from other languages. Hymes states that some linguists have made the assumption that basic vocabulary consists of the names of things "which are likely to be learned early by a child, and, because of frequency, over-learned."[8] He cites studies that support this assumption,[9] although he concludes that further research into the matter is needed.[10] If linguistic research proves that vocabulary items learned earliest by the child are more persistent over generations, then the hypothesis that Bruner formulated for culture generally may be more reasonably expected to hold for another aspect of culture, such as political behavior. Other general support for this notion comes from experimental work by social psychologists that indicates that attitude preferences learned earlier have a long-range advantage over those learned more recently, despite temporary reversals.[11]

The only research applying the early-learning hypothesis to political behavior has been done on American children, but it has important theoretical implications for the comparative study of political orientations acquired in childhood and their functional significance for the American political system. Hess and Easton in a study of children in a Chicago suburb[12] and Greenstein in a study of New Haven school children,[13] found that affective and evaluative orientations toward political authority roles precede the acquisition of factual knowledge about the behavior involved in role performance. Greenstein found that children as young as seven years old, who

[7] Edward M. Bruner, "Cultural Transmission and Cultural Change," *Southwestern Journal of Anthropology,* Vol. 12 (1956), pp. 191–199.

[8] D. H. Hymes, "Lexiocostatistics So Far," *Current Anthropology,* Vol. 1 (1960), p. 5.

[9] Hymes, p. 7.

[10] Hymes, p. 32.

[11] Cf. Carl I. Hovland *et al., The Order of Presentation in Persuasion* (New Haven: Yale University Press, 1957), and Norman Miller and Donald T. Campbell, "Recency and Primacy in Persuasion as a Function of the Timing of Speeches and Measurements," *Journal of Abnormal and Social Psychology,* Vol. 59, (1959), pp. 1–9.

[12] Robert D. Hess and David Easton, "The Child's Changing Image of the President," *Public Opinion Quarterly,* Vol 24 (1960), pp. 632–644.

[13] Fred I. Greenstein, "The Benevolent Leader: Children's Images of Political Authority," *American Political Science Review,* Vol. 54 (1960), pp. 934–943.

were practically devoid of information about what political leaders do, nevertheless evaluated fairly accurately the relative importance of various political positions and socially prestigeful occupational roles. In both studies evidence is produced to support the assertion that the earliest affective-evaluative images of political authority are derived from parents and familial relations; for example, Greenstein notes that the New Haven children described themselves as Republicans or Democrats, apparently following the party preferences of their parents, "long before they were able to make any meaningful statements about the parties, or even to link the party labels with the names of conspicuous party leaders such as the President and Mayor.[14] Hess and Easton found that the youngest children in their sample characterized their fathers as similar in many respects to the President of the United States.[15] Thus, political preferences and emotional tendencies reflecting parental influence are established in the individual before he acquires objective information about the political system.

Are these early affective and evaluative tendencies toward political objects relevant to the operation of the political system? The authors of these studies suggest that they serve important functions. The younger children in the Chicago suburb and New Haven had strongly positive images of the President of the United States. Hess and Easton comment:

> Our conclusions suggest the possibility that if the Presidency is a major link between the child and the structure of the regime, an attachment may be generated that is of a peculiarly potent sort. A consequence for the political system of a child's acquiring his attitude toward the President in this way is that one of the strongest bonds between human beings—that between parents and child—may mediate between maturing individuals and the political structure. If this is so it would contribute in a significant way to the stability of a regime by establishing strong emotional ties at a very early age of a sort that are known to be hard to dislodge.
> Furthermore, from the point of view of the stability of the American political structure, some such attachment early in life has positive consequences. As the child grows to adulthood, he is exposed to considerable debate and conflicts over the merits of various alternative incumbents of the Presidency and of other roles in the political structure. There is constant danger that criticism of the occupant will spill over the role itself. Were this to occur under certain circumstances, respect for the Presidency could be seriously impaired or destroyed. But the data here suggest that one of the factors that prevents this from occuring is a strong parental-like tie with respect to the President's role itself, developed before the child can become familiar with the contention surrounding the incumbent of the office.[16]

Greenstein contrasts the children's affection for and trust of political authority figures with the widespread finding that adult Americans distrust politics and politicians:

> The cynical imagery of Americans seems to be less functionally relevant to their political behavior than the positive side of their responses—their respect for high political leaders and their frequent willingness to hold individual

[14] Greenstein, p. 936.
[15] Hess and Easton, pp. 640–642.
[16] Hess and Easton, p. 644.

leaders in great esteem. This is evident not merely from such relatively narrow mechanisms as the *fait accompli* effect[17] and the general willingness to accept the verdict of elections. The oft-proclaimed stability of the American political system—in spite of a remarkably heterogeneous population—suggests more broadly that powerful psychological mechanisms encouraging political obedience are present in the citizenry. These mechanisms may be as important as many of the more familiar historical, political, economic, and social factors which are drawn on to explain the complex phenomenon of political stability.[18]

If these authors have indeed found, as they claim, a psychological antecedent for political stability, then the comparative study of the images of children in new nations should reveal striking and enlightening variations as well as providing a test of their hypothesis. One prediction would be that in many of the new nations local figures and roles would have greater salience for children than national ones, and the emergence of national figures into the early awareness of individuals might be of crucial significance for future political developments.

The view that certain fundamental political orientations will persist after they cease being appropriate does not necessarily imply that peoples in the newly independent countries of Africa and Asia will be consciously conservative or overtly reject political innovation. Even when innovations in political institutions are greatly desired and eagerly accepted, traditional patterns may intrude themselves into the new forms—a phenomenon that is not unknown to students of European and American political history. It is a matter of political syncretism, of old wine in new bottles. Informal organizational behavior, images of authority, modes of orientation toward leaders, opportunities for intergroup rivalry—these serve as the media through which traditional political patterns have an impact on the present. This kind of persistence can be seen in African separatist religious movements, which not only appear to be promoted in their development by frustrations in the political sphere but which also strikingly reflect traditional authority patterns in a novel institutional setting.[19] Bradburn's analysis of Turkish factory behavior in terms of interpersonal values derived from the traditional family is another example of this.[20] It may be that the novel institutional means of mobilizing people for action is of greater significance for certain kinds of political analysis, but the impact of traditional modes of political behavior should not be overlooked. One would expect, for example, that the influence of traditional patterns on *national* government would be greater in ethnically homogeneous countries such as Somalia and Basutoland, or in countries in which national government is dominated by a single ethnic group, than it would be where several ethnic groups of differing political traditions share the reins of power.

[17] This refers to the increased popularity of a presidential candidate just after he has been elected.

[18] Greenstein, p. 942. Greenstein also proposes a regression hypothesis, that is, that, although later learning intervenes, conflict or crisis results in the individual falling back on the earlier attitudes.

[19] Cf. Bengt Sundkler, *Bantu Prophets in South Africa* (London: Oxford University Press, 1948), and Walter H. Sangree, "The Dynamics of African Separatist Churches," unpublished MS, 1960.

[20] Bradburn, "Interpersonal Relations. . . ."

SOCIALIZATION AND AUTHORITARIANISM

If one accepts as probable that political orientations derived from ethnic group traditions will have a continuing impact in the new states, then the content of these traditions and the psychological mechanisms involved in their transmission become pertinent objects of comparative study. This discussion is limited to patterns of authority, and is conceptually derived from social-psychological analyses of "authoritarianism" and "authoritarian personality" in Western societies.[21] From the viewpoint of contemporary American values, the political and social patterns of most peoples of Asia, Africa, Latin America, and even Europe seem "authoritarian" since they involve more pronounced status distinctions and deferential attitudes than our own. A closer and more informed look, however, reveals vast differences in authority behavior among peoples of the world, suggesting that the concept of authoritarian personality may prove more applicable and useful cross-culturally than it has at the level of individual differences in our own society. Any such application, however, must be preceded by a careful analysis of social decision-making patterns and the amount of command and sanction power vested in leadership roles, a kind of analysis that has been rare in anthropological studies of political organization.

To illustrate the psychological mechanisms involved in the learning of authority patterns, it is useful to examine groups with contrasting authority systems for differences in political socialization. The first comparison presented is one of extremes: the East African kingdom of Buganda (in its nineteenth-century form)[22] and a utopian communist *kibbutz* in Israel (as described by Spiro.)[23]

Buganda, with a population of approximately one million, was one of the most centralized monarchies in Africa. The king was a supreme ruler possessing arbitrary powers,[24] he appointed his favorites as governors of the districts without regard to hereditary qualification; he commanded a standing army, collected taxes from the whole country, and lived in a capital with a population in the tens of thousands. He was the top judicial authority and used extremely severe physical punishments like burning alive, mutilation, and destruction of property at will and frequently. All official positions in the Buganda political system, at national, regional, and local levels, were hierarchically ranked in a chain of command, so that each incumbent oriented

---

[21] Cf. T. W. Adorno, E. Frenkel-Brunswik, D. J. Levinson, and R. N. Sanford, *The Authoritarian Personality* (New York: Harper & Row, 1950), and E. Fromm, *Escape from Freedom* (New York: Holt, Rinehart and Winston, Inc., 1941).

[22] This comparison was suggested by S. J. L. Zake, "Child Rearing and Political Organization," seminar paper, Department of Anthropology, Northwestern University, 1959. Most of the material on Ganda child rearing comes from this paper, the author of which grew up in Buganda.

[23] Melford E. Spiro, *Kibbutz: Venture in Utopia* (Cambridge, Mass.: Harvard University Press, 1955), and *Children of the Kibbutz* (Cambridge, Mass.: Harvard University Press, 1958).

[24] This description of the nineteenth-century political system of Buganda is based on L. A. Fallers, "Despotism, Status Culture, and Social Mobility in an African Kingdom," *Comparative Studies in Society and History*, Vol. 2 (1959), pp. 11–32, and A. I. Richards, *East African Chiefs* (London: Faber and Faber, 1960), chap. II.

himself to those above and below him, showing loyalty to the former and demanding it from the latter. There were, as Fallers points out, great differences in power, honor, and wealth that followed the distribution of authority, but no status groups such as social classes, since the king was able to facilitate social mobility through appointments and the distribution of benefices. The hierarchy was an ordering of individuals rather than groups.

> The Buganda simply do not think of people as being arranged in social layers; they think of social differences instead in terms of dyadic relations of inferiority. There is great sensitivity to distinctions of honor, wealth, importance, and authority as between particular persons, but no conception of broad groups of persons who are essentially equal with respect to these qualities.
> . . . The Buganda were . . . ideologically "nonegalitarian." There were clearly-defined roles for superior and subordinates and an elaborate body of terminology and gesture for talking out these roles.[25]

The top official serving the king had traditional titles that were ranked in a well-known order; according to Richards, these titles "formed the basis of a precedence scale and were used by anyone in authority such as a governor, sub-governor or holder of a benefice to grade those working under him."[26] In other words, the ranked status system operative at the highest level of the political system was explicitly imitated at lower levels. The despotism of the monarch was thus replicated, although in weaker form, throughout the political system.

Kiryat Yedidim, the *kibbutz* studied by Spiro, is a community of five hundred in Israel, and thus is not comparable in size and scale to Buganda. Nevertheless, as a largely self-governing unit with a coherent political ideology, it may be contrasted with Buganda for the limited purposes of this discussion. The community was founded as an agricultural settlement based on collectivistic principles thirty years prior to the field study. The internal authority system of Kiryat Yedidim is summed up as follows:

> The distribution of goods is determined by the principle of "from each according to his ability, to each according to his needs," the latter being determined to a great extent by the entire group assembled in Town Meeting. This biweekly Meeting is the ultimate authority on all other matters which affect the kibbutz or any of its individual members. Authority is delegated by the Meeting to democratically elected officials who carry out policy determined by the Meeting, and who administer the various economic and social institutions of the kibbutz. Tenure of office is brief—never more than three years—which, it is believed, prevents the rise of a leadership cast or an entrenched bureaucracy.[27]

Social control in Kiryat Yedidim is achieved through expressions of public opinion and the ultimate threat of expulsion. Cooperation and voluntarism are stressed in the operation of the *kibbutz;* "labor is performed in work crews under the leadership of a foreman who, perceived as a *primus inter*

[25] Fallers, p. 23.
[26] Richards, p. 48.
[27] Spiro, 1958, pp. 4–5.

pares, serves his tenure of office at the pleasure of his peers."[28] Thus, the authority structure of the community is egalitarian in the sense that leadership roles are rotated among various group members and are vested with little decision-making authority, command power, or special social status. Leaders occupy their positions at the sufferance of the assembled community and must orient themselves to the approval of those whom they lead, while the average member of the *kibbutz* need not pay deference to the leader as a person but only to the expressed will of the group. Like Buganda, Kiryat Yedidim has no social strata differentiated with respect to status and status culture, but, unlike Buganda, its authority system represents a conscious attempt to minimize hierarchy and superior-subordinate relations and to emphasize the consensus and cooperation of a group of peers.

Both Buganda and Kiryat Yedidim have socialization patterns designed to produce adults who have values and behavior patterns appropriate to the functioning of their respective political systems. They will be compared in regard to three aspects of socialization:

   1. The conscious shaping of the child's interpersonal behavior by adults, in conformity with an ideal authority pattern.

   2. The disciplinary techniques used to enforce conformity in childhood.

   3. The authority structure of the primary interpersonal environment of the child.

In Buganda the learning of obedience and deference to superiors is a primary objective of child training. Children are trained to respond immediately to orders from an adult. They also learn to be quiet and inconspicuous in the presence of elders, to sit respectfully, that is, with the feet concealed underneath the body, and to walk past elders in a special manner commensurate with the respect in which they must be held. Questioning of parents is regarded as gross impertinence. Children are taught to call their fathers *Mwami,* a term that means chief or person of power and wealth in the adult political system. In the nineteenth century, this training as applied to boys was consciously regarded by parents as preparation for the possibility of being sent as a page to the court of a chief or the king, where the qualities of obedience, loyalty, and deference to a superior were favored and could lead to political success. It is notable that Margaret Read in describing childhood among the traditional Ngoni political elite, in a less despotic but nevertheless monarchical state in Central Africa, indicates their similar emphasis on inculcating obedience, deference, and decorousness in young children[29] One point of contrast, however, consistent with political differences between the two groups, is that the Ngoni encourage their children to share food and other valued objects equally among themselves, while the Buganda allow and expect the eldest to take the largest share and apportion the rest as he sees fit among the others. Thus, Ganda parents

---

[28] Spiro, p. 4.

[29] Margaret Read, *Children of Their Fathers: Growing Up among the Ngoni of Nyasaland* (New Haven: Yale University Press, 1960).

emphasize obedience and deference to superiors but not sharing among relative equals, in shaping the behavior of their children.

Disobedient or disorderly children in Buganda are severely punished with beatings and dire threats. The hard stem of a banana leaf is often used in beating children for infractions of parental rules, and they grow particularly to fear their fathers as strict disciplinarians.

The Ganda family environment to which the young child is exposed is characteristically hierarchical, with very pronounced dominance-submission relationships. Wives must be extremely submissive to their husband; traditionally, they might not rise in his presence. In a polygynous homestead, the wives are ranked among themselves. Siblings of the same sex are also graded in order of age, and the eldest, in addition to taking the lion's share, is held responsible for the conduct of the others. In children's groups the traditional titles of the king's officials are used as a precedence scale to create a hierarchical order among playmates. All these ranking patterns in family relationships appear to have been more pronounced among chiefly families than among ordinary peasants, which means that those individuals more likely to occupy important political offices by virtue of opportunity were also more likely to be raised in a strongly hierarchical family environment.

In Kiryat Yedidim, learning to participate in the community on an equal and cooperative basis may be said to be the primary objective of child training. On a questionnaire concerning values they hoped to inculcate in their children, *kibbutz* parents put "work" and "love of humanity" first and second, and "good manners" and "respect for parents" last (that is, twelfth and thirteenth in a list of thirteen); "responsibility to kibbutz" was third.[30] They also responded overwhelmingly with "Definitely no," to the question of whether children should blindly obey their parents.[31] In the system of collective education that is employed, children do not live with their parents, are not under their legal control, and are not economically dependent on them. All this is deliberately designed to "emancipate" the child from parental authority and to establish an egalitarian relationship in which fathers and children are peers. Younger children are under the supervision of nurses who direct their activities and discipline them. Obedience is not an emphasis in the training given by the nurses, and a great deal of childhood activity is voluntary and spontaneous. Even concerning the highly valued activity of agricultural work. Spiro states:

> Though these chores are now expected of them, no inducement, other than intrinsic satisfaction, is required for their performance. As in the case of other responsibilities, however, the nurses reinforce successful performances with praise.[32]

In regard to sharing, Spiro makes the following comments:

> One of the primary values that the nurse attempts to transmit, beginning with the very young children, is sharing. . . .
> In the Kindergarten the teacher perceives her most important goals to

[30] Spiro, 1958, pp. 20–21.
[31] Spiro, p. 12.
[32] Spiro, p. 211.

consist in helping her charges to be "human beings"—to help each other, and to have no feeling of "mine and thine"—and to become an "organized" group.[33]

Although there are very few instances in which the nurse reinforces an act of sharing, many situations arise in the context of the daily routine which enable the nurse to stress the value of sharing or the subordination of personal desire to the desire of others.[34]

Thus, by contrast with Buganda, the socializing agents of Kiryat Yedidim lay little stress on obedience and emphasize sharing to a very great extent. The contrast with respect to physical punishment as a disciplinary technique is equally clear. Spiro states:

The philosophy of collective education is opposed to punishment in general and to physical punishment in particular.... In the course of their training nurses are taught to eschew physical punishment, and no nurse in the kibbutz was ever observed to spank, hit, or slap a child.[35]

The most severe punishments administered in Kiryat Yedidim are threats of physical punishment, withdrawal of privilege, and shaming; nonpunitive disciplinary techniques are also used. The children's groups themselves exert powerful pressure toward conformity.

Finally, there is the question of the primary interpersonal environment to which the child is exposed in his early years. In Kiryat Yedidim, this environment for any growing individual consists largely of his age peers. Children live apart from their parents from a few days after birth onward, and they live in a series of age-graded nurseries and dormitories, whose egalitarian character has already been indicated in general terms. They also spend a good deal of time with their parents; thus the husband-wife relationship is relevant. Since the wives are not economically dependent on their husbands, do not even cook for them, work full time and are treated equally in the kibbutz, the husband-wife relationship cannot be thought of as a model for authority behavior that is at all at variance with the egalitarianism of the kibbutz as a whole. In fact, collective education in the kibbutz is predicated on the egalitarian character of every institution within the community so that the child will have no role models for authoritarianism.

This comparison suggests that extremely divergent authority systems have extremely divergent socialization patterns, if one takes adult aims in shaping children's behavior, disciplinary techniques, and the authority structure of the child's primary interpersonal environment as the points of comparison. Emphasis on obedience training, the use of severe physical punishment, and a hierarchically arranged interpersonal environment seem to be correlated with an authoritarian political system, while emphasis on training in sharing and cooperative effort, the use of nonphysical discipline, and a peer-group environment with no pronounced status distinctions, seem to be correlated with an egalitarian political system.

[33] Spiro, p. 43.
[34] Spiro, p. 188.
[35] Spiro, p. 185.

What kind of impact can differences of this kind have on contemporary political behavior in new nations? This can be illustrated by a second comparison, made previously by the present writer,[36] of authoritarianism among the Nuer of the southern Sudan and the Gusii of southwestern Kenya. Since these two East African ethnic groups are located only about one thousand miles apart, in what many anthropologists would consider the same culture area, and since they are also similar in social structure, the comparison involves a narrower range on the authoritarian dimension, one more likely to be found among the ethnic groups of a single nation. Both are traditionally uncentralized tribes of more than a quarter of a million (and less than half a million) population, with segmentary patrilineages as the major form of sociopolitical grouping, and a combination of agriculture and animal husbandry as a subsistence base. Both were characterized by blood feuds among territorial segments before being "pacified" by a British administration that introduced chieftainship and a court system. Despite the broad similarities, available data indicate that traditional decision making, deference, and aggression patterns were quite different in the two groups. The Nuer were democratic in local affairs, rarely behaved in a deferential way to occupants of such local leadership positions as existed, and were prepared to engage in combat on slight provocation. The Gusii, on the other hand, had wealthy "men of power" who dominated local affairs in many communities, displayed elaborate deference and obedience to the most prominent of such men, and granted them a major role in the settlement of disputes.

Patterns of political socialization in the two groups were consistent with their differing patterns of authority and aggression. In the father-son relationship, for example, the Nuer father tended to be affectionate and nonpunitive, while the Gusii father was emotionally aloof and used severe physical punishment in discipline. The husband-wife relationship the Nuer child observed in his early years was one in which the husband was dominant but respectful, so that he considered striking his wife contemptible; the Gusii child grow up in a home in which beating and other displays of temper against the wives by the *paterfamilias* were expected and in which wives had to pay deference to their husband in a number of conspicuous ways. Concerning aggression, Nuer adults encouraged children to fight when attacked by other children, while Gusii parents rewarded their children for reporting attack to adults rather than settling it themselves in combat.

Under colonial administration, when courts were introduced for the peaceful settlement of disputes, the Nuer and Gusii reacted quite differently. Some Nuer were recruited to be judges but they were reluctant to give definite verdicts and sentence their fellow men to legal punishment. Also, despite an overwhelming show of British military force at the onset of colonial rule, the Nuer continued to engage in the prohibited blood feuds, requiring extensive police intervention years after their initial pacification and the establishment of courts. With the Gusii there was never any difficulty about finding elders who were willing to operate decisively in judicial office and

[36] Cf. LeVine, "The Internationalization of Political Values in Stateless Societies," pp. 51–58.

inflict severe punishments when necessary. The people as a whole were quite ready to give up blood feuds for court litigation, and from the very beginning the courts were overloaded with cases, as they are today despite valiant efforts to expand judicial facilities. Thus, traditional ethnic variations in authoritarianism, transmitted to new generations in the socialization process after their structural forms have been superseded by a national governmental structure, cause consistent variations in political behavior under new conditions.

The validation of such analyses awaits comparative study by more objective methods. Although no adequate research instrument exists for the measurement of authoritarianism, some suggestive data are available to indicate that cross-cultural variations of this type have significant psychological correlates. In a large scale quantitative study of young adults in Egypt and the United States, Melikian, using the controversial F scale and a questionnaire measure of adjustment, concludes:

> The relationships between positive attributes of personality and authoritarianism tend to be opposite in Egypt and the United States. They suggest that in Egypt the authoritarian Moslem may be more healthy psychologically, this perhaps because he is conforming to the general culture pattern. On the other hand the Egyptian Christian who is authoritarian, whose subculture is more fluid, presents a less healthy picture. Similarly in the United States, the more authoritarian Catholic may be somewhat better adjusted than the Protestant authoritarian whose subculture tends to be more liberal. Thus it appears that when the personality picture of the authoritarian is taken into account, the general culture as well as the religious context must be defined.[37]

Enough cross-cultural regularities emerge from studies of this kind to warrant attempts to operationalize the authoritarian syndrome in cultural terms and to test in comparative research hypothesized covariations between degree of authoritarianism and patterns of socialization.[38]

LEARNING PROCESSES
AND POLITICAL SOCIALIZATION

Broadly speaking, three mechanisms[39] seem to be involved in the acquisition of political orientations in childhood:

1. *Imitation* The child learns adult roles in large measure through imitating adult behavior; thus the authority structure of the family or domestic group can be vewed as a set of role models. This is also true of the authority struc-

[37] Levon H. Melikian, "Authoritarianism and Its Correlates in the Egyptian Culture and in the United States," *The Journal of Social Issues,* Vol. 15 (1959), p. 68.

[38] Cf. Robert E. Lane, "Fathers and Sons: Foundations of Political Belief," *American Sociological Review,* Vol. 24 (1959), pp. 502–511, for suggested covariations among Western political systems.

[39] The three mechanisms presented are outgrowths of the trichotomy of *role practice, tuition,* and *trial and error* set forth by Robert Sears, E. E. Maccoby, and H. Levin, *Patterns of Child Rearing* (New York: Harper & Row, 1957). I am indebted to Edward T. Hall for his suggestion that his distinction of *formal, informal,* and *technical* learning bears a resemblance to the distinction discussed here; cf. Edward T. Hall, *The Silent Language* (Greenwich, Conn.: Premier Books, 1961), pp. 69–73.

tures of the school classroom, the children's group, and other organized interpersonal situations that are part of the immediate social environment of the child.

2. *Instruction*   Political ideologies or politically relevant moral values are sometimes taught to children; or they become exposed to adult knowledge concerning political leaders, parties, ethnic groups, and so on. In other words, adults may give children a cognitive map of the political world and also explicitly tell them to which parts of that map they are supposed to attach positive and negative values. The process that Hess and Easton term "role specification" is relevant here; this is the increasing differentiation of the images of authority figures as the child grows older. In their own study they describe the prespecification phase as follows:

> Attitudes toward figures such as the President are initially attitudes that have been held toward other authority figures. These attitudes are transferred to political persons who, to the child, are defined as standing in a position with respect to his family and community in something of the fashion that the father, and perhaps the mother, stand with respect to the children in the family. We propose, then, that the first step of political socialization is initially completed with essentially no information about the political figure himself except that he is an authority figure whose status exceeds that of the authorities with whom the child has been familiar. Obviously, an essential part of this first step is the definition of political authority which the adult world first presents to a child. However, this definition is probably an evaluative one, presented in terms of positive or negative emotional tone.[40]

They show that the children in their sample are increasingly able to differentiate the role performance of the American President and another (foreign) chief executive political official from that of their fathers with increasing age (from second to eighth grades). This indicates the effect of political information in producing a progressively differentiated political cognitive map, and suggests that a mechanism akin to discrimination learning (as discussed by learning theorists) is involved. The degree of differentiation of political from familial authority figures as the child grows older may turn out to be a major dimension of cross-cultural variability.

3. *Motivation*   Through trial and error, children learn appropriate behavior. When they do the "wrong" thing, they are punished or otherwise corrected, and when they do the "right" thing, there may be some consequent reward. Some of the habits thus acquired have a "drive" character; that is, they come to have reward and punishment value on their own. The strongest anxieties and positive social motivations appear to be of this nature. Motives concerning achievement, aggression, and dependence may be relevant to political systems, in that the individual may respond to aspects of it not only in terms of which he has learned through imitation and instruction but also in terms of his emotional needs. For example, in Buganda, overt submission to a higher authority is not only a learned response sequence; it also serves to reduce anxiety concerning possible disapproval by a superior and to gratify the drive toward upward mobility that can be achieved only with the help of important persons. The motivational element adds intensity to political

[40] Hess and Easton, p. 643.

behavior. In relating adult political behavior patterns to motives originating in childhood, dependency and affiliative motives to intergroup behavior, and achievement and power motives to the competition for political position. Empirical cases, however, should be expected to reveal numerous motives underlying each culturally patterned aspect of political behavior.

Changing Political Behavior

The preceding discussion has centered about the transmission of traditional political patterns to developing children, but the concept of socialization is limited neither to childhood nor to stable intergenerational transmission. What about the learning processes involved in rapid political change? The types of learning involved are no different, but their institutional form—the socializing agencies—may be quite different. Lane, referring to the intergenerational replication of political beliefs and loyalties within the family as the "mendelian law" of politics, states, "While imitation and common social stakes tend to enforce this law, the socialization process may work to repeal it."[41] Although individual cases of repeal may have their motivational roots in disturbed family relationships, it is ordinarily extrafamilial institutions that provide the new values and behavior patterns involved in political change. Especially in new nations, where family, local community, and ethnic group are likely to be working for the enforcement of this Mendelian law, political leaders striving for change will attempt to create national institutions for the countersocialization of individuals whose orientations have already been formed to some extent along traditional lines. The kinds of institutions that have been used in this way are youth movements, schools and universities, military forces, and special training villages. Any of these can become an assimilating institution, attempting to reorient young adults, adolescents, or even children, and resocialize them to a new national ideology and a new way of life. In their more coercive forms, associated with totalitarian governments, such institutions explicitly attempt to destroy family and other traditional groups as well as inculcating new values. There is evidence to indicate that these institutions for adult socialization are most effective in achieving this aim when they manage to exclude counteracting social stimuli through isolation of the trainees, to maintain consistent goals within the institution, to manipulate rewards and punishments in the service of official training goals, and to use both formal instruction and opportunities for imitation and practice of new roles.[42] In other words, a complete social environment in which the individual becomes temporarily involved may be necessary to effect drastic alterations in his motives, habits, and values after childhood.

One of the few systematic studies of political socialization of American college youth is the famous one by Newcomb, who showed that girls from conservative families who came to Bennington College with conservative

---

[41] Robert E. Lane, p. 502.

[42] For a more thorough discussion of the effectiveness of these factors in adult socialization, cf. Robert A. LeVine, "American College Experience as a Socialization Process," in R. B. Clarke et al., The Study of College Peer Groups: Problems and Prospects for Research (New York: Social Science Research Council MS., 1961).

political and economic attitudes changed over their years as students and acquired more liberal attitudes.[43] Although Bennington College may seem a far cry from any situation one is likely to find in Africa or Asia, its institutional setting for attitude change in young adulthood would seem to be generalizable: isolation of students in an atmosphere of homogeneous political values, with conformity pressures and rewards for acquisition of the new values, and a great deal of exposure to and practice with the novel political orientations.

In every new nation, including those that are making no strenuous efforts to modernize their populations, there are assimilating institutions operating to introduce at least part of the population to new ways of life and to new political ideologies and images. These include schools, universities, industrial and bureaucratic organizations, and religious groups. Very little research has been done to assess empirically the effects on individual political attitudes and values of these institutions, and this would seem to be a task of high priority for students of the political modernization process in the new states.

SUMMARY

Rather than dealing with a variety of political orientations, this chapter has been concentrated on authority patterns. The following kinds of hypotheses for comparative research on political socialization in new nations have been mentioned:

1. Propositions linking the age at which a given political behavior pattern is acquired by the child, and (a) its resistence to change in a situation in which it is no longer adaptive, (b) its functional importance for the maintenance of the political system (or some unit within the political system), (c) its greater strength under conditions of political crisis.

2. Propositions linking certain traditional political syndromes such as "authoritarianism" to cultural patterns of child training in the family and other primary groups.

3. Propositions linking the individual's degree of deviation from the traditional political behavior patterns into which he was socialized with (a) the degree of his involvement in extrafamilial institutions of a modernizing nature, and (b) the nature of the socialization patterns of the modernizing extrafamilial institutions in which he is or has been involved.

[43] Theodore M Newcomb, *Personality and Social Change* (New York: Holt, Rinehart and Winston, Inc., 1943).

18

The Assassination
of President Kennedy:
Public Reactions
and Behavior *

PAUL B. SHEATSLEY
JACOB J. FELDMAN

The assassin's bullet that so abruptly ended the life of John F. Kennedy on November 22, 1963, created a public event unique in the lives of contemporary Americans. The networks of mass communications and personal contact spread the news with a speed that was in all likelihood unprecedented, and, instantaneously, public attention turned away from everyday personal concerns to the details and meaning of the improbable event. Probably never before were the sentiments of the American public engaged so deeply by a happening on the political scene.

The unique character of the event centered around both its sudden swiftness and the personality of the man who was killed. Other events in recent times had some of the same elements, but not in the same combination. Attempts had been made upon the lives of Presidents Truman and Roosevelt, but no American President had actually been assassinated for more than sixty years, long before most current adults were born. Almost twenty years ago, within the memory of most of the public, President Roosevelt had died in office, but the Kennedy assassination was qualitatively different in two major respects: Roosevelt died of natural causes, while Kennedy

* Reprinted by permission from *The Public Opinion Quarterly*, 28 (Summer 1964), pp. 189–215.

was murdered; and Roosevelt, in his fourth term of office, was in his sixties, whereas Kennedy, in his first term and not yet fifty years of age, was the very image of youthful energy and vigor. Among contemporary public events, perhaps the closest parallel to the assassination, in its suddeness and its impact upon the population, was the unexpected Japanese attack on Pearl Harbor twenty-two years ago, which precipitated U.S. entry into World War II, but this event lacked the personal element that attended the unbelievable killing of the nation's President.

As unique an event as the assassination was, it nevertheless provided an opportunity to learn something about more normal phenomena. For instance, we know surprisingly little about the meaning of the presidency to the American public. Many studies have been made of electoral behavior with respect to that office, yet we haven't much idea of just what it is that people feel they are electing. Just as a newspaper strike enabled Berelson to gain considerable insight into the function served by newspapers during normal times, the death of a chief of state can reveal a great deal about the sentiments which normally surround the incumbent of that office.

A survey of reactions to the assassination could also contribute to our knowledge of the bereavement process. Although mourning and grief have been studied intensively in highly select populations, they have not previously been investigated epidemiologically over a broad population. Admittedly, there might be little correspondence between the emotional patterns elicited by an event of potentially appreciable psychological remoteness and those elicited by an unequivocally personal loss like the death of a loved one. Still, this was clearly a good chance to learn at least a little about the variation among different segments of the population in the symptomatology experienced in response to more or less the same stressful situation.

Here was a golden opportunity, then, to collect a body of data with both immediate and long-term significance. None of the other major events of our time had been subjected to detailed investigation; no comprehensive study of reactions to President Roosevelt's death[1] or the attack on Pearl Harbor had been made. Our obligation to the historian of the future would not be fulfilled unless we acted. Consequently, when a meeting was called in Washington by social scientists of similar opinions, the National Opinion

---

[1] Several studies of reactions to Roosevelt's death were published, but they were all based on data that were far from systematically collected. In fact, Orlansky, in his analysis of press reports concerning public reactions to the event, expressed considerable regret that more systematic data had not been collected by anyone. Among the discussions on Roosevelt's death were: Sebastian de Grazia, "A Note on the Psychological Position of the Chief Executive," *Psychiatry*, Vol. 8 (1945), pp. 267–272; Dorthea E. Johannsen, "Reactions to the Death of President Roosevelt," *The Journal of Abnormal and Social Psychology*, Vol. 41 (1946), pp. 218–222; Kurt H. Wolff, "A Partial Analysis of Student Reaction to President Roosevelt's Death," *The Journal of Social Psychology*, Vol. 26 (1947), pp. 35–53; Harold Orlansky, "Reactions to the Death of President Roosevelt," *The Journal of Social Psychology*, Vol. 26 (1947), pp. 235–266; Sebastian de Grazia, *The Political Community* (Chicago: University of Chicago Press, 1948), pp. 112–115. A forerunner of these studies with the death of George V: W. Ronald D. Fairbarin, "The Effect of a King's Death upon Patients Undergoing Analysis," *The International Journal of Psychoanalysis*, Vol. 17 (1936), pp. 278–284.

Research Center (NORC) was quick to respond.[2] Peter H. Rossi, NORC Director, attended this meeting on Sunday, November 24, and a series of studies was planned, one of which was to be national in scope. He returned to Chicago Sunday evening with a preliminary draft of a questionnaire. Although at the time there was no firm prospect of financing the study, it was decided to go ahead in any case. Hopefully, financial support would be obtained somehow later on.

To capture the mood and engagement of the American public in all its immediacy, it was necessary to start our field work as quickly as possible. NORC staff volunteered their services to work around the clock to set the machinery of a national sample study in motion.

The capability to carry out rapidly a "flash" study is a characteristic of a national survey organization such as NORC. A nationwide corps of trained and experienced interviewers is available; national samples are already drawn and ready for use; and printing and duplicating facilities exist on the premises. Perhaps most important is the cadre of professional study directors with years of experience and encyclopedic memories. At 11 P.M. Sunday, with the preliminary questionnaire at hand, a team of four study directors worked through the night on a final round of questionnaire construction. New questions about the assassination were invented, and old files searched for past questions that might now have value for trend purposes. By early morning Monday an acceptable draft had been completed. Meanwhile, the Field Department spent Sunday night and Monday morning alerting interviewers around the country by means of telephone and telegraph.

Because of the delay involved in callbacks on designated respondents who are not available on first call, a modified probability sample was used, of the type known as "block sample." Interviewers are directed to randomly chosen blocks or rural segments, given a prescribed route, and instructed to call at every dwelling unit, seeking to fill age-sex quotas. To ensure an adequate number of working women, the female quota is divided between housewives and employed women. Sampling materials for this type of assignment were already available from past surveys, and these were made ready by the Sampling Department by Monday noon. Following a final conference on the questionnaire at 10 o'clock Monday morning, that document was turned over to typists, and work began on drafting instructions for the interviewers. Copies of our final questionnaire were sent to other participants in the Sunday conference in Washington, for use in modified form in their own substudies. Materials were completed by early afternoon, and, thanks to the work of many volunteers who forewent the holiday occasioned by the President's funeral, all assignments were in the mail at O'Hare Airport by 2:45 Tuesday morning. In spite of the fact that no interviews were attempted on Thursday, Thanksgiving Day, 97 percent of the 1384 interviews were completed by Saturday, November 30.

What follows is a summary of the major findings as gleaned from the

---

[2] The meeting was called by Dr. Leonard Duhl of the National Institutes of Health, acting primarily in his private capacity as a social scientist, and was attended by Henry Riecken, Leonard Soskin, Marc Fried, Robert Bower, Eric Lindeman, Robert Leopold, and Ivor Wayne.

first marginal tabulations, together with a limited analysis based on the reactions of five population groups: (1) Negroes, (2) Northern whites who "preferred" Kennedy in the 1960 election, (3) other Northern whites, (4) Southern whites who "preferred" Kennedy in 1960, and (5) other Southern whites.[3]

HOW THE NEWS SPREAD, AND FIRST REACTIONS

The President was shot at 12:30 P.M. (CST) on Friday; he was pronounced dead at 1 o'clock. By that time 68 percent, or two out of every three adult Americans, had heard the news. Within another hour, an additional 24 percent learned of the assassination, so that in less than two hours it appears that 92 percent of the public was aware of the event. By 6 P.M. the penetration had reached 99.8 percent.[4] (Two of the 1384 respondents told interviewers they did not hear of the assassination until the following day.) This abnormally fast and deep penetration of the news is probably without parallel in the past, although we have no comparable data concerning Pearl Harbor or the death of Roosevelt.[5] Certainly the fact that two-thirds of the public were reached in one hour, nine out of ten in two hours, and almost everybody in less than four hours contrasts sharply with findings by Gallup and others that only rarely are more than 80 percent of the population *ever* aware of any given personality or event.[6]

About half of the people (47 percent) received word of the assassination by means of radio or television, the other half (49 percent) through telephone calls or personal messages. (Four percent first learned from newspapers or other sources.) Here we do have comparable data from a telegraphic survey

[3] Admittedly, retrospective "preference" for Kennedy in the 1960 election is not the same as feeling positively toward him and his program in 1963, but, since we obviously lack any measure of the attitudes of these respondents immediately before the assassination, it is probably the best measure available to us. It correlates well with respondents' current ratings of Kennedy's stature as President. More people now claim to have favored him in 1960 than actually voted for him, but this is a common phenomenon in public opinion surveys. Though he was elected by little over 50 percent of the popular vote, 59 percent in a June 1963 NORC survey said they favored him in 1960, and in the current study 65 percent claimed him as their 1960 preference.

[4] Respondents were asked, "When did you first hear of the assassination of President Kennedy? (About what time of day was it?)" and all replies were converted into Central Standard Time.

[5] A 1945 paper by Miller reports that 91 percent of 143 students at Kent State University heard about the death of Roosevelt within half an hour of the first news flash, Delbert C. Miller, "A Research Note on Mass Communication," *American Sociological Review*, Vol. 10 (1945), p. 692. In contrast, Larsen and Hill, studying diffusion of the news of the death of Senator Robert A. Taft, found that eleven hours had elapsed before 90 percent of a university faculty community heard of the event, and fourteen hours before 90 percent of the eventual knowers among residents of a low-rent housing project heard of it, Otto N. Larsen and Richard J. Hill, "Mass Media and Interpersonal Communication in the Diffusion of a News Event," *American Sociological Review*, Vol. 19 (1954), p. 429. The homogeneous and geographically limited nature of these samples and the obviously lesser impact of the death of Senator Taft rule out any comparisons with our findings.

[6] Gallup release dated December 15, 1963, notes a survey by the Gallup affiliate in Greece, which found that "Just 24 hours after the assassination, 99 percent of Athenians were found to be aware of the tragic occurrence—a remarkably high awareness score when compared, for example, with the fact that one-fourth of the people of that city were unable to identify Premier Charles de Gaulle of France just a few days before his arrival in Athens."

that NORC conducted immediately after the death of President Roosevelt in 1945, and the results are remarkably similar. At that time, 47 percent of the public first heard of the event through radio or the press, while 53 percent got the word from other people. Half the adult population (50 percent) were at home when they first got news of Kennedy's assassination; 29 percent were at work, and the remainder were outside shopping, having lunch, driving, or elsewhere. Only a third (32 percent) were alone when they first heard the news; all the others were with someone, usually family members at home, or co-workers on the job or at lunch.

Some measure of the impact of the event upon the public may be gathered from the fact that the majority (54 percent) said they did not continue their usual activities after they heard the news; and of those who did, most said they found it more difficult. Only 19 percent reported that they were able to carry on "pretty much as usual." Of those who dropped what they were doing, 5 out of 6 said they turned to television or the radio. Others hurried home, presumably also to attend the radio or TV; or they phoned and visited friends and relatives to discuss the event; or they explained that they just grieved, mourned, or "sat and thought about it." In reply to another question, 54 percent of the public said they "felt like talking with other people about it," while 40 percent "felt more like being by myself"; 6 percent could not decide. It appears that the more people admired the late President, the more likely they were to want to be alone after they heard of his death. For example, 51 percent of the Negroes, but only 28 percent of Southern whites who were opposed to Kennedy in 1960, said they "felt more like being by myself." Thirty-seven percent of the adults interviewed said they phoned or went to talk to somebody about the event; and, curiously, 38 percent said that somebody phoned or came to talk to them about the assassination. These calls, in both directions, seem to be divided approximately equally between relatives and nonrelated persons. Asked to compare their own reactions with those of other people, 30 percent believed they were *more* upset than "most people," while only 8 percent said they were less upset than others. Among Negroes, 49 percent were "more upset," only 3 percent less upset, whereas among Southern whites who did not prefer Kennedy in 1960, only 14 percent felt more upset, while 17 percent told interviewers they were less upset than most people.

The majority of all respondents could not recall any other time in their lives when they had the same sort of feelings as when they heard of President Kennedy's assassination. Of those who could think of such an occasion (47 percent of the public), the majority referred to the death of a parent, close friend, or other relative. Only a third of the group mentioned the death of any other public figure; F.D.R. was specifically named by about a fourth. And only 8 percent of those who could recall a similar event referred to Pearl Harbor. Negroes and pro-Kennedy Northerners were much the more likely to compare Kennedy's death with that of a close friend or relative; a full 80 percent of the Negro references were to such an occasion of personal grief. Southerners and non-Kennedy Northerners, when they thought of a similar event, referred more often than other groups to the death of Roosevelt or to Pearl Harbor.

In reply to the open-ended question, "When you first heard that the President had been shot, who did you think probably did it—that is, what sort of person?" only 1 person in 5 failed to name an immediate suspect. Almost half thought right away that it was the work of a crazed or fanatic individual. Twenty-nine percent specifically mentioned mental illness (madman, crazy person, insane, mentally unbalanced, etc.), while an additional 17 percent answered, "Some kind of crackpot," "nut," "fanatic," "extremist," and the like. In ideological terms, about a quarter of the population immediately suspected the work of a Communist, Castroite or other leftist, while only half that number had the immediate reaction that the shot was probably fired by a segregationist or other representative of the right wing. Negroes provided the only exception in the latter case. Of the one-third of all Negroes who suspected an ideological motive for the assassination, 2 out of 3 blamed a segregationist; whites, whether North or South, pro-Kennedy or anti-, were much more likely to attribute the deed to a Communist or Castro supporter.

Interviewers next read a list of seventeen statements representing "the ways that some people felt when they first heard that the President was dead," and Table 18.1 shows the responses of the national sample. Perhaps the most striking finding, already foreshadowed by the comparison of Kennedy's death with that of a close friend or relative, and by the general failure to respond in ideological terms to the question of who killed him, is the immense tide of grief, loss, sorrow, shame, and anger that people felt when they first heard the news, and the relative infrequency with which political or personal concerns were mentioned.

The first reactions of nine out of ten Americans were sympathy for Mrs. Kennedy and the children and deep feelings of sorrow that "a strong young man had been killed at the height of his powers." Four out of five "felt deeply the loss of someone very close and dear." Five out of six admitted to deep feelings of "shame that such a thing could happen in our country," and approximately three out of four "felt angry that anyone should do such a terrible deed." These feelings were characteristic, in only slightly less degree, of those who opposed the late President politically as well as of those who supported him.

These five immediate reactions, each one held by at least 73 percent of the total public, were quite clearly dominant; in fact, none of the other twelve responses was characteristic of as many as half of the people. In retrospect, it is unfortunate that we did not include some such item as, "I could hardly believe it; I thought there must be some mistake." Grief has been said to include "an initial phase of shock and disbelief, in which the sufferer attempts to deny the loss and to insulate himself against the shock of reality,"[7] and it is probable that the response of disbelief was as prevalent as those of loss, sorrow, pity, shame, and anger. Almost half the *volunteered* comments to the question, "Were you more or less upset than most people?" included some reference to this reaction: "I couldn't believe that he was

---

[7] G. L. Engel, citing Freud and others, "Is Grief a Disease?" *Psychosomatic Medicine,* Vol. 23, No. 18 (1964).

TABLE 18.1 IMMEDIATE REACTIONS TO NEWS OF ASSASSINATION (IN PERCENT)

REACTION	VERY DEEPEST FEELING	FELT QUITE DEEPLY	CROSSED MY MIND	NEVER OCCURRED TO ME	TOTAL
Felt so sorry for his wife and children	61	31	6	2	100
Felt sorry that a strong young man had been killed at the height of his powers	52	36	8	4	100
Felt ashamed that this could happen in our country	50	33	10	7	100
Felt the loss of someone very close and dear	45	34	9	12	100
Felt angry that anyone should do such a terrible deed	44	29	14	13	100
Worried about how his death would affect the political situation in this country	19	28	32	21	100
Worried about how his death would affect our relations with other countries	16	28	33	23	100
Felt worried about how the United States would carry on without its leader	16	25	29	30	100
So confused and upset, didn't know what to feel	18	20	14	48	100
Thought it was done by some Communist or other radical to get rid of the President	13	15	40	32	100
Wondered if anybody could really be safe in this country these days when the President himself can get shot	10	11	29	50	100
Worried how this might affect own life, job and future	9	11	17	63	100
Thought it was done by a segregationist or extreme right-winger	8	10	32	50	100
Hoped the man who killed him would be shot down or lynched	6	5	13	76	100
Worried whether person who did it would be a member of my race or religion and bring on persecution	3	3	12	82	100
Felt that in many ways the President had brought it on himself	2	2	11	85	100

NOTE: A seventeenth statement was, "Thought about the many tragic things that have happened to them and this was just another of them." The item was intended to measure self-pity, a tendency to see the loss of the President only as another cross the respondent must bear. As seems obvious now, however, many or perhaps most respondents interpreted it as referring to the Kennedy family, and the meaning of the results is obscure.

dead," "It seemed like a bad dream," "I just couldn't believe it," "It couldn't happen," "We thought it must be a joke," etc.[8]

The three next most frequent reactions were of worry and concern

---

[8] Since the above sentences were written, we have seen a February 5 report by The Texas Poll of answers to the open-ended question, "What was your first reaction to the news of the President's assassination?" "Disbelief" and "Shock" were each mentioned by 42 percent of the state-wide sample. Sixteen percent answered, "sorrow, tears," and no other single emotion was given as first reaction by more than 10 percent.

about the future of the nation. Forty-seven percent immediately worried about the effect of the assassination on "the political situation in this country"; and the fact that this was mentioned by almost two-thirds of the Negroes and a solid majority of Southern white supporters of Kennedy suggests that they were thinking of the fate of the civil rights program rather than of Presidential politics. Forty-four percent worried about "our relations with other countries" and 41 percent about "how the United States would carry on without its leader." The intensity of Negro reaction to the event is further underscored by the finding that two-thirds of this group, as compared with only 38 percent of the general public, were "so confused and upset, they didn't know what to feel"; and that a full half of the Negro population, as compared with only 20 percent of the general public, "worried how this might affect my own life, job and future." One American in five "wondered if anybody could really be safe in this country these days, when the President himself can get shot," and this reaction, too, was voiced by more than twice as many Negroes as whites. Only one person in nine said his first reaction was to "hope the man who killed him would be shot down or lynched."

THE FOUR DAYS

The intensive coverage that radio and TV gave to the events following the assassination was unprecedented, and it is doubtful if the American public was ever before so saturated with details of a single event. The fact that most places of employment closed early Friday afternoon, the intervention of a weekend between the assassination and the funeral, and the proclamation of Monday as a day of national mourning permitted most people to devote full time for four days, if they chose, to the accounts broadcast by the media. And they chose. By his own estimate, the average adult spent eight hours on Friday, ten hours on Saturday, eight hours on Sunday, and another eight hours on Monday, watching television or listening to the radio. These are median times. We did not even attempt to measure the additional hours people must have spent reading the newspaper accounts and discussing the tragedy with family and friends. One would have perhaps expected attention to the media to flag somewhat as the days progressed, but this does not seem to have happened to any significant extent. On any one of the four days, a minimum of 95 percent of the public spent some time attending the radio or television, and on Saturday, Sunday, and Monday, approximately a quarter of the people devoted thirteen or more hours to this activity.[9]

Political opponents of Kennedy spent less time with radio and TV than did his supporters, but even this group averaged six or seven hours per day. Fourteen percent of the public said they "had to turn off their sets at times because they couldn't stand hearing so much tragic news"; 34 percent said they "wanted to stop hearing about the news but just couldn't get themselves

---

[9] In the telegraphic survey following the death of Roosevelt on a Thursday, only 88 percent said they listened to the radio *at any time* on Friday, Saturday, or Sunday.

to turn off the set"; 18 percent said they found themselves watching or listening "more than they really wanted to," and 15 percent (28 percent of the Negroes) said they were not able to watch or listen as much as they would have liked to.

Following the initial phase of shock and disbelief and "a stage of developing awareness of the loss, marked by the painful effects of sadness, guilt, shame, helplessness, or hopelessness," the process of grief is characterized "by crying; by a sense of loss and emptiness; by anorexia (loss of appetite), sleep disturbance, sometimes somatic symptoms of pain or other discomfort. . . ."[10] Table 18.2A indicates the prevalence of a variety of physical and emotional symptoms among the adult population during the period between the President's assassination and funeral.[11] It will be noted that only 1 person out of 9 reported none of the fifteen, that 2 out of 3 said they "felt very nervous and tense," 57 percent "felt sort of dazed and numb," and a majority confessed that there were times during the period when they cried. Almost half the public reported trouble getting to sleep, and over 40 percent said they "felt more tired than usual" and "didn't feel like eating." Negroes and Kennedy supporters were more likely to experience such symptoms than persons politically opposed to the late President, though few even of the latter were entirely immune.

Of course, one cannot assume that all these symptoms stemmed directly from the assassination. At any given time, there are doubtless millions of Americans who feel nervous and tense, have trouble sleeping, or feel more tired than usual. But that a very large proportion of the ailments reported above were indeed a response to the unusual strains of the four days is indicated by Table 18.2B, which reports the proportions who still manifested the various conditions at the time of the interview, from two to five days after the funeral. A prompt and marked recovery had clearly occurred. A full half of the population were by this time free of all the symptoms inquired about; no more than a quarter of the people reported any one of them, and the majority of conditions were now characteristic of only 1 person in 10 or less. Again, the symptoms were more long-lived among Negroes and Kennedy supporters than among his opponents. For example, only 1 in 3 anti-Kennedy Southern whites now reported any of the conditions, while more than 2 out of 3 Negroes were still suffering one or more of them.

Although hardly unaffected by the four days' events the nation's children do seem to have been considerably less upset than their parents. It was presumed that teenagers would react in much the same manner as adults and that children under the age of four would not be directly affected. But we were curious about the emotions of the four-to-twelve age group and the way in which parents of such children attempted to explain the assassination. A little over a third of the households (36 percent) included one or more children of these ages, and, after ascertaining the sex and age of each such child,

---

[10] Engel.

[11] Many of these items were included in the present questionnaire because they had been asked earlier in the course of another study, and base line were therefore available. The data from the two studies are not readily comparable, however, and further analysis is required.

TABLE 18.2 PERCENTAGE REPORTING SELECTED SYMPTOMS AMONG THE ADULT POPULATION

Symptom	A. DURING THE FOUR DAYS						B. AT TIME OF INTERVIEW					
	National Sample	Total Negro	White Pro-K North	White Pro-K South	White Non-K North	White Non-K South	National Sample	Total Negro	White Pro-K North	White Pro-K South	White Non-K North	White Non-K South
Didn't feel like eating	43	58	52	38	31	26	12	25	14	8	7	6
Smoked much more than usual	29	40	33	34	19	21	10	16	11	10	6	4
Had headaches	25	43	28	24	17	12	9	23	10	8	4	4
Had an upset stomach	22	26	28	17	14	14	5	6	7	6	2	4
Cried	53	62	61	53	42	34	20	31	26	16	12	6
Had trouble getting to sleep	48	68	50	53	36	39	18	32	20	17	10	9
Felt very nervous and tense	68	80	72	69	57	56	24	44	26	25	14	15
Felt like getting drunk	4	11	4	1	3	1	1	4	1	1	1	—
Felt more tired than usual	42	61	43	46	32	34	15	23	17	19	9	10
Felt dizzy at times	12	30	12	12	6	5	4	10	4	4	2	2
Lost temper more than usual	19	28	23	13	13	10	4	9	6	2	1	3
Hands sweat and felt damp and clammy	17	26	19	20	8	10	4	9	6	6	1	3
Had rapid heart beats	26	44	30	28	13	16	6	17	6	9	2	4
Felt sort of dazed and numb	57	57	65	64	46	47	20	29	25	18	13	10
Kept forgetting things	34	56	39	35	19	22	12	26	14	12	6	7
Felt none of these	11	4	8	11	18	18	50	29	43	56	63	66
Number of cases	(1384)	(165)	(568)	(184)	(329)	(138)	(1384)	(165)	(568)	(184)	(329)	(138)

interviewers asked: "How upset was (each child)—very upset, somewhat upset, or not upset at all?" Adding together all children aged four to twelve, we find that 23 percent were described as very upset, 45 percent as somewhat upset, and 30 percent as not upset at all. (The reactions of 2 percent were not known to the respondent.) While a total of 68 percent were thus described as upset to some extent, it is perhaps more appropriate, in the light of adults' reports of their own reactions, to note that approximately a third of the children of this age were not upset at all and that only about 1 in 4 was "very upset" by the assassination.[12] And, like the adults, they seem to have recovered quickly. Asked whether, at the time of interview, any of the children were still upset or whether they had all "gotten over it by now," only 15 percent of the respondents with such children in the household said that any of them were still upset.

Two-thirds of respondents with children aged four to twelve in the household said they attempted to explain to the children what had happened, but the nature of the explanations seems to have varied widely. The most frequent response, offered by 39 percent of those who said they tried to explain, was not really an explanation at all, but simply a recital of the facts: "A man shot the President," "President Kennedy is dead," etc. In another 16 percent of the cases, the answer was either vague or irrelevant ("We tried to explain," "I showed him the newspaper"), or it developed that the child had actually received his explanation by means of radio or TV or at school. Thus, personal explanations of what had happened appear to have been attempted in fewer than one-third of the households with children in this age group. Six percent of those who say they tried to explain gave religious explanations ("President Kennedy is in heaven," "It was God's will"); 9 percent explained that he had been killed by someone mentally ill ("He was shot by a crazy person"); 13 percent explained that a "bad," "mean," "cruel," "wicked" man had done the deed. Five percent explained to the children what a great man Kennedy was, and 6 percent told them how terrible and tragic was his death ("We should all feel sad"). Four percent stressed the historic nature of the event ("Something always to remember," "Something to tell your children about"), and the same proportion used the occasion to explain the American form of government and, in particular, the fact that the Vice President would now assume the office.

Probably from very earliest times, a major function of religion has been to provide solace to the bereaved; and the United States, at least as far as church attendance is concerned, is a more religious nation than most.[13] Even aside from the spontaneous prayers and meditation occasioned by the violent death of a beloved President, the frequent references to the deity by national leaders and the ecclesiastical elements of the funeral would lead one to expect an upsurge of religious feelings and behavior among the general

---

[12] "Upsetness" increased with the age of the child. Only 39 percent of the preschoolers, but 72 percent of the six-to-nine age group and 85 percent of the ten-to-twelve group, were described as very or somewhat upset. Girls were more inclined to be upset than boys up to age ten, but thereafter no sex difference is observed.

[13] At a time when Gallup found 50 percent of the American public attending religious service in a particular week, his British affiliate reported only 14 percent in that country (AIPO release April 15, 1957).

public. Unfortunately, there seem to be no national data concerning the frequency, occasions, and content of people's prayers. But, in response to the question, "Did you yourself say any special prayers at any time during this period?" three-fourths of the national sample answered "Yes."[14] By far the most frequent objects of prayer (of 59 percent of those who prayed) were the late President's wife, children, and immediate family. One-third of those who prayed said their prayers for the repose of the late President's soul. About a third of the group prayed for the country, the welfare of the nation, and about a fourth for the new President, that he might have the strength and wisdom required to carry on. Many in the group, of course, prayed for more than one of these objects.

Yet, in contrast to the impression one may have received that the churches were flooded with people during this period and that there was a deepening of religious conviction among Americans as a result of the event, neither of these seems to have occurred. When asked, some days after the post-assassination Sunday and the national day of mourning on Monday, "Have you attended any church or religious service since President Kennedy was assassinated?" half the sample answered "No." The 50 percent affirmative is thus very little higher than the 46 percent average church attendance reported by Gallup in 1962 and 1963.[15] It is true that there was some increase in frequency of attendance during the period. Almost half of those who did attend said they went to more than one service, and a third of the attenders (one-sixth of the population) said their attendance was greater than usual. No significant change, however, was observed in response to the question, "How strongly do you feel about your religious beliefs—very strongly, strongly, moderately, not so strongly, or not strongly at all?" The proportion answering "very strongly" rose only from 40 percent on a June 1963 national survey to 43 percent on the present study, and the proportion answering "strongly" stayed constant at 26 percent.

ATTITUDES TOWARD THE ASSASSINATION

While the major purpose of the NORC survey was to obtain a quick reading on the emotions and behavior of the American people in the days immediately following a sudden national crisis, a number of other questions probed the public's attitudes toward the assassin and the assassin's own killer, and toward the basic causes, if any, of the tragic events. Because of the speed with which the questionnaire was constructed and the lack of opportunity to pretest, these questions were often of the broad open-minded type

[14] Though neither the samples nor the question wordings are identical, two other studies have produced very similar results. In reply to a questionnaire self-administered in late 1963 by a random sample of Christian church members in the California Bay Area, 75 percent said they prayed "quite often" or "regularly, once a week" or more (unpublished data from "A Study of Religion in American Life," University of California, Survey Research Center). And in the 1958 Detroit Area Study, it was found that 71 percent told interviewers they pray more often than once a week (personal communication from Gerhard Lenski, Study Director). A just-published Gallup report (Feb. 7, 1964) states that 63 percent of a national sample pray "frequently."

[15] AIPO released dated Dec. 29, 1963.

and were not always well pointed toward a specific issue. Certain of the findings are of some consequence, however, and we summarize them briefly here.

As indicated by the earlier presentation of the immediate reactions of the public, there was no consensus concerning the ultimate responsibility for the assassination. When asked, "In your own opinion, who or what should really be blamed for the assassination of President Kennedy—aside from the man who actually fired the gun?" 41 percent either had no opinion or blamed only the assassin. Only 1 person in 5 answered in ideological terms, 15 percent blaming Communists or leftists, and 5 percent assigning the blame to right-wingers or segregationists. A total of about 1 person in 4 placed the ultimate blame on the public generally or on the environment. Thus, 10 percent referred to a "climate of hatred" in the country, 8 percent said, "We're all to blame, we must all share the responsibility," and 6 percent spoke of social tensions, declining morality, social unrest, and other environment factors.[16] Fourteen percent specifically blamed the assassination on poor security measures. The lack of consensus apparent in the spontaneous replies to the open question is evident also in the responses to direct questions that asked whether specific groups were in any way to blame. At the time of interview, 37 percent thought Castro or Cuba was in some way to blame, and 32 percent believed Russia in some way responsibile. Twenty-six percent attached some blame to "segregationists," 15 percent to "the people of Dallas," and 15 percent to "John Birchers or other right-wing extremists." Twenty-two percent thought the Secret Service was to some extent at fault, and only 6 percent attached any blame to "Negroes in this country."

Two other open-ended questions asked whether respondents thought the assassination had "taught the American people a lesson of any kind" and whether they could see "any good at all coming from the events of last week." Three-fourths of the public thought some kind of lesson had been learned, 25 percent specifically stating that there must be less hate and intolerance, more love and understanding, among all Americans. Other answers were scattered. Sixteen percent pragmatically said that the lesson was to adopt better security measures to protect our leaders. Nine percent saw the lesson as a blow to American complacency and pride, and a spur to greater humility henceforth; while an equal number drew the opposite conclusion and stressed in their answers the need for more patriotism and harsher treatment of subversives. In response to the other question, half the public could see no good at all emerging from the events in Dallas. Eighteen percent thought there would be less hate and greater unity among Americans, while 10 percent expected that Kennedy's program would be carried on. No other "good" was mentioned by more than 5 percent of the people. On neither of the two questions were there any large intergroup differences, save that Negroes were more likely to say that the events taught people the consequences of hate and intolerance.

<hr/>

[16] This group of answers seems to provide the only possible evidence of guilt feelings on the part of the public in this survey. If guilt is indeed a typical grief reaction, either the public failed to experience it in the case of President Kennedy or it is too subtle an emotion to be revealed by normal survey research methods.

At the time of interview, 72 percent were "pretty much convinced" that Lee Harvey Oswald was the assassin; 28 percent had some doubt that he fired the gun. There was no consensus on why the assassin, whoever he was, had done the deed. A third attributed the action to mental illness, 16 percent blamed communism or left-wing sympathies, 3 percent blamed right-wing sympathies. Twelve percent thought the assassin had a grudge against the President or against the government, and another 12 percent answered generally that he hated everybody, was disgruntled, unhappy, or seeking an unspecified revenge. Interestingly, 12 percent of the public volunteered the opinion that the assassin was paid to do the job and another 11 percent thought he had been ordered or persuaded to do it by some unspecified group. Somewhat surprisingly, only 24 percent said, in reply to a direct question, that the assassination was the work of one man; 62 percent of the public were uncertain. The overwhelming majority (81 percent) were convinced that the assassin's target was really the President; 10 percent thought "he might have been after somebody else," and 9 percent had no opinion.

Reactions to the shooting of Oswald himself provide reassuring evidence of the continued faith and belief of the great majority of Americans in the traditions of justice and fair play. We noted earlier that very few people indeed mentioned hatred of the assassin or a desire for revenge among their first reactions to the assassination of the President. Now, when asked to describe in their own words their feelings when they first saw or heard of the shooting of Oswald, fewer than 1 person in 5 gloated over his death or expressed regret that he did not suffer more. About a third specifically stated their sorrow that he had been deprived of due process and a fair trial, while another third regretted that his death now made it impossible ever to learn the truth.[17] With respect to his slayer, Jack Ruby, a majority (53 percent) specifically stated in their own words that he should stand trial, receive due process, and let the court decide his fate; 15 percent said he should be executed, and 20 percent that he should be punished or treated just like anyone else. Only 4 percent expressed the belief that he should be punished lightly or go free. Asked about their expectations of Ruby's fate, the majority felt he would be severely or appropriately punished, 13 percent thought he would probably be punished lightly or go free, while 9 percent foresaw a successful plea of insanity. A comparison of respondents' wishes with their expectations concerning Ruby reveals, among those for whom such comparison was possible, that 27 percent expected him to get off more easily than they would like, while 9 percent expected him to be punished more severely than they believed he should. The majority (63 percent) expected him to be treated appropriately.

Asked to rate Kennedy as President, a full half of the adult population, during the days after his funeral, called him "one of the two or three best Presidents the country ever had," and an additional 28 percent described him as "better than average." Only 2 percent termed him "somewhat below

[17] Many of the foregoing findings have been reported by Gallup and Harris in their December news releases. Thus, Gallup found only 29 percent who believed the assassin "acted on his own." Harris found 26 percent who had doubt that Oswald fired the gun, and only 5 percent who were "glad Oswald got his due."

average" or "one of the worst Presidents the country ever had." Ninety-seven percent of Negroes considered him above average, as did 90 percent of his white Northern supporters and 78 percent of his white Southern support-ers. Among those whites who had other political preferences in 1960, 65 per-cent of Northerners and 44 percent of Southerners at the time of interview called him better than average. This, of course, contrasts strongly with the last Gallup reading of the late President's popularity while he was yet alive. In a release dated November 10, it was reported that a relatively modest 59 percent approved of "the way Kennedy is handling his job as President," while 28 percent disapproved and 13 percent were undecided. When shown a card listing sixteen adjectives and asked which four best described the late President, he was seen by large majorities in the NORC survey as "intelligent" (80 percent) and "courageous" (66 percent).[18] About half the public chose the words "hard-working" (52 percent), "sincere" (48 percent) and "a good speaker" (47 percent). Thirty percent perceived him as "strong" and 22 per-cent as "wise." Only about 1 person in 5 selected the adjective "young" to describe him; only 10 percent, "liberal," and only 4 percent, "conservative."

Finally, it may be stated that the American public revealed an astonish-ing command of Presidential history at this time, although public opinion surveys have long shown considerable ignorance of political facts. Eighty-eight percent correctly named F.D.R. as the last President to die in office and, when asked to name other Presidents who had been assassinated, 91 percent named Lincoln, 62 percent named McKinley, and almost half (47 percent) named Garfield. This high level of knowledge undoubtedly reflects the edu-cational effects of the mass media to which the public was so heavily ex-posed during the four days.

DISCUSSION

What can we conclude from these data based on personal interviews with a national sample in the days immediately following President Kennedy's assassination and funeral? Further analysis is obviously required, but a num-ber of important findings are already apparent. In no particular order of importance, the following conclusions seem warranted:

1. The increasing size and urbanization of the population, and the ubiquity of radio and television, now make it possible for virtually 100 percent of the public to become aware of a crucial event within a very few hours. Hardly anyone is so isolated from his fellow citizens or so cut off from the mass media that he will not quickly receive the word. It is to be doubted that this was the case even twenty years ago, at the time of Pearl Harbor or of the death of Roosevelt.

---

[18] Courageousness was apparently also attributed to Roosevelt with considerable frequency upon his death. "Many commentators and newspapers remarked that the Presi-dent was a 'fearless man' and Congressman Lyndon Johnson said, 'He was the one person I ever knew—anywhere—who was never afraid' " (Orlansky, p. 253).

2. The Presidential assassination seems clearly to have engaged the "gut feelings" of virtually every American. Events of this order are extremely rare. Survey after survey has consistently shown that most people are normally preoccupied with their own health, their own families, their own problems, and those of their friends and neighbors. These are the things they talk about and worry about. A sizeable proportion follow national and international events, many of them very closely, but their interest is largely that of a spectator watching a game. The election of an Eisenhower, the defeat of a Stevenson, a revolution in Cuba, the death of a Stalin—the surprise drop of an atomic bomb or the launching of a sputnik—such infrequent events, in contrast to the ordinary run-of-the-mill news, arouse the interest of almost everyone, but even they do not produce the cessation of ordinary activities, the almost complete preoccupation with the event, and the actual physical symptoms we have here described.

3. It is important to note that even political opponents of the late President shared the general grief. Despite stories of elementary school children being asked, like those in China, to applaud the assassination, it is clear that any such reactions were quite deviant. Sixty-two percent of the Southern whites who opposed Kennedy in 1960 "felt the loss of someone very close and dear." At least 2 out of 3 of this group felt sympathy, sorrow, anger, and shame for their country. Despite the acrimony of political debate, not only do few Americans condone violence as a civic weapon, but the great majority actually seem to come to the support of political opponents in times of national crisis. Gallop Polls, for example, showed a sharp rise in Eisenhower's "approval rating" after the U-2 incident and the collapse of the Paris summit meeting in 1960, and a similar increase in Kennedy's rating immediately after the disastrous "Bay of Pigs" Cuban invasion in 1961.

4. We may note the tendency to personify the event. The assassination generally evoked feelings similar to those felt at the death of a close friend or relative; rarely was it compared to other times of national crisis. Immediate reactions were most often of sympathy for the President's wife and children, sorrow that "a strong young man had been killed," anger at the assassin, personal shame that such a thing should happen, and feelings of loss of a capable leader—rather than a concern for the political consequences of the event. Perhaps great events can be meaningfully grasped only through personal symbols, such as Colin Kelly became in the days following Pearl Harbor, General MacArthur in the Philippines defeat, or Dwight D. Eisenhower on D-Day. The multitudinous political ramifications of such events are too complicated and diffuse to comprehend; we seek instead a more familiar referent. At such times, too, our attitudes are strongly swayed by emotion, and our emotions tend to seek a human object rather than an abstraction.

5. Perhaps because people responded to the assassination in personal terms, their reactions appear to have followed a well-defined pattern of grief familiar to medical practice; an initial phase of shock and disbelief; a developing awareness of the loss coupled with feelings of sadness, sorrow, shame, and anger; the onset of physical symptoms such as tears, tenseness, sleeplessness, fatigue, and loss of appetite; and, finally, a gradual recovery in the course of which these symptoms disappear and a normal state of well-

being re-established. Had the public *not* reacted to the assassination in some such terms as these—had substantial segments rejoiced over the event, had the people been obsessed by guilt, had they cynically brushed off the shocking news, or had their physical symptoms of grief unduly persisted—there would be some cause for alarm. But the immediate reactions seem normal, and the rapid recovery of both adults and children from the symbols of grief that were so strikingly prevalent during the four days appears to be quite consistent with usual reactions to the death of a loved one.

6. The well-nigh universal expressions of regret and grief and the deification of President Kennedy, even by political opponents, are not at all unique under the circumstances. William McKinley, for example, is today generally regarded as a rather mediocre President, but the world-wide tributes to his administration and character immediately following his assassination are startlingly familiar. "A universal spasm of grief passed from end to end of the land. From far eastern Maine to the western land of gold, from the great lakes of the north to the great gulf of the south, the sentiment of deep regret, the feeling of intense sadness, filled every soul. Never was a man more deeply and widely mourned, not even the sainted Lincoln, nor the warmly esteemed Garfield. . . . The whole nation swung downward into the vale of grief, only slowly to rise again from under the force of that dread blow."[19] "The awful sound of the assassin's bullets seemed to reverberate throughout the world. To every American home the news brought a sense of personal bereavement. To the royal palaces of Europe it brought a shock of horror and amazement. . . . The State Department was flooded with cable messages of anxious inquiry and sincere sympathy from the King of England, the Emperor of Germany, and the governments of all parts of the world."[20]

Lest the reader conclude that such intense sorrow is reserved for assassinated presidents, it should be pointed out that the deaths from *natural causes* of presidents and other chiefs of state also have tended to elicit waves of anguish throughout the populace. There is very little doubt that the demise of President Roosevelt brought forth reactions of nearly the breadth and intensity as those brought forth by the Kennedy assassination.[21] This is hardly surprising because Roosevelt was indeed a heroic figure for much of the public. What really jolts the situation into perspective, though, is the evidence of rather extravagant displays of grief attendant on the death of President Harding, a man of far less heroic stature. "Nothing could have been a more shocking surprise. At the big hotels dancing was immediately stopped and a hush and gloom settled over the crowds who slowly began to leave. . . . Cabarets and hotel dining rooms were quickly deserted." "Meyer London, Socialist Congressman: 'Oh what a calamity. This is a tremendous

[19] Alexander K. McClure and Charles Morris, *The Authentic Life of William McKinley* (W. E. Scull, 1901), p. vii.

[20] Charles S. Olcott, *The Life of William McKinley*, Vol. II (Boston: Houghton Mifflin, 1916), p. 321.

[21] See Orlansky, for a vivid description of public reactions. (The degree of correspondence between the Orlansky account and the present report is remarkable.) See Filmore H. Sanford, "Public Orientation to Roosevelt," *The Public Opinion Quarterly*, Vol. 15 (1951), pp. 189–216, for an indication of the esteem in which Roosevelt was held.

shock. . . . Politics are now forgotten in the love all factions had for him as a man.' " "Colonel Theodore Roosevelt, Acting Secretary of the Navy: 'He gave his life to the service of our country as truly as any one in our history.' " "Jewish leaders compared Harding with Moses dying before he reached the Promised Land."[22]

Unfortunately, no surveys were conducted following the deaths of presidents like Harding and McKinley, and we do not know how much credence to place in the admittedly impressionistic contemporary accounts. We really cannot judge from such accounts how widespread intense emotional responses actually were; journalists and eulogists may well tend to exaggerate the extent of such phenomena for effect. In any case, the widely experienced sense of bereavement following Kennedy's death was not nearly as unusual a phenomenon as many of us believed at the time.

Of course, even if the distribution of the population by level of grief tends to be roughly the same regardless of the personal characteristics of the chief of state who dies, it does not follow that it would necessarily be the same types of people in each instance who feel the loss most intensely. One might speculate that practically every president has tremendous appeal for certain segments of the population and is accepted with only a moderate degree of enthusiasm by the remainder. It would seem likely that the deaths of certain presidents might bring forth the most intense emotional reactions from, for instance, older people residing in small towns, while the deaths of others would affect mainly younger groups residing in the metropolises. The fact that the Negro population seemingly reacted more intensely than the white population in the case of both Kennedy's and Roosevelt's deaths does not necessarily result from greater emotional lability on the part of Negroes. Both these presidents happened to have an unusual appeal for members of minority groups.

There is not space here to examine and comment on all the various explanations for the intensity of affect brought out by the death of a "ruler." We shall restrict ourselves to one of the more popular models. This involves the displacement of childhood feelings of dependency from one or both the subject's parents onto the incumbent chief of state. Anxiety, the manifestations of which are difficult to distinguish from grief, is practically an inevitable consequence of the separation through death from the source of succor. It should be noted, though, that this explanation derives primarily from the observation of patients undergoing psychoanalysis. Such an interpretation is probably useful in accounting for the post-assassination behavior of such patients. It may also give us insight into the feelings of certain limited parts of the general population. Nevertheless, it seems to us that this view of the relationship between a citizen and the chief of state is far less appropriate in the case of President Kennedy than it was in the case of President Roosevelt.[23] It is more difficult to picture the youthful, fun-loving Kennedys as serving *in loco parentis* than it was the Roosevelts or the Eisenhowers. The

---

[22] Orlansky, pp. 263–264.

[23] Democratic Representative Lyndon B. Johnson of Texas was quoted as having made the following statement upon receiving the news of President Roosevelt's death: "He was just like a daddy to me always; he always talked to me just that way." Orlansky, p. 243.

apparent similarity of the reactions to the deaths of Roosevelt and Kennedy may mask appreciable dissimilarity in the feelings toward the two men. The following quotations point up facets of the leader's appeal that may be of particular relevance in understanding the appeal of Kennedy and the meaning of his loss.

> Perhaps a more important source [than the parental surrogate function] of appeal made by the leader to his following lies in the vicarious gratification of their yearnings through his presumed traits and achievements. The splendor, the power, the flame of the leader are shared imaginatively. New elements of meaning enter the lives of those who are emotionally impoverished. The everyday disparities and injustices of social life, and sometimes the lacks and incapacities of personal life, fade out of the center of concern. . . . The tendency to compensate for one's deficiencies by sinking them in the glorious achievements of more fortunate mortals may be an ever-present feature of social life.[24]
>
> The President, in short, is the one-man distillation of the American people just as surely as the Queen is of the British people; he is, in President Taft's words, "The personal embodiment and representative of their dignity and majesty."[25]
>
> Lincoln is the supreme myth, the richest symbol in the American experience. He is, as someone remarked neither irreverently nor sacrilegiously, the martyred Christ of democracy's passion play. And who, then, can measure the strength that is given to the President because he holds Lincoln's office, lives in Lincoln's house, and walks in Lincoln's way? The final greatness of the Presidency lies in the truth that it is not just an office of incredible power but a breeding ground of indestructible myth.[26]

7. It is good to document the relative infrequency of ideological fervor in the public's replies. One wonders what would have been the reaction ten years ago, in 1953, if an active leftist with a Russian wife had been charged with the assassination of the President of the United States. Perhaps one of the accomplishments of John F. Kennedy, in his few years as America's leader, was to dampen the fires of extremism rather than to feed them. It would seem that, even at the most generous estimate, only a minority of the public blamed the assassination even indirectly on Communists, and no more than a fourth, at the most, attributed it to the activities of right-wingers or segregationists. The "lesson" of the assassination was seen much more often as the evil harvest of hatred and intolerance than as a demonstration of need for harsher security measures and stepped-up efforts to "catch the communists."[27]

[24] Sidney Hook, The Hero in History (New York: John Day, 1943), p. 22.

[25] Clinton Rossiter, The American Presidency, rev. ed. (New York: Mentor, 1960), p. 16.

[26] Rossiter, pp. 102–103.

[27] Cf. McClure and Morris, p. 447: "Immediately upon the arrest of the assassin of President McKinley and the news that it was an attempt of anarchists, active and strenuous measures were taken to ferret out the conspiracy, if there were any, and to arrest the conspirators. Immediately, in Chicago, Ill., Paterson, N.J., and other large cities, the police located suspicious characters and those affiliated with anarchistic organizations. In Chicago nine men were arrested and lodged in jail upon very strong suspicion that they had criminal knowledge, at least, of the crime. Emma Goldman, whom the assassin had named as the author of writings and speeches by which he was inflamed, was also arrested and held to answer to the charge of inciting to murder, but was later discharged for lack of evidence."

8. The attitudes toward Oswald and toward his own slayer, Ruby, are heartening in their evidence of the public's sense of justice and fair play At the time of the assassination, when it is evident that Americans were under great emotional strain, only 11 percent "hoped the man who killed him would be shot down or lynched"; the thoughts of 9 out of 10 lay quite elsewhere. The great majority expressed an evidently sincere sorrow and regret over the murder of Oswald. And, far from acclaiming the man who shot him, only 4 percent held the view that Ruby should be punished only lightly or set free—not that he himself should be summarily executed, but that he was entitled to his day in court and should be treated just like anyone else charged with a similar crime. The public's expectations that justice would be done—in spite of the two shocking acts of violence—are also noteworthy. Relatively few believed that Ruby would be punished unduly severely or unduly lightly.

9. The over-all consistency of our findings is marred by one anomaly—the fact that a majority of the public expressed the belief that the assassin did not act alone, that "other people were involved." A fact-finding committee of the Anti-defamation League of B'nai B'rith has taken similar results from Gallup and other surveys to mean that most Americans believe the slayings of Kennedy and his alleged assassin "were the result of organized plotting"; and they attribute this situation to the activities of extremist groups, "which for years have been preaching the existence of plots and conspiracies in United States life."[28] A "conspiratorial" orientation toward public events was undoubtedly quite common during the McCarthy era and even now is readily employed by a substantial portion of the population. As one observer recently put it, "It takes a high degree of sophistication, Freud wrote, to believe in chance; primitive fears are allayed more easily by a devil theory of politics."[29] Resort to a conspiratorial diagnosis would seem to be particularly functional in the case of the Kennedy assassination because most people do not make easy use of the concept of mental illness in explaining behavior—especially if the actor displays self-control and appears to be cognitively rational.

But aside from the lack of any other evidence in our survey to support a conspiratorial interpretation of the assassination, what makes the particular finding anomalous is that the majority who do say "other people were involved" do not seem to take their belief very seriously. Were people truly convinced that a ring of plotters and assassins had carried out the acts, one would expect a public outcry and official actions designed to bring the malefactors to justice. But even though the presumed accomplices of the assassin were still at large, few people seemed particularly concerned about discovering their identities and capturing them. In another survey conducted by NORC one month later, hardly anyone mentioned the apprehension of the plotters as one of the "important problems facing the country."

Rather than indicating widespread paranoia and demonstrating the consequences of extremist propaganda, expression of the belief that others be-

---

[28] New York Times, Feb. 1, 1964.
[29] Daniel Bell, The End of Ideology (New York: Free Press, 1960), p. 193.

sides Oswald were involved would seem to us to have a more mundane foundation. People need to have explanations of important events and, in many cases, "cabalism" provides the most easily understandable and acceptable one.[30] It is hard for most people to understand the psychic processes of a mentally ill person who seemingly acts at random, much easier to ascribe the event to an organized conspiracy with a conscious goal. Moreover, the conclusion that mentally ill people not responsible for their behavior are at large among us, and are capable of capriciously ending the life even of a President, is both bizarre and threatening. Presumption of some sort of conspiracy removes some of the caprice from the situation and thus provides a less threatening interpretation, especially, if one does not really take it too seriously.[31] It is, of course, recognized that many extremists of both right and left normally interpret the course of events as a series of intrigues and have vigorously espoused such a view of the assassination. Our point, however, is that mere assent to such an interpretation in no way implies the effectiveness of extremist propaganda.

10. Finally, we introduce a table suggesting that the assassination of the President and the subsequent televised shooting down of his assassin in a police station had practically no effect at all, even in the short run, on certain basic beliefs and values of the American people that one might have thought to be profoundly upset by such startling and bizarre events. We have already noticed that people felt no more or less strongly involved in their religion after the assassination than they did before. Table 18.3 shows also the results of certain other questions that we included in our interview

TABLE 18.3   EFFECT OF ASSASSINATION ON SELECTED BASIC BELIEFS (PERCENTAGE ANSWERING "YES" OR "AGREE" TO EACH ITEM)

Item	BEFORE ASSASSINATION		AFTER
	Date	Percent	Percent
Feel strongly or very strongly about religious beliefs	6/63	66	69
Most people can be trusted	4/57	75	77
Communist Party members should be allowed to speak on the radio	4/57	17	18
Death is like a long sleep	1/63	55	59
Death is not tragic for the person who dies, only for the survivors	1/63	82	82
White students and Negro students should go to the same schools (whites only)	6/63	63	62

[30] Robert E. Lane, *Political Ideology: Why the American Common Man Believes What He Does* (New York: Free Press, 1962), pp. 113–130.

[31] Almost every crime in the Chicago area that cannot be explained by some such obvious motive as sex or robbery is commonly ascribed to the conspiratorial activities of the "mob" or syndicate. Winick has reported that only 14 percent of his sample failed to associate "the mad bomber" of New York City with some political group and that almost three-quarters pictured him as a Communist, Socialist, Anarchist, or Fascist (Charles Winick, "How People Perceived 'The Mad Bomber,'" *Public Opinion Quarterly*, Vol. 25, 1961, p. 33).

schedule because earlier national norms were available and because responses to them seemed highly susceptible to influence by the assassination.

It may be seen that none of the items registers any marked change, and this is perhaps the most important finding of all. One might have expected an increase in anti-Communist feelings or a sharp decline in the belief that "most people can be trusted." But, in spite of their almost total preoccupation with the event and the strong emotions and even physical symptoms that it produced, Americans did not change their views of the world. The assassination of their President did not seem to make them more or less anti-Communist, it did not affect their attitudes toward civil rights, nor did it erode their basic optimism about other people's motives. And these attitudes are not inflexible; three of them, at least, have shown substantial changes in the past. Willingness to allow Communist Party members to speak on the radio dropped from 45 percent in 1946 to 36 percent in 1948 to 19 percent in 1953. White support of public school integration increased from 30 percent in 1942 to 48 percent in 1956 to 63 percent before the assassination. Belief that most people can be trusted dropped from 68 to 57 percent between the summer of 1952 and the fall of 1953, and then went back up to 75 percent by 1957.

We can only speculate why the particular items shown in Table 18.3 did not register any measurable change in response to the assassination. It should be noted, though, that each of the earlier changes referred to took place over an interval of at least two years. Since the items were not administered either frequently or regularly, we cannot altogether rule out the possibility that our smooth trend line may mask some sharp fluctuations in the response. But from all we know about the behavior of those items, it seems much more likely that short-run changes in the past have been quite small, and that the larger shifts we have cited over time represent the cumulation of many smaller changes in the directions indicated.[32]

Our experience with sharp shifts of opinion in response to major events is based almost entirely upon rather different types of questionnaire items from those at issue here. Cantril's paper on opinion trends in World War II offers some cases in point.[33] For instance, the percentage expecting that Britain and France would win the war dropped over 15 percent in about one week's time in May 1940, in response to the German invasion of the Low Countries. A similar drop was recorded over about a two-week period in April 1941, when Athens fell to the Axis. Such questions have a large cognitive component and it is probably not surprising that responses to them should have been highly sensitive to the day-by-day news of the war. Had we asked in the present study about the need for increased security of the Presidential person or about reactions, favorable or unfavorable, to Lyndon

[32] We know so little about how such items behave normally because they are almost never repeated over short intervals. Most investigators apparently assume that they are too stable to warrant frequent inclusion in interview schedules. A clear lesson from the present research endeavor is that such inquiries should be replicated frequently so as to establish norms of change for a variety of survey items. Then, when we wish to assess the impact of a particular event, we shall have available a better-understood instrument.

[33] Hadley Cantril, "Opinion Trends in World War II: Some Guides to Interpretation," *Public Opinion Quarterly*, Vol. 12 (1948), pp. 30–44.

B. Johnson, or about the prospects of Goldwater for President in 1964, we, too, might have found 10, 15, or even larger percentage-point shifts from earlier findings. We have already noted that approval of Kennedy's performance as President showed a notable climb after the assassination.

But we also note in Cantril that there was a sudden 10-point increase in the proportion who thought it "more important to help England than to keep out of war" during a brief period in July-August 1940, immediately following the initiation of mass air raids on Great Britain. This question has far less cognitive component than "Who will win the war?" and indeed seems somewhat comparable to our question on school segregation in the intensity with which opinions were held and the deep-seated attitudes it engaged. A possible explanation of the disparate behavior of the two items lies in the fact that responsible leadership—notably Roosevelt—interpreted the events of the summer of 1940 to the public in a way that made wartime intervention seem more relevant and necessary. In contrast, no responsible leader interpreted the assassination to the public in a way that made changes in the items we are here considering seem relevant or necessary. Had a responsible Senator or FBI official urged the need of an anti-Communist crusade; had a charismatic evangelist used the occasion to call for a "return to religion"; had some leader on either side of the race issue managed to relate the assassination to civil rights in a way that the public could comprehend— then, some of these items might have changed. But none of this happened.

Finally, though relatively few Americans condone political violence, they are not unaware of its past occurrence or its future possibility. Assassination of a British King or Prime Minister would be unprecedented in modern times, and English reactions might well be different in several respects. But the United States has a relatively recent history of lawlessness on the Western frontier; practically every American knows that Lincoln was shot, and other Presidents too; and there were probably few who would have denied the possibility of a Presidential assassination some time in the future. If so, it would follow that when the majority said, "Most people can be trusted," in 1957, they were allowing for the violence and disorder that from time to time are reflected in the society. The assassination, then, was such an incident, but it required no change in the basic belief that most people can be trusted.

V

OPINIONS, LINKAGE AGENCIES, AND THE POLITICAL SYSTEM

The concluding set of readings examine the process of communicating opinions within the political system. The initial essay (Selection 19), by Stanley Kelley and his associates, makes a study of the effect of legal requirements in restricting those eligible to participate in the voting process, one of the most fundamental forms of political communication. In analyzing returns for 104 of the nation's largest cities, the authors found that 78 percent of the variation in voting could be accounted for by the proportion of the population registered. The qualification procedures facilitating or inhibiting registration represent the most successful, and one of the least appreciated, vehicles for limiting participation in policy making. The researchers contend that "registration requirements are a more effective deterrent to voting than anything that normally operates to deter citizens from voting *once they have registered.*"[1]

[1] Stanley Kelley, Jr., Richard E. Ayres, and William G. Bowen, "Registration and Voting: Putting First Things First," *American Political Science Review*, 61 (June 1967), p. 326. Emphasis added.

The ability of a system to respond to social problems and to cultivate faith in the fairness and sensitivity of its institutions to the needs of its citizens is limited by unnecessarily restrictive qualfications as to who votes. Such barriers appear inimical to the long-run interests of a democratic society.

Selection 20, by Charles O. Jones, examines a most unusual election. Jones graphs the response of the electorate to a presidential candidate whose policies held little attraction for the vast majority of voters. He also traces the road taken by the candidate, Barry Goldwater, to achieve his party's nomination and the impact this candidate's race had on other Republicans seeking elective office. The vote is the conventional means for registering approval of a set of policy programs that citizens would like to see enacted. A series of questions as to the representativeness and rigidity of the procedural outlets provided by the political system is suggested by the situation in which one of the two major political parties puts forward a candidate for the presidency who has a decidedly limited issue appeal. The choice facing the voter was too clear, in reality allowing him little discretion—that is, little grounds for deciding between two candidates in general agreement on most issues, but differing on the means to specified policy ends. A vote for Goldwater appeared to mark a decided reversal of national priorities. Since there was little pressure for such profound policy change, the Republican candidate, predictably, did quite poorly.

Selection 21 approaches communication from the perspective of the candidate attempting to acquaint voters with his views and his personal qualifications and to motivate them to translate their approval into a vote on Election Day. The report by Elihu Katz and Jacob Feldman assesses public reaction to the 1960 Kennedy-Nixon debates, which possibly exerted a decisive effect on the election outcome. Katz and Feldman explore the images communicated by the contenders, the information on issues generated from the debates, and the viewers' evaluation of the importance of the encounter in determining their own vote. The authors then review the general implications of the mass media—television, in particular—as a communications vehicle of political consequence.

19

Registration
and Voting:
Putting
First Things First*

STANLEY KELLEY, JR.
RICHARD E. AYRES
WILLIAM G. BOWEN

In their book *Non-Voting*, published in 1924, Charles E. Merriam and Harold F. Gosnell reported that many persons otherwise eligible to vote had been disfranchised by Chicago's registration requirements. Their data showed that "there were three times as many adult citizens who could not vote because they had failed to register as there were registered voters who had failed to vote in the particular election[1] and that "entirely different reasons [for not voting] were emphasized by those who were not registered than by those who were registered but did not vote . . ."[2] Their observation can hardly be said to have been influential. Until very recently most students of voting have paid little attention to the temporally prior act of registration.[3]

* Reprinted by permission from *The American Political Science Review*, 61 (June 1967), pp. 359–379.

[1] Charles E. Merriam and Harold G. Gosnell, *Non-Voting Causes and Methods of Control* (Chicago: University of Chicago Press, 1924), p. 251.

[2] Merriam and Gosnell, p. 232.

[3] Angus Campbell and his associates at the Survey Research Center of the University of Michigan discuss the relation of voting to certain of the legal arrangements governing sufferage in *The American Voter* (New York: Wiley, 1960), 276–286, and Warren Miller has reported additional findings on the subject in a memorandum to the President's Commission on Registration and Voting Participation. V. O. Key examined the effect of poll

Failure to do so has had important consequences. It has made it easy to discount unduly the significance of *political* influences on the size and composition of electorates; easy to argue unrealistically about the value of efforts to increase the turnout of voters; and easy to be puzzled about some aspects of the behavior of voters.

THE DESIGN OF THE STUDY

The study out of which this article grows was undertaken in an effort to find answers to two questions: To what extent can differences from place to place in the turnout of voters in elections be accounted for by differences in the number of those registered to vote? What factors are most strongly associated with variations in the percentage of those of voting age who do register to vote in different localities? We tried to find answers to these questions by analyzing registration and voting in 1960 in 104 of the nation's largest cities.[4]

Our analysis was guided by Anothony Downs' discussion of voting in his *An Economic Theory of Democracy*. Downs assumes that "every rational man decides to vote just as he makes all other decision: if the returns outweigh the costs, he votes; if not, he abstains,"[5] and that assumption enables him to make a number of interesting deductions about which voters are likely to vote and which are not. We decided to assume that both the voter's decision to register and decisions made by party organizations about

---

taxes on voting in his *Southern Politics* (New York: Knopf, 1950), 599–618, and Howard Freeman, Arnold Simmel, and Murray Gendell discuss the turnout of registered voters in William N. McPhee and William A. Glaser, *Public Opinion and Congressional Elections* (New York: Free Press, 1962), 240–250. Donald R. Matthews and James W. Prothro report findings about rates of registration among Negroes in the South in two articles: "Social and Economic Factors and Negro Voter Registration in the South," *American Political Science Review*, 57 (March 1963), 24–44, and "Political Factors and Negro Voter Registration in the South," *American Political Science Review*, 57 (June 1963), 335–367.

Much earlier, Gosnell presented some interesting information on the relation of registration procedures to turnout in elections in *Getting Out the Vote* (Chicago: University of Chicago Press, 1927) and *Why Europe Votes* (Chicago: University of Chicago Press, 1930), as did Joseph P. Harris at about the same time in his *Registration of Voters in the United States* (Washington: The Brookings Institution, 1929), 106–108. There are of course comments on the relation of registration to voting in works not cited here, but very few additional sources of systematic information about that relationship.

[4] Originally we planned to study factors affecting rates of registration in all cities in the United States with populations above 100,000; we were unable to proceed as planned, however, because we were unable to secure information about registration or registration procedures in some of these cities. Most commonly we could not secure accurate data regarding the percentage of the population of voting age registered to vote or verify the accuracy of such data as we could get. This was the case for 16 cities: Mobile, Montgomery, Tucson, Savannah, Chicago, Evansville, Indianapolis, Shreveport, Jackson, Albuquerque, Knoxville, Amarillo, Beaumont, El Paso, Lubbock, and Wichita Falls. We could not get accurate information regarding times and physical arrangements for registration in eight additional cities: Phoenix, Anaheim, Long Beach, San Jose, Denver, Providence, Madison, and Milwaukee. A figure for the percentage of recent migrants from out of state was missing for Yonkers, New York. Washington, D.C., had no procedures for registering voters in 1960, since, at that time, it had no voters.

[5] Anthony Downs, *An Economic Theory of Democracy* (New York: Harper & Row 1927), p. 260.

efforts to induce citizens to register are made after a similar rational calculation of benefits and costs. If one makes that assumption, it follows that variations in rates of registration among cities are the consequence of differences among them in the way voters assess the value of registering, in the interest politicians have in adding new names to the registration rolls, in costs voters perceive to be associated with the act of registering, and in costs of mounting registration drives. About such assessments, interests, and perceptions we had no direct information, but they could reasonably be supposed to be affected by several factors about which information was available.

The value that voters attach to the act of registering and that politicians put on registration drives should vary, for instance, with the competitiveness of a state's party politics and with the offices that are at stake in an election. As the probable division of the vote for the major parties in a state approaches 50–50, presidential candidates and all candidates for state-wide office have an increasingly strong incentive to induce their partisans to register, and the voter has an increasingly large (if still very small) chance to cast a ballot that will decide the outcome of a contest. As the number of officials to be elected in any given election rises, or, perhaps more accurately, as the scope of governmental power at stake in any election increases, so should the voter's estimate of the importance of the election. We therefore decided to examine the relationship of registration to both these variables.

There are three rather different sorts of costs that voters may see as involved in the act of registering to vote. In the first instance there are *monetary* costs. In 1960 some southern cities literally charged a fee, the poll tax, for putting one's name on the list of eligible voters; but in other places registering might also mean a loss of income through loss of time on the job or time away from a business.[6] Perhaps a more important cost is simple *inconvenience*. To get their names on a registration roll almost all voters must go out of their way to a greater or lesser extent and in some places the bother involved is very considerable indeed. Finally, there are costs of *obtaining information* about registering to vote. A voter must find out where and when he can register and if he is eligible to do so, and acquiring this information may take an appreciable amount of time and effort. We postulated that the magnitude of one or more of these sorts of costs would be greater, and would be seen as greater, in cities where citizens must take a literacy test;[7] where all voters must reregister at frequent intervals; where it is necessary to register considerably in advance of election day; and where the hours during which, and places at which, one can register are restricted.

The findings of the major studies of voting were a second important influence on our early speculation about factors that might account for differences among cities in rates of registration. Registration is hardly ever represented as anything but a purely instrumental act: one registers in order to vote. One would suppose, therefore, that most of the factors that en-

---

[6] Merriam and Gosnell reported that a substantial number of the nonvoters they studied had given fear of loss of income through loss of time away from work as an important reason for not voting; see *Non-Voting*, 86–95.

[7] Literacy tests tend to lower registration, of course, not only because they are a bother but also because they disqualify a certain number of voters.

courage or discourage voting also encourage or discourage registering to vote. Proceeding on that supposition, we posited a strong relationship between registration and those socioeconomic and psychological factors that have figured prominently in explanations of the turnout of voters in elections.[8] We could not of course, hope to discover whether a relationship actually existed between registration and each such factor; no data were available to us on the psychological states or personal traits of persons of voting age in the cities we studied.[9] We could and did, however, try to find out if the proportion of citizens of voting age who were registered to vote in a city was associated with the median income and average educational attainment of the city's residents and with the numbers of recent migrants, young people, males, and Negroes in its population.

There has been less agreement on why various socioeconomic factors are related to turnout in elections than on the fact that they are related, but such is the present state of the literature on voting. Downs attributes differences in the turnout rates of various classes of citizens to their varying abilities to bear the costs of voting or variations in what voting costs them. Thus, to make sense of the choices an election offers him, the educated man needs less additional information than someone who is poorly educated, and higher income groups are in a better position to pay the costs of finding out how their interests are affected by alternatives (and to pay other costs of voting) than are low income groups.[10] S. M. Lipset offers very similar explanations for the relationship of income and education to turnout, and both Downs and Lipset note also that the turnout rates of low-income groups may be lowered by confusion resulting from exposure to a largely conservative press.[11] Campbell and his colleagues argue that "The educated person is distinct from the less educated not only in the number of facts about politics at this command, but also in the sophistication of the concepts he employs to maintain a sense of order and meaning amid the flood of information";[12] the educated man is therefore less likely to abstain from voting out of a feeling that politics is too complicated to understand. Low rates of participation in elections among young voters have been explained by reference to their fluid occupational interests, greater mobility, lack of firm attachments to political parties, and absence of clear positions in the social life of their communities.[13] The low turnout of women relative to men is usually at-

---

[8] The most important have been race, place of residence, education, age, income, marital status, sex, ethnic group affiliation, occupation, geographical mobility, intensity of partisan preferences, perceived closeness of the election, interest in the campaign, concern with the outcome of the election, sense of the efficacy of voting, sense of civic duty, attitudes with respect to issues of public policy, attitudes toward candidates, and level of political information.

[9] Nor could we study the relationship of urban and rural residence to rates of registration, since we limited ourselves to the study of registration in large cities.

[10] See Anthony Downs, 232–236, 260–273.

[11] Downs, p. 235, and Seymour Martin Lipset, *Political Man* (New York: Doubleday, 1960), p. 205.

[12] Angus Campbell, Philip Converse, Warren Miller and Donald Stokes, *The American Voter*, p. 476.

[13] See particularly Seymour Martin Lipset, 202, 209–211; Robert Lane, *Political Life* (New York: Free Press, 1959), 48–49; Angus Campbell et al., *The American Voter*, 496–497; and Lester W. Milbrath, *Political Participation* (Skokie, Ill.: Rand McNally, 1965), p. 135.

tributed to the cultural definition of politics as the concern of men, and that of Negroes relative to whites is attributed to deliberate efforts to discourage Negro voting and to the status of Negroes as a low-income group. It has been argued that newcomers to a community are less likely to vote than old residents because they have less contact with locally dominant groups, because their mobility is likely to have exposed them to politically relevant cross-pressures, and because they are likely to be disqualified for voting by local residence requirements.[14]

Certain common sense considerations were a third influence on our guesses about the factors that might make for higher or lower levels of registration. States require varying periods of residence in the state, and in the county and voting district, before a person is eligible to register even if he is otherwise qualified to do so. All states also require voters to be citizens of the United States. One would therefore expect that variations from place to place in residence requirements and any local variations in numbers of resident aliens would make a difference in the proportion of persons of voting age who are registered to vote in different cities. Further, rates of registration are known to vary regionally. This relationship might reflect differences in the culture of regions rather than regional differences in the values of the variables so far discussed. Finally, those cities having systems of permanent registration employ methods of differing efficiency to remove from registration rolls the names of voters who have died, moved away, or failed to vote for a specified period, a fact which could also account for some of the variation in registration rates from city to city.

It should be apparent that testing some of the hypotheses of interest to us entailed formidable problems in gathering data. We chose to study registration in 1960 because we were able to secure data on registration for a number of jurisdictions from the national committees of the two major parties; moreover, the presidential election of 1960 coincided with a decennial census year. We chose the nation's large cities as units of observation because there were a sufficient number of them to make statistical analysis fruitful and because we could secure data for them that was unavailable either for states or counties. Several of the states, for instance, collect no information on the numbers of their citizens registered to vote. Registration, voting, and census data are reported by counties, but the hours, days of the week, and kinds of places where citizens can register are frequently determined at lower levels of government, and so may vary considerably within counties.

Cities are units of observation well suited to examining the effects on registration of differences among localities in the extent of interparty competition, residence requirements, closing dates for registration, and the availability of places to register. Inter-city analysis is less appropriate for an examination of the effects on registration of individual characteristics such as sex, age, education, and income, which can be better studied by treating the individual as the unit of observation. For instance, it is obviously better to draw inferences about the effects of sex on registration from a direct com-

[14] See Seymour Martin Lipset, pp. 202–208.

parison of registration rates between males and females (after allowing for the effects of other variables) than from a comparison of inter-city differences in registration associated with inter-city differences in sex-ratios. The main reason for including variables which measure individual characteristics in our inter-city analysis was to guard against the possibility that substantial differences among cities in, for example, the proportion of men in the population, might obscure the true effects on registration of variations in such factors as the degree of inter-party competition, residence requirements, and so on. It was also of interest of course, to see if the variables which measure individual characteristics were sufficiently powerful to cause differences among cities in registration rates.

In analyzing differences among cities in the percentage of the voting-age population registered to vote, we used ordinary multiple-regression techniques, and we assumed that linear fits could be used to approximate the true relationships among our variables. Other aspects of our procedures can be explained most conveniently as we present our findings.

FINDINGS

Registration Related to Turnout

Our findings with respect to the first of the two major questions in which we were interested—that concerning the relationship of registration to the turnout of voters in elections—can be reported in a few sentences. In the full sample of cities, 78 percent of the variation in the percentage of the population of voting age that voted could be accounted for by variations in the percentage of the population of voting age that was registered to vote.[15] As one would expect, the relationship was almost one-to-one; that is, if the percentage of the population of voting age registered to vote in city A was one percent higher than in city B, then the percentage of the population of voting age actually voting in city A was, on the average, almost exactly one percent higher than in city B.[16] Moreover, it seems clear that registration requirements are a more effective deterrent to voting than anything that normally operates to deter citizens from voting once they have registered, at least in presidential elections. The mean percentage of *those of voting age who were registered to vote* in the full sample of cities was 73.3 percent and the standard deviation was 14.3 percent. In contrast, the mean percentage of *those registered to vote who voted* was 81.6 percent with a standard deviation of 11.7 percent. Thus the latter was not only higher but also varied within a narrower range.

Variations in Proportion Registered

What factors account for the wide range of differences among cities in the proportion of the population of voting age that is registered to vote? Discussion of our findings with respect to this second question must be con-

[15] The F-ratio for the regression was 361.39.

[16] The regression coefficient of the rate of registration in this regression was 0.96, its standard error was .05, and its "t" value was 19.01.

siderably more extensive. To begin with, we will report what we found to be the most important influences on rates of registration in our full sample of cities. We will then present additional information obtained by examining registration only in those cities with systems of permanent registration (the reason for this separate analysis of cities with systems of permanent registration will be apparent later), by controlling for regional influences, and by analyzing the pattern of residual variance.

Findings with Respect to the Full Sample of Cities

Table 19.1 summarizes the results of our analysis of the registration of voters in the full sample of cities.[17] It seems clear that we included among our explanatory factors a number of highly significant ones: Together, the twelve independent variables in Regression I.1 "explain" (in the sense usual when interpreting multiple regression equations) nearly 80 percent of the variation among cities in percentages of the population of voting age registered to vote. Only one of these twelve variables (the percentage of males in the population of voting age) failed to have the expected sign, and six had "t" values large enough to imply that their regression coefficients were significantly different from zero at a level of confidence of 95 percent or better. In a second regression (I.2 in Table 19.1) that included only these six variables, the value of R^2 fell just three percentage points, and all six continued to show statistically significant relationships to the dependent variable.[18]

Socio-Economic Factors

Regression I.1 included six socio-economic variables—age, race, education, income, sex, and length of residence.[19] Only three—age, education, and race—were significantly related to variations among cities in rates of registration. The implications of the regression coefficients of these variables may be stated as follows:

> A. If the number of persons in the age-group 20 to 34 relative to the number of persons of voting age in a city was larger than the average of all cities in the sample by one percent, the city's rate of registration tended to be one-half of one percent below the average of all cities in the sample.

[17] The results in all of our text tables are reported in terms of partial regression coefficients, standard errors of these coefficients, and t-values. Appendix III contains partial correlation coefficients and Beta-weights.

[18] The R^2's reported in Table 19.1 are not corrected for degrees of freedom; the R^2's for Regression I.1 must therefore be larger than the R^2 for Regression I.2, since the latter contains only six of the twelve independent variables included in the former. Actually, as the F-ratios indicate, Regression I.2 gets higher marks on the statistical significance scale than does Regression I.1, although it is important to remember that we already knew something about the behavior of the variables included in Regression I.2 before it was run. A "t" value significant at the 95 percent level in Regression I.1 was the criterion for the inclusion of variables in Regression I.2, and in such circumstances the meaningfulness of standard significance tests is open to some question.

[19] Precise definitions of these and other variables are given in Appendix I in order of which the variables are discussed below.

TABLE 19.1 REGRESSION ANALYSIS OF DIFFERENCES AMONG CITIES IN PERCENTAGES OF THE POPULATION OF VOTING AGE REGISTERED TO VOTE (104 CITIES, 1960)

VARIABLES[a]	EXPECTED SIGN	REGRESSION I.1[b]			REGRESSION I.2[c]		
		b	(s)	t	b	(s)	t
Independent Variables:							
Socio-Economic Factors							
Age (percent 20–34)	—	—0.47	(0.20)	2.33*	—0.50	(0.18)	2.79**
Sex (percent male)	+	—0.18	(0.63)	0.28			
Race (percent nonwhite)	—	—0.14	(0.07)	2.05*	—0.17	(0.07)	2.46*
Education (median yrs. completed)	+	2.13	(0.99)	2.16*	2.88	(0.72)	4.02*
Income ($100/Yr.)	+	0.23	(0.16)	1.43			
Length of residence (percent from out of state)	—	—0.20	(0.15)	1.33			
Factors Affecting the Value of the Vote							
Inter-party competition (percent)	—	—0.30	(0.10)	3.02**	—0.41	(0.07)	5.60**
Factors Affecting the Costs of Registration[d]							
Provisions regarding literacy tests	+	0.09	(0.04)	2.17*	0.12	(0.04)	3.29**
Closing date for registration	+	0.13	(0.04)	3.45**	0.15	(0.03)	4.28**
Times and places of registration	+	2.20	(2.00)	1.10			
Registration system (permanent or periodic)	+	0.06	(0.04)	1.52			
Other Factors[d]							
Residence requirements	+	0.04	(0.04)	0.96			
Dependent variable: percentage of population of voting age registered to vote							
Mean			73.3			73.3	
Standard deviation			(14.3)			(14.3)	
F-ratio			28.05			52.20	
Standard error of estimate			7.0			7.2	
Number of cities			104			104	
R²				.79**			.76**

Notation: b = Net (partial) regression coefficient;
            (s) = Standard error of regression coefficient;
            t = t-value of regression coefficient (t-values may differ from b/(s) ratios in table because of rounding);
            ** = Significant at 99 percent;
            * = Significant at 95 percent.

[a] Defined in Appendix I.

[b] Includes all variables.

[c] Includes only variables significant at 95 percent level in Regression I.1

[d] As we indicate in Appendix I, these sets of variables are measured by indices whose scales are arbitrary. Thus, no units of measurement are shown in parentheses, and no meaning can be attached to the absolute values of the regression coefficients of these variables without bearing in mind how each index was scaled. The "t" values can, however, be interpreted in the usual way as indicators of statistical significance.

B. If the residents over 25 years of age in a city had a median educational attainment one year above the average of all cities in the sample, the city tended to have a rate of registration that was two to three percent above the average of all cities in the sample.

C. If the percentage of nonwhites in a city's population was greater by one percent than the average in all cities of the sample, the city tended to have a rate of registration that was a little less than one-fifth of one percent below the average of all cities in the sample.

The relationship described in (C) is of particular interest, since it held even when allowances had been made for the use of literacy tests in some cities and even when our race variable was included in the same regression with variables that reflected differences between whites and nonwhites in average income, average educational attainment, and ratios of younger to older persons of voting age.

That we did not find variations in the median income of the populations of cities to be significantly related to rates of registration is also of some interest. Although higher median incomes for the populations of the cities of our sample were associated with higher rates of registration in our multiple regression, the regression coefficient for the income variable was not quite significant at the 90 percent level of confidence. We did find that we could easily push the "t" value for the income variable high enough to indicate a relationship significant at the 99 percent level of confidence if we dropped our race and education variables from the analysis, since both of these had fairly high correlations with the income variable.[20] But various experiments of this kind showed that the income variable, by itself, had less explanatory power than either of the other two. Where intercorrelations of this kind exist, it is impossible on the basis of the statistical techniques we used to sort out the "independent" effect of any of the variables in a precise way. Nevertheless, our results do give some further support to the conclusion of the authors of The American Voter that a voter's education has more directly important consequences for his participation in elections than does his income.[21]

We found that differences in the relative numbers of men and women of voting age in the populations of the cities of our sample had no observable effect on rates of registration in our cities. There were, we think, several reasons for this result. In the first place, differences in the ratios of men to women in the population of voting age in the cities of our sample were relatively slight: The standard deviation of the variable was only 1.49 percent around the mean percentage of males in the population of voting age. Secondly, our data concerned registration in large cities, and the differences between men and women in turnout in elections have been found to be smaller in metropolitan areas than elsewhere.[22] Finally, colinearity of our sex variable with other variables tended to obscure any relationship it might otherwise have shown to rates of registration; those cities in the sample with the largest percentages of males in their population of voting age, it turned out, also

[20] See Appendix II for the matrix of simple correlations.

[21] Angus Campbell et al., The American Voter, pp. 475–476.

[22] Campbell, p. 487.

tended to have unusually large concentrations of young voters and recent migrants from out of state.

The last of the socio-economic variables included in Regression I.1 length of residence, was positively related to rates of registration, but the relationship was not statistically significant. The authority of this finding is compromised somewhat, however, by our reliance on a rather imprecise measure of length of residence, and it is entirely possible that we would have obtained a significant result if we had been able to use a better one.

Factors Affecting the Value of the Vote

From our efforts to detect any effects on rates of registration of factors affecting the value of the vote, we can report two findings. The first, made at an early point in our study, is that differences from city to city in the offices that were at stake in the election of 1960 had very little, if any, impact on registration; the correlation between rates of registration and an index we constructed to reflect such differences was small and not significant. What this result suggests is what the marked differences in turnout for presidential or other elections would also seem to indicate: That the interest of voters in presidential races in the United States is so great that few additional voters are attracted to the polls by an interest in the outcome of other contests.

Rates of registration in our sample of cities were, however, very strongly related to another factor affecting the value of the vote: The normal degree of competitiveness of partisan politics in statewide contests. As Table 19.1 indicates, the regression coefficient of our index of inter-party competition was easily significant at the 99 percent level of confidence in both regressions.[23] This result is consistent with evidence bearing on the relationship of turnout in elections to party competition that has been presented by a number of students of voting[24] and with our own expectation that a high level of competition between parties would increase the incentive for people to register and for politicians to get them to register. It is somewhat at variance, however, with conclusions that Robert Lane and that Angus Campbell and his associates have reached about the relationship between turnout and party competition.

Lane has argued that "although closeness of contest tends to enlist certain politicizing motives and, where habitual, to create stronger parties, the relationship between closeness of contest and turnout in the United States and Britain is small."[25] His conclusion with respect to Great Britain is hardly compelling, since Gosnell has offered equally good evidence for the contrary view.[26] With respect to the United States, Lane acknowledges the close-

[23] Because of the way this variable was measured (See Appendix I), low values imply a high level of competition in a state's party politics; hence, the correlation between the variable and rates of registration is negative.

[24] See especially Harold F. Gosnell, Why Europe Votes, pp. 182–183, 199–203; Lester W. Milbrath, "Political Participation in the States," p. 43 in Herbert Jacob and Kenneth N. Vines (eds.), Politics in the American States (Boston: Little, Brown, 1965); and Herbert Tingsten, Political Behavior (London: P. S. King and Son, 1937), p. 216.

[25] Robert Lane, p. 310.

[26] Lane's data for the election of 1950 are as reported in H. G. Nicholas, The British General Election of 1950 (New York: St. Martin's Press, 1951), p. 318; Gosnell's data were for the election of 1924.

ness of elections in states to be related to turnout but makes much of the fact that variations among *counties* in rates of nonvoting did not appear to be associated with variations among *counties* in the Democratic percentage of the two-party vote in the 1952 presidential election.[27] That fact is quite consistent with our own hypothesis about the relationship of party competition to participation in elections, however, since we expected the relative closeness of contests to affect rates of participation only when the former had relevance to the value of voting; and the level of partisan competition in counties has no meaning for the value of voting in presidential elections.[28]

Angus Campbell and his colleagues found that voters in the election of 1956 with only a weak preference for one party or the other were no more likely to go to the polls whether they saw the election to be one-sided or close. Voters with strong partisan preferences were more likely to vote if they expected the election to be close, but, according to the authors of *The American Voter*, "The question we have used to classify respondents according to their expectations about the election have referred to the contest *in the nation as a whole* . . . the analysis of answers to a question referring to the presidential race within the respondent's state indicates that it is the election *as a whole* that has cognitive and motivational significance, despite the existence of the electoral college."[29]

These findings are not easy to reconcile with our own. It could be that differences in the behavior of highly motivated voters from place to place are indeed an important source of local variations in rates of registration, but it does not seem likely that this is true, and it would not account for our result in any case of such voters do not pay attention to the closeness of the presidential race in their states. It could also be, and this seems more probable, that the factor intervening between the greater competitiveness of a state's party politics and higher turnout is not, for most voters, any conscious assessment of the likely outcome of the current election (such as is assumed by the analysis of *The American Voter*) but rather generalized feelings about how much votes have counted in the past; these generalized feelings may in turn be shaped by campaigning as this typically varies from state to state. Such an hypothesis would be consistent with data which show that Southern voters attribute less efficacy to voting than do Northerners,[30] and not inconsistent with either our own findings or those of Campbell and his co-authors. Finally, it could be that differences in rates of registration between cities of competitive and noncompetitive states should be attributed largely to the

[27] Robert Lane, p. 309.

[28] It does have meaning for the value of the vote in county elections, of course; and if county elections were held in years when major state and national offices were not at stake, one would expect to find a relationship between the competitiveness of a county's politics and the turnout of voters.

[29] Angus Campbell et al., *The American Voter*, p. 100 f.n.

[30] Angus Campbell, Gerald Gurin, and Warren E. Miller, *The Voter Decides* (New York: Harper & Row, 1954), p. 193.

A rearrangement of data presented in *The American Voter*, Table 17.4, p. 479, yields the following results:

SENSE OF POLITICAL EFFICACY	NONSOUTH	SOUTH
High	43%	32%
Medium	28	24
Low	30	44

actions of party activists; they undoubtedly are quite aware both of the level of party competition in a state and of its significance for the value of efforts to entice voters to register.

Factors Affecting Costs of Registration

The four variables we inserted in Regression I.1 in order to examine the relationship between rates of registration and practices or procedures affecting the costs of registering were indices especially constructed for that purpose.[31] All were so scaled as to lead us to predict positive correlations of each variable with the percentage of the population of voting are registered to vote. While all showed the predicted relationship, it was statistically significant in two cases only.

The use of literacy tests was associated with lower rates of registration, as those who put provisions for such tests into election codes doubtless intended it to be.[32] In William Riker's words, "Eighteen states have adopted the [literacy test], seven to disfranchise Negroes, five to disfranchise Indians and Mexicans and Orientals, and six to disfranchise European imigrants."[33] The disfranchising effect of literacy tests appears to have been considerably less severe in cities outside the South, however, than in Southern cities. In one regression involving data from non-Southern cities only, literacy tests continued to be correlated with lower rates of registration, but the relationship was no longer significant even at a level of confidence of 90 percent.

A more striking finding is the extremely strong relationship between the date at which registration rolls are closed and the percentage of the population of voting age that is registered.[34] This variable had the largest "t" value of any of the twelve in Regression I.1, and the second largest "t" value in

[31] The assignment of values in these indices was arbitrary, as has been indicated in the notes to Table 19.1, but a few words about the kind of arbitrariness involved are in order here. This can best be done, perhaps, by indicating how we arrive at the scale of values for one of these indices, that for the variable we have called "registration system." The four positions on that index were assigned values of 10, 25, 34, and 100. This set of values was chosen because it was our guess that a system of permanent registration (valued at 100) was ten times less demanding on voters than a system which combines a cumulative poll tax with annual registration (valued at 10), four times less demanding than a system of annual registration coupled with a noncumulative poll tax (valued at 25), and three times less demanding than a system of annual personal registration (valued at 34).

In a moment of less boldness, we eschewed estimates of how much more restrictive one system was than another and constructed a simple ordinal scale which involved only guesses as to which systems had a greater, and which had a lesser, tendency to restrict registration. The substitution of the ordinal indices had little effect on our results. The cardinal indices showed somewhat stronger relationships to registration than those with ordinal scales, but if one of our cardinal indices was significantly related to registration, so was its ordinal equivalent, and if one of our cardinal indices was not significantly related to registration, neither was its ordinal equivalent.

[32] Cf. Lester Milbrath, "Political Participation in the States," p. 48 in Jacob and Vines, and Donald R. Matthews and James W. Prothro, "Political Factors and Negro Voter Registration in the South," American Political Science Review, 57 (June 1963), at p. 358.

[33] William H. Riker, Democracy in the United States (New York: Crowell-Collier-Macmillan, 1953), p. 66.

[34] To the best of our knowledge only Warren Miller has previously presented systematic evidence tending to show nonvoting to be related to an early closing date for registration. In his memorandum to the President's Commission on Registration and Voting Participation, Miller reported that "One out of every four or five citizens lives in a state where registration closes in September, before an election campaign is well under way. . . . Nonvoting by two or three percent of the population is associated with the September closing dates, both North and South."

Regression I.2. Its regression coefficient of .15 in Regression I.2 implies that extending the closing date for registration from, say, one month to one week prior to election day would tend to increase the percentage of the population registered by about 3.6 percent. For politicians, varying the closing date for registration would thus appear to be a very effective way in which to manipulate the size of the potential electorate.

Why this should be so can be suggested here, if not demonstrated. A longer period in which one may register increases considerably the convenience of doing so, of course, but we doubt that that is all there is to the matter. A late closing date for registration also probably tends to increase rates of registration because it allows the campaign to serve as a reminder to weakly motivated voters that they need to register and as a stimulus to find out from others how they can do so. Such an interpretation of our finding would be consistent with the results of Gosnell's experimental efforts to stimulate registration in Chicago, and with his observation that "... if all the adult citizens in the city had been properly informed regarding registration dates, 10 percent more of them would have registered."[35]

Even though the index we constructed in an effort to assess the effect on rates of registration of differences in systems of registration (permanent or periodic) failed to show a statistically significant relationship to variations in percentages of the population of voting age registered to vote, we are unwilling to deprecate the importance of such differences. Though it is by no means wholly persuasive, there is other evidence that systems of permanent registration are associated with higher rates of registration than are systems of periodic registration.[36] Moreover, our examination of these relationships could not in the nature of the case be very conclusive. For one thing, only fifteen of the cities in our sample had a system of periodic registration or its equivalent. For another, variations in systems of registration were highly correlated with variations in closing dates for registration ($+0.64$). With both these factors working to obscure any relationship that our registration-systems variable might have to rates of registration, that relationship nonetheless just missed significance at a level of confidence of 90 percent.

The variable labelled "times and places of registration" failed to correlate significantly with rates of registration in the full sample of cities. Our index was constructed to reflect the relative difficulty that the average citizen in each city would face in finding a registration place open at hours convenient to him. In constructing it, however, we did not take into account the fact that cities face different tasks in registering voters, depending on whether they use systems of permanent, or periodic, registration. In cities with periodic registration, about one-half of the adult population succeeds in registering, on the average. Cities with permanent registration, again on the average, do not have to deal with anything like this many people; in such cities, at any given time, most potential registrants are already registered. Thus, the convenience of equal facilities in cities having registration systems of the two different sorts cannot be equated. We therefore decided to analyze

35 Harold F. Gosnell, *Getting Out the Vote*, p. 104.

36 See Joseph P. Harris, 106–108, and Robert Lane, p. 315. Warren Miller reported to the President's Commission on Registration and Voting Participation that "The absence of any prevoting registration requirement and the provision for permanent registration are clearly associated with higher turnout at the polls." V. O. Key has shown the poll tax to depress turnout in *Southern Politics*, 599–618.

the effect of variations in the times and facilities for registration in cities using systems of permanent registration—that is, in a set of cities facing really comparable problems in registering voters. The results of that analysis are reported below.

We found that differences among cities in rates of registration were not significantly related to differences in the length of residence in states and localities required of voters. This finding is surprising. No other aspect of the legal provisions relevant to voting has received nearly so much attention from students of voting as residence requirements; indeed, some writers have seemed to regard residence requirements as prototypical of requirements of registration.[37] We may have obtained these results because differences from place to place in requirements of residence were not sufficiently great to make any great difference in the relative percentages of the population of voting age qualified to vote; or it may have been that the differences in the proportion of recent migrants in the populations of our sample of cities were not great enough to affect rates of registration.

It seems to us, however, that some aspects of the reasoning that leads one to expect residence requirements to make a difference in registration rates may be faulty. It is a fact that, in any given year in the United States, many people change residence and are therefore disqualified for voting in many localities. It is true also that respondents to opinion surveys will frequently cite an inability to meet local requirements of residence in explanation of their failure to vote or register,[38] and that survey data show recency of residential change to be negatively correlated with turnout in elections. It does not follow from these facts that residence requirements must keep large numbers of adults from voting who would vote if such requirements did not exist. Residence requirements may disqualify recent migrants as voters, but there are other reasons why they might not vote, some peculiar to their status as recent migrants and some not. Moreover, their own explanations of their conduct can hardly be taken at face value; inability to meet legal qualifications is a "good" reason for not voting and one that is therefore likely to be invoked frequently. Thus, we may have exaggerated the significance of residence requirements not only for differences among cities in rates of registration but also as a cause of nonvoting and nonregistration.

Findings with Respect to Cities with Systems of Permanent Registration

The results of our analysis of registration in the 89 cities of our sample having systems of permanent registration are given in Table 19.2. The twelve

---

[37] This seems to be the sense of Lipset's statement that he does not wish to consider the effects of "legal and technical restrictions like residence requirements, poll taxes and property qualifications, literacy tests (often used as a cover for racial discrimination) and burdensome registration requirements" on the ground that his interest is in *voluntary* (his emphasis) nonvoting. (See Seymour Martin Lipset, p. 181 f.n.) But for the greatest numbers of those who fail to register, nonregistration is just as voluntary or nonvoluntary as is failure to vote.

[38] See Angus Campbell et al., *The Voter Decides*, p. 37; Charles E. Merriam and Harold F. Gosnell, 76–86; and Phillips Bradley and Alfred H. Cope, "A Community Registration Survey," *American Political Science Review*, 45 (September 1951), at p. 777.

TABLE 19.2   REGRESSION ANALYSIS OF DIFFERENCES IN RATES OF REGISTRA-
TION AMONG CITIES WITH SYSTEMS OF PERMANENT REGIS-
TRATION (89 CITIES, 1960)

VARIABLES[a]	EX-PECTED SIGN	REGRESSION II.1[b]			REGRESSION II.2[c]		
		b	(s)	t	b	(s)	t
Independent Variables:							
Socio-Economic Factors							
Age (percent 20–34)	—	—0.42	(0.22)	1.94*	—0.19	(0.18)	1.05
Sex (percent male)	+	—0.13	(0.71)	0.18			
Race (percent nonwhite)	—	—0.17	(0.08)	2.26*	—0.25	(0.07)	3.74**
Education (median yrs. completed)	+	1.11	(1.10)	1.01			
Income ($100/yr.)	+	0.26	(0.18)	1.46			
Length of residence (percent from out of state)	—	—0.19	(0.16)	1.23			
Factors Affecting the Value of the Vote							
Inter-party competition (percent)	—	—0.28	(0.14)	2.05*	—0.51	(0.09)	5.54**
Factors Affecting the Costs of Registration[d]							
Provisions regarding literacy tests	+	0.07	(0.06)	1.21			
Closing date for registration	+	0.15	(0.05)	3.43**	0.17	(0.04)	4.09**
Times and places of registration	+	7.86	(3.67)	2.14*	9.71	(3.31)	2.93**
Other Factors[d]							
Methods of purging registration rolls	+	0.004	(0.05)	0.08			
Residence requirements	+	0.05	(0.05)	1.01			
Dependent variable: percentage of population of voting age registered to vote							
Mean			76.3			76.3	
Standard deviation			(11.6)			(11.6)	
F-ratio			14.80			31.00	
Standard error of estimate			6.8			7.0	
Number of cities			89			89	
R^2			.70**			.65**	

Notation: b = Net (partial) regression coefficient;
(s) = Standard error of regression coefficient;
t = t-value of regression coefficient (t-value may differ from b/(s) ratios in table because of rounding);
** = Significant at 99 percent;
* = Significant at 95 percent;

[a] Defined in Appendix I.

[b] Includes all variables listed.

[c] Includes only variables significant at 95 percent level in Regression II.1

[d] As we indicate in Appendix I, these sets of variables are measured by indices whose scales are arbitrary. Thus, no units of measurement are shown in paraentheses, and no meaning can be attached to the absolute values of the regression coefficients of these variables without bearing in mind how each index was scaled. The "t" values can, however, be interpreted in the usual way as indicators of statistical significance.

independent variables included in Regression 11.1 account for 70 percent of the variation in rates of registration among these cities; the five variables retained in Regression II.2 account for 65 percent of the variation.

For reasons already cited, we included in this analysis a variable not included in Regression I.1: methods of purging registration rolls. To "purge" a registration roll is to remove from it the names of voters no longer qualified to vote. State laws usually specify the circumstances in which a voter's name is to be purged; in most states it will be purged when a voter dies, moves away, or fails to vote within a certain period of time. Both the reasons for purging a voter's name and the procedures for discovering whether there is cause for purging the name of any particular voter, however, vary considerably from city to city. We expected such variations to be related to differences among cities in rates of registration, but they were not significantly related, as Table 19.2 indicates.[39]

Variations in our index of the convenience of the times and places of registration were significantly related to variations in rates of registration. The relationship was significant at the 95 percent level of confidence in Regression II.1 and at the 99 percent level of confidence in regression II.2. This finding is important, for it suggests that local officials, by varying the convenience of registration procedures, may be able to affect appreciably not only the size, but also the composition, of local electorates.

The education variable explained much less of the variation in rates of registration among cities with systems of permanent registration than it did among the cities in our full sample. In our analysis of registration in cities with systems of permanent registration, the regression coefficient of this variable was not significant even at the 90 percent level of confidence. Moreover, changes in its value were associated with changes in rates of registration only about half as great as in Regression I.1

These last two findings—together with analyses of registration of Northern cities, in cities with rates of registration above 78 percent, and in cities with late closing dates for registration—lead us to propose the following generalization: When the costs of registering are generally high, differences from place to place in the value of variables affecting the motivation to vote— education, for example—will account for a considerable part of the variation in rates of registration; when the costs of registering are generally low, differences from place to place in the value of such variables will be relatively less important, and differences in the convenience of arrangements for registration relatively more important, in their effects on rates of registration.

Controlling for the Effects of Region

A classification by region of the 104 cities of our sample reveals a considerable difference among the cities of the various regions in average rates of registration. Those averages were as follows:

[39] It is possible, of course, that the index we constructed did not reflect with sufficient exactness the actual differences in purging practices that exist from city to city. The procedures for purging were difficult to document.

REGION	AVERAGE RATE OF REGISTRATION
Midwest	82.5
West	80.7
Northeast	76.1
Border	70.7
South	55.9

In order to discover if these differences might stem from some difference in the culture of regions rather than from regional variations in the values of the variables discussed so far, we re-computed Regressions I.1 and I.2 with a set of regional dummy variables included. (That is, we re-computed these regressions after having denoted whether a city was in, or not in, each of the five regions by assigning a "1" in the first case and a "0" in the second.) Following is the matrix of t-values needed to show in which instances the regional dummies were significantly different from each other.[40]

	WEST	NORTH-EAST	BORDER	SOUTH	MID-WEST
West	—	1.63	2.23[a]	0.81	0.07
Northeast	1.63	—	0.99	0.43	1.53
Border	2.23[a]	0.99	—	1.25	1.97[a]
South	0.81	0.43	1.25	—	0.37
Midwest	0.70	1.53	1.97[a]	0.37	—

[a] Significant at the 95 percent level of confidence.

Two findings revealed by this matrix warrant comment. First of all, the relationship of the South dummy to registration was not significantly different from that of any of the other four regional dummies. This result is important, because it implies that the low rates of registration characteristic of Southern cities (on the average, 17.4 percent below the mean registration rate for all 104 cities) can be explained mainly in terms of the variables included in Regression I.1.

Secondly, only two pairs of regional dummies did differ significantly from each other in their relationship to registration, Border-West and Border-Midwest. The regression coefficients for the regional dummies shown in Table 19.3 (Regression III.1) indicate that our regression equation over-predicts the rate of registration in the cities of the Border states by about seven percentage points relative to that in Midwestern cities and by about 10.5 percentage points relative to that of Western cities. The equation also tends to under-predict registration in Western cities relative to registration in the rest of the country. We have no ready explanation. It may be that statutes which on their face are not particularly discouraging to registration are administered in a way that does discourage registration in the cities of the Border states. It may also be that voters in the West are more likely than those elsewhere to regard voting as a civic duty. These are mere conjectures, however, which cannot be tested with the data available to us.

[40] These "t" values were obtained by running five versions of Regression III.1, dropping a defferent regional dummy each time, and using the t's for other dummies to find whether or not they are significantly different from the omitted dummy.

TABLE 19.3 REGRESSION ANALYSIS OF DIFFERENCES AMONG CITIES IN PERCENTAGES OF THE POPULATION OF VOTING AGE REGISTERED TO VOTE, WITH REGIONAL VARIABLES (104 CITIES, 1960)

VARIABLES[a]	EX-PECTED SIGN	REGRESSION III.1[b]			REGRESSION III.2[c]		
		b	(s)	t	b	(s)	t
Independent Variables:							
Socioeconomic Factors							
Age (percent 20–34)	—	—0.39	(0.21)	1.89	—0.43	(0.18)	2.36*
Sex (percent male)	+	—0.38	(0.66)	0.57			
Race (percent nonwhite)	—	—0.17	(0.08)	2.25*	—0.18	(0.07)	2.52*
Education (median yrs. completed)	+	1.07	(1.16)	0.92	2.13	(0.91)	2.36*
Income ($100/year)	+	0.19	(0.18)	1.08			
Length of residence (percent from out of state)	—	—0.25	(0.16)	1.58			
Factors Affecting the Value of the Vote							
Inter-party competition (percent)	—	—0.29	(0.12)	2.37*	—0.37	(0.08)	4.68**
Factors Affecting the Costs of Registration[d]							
Provisions regarding literacy tests	+	0.10	(0.04)	2.39*	0.14	(0.04)	3.73**
Closing date for registration	+	0.15	(0.04)	3.83**	0.16	(0.04)	4.62**
Times and places of registration	+	1.50	(2.12)	0.71			
Registration system (permanent or periodic)	+	0.04	(0.04)	0.93			
Other Factors[d]							
Residence requirements	+	0.02	(0.05)	0.38			
Regions							
West		2.20	(3.15)	0.70	3.06	(2.53)	1.21
Northeast		—3.56	(2.32)	1.53*			
Border		—7.05	(3.58)	1.97*	—5.50	(3.04)	1.81
South		—1.65	(4.48)	0.37			
Dependent variable: percentage of the population of voting age registered to vote							
Mean			73.3			73.3	
Standard deviation			(14.3)			(14.3)	
F-ratio			22.09			40.99	
Intercept			67.5			48.2	
Standard error of estimate			6.9			7.0	
Number of cities			104			104	
R²			.80**			.78**	

Notation   b = Net (partial) regression coefficient;
  (s) = standard error of regression coefficient;
  t = t-value of regression coefficient;
  ** = significant at 99 percent;
  * = significant at 95 percent.

a Defined in Appendix I.

b Includes all variables listed.

c Includes only variables significant at 95 percent level in Regression I.1, plus the two regional dummies whose coefficients were significantly different from each other.

d As we indicate in Appendix I, these sets of variables are measured by indices whose scales are arbitrary. Thus, no units of measurement are shown in parentheses, and no meaning can be attached to the absolute values of the regression coefficients of these variables without bearing in mind how each index was scaled. The "t" values can be interpreted in the usual way as indicators of statistical significance.

Comparisons of the regressions reported in Tables 19.1 and 19.3 indicate one additional fact of importance: When regional dummies are included in the regression, the explanatory value of the age and education variables is appreciably lessened. A part of the apparent effect on registration of these two variables thus seems to be associated with factors varying by region that were not taken into account in Regressions I.1 and I.2. For the rest, however, findings already reported can stand without further qualification.

Results for Particular Cities and the Pattern
of Residual Variance

Figure 19.1 shows the relationship between the actual rates of registration for the cities of our full sample and the rates of registration predicted on the basis of Regression I.2. If the predictions had been perfect, all of the 104 observations would lie on the 45 degree line. They do not, but it is encouraging that the regression equation predicts about equally well over the whole range of values for the dependent variable.

Table 19.4 reports actual and predicted rates of registration for each of the cities of the full sample. Cities are listed according to the size of their residuals, starting with Memphis, which had the largest positive residual, and ending with Wichita, which had the largest negative one. The reader may use this table, as we did, as a starting point for efforts to thing of variables that will account for the pattern of residual variance.

We found two variables that seem to account for a very small part of it. The regression equation led us to under-predict registration in cities with large percentages of Catholics in the population.[41] It also led us to over-predict registration in the relatively few cities where there were substantial number of resident aliens.[42]

By far the most important statement we can make about our effort to explain the pattern of residual variance, however, is simply this: Not much came of it. The size or sign of a city's residual had little if any relation to the size of the city,[43] the state in which it was located, its provisions for absentee registration,[44] the percentage of its population that was foreign born,[45] or whether or not it had less stringent residence requirements for voting in presidential elections than it did for voting in state and local elections. There were no substantial differences in the residuals of Southern

[41] Actually, for cities in *counties* with large percentages of Catholics in their populations. Our source was National Council of the Churches of Christ in the United States of America, *Churches and Church Membership in the United States,* New York, 1956–1958.

[42] Our source for percentages of aliens in the population of our cities was U. S. Department of Commerce, Bureau of the Census, *U. S. Census of Population 1960: Characteristics of the Population,* Table 55.

[43] To avoid forcing a linear pattern on this variable, we used a set of dummy variables; however, none had a "t" value as high as 1.00

[44] *Cf.* Lester W. Milbrath, "Political Participation in the States," p. 47 in Jacob and Vines.

[45] This variable had the expected negative sign, but the "t" value of its regression coefficient was only 1.19.

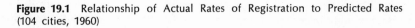

Figure 19.1 Relationship of Actual Rates of Registration to Predicted Rates (104 cities, 1960)

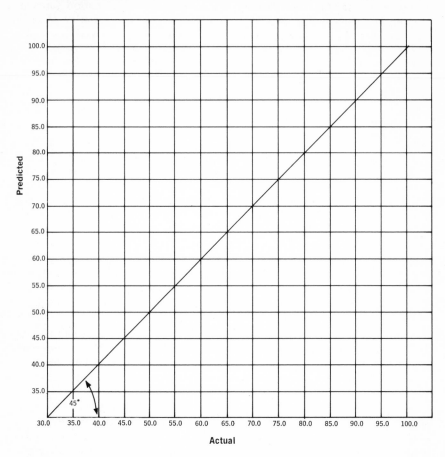

cities as between those with larger or smaller concentrations of Negroes.[46] Our predictions were neither markedly better nor markedly worse for cities that used roving deputy registrars or mobile registration units and those that did not, for cities with high and low percentages of college graduates in their populations,[47] and cities with the most and the least stable populations.[48] Finally, cities with unusually small or unusually large concentrations of young voters, males, and nonwhite residents showed no common tendency, and

[46] *Cf.* Donald R. Matthews and James W. Prothro, "Social and Economic Factors and Negro Voter Registration in the South," *American Political Science Review*, 57 (March 1963), 28–32.

[47] Our source for this variable (actually the percentage of those over 25 years of age who are college graduates) was U. S. Department of Commerce, Bureau of the Census, *County and City Data Book 1962*, Table 6.

[48] Stability of population was measured by the percentage of persons in a city's population over five years of age that were living in the same house in 1960 as they had in 1955. The source for these figures was U. S. Department of Commerce, Bureau of the Census, *County and City Data Book 1962*, Table 6.

TABLE 19.4 ACTUAL AND PREDICTED[a] REGISTRATION RATES AND RESIDUALS (104 CITIES, 1960)

CITY	AC-TUAL	PRE-DICTED	RESID-UAL	CITY	AC-TUAL	PRE-DICTED	RESID-UAL
1. Memphis	84.7	69.3	15.4	54. Salt Lake City	87.0	88.2	—1.2
2. Berkeley	90.5	75.2	15.3	55. Fort Wayne	81.7	82.9	—1.2
3. Gary	87.3	72.4	14.9	56. Oklahoma City	80.4	81.7	—1.3
4. Detroit	92.0	78.2	13.8	57. Topeka	81.9	83.3	—1.4
5. South Bend	96.4	83.5	12.9	58. Tampa	68.8	70.2	—1.4
6. Baton Rouge	64.7	52.4	12.3	59. Elizabeth	75.6	77.1	—1.5
7. Torrance	87.7	76.9	10.8	60. Dayton	73.6	75.1	—1.5
8. Camden	81.3	70.8	10.5	61. Rockford	82.0	83.5	—1.5
9. Dallas	65.0	55.1	9.9	62. Syracuse	79.3	81.0	—1.7
10. Seattle	92.0	82.5	9.5	63. Akron	77.0	78.8	—1.7
11. New Orleans	55.6	46.4	9.2	64. Sacramento	77.3	79.1	—1.8
12. Corpus Christi	61.8	52.8	9.0	65. Toledo	76.9	78.7	—1.8
13. Houston	60.0	57.3	8.7	66. Richmond	46.5	48.5	—2.0
14. Scranton	90.4	81.7	8.7	67. Atlanta	33.8	35.8	—2.0
15. Lansing	91.9	84.6	7.3	68. Norfolk	43.6	45.8	—2.2
16. New Bedford	82.4	75.6	6.8	69. Santa Ana	75.1	77.3	—2.2
17. Tacoma	87.3	80.6	6.7	70. Erie	78.8	81.2	—2.4
18. Des Moines	92.6	86.0	6.6	71. Utica	77.1	79.8	—2.7
19. Jersey City	81.1	74.7	6.4	72. Columbus (O.)	72.4	75.2	—2.8
20. Buffalo	83.0	76.7	6.3	73. Springfield	77.1	80.1	—3.0
21. Albany	88.4	82.2	6.2	74. Duluth	85.1	88.8	—3.7
22. Spokane	89.4	83.4	6.0	75. Greensboro	66.6	70.4	—3.8
23. Cincinnati	79.4	73.8	5.6	76. Patterson	68.4	72.2	—3.8
24. Peoria	87.4	81.8	5.6	77. Cambridge (Mass.)	73.8	77.8	—4.0
25. Minneapolis	82.5	87.2	5.3	78. Oakland	71.9	76.0	—4.1
26. Winston-Salem	71.2	65.9	5.3	79. Louisville	59.0	63.2	—4.2
27. Youngstown	81.0	76.0	5.0	80. Little Rock	61.2	65.5	—4.3
28. Fresno	81.1	76.8	4.3	81. Hartford	70.7	75.0	—4.3
29. St. Paul	91.2	86.9	4.3	82. Lincoln	79.4	83.7	—4.3
30. Philadelphia	77.6	73.6	4.0	83. Rochester	74.9	79.3	—4.4
31. Canton	80.9	77.0	3.9	84. Austin	48.3	52.8	—4.5
32. New Haven	79.2	75.8	3.4	85. Bridgeport	70.6	75.6	—5.0
33. Trenton	75.8	72.4	3.4	86. Boston	74.0	79.2	—5.2
34. Hammond	84.0	80.7	3.3	87. St. Louis	68.5	74.7	—6.2
35. Chattanooga	70.7	68.1	2.6	88. Portsmouth	38.0	44.3	—6.3
36. Birmingham	39.1	36.8	2.3	89. Fort Worth	48.4	54.7	—6.3
37. Waterbury	81.4	79.2	2.2	90. Honolulu	60.0	66.9	—6.9
38. Kansas City (Kans.)	78.9	76.7	2.2	91. Newark	61.4	68.6	—7.2
39. Pasadena	83.2	81.5	1.7	92. Omaha	79.8	87.1	—7.3
40. Pittsburgh	81.2	79.6	1.6	93. San Antonio	42.6	50.1	—7.5
41. Flint	79.6	78.6	1.0	94. Nashville	55.9	64.0	—8.1
42. Glendale	84.9	84.2	0.7	95. Jacksonville	54.9	63.5	—8.6
43. Grand Rapids	83.2	82.9	0.3	96. St. Petersburg	69.7	79.4	—9.7
44. Cleveland	71.5	71.6	—0.1	97. San Francisco	68.0	78.4	—10.4
45. Baltimore	68.1	68.7	—0.6	98. Newport News	35.0	45.5	—10.5
46. Tulsa	82.4	83.0	—0.6	99. Niagra Falls	67.7	78.6	—10.9
47. Columbus (Ga.)	32.1	32.7	—0.6	100. Miami	59.2	71.1	—11.9
48. Worcester	81.0	81.6	—0.6	101. New York	65.7	77.7	—12.0
49. Los Angeles	77.0	77.7	—0.7	102. Allentown	67.7	80.6	—13.0
50. San Diego	73.9	74.7	—0.8	103. Kansas City (Mo.)	65.8	83.8	—18.0
51. Charlotte	69.9	70.9	—1.0	104. Wichita	62.2	82.7	—20.5
52. Dearborn	89.3	90.3	—1.0				
53. Portland (Ore.)	85.8	86.9	—1.1				

[a] Based on Table 19.1, Regression I.2.

neither did cities whose populations had an unusually high or low median educational attainment. Thus, it seems that our simplifying assumption of linear relationships between these variables and the rate of registration did not lead to serious error.

CONCLUDING OBSERVATIONS

One conclusion to be drawn from our study of registration can be put as follows: Local differences in the turnout for elections are to a large extent related to local differences in rates of registration, and these in turn reflect to a considerable degree local differences in the rules governing, and arrangements for handling, the registering of voters. Some of our other conclusions may be of greater interest to practicing politicians, but this one contributes most to a better understanding of the electoral process.

This conclusion lends support, first of all, to Gosnell's explanation for the difference in the normal rates of turnout of voters in the United States, on the one hand, and in other democracies, on the other. This difference, one that has produced considerable commentary on the civic virtues of Americans relative to those of other peoples, was thought by Gosnell to be due in large measure to differing practices in the registration of voters:

> In the European countries studied, a citizen who is entitled to vote does not, as a rule, have to make any effort to see that his name is on the list of eligible voters. The inconvenience of registering for voting in this country has caused many citizens to become nonvoters.[49]

The probable accuracy of this observation is strongly suggested not only by findings that we have already reported but also by a comparison of turnout rates in Canada, France, and Great Britain (all of which have systems of automatic registration) with those in the cities of our sample where more than 90 percent of those of voting age were registered to vote. In 1960 the rate of turnout of registered voters in such cities was, on the average, 78.5 percent. In postwar elections in Canada, France, and Great Britain it has been, again on the average, 74.3, 77.4, and 77.6 percent, respectively.[50]

Secondly, our findings regarding the interrelation of turnout, registration, and registration procedures suggest the solution to a problem discussed by V. O. Key:

> A major question posed by the trend of voting [in U.S. presidential elections] is why the decline in electoral interest since the 1890s. The blunt truth is that nobody knows the answer. A frequent explanation has been that the enfran-

---

[49] Harold F. Gosnell, *Why Europe Votes*, p. 185. That differences in turnout for elections in Europe and America may be largely a function of differences in systems of registration has also been suggested by Seymour Martin Lipset, p. 181 *f.n.*, and Philip E. Converse and George Dupeux, "Politicization of the Electorate in France and the United States," *Public Opinion Quarterly* (Spring 1962), 8–9 *f.n.*

[50] These averages were for six postwar Canadian elections (1945, 1949, 1953, 1957, 1958, 1963), five postwar elections for the French National Assembly (1946, 1951, 1956, 1958, 1962), and six postwar elections in Great Britain (1945, 1950, 1951, 1955, 1959, 1964). The average rate of turnout of registered voters in the cities of our full sample was 81.6 percent, and in Northern cities only it was 84.6 percent.

chisement of women in 1920 brought into the electorate large numbers of persons not in the habit of voting. Yet popular interest began to shrink before the adoption of the women suffrage amendment.[51]

We suspect that a major part of the explanation for the trend of voting in presidential elections lies in the following facts: In the latter half of the nineteenth century, when the turnout of eligible voters was between 75 and 85 percent, voters were not required to register in many parts of the country, and in many places where they were, there were systems of automatic registration. In the period from 1896 to 1924, when the turnout declined almost steadily, state after state enacted registration laws which typically required registration annually and in person of all voters in the nation's large cities; the registration procedures of this era have been described by one student of registration practices as "expensive, cumbersome, and inconvenient to the voter."[52] In the period from 1924 until the present, during which time the turnout has gradually risen, more and more states have been liberalizing their registration laws, particularly as these apply to the larger cities. In short, turnout in presidential elections in the United States may have declined and then risen again, not because of changes in the *interest* of voters in elections, but because of changes in the *interest demanded* of them.

Thirdly, our findings suggest a quite different view of the electorate from that implicit of explicit in many discussions of voting. It is fair to say that the electorate is treated by many students of voting, especially Lazarsfeld, Berelson, and their co-authors, as if it were the product of socio-economic forces. In *The People's Choice* they conclude that ". . . three-quarters of the nonvoters stayed away from the polls deliberately because they were thoroughly unconcerned with the election. . . . A long range program of civic education would be needed to draw such people into the orbit of political life. . . ."[53] In *Voting* they observe that "It is often a mistake to give purely political explanations for nonparticipation. . . . Nonvoting is related to persistent social conditions having little do do with the candidates or the issues of the moment."[54]

While no one could quarrel with the above statement if enough weight were put on the "purely," our study indicates, not only that electorates are much more the product of political forces than many have appreciated, but also that, to a considerable extent, they can be *political artifacts*. Within limits, they can be constructed to a size and composition deemed desirable by those in power. Our matrix of simple correlations (Appendix II), for instance, shows a definite association between restrictive rules and procedures for registration and limited competition between major parties in the states

[51] V. O. Key, *Politics, Parties, and Pressure Groups*, fifth edition (New York: Thomas Y. Crowell, 1964), p. 578.

[52] Joseph P. Harris, p. 89.

[53] Paul F. Lazarsfeld, Bernard Berelson, and Helen Gaudet, *The People's Choice* (New York: Columbia University Press, 1948), p. 47. This conclusion is not well supported even by the data adduced as evidence for it. Some 27 percent of the voters who said they had no interest at all in the campaign nonetheless voted. See Lazarsfeld, p. 46.

[54] Bernard Berelson, Paul F. Lazarsfeld, and William N. McPhee, *Voting* (Chicago: University of Chicago Press, 1954), p. 32.

in which the cities of our sample are located. Presumably, it is easier for a party in power to pursue a restrictive policy toward registration if its opposition is weak. Conversely, success in restricting registration presumably indicates some success in influencing the composition of the population of registered voters, which in turn makes it easier for the party in power to stay in power. While the abilities of Southern politicians to construct electorates have long been appreciated, relatively little curiosity has been shown about any similiar endeavors on the part of their Northern colleagues. It seems unlikely that the latter, any more than the former, have always acted without design in establishing rules for registration.[55]

Finally, the findings of this study have a bearing on the continuing debate between those who favor and those who oppose efforts to get out the vote. A frequent objection to such efforts is that voters not interested enough to vote are not apt to vote wisely and so should be left alone. This view recalls the statement of a New York voter regarding the adequacy of the facilities for registering in New York City in 1964: "I sure do want to vote against that man [Senator Barry Goldwater], but I don't think I hate him enough to stand on that line all day long."[56] How much interest should a voter have to qualify him for voting? Enough to stand in line all day? For half a day? For two days? We cannot say, but those who think voting should be limited to the "interested" ought to be prepared to do so.

APPENDIX I

Definitions of Variables and Sources of Data

1. Age: the number of persons in the age group 20 to 34 divided by the number of persons over 21 years of age. Source: U.S. Department of Commerce, Bureau of the Census, *1960 Census of Population: Characteristics of the Population*, Table 20.

2. Education: median school years completed by persons over 25 years of age. Source: U.S. Department of Commerce, Bureau of the Census, *County and City Data Book 1962*, Table 6.

3. Race: percentage of nonwhites in the population. Source: U.S. Department of Commerce, Bureau of the Census, *County and City Data Book 1962*, Table 6.

4. Income: dollars received per year per family unit divided by 100. Source: U.S. Department of Commerce, Bureau of the Census, *County and City Data Book 1962*, Table 6.

5. Sex: percentage of males in the population over 21 years of age. Source: U.S. Department of Commerce, Bureau of Census, *1960 Census of Population: Characteristics of the Population*, Table 20.

---

[55] One of the authors of the present study found, for instance, that there was a very high positive correlation between an index of the convenience of registering in Chicago wards and differences among wards in the Democratic percentage of the two-party vote, a fact which suggests that Mayor Richard J. Daley's organization is alert to the possibilities of manipulating the composition of Chicago's registered voters: See Richard E. Ayres, *Registration 1060: Key to Democratic Victory?* (Princeton University senior thesis, 1964), pp. 34–35.

[56] *New York Times,* September 6, 1964.

6. Length of Residence: the number of persons over five years of age in the state economic area in which a city is located who resided in another state in 1955, divided by the total number of persons over five years of age in the state economic area in which that city is located. "State economic areas" are as defined in our source of these data: U.S. Department of Commerce, Bureau of Census, *U.S. Census of Population 1960: Selected Area Reports, State Economic Areas,* Table 2.

7. Offices at Stake: the number of contests for the offices of President, U.S. Senator, U.S. Representative, Governor, and Mayor in which any one voter might vote. Source: Richard M. Scammon, ed., *America Votes 4* (Pittsburgh: University of Pittsburgh Press, 1962).

8. Inter-Party Competition: the difference between 50 and the average percentage of the two-party vote received by Democratic candidates in elections for Governor from 1956 to 1960 inclusive and for President in 1956 and 1960. Source: Richard M. Scammon, ed., *America Votes 4* (Pittsburgh: University of Pittsburg Press, 1962).

9. Provisions Regarding Literacy Tests: values of this variable were assigned as follows: test of literacy lending itself to discriminatory administration, 20; simple and straightforward test of literacy, 80; no test of literacy, 100. Where a "20" was assigned, the test required a registrant to show "understanding" or give a "reasonable interpretation" of sections of the U.S. Constitution or state constitutions or to make application without "aid, suggestions or memorandum"; or a registrant might qualify without showing literacy provided he was of "good character" or owned a stated amount and kind of property. Where an "80" was assigned, registrants were not required to interpret passages from the Constitution, and members of minority groups were not at a disadvantage in qualifying for any exemptions to the requirements of literacy. Source: Constance E. Smith, *Voting and Election Laws* (New York: Oceana Publications, Inc., 1960), and the election codes of the relevant states.

10. Closing Date for Registration: in all cases in which registration (or period in which the poll tax could be paid) closed 100 or fewer days before the election, the value assigned was the number of days before the election at which registration was closed subtracted from 100. In all other cases, the value assigned was zero. Source: Constance E. Smith, *Voting and Election Laws,* election codes of relevant states, and answers to questionnaires sent to local boards of elections.

11. Registration System: values for this variable were assigned as follows: annual payment of cumulative poll tax required, 10; annual payment of a noncumulative poll tax required, 25; annual personal registration required (with no requirement for the payment of a poll tax), 34; system of permanent registration, 100. Source: Constance E. Smith, *Voting and Election Laws,* election codes of the relevant states, and answers to questionnaires sent to local boards of election.

12. Times and Places of Registration: assignment of values for this variable involved calculating an index of convenience for each *kind* of registration place open in 1960 and summing the values of such indices to arrive at a convenience score for the registration facilities of the city as a whole. For example, a value for the index of convenience for precinct registration places alone was arrived at by adding the number of hours that precinct registration places were open in 1960 during working hours to two times the number of hours that they were open during the nonworking hours, multiplying this number by the number of precinct registration places, and dividing the whole by the number of persons of voting age. Other kinds of registration places for which we calculated indices of convenience were central (County Court House or City Hall); branch; ward; hospital, plant, or other institutions; mobile units; and roving deputy registrars. "Nonworking" hours were defined as hours before 8 a.m. or after 6 p.m. on week days and all hours on Saturday and Sunday. We also treated all hours during which mobile units were in service, all hours put in by roving deputies, and all hours in hospitals, plants, and other institutions as "nonworking hours." Sources: Constance Smith, *Voting and Election Laws,* election codes of relevant states, answers to questionnaires sent to local Leagues of Women Voters and local Boards of Elections, and telephone interviews with officials of local Board of Elections.

13. Residence Requirements: the values of this variable were assigned as follows: residence of two years or more required in the state, 20; residence of one year required in the state and of more than three months in the county or city, 56; residence of one year required in the state and of three months or less in the county or city, 60; residence of six months required in the state and of more than thirty days in the county or city, 96; residence of six months required in the state and of thirty days or less in the county or city, 100. Source: Constance E. Smith, *Voting and Election Laws,* and the election codes of the relevant states.

14. Methods of Purging Registration Rolls: high values of this variable were assigned to cities where it is easy for a voter to keep his name on the registration rolls, low values to cities where it is not. Two steps were involved in assigning values. An initial score was assigned as follows: provision is made for a mandatory general canvass *or* for a mandatory canvass by mail *or* for public agencies to notify boards of elections of deaths and changes of residence *and* a voter's name is removed upon his failure to vote during a period of less than four years, 15; provisions as just stated except that a voter's name is removed upon his failure to vote during a period of four years or more, 25; provision is made for an optional general canvass *or* for an optional canvass by mail *and/or* for public agencies to notify boards of elections of deaths but not of changes of residence *and* a voter's name is removed upon his failure to vote during a period of less than four years, 45; provisions are as just stated except that a voter's name is removed upon his failure to vote during a period of four years or more, 55; provision is made for an optional general canvass *or* for an optional canvass by mail *and/or* there is no provision for public agencies to notify boards of elections of deaths or changes or residences *and* a voter's name is removed upon his failure to vote during a period of less than four years, 65; provisions are as just stated except that a voter's name is removed upon his failure to vote during a period of four years or more, 75; no provision is made for a canvass, either general or selective, optional or mandatory, *and* there is no provision for public agencies to notify boards of elections of deaths of charges of residence *and* a voter's name is removed upon his failure to vote during a period of less than four years, 90; provisions are as just stated except that a voter's name is removed upon his failure to vote during a period of four years or more *or* there are no provisions of any kind with respect to canvasses, notification of boards of deaths and changes of residence, or removal of names for nonvoting, 100.

Scores assigned as follows were then *subtracted* from scores assigned in accordance with the scheme just described: provision is made for removing the names of all nonvoters, deceased persons, and those who have changed residence automatically and there is no requirement that notice be given the person whose name is being removed, 15; provisions are as just stated except that boards of elections are required to give notice to persons whose names are being removed for a change of residence *and* such persons must apply in person to prevent the removal of their names, 12; provisions are as just stated except that those alleged to have changed residence may testify to the contrary by mail and so prevent removal of the names, 10; boards of elections are required to give notice to persons whose names are being removed either for an alleged change of residence or for nonvoting and such persons must apply in person to prevent removal of their names, 7; provisions as just stated except persons whose names are being removed may prevent such action by applying for reinstatement by mail, 5; provisions as just stated except boards of elections are required to give notice twice to persons whose names are being removed, 0.

Source: Constance Smith, *Voting and Election Laws,* election codes of the relevant states, answers to questionnaires sent to local boards of elections and local Leagues of Women Voters, telephone interviews with officials of local Boards of Elections.

14. Region—West: Montana, Idaho, Wyoming, Colorado, Utah, Nevada, New Mexico, Arizona, Washington, Oregon, California, Alaska, Hawaii.

15. Region—Northeast: Maine, New Hampshire, Vermont, Massachusetts, Rhode Island, Connecticut, New York, New Jersey, Pennsylvania.

16. Region—Border: Delaware, Maryland, West Virginia, Kentucky, Missouri, Oklahoma.

17. Region—South: Virginia, North Carolina, South Carolina, Georgia, Florida, Tennessee, Alabama, Mississippi, Arkansas, Louisiana, Texas.

18. Region—Midwest: Ohio, Michigan, Indiana, Illinois, Wisconsin, Minnesota, Iowa, Nebraska, Kansas, North Dakota, South Dakota.

APPENDIX II REGRESSION I.1: MATRIX OF SIMPLE CORRELATIONS (104 CITIES, 1960)

	(1)	(2)	(3)	(4)	(5)	(6)	(7)	(8)	(9)	(10)	(11)	(12)	(13)
1. Registration	1.00	—0.46	—0.05	—0.54	0.26	0.57	—0.28	—0.71	0.40	0.56	—0.10	0.65	0.57
2. Age (percent 20–34)	—0.46	1.00	0.39	0.34	0.21	—0.11	0.15	0.38	—0.11	—0.32	—0.33	0.13	—0.32
3. Sex (percent male)	—0.05	0.39	1.00	0.05	0.12	0.30	0.23	—0.18	0.11	—0.08	—0.12	0.06	—0.15
4. Race (percent nonwhite)	—0.54	0.34	0.05	1.00	—0.29	—0.41	0.23	0.39	—0.22	—0.36	—0.22	—0.10	—0.17
5. Education (median years completed)	0.26	0.21	0.12	—0.29	1.00	0.54	0.19	—0.00	0.08	0.02	0.08	0.19	0.01
6. Income	0.57	—0.11	0.30	—0.41	0.54	1.00	—0.17	—0.55	0.30	0.19	0.27	0.02	0.27
7. Length of residence	—0.28	0.15	0.23	0.23	0.19	—0.17	1.00	0.24	—0.07	—0.24	—0.18	0.03	—0.04
8. Inter-party competition	—0.71	0.38	—0.18	0.39	—0.00	—0.55	0.24	1.00	—0.39	—0.39	—0.56	0.28	—0.55
9. Residence requirements	0.40	—0.11	0.11	—0.22	0.08	0.30	—0.07	—0.39	1.00	0.43	0.28	—0.14	0.23
10. Literacy tests	0.56	—0.32	—0.08	—0.36	0.02	0.19	—0.24	—0.39	0.43	1.00	0.43	0.07	0.37
11. Closing date	0.66	—0.33	—0.12	—0.22	0.08	0.27	—0.18	—0.56	0.28	0.43	1.00	—0.31	0.64
12. Times and places of registration	—0.10	0.13	0.06	—0.10	0.19	0.02	0.03	0.28	—0.14	0.07	—0.31	1.00	—0.32
13. Registration system	0.57	—0.32	—0.15	—0.17	0.01	0.27	—0.04	—0.55	0.23	0.37	0.64	—0.32	1.00

APPENDIX III PARTIAL CORRELATION COEFFICIENTS AND BETA-WEIGHTS

VARIABLES	REGRESSION											
	I.1		I.2		II.1		II.2		III.1		III.2	
	P	β	P	β	P	β	P	β	P	β	P	β
Age (percent 20–34)	−0.24	−0.16	−0.27	−0.17	−0.22	−0.16	−0.11	0.07	−0.20	−0.13	−0.24	−0.14
Sex (percent male)	−0.03	−0.02			−0.02	−0.02			−0.06	−0.04		
Race (percent nonwhite)	−0.21	−0.13	−0.24	−0.15	−0.25	−0.19	−0.38	−0.28	−0.23	−0.15	−0.25	−0.16
Education (median years completed)	0.22	0.17	0.38	0.22	0.12	0.11			0.10	0.08	0.24	0.17
Income ($100/yr.)	0.15	0.12			0.17	0.17			0.11	0.10		
Length of residence (percent from out of state)	−0.14	−0.08			−0.14	−0.09			−0.17	−0.10		
Inter-party competition	−0.30	−0.26	−0.49	−0.36	−0.23	−0.24	−0.52	−0.44	−0.25	−0.25	−0.43	−0.33
Provisions regarding literacy tests	0.22	0.14	0.32	0.19	0.14	0.11			0.25	0.16	0.36	0.22
Closing date for registration	0.34	0.24	0.40	0.28	0.37	0.25	0.41	0.28	0.38	0.28	0.43	0.30
Times and places of registration	0.11	0.06			0.24	0.16	0.31	0.19	0.08	0.04		
Registration system	0.16	0.12							0.10	0.08		
Residence requirements	0.10	0.05			0.12	0.08			0.04	0.03		
Purging methods					0.01	0.005						
South									−0.04	−0.05		
West									0.07	0.06	0.12	0.08
Northeast									−0.16	−0.11		
Border									−0.21	−0.12	−0.18	−0.09

Notation: P = Partial correlation coefficient.
β = Beta-weight.

20

The 1964 Presidential Election: Further Adventures in Wonderland*

CHARLES O. JONES

In his essay on the 1960 presidential election, Stanley Kelley, Jr., makes reference to "this unsual election," characterized by television debates between the candidates, a Roman Catholic's gaining the Presidency for the first time, and the narrowest winning margin since 1884.[1] In 1964 America treated itself to another unusual election—perhaps the most unusual in contemporary American politics.[2] The Republican party decided to test the "conservative" nostrum for capturing the White House, thus reversing a tradition of selecting moderate candidates. The Democratic party ran its "interim" President—a man who had compiled an incredible record of success with Congress in the short period he had occupied the White House. The election resulted in one of the greatest victories in history for either party. In victory, the Democratic candidate won Vermont, the only solidly Republican state left in the

---

* From *American Government Annual*, 1965–1966 edited by Donald G. Herzberg. Copyright © 1965 by Holt, Rinehart and Winston, Inc. Reprinted by permission of Holt, Rinehart and Winston, Inc.

[1] Stanley Kelley, Jr., "The 1960 Presidential Election," *American Government Annual, 1961–1962* (New York: Holt, Rinehart and Winston, 1961), p. 50.

[2] I must acknowledge a debt of gratitude to the *Congressional Quarterly Weekly Report* and *The New York Times*. An essay of this type would not be possible without these publications.

Union, by a 2–1 margin. In defeat, the only section of the country which was safe for the Republican candidate was the Deep South, the one-time stronghold and retreat of the Democratic party. It was as though the Hatter from Alice's Wonderland had written the script.

It was a year in which "things were not quite right." Senator Barry M. Goldwater suggested that "something is wrong in your land and in your world." He sensed that all was not well in American politics, and he was certain that he would benefit from the dissatisfaction. Senator Goldwater was wrong in his assessment of which candidate would benefit from the nation's uncertainty, but he was right in sensing that there was uncertainty. The source of this curious and undefinable national mood cannot be precisely identified, but no explanation is complete that does not consider the darkness which settled over the nation on November 22, 1963, when an assassin's bullet ended the life of President John F. Kennedy.

This article will describe the 1964 presidential election and evaluate its importance for American politics. The major questions to be considered are: Why and how did Senator Goldwater win the Republican nomination? Why and how did President Lyndon B. Johnson win the election? What are the implications of these events for America's two-party system?

Deciding where in time to begin the description is difficult. Does one begin on July 27, 1960, when Senator Goldwater addressed the Republican national convention—imploring his supporters to "grow up" and organize so that they might win on another day? Or when John F. Kennedy decided that Lyndon B. Johnson should be his running mate? Or, even earlier in time, when General Dwight D. Eisenhower defeated Senator Robert A. Taft for the nomination at the Republican convention in 1952? Or in 1948 when a young Texas congressman won the Democratic nomination for the U.S. Senate by eighty-seven votes in a runoff primary? This description will begin with November 22, 1963. Before that date, the Republican presidential candidate had to defeat the young President. After that date, Republicans had to overcome Lyndon B. Johnson and his record as President, the memory of the young President, and their own disunity. .

There are three major events in a presidential election year: the nomination of candidates, the campaign, and the election itself. The latter is brief—it is all over in one day. The nominating and campaign periods, however, are unmercifully long. These periods have definite phases. The nominating period has *preconvention* and *convention* phases. The campaign period has *planning, testing,* and *critical* phases. Each of these phases will be examined in turn.

NOMINATIONS: THE PRECONVENTION PHASE

Before the assassination of President Kennedy, three Republicans in particular were in the forefront in the race for the Republican nomination in 1964.[3] Because of the defeat of Richard M. Nixon in 1960 by a mere 112,000

[3] See Robert J. Huckshorn, "Presidential Politics, 1963—Prelude to Uncertainty," *American Government Annual, 1964–1965* (New York: Holt, Rinehart and Winston, 1964), pp. 27–36, for a review of preconvention campaigning in 1963.

votes, it seemed logical that he should be given a second try in 1964. After his resounding defeat in the California gubernatorial race in 1962, however, Nixon took himself out of the race for the nomination. Governor Nelson A. Rockefeller of New York won a second term by an impressive margin in 1962 and as a result was touted as the probable winner in the race for the Republican presidential nomination in 1964. His personal life, particularly his remarriage, was soon floodlit by publicity, however, and therefore became a political liability. Senator Barry M. Goldwater from Arizona then became the favorite. But the assassination dealt a severe blow to his chances since the Goldwater strategy was to combine a southern revolt against President Kennedy with midwestern and western support. A Lyndon B. Johnson in the White House neutralized the possible effectiveness of this strategy since Johnson was from the south and had considerable popularity in western and midwestern states.

Thus, the death of President Kennedy made an already ambiguous Republican leadership situation even more unclear. Senator Goldwater's lead over other contenders in the Gallup Poll was reduced considerably after the assassination and at one point he even fell behind Nixon. He never received a majority support from Gallup Poll respondents and later, when pitted against individual candidates in a two-man race, trailed all major candidates. Other names began to receive attention—Henry Cabot Lodge of Massachusetts, Governor George Romney of Michigan, Governor William Scranton of Pennsylvania. Governor Nelson Rockefeller had announced his candidacy before the assassination, but no one gave him much of a chance to win the nomination.

In most presidential election years, it is either clear long in advance of the convention who the candidate will be, or a candidate emerges during preconvention maneuvering. There was no obvious Republican candidate as the election year began. Senator Goldwater announced his candidacy on January 3, 1964, making him the second major willing candidate. Before this announcement, there was serious speculation that he would not run for the nomination—contenting himself to seek reelection to the U.S. Senate. Though no one was certain in January who would win the nomination, most analysts were confident that it would be neither of the two announced candidates—Goldwater nor Rockefeller.

The goal of presidential contenders in preconvention campaigning is to garner the support of 51 percent of the convention delegates. There are several strategies that may be employed to achieve this goal because there are several methods used by states to select delegates to a national convention. Delegates are selected by state party conventions, district party conventions, state party committees, and presidential primaries. Some states use a mixture of these procedures. There are several variations in types of presidential primaries—some allow delegates to indicate on the ballot a commitment to candidates, others do not. Several states provide for presidential preference polls in conjunction with presidential primaries; in some states these polls are only advisory to the delegates, in other states, a mandate to vote for the candidate who wins. There are countless other variations in procedure for delegate selection.[4]

A *willing* candidate may adopt the strategy of working only for delegate support in states where delegates are selected by conventions or committees; alternatively he may try to win presidential primaries and preference polls and then work on other delegates to support him because of his demonstrated popularity in the primaries; or he may rely on a mixture of strategies. Those candidates who are shy about announcing their intentions early will no doubt try to get delegate support in state conventions and committees and work on other delegates at the national convention. Other candidates may rely on the risky strategy of waiting for the convention to come to them in a deadlock between the principal candidates.

The most spectacular preconvention campaigns in recent years were those of Dwight D. Eisenhower in 1952 and John F. Kennedy in 1960. Both relied on what might be called an outside strategy. They demonstrated their popularity in presidential primaries and preference polls in order to convince the press, the public, and, ultimately, convention delegates that they should receive the nomination. Through more "public" means Eisenhower and Kennedy sought to become the "obvious" candidate—the popular favorite.[5] By 1964 it seemed that this outside strategy had become the only method which would be successful. When Governor Rockefeller announced his candidacy, it was evident that he would employ this strategy for winning the nomination.

Though Senator Goldwater announced his intention to run in several presidential primaries and preference polls, it became apparent that the principal strategy of the Goldwater forces was to collect convention delegates by capturing state and local party organizations in those states where these organizations would be selecting delegates. This strategy of working within the party to capture delegate strength might be called an inside strategy.[6] At a time when it seemed that a contender would be nominated only if he relied on the more public route to victory, Senator Goldwater's organization perfected the inside strategy.

[4] For details on delegate selection see Richard Hupman and Eiler C. Ravnholt, *Nomination and Election of the President and Vice-President of the United States* (Washington, D.C.: Government Printing Office, 1964), and Paul David et al., *The Politics of National Party Conventions* (Washington, D.C.: Brookings, 1960).

[5] For descriptions of the Eisenhower strategy see David, et al., chap. 12, and Charles O. Jones. *The Republican party in American Politics* (New York: Crowell-Collier-Macmillan, 1965), chap. 3. For descriptions of the Kennedy strategy see Theodore White, *The Making of the President, 1960*) (New York: Atheneum, 1961) and Paul Tillett, ed., *Inside Politics: The National Conventions, 1960* (Dobbs Ferry, New York: Oceana, 1962).

[6] I have borrowed these useful terms from Nelson W. Polsby. He discusses the "inside" and "outside" strategies used by contenders in the majority leadership fiight in the House of Representatives in 1962. See "Two Strategies of Influence: Choosing a Majority Leader, 1962," in Robert L. Peabody and Nelson W. Polsby, eds., *New Perspectives on the House of Representatives* (Skokie, Ill. Rand McNally, 1963), pp. 237–270. See Richard Dudman. "Ultrarightist Drive to Take Over GOP Was Started Four Years Ago," *St. Louis Post Dispatch*, December 6, 1964, for details of Goldwater's effort to take over the Republican organization.

The success of Goldwater's strategy becomes clear when one examines his progress in collecting delegate strength even though his performance in presidential primaries was unimpressive. By March 10, the date of the first presidential primary in New Hampshire, Goldwater and his associates were already claiming a delegate strength of 400. By June 2, the date of the last presidential primaries in South Dakota and California, it was obvious to everyone that he did indeed have between 400 and 500 delegates—perhaps more. Before the California primary, *none* of these delegates were won in primary contests with major opponents. In point of fact, there were only three primaries that tested the popularity of the major contenders—New Hampshire, Oregon, and California (see Table 20.1). In 1954, as in the recent past, the press followed the presidential primaries and preference polls carefully for an indication of which candidate was emerging as the popular favorite for the nomination. As is shown in Table 20.1, no such candidate emerged in the public tests between contenders. Goldwater, Rockefeller, Representative John Byrnes of Wisconsin, Governor James Rhodes of Ohio, and Ambassador Henry Cabot Lodge of Massachusetts all won contests.

A brief review of the presidential primary and preference poll contests illustrates the confusion. Lodge defeated a field of candidates with write-in votes in New Hampshire—he never left his post as Ambassador to South Vietnam during the primary campaign while Goldwater and Rockefeller both spent considerable time, money, and effort in the state. Representative John Byrnes won the Wisconsin primary on April 7 against no opposition. In other contests in April, Goldwater defeated Senator Margaret Chase Smith (Maine) in Illinois, Lodge won with write-in votes in New Jersey and Massachusetts, and Governor William Scranton won with write-in votes in Pennsylvania. During May, Goldwater defeated former governor and perennial candidate Harold Stassen (Pennsylvania) in Indiana, Governor James Rhodes won control of his delegation in Ohio, Goldwater defeated a write-in effort for Richard M. Nixon in Nebraska, Rockefeller defeated the field of candidates in Oregon, and the slate of delegates endorsed by Goldwater was defeated by a competing unendorsed Goldwater slate of delegates in Florida. In this long period of pre-convention maneuvering only one development stands out in retrospect—Senator Goldwater was progressing steadily beneath his cloud of confusion toward his goal of collecting a majority of those delegates selected by means other than direct public contest with other candidates.

June showed one candidate clearly in the forefront—Barry M. Goldwater. It was possible that Goldwater could win the nomination even if he lost the California primary to Rockefeller. Victory in California, however, would add a certain legitimacy to his whole effort. The outside strategy of demonstrating one's popularity in primaries had not only become the accepted route to the nomination, it seemed like the "democratic" way to do it. To lose the California primary and yet win the nomination would have cast grave doubts on how "democratic" was the Republican nominating process and added weight to the argument that Goldwater was not the popular choice of the rank-and-file Republican voter. Thus, the California primary was important for Goldwater, for Rockefeller, and for the Republican party.

Both candidates campaigned vigorously in California. Goldwater held

TABLE 20.1 REPUBLICAN PRESIDENTIAL PRIMARY AND PREFERENCE POLL RESULTS, 1954

	DATE	VICTOR	NUMBER OF DELEGATES FORMALLY PLEDGED IN PRIMARY
Goldwater vs. Major Opponents			
New Hampshire	March 10	Lodge	14—Lodge
Oregon	May 15	Rockefeller	18—Rockefeller
California	June 2	Goldwater	86—Goldwater
Goldwater vs. Minor Opponents			
Illinois	April 14	Goldwater	0 [a]
Indiana	May 5	Goldwater	0 [b]
Goldwater Unopposed or Opposed by an Unpledged Slate			
Nebraska	May 12	Goldwater	0 [a]
Florida	May 26	unpledged slate	0
South Dakota	June 2	unpledged slate	0
Goldwater Not Entered			
Wisconsin	April 7	Byrnes	30—Byrnes
New Jersey	April 21	no candidates entered	0
Massachusetts	April 28	no candidates entered	0
Pennsylvania	April 28	no candidates entered	0 [a]
District of Columbia	May 5	no candidates entered	0 [a]
Ohio	May 5	Rhodes	58—Rhodes
West Virginia	May 12	Rockefeller	0 [a]
Maryland	May 19	no candidates entered	0 [b]

[a] Candidates for delegate in these states may not indicate a preference on the ballot among presidential candidates and therefore are not formally pledged to a candidate. Presidential candidates oppose one another in preference polls.

[b] Delegates in these state are actually selected in conventions, Presidential candidates oppose one another in preference polls.

an early lead in the polls, Rockefeller led after his victory in Oregon, and Goldwater closed the gap at the last minute. Just twenty-two minutes after the polls had closed in Southern California, the electronic computer for one of the major television networks declared that Goldwater had won California's eight-six delegates. Though a long night of counting resulted in a see-saw battle between the two candidates, Goldwater did win—by 51.4 percent of the vote. There would be minor skirmishes before his victory at the convention in San Francisco, but the battle was over. Senator Goldwater would be the Republican candidate for President.

The minor skirmishes which occurred between the California primary and the Republican convention were the result of a realization on the part of hitherto "shy" candidates that there would be no deadlock between Rockefeller and Goldwater at the convention. The deadlock, if it ever existed, was broken on June 2, and the Arizona Senator was moving rapidly to a position of full control of the Republican party. These "shy" candidates began to speak out at the Annual Governors' Conference in Cleveland, June 8–10.

Governor William Scranton of Pennsylvania, Governor George Romney of Michigan, and Richard Nixon all held press conferences, but their efforts at stopping Goldwater were to no avail. On June 12 Governor Scranton announced his candidacy for the Republican nomination in a speech to the Maryland Republican state convention. He gained the support of Lodge and Rockefeller and immediately launched a last-minute outside strategy for winning the nomination. There were no preconvention contests left, however, in which Scranton could demonstrate his popularity. Thus, he was forced to try and capitalize on public opinion polls that showed him leading Goldwater among the Republican rank-and-file when the two candidates were pitted against one another. Scranton's only hope was to spark a grass-roots movement in his favor which would result in unpledged delegates' voting for him and Goldwater delegates' switching allegiances. It was much too late, as Governor Scranton must have known, for any such effort to succeed. By June 16 it was estimated that Goldwater had approximately 650 of the 655 votes needed to nominate him on the first ballot.

Meanwhile, in the Democratic party President Johnson was doing a little preconvention campaigning of his own. He was not campaigning for the nomination, however, which was assured him. He could concentrate on the general election and rely on a most effective strategy—fulfilling his responsibilities as President. As President, he was guaranteed front-page publicity every day. He was not satisfied with just fulfilling his responsibilities, however. By August, when the Democrats convened in Atlantic City to nominate him, President Johnson could point to an impressive list of problems that had received attention by his Administration and by Congress. Leading the list, of course, was the Civil Rights Act—the most comprehensive piece of civil rights legislation in history. Other accomplishments included passage of important legislation in the areas of tax reform, mass transportation, agriculture, conservation, and education. In addition, he used the White House effectively in helping to solve the crisis in the railroad industry. These accomplishments, the nation's continuing sorrow for John F. Kennedy, and President Johnson's own popularity, resulted in unprecedented margins in the Gallup Poll for Johnson (see Table 20.3). There was remarkably little change in the polls between July and November. Thus, by July 10 (the conclusion of the Republican preconvention phase of the campaign), two outcomes were certain. Senator Goldwater would win the Republican nomination by a large margin and President Johnson would win the election by a wide margin.[7]

NOMINATIONS: GUARANTEED CONFLICT
FOR REPUBLICANS

The Republicans held their convention rather early in 1964—July 13–16. It is wise to schedule the convention early if there is to be a high degree of

[7] Governor George Wallace of Alabama waged an impressive campaign to demonstrate disapproval of the Civil Rights Act by entering primaries and preference polls in Wisconsin, Indiana, and Maryland. He was defeated by the Democratic governors in Wisconsin and Indiana and by Senator Brewster in Maryland. His best showing was in Maryland.

conflict so that there will be time before the general election to heal the party's wounds. Conflict was guaranteed in 1964. Perhaps because of the internal divisions in the party, Republicans selected a convention site designed to discourage conflict. San Francisco is one of the most beautiful cities in the world—and should have served to distract the combatants. It did not seem to have this effect, however.

The Committee on Resolutions, or Platform Committee, held its hearings during the week before the convention. The moderates, led by Scranton, Romney, and Rockefeller, were intent upon writing a moderate rather than a conservative platform. If they could not have a candidate of their choosing, they would try to force the candidate they were getting to change some of his views. Since the Platform Committee is composed of two delegates from each state, and since Senator Goldwater had firm control over a large majority of state delegations, it was to be expected that he would be able to write the kind of platform he wanted. Such was the case. The moderates attempted to strengthen the civil rights section of the platform and to have included a section that would condemn extremist groups—notably the John Birch Society, the Ku Klux Klan, and the Communist party. The Goldwater forces interpreted these efforts as direct attacks on their candidate. They were impressed with the fact that Senator Robert A. Taft of Ohio had compromised with the moderates in 1952 and lost. They were not going to repeat the same mistake—especially since they were in such complete command of the convention. They steamrollered all major attempts by the moderates in the Platform Committee to change the platform. The moderates then shifted their efforts to the convention floor.

The first sessions of any convention are invariably dull. The convention is formally the principal unit in party organization. It must spend some time in the first two or three sessions going through the motions of taking over its position as chief party agency. Normally the first important business is the consideration of the platform. In 1964 the presentation of the platform was virtually the last opportunity that the moderates had to score a victory. They intended to present a minority report with amendments. Though the platform was to have been presented early in the evening of the third session, it was postponed until after former President Dwight D. Eisenhower's address so that his speech would not be delayed. Then the entire platform was read.

It was well past midnight in the East by the time the moderates were able to present their minority report containing five amendments. Two would have expanded the civil rights section in the platform, two would have condemned extremist groups, and one would have stated that the President is solely responsible for the use of nuclear weapons, a result of an interview of Senator Goldwater published in *Der Spiegel*, a German news magazine, where he suggested that the Supreme Commander of NATO be given more latitude in using nuclear weapons. The debate on these amendments was vigorous, and, on occasion, the convention was unruly. Governor Rockefeller in particular, had a difficult time presenting his remarks. He was booed often and with great fervor.

The Goldwater forces opposed all five amendments as unnecessary. All five were defeated by large margins. There was only one roll-call vote, that on the principal civil rights amendment. The amendment was defeated 897 to 409—an indication of Goldwater's strength. The moderates were able to garner a majority of delegates in only 16 of the 53 delegations represented at the Convention.

During the fight over the platform, the Scranton forces were struggling against impossible odds to increase their delegate strength. Goldwater was working hard to hold all of his delegates in line and pick up delegates from those few states that were still uncommitted or committed to a favorite son. Meanwhile the usual number of irrelevant, rallies, parades, and demonstrations were being conducted by the young supporters of the two major candidates.

Scranton's principal strategy remained that of demonstrating that he was the popular candidate, that Goldwater's views were too extreme to qualify him as a presidential candidate.[8] He wanted an opportunity to meet Goldwater in a public appearance to prove his point. It was totally unnecessary for Goldwater to accommodate Scranton's strategy, however. He had the votes. In a last minute attempt to "smoke out" Goldwater, Scranton sent him an intemperate letter which, among other things, stated that "Goldwaterism has come to stand for a whole crazy-quilt collection of absurd and dangerous positions that would be soundly repudiated by the American people in November." The Senator was not taking the bait, however, and refused to answer the letter. Scranton later said that he had not written the letter or seen it before it was sent.

On July 15, 1964, the balloting began for nominating the Republican candidate for President. The results were the happy culmination for conservatives of their four-year effort to capture the party's top prize. The conservatives had done a great deal of "growing up" since Goldwater had advised them to do so on July 27, 1960. Table 20.2 presents the results of the balloting. Senator Goldwater's victory was thorough, but not uniformly so throughout all regions of the country. As is indicated in Table 20.2, Goldwater's greatest support came from southern and border states, his least support from eastern states. He received only 17.2 percent (57 of 332) of the delegates' votes from the East while receiving 95.6 percent (347 of 363) of the votes from southern and border states. Goldwater received strong support from the midwest (74.1 percent of the votes) and the west (84.8 percent).

Table 20.2 also shows the importance of the south to Goldwater's total vote. Nearly 40 percent of his support came from this region. The midwest contributed 29.2 percent, the west 24.6 percent, and the east a mere 6.5 percent. The other candidates, on the other hand, received 64.7 percent of their votes in the east—Scranton 76.2 percent and Rockefeller 79 percent.

Following the nomination of Senator Goldwater for President, the convention nominated William E. Miller, congressman from New York and Republican national committee chairman, for Vice President. Miller received 1305 votes—three Tennessee delegates abstained. Miller apparently was selected because of his reputation as a tough campaigner, his familiarity with

---

[8] If the polls were accurate in this preconvention period, the fact that Goldwater won the nomination despite his poor showing in polls supports the conclusions of Herbert McClosky et al., concerning the differences between Republican party leaders and followers. See "Issue Conflict and Consensus among Party Leaders and Followers," American Political Science Review, 54 (September 1960), pp. 406–427.

the regular Republican organization throughout the country, the fact that he was from New York, was a Catholic, and, according to Senator Goldwater, "he drives Johnson nuts."

Their work done, the delegates left San Francisco after hearing an acceptance speech by Senator Goldwater which caused more controversy in an already divided convention (see below). On July 17, the day after the adjournment of the convention, Goldwater moved swiftly to take over the Republican national organization. To the dismay of many Republicans, and some of his own supporters, he selected one of his aides, Dean Burch from Tucson, Arizona, to be Republican national committee chairman. The national committee confirmed his selection. He named another aide, Denison Kitchel, as the campaign manager.

In reviewing the work of the 1964 Republican national convention, several deviations from past convention behavior are noted.[9] First, no successful candidate for the Republican nomination has ever virtually ignored the important eastern states in his quest for victory. In those recent conventions where there was important conflict for the nomination (1940, 1948, 1952), the winning candidate received most of his delegate support from the east—Willkie 45 percent in 1940, Dewey 45 percent in 1948, and Eisenhower 50.5 percent in 1952.[10] As previously noted, Goldwater got 6.5 percent of his vote from the east. Conversely, successful candidates have not received much of their support from the south—Willkie 14.4 percent, Dewey 20.8 percent, and Eisenhower 17.3 percent—or from the west—Willkie 11.2 percent, Dewey 13.8 percent, and Eisenhower 12.6 percent. Goldwater received 63.9 percent of his support from these regions (39.3 percent in the south, 24.6 percent in the west). Very clearly, the Republican party "moved south and west" at the convention in 1964. The eastern Republicans no longer dominated.

Second, Senator Goldwater employed an inside rather than an outside strategy for winning the nomination. Though he was entered in several primaries and preference polls, he did not attempt to capture delegates by demonstrating his popularity in these contests. He relied principally on his advantage with state party organizations in states that selected delegates in other ways. As noted earlier, Goldwater had major opponents in only three contests and he won one of these—California.

Third, these "new" Republicans in the party's power structure had a different plan for capturing the White House. The prevailing theory in recent years had been that only a moderate Republican candidate could win because most Americans are moderate. The conservatives challenged this thesis. Their theory was that the majority of Americans are conservatives. If offered a truly conservative candidate espousing a truly conservative program, this majority would make itself heard by electing such a candidate to the White House. Basic to this theory is the notion that the present political party alignment is unnatural. A conservative appeal would cut across party lines—perhaps drawing in southern Democrats and losing a number of eastern Republicans. The theory was not a new one—it has been argued for decades.

---

[9] For details of the Republican national convention—major speeches, the platform, proceedings, analysis—see *Congressional Quarterly Weekly Report*, July 17, 1964.

[10] Kelly, *American Government Annual*, p. 55.

TABLE 20.2 BALLOTING FOR PRESIDENTIAL NOMINATION, REPUBLICAN NATIONAL CONVENTION, 1964

Region and State	DELEGATES FOR				REGIONAL PERCENTAGES		
	Gold-water	Scranton	Rocke-feller	Other [a]	Percent of Votes in Region for Goldwater	Percent of Gold-water Vote (883) from Region	Percent of Others (425) Votes from Region
East	57	163	90	22	17.2	6.5	64.7
Conn.	4	12	—	—			
Del.	7	5	—	—			
Me.	—	—	—	14			
Md.	6	13	1	—			
Mass.	5	26	—	3			
N. H.	—	14	—	—			
N. J.	20	20	—	—			
N. Y.	5	—	87	—			
Pa.	4	60	—	—			
R. I.	3	11	—	—			
Vt.	3	2	2	5			
South	347	13	3	0	95.6	39.3	3.8
Ala.	20	—	—	—			
Ark.	9	2	1	—			
Fla.	32	2	—	—			
Ga.	22	2	—	—			
Ky.	21	3	—	—			
La.	20	—	—	—			
Miss.	13	—	—	—			
Mo.	23	1	—	—			
N. C.	26	—	—	—			
Okla.	22	—	—	—			
S. C.	16	—	—	—			
Tenn.	28	—	—	—			
Texas	56	1	—	—			
Va.	29	2	2	—			
W. Va.	10	—	—	—			

Midwest	258	13	3	66	74.1	29.2	19.3
Ill.	56	—	2	—			
Ind.	52	—	—	—			
Iowa	14	10	—	1			
Kan.	18	1	—	40			
Mich.	8	—	—	18			
Minn.	8	—	—	—			
Neb.	16	—	1	6			
N.D.	7	—	—	1			
Ohio	57	2	—	—			
S.D.	12	—	—	—			
Wis.	30	—	—	—			
West	217	12	18	9	84.8	24.6	9.2
Alaska	—	8	—	4			
Ariz.	16	—	—	—			
Calif.	86	—	—	—			
Colo.	15	3	—	—			
Hawaii	4	—	—	4			
Idaho	14	—	—	—			
Mont.	14	—	—	—			
Nev.	6	—	—	—			
N.M.	14	—	18	—			
Ore.	—	—	—	—			
Utah	14	1	—	—			
Wash.	22	—	—	—			
Wyo.	12	—	—	1			
Other	4	13	0	0	23.5	.4	3.1
D.C.	4	3	—	—			
Puerto Rico	—	5	—	—			
Virgin Islands	—	5	—	—			
	883	214	114	97			

[a] Other candidates receiving votes included Senators Margaret Chase Smith (27) and Hiram Fong (5), former Congressman Walter Judd (22), Governor George Romney (41), and former Ambassador Henry Cabot Lodge (2).

SOURCE: Compiled from data in *Congressional Quarterly Weekly Report*, July 17, 1964, p. 1482.

What was new in 1964 was that those who endorsed this particular nostrum were successful in capturing the party and therefore were in a position to test their theory.

Fourth, since collecting a conservative majority would necessitate cutting across party lines, there was no need to compromise in San Francisco with those who refused to accept the conservative nostrum. Specifically there was no need to compromise with those moderate Republicans who so often had had an opportunity to test their theory. Thus, the Goldwater forces refused to concede anything to what had been the center of power in the Republican party. Moderate Republicans were defeated in all of their attempts to revise the platform in committees and on the convention floor; they were not given a vice-presidential candidate to their liking; and in his acceptance speech Senator Goldwater seemed in no mood to win back those whom he had just defeated. "Anyone who joins us in all sincerity we welcome. Those who do not care for our cause, we don't expect to enter our ranks in any case." And then the Senator repeated two sentences that were interpreted as direct blows at moderate attempts to condemn extremism in the platform. "I would remind you that extremism in the defense of liberty is no vice. And let me remind you also that moderation in the pursuit of justice is no virtue." The moderates and liberals were given nothing to soften the humiliation of their lopsided defeat. One function of a national party convention is that of rallying the party to a single cause. In order to accomplish this function, attempts are made to articulate the cause in such a way that unity is achieved. The 1964 Republican convention, however, adjourned as divided, if not more so than when it convened. A disunified majority party faces great odds in achieving victory. A disunified *minority* party has virtually no chance at all.

Following the convention, efforts were made by Goldwater, Miller, Nixon, and Eisenhower to unify the party for the coming campaign. A so-called unity conference was held in Hershey, Pennsylvania, on August 12. Governor Scranton was host to the meeting which was attended by most of the party notables. Though several of those attending announced that they would support the national ticket, it was clear that support from such individuals as Rockefeller would be verbal only—and even then not repeated often. Apparently Rockefeller was successful in getting something in return for his endorsement. Clare Boothe Luce had indicated that she might enter the Senate race in New York as a candidate of the Conservative party. Rockefeller and Keating were hoping that Goldwater would convince her not to do so. She withdrew her name.

During August national chairman Dean Burch moved swiftly to transform the Republican national committee headquarters into a national Goldwater campaign headquarters. In so doing, several experienced party professionals were demoted, assigned new jobs, or forced to resign. Thus, at a very late date in the presidential election year, the Republican national headquarters underwent a major reorganization.[11]

[11] For details of this reorganization see *Congressional Quarterly Weekly Report,* September 25, 1964, pp. 2221–2229, and two articles in the *St. Louis Post-Dispatch*: William K. Wyant, Jr., "Stakes High as Factions Fight for Control of Republican party," December 7, 1964; and Richard Dudman, "Right-Wingers Swarmed into Goldwater Camp with His Full Approval," December 8, 1964.

NOMINATIONS:
STRUCTURED HARMONY FOR DEMOCRATS

Though it was necessary for the Republicans to meet early in order to attempt to resolve their conflicts before the campaign, the Democrats found that they could delay their convention until late August. They had their candidate and therefore could concentrate on presenting a unified front to the television audience. Every effort was made by Democratic leadership to "structure harmony" in the 1964 convention—contrasting their meeting with that of Republicans. The best time for presenting this picture of harmony to the American public would be close to the general election. In fact, it would indeed be an excellent way to "kick off" the 1964 campaign. President Johnson and his vice-presidential candidate would be able to incorporate the free television time accorded them at the convention into their campaign for election in November.

Hearings on the Democratic platform were held in Washington, D.C., during the week before the convention. Cabinet members, congressmen, senators, state officials, and interest-group representatives testified. The result of the week-long deliberations was a document that emphasized the accomplishments of the Kennedy and Johnson Administrations and included something for every major interest. The platform was offered as a "covenant of unity" and was adopted by the convention without controversy on August 25. As might be expected, the Democrats incorporated into their platform statements condemning extremism—specifically naming the John Birch Society, the Communist party, and the Ku Klux Klan—and declaring that control of nuclear weapons "must remain solely with the highest elected official in the country—the President of the United States." Both of these statements had been rejected by the Republican convention.

Only credentials problems disturbed an otherwise placid conclave. The Alabama delegation was challenged before the Committee on Credentials since, as a result of the election of unpledged presidential electors in the May 5 primary, President Johnson's name would not appear on the ballot in November. It was charged that this violated the loyalty provision of the Democratic national convention which required that a state party had to take steps to insure that the Democratic candidates appear on the ballot. The right of the Alabama delegates to be seated was challenged by a Negro attorney from Birmingham, Mr. Orzell Billingsley. The Credentials Committee decided that the delegates could be seated if they signed a personal loyalty oath. Eleven of the fifty-three delegates and alternates did sign the oath—the rest eventually announced that they would leave the convention.

The Mississippi delegation was challenged by a rival delegation from the Mississippi Freedom Democratic party (MFDP). The MFDP charged that the regular Democratic party in Mississippi excluded Negroes from participation and did not support the national party. The MFDP had considerable support among other delegations at the convention and was therefore able to take its challenge to the floor of the convention if necessary. After dramatic testimony before the Credentials Committee, and several delays, the Committee announced its decision: the Mississippi delegates could take their seats if they signed a personal loyalty oath, an antidiscrimination requirement would be in effect for selecting delegates in 1968, two MFDP delegates were seated as "delegates at large," the remaining MFDP representatives were welcomed as "honored guests" of the convention. Four of the regular Mississippi delegates signed the oath—the rest left the convention.

With the conflicts over credentials settled (there were also contests in Oregon, Puerto Rico, and Virgin Islands), the convention moved swiftly to complete its business. The platform was adopted without controversy. Then, in a demonstration of unity, Alabama yielded to Texas on the call of the states for nomination for President, and Governor John B. Connally of Texas, with a conomination speech from Governor Edmund G. Brown of California, nominated Lyndon B. Johnson. Following the seconding speeches, a motion was made to suspend the rules and nominate Johnson by acclamation. The convention roared its approval and President Johnson became the second presidential candidate in the history of the Democratic party to be so nominated (Roosevelt was nominated by acclamation in 1936).

President Johnson decided to go to Convention Hall in Atlantic City on the evening of his nomination to announce that Senator Hubert H. Humphrey from Minnesota was his choice for the vice-presidential nomination. In essence, Johnson had nominated his candidate—though Senator Eugene McCarthy from Minnesota, considered a major contender for the nomination before the convention, delivered the formal nominating speech. Following the usual excessive number of seconding speeches, Senator Humphrey was nominated by acclamation.

Two items of business remained for the thirty-fourth Democratic national convention—a tribute to John F. Kennedy and the acceptance speeches by the candidates. The tribute to President Kennedy was in the form of a movie entitled "A Thousand Days." But the delegates and spectators, could not express their pent-up emotion for the late President by watching a film. They chose to demonstrate when Attorney General Robert F. Kennedy was introduced to present the film. The Convention Hall rocked to the cheers, applause and impressive demonstration of emotion by Democrats. The spontaneous outburst lasted for nearly a quarter of an hour. The intensity of this show of affection for the late President suggested that President Johnson had wisely shifted the tribute to Kennedy to the last day. If it had occurred earlier, the convention might well have insisted that Robert F. Kennedy be given second place on the ticket.

The acceptance speeches by Johnson and Humphrey presaged the pattern to be followed during the campaign. President Johnson emphasized the accomplishments of the Kennedy and Johnson Administrations, the degree to which moderation and good sense would predominate in a future Johnson Administration, and the efforts which would be made to construct the "Great Society." Senator Humphrey attacked the Republican presidential candidate as the temporary spokesman for his party—stating that Goldwater was "not in the mainstream of his party. In fact, he has not even touched the shore." Thus, in the ensuing campaign, President Johnson would accentuate the positive by campaigning for the Kennedy-Johnson accomplishments.

Senator Humphrey would campaign against Senator Goldwater.[12] The situation was somewhat like that in 1956 when President Eisenhower talked of his accomplishments and the problems ahead while Vice President Nixon engaged Democratic candidate Adlai Stevenson.

CAMPAIGNING: THE SPECTACULAR ORDEAL

Having completed the business of formally selecting their candidates, the two parties could concentrate on attacking one another directly. It has been noted that both the preconvention and convention phases are important in election year politics because both publicize the candidates, and most voters have decided by the end of the convention phase how they will vote in November. The campaign period is a spectacular ordeal. Perhaps it is unnecessary, perhaps no one is convinced one way or the other, but no candidate is willing to test such a theory by not campaigning. For at least two months, the United States pauses to pay attention to four men as they crisscross the nation pleading their case to the voter. The presidential campaign is an "unreal" event—both for the participants and the spectators. There is nothing quite like it anywhere in the world. It is characterized by comedy, tragedy, and serious purpose. In the same day presidential campaigns have been known to hit the heights of intellectual encounter and the depths of "gutter-sniping" personality assassination. The 1964 presidential campaign was perhaps a little more "unreal" than most.

Normally there are three campaign phases in a year when there are contests for the nomination. These phases roughly correspond to the three months between the conventions, and the election. It has been typical to hold conventions in July—as the Republicans did in 1964 and both parties did in 1960. August has been devoted to planning the campaign, September to testing the plan, and October to carrying out the most effective plan. Thus, the three campaign period phases might be called the *planning, testing,* and *critical* phases. In 1964, however, both the Democrats and the Republicans knew who the Democratic candidate would be. Thus, the Democrats could begin planning their campaign as soon as they were certain of the identity of the Republican candidate. And they were certain even before the Republican convention. Goldwater could do some planning in advance as soon as he was assured of the Republican nomination, but, of course, a first order of business for him was winning in San Francisco. Goldwater's activities during the campaign generally conform to the three phases noted above. Johnson, however, did not need to wait until August to plan his campaign.

Before discussing the details of the campaign, it is important to examine public opinion poll results. Certainly the fact that President Johnson held such a consistently commanding lead in all national polls, and the vast majority of statewide polls was a major determinant in campaign behavior—

---

[12] For details of the Democratic national convention—major speeches, the platform, the credentials fight, analysis—*Congressional Quarterly Weekly Report,* August 28, 1964.

especially for the Democrats. President Johnson apparently considered the poll data significant. He spoke to the Democratic national committee on August 28, following his nomination in Atlantic City, and cited poll data prepared by Louis Harris, George Gallup, and Elmo Roper—all of which showed him with a large lead. He observed that the "frontlash" vote of Republicans for him would far exceed the "backlash" vote of Democrats for Goldwater.

Table 20.3 presents the Gallup Poll data for the period January 9 to November 2. Johnson held nearly 4–1 leads over Goldwater before the Republican convention. As might be expected, his advantage dropped after the convention but the dip was much less than would be expected and the percentage of undecideds was unusually high (10 percent compared to 6 percent in 1960 at this time). Though the Republican candidate and his supporters were certain that as the campaign proceeded, this margin would be reduced, in fact it remained remarkably steady throughout the three months of the campaign. On July 1, Johnson had 60 percent, on November 2, he had 61 percent, and on November 3, he actually received 61 percent.

The importance of these astounding poll results is that the President did not have to engage his opponent—he could ignore him and concentrate on his own record. Further, Goldwater had to devise some means for making enough impact so as to reduce the margin. But with Johnson remaining aloof, Goldwater had difficulty finding a weak spot. The result was that the "testing" month of September was spent by Goldwater and Miller attacking on a variety of domestic, foreign, and personal issues. But just as Goldwater would not accept the "bait" in San Francisco when moderate Republicans were flaying away trying to find a soft spot, Johnson was not "biting" in September. The chore of answering Goldwater and counterattacking was left to Humphrey. Thus, Johnson ran "against" no one—rather "for" his election. Goldwater ran against Johnson but encountered Humphrey at

TABLE 20.3   GALLUP POLL RESULTS, JANUARY 9–NOVEMBER 2, 1964

DATE	JOHNSON	GOLDWATER	UNDECIDED	JOHNSON CHANGE	GOLDWATER CHANGE
January 9	75	20	5		
January 21	75	18	7	0	− 2
July 1	77	18	5	+ 2	0
July 9	76	20	4	− 1	+ 2
July 12	77	20	3	+ 1	0
Republican Convention					
July 22	60	30	10	−17	+10
August 8	59	31	10	− 1	+ 1
August 23	65	29	6	+ 6	− 2
Democratic Convention					
September 16	65	29	6	0	0
October 4	62	32	6	− 3	+ 3
October 18	64	29	7	+ 2	− 3
November 2	61	32	7	− 3	+ 3

SOURCE: "How the Polls Fared," *Christian Science Monitor*, November 14, 1964.

every turn. Miller ran against both Johnson and Humphrey but found that there was no one left on the Democratic side to engage him.

During the *testing* month of September, the Democrats established a pattern that was relied on throughout the campaign. President Johnson spoke of the Kennedy-Johnson record, the future of America in a Johnson Administration, and, as President, addressed himself to any national or international crisis which developed during the campaign. But he did not begin to campaign too soon. He made a number of "nonpolitical" appearances in early September and began to campaign vigorously toward the end of the month. Senator Humphrey responded to Goldwater's attacks and, in turn, established a theme that would be repeated many times in October. Humphrey characterized Senator Goldwater, as a dangerous man who did not even represent his own party.

Goldwater and Miller discovered a basic theme in September which came to dominate their October campaign. Since Goldwater was never able to engage President Johnson directly, however, this theme had to be developed without clear indications as to whether it was the most effective approach to take. In 1960 "underdog" Kennedy had the advantage of meeting Nixon in debate. Kennedy was able to dispel the notion that he lacked experience and knowledge about the affairs of government. "Underdog" Goldwater never had any such opportunity to meet his adversary before the nation.

The principal Republican theme was decided on after considerable probing. A review of major topics discussed by Goldwater and Miller during September reveals the following:

> Foreign policy: Vietnam, Cuba, United Nations and Red China, general attacks on Administration's foreign policy, retorts to speech by Senator William Fulbright of Arkansas on foreign policy, danger of communism, peace, defense policy.
> Domestic policy: Socialism and big government, law and order, corruption in government, the draft, civil rights, immigration, moral decay of society, taxes, the "bracero" program, medicare, social security, reapportionment, the Supreme Court, the Tennessee Valley Authority, agriculture, poverty, labor unions, nuclear threat.
> Personalities: Johnson's ability, Johnson's war record, Johnson's wealth and how he got it, Johnson Administration is "soft on communism," Johnson's auto driving habits, Johnson had restrictive covenant in property sold, Humphrey and the Americans for Democratic Action.

By October, the *critical* month, though many of these topics were still discussed, a clear pattern had emerged. The October theme went something like this: America is threatened by big government, socialism, and communism. Big government kills initiative and individualism. It leads to corruption among those with authority. If those with authority are corrupt, and the Johnson Administration is characterized by corruption (Bobby Baker, Matthew McCloskey, Billie Sol Estes), then the morals of the whole society are affected. The result is a breakdown in law and order, as is evidenced in America by riots in the streets, raping, murders, and a disinterest among the citizenry in correcting these disorders. Morality and individualism may be restored by electing a President who is honest, acts on his convictions, does not seek political advantage for himself.

One event during the campaign caused concern among Democrats because it seemed to illustrate the Republican argument. On October 14 the White House announced the resignation of Walter W. Jenkins, special assistant to President Johnson. It was soon revealed that Jenkins had been arrested on October 7 for disorderly conduct involving "indecent gestures." Many Republicans were certain that this arrest would have an impact on the election. As it happened, however, several major international events occurred almost simultaneously: the British election on October 15, the resignation of Premier Nikita Khrushchev on the same day, and the detonation of a nuclear device by Communist China on October 16. These developments filled the newspapers and pushed the Jenkins matter out of the headlines. Further, President Johnson seized the opportunity to address the nation on television on October 18 regarding the international crises. Public opinion polls showed that far from being hurt during the eventful week, President Johnson actually gained in popularity.

October was also marked by increasing defensiveness by the Republican candidates. Democratic charges that Goldwater was "reckless," "trigger happy," and against social security, were having an effect. Goldwater, Miller, and Nixon, made a concerted effort during October to counter these charges.

On the Democratic side, Johnson continued to stress what his Administration would do for America and the importance of caution in dealing with nuclear weapons. He seldom, if ever, mentioned Senator Goldwater by name. Humphrey always attacked Goldwater by name—emphasizing the theme that Goldwater was dangerous for America, the Presidency, the Republican party, and was even harmful to real "conservatism" in America. Senator Goldwater and his supporters "have kidnapped the conservative tradition." Their views "are irrelevant to the realities of American life." Goldwater was frequently referred to as "the temporary leader of the opposition." "In his heart," Goldwater "is neither a loyal Republican nor a true conservative." Goldwater was charged with "recklessness," "radicalism," "irresponsibility," "selfishness." If Goldwater were elected, the United States would become a "garrison state in a nightmare world, isolated from everything but a nuclear reign of terror."

Johnson and Humphrey were attempting to capture (or perhaps more accurately, retain) support from the American moderates—those in the "middle of the road." Johnson posed as the man of peace, the moderate who would continue the policies of past administrations. Humphrey even classed himself as a "conservative" in a speech in Ashtabula, Ohio. More importantly, however, Humphrey spent the critical month of October hammering away on the notion that Goldwater was the "radical"—a label frequently reserved for Senator Humphrey in the past. Thus, the Democrats in 1964 were relying on campaign themes previously used by Republican candidates—that the election of Democrats would mean war abroad and radicalism at home.

Public opinion poll data supported this "middle of the road" strategy of Johnson and Humphrey. In one of the most interesting polls taken during the campaign, Louis Harris discovered that a great many Americans tended to view Goldwater as a "radical," while Johnson was viewed by most as a "conservative" or "middle of the roader." The results, as presented in Table 20.4, show that only 1 percent of the respondents considered themselves as "radical" but 45 percent considered Goldwater a "radical." Eighty percent of the respondents considered themselves either "conservatives" or "middle of the road," and 67 percent considered Johnson as belonging to one of these groups.

Early in the campaign, it was assumed by many that the major issue would be civil rights. The most comprehensive civil rights legislation in history had passed the Congress, there had been race riots in northern cities, continued nonviolent action by civil rights workers in the south, church bombings and murders in the Deep South, and Governor Wallace had polled an

TABLE 20.4   VOTER PERCEPTION OF POLITICAL POSITIONS, 1964

Voters' Perception of	POLITICAL POSITION			
	Conservative	Middle of the Road	Liberal	Radical
Goldwater	40	8	7	45
Johnson	25	42	30	3
Themselves	36	44	19	1

SOURCE: "The Harris Survey," *Washington Post*, Washington, D.C., September 8, 1964, p. 1.

impressive vote in the Wisconsin, Indiana, and Maryland presidential primaries. The term *backlash* was employed by commentators to indicate that many Democratic voters in northern states would vote for Senator Goldwater as a protest against the civil rights drive by Negroes. One study during the campaign did indicate that many whites were of the opinion that things had gotten out of hand—that the drive for civil rights had gone too far. In answer to a question about the pace of the civil rights movement, 54 percent of the respondents thought that it should slow down; 49 percent thought that nonviolent demonstrations hurt rather than helped the Negro cause.[13] Students of voting behavior warn, however, that it is risky to assume that public reaction on issues will automatically aid one or the other of the candidates. For Senator Goldwater to benefit from these opinions on the civil rights movements, Democrats would have to connect President Johnson with the bad effects of the movement, be aware of Senator Goldwater's views, conclude that Senator Goldwater's election would improve the situation, and then vote for Goldwater. This same study indicated that only a small number of the respondents were willing to change their vote because of the civil rights issue. And the election returns indicate that, outside the Deep South, any backlash vote for Goldwater was inconsequential compared to the frontlash vote of Republicans for Johnson.

[13] Survey conducted by *The New York Times*, September 21, 1964.

Though nearly every state was visited by one of the major candidates, certain key states received special attention in 1964. Goldwater hoped to win by combining his strength in the west and south with victories in certain key midwestern states. He was convinced that if he won certain large states in these three areas, he would do well in surrounding states. Thus, in the midwestern states he concentrated his efforts in Illinois, Indiana, and Ohio—making four major appearances in Illinois. Since the polls indicated that he had his greatest strength in the Deep South, Goldwater concentrated on the fringes—Florida, North Carolina, Tennessee, and Texas—making four major appearances in Texas, three in North Carolina. In the west, California got most of the attention—four major appearances by Goldwater and three by Miller. Though Goldwater did not spend a great deal of time in eastern states, he did make several major appearances in Pennsylvania and one in Madison Square Garden in New York City. Goldwater complemented this geographical emphasis with extensive use of television and radio—more than any other candidate for the Presidency in history. He taped his most successful campaign appearances to show at later dates. He appeared with General Eisenhower. He relied on television personalities such as Ronald Reagan to support his cause and used countless television spot advertisements.

Johnson and Humphrey gave most of their attention to eastern and midwestern states, and California. In the east, New Jersey, New York, and Pennsylvania, were visited often. In the midwest, Ohio, Michigan, Indiana, and Illinois, received a total of approximately 20 visits by either Johnson or Humphrey. California was visited by one or the other of the two candidates at least seven times. Texas and Florida in the south received considerable attention. The Democrats also relied on television—including some controversial advertisements which associated Goldwater with nuclear war—but not nearly to the same extent as the Republicans.

One of the most curious, and scurrilous, aspects of the campaign was the widespread circulation of paperback books attacking both candidates. President Johnson and other Democrats received the most attention by these writers. The top three best-sellers were A Texan Looks at Lyndon, by J. Evetts Haley; None Dare Call It Treason, by John A. Stormer; and A Choice Not An Echo, by Phyllis Schafly. It is estimated that nearly 10 million copies of these books were sold or distributed during the campaign. Sales of the two principal anti-Goldwater books—Barry Goldwater: Extremist on the Right, by Fred Cook, and Goldwater from A to Z, by Arthur Frommer—were puny by comparison (perhaps because they were more moderate in tone). In addition to these books, there were the usual number of books by the candidates themselves—now in paperback—and laudatory biographies of both candidates.[14]

---

[14] For example see Stephen Shadegg, Freedom Is His Flight Plan (New York: Fleet, 1962); Jack Bell, Mr. Conservative: Barry Goldwater (New York: Doubleday, 1962); Edwin McDowell, Barry Goldwater: Portrait of an Arizonan (Chicago: Regnery, 1964); William S. White, The Professional: Lyndon B. Johnson (New York: Houghton Mifflin 1964); Booth Mooney, The Lyndon Johnson Story (New York: Farrar, Straus, 1964); Michael Amrine, This Awesome Challenge: The Hundred Days of Lyndon B. Johnson (New York: Putnam, 1964). See also the two books by Goldwater, Why Not Victory? (New York: McGraw-Hill, 1962) and The Conscience of a Conservative (New York: Hillman, 1960).

Another "upside down" feature of the 1964 presidential campaign was the failure of the Republican candidate to receive the endorsement of a majority of newspapers. *Editor and Publisher* has been surveying newspaper endorsements of candidates since 1932. Until 1964 the Republican presidential candidate had a sizable majority of newspapers backing him—even Alfred M. Landon in 1936 received the support of 57 percent of the papers responding to the poll. In 1952 Eisenhower received endorsement from a record 67 percent of those responding. In 1960 Nixon was endorsed by 57 percent of the newspapers, a group with a combined circulation of 38 million. Those newspapers endorsing Kennedy in 1960 had a combined circulation of only 8.5 million.

In 1964 President Johnson not only received endorsement from more newspapers than did Goldwater (42.4 percent compared to 34.7 percent, and 22.9 percent independent), but the combined circulation of the pro-Johnson newspapers was nearly 27 million—three times that of the pro-Goldwater newspapers.[15] Many staunch Republican newspapers backed a Democrat for the first time (notably the *New York Herald Tribune*) or declined to support either candidate. Some southern newspapers endorsed a Republican for the first time. It was not altogether surprising that many eastern Republican newspapers endorsed Johnson. It was astounding, however, that so many midwestern and western papers endorsed the President or refused to endorse either candidate. For example, the conservative Republican *Omaha World-Herald* expressed disappointment in Goldwater in an editorial:

> As readers of this page are well aware, our own political convictions are much nearer to those of Barry Goldwater than those of Lyndon Johnson. . . .
> We think it fair to say that in this campaign neither candidate has revealed an impressive, inspiring statesmanship. Neither has shown the calm, poised, responsible judgment that the people wish for in their Commander-in-Chief. Among other things, Mr. Goldwater has seemed a little too contentious, a little too hasty in arguing about trivialities; Mr. Johnson has seemed a little too willing to exploit the Presidency for strictly campaign purposes, and too slow to anger in dealing with wrong-doers.
> Since we do not feel that either candidate thus far has shown outstanding talent for leadership, we do not feel either that we are warranted in urging our more than 250 thousand subscribers to vote for one or the other.[16]

Nebraska had given Nixon a majority of 62.1 percent of its vote in 1960—more than any other state. The disillusionment with Goldwater expressed in this editorial indicated that the state might well go Democratic in 1964—as it did.

There were many other indications that President Johnson was headed for a landslide victory. Not only did the national polls give him wide leads over his opponent but statewide polls also showed Johnson with wide leads in many Republican states. Only two statewide polls picked the wrong man—the Arizona poll had Johnson with a narrow 1 percent lead, with 9 percent undecided, and the South Dakota poll had Goldwater with a small

[15] *Editor and Publisher*, October 31, 1964, pp. 9–13.
[16] *Omaha Sunday Herald*, October 25, 1964.

lead. Sixteen other statewide polls picked the winner—though some had large errors in the margin of victory.

In summary, the Republican campaign in 1964 never really "got off the ground." It lacked confidence and a sense of central purpose compared to recent Republican campaigns. On occasion it was amateurish. The polls indicated that most American voters preferred Johnson and Humphrey. No amount of effort by Goldwater and Miller, the Republican campaign organization, or "assistant campaigners" such as Nixon and Scranton, seemed to change the voters' preferences.

Conversely, the Democratic campaign was characterized by what might be called "cautious smugness." The poll data told them not to worry— and advised them not to spend time engaging the Republican candidates. A lifetime of political experience told them not to be overconfident but to campaign hard up to election day.

ELECTION RESULTS

A record number of Americans voted on November 3, 1964—70,621,479 —though not a record percentage of eligible voters. An overwhelming majority of these voters cast their ballots as the polls indicated they would— for Lyndon B. Johnson and Hubert H. Humphrey. The Democratic candidates received the greatest total vote ever received (nearly 8 million more than Eisenhower-Nixon received in 1956), the greatest percentage of the total vote (61.06 percent), and the greatest plurality (nearly 5 million more than Roosevelt received in 1936). For the Republicans, it was their second lowest electoral count and percentage of the total popular vote in their history (1936 still retained the records for both).[17]

How many ways are there to demonstrate a landslide? If it is complete, the possibilities are limitless. The Democratic triumph in 1964 was about as complete as either party will ever enjoy during a period of relative national stability. I will select a number of means for demonstrating the completeness of the victory, introducing the caveat that in some instances the analysis is based on incomplete returns.

Table 20.5 presents comparative state figures for 1960 and 1964. The advantage in choosing 1960 for comparison is that it is a good year for determining the potential vote of a candidate who is strongly identified with the Republican party. Though Richard M. Nixon undoubtedly picked up votes because of Kennedy's Catholicism,[18] still it can be argued that his total—much more so than Eisenhower's in 1952 and 1956—represents what a Republican candidate may expect in an election if he conducts a well-financed and efficiently organized campaign which capitalizes on his ad-

---

[17] This does not include 1912 when the party was split between Roosevelt and Taft.

[18] The exact number cannot be determined but the Survey Research Center at the University of Michigan estimates that Kennedy lost about 2.2 percent nationally because of his religion (balancing losses of Protestant Democrats against gains from Catholics). See Philip E. Converse et al., "Stability and Change in 1960: A Reinstating Election," American Political Science Review, 55 (June 1964), pp. 269–280.

vantages and his opponent's disadvantages. In a day in which a majority of Americans still identify with the Democratic party, a Republican candidate who is identified by the voters as a Republican could not expect to do much better than Nixon did in 1960. His total, therefore, represents a reasonable potential for a Republican candidate.

As Table 20.5 indicates, Goldwater ran behind Nixon in all states outside the south, and behind him in seven of the thirteen southern states. The range is from 2.6 percent behind Nixon in Florida to 28.8 percent behind him in Hawaii. On an average, Goldwater ran 17.3 percent behind Nixon in eastern states, 14.1 percent behind in midwestern states, and 12.3 percent behind him in western states. In the south, Goldwater ran 6.1 percent ahead of Nixon when Alabama and Mississippi are included, 1 percent behind if they are excluded (Johnson was not on the ballot in Alabama. Nationally, Goldwater trailed Nixon by an average of 9.2 percent per state. Johnson ran ahead of Kennedy by roughly the same percentages as Goldwater ran behind Nixon in all regions but the south. When Alabama is excluded from analysis, Johnson ran, on the average, 1.4 percent ahead of Kennedy in the south.

Until 1964, Republicans had reason to be encouraged by presidential election returns. After so many years of "drought," Eisenhower won thirty-eight states in 1952 and forty-two in 1956; Nixon won twenty-six in 1960.

TABLE 20.5 COMPARISON OF 1960 AND 1964 PRESIDENTIAL ELECTION, PERCENTAGES BY REGION

Region[a] and State[b]	1960		1964		CHANGE	
	Democrat	Republican	Democrat	Republican	Democrat	Republican
East						
Conn.	53.7	46.3	67.8	32.1	+14.1	—14.2
Del.	50.6	49.0	60.9	38.8	+10.3	—10.2
Me.	43.0	57.0	68.8	31.2	+25.8	—25.8
Md.	53.6	46.4	65.5	34.5	+21.9	—21.9
Mass.	60.2	39.6	76.2	23.4	+16.0	—16.2
N. H.	46.6	53.4	63.6	36.4	+17.0	—17.0
N. J.	50.0	49.2	65.6	33.9	+15.6	—15.3
N. Y.	52.5	47.3	68.6	31.3	+16.1	—16.0
Pa.	51.1	48.7	65.0	34.7	+13.9	—14.0
R. I.	63.6	36.4	80.9	19.1	+17.3	—17.3
Vt.	41.4	58.6	66.3	33.7	+24.9	—24.9
W. Va.	52.7	47.3	67.9	32.1	+15.2	—15.2
Average Change					+17.4	—17.3
South						
Ala.	56.9	41.8	—	69.5	—	+27.7
Ark.	50.2	43.1	56.1	43.4	+ 5.9	+ .3
Fla.	48.5	51.5	51.1	48.9	+ 2.6	— 2.6
Ga.	62.6	37.4	45.9	54.1	—16.7	+16.7
Ky.	46.4	53.6	64.0	35.7	+17.6	—17.9
La.	50.4	28.6	43.2	56.8	+ 4.1	— 4.1
N. C.	52.1	47.9	56.2	43.8	— 7.2	+28.2
Miss.	36.3	24.7	12.9	87.1	—23.4	+62.4
Okla.	41.0	59.0	55.7	44.3	+14.7	—14.7
S. C.	51.2	48.8	41.1	58.9	—10.1	+10.1
Tenn.	45.8	52.9	55.5	44.5	+ 9.7	— 8.4
Texas	50.5	48.5	63.3	36.5	+12.8	—12.0
Va.	47.0	52.4	53.5	46.2	+ 6.5	— 6.2
Average Change					+ 1.4	+ 6.1

(Continued on next page)

TABLE 20.5 1960 AND 1964 PRESIDENTIAL ELECTION *(CONTINUED)*

REGION[a] AND STATE[b]	1960		1964		CHANGE	
	Democrat	Republican	Democrat	Republican	Democrat	Republican
Midwest						
Ill.	50.0	49.8	59.5	40.5	+ 9.5	− 9.3
Ind.	44.6	55.0	56.0	43.6	+11.4	−11.4
Ia.	43.2	56.7	61.9	37.9	+18.7	−18.7
Kan.	39.1	60.4	54.1	45.1	+15.0	−15.3
Mich.	50.9	48.8	66.7	33.1	+15.8	−15.7
Minn.	50.6	49.2	63.8	36.0	+13.2	−13.2
Mo.	50.3	49.7	64.0	36.0	+13.7	−13.7
Neb.	37.9	62.1	52.6	47.4	+14.7	−14.7
N. D.	44.5	55.4	58.0	41.9	+13.5	−13.5
Ohio	46.7	53.3	62.9	37.1	+16.2	−16.2
S. D.	41.8	58.2	55.6	44.4	+13.8	−13.8
Wis.	48.0	51.8	62.1	37.7	+14.1	−14.1
Average Change					+14.1	−14.1
West						
Alaska	49.1	50.9	65.9	34.1	+16.8	−16.8
Ariz.	44.4	55.5	49.5	50.4	+ 5.1	− 5.1
Calif.	49.6	50.1	59.2	40.8	+ 9.6	− 9.3
Colo.	44.9	54.9	61.6	38.4	+16.7	−16.5
Hawaii	50.0	50.0	78.8	21.2	+28.8	−28.8
Idaho	46.2	53.8	50.9	49.1	+ 4.7	− 4.7
Mont.	48.6	51.1	58.9	40.6	+10.3	−10.5
Nev.	51.2	48.8	58.6	41.4	+ 7.4	− 7.4
N. M.	50.2	49.4	59.2	40.2	+ 9.0	− 9.2
Ore.	47.4	52.6	63.9	36.1	+16.5	−16.5
Utah	45.2	54.8	54.9	45.1	+ 9.7	− 9.7
Wash.	48.3	50.7	62.0	37.4	+13.7	−13.3
Wyo.	45.0	55.0	56.5	43.5	+11.5	−11.5
Average Change					+12.3	−12.3

[a] The regions are those relied on by the Congressional Quarterly Service.

[b] District of Columbia not included because residents did not vote in 1960. Johnson received 85.5 percent in 1964.

SOURCE: Associated Press final tabulations as reported in the *Arizona Daily Star,* Tucson, Arizona, December 13, 1964.

In fact, *twenty-five states* supported the Republican candidate in all three elections, 1952–1960. Clearly, the Republican party had proved itself to be highly competitive in the race for the Presidency. In 1964 *Senator Goldwater won only one of these twenty-five states* that had established a pattern of voting Republican. He won his own state of Arizona by a narrow margin— the smallest by a Republican since 1948.

Table 20.6 breaks down the regional figures to identify differences among subregions. Goldwater's poorest showing is in New England—an average per state of 19.2 percent behind Nixon—but his performance in all but the Deep South is uniformly bad. In seven of the ten subregions, he ran an average per state of greater than 13 percent behind Nixon.

Since Goldwater ran his best race in the south, it is worthwhile to spend some time on that region. Certain observations are necessary in order to put his performance there in perspective. First, 1964 did not mark the first invasion of a Republican candidate into that region. Hoover carried seven south-

TABLE 20.6   REGIONAL AND SUBREGIONAL BREAKDOWN OF AVERAGE REPUB-
LICAN CHANGE IN STATEWIDE PRESIDENTIAL VOTE, 1960–1964

REGION AND SUBREGION	AVERAGE REPUBLICAN CHANGE PER STATE, 1960–1964	
East	—17.3	
New England (Conn., Me., Mass., N.H., R. I., Vt.)		—19.2
Middle Atlantic (N. J., N. Y., Pa.)		—15.1
East Border (Del., Md., W. Va.)		—15.8
Midwest	—14.1	
Central (Ill., Ind., Ia., Mich., Mo., Ohio, Wis.)		—14.0
Plains States (Kan., Neb., N. D., S. D.)		—14.3
South	+ 6.1	
West Border (Okla., Tex.)		—13.4
South Border (Fla., Ky., N. C., Tenn., Va.)		— 7.8
Deep South (Ala., Ark., Ga., La., Miss., S. C.)		+24.2
West	—12.3	
Pacific (Alaska, Calif., Hawaii, Ore., Wash.)		—16.9
Mountain (Ariz., Colo., Ida., Mont., Nev., N. M., Utah, Wyo.)		— 9.3

SOURCE: Derived from election tabulations.

ern states in 1928 (eight-five electoral votes); Eisenhower carried five in 1952 (sixty-five electoral votes) and seven in 1956 (eighty-five electoral votes); and Nixon carried five in 1960 (fifty-one electoral votes). In 1964 Goldwater carried five for a total of forty-seven electoral votes—four fewer electoral votes than Nixon and nearly forty fewer than Hoover in 1928 and Eisenhower in 1956. Only one of the states Goldwater won had previously been won in this century by a Republican—Louisiana. Thus, his victory in the Deep South states was expensive indeed since other southern border states were lost and all traditionally Republican northern states as well.

Second, those states Goldwater won are usually labeled solid Democratic states. It is a fact, however, that with the exception of Georgia, these states have been flirting with alternatives to the Democratic party in presidential elections since 1948. Until 1964 the Republicans had not offered a candidate who was to their liking on the civil rights issue. Goldwater had voted against the 1964 Civil Rights Act, however, and thus became a favorite in the Deep South. If one examines each state's electoral record, 1948–1964, it is possible to conclude that the Deep South was prepared to defect—not a bulwark of the Democratic party. In 1948 Alabama gave its electoral votes to Strom Thurmond, the Dixiecrat presidential candidate; in 1956 Eisenhower got nearly 40 percent of the vote; in 1960, six of Alabama's eleven electors voted for Senator Harry Byrd for President. Louisiana went for Thurmond in 1948, gave Eisenhower over 47 percent of its vote in 1952, 53.3 percent of its popular vote and all of its electoral vote in 1956, and gave an unpledged States Rights slate of electors 21 percent of its vote in 1960 (Kennedy got 50.4 percent). Mississippi went overwhelmingly for Thurmond in 1948 87.3 percent, Goldwater got 87.1 percent in 1964), gave Eisenhower nearly 40 percent of the vote in 1952, gave an unpledged States Rights group of electors over 17 percent in 1956, and elected an unpledged slate of electors that voted for Senator Byrd in 1960. South Carolina has followed a similar pattern:

Thurmond won in 1948 (over 72 percent of the vote), Eisenhower got over 49 percent in 1952, an unpledged slate of electors got nearly 30 percent in 1956, and Nixon got nearly 49 percent of the vote in 1960. This record in presidential elections is hardly one which can be described as solidly Democratic. Since 1948 these states have seemed to be ready to accept any other alternative which was attractive to them.

Who voted for President Johnson? Outside of the south, practically everyone did. Johnson's majority in the east approached 70 percent, in the midwest 62 percent and in the west, 60 percent. Thus, outside the south, Johnson had nearly a 64 percent majority and nearly a 63 percent majority if all but the five Deep South states that Goldwater won are included.

President Johnson garnered impressive support from groups that normally vote Republican and got increased support from those that normally vote Democratic. Outside the south, he won large majorities in the central city, the suburbs, and the farm. In some cases, his increase over Kennedy in usually Republican suburban areas approached 20 percent. Negroes were almost unanimous in their support of the President and their vote in both the north and the south is becoming increasingly significant in presidential elections due to greater voter registration and turnout.[19] Among ethnic groups, the Jews voted about 9–1 for Johnson—other groups gave him overwhelming support but, in some cases, less than they gave Kennedy. Johnson increased Democratic percentages in all income groups—including the high-income group.[20]

Table 20.7 presents the results of the Gallup Poll estimates of group voting in 1964. As is indicated, President Johnson received a greater percentage of the vote than did Kennedy in *twenty-three* of the *twenty-four* groups listed. Only the Catholics gave Johnson less support than they gave Kennedy. The range of increase is from a 1 percent gain in the south to a 26 percent gain among "nonwhite" voters. An amazingly high percentage of Republicans crossed over to vote for Johnson—an increase of 15 percent over 1960. Thus, with the exception of the five Deep South states won by Goldwater, Johnson's victory was truly national.

Lyndon B. Johnson won overwhelmingly throughout most of the nation, and so did his party. In races for the Senate, the Republican party had its best opportunity in years to gain seats. The 1958 election had been disastrous for the Republican party in the U.S. Senate. Before that election there were forty-seven Republicans and forty-nine Democrats and the Senate Republican party was able to act with strength. After the election there were thirty-four Republicans and sixty-six Democrats—a record number of Republicans had been defeated. Many of the Democrats elected in 1958 won in normally Republican states. Thus, the Republican national organization had anxiously awaited 1964 in order that it might recoup the losses sustained in 1958. The advantage seemed clearly on its side—of the thirty-five Senate

[19] See *The New York Times*, August 23, 1964, where Claude Sitton reports on increased registration of Negroes in the South—well over one-half million increase between 1960 and 1964.

[20] For a summary of voting percentages among principal groups see "The Story of the '64 Ellection," *U.S. News and World Report*, November 16, 1964, pp. 38–45.

TABLE 20.7   GROUP VOTING FOR DEMOCRATIC PRESIDENTIAL CANDIDATE, 1960 AND 1964

GROUP	1960	1964	CHANGE
Men	52	60	+ 8
Women	49	62	+13
White	49	59	+10
Nonwhite	68	94	+26
College	39	52	+13
High school	52	62	+10
Grade school	55	66	+11
Professional and business	42	54	+12
White collar	48	57	+ 9
Manual	60	71	+11
Farmers	48	53	+ 5
21–29 years	54	64	+10
30–49 years	54	63	+ 9
50 years+	46	59	+13
Catholic	78	76	− 2
Protestant	38	55	+17
Republicans	5	20	+15
Democrats	84	87	+ 3
Independents	43	56	+13
East	53	68	+15
Midwest	48	61	+13
South	51	52	+ 1
West	49	60	+11

SOURCE: Gallup Poll results as reported in *Congressional Quarterly Weekly Report,* December 25, 1964, p. 2846.

seats up for reelection, twenty-six were held by Democrats, and many of these Democrats (Hartke, Indiana; Muskie, Maine; Hart, Michigan; Moss, Utah; McGee, Wyoming; Young, Ohio) were among those who had won Republican seats in 1958.

Despite the odds, the Democratic "Class of 1958," which was supposed to be so vulnerable, was returned to the Senate en masse in 1964. Only in California did the Republicans gain a seat. On the other hand, two Republicans who had won in 1958 were defeated—Keating, New York, and Beall, Maryland—as was Mechen in New Mexico (appointed to the seat on the death of Senator Dennis Chavez). The Republicans who did win had very slim margins (an average majority of 53 percent compared to an average majority of 61 percent for the Democrats who won). Thus, an opportunity passed, and the Democrats are assured of controlling the Senate at least until 1970.

The major bright spot in the election for the Republican party came in gubernatorial elections. There was actually a gain of one seat for Republicans and several Republican candidates won reelection despite a Democratic landslide in the state. The most impressive victories were those gained by John A. Volpe in Massachusetts, George W. Romney in Michigan, John H. Chafee in Rhode Island (bucking an 81 percent Johnson majority), and Daniel J. Evans in Washington. These Republican governors will no doubt exert more influence in the Party than they have in the immediate past.

For the first time since 1948 the Democratic candidate "led" his ticket and the Republican candidate "trailed" his ticket. As Table 20.8 indicates, Goldwater ran behind twenty-seven of the thirty-four Republican candidates for Senate seats, and behind fifteen of the twenty-five candidates for governor. Republican Senate candidates ran an average of 4.0 percent ahead of Goldwater in all races and an average of 5.5 percent ahead of him in races outside the south. As shown in Table 20.8 the range of difference was between + 31.6 percent (Hiram L. Fong, Hawaii) and − 23.6 percent (Richard A. May running against Senator Harry Byrd, Virginia).

The Republican candidates for governor ran even further ahead of Goldwater on the average. In all races they ran an average of 5.8 percent ahead and an average of 7.8 percent ahead in races outside the south. The range was from the incredible performance of John H. Chafee of Rhode Island—42.2 percent ahead of Goldwater—to the poor showing of Evan Hultman in Iowa—11.6 percent behind Goldwater, who also ran poorly (38.1 percent of the two-party vote).

In the three previous presidential elections, the results had been just the opposite. Eisenhower and Nixon led their tickets. In 1960, Nixon ran ahead of twenty-one of twenty-seven Republican senatorial candidates (an average of 3.9 percent) and ahead of nineteen of twenty-seven Republican candidates for governor (an average of 3.4 percent).

The 1964 election was an unfortunate event for Republicans in other races as well. Supreme efforts had been made by the Republican party in 1960 and 1962 to win back seats in the House of Representatives lost in the 1958 debacle (when forty-seven fewer Republicans returned to the House). Twenty seats were gained in 1960, and though only two seats were gained in 1962, it was the second time since 1920 that Republicans gained House seats in two consecutive elections. It was hoped that 1964 would continue the trend toward reestablishing a strong opposition party in the House. On November 3, 1964, however, only 140 Republicans were elected to the House—the fewest since 1936, when 89 were elected. Most of the gains for the Democrats were in those regions where Johnson swamped Goldwater— sixteen seats gained in the east, and nineteen in the midwest.

The majority of those Republicans who were defeated were conservatives—many closely identified with Goldwater. On June 17, 1964, fifty-three Republican congressmen issued a statement that the nomination of Senator Goldwater would result "in substantial increases in Republican membership in both houses of Congress." Of these, seventeen were defeated; three retired, but their districts were won by Democrats; one was defeated in his attempt at winning a statewide office; twenty-six had reduced margins compared to 1962. Only six had increased margins over 1962.[21]

A number of the Republicans defeated in 1964 had considerable seniority in the House. For example, Ben. F. Jensen, Iowa, was the ranking Republican on the Committee on Appropriations; August E. Johansen, Michigan, ranking Republican on the Committee on Un-American Activities; J. Edgar Chenoweth, Colorado, third ranking Republican on the Committee on Science and Astronautics; Katharine St. George, New York, second ranking Repub-

21 Congressional Quarterly Weekly Report. November, 6, 1964, p. 2643.

TABLE 20.8 PERCENTAGE OF TWO-PARTY VOTE RECEIVED BY GOLDWATER AND BY REPUBLICAN CANDIDATES FOR SENATOR AND GOVERNOR, 1964

STATE	GOLD-WATER PERCENT	REPUBLICAN CAND. FOR SENATE PERCENT	DIFFERENCE	REPUBLICAN CAND. FOR GOV. PERCENT	DIFFERENCE
Ariz.	50.3	51.3	+ 1.0	46.6	— 3.7
Ark.	43.4	—	—	42.6	— .8
Calif.	40.2	51.3	+11.1	—	—
Conn.	32.2	35.3	+ 3.1	—	—
Del.	38.9	51.7	+12.8	48.6	+ 9.7
Fla.	49.0	36.3	—12.7	42.4	— 6.6
Hawaii	21.3	52.9	+31.6	—	—
Ill.	40.5	—	—	48.1	+ 7.6
Ind.	43.9	45.6	+ 1.7	45.9	+ 2.0
Iowa	38.1	—	—	26.5	—11.6
Kans.	45.6	—	—	52.1	+ 6.5
Me.	31.2	33.4	+ 2.2	—	—
Md.	33.6	36.7	+ 3.1	—	—
Mass.	23.6	25.6	+ 2.0	50.5	+26.9
Mich.	32.3	35.6	+ 3.3	56.3	+24.0
Minn.	36.0	39.8	+ 3.8	—	—
Mo.	35.4	32.5	— 2.9	38.1	+ 2.7
Mont.	40.7	35.5	— 5.2	51.3	+10.6
Nebr.	47.2	61.1	+13.9	40.1	— 7.1
Nev.	41.6	49.9	+ 8.3	—	—
N. H.	36.1	—	—	33.2	— 2.9
N. J.	34.0	37.5	+ 3.5	—	—
N. M.	40.9	45.3	+ 4.4	39.9	— 1.0
N. Y.	31.8	44.0	+12.2	—	—
N. D.	42.0	42.7	+ .7	44.3	+ 2.3
N. C.	44.0	—	—	43.8	— .2
Ohio	37.2	49.8	+12.6	—	—
Okla.	44.2	48.9	+ 4.7	—	—
Pa.	35.1	50.6	+15.5	—	—
R. I.	19.1	17.1	— 2.0	61.3	+42.2
S. D.	44.3	—	—	51.5	+ 7.2
Tenn.[b]	44.5	46.4	+ 1.9	—	—
	—	47.6	+ 3.1	—	—
Texas	37.1	43.5	+ 6.4	26.2	—10.9
Utah	45.3	42.6	— 2.7	43.0	— 2.3
Vt.	33.7	53.3	+19.6	35.2	+ 1.5
Va.	46.3	22.7	—23.6	—	—
Wash.	37.6	27.8	— 9.8	60.1	+22.5
W. Va.	32.3	32.4	+ .1	45.3	+13.0
Wisc.	37.9	46.6	+ 8.7	50.7	+12.8
Wyo.	43.6	46.3	+ 2.7	—	—

[a] Share of major party vote.

[b] Two Senate races in Tennessee in 1964.

SOURCE: *Congressional Quarterly Weekly Report*, November 6, 1964, p. 2628.

lican on the Committee on Rules; R. Walter Riehlman, New York, ranking Republican on the Committee on Government Operations; George Meader, Michigan, second ranking Republican on the Committee on Government Operations; Paul F. Schenck, Ohio, ranking Republican on the Committee on House Administration and third ranking Republican on the Committee on Interstate and Foreign Commerce; J. Ernest Wharton, New York, second ranking Republican on the Committee on Interior and Insular Affairs; William K. Van Pelt, Wisconsin, second ranking Republican on the Committee on Merchant Marine and Fisheries.

Other Republicans won despite tremendous majorities built up by President Johnson in their districts. The most notable of these victories was that of John V. Lindsay of New York, who garnered over 70 percent of the vote in 1964 despite Johnson's huge majority in Lindsay's Manhattan district.

Goldwater's coattails in the Deep South carried in seven new Republican congressmen—five from Alabama and one each from Georgia and Mississippi. As was true at the presidential level, however, victory in the southern congressional districts proved costly in the rest of the nation.

The thoroughness of the Republican defeat in House races is not told merely in the number of seats gained and lost. An analysis of election returns available at this writing shows that most Republicans who managed to survive did so with reduced margins—101 Republican districts were won by smaller margins than in 1962, 25 with increased margins. The opposite was the case for Democratic districts—148 had increased margins over 1962, 26 had reduced margins.

Table 20.9 indicates the problem that Republicans will face in 1966 as a result of the 1964 defeat. There were contests (that is, Republican *and* Democratic candidates in *both* 1962 and 1964 in 358 congressional districts. In 1962 eighty-seven Republican candidates in these contested districts won by 60 percent or more of the vote. In 1964 only thirty-six had winning margins of 60 percent or more. In 1962 ninety-five Democrats in contested districts won by 60 percent or more—only eight more than the Republicans

TABLE 20.9   REPUBLICAN AND DEMOCRATIC CONGRESSIONAL DISTRICTS WON BY 60 PERCENT OR MORE, 1962 AND 1964[a]

Winning Margins	1962		1964		CHANGE	
	Gop Dists.	Demo Dists.	Gop Dists.	Demo Dists.	Gop Dists.	Demo Dists.
60–69.9%	77	54	34	72	—43	+18
70–79.9	10	37	2	47	— 8	+10
80–100	—	4	—	20	—	+16
Totals	87	95	36	139	—51	+44

[a] Only those 358 districts which were contested by both parties in both 1962 and 1964 are examined.

SOURCE: Derived from data in *Congressional Quarterly Weekly Report,* November 13, 1964, pp. 2701–2706.

(though forty-one of these were won by 70 percent or more compared to ten for Republicans). In 1964 Democrats won *139* contested districts by greater than 60 percent—*103* more than the Republicans. *Sixty-seven* of these 139 were won by 70 percent or more, compared to only 2 for the Republicans. Thus, not only did Democrats defeat Republicans in 1964, but many Democratic seats that were marginal are now safe and many Republican seats that were safe are now marginal. Such are the repercussions of a landslide victory.

The Democratic sweep also reached into state legislative races. In 1962 Republicans increased their numbers in state legislatures by 50 Senate and 101 House seats. In 1964 over 100 Republican Senate seats and over 450 Republican House seats were lost. Again the principal losses were in the east and midwest—213 House and Senate seats lost in eastern states, none gained; 277 lost in midwestern states, 1 gained. Losses were less severe in the south and west and were offset in part by small gains. Both houses were lost to the Democrats in Indiana, Iowa, Maine, Michigan, New York, and Utah. Democrats won the lower house from Republicans in Colorado, Illinois, Montana, North Dakota, Pennsylvania, Wisconsin, and Wyoming. The lower house in normally Republican Iowa is now under Democratic control by the incredible margin of 101–23.[22]

The loss of so many state legislative seats by Republicans will doubtless have repercussions for some time. With continued pressure to reapportion state legislative and congressional districts, the Democrats are in a good position to ensure their continued control of legislative bodies. Certainly one may expect that a Democratic state legislature will do what it can to favor that party in drawing district lines. In 1965 Democrats will control both houses of the legislatures in thirty-two states—Republicans will control the legislature of six states (the rest are divided in control or are nonpartisan).

Normally, it is possible in a general election for both parties to glean some satisfaction from the results. There are so many contests that even the minority party is bound to win enough to be encouraged by the results. In 1964, however, aside from certain gubernatorial results, there was little or nothing to encourage Republicans. The Democratic victory was complete. In one sense, it might be said that the 1964 victory was even more impressive than the 1936 victory. In 1936 the nation was staggering under a Great Depression for which the Republicans were held responsible. In 1964 there was no similar crisis—the Democratic candidates across the nation simply administered a thorough "shellacking" to Republican candidates.

CONCLUDING OBSERVATIONS

Until November 3 the presidential election belonged to the candidates, their supporters, and the voters. They all performed their functions as expected. The event now belongs to the scholar. It is too early to offer the final judgment on the impact of this important event for the American political system but scholars must begin to perform their expected function of analysis. This essay provides, in an initial analytical description, a number of observations that should serve to stimulate scholarly discussion.

First, it seems clear that when there is a contest for the nomination a presidential candidate who relies on an inside strategy to get the nomination will have difficulty winning in November. It is quite possible that a

[22] *Congressional Quarterly Weekly Report,* November 20, 1964, p. 2709.

future candidate may again win the nomination as Goldwater did in 1964, but at some point a winning candidate must demonstrate his popularity. An outside strategy is more than just "democratic"; it is a test of a candidate not unlike the general election itself. While the nomination can be won by the inside strategy, the election cannot. Presidential elections are very much "public" events—a candidate who wins the nomination despite his unpopularity with the voters has indeed won a Pyrrhic victory.

Second, the Republican national convention chose a candidate who was not acceptable to several important party leaders. The party was never able to achieve unity following the convention. If the party wants to win the Presidency, it appears that a candidate who is highly controversial within the party should not be selected. This generalization is particularly applicable to the minority party. A minority party victory can only be fashioned if the party is unified enough to take advantage of majority party defections. In 1964 the Republicans courted calamitous defeat by selecting a candidate who divided the party. It is possible that Governor Rockefeller's nomination likewise would have resulted in a serious defeat because of his unacceptability to the Goldwater faction.

The selection of a candidate who divides rather than unifies the party and is defeated by a large margin will likely have a continuing effect on the party. In 1964 there was an intense postelection effort to oust national party chairman Dean Burch. Burch was Goldwater's choice for chairman when he became the nominee of the party. He became the symbol of Goldwater's continued control of the party apparatus and therefore the moderates insisted on his resignation. Other party struggles are guaranteed because of the manner by which Goldwater won the nomination. His organization was successful in capturing many regular state and local party units and creating party units where none existed. Wresting control from the conservative group will be difficult in all sections of the country but virtually impossible in parts of the south where conservatives have created a Republican party organization for the first time in decades. No rival moderate group exists in many southern states.

Third, one is led to observe that regardless of what the minority party does at its national conventional, it faces enormous odds in winning control of the national government. There are long periods of one-party dominance in American political history. The Republican party was dominant between 1860 and 1930; the Democratic party since that time. Being the dominant party means more than winning elections. It means that most American voters tend to identify with the dominant party.[23] Thus, the Republican party will win national elections only when enough voters who identify with the Democratic party vote for Republican candidates. President Eisenhower was highly successful in convincing Democrats to vote for him. But he was a very special sort of candidate. Eisenhower was not identified as a partisan Republican by many Democrats and therefore they had little trouble rationalizing their vote. In 1960, Republicans offered a man who was very much identified with the Republican party—Richard M. Nixon. Still, through hard campaigning, good organization, and certain disadvantages of his opponent

[23] For details on the extent of Democratic party preference among voters see Angus Campbell et al., The American Voter (New York: John Wiley & Sons, Inc., 1960).

(notably religion), Nixon came close to victory. In 1964, Republicans selected a man unacceptable not only to Democrats but also to many Republicans. The Democrats, on the other hand, nominated a man with whom many Republicans could identify.

In short, the Republican party requires certain special conditions to win and even when it does win the White House, it will likely face a Democratic Congress. Confronting this prospect over a period of years, Republicans develop a variety of nostrums for becoming the majority. The moderates emphasize that most Americans are moderates and an appeal to them will result in victory. The conservatives claim that most Americans are conservative and if the Republican party offers a candidate and a program that reflect this viewpoint, it will once more be the majority party. A number of liberals support their interpretation of American majority sentiment on the same basis. In 1964 the conservative nostrum was tested and the result was disastrous. The fact is that none of these plans will actually result in the Republican party becoming the dominant party in one election. A dominant or majority party is preferred by a majority of voters not just on election day but over a long period of time. Aside from a jolting calamitous event (such as the Civil War or the Great Depression) only national and state party organizations, which are integrated enough to develop unified goals and efficient enough to achieve these goals, can tip the balance toward the Republican party. No such organization presently exists.

Fourth, while voters have rejected the Republicans, they have clearly given the Democrats control of the national government. There can be no ambiguity following the 1964 election as to which political party is responsible for national policy making. Some observers suggest that such an overwhelming victory results in internal party division and point to President Roosevelt's experience following the 1936 election as evidence. Students have an opportunity in the next two years to examine how President Johnson uses his great victory and the office of the Presidency to avoid internal party conflict in enacting his program. Comparisons can and should be made with the Roosevelt Administration.

The Democratic majorities in Congress will also require continuing analysis. In contrast to 1937–1938, the House and Senate Democratic parties are quite different groups. Reapportionment, Republican victories in the south, greater seniority of northern and western Democrats than in 1937, these and other developments have changed the "face" of the congressional Democratic parties. Further, President Johnson, unlike President Roosevelt, had his political training in Congress. He deals in the type of political currency familiar to legislators. He also led his ticket in 1964 and can argue that many members of Congress owe their allegiance to him. It may well be that executive-legislative relations in the Johnson Administration will be characteristic of what reformers have called responsible party government—where the responsibility for policy making is definite and those with this responsibility have the tools for implementing their solutions to public problems.[24]

[24] See Committee on Political Parties, American Political Science Association, "Toward A More Responsible Two-Party System," *American Political Science Review,* 44 (September 1950), Supplement; James M. Burns, *The Deadlock of Democracy: Four Party Politics in America* (New York: Prentice-Hall, Inc., 1964); E. E. Schattschneider, *Party Government* (New York: Holt, Rinehart and Winston, Inc., 1942).

Fifth, the success of public opinion polling, particularly in the last two presidential elections, has been impressive. Not only have the polls predicted the outcome with amazing accuracy but they have reflected changes in opinion during the course of the campaign. Though there is an increasing literature on polling, their greater use suggests that students need to inquire further into the effect of these surveys on campaigning and voting behavior. It was evident that poll data were important in determining the strategies of both candidates in 1964—particularly so for the Democrats.

Sixth, the significance of this election for the south will be pondered for a number of years. Despite his support of the most sweeping civil rights legislation in history, the majority of southern states gave their electoral votes to President Johnson. As more Negroes are registered to vote and industrial development continues at an ever increasing rate in most southern states, these states will continue to be "nationalized"; that is, less distinct from states in other regions. Other southern states, in particular Alabama and Mississippi, demonstrated in 1964 that they are increasingly isolated from national trends. These two states gave Senator Goldwater fantastic majorities. If Vermont, or South Dakota, or Kansas, had given Goldwater such majorities, it would have been unusual, but conceivable. Alabama and Mississippi, however, have had no Republican tradition. In 1964, they were demonstrating their virtually unanimous opposition to national policy making in the area of civil rights. Georgia, Louisiana, and South Carolina also gave their votes to Goldwater but the margins were considerably smaller. What the future holds for these states is not certain but if there were any doubt before the election, it should be clear now that, like the "cheese" in the familiar children's game, Alabama and Mississippi now "stand alone."

I have subtitled this essay, "Further Adventures in Wonderland." The 1964 presidential election is reminiscent of Alice's experiences. It was "upside down," "curious," a "mad tea party" often characterized by unbelievable dialogue. As with all analogies, however, there are important differences as well as similarities. Alice finally awakened to discover that her adventures were the result of a "curious dream." And Lewis Carroll tells us that Alice then "got up and ran off, thinking while she ran, as well she might, what a wonderful dream it had been." Dreams do not have to have meaning—they can be fanciful and soon forgotten.

Though many may have convinced themselves that the 1964 presidential election was a dream—or perhaps a nightmare—it did, in fact, take place. All of those improbable things did happen—roughly in the sequence described in this essay—and must now be analyzed by students of politics—not dreamers.

21

The Kennedy-Nixon
Debates: A Survey
of Surveys*

ELIHU KATZ
JACOB J. FELDMAN

To date we have been able to locate thirty-one independent studies of public
response to the Kennedy-Nixon TV debates and there may well be more.[1]
Although relatively little advance notice was given, the speedy response of
opinion pollsters, market research organizations, journalism professors and
a variety of other individuals and organizations adds up to what is almost certainly the largest number of studies of a single public event in the history of
opinion and attitude research. Table 21.1 is an inventory of the main features
of the design of these studies.

In this article, we propose to compare and contrast the various studies
and, hopefully, to arrive at some general conclusions concerning the impact
of the debates. The place to begin, of course, is with the audience. Who
heard the debates? Who was available to be influenced?

THE AUDIENCE

Most of the studies have an answer to this question, at least in terms
of the over-all total of viewers and listeners. As Table 21.2 demonstrates, the

* Reprinted by permission from *Studies in Public Communication*, No. 4 (Autumn
1962), pp. 127–163.

[1] This is an abridged version of a chapter prepared for *The Great Debates*, Sidney
Kraus, ed., Bloomington: Indiana University Press, 1962. . . .

TABLE 21.1 THE STUDIES

NO.	NAME AND LOCALE	SIZE OF SAMPLE	TIMING[a]
1[b]	Arbitron (National)	1400	Coincident
2	R. H. Bruskin (National)	2500	V_2
3	California Poll (State of California)	Varied from 619 to 1270 (A_2)	P_2 (twice), $A_2 D_2$
4	Canadian Broadcasting Corporation (7 Major Canadian cities)	4800	D_2
5	Richard F. Carter, Institute for Communication Research, Stanford (4 cities near Stanford, California)	Approximately 100	$A_1-A_2-D_2$
6	Creative Research Associates (Chicago)	996[c]	B_1-B_2, C_1-C_2, D_1-D_2
7	Paul J. Deutschmann, Communication Research Center, Michigan State University (Lansing and East Lansing, Michigan)	159	$P_1-A_1-A_2$
8[b]	Alex Edelstein, School of Communication, University of Washington (Seattle, Washington) (campus)	407	V_1
9A	Gallup Poll (National)	Varied from about 1500 to 8000	P_2, A_1, A_2, D_2
9B	Gallup Poll (Hopewell, N.J.)	60 in televote Sample, 65 interview only	A (coincident)
10[b]	Louis Harris and Associates		
11	Iowa Poll (State of Iowa)		P_2, B_2, V_1
12[b]	Noel W. Keys and Alan Whiteleather, University of North Carolina (Chapel Hill, N.C.) (campus)	28 (students)	V_1 (kinescope of 3rd debate)
13[b]	Frederick Koenig and Carol Thometz, Southern Methodist University (Dallas, Texas) (campus)	223 (students)	$A_1-A_2-B_2$
14	John F. Kraft, Inc. (National)	2200[d] interviews at P_2; about 300 at A_2; 300 at B_2; 500 at C_2; 1000 at D_2	$P_2 \rightleftarrows {A_2 \atop B_2 \atop C_2} \rightleftarrows D_2$
15	Sidney Kraus and Raymond G. Smith, Indiana University (Indianapolis)	142	$A_1-A_2-D_1-D_2-V_2$
16	Gladys E. Lang and Kurt Lang, Queens College (New York City and college campus)	95	$A_1-A_2-D_2$
17	Market Psychology Inc. (New Brunswick, N. J.)	231	D_2
18	Minnesota Poll (State of Minnesota)	1000	$C_2-D_2-A_1$
19[b]	Roger E. Nebergall and Muzafer Sherif, University of Oklahoma (campuses in Oklahoma, Kansas, Washington and elsewhere)	Over 1500	V_1
20	A. C. Nielsen Company (National)	1100	A, B, C, D (coincident)
21	Opinion Research Corporation (National)	2672[d]	$P_2 \nearrow {A_2 \atop B_2} \rightarrow C_2 \searrow {D_2 \atop V_2}$

TABLE 21.1 THE STUDIES (*CONTINUED*)

NO.	NAME AND LOCALE	SIZE OF SAMPLE	TIMING[a]
22	Elmo Roper & Associates (National)	Approximately 3000	P_2, D_2
23	Schwerin Research Corporation (New York City)	About 250–300 after each debate	A_2, B_2, C_2, D_2
24	Hans Sebald, Ohio State University (Columbus, Ohio) (campus)	152 (students)	V_1
25	Sindlinger & Co. (National)	About 3000 at each point in time	A_1, A_2, B_2, C_2, D_2
26 [b]	Individuals associated with Social Research, Inc. (6–10 cities—different for each debate)	70–120 each time	A_2, B_2, C_2, D_2
27	Survey Research Center, University of Michigan (National)	1803	$P_1–P_2–V_2$
28	Percy H. Tannenbaum, Bradley S. Greenberg and Fred R. Silverman, Mass Communication Research Center, University of Wisconsin (Madison, Wisconsin) (campus)	187	$A_1–A_2–D_2$
29	Texas Poll (State of Texas)	520	B_2
30	Malachi C. Topping and Lawrence W. Lichty, Ohio State University (Columbus, Ohio) (campus)	114	$D_1–D_2$
31	David Wallace, Bureau of Applied Social Research, Columbia University (Westport, Connecticut)	About 500	P_2, V_2

[a] P_1 = previous election (same respondents); P_2 = early in 1960 campaign; $A_1, B_1, C_1, D_1,$ = just before 1st, 2d, 3d, 4th debate; A_2, B_2, C_2, D_2 = just after 1st, 2d, 3d, 4th debate; V_1 = before election day; V_2 = after election.

[b] Several of these studies are cited in the text only rarely or not at all. This is because, at the time of writing, they had not yet been formally analyzed (19, 26); or because they were not in a form that was immediately amenable to our purpose (1); or because we discovered them too late (8, 12, 13, 30); or because they were not made available to us (10).

[c] About one-third of the total interviewed before and after each debate.

[d] In both Kraft and ORC, a sub-sample of the original sample was reinterviewed on each of the successive waves.

national studies are virtually unanimous in placing the figure for the first debate at 60 to 65 percent of the total adult population (9A, 14, 20, 21, 25)[2] Some of the local studies show higher figures (5, 7, 28) because they tend to include respondents with higher education and greater political interest. Altogether some 70 of the 107 million U.S. adults—and perhaps another 10 to 15 million younger people—watched or listened to the first debate.

Compared with the first debate, the figures for the various studies are less consistent concerning the subsequent debates. Furthermore, it is difficult to know how to account for the effect of the different days of the week (Monday, Friday, Thursday, Friday) and the different hours of the day (9:30, 7:30, 7:30, 10:00 Eastern Time). The Nielsen ratings (20) show a decline in

[2] Numbers in parentheses refer to studies described in Table 21.1.

percent of TV homes tuned in[3] (measured by coincident metered readings) but, interestingly, a larger total audience (measured by diary records) for the second and third debates (80 and 82 million individuals) than for the first (77 million) or the last (70 million). This is almost certainly due to the fact that the second and third debates were on the air early enough in the evening to have included more children and, possibly, more adults with early bed-times. In any event, a conservative estimate would be that at least 55 per-cent of the total adult population watched or listened to each of the debates and, altogether, that upwards of 80 percent of the population saw or heard at least one of the debates (9A, 14, 20, 22, 27). The average debate viewer was in the audience for some 2 1/2 hours—that is, for three of the debates.

Surely this is one of the great political assemblages of all time. Still, there are some other facts which ought to be noted for the sake of a bal-anced perspective. First, it should be borne in mind that the proportion of adults who turn on their sets on an average weekday evening—according to a study made in July 1960 (25)—is in the neighborhood of 70 percent and, from another study, that about 45 percent of adults are at their sets during an average evening hour.[4] In other words, a very large proportion of the debate audience was immediately accessible; little effort had to be exerted to rally them. Moreover, there is little doubt that the relative absence of alternative program choices inflated the debate audiences. Among the Canadian cities studied, for example, audiences ranged between 50 and 60 percent for the fourth debate, except in Calgary—the only city among those surveyed offering an alternative program—where the figure dropped to 35 percent (4). Again, two studies (7, 25) suggest that the attention-span of the audiences is an important factor to reckon with. There is reason to believe that as much as one-third of the audience for each of the debates watched less than the entire program (25). The fact that the Nielsen (20) figures for TV homes reached by the first debate does not decline similarly (68.5 per-cent for the first half hour, 64.2 percent for the second half hour) may mean only that the set remained on even though family members drifted away, or that the tune-outs only slightly exceeded the tune-ins.

Nevertheless, it is evident that the audiences for the debates were exceedingly large. A comparison of Monday, September 26—the evening of the first debate—with the previous Monday evening reveals a higher pro-portion of sets in use throughout the evening and a *rise* in the size of the audience when the debate began at 9:30 P.M. (65.9 to 68.5 percent of TV homes) in contrast to the previous week's *decline* (59.5 to 55.0 percent). As

---

[3] Since the debates were carried by the three major networks, there was little choice open to the viewer if his set was on at all. About 88 percent of sets in use during the hours of the debate were tuned to the debates (20).

[4] *Report on Audience Composition,* Television Bureau of Advertising, 1959. Note that this study is somewhat dated and, moreover, that seasonal fluctuations are tremendous. According to the A. C. Nielson Co. report, *Television '61,* the average evening audience for January–February (when 55 percent of TV homes tune in their sets for an average of about 6 hours per day) is 64 percent greater than the July–August audience.

TABLE 21.2 PERCENT OF ADULTS VIEWING (OR LISTENING TO) DEBATES[a]

STUDY NO.	NAME AND LOCALE	FIRST DEBATE	SECOND DEBATE	THIRD DEBATE	FOURTH DEBATE	ONE OR MORE	ALL 4	REMARKS
3	California Poll (state)	65						Registered voters
4	Canadian Broadcasting Corporation				54 (weighted)			Percent of TV households
5	Carter (local)	81	76	67	61			
6	Creative Research Associates (local)		71	64	64			
7	Deutschmann (local)	75						44 percent stayed tuned throughout
9A	Gallup (natl.)	60				80		Registered voters
14	Kraft (natl.) [b]	65	66	65		87		
18	Minnesota					88		
20	Nielsen (natl.)	60	62	64	54			percent of population 12 years and over
21	Opinion Research Corp. (natl.)	66	49	51	49			1st debate viewing only; others viewing plus listening
22	Roper (natl.)				56	83	30	Viewing only ("seen on television")
23	Schwerin (local)	65	47	47	59			

(Continued on next page)

TABLE 21.2   ADULTS VIEWING DEBATES *(CONTINUED)*

STUDY NO.	NAME AND LOCALE	FIRST DEBATE	SECOND DEBATE	THIRD DEBATE	FOURTH DEBATE	ONE OR MORE	ALL 4	REMARKS
25	Sindlinger (natl.)	66	69	58	61			12 yrs. or older; approx. 45 percent stayed tuned through-out each debate
27	Survey Re-search center (natl.)					79		
28	Tannen-baum (local)	87						

ᵃ Viewing plus listening unless otherwise noted (see Remarks). Approximately 10 percent of total are listeners rather than viewers.

ᵇ Figures for debates 2 and 3 on the assumption that those (about 1/3) who could not be contacted watched or did not watch in same proportions as those who were contacted.

Stanley Kelley, Jr., infers from his examination of these figures, it seems clear that people stayed home (and stayed up) to watch the debate.[5]

Concerning the composition of the audience, several studies found almost equally high proportions of both Nixon and Kennedy supporters attending (9, 18).[6] While there was a correlation between educational level and viewing, over 50 percent of those with a grade school education or less were there (9), although the first debate was much more successful in this respect than subsequent debates (21). And several studies show (7, 25) that those who did not actually see the programs read about them or heard about them. Sindlinger (25) reports that 67 percent of all newspaper readers (which consists of virtually the entire adult population) read about the first debate within twenty-four hours and about half talked about each of the debates within the same time period (7, 25). Naturally, most of these were people who also heard or saw the programs but some also learned about them—and, cer-

[5] For an interesting account of the campaign as a whole, and the debates in the perspective of the campaign, see Stanley Kelley, Jr., "The 1960 Presidential Election," in K. Hinderaker ed., *American Government Annual, 1961–1962* (New York: Holt, Rinehart and Winston, 1961).

[6] Opinion Research Corporation (21) finds somewhat higher proportions of Nixon supporters in the audience for Debates 3 and 4. Interestingly, as we shall show below, these were the debates in which Nixon is thought to have done better. But the more likely explanation is that Nixon supporters, on the whole, were somewhat better educated and therefore more likely to continue in the audience.

tainly, many understood them better—by virtue of exposure to these supplementary sources of information. We have the impression that not more than 10 percent of the population failed to learn about the debates within twenty-four hours.

But listening to the debates, as we have said, did vary according to education (7, 9, 18), ranging for the first debate from three-fourths of the college-educated to just over half of those with grammar school or less. It varied with occupation (80 percent of business and professionals; two-thirds of clerical and sales; half of manual workers and farmers). People in the East and West (and perhaps in the Midwest) listened more than those in the South (9, 25). Most interesting of all, it varied with religious affiliation. Three studies (7, 9, 18) find disproportionately more Catholics in the audience, despite the fact of the generally higher educational and occupational status of the Protestants. Indeed, those Protestants who mentioned religion as the "most important issue of the campaign" were much less likely to be viewers (7).

Research on voting behavior has all but dispelled the myth of the "independent voter"—the ideal citizen who does not make up his mind until election eve, when he retires to the quiet of his study to weigh the opposing arguments of the two parties. The truth is that people who make up their minds late in the campaign are likely to have very little interest in the election.[7] This is reflected in the debate audience, too. Viewing of the debates was related to strength of commitment to candidate or party. "Independent voters" were far less likely to hear the debates (7, 9, 21, 27). It is also worth reiterating that by a wide margin, the first debate drew in larger proportions of the less informed segments of the public than any succeeding debate.

Only two studies (5, 25) report on the context in which the listening or viewing took place. Carter (5) found that viewing was done in the company of family members (usually just the spouse) and, occasionally, of friends and neighbors. Only one-fifth of the respondents listened alone. There is evidence (14, 20, 25) that, over the period of the debates, people were increasingly in their own homes. Radio listeners (some 10 to 20 percent) were much less likely to be at home; indeed, about one-half listened in their cars (25).

INTEREST IN THE DEBATES

A Gallup Poll (9A) taken before the first debates found 55 percent of a national sample of adults looking forward to the debates with "a lot" of interest. Sindlinger (25) found that 90 percent of the population aged twelve and over knew of the debates in advance. Furthermore, compared with both the 1952 and the 1956 campaign, more people were interested in the campaign (9, 25) and more were open to influence than had said so in '52 or '56.

[7] See Bernard Berelson, Paul F. Lazarsfeld, and William N. McPhee, *Voting* (Chicago: University of Chicago Press, 1954).

For example, more people said they "thought a lot" about the campaign in 1960 (9), and there was some tendency to make up one's mind later in the 1960 campaign than in '48, '52, and '56 (76 percent knew whom they would support at the time of the 1956 conventions as compared with 60 percent at the time of the 1960 conventions [27]).

No less important was the overall increase in the use of television as a medium for the presidential campaign (8, 27). In 1952, 31 percent of a national sample credited TV with bringing them "most information" about the campaign; 49 percent of the same respondents said so in 1956, and 60 percent in 1960 (27).[8]

The TV debates, then, were introduced into a campaign which was attracting unusually high interest and were presented via a medium which had emerged as the predominant source of campaign information.[9]

Did people find the debates interesting? Did they think the debates were a good idea? The evidence that the overwhelming answer is "yes" is abundant, though much of it can only be inferred rather than established directly. Only three studies asked directly. Sindlinger (25) asked after each debate, "Do you think these face-to-face meetings between Nixon and Kennedy are a good idea, bad idea, or just what do you think?" The California Poll (3) asked, "Do you feel that this kind of debate between Presidential candidates is a good way or a poor way to get the issues across to the American public?" The Canadian Broadcasting Corporation (4) asked, "Are you glad you had the chance of seeing the debate [fourth debate] on TV, or would you rather have seen something else instead?" In both the United States and Canada, more than two-thirds (in California 83 percent) of those who saw the debates responded positively (3, 4, 25). Indeed, the positive response increased from debate to debate. Women were consistently more positive than men and the largest proportion who thought it was a bad idea, interestingly, favored Nixon (25).

It may well be that the explanation for the greater approval given each successive debate is a product of self-selection and the resultant increase in sophistication and political involvement of the audience. At any rate, this is the suggestion implicit in the Canadian findings, which establish that the *smaller* the audience, and the more *selective* the audience, the more it will be likely to approve. Thus Calgary and Vancouver attracted proportionately fewer listeners than the Eastern cities (and Calgary, as has already been stated, had an alternative program available) but these two Western cities had the highest vote of appreciation for the program (4). Incidentally, 60 to 70 percent of English-speaking Canadians in the seven cities surveyed felt that the debate format should be employed in Canadian politics.

More indirect indices of interests are reflected in the extent to which

[8] Almost all of the decline came from radio; newspapers continued to be credited by about one-quarter of the population as the source that brings "most information."

[9] The crediting of TV with so much importance as a source of information concerning the campaign probably reflects the importance of TV as a medium of up-to-the-minute news. In most other areas of ideas and advice, people tend to choose magazines over TV. As we shall argue below, TV is primarily perceived as a medium of entertainment. For data on this general area, see "A Study of the Magazine Market," Part II, conducted for the Magazine Publishers Associated by the Market Research Corporation of America.

the debates were discussed or read about by those who listened. Deutsch-mann (7) found that 77 percent of those who saw the debates sought additional information about them. Only four or five news events have had comparable audiences in the past few years (25). About half the population discussed the debates within twenty-four hours and, although this is less than the number who discussed such things as Khrushchev's visits to the U.S., or Eisenhower's stroke, or the Russian and U.S. conquests of space, or even the Little Rock episode, it is an important high point in political discussion (7, 25).

Inquiring more specifically into what people liked and disliked about the debates, Carter (5) found that the clash of personalities was what seemed to be most attractive. Thus, the later debates were liked better because they were considered more "direct, lively, emotional, peppy, spirited."[10] Similarly, in the analysis of the high points in the reactions (recorded by machine) of viewers assembled especially to watch the first debate, the Gallup Poll's Hopewell study (9B) found that generalized "inspirational" material (Kennedy: "If we fail, then freedom fails"; Nixon: "A record is never something to stand on, it's something to build on") or effective counterattack (Nixon: "It is very difficult to blame the four Republicans for the eight Democrats not getting something through that particular committee") far outscored the facts and statistics of gross national product, etc.[11] There is no doubt that the immediate response, at any rate, was to the drama of the combat and to the rhetoric. Fifty-four percent of the Schwerin respondents (23) considered the first debate "a considerable improvement" when asked to compare it "with other political speeches on TV." When asked to compare it "with other political programs of the panel or interview type," 37 percent said "considerable improvement" and 40 percent "some improvement."

Just as the audience responded to the rhetoric more than to the statistics, so they responded to the personalities more than to the issues. And many were quite aware of that fact. Asked which were better portrayed, issues or candidates, 19 percent of Carter's respondents (5) said the candidates; only 7 percent said the issues; 50 percent said both. There is little doubt, from this study and others (4, 16), that the audience was busy analyzing the character of the contestants—their "presentations of self." Indeed, several of the academic studies focused exclusively on "images" rather than "issues" as the proper subject for investigation.

There was a minority which did not like the debates. Most of these,

[10] Kennedy voters liked the first two debates better than Nixon voters and the opposite was true for the last two. The obvious explanation for this is below.

[11] The machine graphically records "like" and "dislike" on a moving tape. Given the conceptual limitations of the machine, it is no surprise that the more stirring parts of the exchange scored most positively. It should be pointed out, however, that the facts and figures scored high on "dislike." The Schwerin organization conducted a similar "program analyzer" study during the Korean War, recording audience reactions to a speech by President Truman. "Liking" responses rose during appeals to patriotism, Americans' strength, etc., and dropped with references to sacrifice, higher taxes, etc. Another "program analyzer" study of a film of one of the debates, carried out at the University of North Carolina by Noel Keys and Alan K. Whiteleather (12), focused on party differences in the extent of approval or disapproval of the statements of each candidate. They found that Democratic students (N = 13) allocated approval (of Kennedy) and disapproval (of Nixon) less extremely than the Republicans (N = 14), though the mean differences were small.

as had already been pointed out, did so because they felt that their man had been bettered. Indeed, in anticipation of the first debate, there is some evidence that Kennedy supporters were preparing to discount the outcome of the debate on the ground that competitive performance in the debate is irrelevant to the office of the presidency (16).

Alone among the studies, Carter (5) asked how the debates might be improved. Surprisingly, some 70 percent were able to volunteer suggestions (and even considering that Carter's sample was a politically involved one, this seems like an extraordinary response). Of those who responded, 20 percent thought the debates should be longer; almost that many urged the elimination of the interviewer panel; a smaller number suggested that each debate be limited to only one topic; and there was a large variety of other suggestions.

WHO WON?

In contrast to the paucity of specific questions concerning the format of the debates, it is surely revealing that so many of the studies asked, unabashedly, "Who won?" or words to that effect.

Again, the studies are very consistent concerning the results (see Table 21.3). The first debate was clearly won by Kennedy. That is, a plurality of respondents in every one of the thirteen applicable studies reported this result. The second debate was very close. The third debate was won by Nixon. And the final debate, again, was very close. (Only the Schwerin study [23] disagrees that the second and fourth debates were inconclusive. In both cases, the New Yorkers in the Schwerin laboratories declare Kennedy the winner by large margins.) Overall, when the question was asked about the debates as a whole (5, 9, 11, 14, 18, 22, 31) Kennedy was far ahead.

Table 21.4 provides some insight into the major basis upon which people decide who won. Examining results for the first debate only, several things are evident from the table: (a) With the exception of two local studies (7, 31), individuals with a party affiliation or with a specific voting intention declare their own candidate the winner more often than they choose the opposition candidate. (b) More Republicans and Nixon supporters choose Kennedy as the winner than Democrats and Kennedy supporters choose Nixon; this is true of every one of the studies. (c) More of the former than the latter insist that they cannot decide who won. In other words, there is a marked tendency to choose one's own candidate as the winner, though among the relatively small number who concede to the opposition (5 to 10 percent in the state and national polls), there is a greater proportion of Republicans and Nixon supporters. Republicans, too, are more likely than Democrats and Kennedy supporters to say that they have no choices. (d) Finally, note that the Undecided—those who had not yet made up their minds between the candidates—choose Kennedy more often than Nixon, though most of them report no choice.

Most of the other factors which differentiate between those who thought that Kennedy won and those who thought that Nixon won (education, occupation, age, religion, etc.) are confounded with voting intention and, therefore, we shall not report them. Only sex (happily) tends to be relatively free of statistical contamination. As it turns out, Nixon's debate performance seems to have impressed proportionately more women than men (14, 18, 25).

Roper (22) asked those who named one or the other candidate as having won the final debate, "In what ways would you say that (Kennedy, Nixon) was better?" and the answers were cross-tabulated by voting intention. Three categories of reasons characterize the loyal partisans as compared with those who conceded defeat: they said that the winner was better, first of all, because they *agreed with his views*; secondly, because he was *better informed*; and, finally, because he was more *sincere*, honest, truthful, etc. Those who decided for Kennedy were much more likely than those who decided for Nixon to emphasize that their choice was *specific*, gave facts, answered questions directly rather than evasively. Comparing only the two (very small) groups of conceders, it appears that Nixon supporters who conceded that Kennedy had won did so primarily on personality grounds: they liked his personality, they said. And they concurred in his partisans' admiration for his specificity.[12] Kennedy supporters who conceded that Nixon had won the debate were unique in attributing the victory to his having kept his opponent on the defensive, and they were much more likely than Nixon's own partisans to feel that he had displayed greater confidence in presenting his position.

Although there are various ways in which the many categories of response classified by Roper might be combined and recombined, it seems that a candidate's general informedness and his style of presentation of facts and arguments were more important criteria for judgment than either what he said or his personality as a whole. In other words, if these attributes are separable at all, the Roper data seem to argue that style of presentation was more important than either the content of the presentation (issues) or the personality of the debater (image).[13] This is in contrast to those who have speculated that the audience was interested only in the personalities of the candidates.

The Canadian study (4) feels that *both* personality and style of presentation were important frames of reference and agrees that the subject matter of the debate—the issues—was rarely mentioned as a factor which "counted in favor of" or "counted against" each candidate. Thus, "the ques-

---

[12] Still, pro-Kennedy people and those who leaned toward Nixon (but not those "for" or "strongly for" Nixon) apparently would have liked Kennedy to be even more specific. Asked by Market Psychology, Inc. (17) to complete the sentence, "I would like Kennedy a little more if he would only . . .," large proportions of these groups (in New Brunswick, N. J.) said, "If he would only be more specific," especially about details of his foreign policy. Sizable proportions of the same groups said he should be "less rash, less double-talking, more mature, time his phrases, speak more slowly and more clearly, speak right to us, not end so abruptly, show the sense of the Presidency as an awful trust rather than merely a political goal, etc."

[13] The Kraus-Smith paper (15) finds the "images" attributed to each candidate closer to the "images" of some issues than of others. E.g., it is suggested that the "profile" of the Democratic image of Kennedy matches the "profile" of Catholicism, federal aid to education, and the U. N.

TABLE 21.3   WHO WON? (PERCENT OF ALL VIEWERS[a])

STUDY	QUESTION	FIRST DEBATE		SECOND DEBATE		THIRD DEBATE		FOURTH DEBATE		ALL DEBATES	
		RMN	JFK	RMN	JFK	RMN	JFK	RMN	JFK	RMN	JFK
3 California Poll	"Made better impression"	24	35								
5 Carter	"Who benefited"									11	49
7 Deutschmann	"Won votes"	7	26								
9 Gallup Poll	"Better job"	23	43							30	42
11 Iowa Poll	"Gained most"	23[b]	35[b]							21	32
14 Kraft		31	40	42	41	39	34			30	42
18 Minnesota Poll	"Gained the most"									17	51
21 Opinion Research Corp.	"Best job stating his case"	25	39	31	36	46	28	39	35		
22 Roper	"Best job"							31	36	21	37
23 Schwerin	"Outscored"	23	39	28	44	42	39	27	52		
25 Singlinger	"Who won"	24	26	31	28	40	23	35	36		
29 Texas Poll	"Best job"	26[b]	46[b]								
31 Wallace	"Better impression"									23	54

[a] The difference between sum of totals and 100 represents "no choice."

[b] Question was asked following second debate and referred to first two debates.

tions we asked here were carefully worded so as to allow respondents to talk either about what the candidates said or about the two men themselves and how they performed. . . . The fact that so little comment was directed at the subject matter of the debate or at any of the arguments involved, and so much more at the candidates themselves and the general quality of their respective performance as debaters, would seem to confirm what some commentators have already suggested. That is that a television debate of this kind, which focuses attention so sharply on the contestants themselves, leaves a mass audience with (as we have seen) some very distinct impressions of the capabilities of the two men as debaters and as persons, but (as our results suggest) with very little idea of what the debate was all about." (4)

TABLE 21.4 "WHO WON" FIRST DEBATE: PERCENTAGE DISTRIBUTION OF CHOICE OF WINNER ACCORDING TO VOTING INTENTION OR PARTY AFFILIATION[a] (EACH ROW EQUALS 100 PERCENT)

Study	Question	Intention or Affiliation	WINNER		
			Nixon	Kennedy	No Choice[b]
3 California Poll	"Made better impression"	Republican	39	17	44
		Democratic	11	51	38
7 Deutschmann	"Won votes"	Republican	10	27	63
		Democratic	4	30	66
		Independent	4	19	67
9A Gallup	"Better job"	Pro-Nixon	45	17	38
		Pro-Kennedy	3	71	26
		Undecided	12	26	62
11 Iowa Poll[c]	"Gained most"	Pro-Nixon	39	16	45
		Pro-Kennedy	3	62	35
		Undecided	28	30	62
14 Kraft[c]		Pro-Nixon	59	17	24
		Pro-Kennedy	7	65	28
		Undecided	25	31	44
21 Opinion Research Corp.	"Best job stating his case"	Pro-Nixon	52	8	40
		Pro-Kennedy	2	73	25
		Undecided	4	22	74
23 Schwerin	"Outscored"	Pro-Nixon	47	6	47
		Pro-Kennedy	7	39	54
		Undecided	7	39	54
31 Wallace	"Better impression"	Republican	28	46	26
		Democratic	2	87	11
		Independent	26	48	26

[a] Information on voting intention and party affiliation was obtained during the same interview as evaluation of the debates. It is conceivable, therefore, that some people aligned their party affiliation or voting intention according to their evaluation of who won the debate. Although several studies have pre-debate information available, only the Kraft study actually employs voting intentions obtained in an earlier interview.

[b] No Choice and/or Don't Know.

[c] Question was asked following second debate and referred to first two debates.

LEARNING FROM THE DEBATES: THE ISSUES

That does not mean that people learned nothing from the debates about the issues. Indeed, Carter (5) gave a 16-item information test to his respondents based on statements made by the candidates in the first debate and found not only that at least some of what was said was remembered but, even more, that there was no evidence that a process of "selective recall" was operating. That is to say, Democratic viewers were no more likely to recognize statements made by Kennedy than statements made by Nixon and the same thing holds true for Republican viewers. This is an extraordinary finding, suggesting that the debates not only overcame the well-established tendency toward selective exposure (which insulates one from opposition arguments) but also—at least as far as information is concerned—the tendency to perceive and recall selectively.

A related study by Sebald (24) also finds respondents—sociology students at Ohio State, in this case—equally able to identify correctly statements made by either candidate (regardless of their own preferences). Sebald's concern, however, was rather different from Carter's (5). Respondents were presented with a set of statements made by the two candidates and were asked, first, to agree or disagree with each statement and, second, to name its author. While the overall attribution of statements to the two candidates was equally correct, statements with which a respondent disagreed were most often attributed to the opposition candidate, even when actually made by the respondent's own candidate—while statements with which the respondent agreed were much more accurately attributed to the candidate who made them. This implies that it may be more painful to disagree with one's own candidate than to agree with some statement of the opposition. In still another aspect of the same study, respondents were asked to recall spontaneously statements made by the candidates. Here, the students tended to recall those of their own candidate's statements with which they personally agreed and statements of the opposition candidate with which they disagreed.[14] It is not clear, however, whether the students' opinions on the issues preceded or followed exposure to the candidates.

Of course, there is plenty of other evidence to illustrate the workings of selective perception in audience reaction to the debates. The distribution of votes on "who won" according to voting intention or political affiliation (Table 21.4) provides an obvious example; and there are many others. An especially pertinent example is reported by Kraft (14), who finds that those who say that the most important thing discussed in the (second) debate was foreign policy were much more likely to be pro-Nixon than pro-Kennedy, whereas those who say that some domestic matter was the most important topic discussed tended to be for Kennedy.

The evidence (21, 25) suggests that foreign affairs was the paramount issue during the entire campaign and, according to Sindlinger (25), it increased in importance following the second, third, and forth debates. Since Nixon was generally conceded to be the more expert and experienced in foreign affairs—he was far ahead of Kennedy in perceived ability at "handling the Russians" and "keeping the peace" (9A, 21, 22)—the focus on foreign affairs was clearly to Nixon's advantage. In the debates themselves, the Quemoy-Matsu issue seemed to work for Nixon. Roper (22) asked specifically, "How do you feel about this—that Nixon scored against Kennedy in these discussions about the offshore islands of Quemoy and Matsu . . . or that Kennedy scored against Nixon or that neither one of them handled this issue well?" While partisans said that their own candidate had outscored the other, the Nixon supporters were surer of this than were the Kennedy supporters. Similarly, in Carter's study (5), California Republicans were much surer than Democrats that their man got "the best of the argument" over

[14] This line of analysis is developed in Berelson, Lazarsfeld, and McPhee, *Voting*, chap. 10.

issues such as "peace," "Cuba," "U-2 flights," and "disarmament." Public perception of Kennedy's ability in foreign affairs did increase as a result of the debates (3, 18, 22) but, even so, Nixon might well have won, if perceived ability at handling foreign affairs had influenced more votes.

There seems to be little doubt that the debates made some issues more salient, as all campaigns do. Quemoy and Matsu (from which Nixon profited), U.S. prestige (which benefited Kennedy [5]), and domestic issues such as unemployment, old-age medical insurance, aid to education, and farm policy (all of which benefited Kennedy [5, 21]) were the major ones. But the Krauss-Smith study (15), which investigated the extent of actual changes in opinion on the issues as a result of the debates, found no change at all, while the Carter study (5) found high proportions insisting, on most issues, that neither candidate had gotten "the best of the argument."

Still, it is worth bearing in mind that people seemed to remember some of the content of the debates. Moreover, when asked, 27 percent of the respondents in one study (5) assert that the debates helped them learn something about the issues, and this is not far from the percentage that say they learned something about the candidates (35 percent) or that the debates generally increased the level of their information and interest in the campaign (17 percent).

As far as issues are concerned, then, the debates seem to have (a) made some issues salient rather than others (the issues made salient, of course, may or may not have been the most "important" ones); (b) caused some people to learn where the candidates stand (including the stand of the opposition candidate); (c) effected very few changes of opinion on the issues; and (d) focused more on presentation and personality than on issues.

LEARNING FROM THE DEBATES: THE CANDIDATES

Sixty-one percent of the Kennedy voters said they learned "a great deal . . . about the candidates and what they stand for" from the TV debates (21). Only about half as many said they learned "a great deal" from other TV appearances of the candidates, from news in the newspapers, from columnists or editorials. The Nixon voters are more grudging about the debates—since their outcome is so clearly associated with the victorious Kennedy. Still, 35 percent of the Nixon voters say they learned a "great deal"—as large a percentage as for any other source of information.

We have already seen that viewers learned something about the issues, though perhaps not very much. But there is considerably more reason to believe that they learned something about the candidates themselves. They discovered how well each candidate could perform in a debate and they formed images of each candidate's character and abilities.

Many will argue that this is unfortunate learning in the sense that whether a candidate is perceived as sincere, or tough, or quick on his feet is, first of all, probably not an important qualification for the office of president and, secondly, probably misperceived anyway. (Some would say similar things about the issues as they were presented in the debates.) But is it altogether unfortunate? Is it irrational to assume that the observation of two men interacting (albeit with many restrictions) under extreme pressure may be somewhat diagnostic of performance in a high-pressure job? Is the candidates' manner of handling rhetoric or statistics really so remote from the American voter's task of evaluating the qualifications of the man, as much as of the party, for the presidency? It is certainly much more rational than judging an automobile by its body or a book by its cover, but—as some sympathetic soul has pointed out—even these actions may not be as demented as they seem. People are not so foolish as to equate an automobile with the design of its body but, when mechanical sophistication is lacking, they use the body, and whatever other clues are available to them, as indices of the quality of the car.

Whatever the case, there is evidence from several studies (3, 5, 16, 28) that Kennedy fared far better than Nixon as far as positive images are concerned. Of course, Kennedy had the "advantage" of being all but unknown. Nixon had to maintain his image; Kennedy had to attain his—and the latter (or so it seems after the event) is the easier thing to do.

The most elaborate of the several image studies is that of Tannenbaum (28), in which respondents are asked to choose the attributes of their Ideal President in terms of a set of scales such as weak-strong, agitated-calm, old-young, and the like, and then—before and after the first debate and, once more, following the last debate—they were asked to rate the two candidates in terms of the same scales. The first debate moved the ratings of Kennedy, on all twelve scales, in the direction of the Ideal President, the most important shift being on "experienced-inexperienced." Changes in the before and after ratings of Nixon seemed random and inconsistent by comparison. Both men moved away from Ideal by the end of the debates but Nixon moved away more decisively than did Kennedy. Tannenbaum concludes that "Kennedy did not necessarily win the debates, but Nixon lost them. . . ."

Both Tannenbaum (28) and Carter (5) find that Kennedy's performance in the first debate impressed Democrats and Republicans alike as far as positive images are concerned. Over the entire period of the debates, the Carter findings (5) indicate that the Democrats boosted Kennedy higher and higher while the Republicans' appreciation of Kennedy increased almost as much. Nixon barely maintained his original position. Two studies of university students (12, 13) identified a decline in the favorability of the Nixon image among pro-Kennedy people as the major change and one of the studies (13) found a corresponding improvement in the image of Kennedy among pro-Nixonites.

Not so in Chicago, however, Creative Research Associates (6) found that Nixon's image improved even more than Kennedy's in the second, third, and fourth debates and that Nixon lost ground not so much in the debates but outside them ("between" them).

But this is the only exception and, in any case, CRA (6) does not discuss the first debate, which, apparently, made the most of the difference. The first debate seems to have served, primarily, to rally the doubting Democrats. A respondent in the Lang's study (16) is quoted as saying that, as a

result of the first debate, he "switched from being an anti-Nixon Democrat to a pro-Kennedy Democrat." According to the Langs, many Democrats
expected Kennedy to do less well and, in anticipation, were prepared to discount the connection between performance in the debates and qualification
for the role of president. Kennedy's victory not only strengthened confidence
in him among partisans and potential partisans but, by making the performance criterion universally legitimate, made the institution of the debates
more important than they otherwise might have been and the defeat of
Nixon all the more serious (16).[15]

These changes in the image of Kennedy surely account for the increase
in the overall favorability toward Kennedy over the period of the debates.
Five studies inquire specifically into the generalized attitudes of voters toward the two candidates, and the results are summarized in Table 21.5. Just
as in the evaluation of "who won," it is evident from the table that (a) the
Democrats reported that their opinion of Kennedy had improved more often
than Republicans reported an improvement in their general opinion of
Nixon; (b) Republicans became more favorable to Kennedy than Democrats
to Nixon; (c) indeed, two of the studies (3, 23) suggest that the Democrats
became much more unfavorable to Nixon following the first debate than the
Republicans did to Kennedy; (d) Independents (23, 27) moved more toward
Kennedy than Nixon. Important as these figures are, however, it is no less
important to note that close to half of the respondents in each of these
studies reported no change at all.

IMPACT OF THE DEBATES ON VOTING DECISIONS

But did this affect any votes? That is a hard question to answer.

Ideally, to test for the impact of a given debate on voting intentions it
would be necessary (a) to have before and after measures of the voting
intentions of the same group of respondents; (b) to compare viewers and
nonviewers. And, in order to assess the impact on actual voting, it would be
necessary (c) to establish that a change in voting intention resulting from
exposure to the debate had persisted until Election Day.

But this is very elusive information. Most studies are not based on panels
of the same respondents (trend studies, of course, reveal only changes in
the total distributions and conceal internal changes). Furthermore, even a
panel study cannot focus so narrowly on the debates as to be sure that it
was a debate rather than some other campaign event which best explains
changes in voting intention. Then, too, it is almost impossible to compare

[15] An analysis of the Tannenbaum data (28) tends to confirm the notion that the first
debate was especially influential for Democrats and Independents. Of particular interest
here is the marked improvement in the eyes of Democrats and Independents in Kennedy's
position relative to Nixon's with respect to such traits as "experience" and "strength."
While Kennedy's image as a "TV performer" showed particular improvement with respect
to these traits, there was also improvement in the corresponding components of his "presidential" image. The results are reported in Bradley S. Greenberg, "The Political Candidate
Versus the Television Performer," a paper read at the annual meeting of the Pacific Chapter, American Association for Public Opinion Research, Los Angeles, January, 1962.

TABLE 21.5   IMPACT OF DEBATES ON FAVORABILITY TOWARD CANDIDATES ACCORDING TO POLITICAL PREDISPOSITIONS (VIEWERS ONLY)[a]

Study	Questions		PERCENT MORE FAVORABLE			PERCENT LESS FAVORABLE		
			Rep	Dem	Ind	Rep	Dem	Ind
3 California Poll (First Debate)	"Did seeing the debate make you more favorable or less favorable toward Nixon? Toward Kennedy?	Toward Nixon	33	15		8	33	
		Toward Kennedy	25	54		19	4	
5 Carter (after four debates)	"Did your feelings about either candidate change in any way as a result of the television debates? In what way?"	Toward Nixon	25	14		17	29	
		Toward Kennedy	19	39		32	16	
18 Minnesota Poll (after three debates)	"Has your opinion of Kennedy (Nixon) changed in any way as a result of the debates? In what way?"	Toward Nixon	29	13	20	2	12	8
		Toward Kennedy	6	23	19	17	2	11
23 Schwerin [b] (first debate)	"Having seen this debate, what is your attitude toward Vice-President Nixon? Toward Senator Kennedy?"	Toward Nixon	57	13	16	2	31	11
		Toward Kennedy	25	72	36	14	6	2
27 Survey Research Center [c] (after four debates)	"Was your feeling about (Kennedy) (Nixon) any different after you watched those programs?"	Toward Nixon (against Kennedy)	40	11	17			
		Toward Kennedy (against Nixon)	19	56	40			
		Neither	41	33	43			

     [a] Read this table as follows: Considering the California Poll, for example, 33% of Republican viewers became more favorable to Nixon, 8% less favorable, and (not shown in the table) 59% remained unchanged. Among Democratic viewers, 15% became more favorable toward Nixon, 33% less favorable, and (not shown in the table) 52% remained unchanged.

     [b] In the Schwerin study, political predisposition was indexed by preference for candidates rather than for party.

     [c] Whereas the other studies percentaged changes in favorability separately for each candidate, the SRC study combined pro-Kennedy and anti-Nixon changes and pro-Nixon and anti-Kennedy changes and percentaged these over the total viewers of each party.

viewers and nonviewers since these were somewhat different kinds of people to begin with and, what's more, nonviewers got the word so quickly. For example, Deutschmann (7) finds a certain amount of change presumably as a result of the first debate but no difference between viewers and nonviewers.

     Bearing all these limitations in mind, let us look at the evidence.

     First of all, it seems safe to say that the debates—especially the first one —resulted primarily in a strengthening of commitment to one's own party and candidate. This was much more the case for Democrats than Republicans but the former had much greater room for improvement. Thus, according to

ORC (21), the 63 percent of Republicans who were "strongly committed" to Nixon in August dropped upon re-interview following the first debate to 59 percent, whereas the percentage of Democrats "strongly committed" to Kennedy increased from 39 to 46. Similarly, the Langs (16) found that most of the changes following the first debate were those of undecided Democratic party sympathizers whose votes had "crytallized" as a result of the debates.

Secondly, trend data on changes in strength of commitment from debate to debate follow the pattern of evalution of "who won." Consider Table 21.6, based, again, on the ORC study (21). In the two debates with a clearcut winner (first and third) there is an increase in strength of commitment to the winner and a decrease in commitment to the loser. Between the first and second debates (the second being a tie) both candidates gained strength equally. The fourth debate (also a tie) fits the pattern somewhat less well, though the net gain for Kennedy results from Nixon's loss of Republican strength-of-commitment rather than an increase in commitment among Democrats.

TABLE 21.6   CHANGE IN COMMITMENT FROM DEBATE TO DEBATE[a]

Debate	Winner	PERCENT CHANGE IN "STRONG COMMITMENT" TO OWN PARTY'S CANDIDATE	
		Republicans	Democrats
First	Kennedy	—4	+ 7
Second	Tie	+9	+ 8
Third	Nixon	+7	— 1
Fourth	Tie	—4	+ 2
Net Change		+8	+16

[a] Adapted from ORC study (21).

Finally, still drawing on the same study, Table 21.7 compares the pre- and post-debate positions (on a nine-point scale) of viewers and nonviewers.[16] The first thing to note in the table is that viewers of the debates, if anything, changed *less* than nonviewers. This is not as surprising as it sounds considering the fact that the nonviewers were far less interested in the election and far less committed to a candidate than the viewers. Previous election studies have shown that these are the people who are most open to influence, who are least likely to vote, and whose responses, in any case, are of dubious reliability. The second important point to note in the table is that among those who did change their voting intentions, by and large, neither candidate gained; this is true for both viewers and nonviewers of the final three debates. *Only in the first debate* is there evidence that viewing made a difference for one of the candidates. The net gain for Kennedy among

[16] These data are based on before and after comparisons of the *same* respondents. There are four sets of comparisons, one for each debate. Any movement on the scale (e.g., from "leaners" toward Kennedy to "strongly committed" to Kennedy) is classified as a change—in this case, of course, a pro-Kennedy change.

TABLE 21.7   CHANGES IN COMMITMENT OF VIEWERS AND NONVIEWERS[a]

	FIRST DEBATE		SECOND DEBATE		THIRD DEBATE		FOURTH DEBATE	
	Viewers percent	Non-Viewers percent	Viewers percent	Non-Viewers percent	Viewers percent	Non-Viewers percent	Viewers percent	Non-Viewers percent
Unchanged	58	52	65	66	73	69	70	67
Change to Kennedy	25	25	17	17	14	15	16	16
Change to Nixon	17	23	18	17	13	16	14	17
Net gain for Kennedy	+8	+2	—1	0	+1	—1	+2	—1

[a] Based on special tabulations by ORC (21) of before-and-after interviews with the *same* individuals. Before and after the first debate, for example, 58 percent of the viewers indicated precisely the same commitment (on a 9-point scale), while 25 percent made a change in Kennedy's favor (from "leaning" to "strongly committed") and 17 percent changed in favor of Nixon.

viewers of the first debate is 8 percent, compared with the usual negigible difference (2 percent) among the nonviewers.[17]

As previously noted, Deutschmann's (7) report is rather similar. He found no difference in the extent of change among viewers and nonviewers of the first debate. He also found that 25 percent of his panel made a change (on a seven-point scale) before and after the first debate, of whom 11 percent crossed over from one candidate to the other. Kennedy profited slightly more than Nixon from the net result of these moves. Again, the Creative Research study (6) found that nonviewers changed at least as much as viewers of the second, third, and fourth debates. There is a whisper of a suggestion that there was more movement from undecided to a specific voting intention among the viewers than among the nonviewers.[18]

From these studies (7, 16, 21) it appears a reasonable inference that the debates did have some effect or, more exactly, that at least the first debate accelerated Democratic support for Kennedy among viewers.

To put these findings in a somewhat different perspective, however, it is instructive to consider the long-term trend within which the abovementioned changes were going on. Consider Table 21.8, in which the trend results of the Gallup Poll (9A) are reported for the entire campaign. The results reported on September 25 were obtained immediately before the first debate and the interviewing for the report of October 12 was conducted immediately after the first debate, during the period September 27–October 4. Here, too, it appears that Kenndey scored a net gain in the debates, advancing three percentage points while Nixon lost one. But consider the long-term trend, which suggests that Kennedy was gradually advancing anyway!

[17] The absence of a clear-cut net gain for Nixon among viewers of the third debate conflicts with Table 23.6. It is difficult to reconcile these two sets of data.

[18] The ORC (21) and Deutschmann (7) data just presented were analyzed as "panel" data, comparing the response each individual gave before the debate with his post-debate response. Creative Research Associates (6) also interviewed the same respondents before and after each debate but presented only the overall marginal distributions at each point in time and therefore could measure only the "net change."

   Did the debates really affect the final outcome? Apart from strengthen-
ing Democratic convictions about their candidate, it is very difficult to say
conclusively.

   But if you *ask* people whether the debates influenced their voting
decision, they say yes. As Table 21.9 reveals, a sizable proportion of the
voting population feels that the debates helped them decide. This is more
true for Democrats than for Republicans, as has already been pointed out.[19]
But consider the 6 percent in the national Roper study (22) who say that the
debates "made them decide" or the 39 percent in the Bruskin study (2)

TABLE 21.8   THE GALLUP POLL (9A)[a] (EACH ROW EQUALS 100 PERCENT)

RELEASE DATE	KENNEDY JOHNSON	NIXON LODGE	UNDECIDED
August 17	44	50	6
August 31	47	47	6
September 14	48	47	5
September 25 [b]	46	47	7
October 12 [c]	49	46	5
October 26	48	48	4
November 4 (adjusted for probable voters)	51	45	4
November 7	49	48	3
Actual vote	50.1	49.9	

   [a] "If the election were held today, which ticket would you vote for—Nixon and
Lodge or Kennedy and Johnson?" Results reported above include those registered and in-
tending to vote who were more or less certain of their choice. Note further adjustment of
November 4.

   [b] Before first debate.

   [c] After first debate.

who mention the debates in answer to a very different question concerning
"the one most important thing" that led to Kennedy's victory.[20] Even these
people, almost certainly, were reinforced by the debates in their prior inclinations rather than converted. On the other hand, who is to say that the
doubts and reservations which existed among Democrats regarding Kennedy
might not have been dispelled at all if it had not been for the debates?

   [19] A study of University of Washington students by Edelstein (8) finds 5 to 6 percent
who consider the debates the "most important" factor in their decisions and some 35 percent who feel that the debates were at least "fairly important." There is little, if any, support here, however, for the finding of other studies that the debates were considered more
important by Democrats than by Republicans.

   [20] ORC (21) asked a question only slightly different from Bruskin's (2) but with very
different results. To the question "What do you think were the most important issues or
factors in deciding who won the election?" only 8 percent mentioned the debates, while
18 percent mentioned religion, 12 percent mentioned labor vote, 10 percent mentioned
personality, and, in addition, a large number of specific issues were named. A phenomenon similar to the difference between the Roper (22) and Bruskin (2) results noted in the
text has been often observed in survey research. In studies of medical care, for instance,
very few people ever attribute their own failure to have an illness attended by a physician
to a fear of the diagnosis, while a large proportion of the same people ascribe this motive
to "most people."

TABLE 21.9   PERCEIVED ROLE OF DEBATES IN DECISION-MAKING PROCESS ACCORDING TO VOTING INTENTION[a]

STUDY	QUESTION	ANSWER	PRO-NIXON PER-CENT	PRO-KEN-NEDY PER-CENT	UNDE-CIDED PER-CENT	TOTAL PER-CENT
11 Iowa Poll [b] (after two de-bates)	"Do you feel that these televi-sion debates between Nixon and Kennedy have helped YOU DECIDE which candidate you will vote for or haven't the de-bates made any difference?"	Yes, helped decide	28	42	34	34
		No, no difference	70	57	64	64
		Don't know	2	1	2	2
			100	100	100	100
22 Roper (after four de-bates)	"Different people have said the debates did different things for them. Some say the debates made them decide who they'll vote for; some say they made them more sure their choice was right; some say they left them less sure, and others say the debates had practically no effect on them one way or the other. Which is most true for you?"	Made them decide	3	9	1	6
		Made them more sure	39	49	4	41
		Made them less sure	5	3	24	5
		No effect	49	35	52	43
		Don't know	4	4	19	5
			100	100	100	100

[a] Percent of pro-Nixon, pro-Kennedy, Undecided, and all respondents.

[b] The Iowa Poll also reports on results of a similar question asked after all four de-bates were over: helped, 29 percent; no difference, 63 percent; don't know, 8 percent. No breakdown is given according to voting intention. Note the decline in the proportion claiming that they were helped in their decisions.

SOME POLITICAL AND POLICY IMPLICATIONS

The First Debate

The drawing power of the first debate, particularly its ability to attract almost equal proportions of both parties and large proportions of even the least educated groups, may be a unique occurrence. Later debates showed a decline both in numbers and representativeness—though the audience was still phenomenal. Debates in future years, if they are institutionalized, may have considerably less appeal.

It is interesting to note that, in the present instance, the "primacy" effect was more powerful than the "recency" effect. Though Nixon had the better of the last two debates by common consent, appraisal of the debates as a whole consistently finds Kennedy the victor.[26]

[26] An alternative explanation would be that none of the succeeding debates (even the third—on foreign policy—which Nixon won decisively) produced a difference of the magnitude of the first debate. On "primacy" and "recency," See Carl I. Hovland et al., The Order of Presentation in Persuasion (New Haven: Yale University Press, 1957).

The Issues

There is no doubt that the debates were more effective in presenting the candidates than the issues. If anbody is interested in communicating the issues, it might be well to take account of some of the suggestions made by the viewers, such as the idea of limiting a given debate to a single issue (5).

Social Functions of the Debates

The role of the debates (and of the campaign generally) in focusing public attention on the national drama, for all its intended divisiveness, is probably a highly integrative force in American life. In this connection, one of the extraordinary aspects of the debates was, to everyone's suprise, that voters learned something about the candidate they opposed (even though they very rarely gave him their vote). For one thing, they remembered what he said (5); for another, they learned that he was human, that he could become nervous, tired, etc. (16). And, over the course of the campaign, there is evidence (14) of a decline in the percentage who report "dislike of other candidate" as an explanation of their own choice (though, it should be noted, this may simply be a product of learning better answers to the question as time went by). It seems that the debates might make for a greater acceptance of the winning candidate—even if one voted against him: one knew more about him, one felt that he was more human and more accessible.[27] But these are just guesses, and the pity is that in their concentration on the combat, the studies failed to get so much of either the context or the latent consequences of the institution of the debates.

---

[27] In "Religion and Politics: The 1960 Elections," a paper delivered at the 1961 meetings of the American Sociological Association in St. Louis and based on the SRC study (27), Philip E. Converse suggests that the debates served to combat easy stereotyping of the candidates. He refers particularly to the concern of Protestant Democrats over Kennedy's Catholicism. "The mass media," says Converse, "—and the television debates in particular—filled in more fully an image of Kennedy. They did not modify cleavages by convincing Protestants that Catholicism per se was not black. But they did serve up a host of other items of information about this man. He was not only a Catholic, but was as well (in the public eye, from interview material) quick-witted, energetic, and poised. These are traits valued across religious lines, and act at the same time to call into question some of the more garish anti-Catholic stereotypes. While in the grand scheme of things such perceptions may seem superficial, they are real to the actors, and the fact that such perceptions compete with some success against the initial cognition of the candidate's group membership gives some sense, in turn, of the superficiality of the latter as a cue for many people. Bit by bit, as religiously innocuous information filled in, the Protestant Democrat could come to accept Kennedy primarily as a Democrat, his unfortunate religion notwithstanding. Vote intentions angled away from group lines toward party lines."